THE COMPLETE COPLAND

AARON COPLAND, 1964
Photograph by Victor Kraft

THE COMPLETE COPLAND

by

AARON COPLAND and VIVIAN PERLIS

PENDRAGON PRESS

HILLSDALE, N.Y.

Pendragon Press Musicological Series

Aesthetics in Music
Annotated Reference Tools in Music
Bucina: The Historic Brass Society
The Complete Organ
Dimension & Diversity: Studies in 20th-Century Music
Distinguished Reprints
Festschrifts
Franz Liszt Studies
French Opera in the 17th & 18th Centuries
Harmonologia: Studies in Music Theory
The Historical Harpsichord
Interplay: Music in Interdisciplinary Dialogue
The Juilliard Performance Guides
Lives in Music
Monographs in Musicology
Musical Life in 19th-Century France
North American Beethoven Studies
Opera Studies
Organologia: Instruments and Performance Practice
The Complete Works of G.B. Pergolesi
Polish Music History
RILM Retrospectives
The Sociology of Music
Studies in Czech Music
Thematic Catalogues
Vox Musicae: The Voice, Vocal Pedagogy, and Song
Wendy Hilton Dance & Music

In Memory of
Claire Brook

Cover design by Stuart Ross, drawing by Marcos Blahove

Library of Congress Cataloging-in-Publication Data

Copland, Aaron, 1900-1990.
The complete Copland / by Aaron Copland and Vivian Perlis.
p. cm. -- (Pendragon Press musicological series)
Includes bibliographical references and index.
ISBN 978-1-57647-190-6 (alk. paper)
1. Copland, Aaron, 1900-1990. 2. Composers--United States--Biography. I. Perlis, Vivian. II. Title.
ML410.C756A3 2012
780.92--dc23
[B]
2012013998

CONTENTS

A NOTE TO THE READER

by

Vivian Perlis

The Complete Copland presents the life of this exceptional twentieth-century American composer in one volume, updating the original autobiography that appeared in two volumes in 1984 and 1989. Copland's life and career had a natural flow that followed the rapid and turbulent changes in what came to be called "the American Century." He did not experience a dramatic mid-century reversal or an epiphany in compositional style, as might be implied by the two volume format. (Inevitably, readers chose *Copland Since 1943* first, followed by *Copland: 1900 to 1942*, rather than vice versa.) Now, here is a complete portrait of Copland, from beginning to end (and beyond). The format is still tri- directional: the voice of the composer as the basic text; interludes by me to set the historical scene; and voices of third parties edited to expand and enhance the picture.

The text is pure Aaron, in his own inimitable voice, edited from various sources, primarily oral history interviews made in 1975 and 1976 for Oral History of American Music (OHAM), Yale University. The testimonies of colleagues, relatives, and friends "on Copland" were made for the book publication and were donated to the Yale Music Library in 2008.

Interspersed in the text, the reader will find: a prelude, which traces the genealogy of the Copland and Mittenthal families; twelve interludes which set the historical context; and a postlude prepared for this revision that covers the period from Copland's death in 1990 and traces the life of his music since that time. Footnotes appear directly on the page, prepared and revised according to the addition of fresh data that surfaced with the passage of time.

Familiarity with Copland's papers clearly demonstrates his intention to write an autobiography. It was not only his natural frugality that led him to save letters, lecture notes, and sketches—a researcher in the Copland Collection will soon find numerous "For Autobiog" scribbled in the margins.

In "A Note to the Reader" in 1984, Copland wrote: "My idea was not so much to present a personal memoir as to tell the story of American music as I experienced it in my lifetime." It is an extraordinary story as told by one of the great creative figures in American history.

PRELUDE:
THE MITTENTHALS AND THE COPLANDS

In the world of music, "Aaron" means only one person. But in the Copland family, the name was not so exclusive. A younger cousin, Aaron Levine, lived with the Coplands for several years, so there were "Little Aaron" and "Big Aaron" in the house. Both boys had been named after their grandfather, Aaron Mittenthal. It is tempting to consider whether Aaron Copland had more in common with his maternal grandfather than a name. As young men, both left home to better themselves in a foreign country: in the 1920s, Aaron Copland set out from Brooklyn to further his musical education in France; many years earlier, Aaron Mittenthal left a small village on the border of Russia and Poland in search of freedom and security in America. His wife, Bertha, and four children were to follow later. The youngest of them, Sarah, would become the mother of Aaron Copland.

The Mittenthal side of the family is large and geographically widespread, but they have taken care to trace the family genealogy and to pass down stories and information from one generation to the next. It is said that Joseph Ben Ezra was the founder of the Mittenthal clan. He took the name in the 1850s when the Government of Lithuania decreed that the Jewish populace adopt surnames.[1] In English, Mittenthal means "mid- vale" or "between valley and fields," and this name was chosen because it described the countryside of Vishtinets[2] where Joseph lived with his wife, Bessie.

Three generations of Mittenthal girls have delighted in the story of Bessie's "liberation." It seems that her parents had signed a marriage contract in the traditional manner without the bride seeing the groom, and gifts were exchanged to bind the contract. When Bessie saw the man she was to marry, she refused to go through with the wedding. His family sued. At the court hearing, when the judge asked why she would not honor the contract, Bessie stood up and said, "Look at me—now, look at him!" Bessie was tall and attractive, and the groom was short and unimpressive. Bessie won the case, and the contract was broken. Then came the favorite part of the story—it turned out that Bessie had been in love with a young man named Joseph Mittenthal all the time!

Joseph and Bessie were married and had many children. The eldest was Aaron (nicknamed Archie), and next came Ephraim. These two emigrated to America first; the six younger children followed.[3] When Joseph and Bessie grew old, they came to America (between 1875 and 1880) to see all their children for one last time. They visited New York, Texas, Peoria, and many other small towns where their children had settled, before returning to Russia. Then they sold their belongings and moved to Palestine. Prior to the 1948 war, family members who traveled to Israel could visit their graves in the old cemetery in Jerusalem, but more recently, relatives have been unable to locate the Mittenthal tombstone.

It was after the American Civil War, about 1868, and before the first massive relocation of Russian Jews to America,[4] that Aaron and Ephraim Mittenthal reached New York City. With bits of information and recommendations from cousins who had preceded them, the brothers headed west and south out of New York. Aaron settled first in Chillicothe, Illinois, while Ephraim continued on to Texas. They sold dry goods off their wagons or opened small stores wherever they settled. They were Yankee peddlers, but with a difference—these were Yiddish Yankee peddlers. Settlers came from miles around just to see what a Jew looked like. When their customers were Indians, verbal exchanges must have been a unique mix of Yiddish, English, and Indian. After Aaron Mittenthal established himself in Chillicothe, he sent for Bertha, known as "Boshie," and the four children. Sarah was then six or seven, young enough so that she grew up with no trace of a foreign accent. The family lived in Chillicothe for about two years, where a fifth child was born. Then they moved on to Peoria, opened another store, and had another baby. The older children attended public school in Peoria before the family moved to Texas.

In 1874 and 1875, when Aaron Mittenthal moved across the plains in his wagon, Dallas was a small town. But he settled first in the smaller village of Ladonia and then either in Graham or Jefferson before joining Ephraim in Dallas to open A. & E. Mittenthal, a large

[1] The reason was probably anti-Semitic in origin. Nicholas I was rigorous in his attempts to secularize the Jewish population.

[2] Vishtinets (Polish, Wisztyniec), a small border town in what was East Prussia, now part of Russia east of Kaliningrad (formerly Königsberg). The town is not indicated on modern maps. According to the family, half of the house in Vishtinets was in Germany, the other half in Russia.

[3] They were Jessie, Pauline, Hannah, Philip Nathan, Jacob, and Max.

[4] Only a trickle of several thousand came before 1870, about 40,000 in the 1870s, and approximately 2 million in the 1880s. See Irving Howe, World of Our Fathers, Chapter I: "Toward America" (New York: Harcourt Brace Jovanovich, 1976), 5-25.

H.S. Mittenthal store being moved from Panhandle City to Amarillo, Texas, 1889.
(H.S. was Hyman, son of Ephraim)

wholesale and retail dry-goods store.[5] There, two more children were born.[6] Aaron Mittenthal was well known in Dallas for two reasons: he was a Jew, and he hired Jesse James' brother, Frank, to work in his store. Frank James was a drawing card, but it is said that he took off with the store's profits. This may have been the reason Aaron Mittenthal pulled up stakes and returned to New York in 188.

Aaron Copland's mother, Sarah Mittenthal, born in Russia, grew up in Illinois and Texas, where cowboys and Indians were a natural part of her life. Perhaps this is at least a partial answer to that question so often asked of the composer: "How could a Jewish boy, born and raised in Brooklyn, write 'cowboy' music?" Sarah was nineteen when she came to New York City with her parents and younger siblings. (The older sisters and a brother were established by then in Texas, in Waxahachie and Dallas, and stayed on there.) The family lived first on East Broadway, and then at 413 East 122nd Street. Nathan (there were nine children in all) was born there. New York became family headquarters. Mittenthals came to visit in summers from California, Texas, Illinois, Atlanta, and other places south and west "to get away from the heat." On Friday evenings, Sabbath dinners at Boshie and Aaron Mittenthal's apartment, 939 Longwood Avenue in the Bronx, were in the Jewish tradition. Although the family was not religious in the orthodox sense, they were always proud of their heritage. Jewish holidays and Sabbath dinners served as occasions to bring the family together. Boshie continued in these customs after her husband died in 1896, before Aaron Copland was born.[7] Grandmother Mittenthal was part of Aaron Copland's young life, as she was for others of his generation, among them a cousin who remembers her well:

[5] The family has had a long and successful merchandising history in Dallas. Ephraim's daughter, Hattie, married Meyer Lichtenstein; their daughter, Minnie, married Herbert Marcus, one of the original founders (with Al Neiman) of the Neiman-Marcus store.

[6] They were named Jacob and Abraham. Copland's "Uncle Abe" became the family historian, an unofficial position assumed after Abe's death in 1954 by his son, Arnold Mittenthal.

[7] Since family opinions varied on Aaron Mittenthal's death date, a search was made at the Bureau of Vital Statistics, establishing the fact that he died 12 March 1896 at age fifty-nine.

Selma Gordon Furman[8]

I adored Aaron's Grandmother, "Tanta Boshie." She had great warmth and understanding. My part of the family lived in Atlanta and Charlotte, N.C., and she and I carried on a correspondence all during the winter months. She wrote to me in Yiddish, and I had to find someone to translate for me. We had many trips to New York to visit my mother's four sisters, and I remember the lovely times on Friday nights. Sometimes the children and mothers were away at the beach in Jersey or Long Island, and the men would all come to Grandmother's for Friday night supper—Abe, college-educated and the patriarch of the family, Sam, who lived in Texas and was a charmer, and Ben Brin, a grandson. After supper, the men did the dishes. They all adored their grandmother and took great care with her. I knew only one of her daughters—cousin Sarah, Aaron's mother.

Sarah Mittenthal was not a pretty girl. She was rather tall and very thin, a look not in style in those days. Aaron Copland clearly resembles his mother. She is described as having been somewhat reserved and formal, but with a sweet and warm nature beneath the surface. The Mittenthals consider these traits part of their Southern background. They were brought up not to shout, raise voices, or lose tempers. Copland's quiet manner is called "that Southern charm" by his mother's family. Mittenthal family members were amused by a television tribute for Copland's eightieth birthday, in which Leonard Bernstein, while rehearsing the National Symphony Orchestra in Lincoln Portrait with Aaron as narrator, told the players that if they didn't play more softly, Copland would have to shout to be heard. The composer's rejoinder was typical—"I'm not a shouter."

Music was part of Sarah's upbringing—she took piano lessons, as did her sister Lillian, and it is said that she accompanied herself as she sang the popular songs of the day. Copland does not remember his mother singing or playing the piano, but his niece, Felice Copland Marlin, recalls: "Grandma sang a song to me when I was very young about hanging Jeff Davis to a sour apple tree,"[9] and family legend has it that it was Sarah's singing of "I'll Await My Love" at a social gathering that proved irresistible to the young and dapper Harris Copland.

Harris Morris Copland, Aaron's father, was born on 15 July 1860 in Shavli,[10] a part of Russia that was then Lithuania. The family name, spelled in Russian, would have been Koplan, or in English, Kaplan. Harris was the eldest of eight children of a furrier, Sussman Alexander Kaplan, and his wife, Frieda Leahe. Had it not been for the long history of intolerance that spread over Europe from Poland in the northwest to Armenia in the southeast, Aaron Copland's father would never have come to America. But Harris, like so many young European Jewish boys faced with military conscription, felt the lure of the land of freedom and opportunity. These immigrants crossed the borders illegally—north to Amsterdam or

[8] Interview, Selma Gordon Furman with Vivian Perlis, 13 December 1979, New York City.

[9] Interview, Felice Copland Marlin with Perlis, 12 April 1981, New York City. The song was the sixth verse of "Glory! Glory! Hallelujah!" The first line is, "They will hang Jeff Davis to a tree." See Grand Army War Songs, ed. Wilson Smith (Cleveland: Brainard's Sons, 1886), pp. 54-56.

[10] Shavli (Lithuanian, Siauliai), a town in Lithuania, still has the same name.

by foot through Germany and then by sea to England or Scotland. Young Harris went first to Glasgow and then to Manchester, where he took menial jobs to earn passage for the crossing.

Harris arrived at New York Harbor in 1877, at a time when millions of homeless and penniless Russians were making a mass exodus from Europe. He was a boy of seventeen;; somehow, between Russia and America, his name became Copland.[11] Young Harris was not running away from home, nor did he intend more than a temporary absence from his family. Like many other Jewish immigrant families, the young men came first to earn enough money so that parents and younger children could follow. Some families never saw their sons again, but Harris Copland was determined to bring the entire family to America from Russia. A cousin in Brooklyn helped get him started by supplying a pushcart and a place to live. Harris was plucky and resourceful. Before long he was able to bring over his brothers and sisters one at a time, and then his parents[12] and three younger sisters. Harris helped his brothers, Abe and Alfred, to establish businesses in Brooklyn. When his sister Sadie came over, she lived in Harris's home and was married from there, and another sister, Fanny, worked in his store until she too was married. Later generations of Coplands have been puzzled at the Yiddish newspapers still in their parents' homes, but there was little extra money for school, and certainly not for the women in the family. Many of the immigrant generation never learned to read or write English.

Harris M. Copland was lively, outgoing, and good-looking. He has been described as being "all business," and it is no wonder, considering the intense competition in retail merchandising, and the work hours that stretched from nine to nine every day plus a half-day on Sunday. Later in life, Harris Copland found a second topic of conversation—his son, the famous composer. He would carry newspaper clippings in his vest pocket ready to show at a moment's notice. At family gatherings, knowing relatives would quickly move away from Harris as he reached for the reviews, but the unsuspecting were cornered and bombarded with stories of Aaron's most recent successes. "What?" Harris would exclaim in his Russian accent, "You never heard of the famous Russian conductor who is playing Aaron's music?" And the name "Koussevitzky" would fairly explode from him to the bewilderment of the captive audience.

Sarah Mittenthal, c. 1885

Harris M. Copland, c. 1890

The Copland family at the wedding of Harris' sister Sadie to H. H. Uris, 1899. Top row: the wedding couple between Harris' brothers Abe (left) and Alfred (right); center row (left to right): Harris' sister Becky Abrams, Hyman Abrams, Aaron's grandmother Frieda Kaplan, his brother Leon, Harris M. Copland, Sarah Copland, Aaron's brother Ralph; bottom row: Elsie Abrams, Aaron's sisters Laurine and Josephine

Sarah Mittenthal and Harris Copland were married on 25 October 1885 in Pythagoras Hall on Canal Street. For the first few years of their marriage they lived in an apartment near Washington Avenue and Dean Street. Ralph, their first child, was born there. This was an ordinary middle-class neighborhood with only a few other Jewish families among the predominantly Irish and Italian residents. Stationery from "H. M. Copland's Department Store" in the twenties gives the date of establishment as 1884; therefore, Harris must have had a store a year earlier and for several years after his marriage, before renting the property on the northwest corner of Washington Avenue and Dean Street from Sebastian Vollmuth,

[11] Several theories have been put forth concerning Copland's name. See Edward T. Cone, "Conversation with Aaron Copland," *Perspectives of New Music*, VI: 2 (Spring-Summer 1968), 57-72; repr. in *Perspectives on American Composers*, ed. Benjamin Boretz and Edward T. Cone (New York: W. W. Norton, 1971), 131-46.

[12] Copland's grandparents, Frieda and Sussman Kaplan, lived the rest of their lives in Brooklyn and died in their late seventies only a few months apart in 1918. They had eight sons and daughters, twenty-six grandchildren, thirty-one great-grandchildren, and eighteen great-great-grandchildren.

[13] This and all following data pertaining to Harris M. Copland's real estate interests were obtained from the City Register of Kings County, Brooklyn.

a baker, in 1890.[13] Under the terms of Copland's lease with Vollmuth, he acquired "a five-year tenure [for 626 and 628 Washington Avenue] at the yearly rate or sum of $560. . ." It was not until 1897 that Harris acquired 630 and 632 Washington Avenue, where Vollmuth put up a new building for occupancy by Copland.

In this expanded building, Aaron Copland was born. The house was above and to the side of the store, with three floors and a private entryway. On the first floor were the kitchen, dining room, and maid's room. The parlor and master bedroom were on the second floor, and the children's rooms on the third. There was little that was distinctive about the house, though a curio cabinet with a silver spoon collection sat in the dining room and a Steinway upright piano—"The glory of the household"—in the parlor.[14] The store was a typical dry-goods establishment of the times. There was a shoe section, a toy department, household items, and clothing, such as handkerchiefs and underwear. According to reports, "Corsets and ribbons were big." Vollmuth, being the neighborhood baker, specified in the 1897 lease that Copland "may underlet the whole or any part of the premises for any business except a bakery or for the sale of bread and cake." Subsequent leasing agreements were executed between the two. The store expanded and prospered and Harris acquired 771 and 773 Dean Street in 1907. From 1906 on, Copland's Department Store had a telephone; Aaron recalled the number all his life—Prospect 4666—and a horse and wagon were kept at the local livery. The Coplands were considered people of standing in the neighborhood, and the store was a source of pride to Sarah and Harris, who both worked there with a dozen employees. In April of 1980, Aaron Copland received a letter from a stranger, one John Gallagher:

> My mother and father lived at 745 Dean Street, Brooklyn, in a small row family house, a few doors short of Underhill Avenue. My mother and her mother, and indeed the whole family knew your father well. They were frequent customers at "Coplands" on Washington Ave. My mother used to relate to me how kind your father was. As an example---evidently Copland's would have some sort of a surprise sale. When the announcement was made all the customers would rush over to the counter. Your father would say, "Make room for Mrs. Gallagher. She has a large family." And he would hand goods over the heads of others to my grandmother.. . . I thought you might be interested in knowing how highly regarded your father was from some persons who knew him so well, the Gallaghers, your old neighbors from the dusty but lovely past in Brooklyn. . I remember one time standing at the front basement window in my mother's house. A young boy was walking past the door. He was dressed in black and had a black case under his arm. My mother said, "That's young Aaron Copland. He's studying music in New York. . .

In 1898, when Aaron's aunt Sadie married Harris H. Uris, Grandmother Kaplan came over from Europe for a visit, and soon afterward she returned for good with her husband and the three youngest girls. Harris H. Uris was known as "H.H." in the family, while Harris M. Copland was called "H.M." Sadie and H.H. lived in New York and often entertained the Brooklyn Coplands on Sunday afternoons at home or at a favorite restaurant, Pabst's, on 125th Street. The children were impressed with Sarah's unusual habit of drinking a glass

Aaron's grandmother Frieda Kaplan (1844-1916) and grandfather Sussman Alexander Kaplan (1838-1918) with their three youngest daughters (left to right): Lillian, Rose, and Fanny, 1899.

of beer in the evening. When old enough, the Uris and Mittenthal youngsters traveled to Brooklyn by streetcar to "help out" at Copland's. They were always paid for their services. They all remember that on Christmas night, after the store closed, all unsold toys were distributed among the children.[15] But for them Christmas was not a religious holiday—the celebration was one of relief that the most demanding work time of the year was over. Jewish high holy days were observed, but the regular Saturday Sabbath could not be celebrated, since Saturday was the busiest day of the week and stores were open until nine as on weeknights. "Somehow," according to Aaron Copland, "religion had to accommodate itself to the business of living, especially in neighborhoods such as ours that were not Jewish in character."

There were four or five Copland stores at various times in Brooklyn during the first decades of the century. Harris' was the largest and most successful. Another Copland's at 1794 Fulton Street was run by Fanny and her husband, Arthur Abrams. Smaller than Harris', it ran for the longest period, from 1909 to 1933. A trolley ride between stores cost five cents, and Fanny's son, Irving, recalls the trip to pick up orders made jointly or to deliver merchandise: "Aaron at age sixteen took the streetcar in the other direction to our place to teach my sister Ruth piano."[16] After Fanny Abrams became a young widow, she ran the store and supported her three children alone. Abe Copeland operated a third store. Aaron's Uncle Abe chose

[14] H. M. Copland bought a style I walnut upright with stool on 4 November 1905 for $625 (special price because previous piano was defective). Later, on 23 April 1919, he bought an O ebony grand for Aaron: 5' 10 1/2" long, for $1,050 with a $250 trade for the upright. (Information from Steinway & Sons, New York.) The grand piano was sold in 1921 when Copland was in Paris and the family left Washington Avenue.

[15] For more information, see interview, Harold Uris with Perlis, 25 November 1980, New York City.

[16] Irving Copeland, Fanny and Arthur Abrams' son, took the name Copeland as a youngster after his father died. Interview, Irving Copeland with Perlis, 7 April 1981, New York City.

this spelling, perhaps because his wife, Etta, thought it more distinguished. The result is that Aaron Copland has both Copeland and Copland relatives. Uncle Alfred Copland also acquired stores, first in Brooklyn and later in the Bronx. Alfred married Helen, a sister of Harris Uris, further tying the relationship between the two families.

It was while Aaron was in Paris that his parents sold the store. They had been considering retirement, and after the store was broken into and robbed, their decision was made. Aaron responded to this news (11 July 1921): "I have just received your letter about the robbery and the selling out.. . . I don't suppose there's much hope of recovering the goods. Still don't understand what you will do with the store if you do sell out, because the lease doesn't expire till May. . . ." Aaron heard from home that they planned a big sale. He wrote (15 July 1921): "When do you expect to be out for good?" And (27 January 1922): "The news about your intentions to sell out both businesses[17] was very thrilling but you don't give many details. What are your plans afterwards? How long do you intend to live on Washington Ave. after May 31st? How about your trip to Texas and California? What does Pop intend to occupy himself with (since one can't play pinochle all day long). . ." (15 March 1922): "I was very tickled to hear that being out of the store agrees with you so well. And I was quite

Sarah and Harris Copland in front of Copland's Department Store during the final sale before their retirement, 1922.

[17] Harris had invested in a silk business in addition to the store, probably in Manhattan, that suffered losses in the early twenties.

astounded to hear you asking my advice as to a trip to Europe. . . "(Aaron discouraged this, advising Texas and California instead.)

On 29 June 1923 Harris sublet his interests in 626-32 Washington Avenue as well as 771 and 773 Dean Street. It is not known precisely where Sarah and Harris were living when Aaron returned from Paris in 1924. They rented an apartment briefly on Prospect Place. It was not until 1926 that the name of Harris M. Copland reappeared in the telephone directory at 1745 Caton Avenue; there it remained until 1929. Although Harris had acquired a building at 1176 President Street in October of 1923, the mortgages were not secured until 1928. Sarah and Harris moved into the apartment on the ground floor and rented out those above. It was a peaceful and quiet neighborhood, and Sarah and Harris Copland might have lived there comfortably in semi-retirement had it not been for the Depression. Rents collapsed and Harris lost his savings and had trouble paying off the mortgages. After many years as a successful businessman and head of the Copland family, he was forced to borrow money from his relatives. In 1935 or 1936 Harris and his son Leon went into a "job lot" shoe business together in Manhattan.

Sarah and Harris did not discuss their financial troubles with Aaron. They were a devoted couple, and in 1935 the entire family gathered to help celebrate their fiftieth wedding anniversary. In 1937 the *Brooklyn Daily Eagle* carried an article and picture captioned: "Married 52 years, the Coplands still enjoy going out together. Climax of happiness in their wedded life is acclaim their son has won as a composer." All Harris Copland's seven brothers and sisters died in their middle years. Sarah passed away 17 July 1944 at the age of eighty-three, and Harris less than a year later, 12 February 1945 at eighty-six.

Aaron Copland, the composer, was different from the rest of the family. There had been no artists on either side, Mittenthal or Copland, nor did any follow. Although Copland's life and interests were to lead him far from the family, he never rejected or forgot them. From generations back, when relatives helped each other settle in America, the unwritten rule was for family to help family. Harris Copland had felt that responsibility when he left home as a boy. And after the Uris brothers became financially successful, they generously came to the aid of the "artist" member of the family when he was an unknown and struggling composer.

Aaron Copland, in turn, was always helpful and welcoming to family whenever and wherever he could be. A cousin, Arnold Mittenthal, remembers that Aaron played at his Bar Mitzvah party on a piano that had keys missing, and that later, Aaron wrote from Paris to advise him on his education. Cousin Madeleine Uris Friedman recalls that when she and her husband came to Paris, Aaron met them at the boat and guided them through the city.[18] For many years, at innumerable concerts and receptions, Copland, on spotting a relative, could be seen throwing up his hands in a characteristic gesture and exclaiming, "What? You here! You came all that way just to see me?" Requests from family were always acknowledged with graciousness, from signing photographs to conducting home town orchestras. (In the 1980-81 concert season, Dallas, Las Vegas, and San Diego were added to Copland's full schedule in order to please relatives anxious to show off the celebrity of the family.)

[18] Interview, Madeleine Uris Friedman with Perlis, 4 May 1981, New York City.

BROOKLYN

1900 - 1921

For a long time I harbored the pleasant notion that I was a child of the twentieth century, having been born on 14 November 1900. But some authorities claim that the twentieth century began on 1 January 1901. I calculate therefore that I spent my first forty-eight days in the nineteenth century—an alarming thought! Unlike some creative artists, I have no memory of a lonely childhood. It seems to me I was always surrounded by people. Certainly, at birth, I must have been stared at in my crib by my four considerably older siblings: Ralph, twelve, Leon, ten, Laurine, eight, and Josephine, seven. I might have been stared at more by my father and mother if they hadn't been so preoccupied with the management of the source of our livelihood: a fair-sized department store in Brooklyn, New York.

I mention the store right off because it provided the central core of our lives. It most certainly proved to be influential in the shaping of my formative years. I grew up in the midst of a larger world than would have been supplied by a mere "home." The store's "help"—as our dozen or more employees were called—and the customers themselves provided me, at times, with a wide audience at a tender age. And the family as audience was ever present, for we lived above one section of the store, being the sole occupants on three floors of a red brick tenement-style building. I hasten to add that this seemed luxurious living to me at the time, partly because I always had my own bedroom, and partly because we always had domestic help and plenty to eat. I remember comparatively little surveillance as far as growing up was concerned—everyone was too busy with their own affairs. Moreover, my guess is that by the time I came along, my parents had expended a large measure of their guiding instincts on the four older children, so that I had a sense of being on my own from an early age.

The daily routine at the store was demanding. Saturdays and Sale Days were particularly exhausting, and Christmas was the busiest time of all. I distinctly remember "helping out" in the toy department (after school hours, of course). In retrospect, it occurs to me that I was selling toys to other children at an age when I might well have been playing with the toys myself. In any event, I was always paid for working in the store—an excellent way of feeding a child's ego. In my teens I bought music with my store money. I occasionally acted as relief cashier when the regular employee was off duty. The cashier's perch was a balcony area near the ceiling from which one could survey most of the premises. Cash and sales checks arrived with a bang via a system of wired "trolley cars," which gave this post a certain dramatic punch. But most important was the responsibility and trust the job implied. Artists are usually thought to be nitwits in the handling of money. No one ever accused me of that particular failing.

Both my parents were members of large families, my father being the oldest of eight children and my mother one of nine. All of my fifteen uncles and aunts were either born in the United States or brought here from abroad. Even a child could sort them out, if only because of the way they spoke—with or without a foreign accent. (I mention this detail because it may have had something to do with my later stressing the need for a specifically American speech in our serious music.) On Sundays we generally visited relations in Manhattan or the Bronx, where Grandma Mittenthal lived with her youngest son, Nathan, who married late. I particularly recall visits to our affluent branch, the Uris family, at their roomy apartment on upper Madison Avenue. When spring came, the family went on outings down Ocean Avenue to Brighton Beach in our horse and buggy (the same horse that pulled the delivery wagon on weekdays). By 1914 or thereabouts, we bought our first automobile. One felt like an absolute plutocrat riding around the neighborhood in that new gray Chalmers. Now on Sundays or holidays we were able to travel as far away as Arverne or Rockaway Beach. My older brothers Ralph and Leon drove, of course, but it was when my lively sister Laurine took the wheel that all heads turned to stare at the sight of a girl driving a car. I learned to drive the Chalmers from Laurine when I was about sixteen.

In a brief autobiographical sketch, written in 1939 at the invitation of the *Magazine of Art*,[1] I began: "I was born on a street in Brooklyn that can only be described as drab. . . ." To my surprise, the idea of a composer of so-called serious music being born on a drab street seems to have caught the fancy of many a commentator. But that was the way Washington Avenue seemed in retrospect, long after I had left it. To any boy living there it would have seemed like an ordinary Brooklyn street. There were our neighbors Vollmuth the baker, Peper the painter, Levy the butcher, the candy store man across the street from our house, the large grocery store down the block (no chain stores yet), and, of course, the corner saloon with its occasional neighborhood drunks. Culture could hardly be said to be a familiar word on our street, yet it wasn't entirely absent from the area. A ten-minute walk up Washington Avenue brings you to Eastern Parkway where you will find the Brooklyn Museum. (It was there, aged ten, that I suffered my first "cultural" shock at the sight of a nude statue.) Ten minutes in

[1] Aaron Copland, "Composer from Brooklyn," *Magazine of Art*, 32 (September 1939), 522, 523, 548, 549, 555; repr. in Aaron Copland, *Our New Music* (New York: Whittlesey House, 1941), 212-30; and in rev. edn., *The New Music: 1900-1960* (New York: W. W. Norton, 1968), 151-68.

the opposite direction from our house was the Brooklyn Academy of Music, where I heard my first symphony concert when I was sixteen. How pleasant it is to be able to point out that both the museum and the academy continue to fulfill their cultural mission on their respective sites three quarters of a century later.

Family life in the Copland household might be characterized as lively and industrious; there was little dawdling. My father, Harris Copland, was a strong figure in the eyes of both his family and his employees. Father was justifiably proud of what he had accomplished in the business world. But above all, he never let us forget that it was America that had made all this possible. A longtime member of the local Democratic Club, he voted a straight Democrat ticket at every election. Moreover, he depended on the club for his principal diversion: playing pinochle on many an evening with his fellow members. Once in a while he took me on an outing. I recall especially going together to the Lafayette Baths in Manhattan, topped off with an evening at Minsky's Burlesque!

However, I was closer to my mother. She was affectionate, and a very nice mother to have. More sensitive than my father, she had profited by the experience of bringing up the four older children, and by a seven-year hiatus before I came along. I don't know if our family doctor brought us all into the world, but Mother had great confidence when one of us was sick that all would be well once Dr. Dower arrived. Fortunately for us, she could always be depended upon to act as sympathetic intermediary when my father—referred to as "The Boss" by everyone—had to be swayed. Mother led a busy, fruitful, and sometimes hectic life between overseeing the household and helping my father in the store. If ever she was depressed or irritable, she managed to hide it well. I can only conclude that I must have inherited some of my own comparative evenness of temperament from my mother.

Because of Mother's involvement in the store, we always had a maid-of-all-work to take charge of household affairs. I remember best Lily Coombs, a native of Barbados, who stayed with us longest and left the deepest impression. Of a calm disposition, she had a gift for intuiting the underlying motives of those around her. I was a favorite of hers, and took her seriously when she would prophesy, as she did more than once: "Mr. Aaron, someday you're goin' to be swingin' in circles!" As one way of showing my appreciation for her many kindnesses, I took it upon myself to teach her daughter Ena to play the piano. When I was in Paris in the twenties, I wrote home about a soirée at Mademoiselle Nadia Boulanger's apartment attended by many famous musicians: "Tell Lil I am finally swingin' in circles!"

Another "servant girl" I particularly remember was Tessie Tevyovitch, from Hungary. It was she who was delegated to accompany me on my annual one-day spree to the Amusement Park at Coney Island. What the family never knew was that Tessie had prearranged a rendezvous with a boyfriend at the end of the Coney Island trolley line. That left me free to go off on my own for a glorious day of hair-raising rides, sideshow visits, and hot dog interludes. At the appointed time we met again at the trolley car barn for the ride home, during which, with a far-off gaze, she seemed to be lending only half an ear to my excited recital of the daring exploits of my day.

Top: Aaron with sister Josephine, 1909
Right: Aaron at age six
Above: Aaron at age two

Sometime before I was born, my parents joined Brooklyn's oldest synagogue, Baith Israel Anshei-Emes, situated at Kane and Court Streets in downtown Brooklyn.[2] On high holy days you weren't supposed to ride, and it took us about forty-five minutes to walk there. By the time I was almost thirteen and being readied with Hebrew lessons for my Bar Mitzvah, my father had been president of the synagogue for several years. By curious coincidence our rabbi, Israel Goldfarb, was himself a composer of liturgical music and the possessor of a fine baritone voice. Rabbi Goldfarb[3] was a sensitive human being and an effective leader of his congregation. The part of my Bar Mitzvah I recall most vividly was the banquet—it actually took place in the store! Relatives came from near and far. The merchandise was moved away and an area cleared where we could set up tables. Religious observance in the Copland family was mostly a matter of conventional participation rather than a deep commitment to other-worldly experience. Despite this, one very solemn moment remains vivid in my memory: on Yom Kippur, the Day of Atonement, the elder graybeards of the congregation stretched themselves out prone in the aisles of the synagogue and prayed for forgiveness of man's evil ways. In a lighter vein, it was the small dance bands at Jewish weddings and parties that fascinated me.

School life had begun in the usual way at age six when I was taken by my mother to be registered at Public School No. 111 at Vanderbilt Avenue and Sterling Place. Our school was situated in the midst of a "nice" neighborhood—that is to say, Sterling Place boasted rows of upper-middle-class houses with brownstone fronts. But the trouble was that in walking there I had to pass through a few blocks near St. Patrick's Catholic School on Dean Street, and that was always "dangerous territory." A Jewish boy had to watch out for himself. For whatever reason, I recall the tough trip to school, but I seem to have blotted out the eight years of grammar school attendance—teachers, fellow pupils, and all. I did my homework, moved ahead each term in the usual way, and graduated from P.S. 9 in 1914. What left a deeper impression were the summers I spent at boys' camp between 1910 and 1913. Camp Carey was situated on the shores of Lake Carey, not far from Wilkes-Barre in the mountains of Pennsylvania. It was there that I learned to swim (the guy in charge would throw me in and yell, "Swim, you son of a gun, swim!"), to row a boat, and to play tennis. The last was the only sport I was ever any good at. What I remember with special nostalgia, however, were the overnight hikes we used to take along the banks of the Susquehanna River. I can still hear the wail of the engine whistles of the seemingly endless freight trains on the opposite bank, jangling their way toward Chicago as we slept out under blankets on the low cliffs above the river. Many years later, in 1976, I was giving a concert in Harrisburg and saw views of what I remembered of the Susquehanna, and I stood outside to listen for those sounds I had heard as a boy. One other aspect of summer camp life I still remember with considerable pleasure. Though my record at sports was nothing to write home about, I can recall the satisfaction of being looked up to by the other boys when decisions had to be made. By my third summer at Camp Carey, "What does Aaron think?" became a familiar phrase.

[2]Founded in 1855, Baith Israel Anshei-Emes was known as Brooklyn's "Mother Synagogue."

[3]Israel Goldfarb (1880-1967) founded the School of Sacred Music of the Hebrew Union College-Jewish Institute of Religion. He is known as the father of congregational singing in synagogues.

My Uncle Alfred played the violin, but I don't recall hearing him or even seeing him with his instrument. Whatever music we heard at home was supplied either by my oldest brother, Ralph (violin), or my sister, Laurine (piano). Ralph studied with Heinrich Schradieck, a German violinist of some reputation, while Laurine had her lessons with Mrs. Schradieck. Ralph and Laurine played duets at home—mostly potpourris from operas—but their top accomplishment was a fair rendition of the Mendelssohn *Violin Concerto.* Ralph was more serious about his music than Laurine. Her piano studies were for the purpose of accompanying herself and the rest of us. I clearly recall ragtime and selections from popular shows of the day being played in the evenings at home. One song, "The Pink Lady," made a memorable impression. Music-making at home took on a glow that the development of the phonograph tended to dissipate. The only phonograph I knew about was at the home of my Mittenthal cousins at 41 Convent Avenue, and there I would sit for hours with my ear to the horn listening to popular records. Laurine, or "La," always the lively one, was a good dancer. She and Josephine tried out their latest dance steps on me. I learned them rather easily, and have enjoyed dancing ever since I was a boy.

Laurine traveled to Manhattan for singing lessons at the Metropolitan Opera School. She had access to a seat in a box at the old Met, and whenever she attended a performance, she always brought back a libretto and program for my delectation. These served their purpose when I turned seventeen or eighteen and joined the ranks of standees for performances of Carmen or Tristan at the Met. My brothers and my sister Josephine claimed that they first became aware of my showing an interest in music when I began hanging about the piano whenever Laurine was practicing, much to her annoyance. If Laurine was fifteen years old, I was seven. I used to think that my first attempts at "composition" dated from my eleventh year, but this notion was dispelled when Ralph's wife, Dorothy, whom I had known as a child, produced a letter of mine postmarked "Brooklyn, NY., April 19, 1909." Apparently I had been ill and Dorothy had sent me a present. In my thank-you letter, I am astonished to read the following passage:

> Mother said I should tell you in this letter that you made me very happy this morning when I received your cherry. I even made up a song with your name in it.
>
> I will be very pleased to sing it for you the next time I come down, which I hope will be very soon. With best love to everyone from all, I remain,
>
> Your sweetheart,
> Aaron
>
> These for yourself: X X X X X X X X X X X X X X

The letter is proof-positive that I was beginning to make up songs at age eight and a half. The first written-down notes that have survived consist of about seven measures for chorus and piano, composed when I was about eleven. At the top of the page stands the rather ambitious title: "Music for opera, *Zenatello*, Act I." Also, when I was eleven, I persuaded

In the family automobile, c. 1916 (left to right): Dorothy and Ralph Copland, Sarah Copland, Abe Copeland, Harris Copland, Charlie Marcus, and Laurine Copland

Laurine to start me off on piano lessons, and at about this time I decided to re-set *Cavalleria Rusticana.* Laurine must have brought home the libretto. Having no music paper, I drew a six-line staff and got as far as the offstage women's chorus at the start of the opera, about two pages, before giving up. I must have realized even then that opera was tough going. At about fourteen, I composed part of a song, "Lola," and copied out music by others that I could not afford to buy.[4] These feeble attempts are rather alarming to look at now. I was so naive that I didn't even know how to connect the notes! But before long, Laurine decided she had taught me everything she knew, and it was time for me to find a real piano teacher.

Mr. Leopold Wolfsohn was giving lessons to the Uris children His claim to distinction was that he was a teacher from Manhattan who spent one day a week in Brooklyn, giving lessons in a rented studio in the old Pouch Mansion at 345 Clinton Avenue. It took some convincing for my parents to agree to my piano studies—after all, they had paid for lessons for their other kids without remarkable results. But they finally agreed. It was typical that no one in the family accompanied me when I went to arrange for lessons with Mr. Wolfsohn. My parents always had a kind of basic confidence in me —"If he thinks he can do it, let him do it." Fortunately for me, Wolfsohn was a competent instructor, with a well-organized teaching method. He used the Hanon book of exercises[5] and was responsible for my debut

[4] Daniel B. Mather's research on Copland's juvenilia emphasizes the influence of popular music on the composer's oeuvre. Mather's discoveries of fresh material has resulted in two papers: "I'm on the Way to Mandalay," *American Musicological Society*, November 2008; and "Scenes from Adolescence: Aaron Copland and Tin Pan Alley," American Musicological Society, March 2011.

[5] Charles-Louis Hanon, *The Virtuoso Pianist in Sixty Exercises for the Piano for the Acquirement of Agility, Independence, Strength and Perfect Evenness in the Fingers as Well as Suppleness of the Wrist,* translated from the French by T. Baker (New York: G. Schirmer; Boston: Boston Music Co., 1900). Copland identified some exercises in his juvenilia file as "probably by Wolfsohn."

as a concert pianist, when after studying with him for three years, he invited me to take part in his annual student concert held in the spacious auditorium of the Wanamaker Department Store in downtown Manhattan.

It was ironic that my debut should have taken place in a store, of all places. The year was 1917 and the piece I was to perform was the *Polonaise in B* by Paderewski. The one memory that comes to mind in connection with my debut is that as I approached the stage to make my entrance Mr. Wolfsohn suddenly began boxing my ears and head, exclaiming excitedly: "Don't be nervous, don't be nervous!" I was taken completely by surprise and couldn't imagine what had come over him. Later, he explained that this was a well-tried expedient for taking a student's mind off his stage fright. Despite this contretemps, I think I aquitted myself well enough. In any event, I don't believe I ever really seriously considered the idea of embarking on a career as a concert pianist.

My piano debut was not my first public performance. As a child I recited poems, particularly one that was called "How Would You Like to Be a Dog?" That was spoken with great emotion. I sang in public, too, before my voice changed. I was in the Glee Club at Boys' High on Marcy Avenue, where I was enrolled during the years of piano study with Mr. Wolfsohn. Here again, as in grammar school, despite four years of attendance before

Zenatello, an opera composed at the age of eleven

ation in June of 1918, I recall very little of daily school life. I do remember that there was not much in the way of musical stimulation. Our teacher, Mr. Flint, was a joke—or so the so the students thought—and not an entertaining one. The Latin teacher, when moved to call upon me, always did so by expressively reciting a line from *Julius Caesar*: "Yon Cassius has a lean and hungry look. " An apt description, no doubt, because I was decidely tall and skinny for my age.

My fellow students made a more lasting impression on me than our instructors, perhaps because I still have the photograph of our graduating class. That helps to bring many of them to mind, especially Bob Gordon, Daniel Burns, Gus Feldman, and Frank Carroll. My marks were fairly good, but if I distinguished myself musically in any way it has left no trace. Again, it was the summers away from home that played a significant role in my development. After Camp Carey, the summer of 1915 was spent at a YMHA camp. The first half of the summer of 1916 was occupied berry-picking in Marlboro, New York, to help the war effort by replacing men who were drafted. I went with a small group from Boys' High, picked all day, and slept in the farmer's barn at night.

By August I must have needed a rest, for the family decided to send me off to spend a few weeks at the Fairmont Hotel in Tannersville, New York. This was a gathering place for well-known Jewish literary people. There I became friendly with a niece of the original owner of the hotel, Martha ("Marty") Dreiblatt. We were chums. I taught her how to canoe, and we played tennis together. At the weekly Saturday dances we were both happy to have someone to dance with, and later when we returned to Brooklyn, we occasionally went out dancing or to a show at the Orpheum vaudeville theater.[6] It was also my good fortune to meet Aaron Schaffer at the Fairmont that summer of 1916. He was my senior by seven years, a young intellectual, the son of a respected rabbi in Baltimore, and himself a student at Johns Hopkins University concentrating on French and French literature. Best of all, he was a music lover, who liked nothing better than to have me play the pieces I was studying and beginning to write. After that summer when Schaffer occasionally came to New York from Baltimore, he and Marty Dreiblatt and I would get together, and I would play my latest musical discoveries for them. (Again, there was "Big Aaron" and "Little Aaron," but this time the roles were reversed.)

The summer of 1917 was divided between more berry-picking and a job as a runner for a Wall Street brokerage firm. That job consisted of delivering stocks and bonds to other firms in the area—not too onerous except that the summer heat made it hard on the feet. Nevertheless I went back to Wall Street for a second summer in 1918, but this time I was promoted to an inside job. I looked forward to the lunch periods that year because I had come upon a basement bookstore that sold second-hand books in French. It was there that I invested in my first French book, a battered copy of Alphonse Daudet's play *Sappho*.

As near as I can calculate, it must have been during the winter of 1915-16 when I was fifteen that I came to the decision to spend my life as a musician. It was so startling an idea that I dared not share it with anyone. By this time my brother Ralph was at Columbia University, studying to become a lawyer even though he was not of the right temperament to be a successful one. My other brother Leon followed Pa into the store. But a musician? Music is so uncertain, so few reach the top, and how does one support a family on so shaky a basis? And where did you get such an idea anyway? I asked myself all these things if only because I realized I would hear them from my father sooner or later. But deep down I knew that reasonableness had nothing to do with it. The urge toward spending a life in music was irresistible.

[6] Also described in an interview, Martha Dreiblatt with Perlis, March 1981, New York City.

"Lola," a song composed by Copland at about fourteen years of age

It wasn't quite clear to me as yet what aspect of music I would concentrate on. I seem to remember drifting off from what was meant to be piano practice into improvising music of my own. When I was fifteen I composed a waltz—unfinished, but the written part makes sense. I was a mere novice, but some inner conviction led me to think that someday I might achieve my fondest hopes. In Aaron Schaffer I had a kindred artistic spirit with whom I could share my yearnings and ambitions. My first letter to him was written on the train home after the summer's vacation of 1916. My letters to him are lost, but something of their tone can be surmised from a reply Schaffer mailed me soon after he returned to Baltimore:

> If I have stimulated you just the slightest bit towards continuing in the ennobling work for which you seem now so well fitted, I feel that I have accomplished something worth while and that my

> vacation was anything but a failure. You say that your heart is full of high ideals and great ambitions. I need not tell you that I, too, have certain definite aims which might seem, to the average man, either incomprehensible or useless. . . . Young men with aesthetic qualities and aspirations have always had, and have today more than ever, a terrific battle to fight against the dogged "horse-sense" (a word I almost detest) of the everyday, work-a-day world. So that when I urge you to be firm in your resolution to enter one of the most glorious professions in the gift of God and not be deterred by the carping of small-minded people, I am only strengthening myself for the same task . . .

This was heady stuff for a youngster of sixteen! Schaffer's attitude encouraged me to believe that it was not a foolhardy ambition, this idea of mine to adopt music as a profession. We continued to correspond. My new friend advised me about literature, his own field, and at about this time I began to read voraciously, adding French literature to the Horatio Alger and Mark Twain I was already familiar with. I sat on the "stoop" in front of the store reading while the kids in the neighborhood played street games. No one seemed to think it strange.

It was at Boys' High that I came to know an aspiring young Brooklyn organist named John Kober. We met in the Glee Club. Aaron Schaffer could feed the higher reaches of my artistic aspirations, but John was right there in Brooklyn to share musical experiences by playing four-hand piano arrangements of the symphonic repertoire with me. We familiarized ourselves with the classic literature at a time when these pieces were not yet available on recordings. In a letter to John on 11 October 1917 I wrote: "The four hours was real enjoyment, playing duets together at my sister's home. The slick piano is still there."[7] The music was borrowed from the Montague Street branch of the Brooklyn Public Library. In other letters of 1917 I wrote about seeing *Boris Godunov* at the Metropolitan Opera and hearing Percy Grainger play Grieg's *Piano Concerto*. And after hearing Tchaikovsky's *Symphony No. 6,* I wrote: "Could you get the *Pathetique* for four-hands through your library? I heard the Philharmonic play it and I am sure I can now show you some beauties in it that we missed. It is perfectly ravishing. Need I say more? . . ." I arranged to meet John for a concert (18 October 1917): "I also have the program and in the musical literature that I have are included some of the numbers. These include Beethoven's *Sonata* Op. 110, a Brahms *Intermezzo*, and the Chopin *Valse* and the *Ballade in G minor*. I also have the original song from which Liszt derived the 'On Wings of Song.' It is a song by Mendelssohn and I sing it often. . . "[8] At the end of the year: "I have 4 piano pieces by my teacher [Rubin Goldmark] that I want you to hear. And this confidentially, I have just composed a song that I have not been able to sing to anyone yet, so you will be the first victim.[9] The words, written by a Belgian poet are in my opinion very stirring. . . ."

In 1916 I still had not finished a composition. I sent for a mail-order harmony course, but when I could not complete a *Capriccio* for violin and piano in 1916, I realized that in order to develop I needed a real teacher of harmony and counterpoint. Once again, my parents were good enough to agree to pay for lessons if I found the teacher. Not knowing any harmony teachers myself, I naturally asked Mr. Wolfsohn if he could recommend someone. He did—Rubin Goldmark, whose studio was at 140 West 87th Street in Manhattan. I telephoned for an appointment and at the agreed time approached the brownstone house with a certain trepidation. As I mounted the outdoor steps I noticed a sign in the first-floor window that read: Dr. Goldmark. That's reassuring, I thought to myself; if he earned a doctorate in music, he must be good. The maid who answered the doorbell ushered me into an anteroom and said that Dr. Goldmark would see me shortly. I waited as patiently as I could—so much depended on this visit. After what seemed like a long time, the double doors finally opened and a portly gentleman motioned to me to enter. When we were seated he said, "Well, what's the matter with you?" "Nothing," I replied. "I just want to study harmony." "In that case," he said, "you want to see my brother Rubin on the third floor."

Rubin Goldmark, as it turned out, proved to be an excellent teacher in the fundamentals of musical composition. He was born in New York and came from a musical family—his uncle, Karl Goldmark, was the famous Austro-Hungarian composer of operas in mid-nineteenth-century Vienna. Rubin Goldmark had studied composition at the Vienna Conservatory, and later in New York with Dvořák. The lessons he gave were clearly presented and stayed close to the subject under discussion. He used Richter's *Manual of Harmony* and *Modern Harmony in Its Theory and Practice* by Foote and Spalding.[10] Goldmark had a dry wit, and had earned a well-deserved reputation as after-dinner speaker at musical gatherings. If a student made a real boner, he was invited by Goldmark, with a twinkle in his eye, to become a member of his "Schlemiel" Club. I studied with him for four years, from the winter of 1917 to the spring of 1921. The one drawback—a serious one from my standpoint—was that he had little if any sympathy for the advanced musical idioms of the day, and frankly admitted the fact. I remember seeing on his piano in 1921 a copy of Charles Ives' extraordinary *"Concord" Sonata.*[11] I immediately asked if I could borrow the music, but Goldmark said, "You stay away from it. I don't want you to be contaminated by stuff like that." I didn't see the piece again, actually, until ten years had gone by. Moreover, I never remember his discussing the subject of nationalism or folklorism, and he certainly never suggested them to me as possible influences. Other talented musicians, George Gershwin, Leopold Godowsky II, and Frederick Jacobi studied with Goldmark during my time with him, but I had little contact with them. I don't believe I met Gershwin then, and I saw Jacobi and Godowsky only a few times.[12] I suffered from a sense of musical isolation during

[7] Correspondence from Copland to John Kober was provided by Kober. Seeing these letters in 1980, Copland commented, "I must have been trying to look artistic!"

[8] "Auf Flügeln des Gesanges."

[9] Kober admits that he did not understand Copland's harmonies, but he valued their piano sessions and missed them when his friend went to France. Interview, Kober with William Owen for Perlis, 22 April 1981, Garden City, New York.

[10] Ernst Friedrich Eduard Richter, *Manual of Harmony*, translated from the German by John Morgan (New York: G. Schirmer, 1867); Arthur Foote and Walter Spalding, *Modern Harmony in Its Theory and Practice* (Boston & New York: Arthur Schmidt, 1905).

[11] Ives compiled a list of prominent musicians, Goldmark among them, to whom he sent free copies of his *Second Piano Sonata* ("Concord, Mass., 1840-1860") in January 1921. See Ives Collection, Yale Music Library, New Haven, Connecticut.

[12] "I had my lesson right after his, and Goldmark would tell me, 'Here's this very talented fellow, really extremely musical and gifted, so I give him fugues to write and look what he brings me!' And Goldmark would show me these advanced things of Copland. . . ." For Leopold Godowsky II's memoir of Goldmark's comments on Copland, see interview with Perlis, Oral History of American Music, Yale, September 1970, Westport, Connecticut. Godowsky died 18 February 1983.

those years. Nevertheless, I have always been grateful to Goldmark for the solid basic training he gave me[13] and which accounted, I believe, for the high regard in which he was held. When the Juilliard School of Music was founded in 1924, he was named head of the Department of Composition.

After my initial winter of study we both agreed that I might do well to find a new piano teacher. My own idea was that I had absorbed about as much as I could from Mr. Wolfsohn. Goldmark advised a New York pianist named Victor Wittgenstein. I spent two winters as his student, hoping to gain some insight into the performance of a more contemporary piano repertoire, without any memorable results. Wittgenstein considered me a musical radical, and in that sense, perhaps, too much for him to handle. In any event, I moved on from Wittgenstein to a well-known piano pedagogue, Clarence Adler, and remained with him from the winter of 1919 to the spring of 1921. Mr. Adler was a cultivated and sensitive musician with broad tastes, known for the beautiful tone he drew from the instrument. From time to time his pupils gathered at his studio to perform for their friends and for one another. At one such occasion, I played the Ravel *Sonatine*. The piece was considered so unconventional as to need explanatory remarks from me. It was my first talk about a musical "modernist." Without being aware of it, I was embarking here for the first time on the role of musical commentator, which has afforded me pleasure and income ever since.

These same four years, from the fall of 1917 to the spring of 1921, represented much more to me than the study of piano, harmony, counterpoint, and form. What made them truly stimulating was the sense I had of uncovering a whole cultural world outside the field of music that I gradually became aware of in my growing-up years. This sense of discovery was doubly exhilarating because, for the most part, I found it out for myself. It was at the Brooklyn Public Library on Montague Street that I made my acquaintance with Sigmund Freud, Havelock Ellis, Romain Rolland's *Jean Christophe*, and Walt Whitman's *I Hear America Singing*. Reading became a passion second only to music. Along with this came a broadening of my musical horizons. I can still recall the thrill of coming upon racks of music scores in the dingy upstairs corner room at the library. And what was equally surprising was the fact that music scores, like the books downstairs, could be borrowed for study at home. I learned to orchestrate by borrowing scores from the library. When I knew I was going to hear something performed, I imagined what it would sound like, took the score to the concert, and followed it to see whether it matched what I thought I was going to hear. The difficulty was that they used to turn down the lights very often, so that you couldn't see. I remember an embarrassing incident when I was looking forward enormously to hearing Pelléas et Mélisande for the first time, and I think it was the Chicago Opera Company that came to the Brooklyn Academy of Music with a one-shot guest performance of this "odd" work. I got myself all prepared in my seat up in the gallery with a little searchlight and the score—the piano-vocal score actually, because the other one would have been way out of my price range—and I waited till all the lights went out and then quietly turned my light on. Well, I hadn't gotten beyond two pages when an usher dashed up and said, "Turn that light out, you dope! Turn that light out!," and my whole plan collapsed. That must have been around 1918.

[13] In Copland's juvenilia file are six books (undated) of studies with Goldmark. In book two, Goldmark wrote: "Avoid parallel fourths. Do not let voices be more than one octave apart. . . . the above is not good. Avoid unisons and octaves as much as possible." Also included are a fugue for four voices and a movement of a piano sonata.

Further exploration in Manhattan uncovered another unusually good music collection at the 58th Street branch of the New York Public Library, under the aegis of Miss Dorothy Lawton. She was thought to be a crotchety old character by some borrowers, but to me she couldn't have been more kind, pointing out her latest acquisitions, and on occasion putting them aside until I appeared, as she knew I would be looking for the most recent arrivals of contemporary music. These were war years and printed scores were difficult to acquire, not being exported in quantity from Europe. I found a music store on Livingston Street in Brooklyn where to my delight I could occasionally discover a piano piece by Debussy or Ravel. But my particular passion in those days was Alexander Scriabin, whose scores were practically unobtainable. That fact made them doubly cherished. Suddenly to come upon a copy of his *Vers la flamme* (1914) or the *Tenth Sonata* (1913) was an unbelievable stroke of good fortune.

During 1918, Aaron Schaffer sent me a book of poems he had published[14] (he was by then on the faculty of Johns Hopkins), and I set three of them to music: "A Summer Vacation," "Night," and "My Heart Is in the East." "Big Aaron" had written (23 May 1918) to suggest that we publish a volume of lieder together—"A splendid, foolhardy notion?" As much as Schaffer influenced my thinking in those impressionable years, he admitted to being musically conservative. Of the first of the songs I sent, he wrote, "Too much and too sudden variety? The last song captivated the entire household. Sudden changes of key and occasional discords à la Debussy and Ravel." That letter was signed "Yours in the love of poetry and music." And in June 1918, "The next thing you know we will be collaborating on an epoch-making American opera. You are blessed with a rare gift."

When Schaffer left to study at the Sorbonne in 1919, I was eager to hear about artistic life in Paris. He described his adventures at the opera and theater. From my side I wrote about what meager contemporary musical events I could find in New York. One was a recital by Leo Ornstein, considered the radical "futurist" composer, whose *Danse sauvage* was stirring up so much controversy. I can't say I knew the names of more than a handful of other contemporary American composers at the time. John Alden Carpenter and Charles Griffes stood out. I read about them and other new composers in the pages of *The Dial,* the literary avant-garde monthly of that period (published from 1880 to 1929). Their music commentator was Paul Rosenfeld, and he was considered the one to read for the most recent developments. Rosenfeld's prose style may have been too lush at times, but the important thing was that he wrote perceptively about controversial figures such as Schoenberg, Stravinsky, Ornstein, Mahler, and Sibelius.

This was also the period when I began extending my musical horizons by attending more concerts. Earlier, I had gone with Mother to hear John McCormack sing at the old

[14] Aaron Schaffer, *Selected Poems* (Boston: The Poet Lore Company; The Gotham Press, 1916).

Night, an early song set to a poem by Aaron Schaffer

Hippodrome on Sixth Avenue and 43rd Street, and Jascha Heifetz play at Carnegie Hall. The pinnacle was reached when I attended a Paderewski piano recital in a darkened hall, his head effulgent in a glow of golden hair. I went to hear Walter Damrosch and his New York Symphony performing Brahms and Wagner at Aeolian Hall in Manhattan on Sunday afternoons, or to the Boston Symphony, who came to Brooklyn on Friday nights for a series of five concerts each year. During the season of 1918-19, the French composer Henri Rabaud was at the head of the orchestra. He was an especially intriguing figure to me because his opera *Marouf* had been successfully produced only a few years before at the Opera Comique. I attended one of his Brooklyn Academy concerts with the Boston Symphony and during the course of it determined to go backstage at the end of the performance to see a real composer-conductor close up, and perhaps shake his hand. As the final chord sounded, I hurried outside to the stage entrance, but the attendant wouldn't let me in. I waited where I was until the great man emerged. At the least, I thought, I could shake his hand as he passed. But when the moment came and Maître Rabaud appeared, I lost courage and let him pass without a word or a handshake. Perhaps that explains why I tend to be kind to young aspirants who show up at the green room door after I have conducted one of my own concerts.

I decided not to go to college after high school, but to devote myself entirely to the study of music. Aaron Schaffer was concerned about my plans, for he wrote: "Do not go even temporarily into theater playing! Hold on to youthful ideals!" In the winter that followed graduation, I looked for a part-time job as a pianist in order to spare myself the embarrassment of depending on my parents for pocket and concert money. I noticed an advertisement in the *Brooklyn Daily Eagle* that the Finnish Socialist Hall in our borough needed a pianist to play for dances two nights a week in a trio consisting of violin, clarinet, and piano. I applied and landed the job; as it turned out, there were two unexpected by-products. I made my first contact with what seemed to me then to be "radical" politics, and I gained a new friend in the clarinet player, Arne Vainio. Vainio was a young intellectual who played clarinet and cello and liked to talk about books, politics, music, and poetry. He introduced me to a socialist newspaper, *The Call*.[15] It wasn't long before we were exploring the cello and piano literature together, especially the Beethoven cello sonatas. This stimulated me to write two pieces myself, thereby learning the importance of testing one's work in live performance.[16] Interspersed were discussions of socialism as a political philosophy and of Eugene V. Debs, the American Party's leader. All this, remember, was close to the events of the 1917 Russian Revolution. Coming as I did from a thoroughly bourgeois environment, I found Vainio and his contact with Finnish socialism fascinating. But there was little sympathy for radical politics at home. My father had too vivid a memory of Russian oppression to believe that any theory of socialistic government could possibly establish itself in so backward a country as Russia. Aaron Schaffer, who was a staunch Zionist, considered my friendship with Vainio downright dangerous. He was convinced that my new friend was not only radical but anti-Semitic.

[15] *The Call* was published daily in New York from 1908 to 1923.

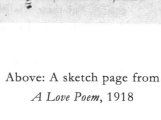

Above: A sketch page from *A Love Poem*, 1918

Left: Detail from high school graduation photograph, Copland, center

As an addition to my job as pianist at the Finnish Socialist Hall, I looked for similar employment during the summers of 1919 and 1920 in what was known as the "borscht belt" of the Catskill Mountains. In July 1919 I was employed at the White Sulphur Springs Hotel in White Sulphur Springs, New York, and in August at the Breezy Hill Hotel in Fleischmanns, New York. During July I met and played with Sidney Roof, violinist (later to become a medical doctor), and at one or the other hotel I made the acquaintance of Miss Minnie Rutenberg, aspiring pianist, who had considerable interest in my early piano pieces. The summer of 1920 was spent working as pianist at Schoharie Mansion in Elk Park, Green County, New York. But by that time my mind was elsewhere; I was dreaming of nothing less than Paris, France. Aaron Schaffer was in Paris for nine months of graduate study at the Sorbonne. "If only you could come to Paris with me," he wrote. "Wouldn't we be two happy Bohemians!"

I began to plan to join my friend in June 1920, but it turned out that Rubin Goldmark thought otherwise. To him, the sonata form was the pinnacle of our work together, and I had yet to write a fully completed four-movement sonata. He considered especially the first-movement sonata-allegro form the key to all future composition, and would not allow me to leave town without it! Reluctantly, I allowed myself to be persuaded to delay departure for a year—until June 1921. And when, finally, I went to France, Goldmark wrote to remind me (26 August 1921):

> I hope you will make some more progress in the Sonata form. Don't get to despise this, even if you should fall into the hands of some radicals. There is no preparation like it—if you once master it—for doing anything you like afterwards. . . .

I had read in the magazine *Musical America* of a plan by the French government to establish a summer school for American musicians in the Palace of Fontainebleau, a short distance from Paris. This was said to be a gesture of appreciation to America for its friendship during World War I. I was in such a rush to enroll that I was the first student to sign up and be accepted. Actually, I was one out of nine awarded scholarships. My parents were less than enthusiastic, but it was known that any well-educated musician had to have the European experience. In the past, that had meant Germany, but since the war, the focus for the arts had shifted to France. Schaffer had returned from Paris by now and taken a position at the University of Texas. When I wrote to him about Fontainebleau, he responded in December 1920: " Need I tell you my answer? You know well what it will be! Cherish the ideals you have formed and carry them away with you. . . ." I must have bombarded Schaffer with questions that he handled as best he could, about passport, hotels, bookstores, plays, restaurants, and so on. And then he wrote:

> Well, old pal, if you are leaving June 9, I am afraid we shall not see each other again for a long time. I sincerely wish for you the finest success. Be sure to write me often and keep me posted on the happenings in the Ville-Lumière. . . .[17]

[16] In Copland's juvenilia file: *Poème* (December 1918) and *Lament* (ca.1919) for cello and piano (incomplete). *Lament* makes use of a traditional Hebrew melody. Both pieces were performed by Yo Yo Ma at Tanglewood in 1981. Also dating from this period are a trio and arrangements of several Chopin *Preludes for cello and piano.*

The winter of 1920-21 in New York before leaving for France was a busy one. I was intent on reading as many books in French as I could lay my hands on; I played quantities of French music borrowed from the Brooklyn Public Library, alone, and with John Kober; and I attended as many concerts as I could afford. I had composed a Prelude for violin and piano in November of 1919; in February of 1921 I decided to try another. They seem to me to be somewhat in the style of César Franck. I had written several early songs in addition to the three settings of poems by Schaffer.[18] These were in the style of Debussy, who I thought was "hot stuff" before Scriabin and then Stravinsky took his place in my mind as the foremost modern composer. During my last months at home, I composed two songs that seem to me to show the beginnings of a musical personality, at least in terms of rhythmic feeling, frequent meter changes, and sense of form. "Pastorale" was set to a text from the Kafiristan translated by E. Powys Mathers. Its brief two pages are dated 4-12 April 1921. This and "Old Poem," dated 1920, with a text translated from the Chinese by Arthur Whaley, I took with me to France; they were performed several times during my first year abroad.

Most of my early music was for solo piano.[19] I composed sonnets and dedicated them to my friends, and my *Waltz Caprice* was a big number. It was six pages long and a show-off work, rather Lisztian and more of a virtuoso piece than anything I had composed up to then. The Sonata was dutifully finished for Goldmark before I left, and went with me to France together with a few more interesting freely written pieces. The first two of my *Trois Esquisses*[20] were composed before leaving—*Amertune* on my twentieth birthday, 14 November 1920, and *Pensif* on 8 January 1921. The third, *Jazzy*, must have been in my mind or sketched out the spring before I left for France, but it was not put to paper until Paris, 3 November 1921.

One short piano piece that was composed before leaving Brooklyn proved to be more important to my career than I could possibly have imagined at the time. *Scherzo Humoristique: Le Chat et la Souris* (*The Cat and the Mouse*) was written after a poem by La Fontaine, "Le Chat et la Souris." Considering its modern harmonies and unconventional rhythms, I decided not to show it to Goldmark. On 12 May, shortly before my departure, Goldmark's composition students honored him with a dinner party at the Restaurant Esplanade at 305 West End

[17] Aaron Schaffer died 24 February 1957, Austin, Texas.

[18] *Melancholy* (4 September 1917), subtitled "à la Debussy," text by Jeffery Farnol; *Simone* (16 September 1919), text by Rémy de Gourmont; *Music I Heard* (1920) text by Conrad Aiken.

[19] Early piano pieces include *Moment Musicale*, subtitled "a poem" (28 May 1917; *Waltz Caprice* (March 1918); *Danse Characteristique for four-hands* (1917 or 1918); and *Sonnets* I, *II, III: Sonnet I,* "*GF* (Gus Feldman); *II*, "*A.V*" (Arne Vainio) with a quotation from Aiken at the head of the page; *III*, also "*A.V.*" with a quotation from Sandburg. The first of these was removed from this series by Copland to become the second of *Three Sonnets.*

[20] Phillip Ramey gave the first performance of No. 1, *Amertune*, 22 November 1980 at "Wall-to-Wall Copland," Symphony Space, New York City; the complete *Trois Esquisses* were performed and recorded in 1981 by Leo Smit to whom they are dedicated. The pieces were published as *Three Moods* (I. *Embittered; II. Wistful; III. Jazzy*) in 1981. Sketches reveal that the group was originally planned as "four moods." Copland labeled the third of the four, *Petit Portrait,* a "supplement." The subject was a school friend, Abe Ginsburg, who, according to Copland, was "rather moody and unhappy with himself." The first three notes—A-B-E—spell his name and are heard as a motive throughout. *Petit Portrait* is published in *Aaron Copland Piano Album*, ed. Leo Smit (New York: Boosey & Hawkes, 1981).

(Above) Manuscript page, *The Cat and The Mouse*, 1920

(Right) Copland at 20 years of age

Avenue. As part of the after-dinner festivities, it was announced that we would hear several different harmonizations of a chorale, without identifying the composer. Example number three bristled with irritating dissonances. Without hesitation, Mr. Goldmark pointed an accusatory finger at me. "You are the culprit." It was a joke, of course, and we all laughed. But I have remembered it after these many years since it stamped me as the "modernist" member of the class.[21]

The news of my upcoming European venture soon spread to the outer reaches of the family. Before long I heard from my cousin, Elsie Abrams, that her husband, Dr. Morris Clurman, had a younger brother about my age who was planning to spend a year in Paris studying French civilization at the Sorbonne. We arranged to meet at Brentano's bookstore in Manhattan. We liked each other from that first encounter and agreed that it would be economically advantageous and less lonely if we shared an apartment in Paris. I was scheduled to arrive in France first, so I offered to look for suitable quarters. The shy young man's name was Harold Clurman. Our friendship started then and lasted for sixty years until his death in 1980.

[21] In June 2012, Professor Stephen Gottlieb came forth with the score and papers relating to the Goldmark dinner. Gottlieb's father, David Gottlieb, was one of Goldmark's students and was responsible for the evening's entertainment. Invitations were sent for 19 May 1921at the Restaurant Esplanade in New York City. Copland's three-line pencil score, titled "A Musical Joke," was written for the occasion, as part of the after-dinner entertainment. The author of the piece was recognized immediately by Goldmark as Copland. Steve Gottlieb, who inherited the papers from his father, sent copies of the score to Vivian Perlis, along with other items from the tribute to Goldmark, including the invitation, the menu, a list of attendees, and a signed photograph of Goldmark. Perlis suggested that Gottlieb deposit the score and papers in the Copland Collection at the Library of Congress.

FONTAINEBLEAU
SUMMER 1921

A Bord de "France"
le Fri. June 10, 1921
9:05 A.M.

Dear Ma & Pa,—

I have decided to write you a little every day and so give you an idea of life on board this boat. After I left the deck for the first time, I looked over some of the numerous presents showered upon me. Harry Brin gave me a fancy book about France, Arnold a swell wallet, and Charlie a brand new camera with plenty of films, so that you shall get plenty of pictures. I got on deck again just in time to wave good-bye to the Statue of Liberty. By that time, dinner was ready. It was very nice and I ate my share. Then I started looking for my deck chair, but I haven't found it yet. We just sit down in any chair until someone puts us out. It seems there aren't enough chairs to go around and I have been advised to get my money back. But, of course, you are anxious to know whether I am sea sick. Everyone agrees that they never saw the seas calmer, but nevertheless, I feel none too sure of myself. You know how it feels to be in the dentist's chair when he is drilling your teeth for 8 minutes. Well, the throbbing of the ship does the same to my stomach, only this is for 8 days! However, I have had no spells or mishaps and so I feel the worst is yet to come. I feel fairly perfect when I stay on deck, it is only when I go below that the foolish feeling comes on me. You can well believe that I fly down those stairs and up again as fast as my long legs can carry me. To my great surprise, I slept quite well last night.

It seems that the fourth fellow missed the boat. So we have a little spare room in that dinky little place. But even if it were a palace, you couldn't get me to *stay* down there! I have met the other two fellows and some more of the students going to Fontainebleau but I haven't felt the need for company yet, and so have been rather by myself, looking out at the sea and resting. The piano is also below deck and so out of the question. I have begun reading my French book, but feel that I can learn more by listening in on some French conversations. There are a great many Frenchmen on board, and I make it a point to speak French to the stewards and waiters, even tho they don't understand me.

Saturday: noon

Today I feel fine. The sea is like a lake and so I am just beginning to enjoy the trip. Let's hope it stays this way. This morning I and a violinist got a pass to get into the first class and played there for an hour. It certainly was a relief to get something to do. Until now the time dragged terribly, but now that I can eat and move off the deck I think things will go better. There is to be a dance this evening to help break up the monotony and then, of course, I read a great deal—I am continuing now, after having eaten my dinner. We had some soup, some omelettes with potatoes inside, some mutton chops and french fried potatoes and coffee. I also ate the whole business for the first time since Thursday noon. They also serve white and red wine at meals. I don't like the white stuff, but the red wine tastes like poor port wine. I am getting used to it. I am very lucky in being seated next to three French people, who always converse in French. One is an old priest, another a painter, and a young woman who has attended college in America. They are very nice to me and always encourage me when I try to splash some French.

Sunday: 6 P.M.

One more day gone, and still nothing but water, water everywhere. On board ship Sunday is exactly like every other day. Last night there was a very dense fog and the fog horn kept on blowing every 2 minutes. It was quite dangerous since we were right in the iceberg zone, but by tonight we shall be out of the way of those unnecessary affairs, they tell me. I have gotten thoroughly accustomed to the movement of the ship and have not been at all sick since Friday, nor do I expect to be in the future. You can just imagine how glad I am. I also sleep and eat well. Tell Lil they serve everything in a peculiar manner. Breakfast is opposite—first coffee, then eggs, and finish with oatmeal! At dinner if we have, say, green peas, they always serve them separately, and never with the meat. And then there is always the wine which everyone drinks like water, and it is little more than that. But best of all at meals are the three French people who have taken me under their care and teach me French while eating. They roar at my funny mistakes, and I learn by leaps and jumps. I spend a great deal of time with one of them, the painter, who is a man of about 30 and has been giving me the most valuable information about Paris, a fellow who reminds me of Aaron Schaffer sometimes.

Monday: 6 P.M.

I don't expect to add much to-day. Everything is about the same. Altho the sea is rougher to-day than it has been, I feel just as if I were at 628. To kill some time I took a bath to-day and so spent my first franc for soap! After putting 3 cakes in my trunk, I find that they do not supply any soap on the ship. Also, I forgot to tell you that there were handkerchiefs in my valise.

Wednesday: 9 A.M.

Well, to-day is our last day on the water, thank heavens! It was all very nice, but—! Yesterday, the sea was at its roughest, and after having decided I would never be sea sick again, I felt it worse than ever. The worst part of it was that I had promised to play a solo, and also accompany a fiddler at a concert in the first class. In spite of feeling punk, I played the solo, tho I was the only one in a room of 400 people that had no dress clothes on. Even if I had had them, I would not have been well enough to change into them. I am enclosing the program.[1] Ask Ralph to tell you who Irene Bordoni is (she was on the programme). I had the exquisite honor of being congratulated on my playing by the Captain of the ship, who is like a king here. So much for that.

We expect to arrive at Havre sometime during the night, and leave for Paris about 7 A.M. to-morrow morning. I expect, then, to go to a hotel that my friend the painter has assured me is fine. I'll mail this letter today in order that it may go off as soon as we land and write you again from Paris. You may write to me as soon as you get this letter in care of the school at Fontainebleau (Viola has the address), since by the time it gets there I will be there also. At any rate, I may send you a cablegram from Paris, as I imagine you must be anxious to hear from me by now. Well, you need never worry. If anything extraordinary should happen (like my giving a concert in Paris) why, I will cablegram to you immediately.

It is impossible for me to name everyone to whom I send my love, but spread it around generally, to yourselves, the folks, Lil and Ena and the girls in the store.

Yours for Paris,
Aaron

P.S. Give my special thanks to La and Charlie who lavished on me book, candy, shirts and camera. To-day I expect to drop Arnold and Uncle Sam a card, tip the waiter and steward. Now that the trip is almost over I can say that altho France may be a Paradise, it is H— to get there. Anyway (at times)! (Save my letters as I have decided not to bother with a diary.)

The painter was Marcel Duchamp. This meant nothing to me, despite the fact that in 1913, at the New York Armory Show, he had sent the art world into a tizzy with his Nude Descending a Staircase. Duchamp took a dim view of me trying to learn anything of importance about music, and especially the music of our time, at Fontainebleau. "Well," I said, "you're probably right, but what am I to do? Since I know absolutely no one in France, it seems like a good idea to spend two and a half months with fellow American music students in a French musical environment such as the school provides."

"Wrong—you are mistaken," said Duchamp. "It will be a waste of your time. You would do better to take your chances in Paris."

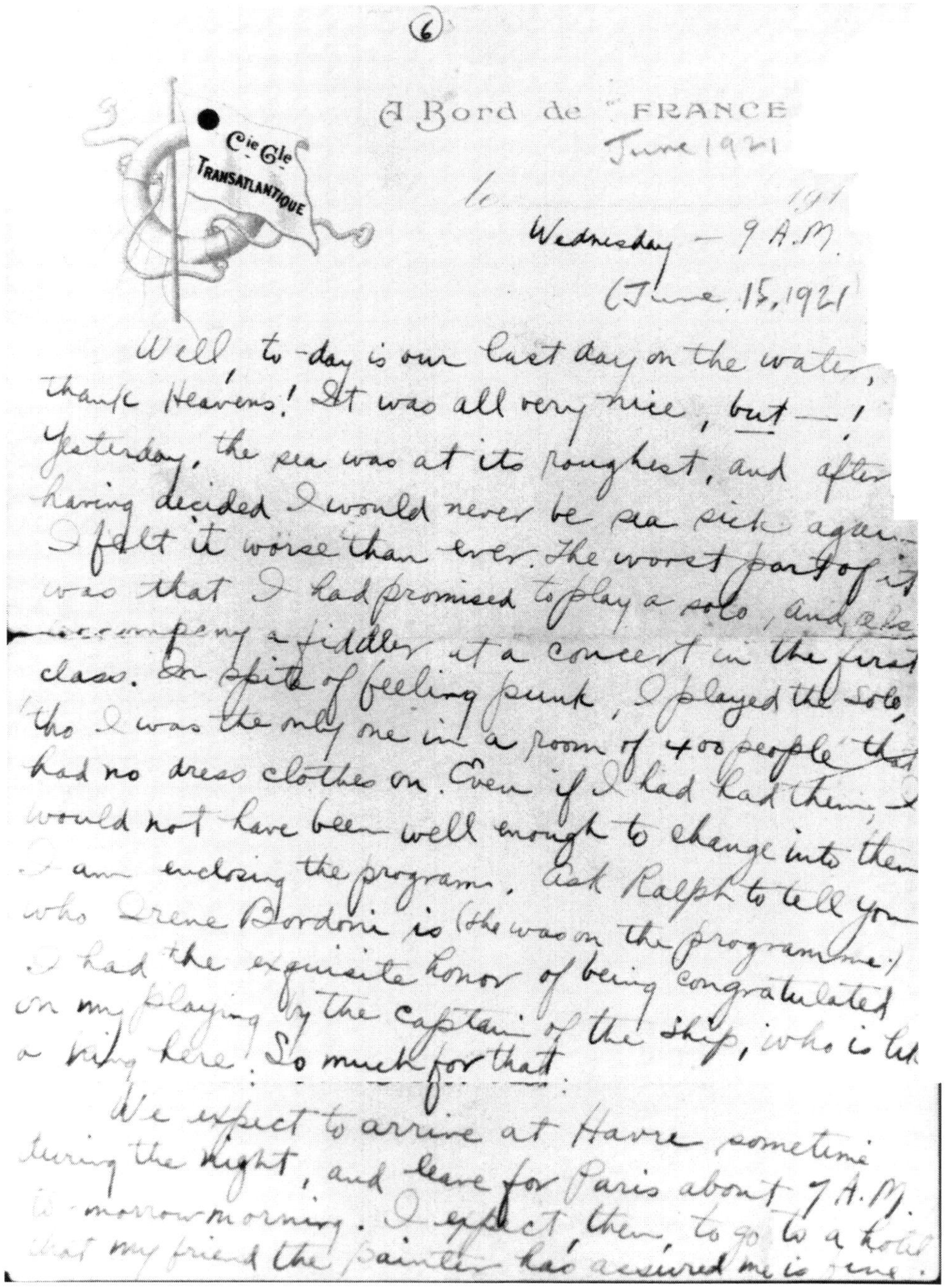

(6)

A Bord de "FRANCE"

Cie Gle Transatlantique

June 1921

Wednesday — 9 A.M.
(June 15, 1921)

Well, to-day is our last day on the water, thank Heavens! It was all very nice, but—! Yesterday, the sea was at its roughest, and after having decided I would never be sea sick again, I felt it worse than ever. The worst part of it was that I had promised to play a solo, and also accompany a fiddler at a concert in the first class. In spite of feeling punk, I played the solo, tho I was the only one in a room of 400 people that had no dress clothes on. Even if I had had them, I would not have been well enough to change into them. I am enclosing the program. Ask Ralph to tell you who Irene Bordoni is (she was on the programme.) I had the exquisite honor of being congratulated on my playing by the captain of the ship, who is like a king here. So much for that.

We expect to arrive at Havre sometime during the night, and leave for Paris about 7 A.M. to-morrow morning. I expect, then, to go to a hotel that my friend the painter has assured me is fine.

The first page of Copland's Wednesday letter home, written on shipboard

[1] Copland played the Beethoven *Sonata*, op. 90.

Duchamp was right, of course, except that he didn't know of the presence at Fontainebleau of a teacher named Nadia Boulanger. But then, neither did I. I was very impressed by Duchamp on the morning of our debarkation. We were due to land at eight. By six all the passengers, as was only natural after eight days at sea, were hanging over the rail, gazing rapturously as the coast of France slowly emerged from the fog, dim on the horizon. All the passengers, that is, except Duchamp. I still see him vividly, pipe in mouth, reclining in his deck chair, oblivous of his fellow passengers, intent on the solution of some tough chess problem. I was terribly impressed by his independence of mind.

Imagine my naiveté—arriving in Paris in mid-June without a hotel reservation! Duchamp had recommended the Hôtel Voltaire on the Quai Voltaire, and he drove there with me in a taxi, but it was full. I then headed for the Hôtel Savoy on the rue Vaugirard where Aaron Schaffer had stayed. Fortunately, they had a vacancy. The rest of that day was spent walking about town. I was the typical American tourist, impressed at how foreign everything seemed. The streets, the taxis, the sidewalk cafés, the sound of the language—so different from my high school French—all produced a certain hectic ambiance not unlike New York's East Side ghetto neighborhoods. While walking about the streets of Paris on that first day, I noticed on the billboards that there was to be a premiere performance of a new ballet by Darius Milhaud, *Les Mariés de la Tour Eiffel*, performed by the Ballet Suédois at the Théâtre des Champs Elysées the night of 19 June. Of course, I decided to go. It was a show put on by Cocteau and a group of composers called *Les Six*. The program included an overture by Georges Auric and new works by Germaine Tailleferre, Arthur Honegger, and Francis Poulenc. The audience was shocked by the modernity of the music and the fanciful nature of the production; they whistled and hooted each time the curtain descended. I recall seeing Milhaud take a bow from the stage to mixed applause and hisses. It was the perfect way to spend one of my first nights in Paris—to get right into the action, where controversial music and dance were happening.

Exciting as this first taste of Paris was, I soon wanted to get to work and found it difficult not to have a piano. The best I could do was to go to the American Women's Club to use theirs at odd hours, and I wrote home that I was ready to leave for Fontainebleau. It seems to me, rereading those first letters from France, that I must have been at least a little homesick. I reminded the folks several times to send my magazines, *The Dial* and *Musical America*, "and be sure to keep me well supplied with letters as this is a very, very long way from home." I made a habit of writing every Sunday and sending a financial report at the end of each month. I wrote to Aaron Schaffer about Cocteau and *Les Six*, but my letters to Ma and Pa tended to be more prosaic—about food and finances:

> . . . Now that I can understand the menus better, I am not forced to order only omelettes.... They never serve butter with meals anywhere, and always charge extra for it if you ask for it. They have no pies at all, and if you ask for coffee they always serve it black, no milk. Then if you are eating dinner, the waiter asks you what kind of wine you want, and if you say no wine, he looks at you as if you were drunk! . . . I find that I can eat my 3 meals a day for a little less than $1.50 including tips, wine and not stinging myself.

During my first week in Paris I saw Duchamp twice again, and he treated me to a show and dinner. On the evening of 24 July before leaving for Fontainebleau, I wrote home:

How silly Prohibition seems from Paris! All the saloons are wide open, with women standing at the bar like the men. And, don't forget this—I have never yet seen anyone drunk in Paris! Everytime I take a glass of beer here, I think of you. . . . It seems strange to think that when I am getting in bed here at 12 o'clock, you are having supper in New York. It's a funny world anyway. Affectionately, Aaron."

Fontainebleau June 25th, 1921

Dear Ma & Pa,

At last I am in Fontainebleau! Everything has turned out splendidly.

There was an autobus at the station to meet us, and we had dinner at the Palace. It certainly is a marvellous place, all surrounded by forests and woods, which are open to the public during the day. The conservatory rooms are on the ground floor, the girls live upstairs, and the boys live with French families around the town. I am living in a room for myself which I like very much. It is as big as our parlor, with 3 windows bigger than ours, is nicely furnished, has running water, and the nicest old lady to take care of me, who speaks French only, so that I am forced to learn by talking to her. I have already hired a piano (at about $5.00 a month). The house is on a very quiet street, about a 20-minute walk from the Palace, where we all eat our meals. The dinner was very good, so I don't think we'll have any trouble on that point. My trunk is going to be sent here tonight. You have no idea how good it is to feel that I am settled, at last.

To-morrow, a great all day affair is being prepared as the formal opening of the school. All the high muck-a-mucks will be here, there are to be concerts, speeches and fireworks. I really can't see why they make so much fuss. The school is really to begin on Monday. All the pupils are not here yet, as one of the boats is late.

Aaron with his landlady at 195 rue St. Merry, Fontainebleau, July 1921

I have been playing on one of the baby grands at the Palace all afternoon, and enjoyed myself immensely, after not having any piano for over 2 weeks. I have decided to study piano here also for 220 francs, (about $20) a month extra. If I don't think I'm getting my money's worth, I'll quit after a month. The piano teacher, Isadore Philipp, is very famous, and known all over Europe and America, and I think it is certainly worth the money.[2]

The town of Fontainebleau itself is very sleepy, but tries very hard to be up-to-date. They have one or two movies even. And by the way, in the Paris moving picture houses, I noticed that they advertised only American pictures, with Charles Ray and Norma Talmadge and Charlie Chaplin. I already noticed that there are a great many tourists who come here daily, to see the Palace and the Forest. And I must say, they are worth coming to see. Someday soon, I shall take my camera and get some pictures to send you.

Now I must get back to the Palace to eat supper. In the mornings I must be up at seven, so it will be a case of early to bed, early to rise. There is nothing to do here at night, anyway.

Well, I'm sure you'll be glad to hear I am so nicely settled. Love to all.

Affectionately,
Aaron

Walter Damrosch was the American founder of the school at Fontainebleau. The director in France was Francis Casadesus (the uncle of Robert and Jules, who was then about my age and who became my friend during that summer). Saint-Saens held the honorary position of general director. In later years, Fontainebleau attracted some very fine students, among them pianists Beveridge Webster, who enrolled as a teenager in 1922, and John Kirkpatrick, who was there for several summers in the twenties. But the student body that first summer of 1921 was not my dream of what a student body might be. The degree of scholarly interest was rather mild, I would say. The Americans were there partly because the school was in France, and to some, it was a pleasant way of spending a vacation in a foreign land. But after all, I also went there because I was concerned about going to France all alone, not knowing a living soul. Most of the ninety-one students like myself had never been to France, and we thought of it as an easy way of making contact with French culture, especially musical culture. But the students were friendly and called me "George" because of the fame of the pianist and Debussy specialist George Copeland. It was, as Duchamp had warned, a rather conventional school, except for the presence there of Nadia Boulanger.

Whatever reservations I had about the school, I had none about Fontainebleau itself. In fact, I fell in love with the quiet town and everything connected with it. I took great pleasure in walking in the beautiful gardens and in renting a bicycle and riding with other students through the countryside and through the Forest, coming into small ancient villages that seemed very quaint to me, considering my Brooklyn background. I was impressed with being served "real, live champagne" on Bastille Day, and with the library at the Palace. I wrote home about the forty thousand volumes of books there, all marked with a gold-leaf "N" for Napoleon, who had lived in the Palace. "It sure does give me a thrill to walk into that marvellous room (It's a block long and all decorated in gold like a ball room). They have all sorts of old books in English and French and if it wasn't for the fact that we can only go in once a week, I would never get out of there." My rented piano had arrived early in the summer. "My piano is an awful tin can," I wrote home. "I do some work on it. There are no pianos in France to compare with the Steinway. America is ahead in that, anyway."

The composition teacher was Paul Vidal, at that time about sixty years of age, who had served in that capacity for many years at the Paris Conservatoire. I had considerable difficulty understanding the French patois he spoke, but in any event it was clear from the outset that he had little or no sympathy for the contemporary musical idiom. In that respect he was not very different from Rubin Goldmark. In the midst of our studies, Maître Vidal took off for three weeks of vacation and we were assigned to his assistant, André Bloch, As it turned out, Monsieur Bloch spoke some English and displayed a certain understanding for the harmonic idiom of the day. I played *The Cat and the Mouse* for him, and a few songs that he seemed to like. Under Bloch's guidance I practiced setting songs to French words, and Jules Casadesus and I translated "Old Poem" (the title was first "Mélodie chinoise;" later, "Vieux Poème"). I worked on arrangements, such as a reduction of Brahms' Second Symphony for violin, cello, and piano. But in retrospect I can't say that the summer's compositional work was anything more than routine.[3]

During the course of the summer, we met for a few times for conducting lessons with Albert Wolff, a well-known *chef d'orchestre* at the Opéra Comique. I had been given a choice between piano instruction and conducting lessons and had chosen the latter. I wrote home to report: "I have had my first conducting lesson and enjoyed it immensely. If ever the opportunity to conduct presents itself, I won't be so green at it. . . . You ought to see me conducting an imaginary orchestra, waving my arms wildly in the air, making faces at empty chairs!" I found myself seated at meals next to a talented and charming harp student, Djina Ostrowska, and a young composer from Cleveland named G. Herbert Elwell. It wasn't long before we became good friends. (In later years Elwell served as music critic for the *Cleveland Plain Dealer.*)

Djina Ostrowska was older than the rest of us, and had come to study with the French harp virtuoso, Marcel Grandjany, who was a member of the faculty at the Paris Conservatoire. (In the thirties Ostrowska became second harpist with the New York Philharmonic, the only woman in the orchestra at that time.) It was she who first began talking to me about Nadia Boulanger, enthusing about a harmony teacher at the school. I had had several years of harmony, so, of course, I wasn't interested in further harmonic studies. It was old stuff to me. I had worked on harmony, counterpoint, and composition with Rubin Goldmark for four years. It's perfectly possible that I might never have had any contact with Nadia Boulanger at the Fontainebleau school if it were not for the enthusiasm of Ostrowska, urging me to visit Mademoiselle's harmony class. "Just go and see the way she does it." I said to her, "I've had three years of harmony. I'm not interested in harmony classes." But she repeatedly urged, "Just go and see the way she does it." So I allowed myself to be persuaded.

[2] For some reason, Copland did not study with Philipp after all.

[3] Among Copland's manuscripts are the pieces mentioned here as well as several exercise books from Fontainebleau with markings in pencil, probably by Vidal or Bloch.

I no longer recall what Mademoiselle Boulanger was doing that day, harmonically speaking, that was so striking, although I remember that the subject was *Boris Godunov*. Her sense of involvement in the whole subject of harmony made it more lively than I ever thought it could be. She created a kind of excitement about the subject, emphasizing how it was, after all, the fundamental basis of our music, when one really thought about it. I suspected that first day that I had found my composition teacher. Later in the summer, I was rather sur-

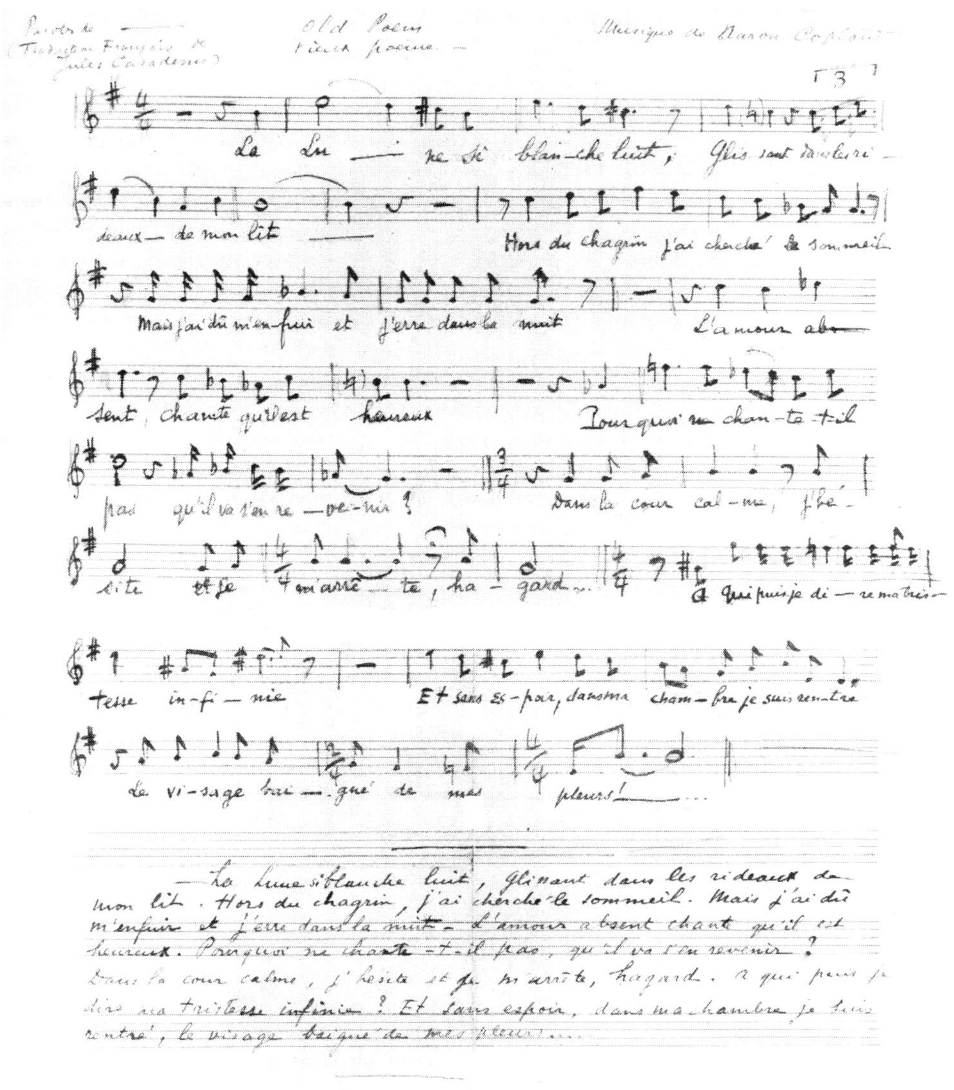

Manuscript page, "Old Poem," with words translated into French by Jules Casadesus

prised and flattered when Mademoiselle invited me with a group of her students to come to the other side of Paris for tea at her summer home in Gargenville. It felt like special attention. So I went, and that day I made the decision to study with her after returning to Paris in the fall.

By the end of July I was playing the short piano pieces that I had brought along to France with me at school concerts. I wrote home (3 August): "Sad to say, my composition made quite a hit; I say it is sad, because I can't get over the idea that if a thing is popular it can't be good." (Needless to say, I was to change that opinion!) By the end of the second month at Fontainebleau, I decided to give up my rented piano. "I have banged all the guts out of it by this time, and will thereby save about $5." By then, I had access to decent pianos in the Palace.

Harold Clurman wrote during the summer urging me to find our apartment in Paris. After a few unsuccessful and exhausting trips into the city, I began to fear that the idea might be impossible. Clurman was to sail on 14 September. His arrival was to coincide with the closing concert of the school in Paris on the twenty-third. That was to be a repeat of one at the Fontainebleau Theatre on the twenty-first, when my "Old Poem" was sung by a Miss MacAllister, and I played several piano pieces. I wrote home: "The last one is based on two jazz melodies and ought to make the old professors sit up and take notice."[4]

One of the pieces was *The Cat and the Mouse*, and the most amazing thing happened during intermission of the Fontainebleau concert. Monsieur Jacques Durand, the music publisher of Debussy, came backstage and asked me to come to see him in Paris about publishing the piece. I wrote home (27 September):

> Let me try to calmly explain to you what this means. In the first place Durand & Son is the biggest music publishing firm in Paris, which means the world. To finally see my music printed means more to me than any debut in Carnegie Hall ever could. . Don't expect me to make any fortunes out of my compositions. Composing is not a business, but a luxury, which you are so good as to allow me to afford. . . . I received a long letter from Mr. Goldmark. What would he have to say to all this!

The last week of Fontainebleau, at the end of September, was filled with excitement after the somewhat lazy and quiet summer. For one thing, just a few days before Clurman arrived, and after despairing that it would ever happen, I found an apartment. I was overjoyed because it was big enough for both of us, although by any standards modest. It was on the fourth floor at 207 Boulevard Raspail, near the Latin Quarter, exactly where I wanted to be. The rent was about $25 a month, to be split between us. After tipping and bribing the right people, I recall coming out on the street and having a wild desire to run up to every stranger I met and howl the marvelous news. I wrote home: "Please don't pronounce Raspail like Raspale, but like this—Raspighy to rhyme with skiey. . . . Now you need never worry. I shall take care of Harold and he shall take care of me. . . ."

That same week, the students at the school were "treated" to a free tour of the battlefields. This was a sobering experience in the midst of gala preparations for the closing fes-

[4] This must have been "Jazzy."

Nadia Boulanger surrounded by students at Fontainebleau (left to right):
Zo Elliott, Harrison Kerr, Copland, Melville Smith

tivities of Fontainebleau. It was terribly disturbing to see the city of Rheims in ruins and to be shown trenches, forests, barbed-wire entanglements, and cemeteries with black crosses. About this experience I wrote to Ma and Pa: "To think that man can be such a beast. One thing is sure—I am absolutely inoculated against war fever, for all time to come, and not if everybody on earth stood on their heads, would I fight in any army for any cause. I'd go to prison first. If everyone did the same there would be no war. . . ."

The apartment and the upcoming concerts quickly took my mind off such matters. It was my first opportunity to wear the tuxedo I had sent over in my trunk. To the outfit I added a hat bought in Paris for 25 francs. "It's very French and makes me look like the giraffe I am. . . ." Clurman arrived, and I met him on the evening of the Paris concert.[5] Harold used to remind me that I was introduced to the audience that evening by the ancient organist and composer Charles Widor as "un jeune compositeur americain de tendences modernes."[6] The program included songs and four piano pieces[7] that I played.

[5] The concert was at the Salle Gaveau for the benefit of the Association Nationale des Anciens Elèves du Conservatoire de Musique et de Déclamation.

Both "graduation" concerts (Fontainebleau and Paris) were well attended and gala, with newspaper announcements in advance and champagne receptions afterward. Not wanting the folks at home to think I was getting too fancy, I wrote: "Don't think I've forgotten Washington Ave. I shall certainly think of you all eating those enormous dinners on Rosh Hashona and groan at the thought of missing the marvellous cakes after the fasting is over on Yom Kippur. . . ."

The day after the Paris concert, Clurman and I returned to Fontainebleau together. Since we could not move into our Paris flat until 1 October, Clurman stayed with friends in Paris while I remained at the Palace at Fontainebleau at the invitation of Jules Casadesus. I was given a room with a good piano and had to pay only for my meals. I walked in the beautiful gardens in the evenings and "felt the presence of Napoleon's ghost." Although Duchamp had not been mistaken about Fontainebleau, it had been a special place for me in many ways. I sent the clippings from the French newspapers home, translating each for the folks, and the diploma, warning them not to bother to frame it. Then I began to pack my trunk for Paris.

[6] Interview, Harold Clurman with Perlis, 20 May 1979, New York City. Clurman died 9 September 1980.

[7] According to a review by E. Gilles in the Paris newspaper *Le Seine et Marnais* on 3 September 1921, which Copland sent to his family with a note that it was "the best" of the reviews, the pieces were *Le Chat et la Souris, Ce qu'a vu le vent d'ouest, Le Rêveur,* and "Jazzy" from *Trois Esquisses.* Copland accompanied a "Miss MacAlister" in his *Melodie Chinoise,* and in songs by Alexander Brackocky, "who had been called home suddenly." M. Gilles described Copland as "having the fine temperament of an artist...." No piece with the title *Le Rêveur* has survived. According to Copland: "It probably became something else, since I never threw anything away!" No information has been found about Miss MacAllister (Copland's spelling) or "Mac Alister" (the newspaper review).

PARIS

1921 - 1924

If there was anything wrong with being twenty in the twenties, it is being eighty in the eighties. From a musical standpoint it was a marvelous time to be alive. In exploring the artistic climate of our times, it would he difficult to exaggerate the importance of the decade 1920 to 1929. I can speak with some authority on the period because I had what might be called a front seat. Because I lived in Paris as a student for three years, from 1921 to 1924, I am able to give an eyewitness account of those incredibly interesting and fascinating years. Of course the twenties are famous! No other decade rivals their appeal. The sheer glamour of the period exerts a magic spell. The very word "modern" was exciting. The air was charged with talk of new tendencies, and the password was originality—anything was possible. Every young artist wanted to do something unheard of, something nobody had done before. Tradition was nothing; innovation everything. The publicized twenties are easy to laugh at. It was the period of the jazz age, of what Americans called the "flappers," and the time of Prohibition. We laughed then too, at all those more grotesque aspects of the twenties—the atmosphere was admittedly somewhat hysterical. But the real twenties that concerned the artist were full of activity and vitality. We profited by this sense of new things happening.

The end of every war seems to bring to artists, as well as the rest of the world, a sense of relief and renewal. The end of World War I was very different from the end of the war in the forties. We were left with no anxiety complex. The German Kaiser was really finished at the end of World War I. In most of Europe and America money and art patrons were plentiful, and there was the conviction that nothing but prosperity and good times lay ahead. I have often thought that all our preoccupations in music since then may be traced back to that period. Nothing really new, with the possible exception of electronic and computer music, has happened since. That is to say, nothing that did not have its origins during the twenties. There seemed a wealth of new voices from all parts of Europe, North and South America. Among them were two dominant musical personalities who would profoundly influence twentieth-century musical thinking: Stravinsky and Schoenberg, or, if you prefer, Schoenberg and Stravinsky. Each represented a distinct aesthetic, a different manner of composing, and a quite different way of thinking about the whole problem of the composer's art.

Paris, of course, was the center of this renewed excitement in the arts. Arriving at twenty on French soil, my expectations were dangerously high, but I was not to be disappointed. Paris was filled with cosmopolitan artists from all over the world, many of whom had settled there as expatriates. It was the time of Tristan Tzara and Dada; the time of André Breton and surrealism; it was when we first heard the names of James Joyce and Gertrude Stein, T. S. Eliot and Ezra Pound, and also of the French writers Marcel Proust and André Gide. The painters were enormously active, with Picasso taking centerstage and interesting figures like Georges Braque and Max Ernst working in Paris at that time. All kinds of artistic activities were bursting around me, and I was determined to take it all in as fast as possible.

Perhaps my three student years in France are so vivid in my memory because they had such enormous influence on my future career. Man has not yet devised a method for measuring influences on an artist—influences can be direct or indirect, positive or negative, sharp or subtle. All this notwithstanding, it was in France in the early twenties that I reached my majority, that my ideas came of age, and it was there I came to know those who were to be the major and continuing influences in my life. I speak of Nadia Boulanger, my teacher, and Serge Koussevitzky, the great Russian conductor. I cannot imagine what my career would have been without them. And of course, Harold Clurman. We were together constantly during the Paris years.

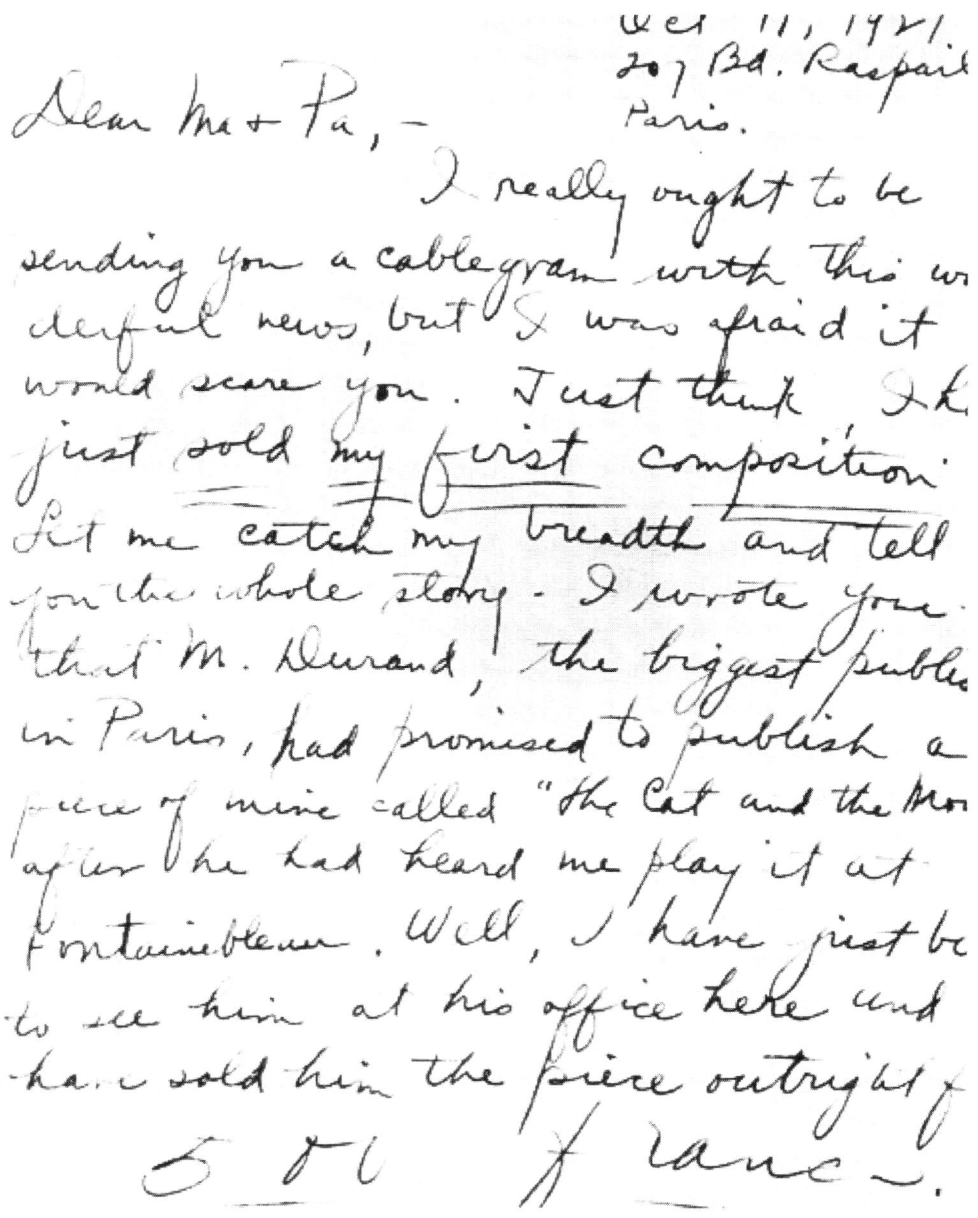
Oct 11, 1921.
207 Bd. Raspail
Paris.
Dear Ma + Pa, —
I really ought to be sending you a cablegram with this wo-
derful news, but I was afraid it would scare you. Just think I h
just sold my first composition!
Let me catch my breath and tell you the whole story. I wrote you
that M. Durand, the biggest publi
in Paris, had promised to publish a piece of mine called "The Cat and the Mo
after he had heard me play it at Fontainebleau. Well, I have just be
to see him at his office here and have sold him the piece outright f
500 francs.

The first page of a letter from Copland to his parents

Harold Clurman[1]

When I look back, it was a crumby apartment. Furnished, but not well. The bed developed bedbugs, and we had to have it fumigated. Aaron tended to be very economical. He had a great sense of the value of the dollar, which I have not. I told him, when he sold his first piece of music outright to that French publisher, that it was the only bad business deal I ever saw him make. He sold it for about 500 francs, and at that time $40 or thereabouts seemed like a fortune to him. I tended always to want to eat more luxuriously than Aaron. And I always used to complain, "I don't understand why your bill comes to less than mine." Well, it was simple. I liked to eat better and more. I was always wanting to go to more expensive places; he to less expensive ones. But we never had a real quarrel—not in all the time we've known each other. We each paid for our own meals very carefully in Paris. He would do the adding because I couldn't add. He was at that time in every way much more used to dealing with the world. We both got money from home—about $20 or $25 a week. It was enough to keep us going and we had money for concerts, plays, and books too.

I was very, very shy in those years—a fact that seems to astonish all who have known me since. Aaron was the same as now—careful, judicious, balanced. I, on the other hand, was impetuous and absolutely impractical. I'm not too practical now either. You see, Aaron was brought up by a father who was a businessman and I by a father who was at the same time a doctor and a dreamer. I can get very assertive and just yell at the top of my voice. Aaron never expressed himself that way. But when he would say very quietly, "I don't like it" about something, it was just as strong as when I yelled. He was able to find a word, one word maybe, and that's why he writes well. Finding what he's saying adequate to what he means. One of the reasons we couldn't quarrel is because I have such faith in his judgment. Anyway, he never says something is no good, only, "I don't care for it." How can you argue with that?

I would spend the days at the Sorbonne or the American Library while Aaron was in the apartment, composing and practicing. I heard certain pieces over and over again. We had lunch and dinner together every day. I'd meet Aaron after his classes with Boulanger. The first thing I'd say was, "What did you learn today?" And as nearly as he could describe it to a layman without technical knowledge of music, he would tell me what he learned. And you know he had a faculty that stood him in good stead as a teacher—making complicated matters clear. He would ask me about my classes and what I was reading. We didn't speak very much to anybody else, since we had established a great friendship and we discussed everything together. In the evenings, I took him to the theater or he took me to concerts. We were very serious about the arts, but we had a lot of fun too, going around to places like Sylvia Beach's bookstore and catching glimpses of famous writers like Hemingway, Joyce, and Pound, and seeing the composers and poets in the cafes and restaurants. When people ask, "What was Joyce like?", or Pound, or Satie, I have to laugh, thinking of us two greenhorn kids. Twenty years old we were! We were pretty well read and knew what was happening, but we didn't know anybody. We kept comparing French culture to what we didn't have at home, wondering why Americans were not as interested in the arts. In our youthful enthusiasm we talked about changing things around.

I had been to college and read a lot. Aaron respected that. He still does. One day he said, "Who is Caligula?" I told him, and he said, "That's the advantage of going to college. You know who Caligula

[1] Clurman interview.

is." Even nowadays when he is on a college campus he always says, "You know, I missed this," and he feels nostalgic about something he never had. But he made up for it. He was a good reader. Sometimes I went with Aaron to Boulanger's place when she had those teas with all the musicians, and her outspoken Russian mother was pouring tea. Aaron was pleased that Boulanger thought me intelligent. She would say, "Tell me, young friend of Copland, you who read everything . . . ." Well, I had to read a lot and to work hard to become a good writer, if I am a good writer. Aaron helped me not only learn music, but with my own writing. He'd say, "This is not bad, but what do you need this passage for?" If he didn't like something, he'd always say so. One time he said, "You know, I really learned a lot from what you wrote, but it's so badly written!" That was in 1927. And it was badly written. Later on when I got better, he'd say, "That's a good article. That's a very good article. But this whole passage is wrong." His sense of fitness, which he has in the writing of music, extended to literature. I always remember his compliments to me because he doesn't give them out injudiciously even to his best friends. Things he knew when he was twenty-one took me till I was forty to know. He said I was a late developer. Aaron knew what he wanted to be when he was fourteen, and I didn't ever know what I wanted to be. In Paris he was already composing mature pieces. I wasn't mature enough to wipe my nose. I still am not sure which I am—critic, writer, director, ladies man, or teacher! I just say I am Harold Clurman. But Aaron always knew. I don't know how he achieved it. It's like a talent for music or mathematics, that enormous balance.

Our second apartment in Paris we rented in the fall of 1922, after I had gone home for the summer and Aaron had spent a few months in Berlin. It was in a private house on the Via d'Alesia. A very nice lady who had been a singer ran it, and it was nicely located on the Left Bank. When we first saw it, Aaron said, "This is going to be too expensive." But it wasn't so expensive, and it was the most pleasant place we lived in together. Aaron's main work with Boulanger that year was the writing of a ballet. We saw a film together, called Nosferatu, *with vampires and graveyards and other gruesome things. Aaron wanted a libretto based on that, so I worked on it. That's why he dedicated* Grohg *to me. I wasn't a libretto writer, and it was a young effort by both of us. Later, Aaron dedicated his book* Copland On Music[2] *to me, and I dedicated* All People Are Famous[3] *to Aaron, since he's on almost every page.*

You ask me if Aaron ever got angry or resentful. He doesn't take time out for that. Even at the time of the McCarthy hearings, which was one thing he really felt passionately against, he only expressed his anger very briefly. When we returned together from France in 1924, and he had no money and had to play at summer hotels, he didn't seem to mind too much. He took everything in his stride. He is a man who knows about acceptance, not in the sense that others do, but a kind of metaphysical acceptance. I get stirred up and very angry and hurt about certain things, but Aaron's indignation is intellectual and unviolently expressed. Through the years I joked that he was not a dramatic character, because he didn't change much. He just got better. He got more mature. He got more knowledge. He got more experience. But his basic character never changed. Once I remember him talking about a fear of being isolated in his old age. I could see he was moved by it, but he said it just once. When I had trouble in my private life, I could talk about it and would repeat myself and repeat myself and become a big bore. Aaron was never that way.

[2] Aaron Copland, *Copland on Music* (Garden City, New York: Doubleday, 1960; repr. New York: W. W. Norton, 1963).

[3] Harold Clurman, *All People Are Famous* (New York: Harcourt Brace Jovanovich, 1974).

Copland with friends in Paris (*left to right*): Melville Smith, Copland, Clurman, and Eyvind Hesselberg

Was he ambitious, you ask? His ambition was to be a great man for himself. The only ambition I ever heard him remark on was, "I want to be remembered." We were open with each other. I would confess personal things to him, but there was nothing for him to confess. His life was not complex. He was always just what you see, not a crazy romantic fella like me. I have such a big admiration for him as a person. To me he's a great man.

After three years in Paris, we sailed home and never lived together after that. We conducted our private lives separately, but we saw a great deal of each other and always kept in touch. When Stella [Adler] and I were married, Aaron got along with her. She liked him, and he liked her. He was too smart ever to interfere when I was unhappy. But I always poured my troubles out to him, including the Group Theatre and money problems. What bothered me, I had to take money from him for a while when I needed it desperately. He got Guggenheims right away, and my affluence did not come until much later. And as I said, he knew how to save money, which I never did.

Aaron was around the Group Theatre a lot, since he was my friend, and also the conception of the Group interested him. We both knew when we returned from Europe in 1924 that we wanted to be spokesmen of our generation in American arts. I tried to do it through the Group, and Aaron tried with his Copland-Sessions Concerts and other efforts. My involvement in the Group was more political than Aaron's. I was moving pretty far to the left. Aaron was not political, but he liked the idea of sharing creative efforts and ideas. That stirred him. He was sociable, and he liked to fit in. Maybe that's why some of his music is popular. He didn't have to push to become popular. Whenever someone would ask why he wrote a particular kind of music, he'd answer, "It came out that way." It was just normal for him.

Aaron is my composer in the sense that he is part of the world I inhabit. I can understand why Nietzsche was made for Wagner. In the theater I would say that Clifford Odets was closest to the way I feel—he has a certain sense of America all through his work which is part of my sense of America and part of my experience with life. As Odets is my playwright, Copland is my composer. His world is parallel with mine.

On the reverse of this snapshot, Copland wrote to his parents:"This is my gorgeous tin pan at 207."

I lost no time after settling into our Paris apartment in going to see M. Durand about the publication of *Le Chat et la Souris*. A contract for 500 francs[4] was offered and I was delighted to sign it. It may not have been a good business deal in the long run, but it seemed wonderful to me in 1921. I felt that at least a start had been made toward a career as a professional composer; best of all, I could write home that I actually was to get paid for my music. I ended that letter (11 October): "So, we have a composer in the Copland family it seems. Who says there are no more miracles!" The proofs were promised in a few weeks, and I planned to send copies of my first published piece to the to the States before my twenty-first birthday. I began to think about how I would spend the 500 francs. But as the weeks stretched into months, and 1921 became 1922, I learned my first lesson in regard to publication dates. Never again would I announce such an event in advance! Pop had already placed an order for twenty-five copies of *The Cat and the Mouse*; what he planned to do with them was a complete mystery.

The time had come to continue my studies. On 26 October I went to 36 rue Ballu[5] to talk to Nadia Boulanger about composition lessons. As the small shaky elevator lifted me to her fourth-floor apartment, I began to have second thoughts. I knew of no other American who had ever studied advanced composition with her. In fact, I had never heard of any composer who had studied with a woman. History, for some unexplained reasons, had not yet produced a great woman composer. How was this going to sound to the folks back home? Standing alone in Mademoiselle Boulanger's imposing presence—the long dark skirt, pince-nez glasses—I was conscious of the stark differences between us: a gawky twenty-year-old from Brooklyn and the self-assured "older woman" who regularly dined with the intellectual Parisian heroes. She glanced at the sonata written for Goldmark and then asked to hear one of my other compositions. I played a short piece rooted in the jazz idiom, so modern that Goldmark earlier had confessed he didn't know what to say about it, Mademoiselle, as all her students called her, simply said, "Yes. Come. We will start tomorrow."

So began the decisive musical experience of my life, for Nadia Boulanger turned out to be one of the great music teachers of her time.[6] I wrote home:

> Now be prepared for a surprise. My teacher is not as you suppose—a man, but a woman of about 40 [she was actually 34], one of the best known musicians in France, a teacher of harmony at the Paris Conservatoire. . . . She understands the kind of modern music I like to write, so that she was the teacher I was looking for. It has been all arranged and I have a lesson on Saturday morning of each week. . . ." To soften the surprise, I added: ". . . she charges only 60 frcs. (about $4.20) a lesson, which compared with the $6.00 I paid Goldmark is not so expensive. . . .

Two other Americans found Mademoiselle at about the same time— Melville Smith and Virgil Thomson. They came to Boulanger for organ lessons, and Virgil for counterpoint as well. I believe that I was the first to study advanced composition with her. Many years later, Virgil wrote that every town in the United States could boast two things: a five-and-ten-cent store and a Boulanger student. As it turned out, he was not far from the truth. Over the years, Mademoiselle taught a host of gifted young men and women, composers and conductors of contemporary music, teachers, writers, and performers. Twentieth-century music was nurtured in her old-fashioned salon. "The composition of music cannot be taught," she used to say—then went ahead and taught it anyway. She knew everything about music—what came before Bach, Stravinsky's latest works, what came after Stravinsky, and everything in between. Technical skills—counterpoint, orchestration, sight-reading—were second nature to her. She believed in strict discipline and she worked hard herself. She might say to a student, "Come at seven," and one would not know whether to arrive in the morning or evening—both were in the range of her work day. She was profoundly committed to music. In her eyes, one had to be wholly committed. Technical mastery was to be rigorously pursued and absorbed, and essentials implanted early. There wasn't anything she couldn't do in a technical sense—read all the various music clefs with ease, play orchestral scores at the piano—all those things that are desirable for a young musician to know, she was able to do easily. She knew that unerring musicianship had to become a reflex so that the mind could be free for the art of composition. "To study music, we must learn the rules," she would say. "To create music, we must forget them." And then she might quote Stravinsky, "If everything would be permitted to me, I would feel lost in this abyss of freedom."

No one ever came to a Boulanger class late more than once; her disapproval could be annihilating. Nor was her praise lavishly given. When Mademoiselle called something good, it was a red-letter day. She never missed student concerts and could be seen applauding with the rest of the audience, but the next day she would enumerate every flaw in the performance. She could look at a score and "hear" the music in her head, understanding at once what the composer was attempting. Mademoiselle could always find the weak spot you suspected was weak in a piece, but had hoped she would not notice. She could also tell you why it was weak. Her critical faculty was unerring. Known to be difficult with those she considered untalented, she felt it her duty to be brutally honest and uncompromising. There must have been some unhappy scenes in that studio at times! I must say that I never witnessed that side of Boulanger's nature, although I do recall having to read torturously through Mahler orchestra scores at the

[4] 7.0400 cents to the franc; in 1921, 500 francs was worth $35.20.

[5] The name was later changed to 3 Place Lili Boulanger in memory of Nadia Boulanger's sister.

[6] Included in Copland's writings on Boulanger are "A Note on Nadia Boulanger," *Fontainebleau Alumni Bulletin,* 5 (May 1930); and "An Affectionate Portrait," *Harper's Magazine,* 222 (October 1960), 49-51.

piano with Mademoiselle insisting I go on to the end without stopping, no matter how slowly; this was a routine requirement of her score-reading classes.

But it was wonderful for me to find a teacher with such openness of mind, while at the same time she held firm ideas of right and wrong in musical matters. The confidence she had in my talents and her belief in me were at the very least flattering and more—they were crucial to my development at this time of my career. Mademoiselle had the sensitivity of the finest musician and the matchless gift of conveying her understanding with such enthusiasm that it made me try harder, which was all she really wanted. Having divined the depth of talent with which each of her students was endowed, she simply proposed to develop it to the full. She had an unusual method of rating her students: the poorest ones were taught on Monday. On each successive day in the week the quality improved, so that by Saturday she was teaching her best students. Then, in each category, she put the poorest students earliest each day, so everyone knew that those who came late on Saturday were Mademoiselle's favorites. I do not know exactly how she taught others; some must have sat at the organ that dominated the far end of the spacious living room of that legendary apartment. For my lessons, we both sat at one of the grand pianos, and at her command, I would prop my most recent composition on the music stand and play it for her. She did not lecture, but she would ask, over and over, "What do you hear?" And constantly searching my own heart and mind, I would play on, ending the hour exhausted, exhilarated.

It might not seem so at first, but perhaps it was an advantage that Nadia Boulanger was not herself a regularly practicing composer. Teaching came first for her; it was not something she had to do in order to free herself for something else. To what extent Mademoiselle had serious ambitions as a composer has never been entirely established. Born 16 September 1887 as Nadia Juliette Boulanger, she came from a musical milieu. Her father, Ernest Boulanger, was a composer and singing teacher at the Paris Conservatoire, and her mother, formerly the Princess Mychetsky, had been his pupil. Nadia had a few short pieces published and had aided the pianist Raoul Pugno in the orchestration of an opera. Mainly she was credited with the training of her gifted younger sister, Lili, who won the first Prix de Rome ever accorded a woman composer. Lili fell ill and died at the age of twenty-four in 1918, and Nadia mourned her the rest of her life. She told me that her dedication to teaching was in Lili's memory and therefore a sacred trust.

Mademoiselle was a very devout Catholic. Her students would sometimes joke that if you wrote a work with religious words for her, you were made. But Nadia considered personal beliefs a private matter. In all the time I knew her, I never recall any remark or discussion about religion. A biographer has accused Boulanger of anti-Semitism, and then to cover any conflicting opinion, such as my own, the writer claimed: "Her self-control was so remarkable that apparently none of her Jewish students ever noticed any tinge of anti-Semitism in her behavior."[7] Nadia's strength and self- control were indeed admirable, but being without family, she relied on her friends in times of

[7] Léonie Rosenstiel, *Nadia Boulanger: A Life in Music* (New York: W. W. Norton, 1982), 198.

Nadia Boulanger at the organ in her apartment, 36 rue Ballu, Paris, 1922

personal need and support. She and I became close friends, and there were other Jewish students who were Nadia's friends. It is impossible that one of us would not have noticed anti-Semitism in her behavior. Especially during the war years, we were very much aware of such things. I feel certain that anti-Semitism was not part of Nadia Boulanger's personality. I also find puzzling the descriptions of Nadia as masculine and dour. I must assume that they come from persons who saw her only in later years. As a young woman, she gave off a kind of reserved warmth, and there was an old-fashioned womanliness about her that was charming. She wore low-heeled, "sensible" shoes, long black skirts, and glasses, but these seemed to contrast pleasantly with her bright intelligence and lively temperament. In later years, as she became smaller and thinner, Nadia was quasi-nunlike in appearance. Her voice was distinctive—it was very low and remained extraordinarily resonant throughout her long life.[8]

It soon became clear that the teaching aspect of our relationship was not the only valuable thing for me. One must not forget that Mademoiselle's intelligence went beyond the subject of music. She was a superior person, knowledgeable about literature

[8] Nadia Boulanger died 22 October 1979 at the age of ninety-two. An international festival-conference was held on the 25th anniversary of her death in Boulder, Colorado, sponsored by the American Music Research Center.

Mademoiselle Boulanger with students, 1923 (*left to right*): Eyvind Hesselberg, unidentified, Robert Delaney, unidentified, Copland, Mario Braggioti, Melville Smith, unidentified, and Armand Marquint

and other arts. Altogether, you had the warmth of her personality, the extensive musical knowledge, and a first- class intellect. The feeling in her Paris studio was of being at the center of what was going on in the artistic life of Paris. You weren't merely studying an art that happened in the past. It was all alive, and being created around you. It was not at all unusual to find the latest score of Stravinsky on her piano, still in manuscript, or those of Albert Roussel, Milhaud, or Honegger. I discovered Mahler through Mademoiselle. How she got on to him I don't know, but she had the score for *Das Lied von der Erde* in 1922, and we pored over it together—especially the orchestration. On Wednesday afternoons she held class meetings for her students, *déchiffrage* classes, where new works were read at the piano by some bright student. They would be discussed and enthused about, or dismissed. At other times we sang Monteverdi and Gesualdo madrigals, which were virtually unperformed at that time. Also, the latest literary and artistic works were examined: Kafka, Mann, Gide, Pound. Those Wednesday afternoons became an institution. After two hours or more of music, tea and cakes were served. The musical greats came to Mademoiselle's Wednesday teas—pianists, singers, and composers—as well as students and journalists. I met Stravinsky there, Milhaud, Poulenc, and Roussel. I saw Ravel and Villa-Lobos, and on one occasion I shook hands with Saint-Saëns. He played the piano and he played well, though he was in his eighties. I came to know Nadia's French students: Jean Françaix, Annette Dieudonné, and Marcelle de Manziarly.[9] Nadia's mother always presided over the tea table, her hand shaking, but never spilling a drop. I never heard Nadia boast about her mother being of the aristocracy as has been stated in some writings about her. Madame was an ebullient type who seemed to take pleasure in shocking visitors with her outspoken language. She was very much in evidence and at times younger in behavior than her daughter. Nadia was quite proper, while her mother was rather Rabelaisian at times; their roles often seemed oddly reversed to me.

When I first knew Nadia, she was already teaching harmony at the Paris Conservatoire; she also taught organ and counterpoint at the Ecole Normale de Musique, and in summers she drove twice a week from her home in Gargenville to teach at Fontainebleau. She was second organist at the Church of the Madeleine and served on several important boards, among them the score-reading and program committees for the Société Musicale Indépendante (SMI)[10] which sponsored contests of contemporary music for little-known and unpublished composers. It was not long after our lessons began that Mademoiselle suggested a performance of my music at a December SMI concert. My songs, "Pastorale" and "Old Poem," were sung by the American tenor Charles Hubbard with Boulanger at the piano. That was my first experience of hearing my music performed by others while I sat in the audience. The concert was favorably reviewed the next day in the *Paris Herald*. Later that season, on 10 January 1922, Hubbard performed the songs again in a recital at the Salle des Agriculteurs.

I can still remember the eagerness of Nadia's curiosity concerning my rhythms in these early works, particularly the jazz-derived ones. Before long we were exploring polyrhythmic devices together—their difficulty of execution intrigued her. Mademoiselle was confident that I could write in larger forms. Within a short time she was able to extract from a composer of two-page songs and three-page piano pieces a full-sized ballet lasting over thirty minutes. At the time when I was her pupil, Boulanger had one all-embracing principle, namely, the desirability of aiming first and foremost at the creation of what she called "la grande ligne" in music. Much was included in that phrase: the sense of forward motion, of flow and continuity in the musical discourse; the feeling for inevitability, for the creating of an entire piece that could be thought of as a functioning entity. Boulanger had an acute sense of contrast and balance. Her teaching, I suppose, was French in that she stressed clarity of conception, textures, and elegance in proportion. Much has happened in music since those years, and perhaps Boulanger's theories seem outdated; but in the early twenties her musical ideas and her confidence in my ability to apply them meant a great deal to my development as a composer.

[9] Marcelle de Manziarly described Copland as she first knew him and during their continuing friendship. Interview with Perlis, 29 August 1979, Paris.

[10] Founded in 1909 by Gabriel Fauré.

Nadia Boulanger [11]

A very long time ago Copland was my student. To let him develop was my great concern. One could tell his talent immediately. The great gift is a demonstration of God. More the student is gifted, more you must be careful not to invade his self. But I hope that I did never disturb him, because then is no more to be a teacher, is to be a tyrant. And it brings nothing. He must learn to write well, read well, understand, see, pay attention, have memory trained—every obligation he has, many obligations. But he must never spoil his personality. The teacher must respect the personality of the student, and the student must submit to what makes life possible: order, rigor, and freedom. If Copland would ask of me, "Is this what you want?" I would say, "I want nothing. I want to answer your questions; I will know what you think about, what you talk about." Since 1921 we are not one year without connection. He is such a faithful human being, and today as warm as when he was a youngster. What is fascinating is to see youngsters develop—to have seen the beginning of Copland with a sense of proportion (already an accomplishment itself), and then his long development. I adore seeing the progress of the very gifted or the small progress—but some change, if only the student is ready to express himself.

I am not interested for people to know what I do or do not. I am interested in the student—to bring people to be themselves, and at the same time, know how to conform to the limits that he may find freedom. We can establish logically all the degrees of education—grammar, calculation, numbers—all that we can. But the real value is not in our hands. I have earned my living since seventeen, but there are things you penetrate only rather late in life, because more you go in life, more you touch the real expression. It is the life of the spirit that counts, but we are not in a society for that. No, it is a life of money, and you cannot avoid it. Everybody is obliged to earn his bread. I have had to earn my living in teaching, and it offends me today as it did when I started in 1904. What has been given me to think is so deep, so authentical, that I am grateful. I can explain the grammar of music, I can make a youngster see if he has any kind of gift— not to become great, but to be a little more himself, a little better, a little more understanding.

My mother was Russian; I adored her. I received much help from her, much affection from my family, my teachers, my students. My mother was not a musician, but her principle was "Have you done all what you could?" But we are so lazy! I confess that I suffer very much not to talk Russian. If for ten years I learned one word a week, I would talk Russian. Have I done it? No. I have worked very much in my life, but would I have died because I learned one word a week? I can't believe it! The greatest influence on my life was the one of my sister Lili. When she was born, I had the impression I had been honored by a responsibility that I must guide, protect her. She was six years younger than I. Very soon she was such an unbelievable personality that she became my guide. She was so pure and inaccessible to any kind of temptation. She led her life in the memory of our father, who died when Lili was six years old. She knew she was to become a composer. When she was already so sick, she said to me, "Be aware when your students will be near you, they will have the age when I quit you." She knew she was to die. I believe she was then already a great composer.

Copland and Boulanger, 1976

Generation after generation have come to me since Copland, and still talented American youngsters come. Yes, they have a certain characteristic. Also, my Japanese students. I say to them, "Don't forget you are Japanese. Remain Japanese. Then know that we exist. Feel at home in Europe. But do not lose your quality." I will have this summer two Korean students, and with them I say the same. But on the very high level, everything is either good or not good. Now, I am tired beyond words and I am sick. I never pay attention to my health, but now I have been stopped. I am glad to have the boys around me. One is fourteen years only! I forget completely when I am with them. Now tonight I write my lesson to prepare for Fontainebleau tomorrow, where I am terrified and delighted to see what I must do. I was happy to talk to you about Copland, but I cannot explain love, I cannot explain music, I cannot explain art. I feel it, but I can only explain the means employed to do what we do.

It must have been cause for profound satisfaction for Nadia that she guided the musical destiny of so many of this century's fine composers: in France, Marcelle de Manziarly, Jean Françaix, and Igor Markevitch; in England, Lennox Berkeley; in America, Walter Piston, Roy Harris, Marc Blitzstein, David Diamond, Elliott Carter, Irving Fine, Harold Shapero, Louise Talma, Arthur Berger, Easley Blackwood, and others, many of whom came to Nadia through my recommendation. We were called the "Boulangerie." I have lost track, if I ever knew, how that got started, but Nadia used the term herself in a letter to me as early as 1925. Honors and awards were bestowed on Nadia Boulanger during her lifetime, but we have no reward in this country commensurate with her contribution to our musical development. I am certain that she had the reward she most coveted—the deep affection and respect of her many pupils. Even those who were critical of her had respect for her profound musical knowledge and devotion to her art and to her students. She wanted them to do well, not out of vanity for herself, but out of the depth of her caring for them. Of course, Boulanger's insistence on discipline and reliance on traditional formulae was not right for everyone. Roy Harris said that except for the strongest musicians it was dangerous to study with Boulanger, because her own personality and talents were so strong.

My relationship with her began in 1921 as student to teacher and grew into an enduring friendship. She always helped me in every way she possibly could, and we were never out of touch with each other for long. Even now, I think of Nadia as still there in that legendary apartment on the rue Ballu where she lived for over seventy years.

[11] Interview in English. Nadia Boulanger with Perlis, Oral History of American Music, Yale. June 1976, Paris.

From my very first lessons, I sensed something special there. I soon realized that I was going to need more than one year abroad, and I convinced my parents to let me stay another year in Paris and then yet another—three in all to study with her and to absorb the unique artistic atmosphere of the times.

Very much on the scene in Paris in the early twenties was a group of composers of diverse talents who realized that they could more easily get heard as a unit than individually; they were first named *Les Six* by the critic Henri Collet. The group represented new attitudes in music and the spirit of the period. They signified the absolute end of the Germanic Brahmsian and Wagnerian approach—the one that seemed to say you had to listen to music in a very solemn and sacrosanct manner with your eyes closed and your head in your hands. They were not long-haired romantic genius types. These six, five men and one woman, were what we would call "regular guys." Francis Poulenc and Georges Auric were young, lively, full of temperament, and to me, very French. Poulenc had a charming personal gift that he knew very well how to use. There is something about his pieces that always brings to mind the joyful period in which they were written. Germaine Tailleferre was a beautiful girl who wrote a kind of post-impressionist music, and Louis Durey seemed to be standing around at the time; his early music sounded modern, but for some reason, he seceded from the group in 1923 and was not heard of again.

The two most striking composers of *Les Six* were Arthur Honegger and Darius Milhaud. Honegger was of Swiss background and closer to German music than the others. It was Milhaud who interested me most.[12] I was amazed at his verve and wit, the ease with which he turned out reams of music, and his confident and outspoken manner. When other people were thinking, "Down with Wagner!" he was the one who yelled "Down with Wagner!" He and other members of the group taunted the critics, who fought back, giving *Les Six* a great deal of notoriety and publicity.[13] Erik Satie was their musical godfather. He had a program for French music: it had to be anti-German, anti-grandiose, anti-impressionist, and even anti-impressive. Virgil Thomson, longtime admirer of Satie, has written:

> . . . during an acquaintance with it of more than forty years his music has never ceased to be rewarding. People take to Satie or they don't. . .[14]

Virgil took to him, as did others who seized on Satie's aesthetic to announce themselves free of romanticism and impressionism once and for all. I saw Satie occasionally in a restaurant in Paris. He was always alone and invariably ate with his face in his plate, casting quick glances from right to left as if he feared somebody might snatch the food away from him. He really was what the French call "un caractère." He was thought of as part mascot, part jester, part primitive, and part sage. If Satie was the spiritual godfather of *Les Six*, Jean Cocteau was their literary spokesman. His well-known pamphlet *Le Coq et l'harlequin* had in it all the shibboleths of the new day. He coined the phrase, "une musique de tous les jours," and *Les Six* insisted on that kind of music—the everyday kind that you listened to with your eyes wide open.

By far the most dynamic musical presence in France was a Russian. I still retain a vivid memory of the first time I laid eyes on Igor Stravinsky. I was walking down the rue Saint-Honoré one day in the fall of 1921 when suddenly I spied a short man approaching from the opposite direction. "Oh Lord," I thought, "that looks like Stravinsky in the flesh." I was much too overawed to dream of speaking with him, but as soon as he passed, I found myself wheeling around and following after him as if drawn by a magnet. It was a reflex action, inspired by admiration for the leading creative spirit of the new decade. I didn't tag after him for long, because I felt embarrassed at the naiveté of my behavior, but the memory of that spontaneous need to pay homage has remained with me for more than half a century. Years later I told him of my first live view of him, and we both had a good laugh about it. It was soon after that incident that I actually did meet Stravinsky in Paris at one of Mademoiselle's Wednesday afternoon classes, and I was one of the dozen or more students who stood about in awe of the Master's presence. More than once during those early years we had the privilege of examining Stravinsky's most recently completed work, even before performance and publication. Because of his close friendship with Boulanger (aided by the fact that her mother was of Russian origin), his latest opus found its way onto her piano rack. Even so, Mademoiselle always referred to him as "Mr. Stravinsky." One of her favorite students, Jean Françaix, said: "Nadia had two polestars, God and Stravinsky. Of course, no one had any objection to the first. The trouble with the second was that he was her close friend and the world's greatest living composer, so she tended to lead her students toward the Stravinsky style. . . ." It was the period of his anti-string pieces, and we examined the scores of the *Symphonies of Wind Instruments*, the *Octet*, and the *Concerto for Pianoforte and Wind Instruments*. I was fascinated to see these works in which he dispensed with strings in order to create just the kind of dry sound he was after.

For me there was no doubt that Stravinsky was the most exciting musical creator on the scene. He was the hero of my student days, and I was relieved to hear at one of Boulanger's classes that he composed at the piano as I had always done. Heading the list of Stravinsky's gifts was his rhythmic virtuosity. The ballets, *Firebird, Petrushka,* and the *Rite of Spring*, had such rhythmic power and unspoiled vigor. There was also much one could learn from Stravinsky's bold use of dissonance and his unusual instrumental combinations that projected sharply defined colors so different from the luminous, soft lines of French impressionism. I was particularly struck by the strong Russian element in his music. He borrowed freely from folk materials, and I have no doubt that this strongly influenced me to try to find a way to a distinctively American music. It was easy to see a parallel between Stravinsky's powerful Slavic rhythmic drive and our American sense of rhythmic ingenuity. The most important thing for me, though, was that Stravinsky proved it was possible for a twentieth-century composer to create his own tradition.

[12] For Copland on Milhaud, see "The Lyricism of Milhaud," *Modern Music, VI:* 2 (January-February 1929), 14-19, repr. in *Our New Music* and *The New Music* 1900-1960; and "The Art of Darius Milhaud," *Saturday Review of Literature,* 31:26 (26 June 1948), 43.

[13] Emile Vuillermoz, an influential critic, was angered by the group's contempt for Debussy and Ravel.

[14] Virgil Thomson, *Virgil Thomson* (New York: Alfred A. Knopf, 1967), 64.

Several of the new Stravinsky works were heard for the first time at the orchestral concerts organized and conducted by Serge Koussevitzky. The "Concerts Koussevitzky" took place at the Paris Opera House each spring and fall between 1920 and 1924 and attracted an international audience of the musical elite. I went to every one and sat high up in the gallery along with the other students. It was my first introduction to Koussevitzky, the conductor who would become so important to my own career. Those concerts were a unique opportunity to hear premieres and performances of contemporary works, among them the neoclassic compositions of Stravinsky that we had discussed in Boulanger's classes. These were not works one fell in love with on first hearing. Their dry sonorities and classically oriented tunes lacked surface charm. When I heard the premiere performance of the *Octet* at a Koussevitzky concert in the fall of 1923, it was a reverse shocker, even after seeing the score at Boulanger's. Its neoclassicism was a curious about-face on Stravinsky's part and indicated a surprising development that nobody could have predicted. Here was Stravinsky—who had created a neoprimitive style that everyone agreed was one of the most original in modern music—now, without any explanation, presenting a piece to the public that bore no resemblance to the style with which he had become identified! We could not have known then, in the early twenties, that Stravinsky was to persist in this neoclassic style, and that it would have so great an influence, not only in Europe, but all over the world. As always with Stravinsky, it was the power of his musical personality that carried one along. This was especially true of the *Piano Concerto* when, as at its first performance with the composer himself as soloist, he played his instrument in a markedly dry and relentless fashion; one was aware of an inner drive that was both irresistible and unforgettable. After Paris, I would see Stravinsky occasionally at concerts and dinner parties. .

Stravinsky and I corresponded occasionally through the years; we sent birthday greetings and developed an informal way with each other. Once in a while, I sent him a score. About my *Clarinet Concerto* he wrote (14 August 1950): "I want to tell you how much I love your *Clarinet Concerto* and how glad I have been to receive it from you. . ." Yet even after we began to address each other as "Cher ami," I never completely lost that awe I felt for Igor Stravinsky from the time I was a young student in Paris.

Clurman and I often went to concerts, ballets, and plays where we saw other young American students, among them, Melville Smith and Virgil Thomson. Virgil says that he never saw our "pad" in Paris,[15] but I seem to recall that he visited us. In any case, Virgil was more at home with the French crowd led by Cocteau, who frequented *Le Boeuf sur le toit,* a bar named after a Milhaud score. Although jazz was featured there, we Americans were more likely to be found around the cafés of Montparnasse and the Left Bank: Le Dome, La Coupole, or Les Deux Magots. We got to know George Antheil after he came to Paris from Berlin in 1923.[16]

[15] Interview, Virgil Thomson with Perlis, 6 June 1979, New York City.

[16] Copland's first contribution to *The League of Composers' Review* (later called *Modern Music*) was on George Antheil in "Forecast and Review," II:2 (January, 1925) 26-28.

Antheil lived with his little Hungarian wife, Boskie, in a tiny room above Shakespeare and Company, Sylvia Beach's famous bookstore at 12 rue de l'Odeon. He was much admired by Ezra Pound and James Joyce. I recall a concert in 1923 where Antheil played, and Ezra Pound, with his striking red beard much in evidence, passionately turned pages.

For me, the bookshops were even more attractive than the cafés, for it was there one might see the great artistic and literary figures of the twenties. I never went to Shakespeare and Company without a sense of excitement. For one thing, it helped me to keep in touch with what was going on back home in literature; for another, it was one of the centers where things were happening. Hemingway was around, a big presence with a surprisingly squeaky voice, and Joyce came there almost every evening at six o'clock to pick up proof sheets of *Ulysses*, which Miss Beach was publishing. One day I got up the nerve to approach him with a question about the source of some music in *Ulysses*, and he answered politely that it was a song his mother had sung when he was a boy. I bought a first edition of *Ulysses* from Miss Beach's and, unfortunately, sold it later for $40. For French books, we went across the street to La Maison des Amis des Livres, presided over by Adrienne Monnier, Sylvia Beach's partner and friend. I familiarized myself with the monthly *La Nouvelle Revue Française*, which featured French writers such as Gide and Proust, and I occasionally saw these figures at the bookshops. Harold and I felt that we were living in a very civilized atmosphere. There was much more than music going on, and we were well aware of it. In an effort to become even more a part of it all, I signed up for free classes twice a week in French literature and history at the Collège de France at the Sorbonne.

Before my twenty-first birthday on 14 November 1921, I received an avalanche of greetings from home, including a rare letter directly from Pa. I answered: "I begin to understand that half the fun in accomplishing anything is to be able to share it with others. . . . It is very nice of you to ask me what I would like for my 21st birthday. Don't you think you have already given me quite enough for a couple of birthdays?" At the end of November, I wrote: "I must tell you how very well satisfied I am with my composition teacher. She is the exact sort of instructor I needed, and knows every musician of any importance in France." On the fifteenth the student quartet I wrote at Fontainebleau was played as a competition piece for an invited audience. I sent the program home with a letter:

> I have been meeting some of the Fontainebleau students at various concerts and they all seem to be much more excited about it than I am. You understand there is only one other contestant, a Mr. [Stanley] Avery, a man of about 40, who is now in Minneapolis, so that the whole burden of the affair rests on my shoulders. By which I mean to say, that to my great disgust, I fear I am to be the center of attraction on Thursday. . . .

In my next letter I enclosed the favorable review from the *Herald* along with my own less enthusiastic description of the results:

> I need only make clear that neither I nor Mr. Avery got the "Prix de Paris" (a fancy name for a mere diploma). For reasons best known to the jury of judges, the prize was not given to anyone and we both got honorary mentions. Anyway I'm glad the whole business is

> over, since I never took any interest in it from the start. Understand that I am not at all disappointed, and that I did not need 10 judges to tell me my quartet was rotten; I knew it myself. . . [17]

Ma and Pa wanted me to continue my piano studies, probably thinking that I would have a better chance of making a living as a performer than as a composer. (I had not as yet told them that I had no intention of being a concert pianist.) In mid-December I chose Ricardo Viñes for my teacher. He was a well-known Spanish pianist who lived in Paris and played the contemporary French and Spanish repertoires. I had some idea that we need not study in the usual way—our lessons were to be a special kind of thing. Viñes, I believed, had the key to the performance of contemporary piano literature; he had introduced several works of Debussy and Ravel to the public and was known to be one of the first to understand them. He was a modest man who didn't say much, and our lessons were somewhat of a disappointment; there weren't many, and they ended when the pianist went on tour in the spring.

Meanwhile Paris was preparing for Christmas. On all the streets and boulevards were hundreds of little extra wooden shops where everything imaginable was sold. It looked like New York's Hester Street on a grand scale. I bought winter gloves and wrote home describing how the "Yiddisher Frenchman" rubbed his hands together just as I had seen merchants do on Canal Street. I thought about the family in Brooklyn, knowing it was the last Christmas for Copland's Department Store, but there was little time for nostalgia. I was preparing to leave for London on 20 December. Since Harold had decided not to go with me, I got in touch with Herbert Elwell, who had left Fontainebleau abruptly during the previous summer to live in London, and he offered to meet me at the Victoria station. After recovering from the Channel crossing—for three hours I was even more seasick than on the Atlantic—I had a fine time seeing the sights in London. There were few concerts or operas due to the Christmas season, but Elwell and I went to the ballet, and saw *The Beggar's Opera* together. When the time came to go back to Paris, I faced the return crossing with cotton in my ears, lemon in one pocket, and Mother Somebody's Pills in the other.

I am told that I began to be known that winter in Paris as "that talented young American composer." If so, it was due to Boulanger's interest in me, and the contract with Durand (I was still waiting for that piece!). At home, my family made sure that the local newspapers reported on my activities regularly, and one Sunday in December, the *Standard Union* ran an article accompanied with pictures. My response was: "I really don't know what to say about all this free advertising. . . . I suppose it's all right, and I hope you are all getting a lot of fun out of it, but I want to warn you that I'm exactly the same tall, lanky lucksh [noodle] who left America seven months ago." A student of Goldmark wrote that my old teacher was as proud of me "as a mother hen," and Alma Harwood, a patroness of music in New York, met Goldmark at a concert where he jokingly remarked that I got more for my piece from Durand than he had ever gotten for one of his. That story made the rounds. In my weekly letter home I wrote:

[17] Rough sketches toward a string quartet, dated 1921, are in Copland's files, but the complete score has never been found.

> It's sad since it shows how much serious music is worth in dollars and cents in America. But at the same time one must remember that most composers in America get royalties while most composers in Europe sell their music outright. But the long and the short of it is that there is no money to be made in composition either way. Therefore, one makes a living some other way (teaching, accompanying, concertizing and so forth).

My big news was non-musical:

> I regret to announce that I have sat the seat of my pants out! The pants of the suit that was new when I left home. When Harold made the discovery I was astounded to think of all the water that must have flowed under the Manhattan Bridge since last I went over it with those pants absolutely new!

We were often cold in our apartment that winter. Harold would pray for warm weather so that we could be comfortable without using gas. We dreaded the arrival of the gas bill and held our breath each time it came, before looking at the amount.

All Mademoiselle's pupils wrote, among other things, motets and a passacaglia. *Four Motets,* written under her instruction in 1921, were settings of biblical texts for an a cappella chorus of mixed voices. Mademoiselle had them sung in class several times, and both she and Melville Smith directed performances of the *Motets* at Fontainebleau in 1924. I think of these works as student pieces that show some influence of Moussorgsky, whom I admired. Mademoiselle conducted the *Motets* again in Paris in 1937[18] and they have recently been dug out and performed at Columbia University.[19] I agreed to the publication of the *Four Motets* with mixed emotions. While they have a certain curiosity value—perhaps people want to know what I was doing as a student—the style is not yet really mine.[20] The *Passacaglia* is a more mature work, reflecting Boulanger's insistence on disciplined writing. In my treatment of an eight-bar theme in C-sharp with eight variations, there is an emphasis on architectural structure. Perhaps because of this, the work appeared cold to some critics when it was first heard, but Mademoiselle recognized the underlying emotion in it right away. The *Passacaglia* is dedicated to her. I am told that it is not an easy piece to play. The last two variations build to such a climax that in places it was necessary to use three staves.

The *Passacaglia* was first performed in January 1923 by Daniel Ericourt at an SMI concert in Paris. I attempted an arrangement of the *Passacaglia* for orchestra in 1923

[18] On 26 January in a concert with works by Boulanger's students, among them Lennox Berkeley, Igor Markevitch, Marcelle de Manziarly, and Jean Françai s. The program lists Copland's piece as : "*Trois Motets,* a first performance."

[19] Jack Beeson, composer and friend of Douglas Moore, found pages of a Copland score among Moore's papers left to Coumbia University after his death. Beeson identified it as *Four Motets* and was responsible for a performance and publication in 1979.

[20] On 3 April 1934 one *Motet* was included in a program at the Euclid Avenue Temple on East 82nd Street and Euclid Avenue, Brooklyn. "An Evening of Hebrew Sacred and Folk Music" concluded with "Modern Compositions" by Ernest Bloch and Aaron Copland. On the program, Copland's work is called "Prayer(Motet)" and Copland is identified as "a brilliant young Jewish Composer.."

and reached the double bar, but the ending is only outlined and not complete.[21] Evidently, I decided not to finish the orchestral version—or perhaps I was only practicing orchestration. Melville Smith transcribed the *Passacaglia* for organ. He performed it, but the edition was never published. (In 1981, the organist William Owen completed Melville's work and played the organ transcription in New York.) In 1931 I was pleasantly surprised when the choreographer Helen Tamiris asked to use the *Passacaglia* for a ballet, *Olympus Americanus*, set in six parts in ancient Greece, which was first performed on 3 February that year.

I finally received *Le Chat et la Souris* from Durand in February 1922. I promptly sent copies home and to Aaron Schaffer, who asked a piano student in Texas to study and play it for him; I mailed a copy to each of my teachers Clarence Adler and Rubin Goldmark. Goldmark wrote (16 May 1922): "I think it very good—clever, musicianly and not too extreme for my tastes." Mademoiselle had written to the publisher, Maurice Senart, about my compositions, and he responded by inviting me to play for him. I arrived at the firm's offices on 7 March, and to my surprise found a committee of seven men, the entire board of Senart publishers, gathered to judge my works. I performed the *Passacaglia* and accompanied myself in three songs on the worst piano I had ever played. Everyone was very polite, arid when I finished, Senart said he would let me know by mail whether they would publish anything. He kept my compositions and then kept me waiting nervously for the decision. Eventually, the pieces were accepted. This time I would not be selling the compositions outright, but on a royalty basis of 10 percent on each copy for the first thousand and 15 percent on the second thousand. I was delighted to be published again, even though I feared that I would not make anything on "Old Poem," because I had to pay the poet $5 for the rights. I sensed that without Mademoiselle's influence these publications would not have come about. As with *The Cat and the Mouse*, she helped me prepare the works for publication.

During the winter I made plans to go to Italy for three weeks in the spring. I began to study Italian to learn the essentials. Harold was going to Berlin over Easter, and since we did not want to leave the apartment untended for long, I decided to leave for Italy by the end of March. Melville Smith went with me; he knew some Italian, and it was more fun than going alone. Melville was an enthusiastic type, even though relentlessly self-effacing. We left for Milan on 26 March. It was a twenty-four-hour train trip and in second class there were no sleeping cars, but my first glimpse of the Alps and the Italian lakes made up for any discomfort. We settled into the Grand Hotel Metropole in Milan, walked everywhere, went to La Scala twice, and then left for Rome. At the Hotel Lugano Pension Fleurie we paid 55 lire a day, or about $2.75, for a room with three full meals with lots of spaghetti. Through Boulanger's contacts, I met two young American musicians who were on scholarship, and I thought that I might follow in

On the right: The first page of a letter home, 1922

[21] This manuscript is in Copland's files at the Library of Congress.

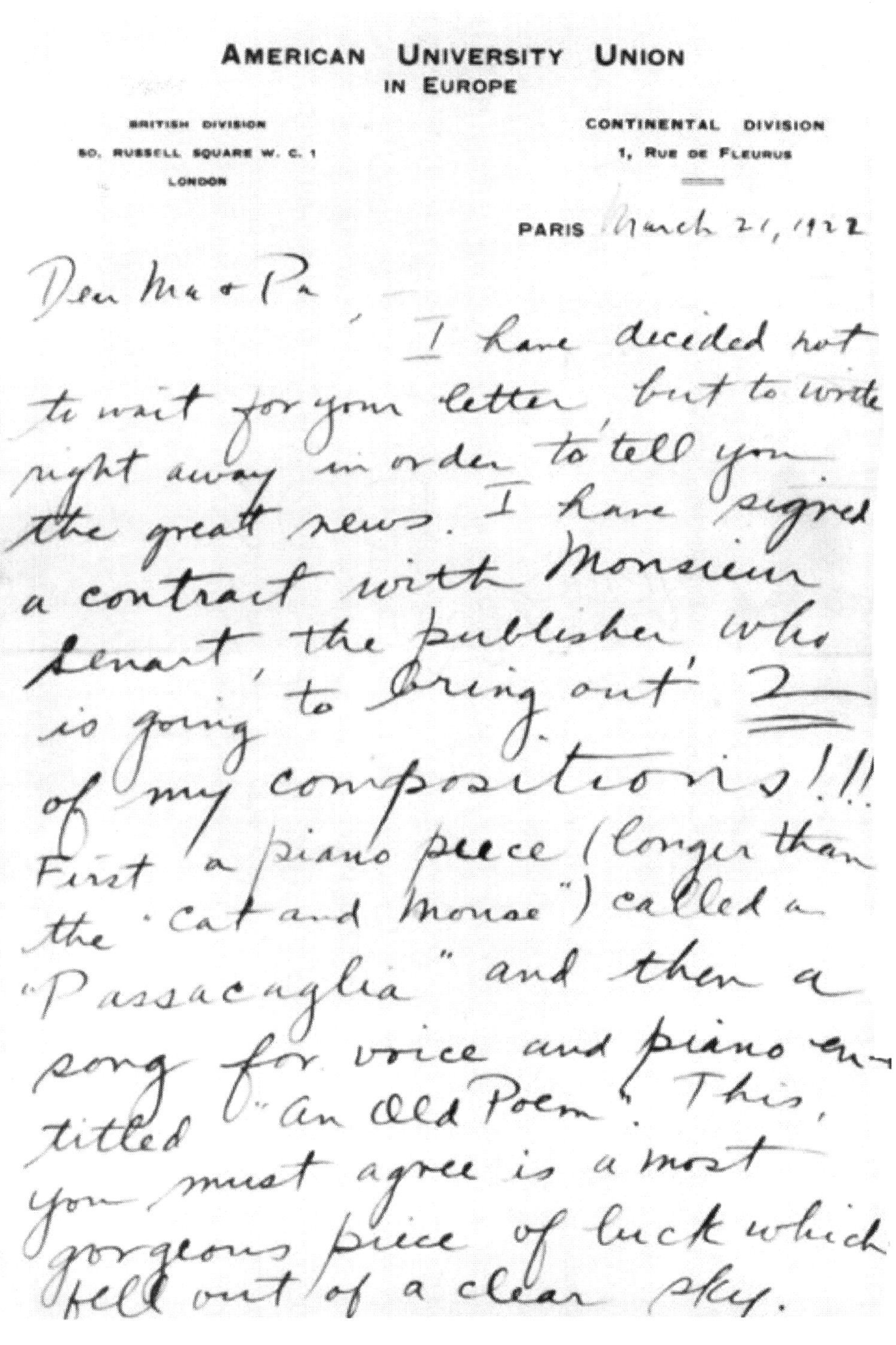

AMERICAN UNIVERSITY UNION
IN EUROPE

BRITISH DIVISION
50, RUSSELL SQUARE W. C. 1
LONDON

CONTINENTAL DIVISION
1, RUE DE FLEURUS

PARIS March 21, 1922

Dear Ma & Pa

I have decided not to wait for your letter but to write right away in order to tell you the great news. I have signed a contract with Monsieur Senart, the publisher who is going to bring out 2 of my compositions!!! First a piano piece (longer than the "Cat and Mouse") called a the "Passacaglia" and then a song for voice and piano entitled "An Old Poem". This, you must agree is a most gorgeous piece of luck which fell out of a clear sky.

their footsteps in order to return to Rome someday. After four days in Florence, we came back to Paris. It was altogether a wonderful trip, and I hastened to explain to the folks that the Italians in Italy were very different from those around Washington Avenue in Brooklyn.

Harold was in Berlin when I got back to Paris, and I missed him. We had really become inseparable friends. I stayed quietly at home with my music and books, and wrote to the family:

> I wonder if you ever realize what a large part the reading of books on all imaginable subjects plays in my existence. I read not to learn anything, but from the pure love of it. Had I gone to college, I should be graduating this year, but I never regret not having done so. Of course, there are plenty of people who must see you with a college diploma to make them believe you are educated, but I feel my extensive reading has done a great deal to make up for any geometry or chemistry they teach one there. I often think, in planning ahead, that rather than teach or concertize to make a living, I should greatly prefer to write on musical subjects. I intend to make an attempt at writing some short articles this summer and sending them to musical papers at home and see what happens.

When Harold returned from Berlin, we had only one month left before he was to sail home for the summer. Harold had been homesick during the gray wintry months, but when the weather changed, he was sorry that he was not going to Germany as I had decided to do that summer. I had only five lessons left with Mademoiselle and wanted to make the most of them. She thought it was time for me to attempt an orchestral work, so I began to search for an idea, and when I showed her a few piano sketches (one was a dance, *Petite Valse*), Mademoiselle suggested that I try to build them into a ballet. Everyone wanted to write ballets due to the enormous popularity and influence of the Diaghilev, Nijinsky, and Stravinsky ballets.[22] I planned to work on the sketches during the summer months in Berlin. While I grappled with the problem of what to do with my belongings (especially all the music), I thought about the changes at home. It's curious that one can sometimes see America more clearly from across the ocean than when living right inside it. I became sentimental about Brooklyn while in Paris in a way that I could never have done while living there. I tried to picture the store closed and the household on Washington Avenue disbanded. What had happened to all the help? And Lil, who had taken special care of me?[23] Ralph and Dorothy had a baby girl I had never seen. And Grandma died that spring. "Dear Ma and Pa," I wrote once again, "It is needless for me to tell you how very deeply moved I was to hear of Grandma's death. I will remember the time I went to the Bronx to say goodbye to her, and something seemed to tell me then that I was seeing her for the last time."

I wrote to Goldmark and Adler for letters of introduction to musicians in Germany, since they had both studied there. Goldmark sent letters to Artur Schnabel in Berlin

Proof page of *The Cat and the Mouse* with corrections and marginalia by Boulanger

[22] In Copland's files are a sketch for a ballet in one act, *Longchamp* (undated, but probably from the period); and a "Plan for *Longchamp*: Intro, Dance I, Interlude, Dance II, Interlude, Dance III, and Finale," with timings for each section.

[23] Lillian Coombs stayed with Sarah and Harris Copland until they both died—she in 1944, he in 1945.

and to a cousin in Vienna who was a music critic. My plan was to spend the summer of 1922 in Berlin and perhaps the following one in Vienna in order to make contact with German and Austrian musical life. I had been aware for some time of Schoenberg, Berg, and Webern, and I thought, to be fair, I should get a sense of the German side of things. I had no clear idea how to get in touch with German musical life, since I knew no one in Berlin at the time. But I took a room in the modest house of a Frau Jurges at BruckenAllee and began to explore the city. My sense of isolation grew, partly because the only German I knew was from the Yiddish I had heard at home.

I cannot say that I got a great deal out of my two months in Berlin. For one thing, it was a politically unstable time. The German mark had collapsed, and every time I changed a dollar, I got more marks. Finally you had to bring a valise to take it all home from the bank. Each day I woke up richer than the day before. I was sitting pretty, but it couldn't go on, and nobody knew what was going to happen next. I just didn't feel good about Berlin. Everyone was getting more prosperous each day, but it was very grim. I called on Schnabel, and he was cordial enough, but depressed about the conditions in Germany, and I did not see him again. I met Kurt Weill—we were both twenty-two years old. He was in an even more precarious position than I, since he didn't have any foreign money to exchange. Weill was studying with Ferruccio Busoni, and he had the idea that he wanted to write a new kind of opera, one that would be closer to contemporary life and preoccupations. Within a few years, his *Threepenny Opera*, so cynical and strangely moving, would present the perfect image of that hopeless and stressful time in Berlin. The concert scene was virtually nonexistent in the summer, but I heard a performance of Mahler's *Das Lied von der Erde* conducted by Bruno Walter that carried me away, and some operas. I was impressed with *Der Freischütz* and Franz Schreker's *Der Schatzgraber*, and it excited my curiosity to hear Schoenberg's *Pierrot lunaire* in Germany, since I had just had my introduction to that unusual work before leaving Paris.

My first letter to Nadia Boulanger was sent from Berlin that summer.[24] It surprises me now to be reminded that I had ever considered spending my second year abroad in Germany. When I wrote to Boulanger asking to return to study with her, she responded: "I am anxious to see the new parts of the ballet whose beginning pleases me so much." She asked me to buy some music for her—Schoenberg's *Traité d'harmonie*, and "anything else that's new and seems interesting to you." I found all except the Schoenberg, and on my own I bought for her "among quelque chose de nouveau, Bela Bartók's *Improvisations* [on Hungarian Folksongs] op. 20 for piano, an exquisite little work, and also Egon Wellesz' *Quatuor des cordes* that I find very interesting. . ." I decided to carry the music back with me instead of sending it. I was lonely in Berlin and impatient to return to Paris; 10 October couldn't come soon enough to please me.

[24] Copland's letters to Boulanger were sent to Copland by Annette Dieudonné in 1981, after Boulanger's death. They are now in the Library of Congress.

Harold and I often saw foreign films in Paris. One evening in the fall of 1922, we went to see the popular German horror film *Nosferatu*. It was about a vampire magician with the power to make corpses come to life. I was still searching for a story for my ballet, and by the time we reached home that night, I decided that this bizarre tale would be the basis for my ballet. Harold had never written a scenario, but he was eager to try. At first we called it *Le Nécromancien*. The title *Grohg* was chosen later. This ballet became the most ambitious undertaking of my Paris years—I had no choreographer, commission, or contact with a major ballet company. Nevertheless, I wrote this for the big time: a one-act, thirty-five-minute ballet for full pit orchestra plus piano. The opening section, "Cortège macabre," calls for four coffins to be displayed before *Grohg*, a magician. Three dances follow: one by one, the magician brings to life the corpses of an adolescent, an opium eater, and a streetwalker.[25] The magician's passions get the better of him, he attempts to embrace the girl, and she slaps him. He loses control, the corpses rise and jeer, and *Grohg* hurls the girl at them. The ballet ends with a return of the "Cortège" as the magician drags the coffins offstage.[26] In addition to these characters, an elaborate retinue of "servitors" dance around the coffins. There was a taste for the bizarre at the time, and if *Grohg* sounds morbid and excessive, the music was meant to be fantastic rather than ghastly. Also, the need for gruesome effects gave me an excuse for using "modern" rhythms and dissonances. In spite of the grotesque nature of the work, Mademoiselle encouraged me. She was taken with my use of polyrhythms and was the first to point out that I had a rhythmic sense that differed from that of the Europeans. She was fascinated with trying to play independent rhythms herself, and I remember sitting together at the piano, with me poking away at one rhythm while she played another.

Until *Grohg*, I had written only short piano pieces using jazz-derived rhythms. Now I was translating those techniques into a larger framework. On one polyrhythmic section of "Cortège," I wrote the following note: "to *le chef d'orchestre*: N.B. To facilitate the task of the conductor, a common bar line has been retained in this polyrhythmic section. The small notes indicate the precise rhythm desired." In the Finale, an *allegro vivo*, I let loose with alternating 5/4, 3/4, and 3/8 measures. *Grohg* as a youthful work had its shortcomings, but it foreshadowed my preoccupation with experiments in jazz for the next few years and was the forerunner of my later ballets.[27] In 1924 before I left Paris, Mademoiselle and I played *Grohg* for piano four-hands at a farewell party at her rue Ballu apartment. I revised the ballet in 1932 but did not release it for publication. *Grohg* has never been choreographed or staged. I arranged the introductory "Cortège macabre" as a separate work; it thereby became my earliest orchestral piece.[28] Other usable material from *Grohg* went into the *Dance Symphony*.[29]

[25] A sketch in Copland's files shows streetwalker as "street girl" in Copland's hand.

[26] From Clurman interview: ". . .we had some hilarious times, Aaron and I, acting out those parts!"

[27] The score of *Cortège macabre* was donated by Copland in 1925 to the Sibley Library, Eastman School of Music, Rochester, New York.

[28] Also extracted from *Grohg* was *Dance of the Adolescents* in a two-piano arrangement.

[29] Seventy years later, British composer Oliver Knussen recnstructed the original *Grogh* score and conducted its world premiere. 6 June 1992, at Aldeburgh with the London Sinfonietta. Pub. Boosey & Hawkes,1993.

Soon after I returned to the States, I submitted *Cortège macabre* to Howard Hanson in Rochester, who chose it and six others from forty-eight pieces submitted to the Eastman Philharmonia for the first of the American Composers Concerts. The date was 2 May 1925, and the occasion received national attention. (These annual concerts became the Festival of American Music in 1930; they were important in introducing works by many young composers through the years.) After *Cortège* was performed again in New York in 1927 by a different orchestra, I decided to withdraw it from my catalogue. In 1971 Hanson asked to conduct *Cortège* once more in a concert marking the last Festival of American Music; I agreed, thinking if Hanson liked it, there must be something good about it!

In 1922 though, the important thing was that the ballet was my chance to work on orchestration with Boulanger. While still in Brooklyn, I had made attempts to reorchestrate standard works, and I wrote songs in several versions with various instrumental accompaniments. (One song, "Alone," I arranged for voice and piano with viola, and in another version for voice and orchestra.)[30] In Boulanger's instrumental class I wrote seven short studies for instruments with piano: flute, oboe, clarinet, bassoon, horn, trumpet, and trombone. While these early efforts were instructive, I had had no formal studies in orchestration before working on *Grohg* with Boulanger.

Many of my evenings in Paris were spent composing. I have always found night hours agreeable for working. The stillness and tranquillity seem to me conducive to composing music. There is something romantic about the night time with its peaceful uninterrupted hours that is appropriate for a slow worker like myself—I have never dashed anything off in a burst of inspiration, even when very young. I tend to work carefully, put things aside, and then take them up again for a fresh look. Because I spend a lot of time and care with a work, once it's done, it's done. I rarely make changes or feel dissatisfied with a finished work. I have only occasionally, as in the case of *Grohg*, made revisions or recalled a piece. I try to make relatively certain that I am satisfied before letting a work go out into the world. In Paris my composing hours often extended into the early morning hours, since the days were filled with classes, practicing, and other practical matters. In my second year abroad, I began to feel more at home. I wrote to my cousin, Arnold Mittenthal, who was about to enter Yale College (10 February 1923):

> . . . The Paris I live in today is very different for me than the Paris of my first weeks. Many things—language, customs, morals which seemed impossibly strange then, I now take for granted. That doesn't mean that I have adopted the Gallic attitude toward "l'amour," but I certainly understand all these things better than when I arrived. After all, I suppose if one lived here long enough, Paris could become as commonplace as Brooklyn. Luckily, I have not arrived at that state yet. The awful smell in the subways, the marvellous pastry shops, a walk on the boulevard, the astounding lack of bathtubs

[30] Three versions are in Copland's unpublished juvenilia. "Alone" (voice and piano) was premiered by Jan DeGaetani, 6 December 1984, Carnegie Hall, New York City. The original version and a second version with viola added was performed by Elaine Bonazzi (mezzo-soprano), Miles Hoffman (viola), William Black (piano), The Library of Congress, April 1987. A third version for voice and orchestra was made by Copland.

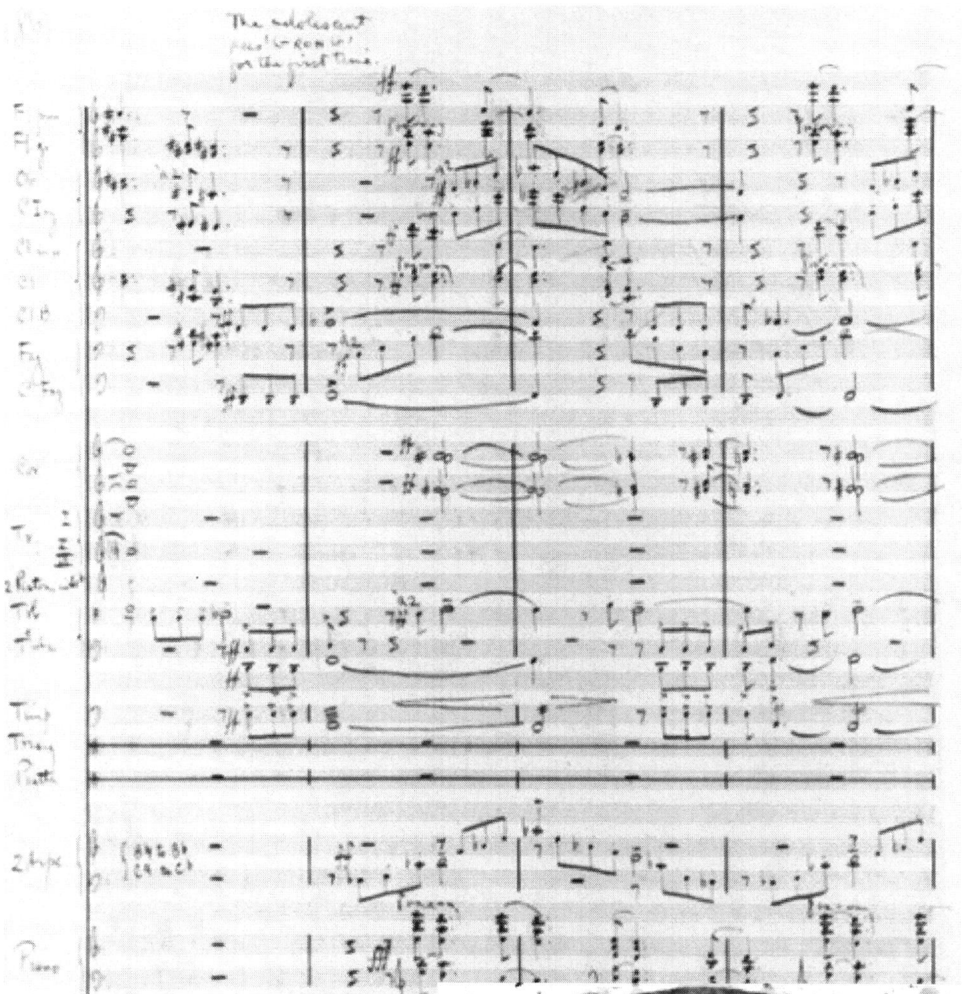

Above: Manuscript page from the ballet *Grohg*
Right: Copland with Harold Clurman, Paris, 1921

> in France, the very atmospheric Café de la Rotunde, those painted things who "once were women,"—all these aspects of Parisian life and many more still strike me as quaint and European. . . .

Determined to experience as much of this European flavor as possible while still abroad, I traveled again in the spring, this time to Bruges and then Brussels, where the wonderful organ recitals at the Consérvatoire Royal were most impressive.

In my catalogue under "Chamber Music" can be found *Two Pieces—Lento Molto* and *Rondino for String Quartet.*[31] The *Rondino* was written in the spring of 1923 in Paris as the second part of an "Hommage à Fauré." (Gabriel Fauré was Boulanger's favorite composer, and I soon shared her admiration for him.) Preceding the *Rondino* had been an arrangement for string quartet of the *Prélude IX* from Fauré's *Préludes pour piano* (op. 103). The *Rondino* was based on the letters of Fauré's name. Mixed with his influence can be heard a hint of American jazz and a bit of mild polytonality. *Rondino* was my first completed work for string quartet. Mademoiselle got together a professional quartet to read through it one Wednesday afternoon. Nadia often did this for students, and the hearing of one's imagined instrumentation did more for learning instrumentation and orchestration than many hours of spoken instruction.

The first performance of "Hommage à Fauré" took place in September 1924 at Fontainebleau. The old master Fauré was then seventy-eight and within a few months of his death. I came to admire his classic sense of order. It is strange that the musical public outside of France has never been convinced of his special charms, the delicacy, reserve, imperturbable calm—qualities that are not easily exportable. One of my first published articles was: "Gabriel Fauré, a Neglected Master."[32] My arrangement of Fauré's *Prélude* was appropriate to the occasion in 1924. In 1928 it was replaced by *Lento Molto*, which, when paired with *Rondino*, became *Two Pieces for String Quartet.*

Harold and I left for Vienna in June 1923. As Goldmark had indicated, Vienna was very different from Berlin, and the summer was rewarding and enjoyable. We found rooms with a Frau Steinhof and explored the delights of the city. Mademoiselle wrote reminding me to work on the ballet and again commissioning me to buy music for her, "for hundred or hundred and twenty francs . . . to be curious of music for a price, but no more, pleases me infinitely." Wanting her to know how much her teaching meant to me, I wrote (25 July 1923):

> I might get really sentimental about the rue Ballu and all that it has meant and still means to me. . . . Not being romantic, I musn't get 'sentimental' about anything, must I? But I am sure you will understand what I feel I owe you after two years of work, just as you understood the emotion in my apparently cold Passacaglia. . . .

[31] *Two Pieces for String Quartet* was arranged for string orchestra and is published in both versions; Copland's files contain an undated sketch toward the orchestration.

[32] The article appeared in *Musical Quarterly*, X:4 (October 1924), 573-86.

I had improved my German enough by then to read through some German literature, and I looked at a lot of music—Bruckner, Reger, and Mahler. Reading through a violin sonata (op. 72) by Reger, I was surprised to find it so good that I wanted to familiarize myself further with his work. But I was not so much impressed with Bruckner. About five hours a day was spent on the ballet and on an assignment for a chamber music piece for clarinet and flute that Boulanger had given her students as a task for the summer. I was determined to do as much as possible on both works before leaving for Salzburg with Clurman at the beginning of August, for the First Festival of the International Society for Contemporary Music (ISCM). I wrote to Boulanger, "Six successive evenings of modern music should prove a big enough feast for even so insatiable a gourmand as myself. . . ."

We were thrilled to be there with so many of the world's leading composers. It was a stimulating experience and one of the checkpoints in time when the place of my own country's music on the international scene became clear to me. I knew then that I wanted to see American music represented with more important offerings than the modest Emerson Whithorne piece that was the only American work. I reported on the festival to Boulanger, relating that Stravinsky and Ravel were still the most popular composers, and that Milhaud, Poulenc, and Honegger were not very well received. I was most excited ("le plus frappé") on hearing Hindemith, Krenek, and Hába, and reported that Hindemith was the most played and talked about. Personally, I found the quartets of Ernst Krenek and Alois Hába the most interesting. One day while in my hotel room, mystifying sounds came from the room adjoining mine. I could not imagine what was going on. At the evening concert I realized that it had been the musicians rehearsing Hába's quarter-tone quartet. When I returned to Vienna from the Salzburg festival, I used quarter tones in the viola solo linking the slow movement of *Grohg* to the Finale.

In Vienna that summer I listened to jazz in the bars, and hearing it in a fresh context heightened my interest in its potential. I began to consider that jazz rhythms might be the way to make an American-sounding music. The Finale of *Grohg* reflects these ideas. I returned to Paris with additional pages for the ballet and a brand new piece. I had been playing around with some ideas for the flute and clarinet assignment when I came upon a poem by the seventeenth-century English poet Richard Barnefield. "As It Fell Upon a Day" had the simplicity and tenderness that moved me to attempt to evoke that poignant expression musically. I got the idea to add a voice part to Boulanger's assignment. The imitative counterpoint between the two instruments in the introduction would satisfy my teacher's request. The harmonies that seem to evoke an early English flavor were suggested by the nature of the text. I am often asked about "modal" writing in connection with "As It Fell. . . ." I can only say that I never learned all about the modes—major and minor were the only modes my generation were taught! If the music sounds modal it is because I wanted to come close to the expression of the poetry. The SMI was once again responsible for a premiere. "As It Fell . . .was played first under their auspices in the Salle Pleyel on 6 February 1924. Ada MacLeish, wife of the poet Archibald MacLeish, was the soprano soloist. The reviewer for *Le Menestrel* called "As It Fell. . . . the best piece on a program that included works by Leo Sowerby, Jean

Deré, and Roussel." This song has been performed often and is usually well received.[33] I recall particularly an all-Copland concert in New York in 1935, perhaps because of the performers—Ethel and Otto Luening and Robert McBride.

In October 1923 Clurman and I moved into our third apartment in Paris at 66 Boulevard Pasteur. A mulatto family were the landlords, and I will never forget the distinguished gentleman of the household, a judge in the French court, asking us politely if we held any racial prejudices. Harold and I were horrified to realize that Americans had the reputation for such bigotry abroad. Soon after we were settled in that fall, I met Mme Genevieve Butez, who invited me to play chamber music with a small group of accomplished amateur string players. We read through the classics, and occasionally I brought along a contemporary piece and got kidded about being a modernist. We became good friends. The quartet gave a farewell party for me when I left Paris in the spring of 1924, and they all wrote to me after I returned to the States.

The "Concerts Koussevitzky" continued to be highlights on the musical scene that season. Maestro outdid himself with unusual programs in both the fall and spring. Only in the atmosphere of Paris in the twenties could an orchestral series like that have taken place, and with such expectation and popularity. We heard Honegger's *Pacific 231* and Prokofiev's *Sept, ils sont sept* in premieres, and Koussevitzky presented an all-Stravinsky program with the composer as soloist in the first performance of his *Piano Concerto.* Koussevitzky's four years of conducting this series in Paris were to end that spring. The announcement came that the famous Russian conductor would lead the Boston Symphony Orchestra the following season. It seemed unbelievable to us. Would he play such ultra-modern music in Boston? When Mademoiselle saw the announcement in the papers, she said, "We must go and visit him." She was on cordial terms with Koussevitzky and took it for granted that he would want to meet a young composer from the country he was about to visit for the first time.

The Koussevitzky house in Paris seemed very grand to me. Under my arm I carried my only orchestral score, *Cortège macabre.* Maestro asked me to play it. Prokofiev was visiting that day (perhaps Dr. Koussevitzky had invited him to see Boulanger) and much to my discomfort, he stood directly behind me at the piano while I played—I wanted to do my selling job alone. When I had finished and before anyone could say anything, Prokofiev blurted out, "Too much bassi ostinati." But Dr. Koussevitzky promised to conduct the piece with the Boston Symphony Orchestra during his first season. And, knowing that Boulanger planned to be in the States at the invitation of Walter Damrosch, Koussevitzky suggested that she appear with the Boston Symphony as organ soloist in a new orchestral work that I would compose.[34] "You vill write an organ concerto, Mademoiselle Boulanger vill play it and I vill conduct!" Koussevitzky pronounced in no uncertain terms. Mademoiselle agreed, but when we left, I exclaimed, "Do you really think I can do it?" (I had never heard a note of my own orchestration or written anything for the organ. Moreover, the organ was not a favorite instrument of

[33] It was first published in *New Music Quarterly*, 11:4 (July 1929).

[34] It is not clear whether Koussevitzky or Boulanger originated the idea for the piece.

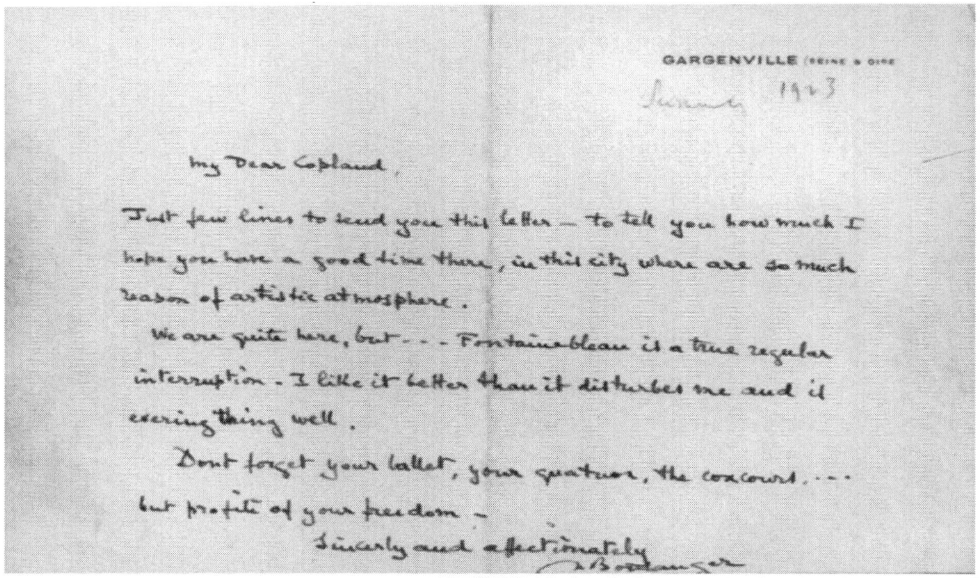
GARGENVILLE (SEINE & OISE)
Summer 1923

My Dear Copland,

Just few lines to send you this letter — to tell you how much I hope you have a good time there, in this city where are so much reason of artistic atmosphere.

We are quite here, but . . . Fontainebleau is a true regular interruption — I like it better than it disturbes me and is carrying thing well.

Dont forget your ballet, your quatuor, the concours, . . . but profit of your freedom —

Sincerely and affectionately
N Boulanger

Above: Letter from Boulanger to Copland, 1923 (the date is in Copland's hand)

Right: Letter from Copland to Boulanger from Vienna, July, 1923

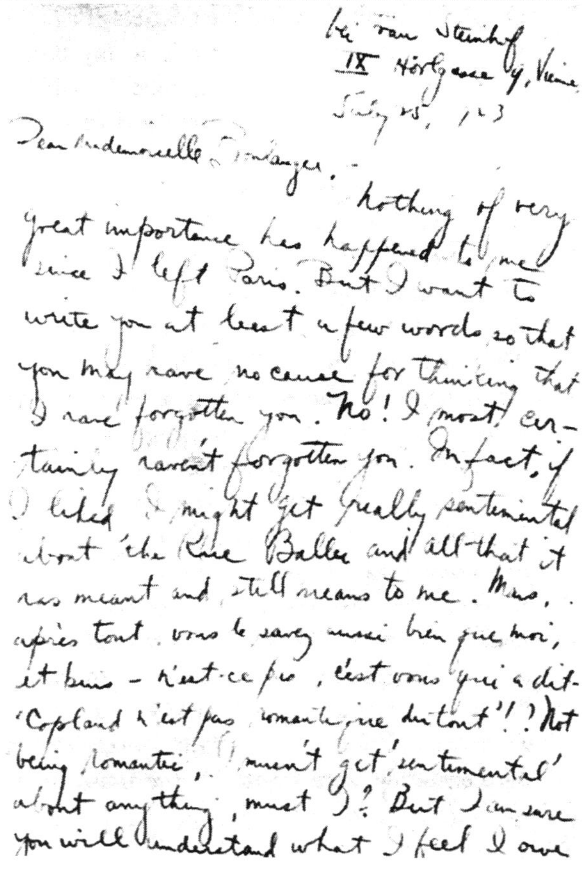
bei van Steinhof
18 Hörlgasse 9, Vienna
July 25, '23

Dear Mademoiselle Boulanger, —

Nothing of very great importance has happened to me since I left Paris. But I want to write you at least a few words so that you may have no cause for thinking that I have forgotten you. No! I most certainly haven't forgotten you. In fact, if I liked I might get really sentimental about the Rue Ballu and all that it was meant and still means to me. Mais, après tout, vous le savez aussi bien que moi, et puis — n'est-ce pas, c'est vous qui a dit 'Copland n'est pas romantique du tout'!? Not being romantic, I mustn't get 'sentimental' about anything, must I? But I am sure you will understand what I feel I owe

mine.) She pointed her finger at me. "You can do it." And when Mademoiselle said, "You can do it," that was the end of the discussion.

I can only assume that Koussevitzky trusted Boulanger's faith in me and that he wanted a new American work with her as soloist. Whatever the reasons, I had misgivings, and it was only my teacher's confidence that gave me the courage to go on. Boulanger must have written immediately to Damrosch, for the next thing I knew, a big unwritten composition for organ and orchestra was scheduled for performance in the 1924-25 season by both Walter Damrosch with the New York Symphony and Serge Koussevitzky with the Boston Symphony Orchestra. Two major performances were at stake. It was very tempting, but very scary. I was confident that if I wrote music that could be played on an organ, Mademoiselle would advise me as to the appropriate organ registrations needed. I would only have to indicate to her what effect I was hoping to obtain. Looking back, I realize how lucky I was, first to have found Boulanger, and then Koussevitzky at just the perfect time for any of this to happen. In a personal way I was pleased, for it meant that my connections with Paris would not be cut off suddenly. I would be constantly in touch with Boulanger about the music, and within a few months she and Koussevitzky would be in America.

Caricature of Aaron Copland by Olga Koussevitsky

INTERLUDE I

What was the state of the arts in America during the years Copland was in France? Little could compare with the ferment of Paris or Vienna, but the explosion of experimentation and innovation abroad had been so strong that its shock waves reached New York and reverberated across the country. In the visual arts as early as 1913, the Armory Show had heralded the arrival of modern art; in literature by the early twenties, Hemingway, Joyce, and Lawrence were being read by those who considered themselves the American avant-garde. But music lagged behind. Contemporary works were programmed only occasionally, giving rise to snickers, giggles, or downright sarcasm from audiences and critics. Arnold Schoenberg's name was familiar among the cognoscenti, but not his music; Charles Ives was not known at all, although by 1920 he had virtually finished composing; and Leo Ornstein, the "futurist" composer, was shocking audiences with performances of his unusual early pieces. It was Igor Stravinsky whose popularity abroad was reflected most strongly on the New York concert scene. The critic Pitts Sanborn wrote, "Inevitably the New York music season of 1923-24 will go down in history as the Stravinsky season. . . ."[1]

Characteristically, the first societies to champion the cause of modern music in America were led by foreigners. In 1920 E. Robert Schmitz, a French concert pianist, founded and directed an international society based in New York that was first called the Franco-American Musical Society, and later Pro-Musica, Inc. It became an influential force in introducing audiences to living composers and little-known music. By 1930 Pro-Musica had established over forty chapters in the States and abroad. American composers were not ignored by Pro-Musica, but its primary objective was to bring European musicians to the United States. The International Composers' Guild (ICG) was obviously international in scope.[2] Founded by Edgard Varèse in 1921 with a small group in Greenwich Village, the ICG ran into difficulties by the end of its second season after several of its leading members had a falling out with Varèse. Claire R. Reis, composers Lazare Saminsky and Louis Gruenberg, and the patroness Alma Wertheim left to form a new society in 1923, the League of Composers. The divorce was not a friendly one, and reasons for it have been disputed through the years by both sides.[3] Varèse and his colleagues, particularly Carlos Salzedo and Carl Ruggles, managed to keep the ICG alive until after its 1926-27 season. During this period, New York had the advantage of two groups in competition, both presenting modern music programs.

Copland was still in Paris during the League's first season of 1923-24. Claire Reis, executive director, and Minna Lederman, editor of *Modern Music*, subsequently brought the League and the publication into positions of prominence. Of course, in the overall musical picture, modern music played a small role. There was very little opportunity for the performance of American contemporary symphonic music until later, when Koussevitzky and Stokowski began to schedule works regularly. As for publication opportunities, only a few of the older established men such as Daniel Gregory Mason, Horatio Parker, and Rubin Goldmark had music in print. For young composers, there was no outlet whatsoever until Henry Cowell's bold experiment of publishing American works in New Music Editions began in 1927[4] and only a very few young Americans were known well enough abroad to have an occasional piece published by one of the big houses. The few existing teaching positions were invariably filled by the older generation of conservative composers. There were no government or foundation grants, competitions, prizes, or commissions for financial remuneration. On the positive side, however, were the wealthy patrons and patronesses who occasionally made it possible for a promising young artist to experience financial freedom for a limited time.

In June 1924 Copland and Clurman sailed home from France. Copland recalls nothing of the return trip, although the crossing to France three years earlier is vivid in his memory. According to Clurman, Aaron was seasick and both were anxious to get home; neither

[1] Pitts Sanborn, "Honors of the Season," *The League of Composers' Review*, I: 2 (June 1924), 3.

[2] For a history, description, and list of performances, see R. Allen Lott, " 'New Music for New Ears,'" *Journal of the American Musicological Society*, XXXVI: 2 (Summer 1983), 266-86.

[3] See Louise Varèse, *Varèse: A Looking-Glass Diary* (New York: W. W. Norton, 1972), 169-91; and Claire R. Reis, "Twenty-five Years with The League of Composers," *Musical Quarterly*, XXXIV : 1 (January 1948), 1-14. Also, for a description of the ICG board meetings before the break, see Claire R. Reis, *Composers, Conductors, and Critics* (New York: Oxford University Press, 1955, repr. Detroit, Michigan: Information Coordinators, 1974), 13-15.

[4] See Rita H. Mead, *Henry Cowell's New Music, 1925-1936: The Society, the Music Editions, and the Recordings* (Ann Arbor, Michigan: UMI Research Press, 1981).

had seriously considered becoming an expatriate. But Aaron had become a Francophile, and in less than two years he would return to France, and then twice again before the end of the decade. Copland's French had become fluent; but even so, he knew what it took for a foreigner to be accepted by the French, and he never felt completely at home there. Moreover, there was an "affirm America" movement under way, spearheaded by young writers Waldo Frank and Edmund Wilson. It was catching on fast, and Aaron and Harold felt its pull.

Copland had gone to Europe to learn how to compose, and had "found" America while viewing it from abroad. He saw European composers take up American jazz and thought that if composers like Debussy and Ravel, Stravinsky and Milhaud could use ragtime and jazz rhythms, the way might be open for American composers. Perhaps, he thought, here finally was music an American might write better than a European. While Copland was in Paris, only a few composers at home had toyed with a polite form of jazz—John Alden Carpenter in the ballets *Krazy Kat* and *Skyscrapers*, and Louis Gruenberg with *The Daniel Jazz*. None made the impact of Stravinsky's *Ragtime for Eleven Instruments* and *Piano Rag Music*, or Darius Milhaud's *Création du monde*, which caused a sensation when premiered in Paris in 1923. (Milhaud had the temerity to lecture Americans on jazz when he visited the States in 1920-21.) The only American piece that came close to the notoriety of Milhaud's was Gershwin's *Rhapsody in Blue*, commissioned by Paul Whiteman and first played on Lincoln's Birthday in 1924 in a concert called, "An Experiment in Modern Music." Jazz was considered a new discovery, as though it had just happened on the scene in time for white composers to use its lively and danceable rhythms in their concert music. Composers made forays to Harlem to hear the way real jazz was played at the Apollo and Small's Paradise, and they suddenly began to talk about "riffs," "blue notes," and "breaks." The terms "African American" and "black" were not yet in use, nor was there any perception of jazz as an indigenous African American art. "Negroes" played jazz in nightclubs, but most of them could not read music, and therefore jazz was only art when incorporated into rhapsodies, symphonies, and ballets by white concert composers. Even then, the issue was hotly debated. Nevertheless, for a brief time it seemed possible that our popular and concert musics, so hopelessly divided, might have found a way of blending. High society went slumming in Harlem to hear jazz in the clubs, and on one memorable evening in the season before Copland returned to America, the League of Composers sponsored a concert in which the adventurous singer, Eva Gauthier, in formal black attire introduced George Gershwin in top hat and tails for a mixed program of popular and art songs at Aeolian Hall. Only black Americans puzzled over all this, wondering how a bandleader with the incredible name of Whiteman had come to be called "The King of Jazz."

Copland was not to enter the mainstream of musical activities in New York immediately. First, he had to fulfill the commission to compose a major symphonic work with organ solo for performances in the upcoming season. Aaron contemplated the changes in his life: never again would he live at home; his student days were over; and he would have to find a job that would allow time to compose. He had no idea how he would support himself, nor did he have any more notion in 1924 of how a composer gets started in America than when he left Brooklyn in 1921. As Copland and Clurman stepped off the gangplank of the France, they solemnly shook hands and turned to greet the Mittenthals, Coplands, Urises, and Clurmans who had come to welcome the young men home from their European adventures. Then they went their separate but inseparable ways, each to achieve in his own art what he had dreamed and talked about in Paris.

After a few weeks of family reunions and kidding from brother Leon about being "Frenchified," Aaron got down to the urgent business of finding a job. He looked up an old friend, Abraham Ginsburg, a violinist with whom he had played chamber music years before. Abe offered him a job as pianist in a trio at a resort hotel in Milford, Pennsylvania, for the summer, and Aaron was delighted to find a job in music in a place that promised quiet and time to compose. The manager of the Hotel Colonial, Signore C. Lauritano, had dabbled in music. Business was slow, so the boss stood over the trio at lunch, dinner, and for dancing in the evenings, making their lives miserable and giving them "hell" for their interpretations of popular Italian opera. Aaron rented a movie theater, and there he worked every morning at the piano in the musty, dark house. He managed to make a final ink draft of the *Cortège macabre* before the young lady who played piano for the movies in the evenings heard him and insisted that he stop banging on her piano.

Progress was slow on the symphony. Mademoiselle wrote impatiently from her summer home, "Les Maisonettes," in Gargenville, "Give me quickly news of the brain child. . ." Copland responded, thanking his teacher for preparing five of his works for performance at Fontainebleau and informing her that in mid-August he was resigning his job as pianist of the Hotel Colonial's music trio because it was impossible to make headway on the "sinfonietta." (At various times the piece was called concerto, sinfonietta, symphony.) Copland fled to Laurine's home in Brooklyn at 557 East 12th Street in order to use her good piano, and set to work full time. He reported to Boulanger:

> Let me tell you how far it is advanced—for several reasons I have decided to make it in three movements instead of four. The first will be a short andante (the one I wrote in May), then the scherzo, and lastly will come the most important movement with which I originally thought I would begin the work. It will take about twenty minutes altogether. (Honegger's first violin sonata has three movements arranged something like that.) So far I have completely finished only the first movement, which is also orchestrated. But the other two movements are, *pour ainsi dire,* finished—that is, they are clear in my mind, but I must still write them down and orchestrate them and fill in the details. If I sent it to you by October 1st, you will still have two full months to prepare it. It goes without saying that any corrections you make, I approve of *a priori.*

Aaron and Harold met often. When Melville Smith returned from Paris, they sat him down and made him talk for hours about all that had happened since their departure. While finishing the first draft of the symphony in October, Aaron moved into his first small studio in Manhattan at 135 West 74th Street. Excitedly he sent out cards with his address, announcing his availability for teaching and stating: "Recently back from Paris." But not a single response ever came in. This was, to say the least, disheartening. His confidence was restored, however, when Mademoiselle wrote her reactions to the *Organ Symphony*:

> I can't tell you my joy—the work is so brilliant, so full of music. . . . I must at once thank you profoundly for the dedication to which, I assure you, I attach a value that surpasses in every-

thing obvious questions. . . . This to me is truly a genuine pride of an artist and the real joy of a friend. . . .

From this time on, New York City became Copland's home base. Travel would satisfy his thirst for a wide range of experience, but the pull back to New York was strong. Even later, when Copland moved to the countryside, he was never far from the city. But wherever he lived, the center of interest was always the room with the piano. A house without one felt bare. (Once, when in Tangier, an instrument that only mildly resembled a piano arrived across the backs of two sturdy mules. Copland would not have stayed without it.) Travel would never be pure vacation, but always stimulated by some sort of musical assignment. Wherever he would find himself—Paris, Mexico, South America, Moscow, Japan, Israel, or Hollywood—Copland would channel his energies and talents to the work at hand. The ability to take music wherever and however he found it would communicate itself to performers. This accounts, at least in part, for Copland's enormous popularity; he would never expect a high school band or South American orchestra to play like the New York Philharmonic.

Returning from a trip, Copland's first activity was always to catch up with musical events at home. After settling into his small studio in 1924, he quickly appraised the current musical scene and became part of it. In Paris Aaron Copland had made a splash as a promising newcomer. But when he moved to New York in the fall of 1924, the name Copland was not known—not until January 1925, when a big new work for organ and orchestra by a twenty-four-year-old American was premiered by the New York Symphony Orchestra.

Copland in the twenties

NEW YORK
1924 - 1926

How I got through the first few months, I really don't know. I had met the American composer Marion Bauer in Paris the season before, and she recommended me to the League of Composers. It was the start of their second season, and they were initiating a series devoted to "The musical youngsters of America, England, and the Continent." I was invited to audition for the board at Claire Reis' apartment. I accompanied myself singing the "Old Poem" and played a few piano pieces. The *Passacaglia* and *The Cat and the Mouse* were accepted for the League's first "Young Composers' Concert." Led for years by Marion Bauer, this series often served to introduce compositions by unknown American composers. On the first program, held at the Anderson Galleries in November 1924, the critic Olin Downes introduced works by George Antheil, Mario Castelnuovo-Tedesco, Alois Hába, Richard Hammond, Ernst Krenek, Bernard Rogers, Alexander Steinert, and me. It was my first public appearance in New York—not a very impressive debut, but the pieces were well received, and when Paul Rosenfeld phoned the next day to tell me he liked my music, I would not have been more surprised if the President of the United States had called. To me, an okay from the critic of *The Dial* seemed better than approval from *The New York Times.*

Paul Rosenfeld is unjustly forgotten nowadays.[1] He was not a newspaper critic in the usual sense and never wrote in a journalistic style. His prose was richly expressive, sometimes even too much so, with occasional sentences in a language all his own. Paul had the unusual ability of being able to write about all of the arts. Anyone interested in new music in the twenties, of course, read him regularly. What made Paul so special was not so much what he said or how he said it, but his complete involvement in the music he was criticizing. The American scene in particular was a consuming interest—he believed passionately in the emergence of an important school of contemporary American composers. Paul was one of the first critics to write perceptively about Ives, Ornstein, Varèse, Ruggles, Cowell, Harris, and Sessions. Rosenfeld's description of my appearance at that first League concert has been quoted often: "A slim, beglassed, shy and still self-assured young fellow with the aspect of a benevolent and scholastic grasshopper. . . ."[2] Rosenfeld lived a bachelor life surrounded by the latest books. He invited me to dinners at his apartment on Irving Place with the most interesting people in the avant-garde literary, music, and art worlds. Among the writers I enjoyed meeting there were Hart Crane, Lewis Mumford, Waldo Frank, e.e. cummings, and Edmund Wilson. I seem to remember that Rosenfeld introduced me to Minna Lederman soon after I returned from Paris. Minna was the brand-new editor of the brand-new magazine *The League of Composers' Review* (soon to become better known as *Modern Music*). Paul became interested in promoting my career and was well aware that I would be in need of financial assistance. I kept him informed about the *Organ Symphony,* and he promised to keep me in mind should a wealthy patron or patroness appear on the scene.

Sections of the *Symphony* were sent off to Nadia as soon as they were composed. Although my student days were over, it was important for me at that time to have such a highly experienced eye look at my work and make suggestions. And, of course, I was relying heavily on Nadia for correcting the organ part and providing registrations. Mademoiselle wrote in October:

> I am sailing December 27, playing in New York January 11—Engles [George, manager of the orchestra] has asked me for my program—I can ask him to be patient for a bit—but will you be ready and what title? When shall I have the music? Will the orchestra parts be ready? There is no more time to lose—above all, don't be too complicated—one cannot rehearse very much and orchestras are not ready to handle certain problems properly. How much pleasure our little parties will give me—I hope to remain a while in New York since I play there the eleventh, I have my first lecture there the nineteenth—and I hope to have a little freedom—it will be necessary to work, it is true, for your organs are different from ours—and I shall have to give some lessons probably, without counting the appearances in society!

[1] See Aaron Copland, "Memorial to Paul Rosenfeld," *Music Library Association Notes*, 4:2 (March 1947); repr. as "A Verdict," *Paul Rosenfeld, Voyager in the Arts* (New York: Creative Age Press, 1948), 166-69.

[2] Paul Rosenfeld, "The Newest American Composers," *Modern Music*, XV: 3 (March-April 1938), 153.

Nadia never expressed doubt about the *Symphony* as a whole, but after I sent the completed score, she wrote again suggesting I compose an alternate ending in case the one I had written didn't work when we got together with the orchestra. Also, she feared that the tempo in the Scherzo was too fast and might lead to "confusion." I accepted some of her suggestions, but decided to take my chances with the ending and with the tempo of the Scherzo.

Walter Damrosch, conductor of the New York Symphony Orchestra, would never have accepted my *Organ Symphony* if I had presented it to him cold. I was just a brash young man from Brooklyn as far as he was concerned, who for some strange reason had attracted Boulanger's attention. He greatly admired her, and if she wanted to perform the piece, well, of course, he agreed. He probably said "Sure," without any idea of what I was going to present to him. I had no idea what Damrosch or his musicians thought of my composition. Undoubtedly, from their standpoint, it was "far out." I have a vivid memory of the first rehearsal, because of all times, I was late due to an unexplained delay on the subway. I was really in a panic, thinking that I was going to miss the entire rehearsal. I dashed from Times Square to Aeolian Hall on 43rd Street near Sixth Avenue. I was in such a hurry to get into the hall that instead of going around the block to the stage entrance, I yanked open the front door of the main hall—suddenly, I got a blast of my own orchestration!

It was a moment I shall never forget. It was the Scherzo movement, very brilliant, brassy, and glamorous-sounding. I had orchestrated the piece for large orchestra: triple woodwinds, full brass, and an array of percussion requiring five players in addition to the timpanist. I was absolutely overwhelmed to hear my own orchestration for the very first time. It sounded so glorious to me, so much grander than I could possibly have imagined. Had I arrived at the beginning of the rehearsal, it might not have been quite so impressive, since the symphony begins quietly with a rather short and reflective Prelude, not much like a traditional symphonic first movement.

All three movements are loosely connected by an unobtrusive recurring theme that becomes more significant as the piece progresses. The first big climax is in the Scherzo, a movement designed to maintain a strong drive all the way through. This second movement interested Boulanger and Koussevitzky most, because of its rhythmic experimentation, irregular note groupings, and uneven accents. The Scherzo was my idea of what could be done to adapt the raw material of jazz. I was not yet using jazz openly and directly; nevertheless, if you listen to the Scherzo even now, you hear rhythms that would not have been there if I had not been born and raised in Brooklyn.[3] The final movement of the Symphony is a modified sonata form, resembling a traditional symphonic first movement.

The *Symphony for Organ and Orchestra* had its premiere as planned on 11 January 1925 with the New York Symphony Orchestra conducted by Walter Damrosch at Aeolian Hall. This was Nadia Boulanger's American debut, and she was very warmly received by the press and audience. Perhaps Nadia had planned the order of the program, for my piece was placed prominently, second from the end, and after the audience had been won over. At its conclusion, there was considerable applause, and when Mr. Damrosch pointed to the upper box where I was seated, I rose to bow. As things quieted down, Mr. Damrosch advanced to the footlights and to everyone's surprise, addressed the audience. "Ladies and gentlemen," he began, "I am sure you will agree that if a gifted young man can write a symphony like this at twenty-three"—and here he paused dramatically, leaving the audience to expect a proclamation of a new musical genius— then continued, "within five years he will be ready to commit murder!"

It was a joke, of course, and I laughed along with the audience; but it was also Damrosch's way of smoothing the ruffled feathers of his conservative Sunday afternoon ladies faced with modern American music. For years after, whenever I met Damrosch, he said apologetically, "Copland, you understood what I meant by that remark?" Far more important to me was that Mademoiselle found the music worthwhile. She was intrigued with certain rhythmic aspects of it, and it pleased me to know that when she asked Virgil Thomson his opinion of the *Organ Symphony*, he said, "I wept when I heard it." Nadia asked, "But why did you weep?" Virgil replied, "Because I had not written it myself!" More recently, Virgil added: "The piece that opened the whole door to me was that *Organ Symphony* of Aaron's. I thought that it was the voice of America in our generation. It spoke in the same way that Kerouac did thirty years later. . . ."[4]

The day after the premiere, a news article proclaimed, "Young Composer to Commit Murder!" But Lawrence Gilman, the open-minded critic of the *Herald Tribune*, quipped:

> Copland does not strike me as one of the murderous kind.. . . The real murderers of music are the unimaginative standpatters among composers. . . . There are pages in Mr. Copland's symphony which have bite and power, both rhythmical and harmonic. . . . Mr. Copland, even though he does present us with some second-hand Stravinsky—his second movement is redolent of *Petroushka*—even though he suggests to us in his first movement a kind of Prospect Park Schoenberg, is nevertheless, on the whole, working out his own musical destiny in his own way, and we shall follow his pursuit of it with lively interest.

Others were not so kind. The *Standard Union* writer commented, "To the names of Cowell, Ruggles and Varèse (potential volcanoes, all three) must now be added that of a new and seething crater, Aaron Copland, of Brooklyn." But no one was indifferent, even the very conservative W. J. Henderson of the *New York Sun*: "The real defect of the symphony is its undisguised search of thrills. This is a pity, for the work discloses the existence of a real talent." Paul Rosenfeld, writing in a characteristic lush prose, was positively rhapsodic.

[3] The Scherzo was arranged for two pianos by John Kirkpatrick. The unpublished manuscript is in the Kirkpatrick collection, Yale.

[4] Thomson interview, and "Notes on Copland's Organ Symphony," unpublished typescript, which, according to Thomson, was probably meant as an article for the *Boston Transcript*; copy sent to Perlis, 1980.

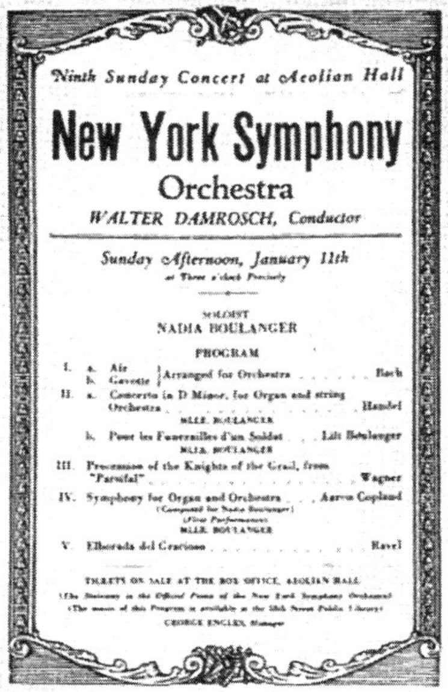
Ninth Sunday Concert at Aeolian Hall

New York Symphony Orchestra

WALTER DAMROSCH, Conductor

Sunday Afternoon, January 11th

SOLOIST
NADIA BOULANGER

PROGRAM

I. a. Air; b. Gavotte — Arranged for Orchestra . . . Bach

II. a. Concerto in D Minor, for Organ and string Orchestra . . . Handel
MLLE. BOULANGER

b. Pour les Funerailles d'un Soldat . . . Lili Boulanger
MLLE. BOULANGER

III. Procession of the Knights of the Grail, from "Parsifal" . . . Wagner

IV. Symphony for Organ and Orchestra . . . Aaron Copland
MLLE. BOULANGER

V. Elborada del Gracioso . . . Ravel

TICKETS ON SALE AT THE BOX OFFICE, AEOLIAN HALL

GEORGE ENGLES, Manager

Above: Piano-duet sketch of the second movement Scherzo from the *Symphony for Organ and Orchestra*

Right: Program of the premiere of Copland's *Symphony for Organ and Orchestra*, Aeolian Hall, 1925

Harold Clurman and I escorted Nadia around New York City, showing her the sights. The Great White Way was particularly impressive in those days. Her reaction amused us: "It is *extraordinaire*, but not very *raffinated*!" The Boston performance of the *Organ Symphony* was not far off. Koussevitzky invited me to come up a week in advance to go over the score. Damrosch and Koussevitzky had both taken my composition on Boulanger's word, but the difference between the two conductors was striking. I was astounded at the attention Koussevitzky gave to the work. He created an atmosphere that implied there was nothing else of importance on the program; my piece was to be the main event of the symphony week. It was quite an amazing experience for a young unknown composer to have the Boston Symphony Orchestra and its famous conductor at his disposal.

I've never seen anything like Koussevitzky's enthusiasm for new music before or since. He showed the same adventurous spirit in Boston as in Paris, and I had the good fortune to be the first American composer on the scene as Dr. Koussevitzky began his musical life in Boston. Others would have similar experiences, William Schuman and Leonard Bernstein among them. We would be invited to spend an entire week at the Koussevitzky home in Boston with the Maestro and his gracious wife Natalie. There, each evening, after orchestra rehearsals during the day, we would go over the score at the piano, working on difficult rhythms that sometimes did not come naturally to Koussevitzky. He was interested in these rhythmic experiments, and even if they made conducting the music more difficult, he was willing to work them out. I'm sure he knew in advance that his rather conservative audience was not likely to enjoy a composition based on jazz materials and avant-garde harmonies, but he was excited to be part of the movement for modern music.

There was an unforgettable occurrence during Boulanger's performance of the *Organ Symphony* in Boston. An organ key got stuck and would not release. While the orchestra kept playing, the tone grew stronger, filling the hall with a loud and insistent sound. Koussevitzky stopped the orchestra. Nobody was playing, but the organ tone continued, becoming more and more unbearable. Mademoiselle motioned to Koussevitzky—something had to be done immediately! Suddenly, Nadia left the stage, while Koussevitzky remained on the podium, looking as dignified as usual. In a few moments, the tone ceased. The silence was deafening! The audience applauded as Nadia returned to proceed with the performance. If it had been an uncomfortable moment for audience and performers, imagine the poor composer! The whole episode probably lasted no more than two minutes, but to me it had seemed like hours.

After Boulanger, organists who played the *Organ Symphony* included Melville Smith, who made an organ and piano arrangement of it that has been published, and E. Power Biggs, who recorded the piece with Bernstein and the New York Philharmonic. In December 1982 William Owen was the soloist when I conducted the New Haven Symphony Orchestra in Woolsey Hall, where there is a large and wonderful-sounding instrument. I was reminded of a difficulty inherent in music for this combination when Bill Owen informed me that the delay between depressing the key and the actual sound can be as long as a full second. This means that the organist must anticipate the conductor's beat by just that much time if organ and orchestra are to play together. This delay factor is not the only drawback

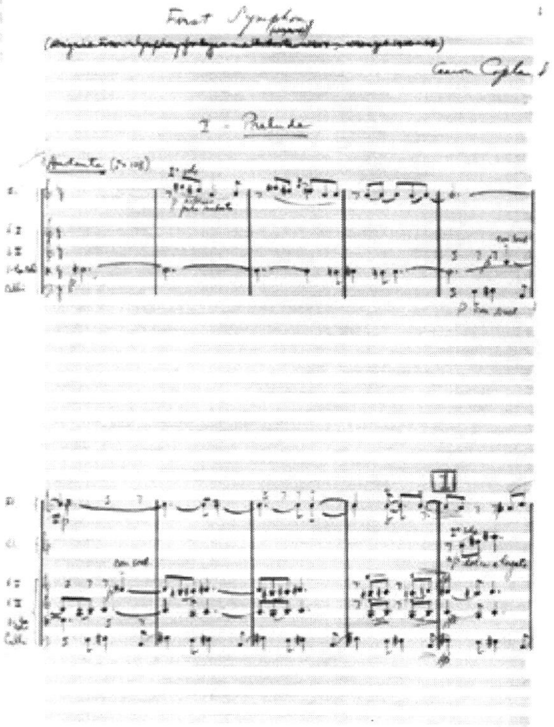

Above: Manuscript page of the Prelude from the *Symphony for Organ and Orchestra*

Right: The revised version without organ of the *First Symphony*

in composing works for organ and orchestra. Not every concert hall has an organ, and the composer limits himself seriously in performance possibilities. Practical considerations, therefore, dictated a version of the piece without organ. It was not that I was dissatisfied with the original, and I am still delighted when the piece is performed with organ and orchestra.

In the summer of 1926, when I was staying in Guéthary, a Basque village in France, I tried out an arrangement of the Scherzo without organ, using an amateur orchestra. Fritz Reiner conducted it in this form with the Philadelphia Orchestra at Carnegie Hall on 4 and 5 November 1927. Reiner considered the work "very American." I decided to rescore the entire symphony; the result was a revised version that became my *First Symphony*. In it, the organ part is replaced with additional orchestration—woodwinds in lyrical passages, and piano elsewhere. Additional brass add necessary punch to sections that depended on massive organ chords, such as the closing bars of the Finale. The *First Symphony* was premiered in Berlin with the Berlin Symphony Orchestra conducted by Ernest Ansermet in 1931. Later on, I arranged the Prelude from the *Symphony* as a separate piece for chamber orchestra.[5]

In a tribute to Koussevitzky in 1944 on the occasion of his twentieth anniversary with the Boston Symphony Orchestra (BSO), I wrote, "The story of Serge Koussevitzky and the American composer will someday take on the character of a legend."[6] And so it has. Everyone who knew him has stories about "Koussie." (I doubt anyone ever called him that to his face, and I sometimes wondered if he knew how often and how hilariously his expressions and speech were imitated.) Koussevitzky was a unique combination—awesome as a musician, dignified and elegant as a man—but unintentionally funny when he spoke English. Part of the Koussevitzky legend has to do with the Maestro's strong support of new music, and his outspoken reactions to it. If he didn't like a piece, he would say so in no uncertain terms. Some other conductor might perform a new work if Koussevitzky turned it down, but the special atmosphere that surrounded a Koussevitzky premiere would be lacking. But if he liked a work, he liked it wholeheartedly, and that meant a performance by the BSO, every young American composer's dream.

Players in the orchestra who worked under Koussevitzky, had their special stories about him. All agreed that he was a benevolent despot. Whatever the piece, no matter how the orchestra felt about it, Koussevitzky would demand the same attention as for a recognized masterpiece. He would say to the orchestra, "The next Beethoven vill from Colorado come!" He felt responsible, as musical leader of the community, for convincing both orchestra and public of the value of the new music which he accepted for performance.

Koussevitzky's programs in Boston were planned so that the major portion of rehearsal time could be devoted to a new work, and when he invited composers to rehearsals, usually Thursday

[5] The score for Copland's *Prelude* for chamber orchestra was donated to the Sibley Library, Eastman School of Music, by David Diamond, November 1943. A version for piano trio is in the Kirkpatrick papers, Yale, unpublished. See Perlis, "Aaron Copland and John Kirkpatrick: 'Dear John, Can you help me out?'" paper presented 18 November 2000 at the Library of Congress.

[6] See Aaron Copland, "Serge Koussevitzky and the American Composer," *Modern Music*, XXX:3 (July 1944), 255-69.

mornings, the orchestra members were on special guard—they knew the Maestro would be particularly demanding. He had the kind of authority over his men that no longer exists in American orchestras. One likes to think that it was his enthusiasm for the music that caught on to the players, but if not, his hold on them was so secure that we as composers felt supported by the entire BSO as well as by its conductor. It is not by chance that during the twenty-five years of Koussevitzky's leadership, from 1924 to 1949, American symphonic music came of age. During that time he gave the first performances of sixty-six American pieces. Moreover, once a work was performed, it was often repeated several times, even on the heels of adverse comment. In 1981, a Sunday *New York Times* article summed up that year's musical activities. The title was "Is There Life After Premieres for New Music?"[7] The answers were overwhelmingly negative. It would not please Koussevitzky to know that he set no precedent by his custom of keeping contemporary works in the repertoire. Koussevitzky's profound commitment to contemporary music extended to the economic and physical well-being of each composer. He felt personally responsible for us. I recall being surprised to discover that in the late twenties Koussevitzky had spoken privately to Claire Reis, asking her not to urge me to join the board of the League of Composers because it might infringe on my composing time. He could never accustom himself to the fact that in a country as rich as ours, composers could not devote themselves full time to writing music. He had a reverential attitude toward the act of composing that seemed positively romantic, even though it was often directed toward twentieth- century music.

Koussevitzky was determined to support his ideas with more than talk. In 1942 he established a foundation in honor of his wife, Natalie, who died that year. The Koussevitzky Foundation's basic aim is to assist composers. I was on the board of the foundation for many years, and I recall Koussevitzky, at one of the earliest meetings, making a plea for a composers' fund to be started by musicians, who would donate one dollar each, because, as he said, "We musicians must be first to stand by the composer because we owe him most. . ."[8] The Koussevitzky Foundation awarded many scholarships to gifted students of the Berkshire Music Center;[9] it aided composers and commissioned new works. In addition, it is a continuing tribute to Serge Koussevitzky, friend of the American composer. He was certainly a friend to me—in fact, Koussevitzky's support was crucial to my development as a composer. When the *Symphony for Organ and Orchestra* caused a furor in the Boston papers and was called "ultra-modern," Koussevitzky was unfazed. After all, he pointed out, if everybody loved it from the start, there would be no challenge. He promptly invited me to write another work for the Boston Symphony Orchestra to be premiered the following season. His confidence in me seemed unshakeable, perhaps because it was part of an unswerving belief in the creative musical force of our times. Sometime later I discovered that Koussevitzky was somewhat a frustrated composer himself; I am convinced that this must have accounted for his deep understanding for what it means to write music.

[7] Allan Kozinn, "Is There Life After Premieres for New Music?" *The New York Times*, Arts and Leisure Section (29 December 1981), 19-20.

[8] See minutes of the Koussevitzky Foundation meetings in Copland's files in the Library of Congress.

[9] The Koussevitzky Foundation of New York City and the Serge Koussevitzky Music Foundation in the Library of Congress commission approximately eight new works annually. Jointly granting the commissions are the organzations who will perform the new works.

After the performances of the *Organ Symphony*, Paul Rosenfeld discussed my financial problems with Minna Lederman, and they worked out a sketchy little plan. Several affluent women known to both of them were invited to her parents' house, and I came there to play my piano pieces for them. After I left, a collection was taken, but the amount was so small that Minna said to Paul, "Now you must go to Alma." Alma Wertheim, the daughter of Ambassador Morgenthau and a wealthy patron of the arts, invited me to play for her twice. After some consideration she gave me a check for $1,000. Without that, I don't know how I would have managed in the year that followed while I was composing *Music for the Theatre*.

Minna Lederman Daniel[10]

I was at the concert when Damrosch made his splashy statement. The piece didn't seem to me in any way shocking. But it's true, from that very moment Aaron became a public figure. His parents were present and I was struck by his resemblance to his mother. She was slender, tall, had blue eyes and a kindly expression. Something of that look is in Copland's face too, but it's a little misleading, I think. It's partly due to his thick eyeglasses. He's not all so benevolent. He's really a little sharper than that.

When he first came to my parents' house, it was for help to get him survival money for the rest of the year. He now had a commission from the League for a new piece—and commissions in those days were seldom for money, mostly they were promises for public performance. I remember how he looked. Even then he had an extraordinary presence. Being young myself, I didn't think of him so much as a young man. The image of Stravinsky came to me immediately because the face had a similar irregularity of features, although it was not at all so composed and balanced as Stravinsky's. His clothes were very catch-as-catch-can, hanging loosely around him. Though of a very much better quality today, they often give the same casually-put-together air.

Aaron, when young, was sensitive about his appearance but I never could understand why. For artists and photographers he was always the perfect subject, the face one could never forget—after Stravinsky's, THE face. All in all he had, as the cartoonist Al Frueh said, a triangular look. A long, lean body gave the perfect balance to his impressive beaked head. Even then there was an air of unstudied elegance about him. A hawk, yet not predatory. Not what you would call good-looking—something much better, more striking.

Aaron wrote his first piece for me for the January 1925 issue of the Review. *From then on, he became my unofficial associate. Although he did not join the League's board until almost a decade later, he had an immediate effect on the magazine. In a talk we had soon after that article appeared, he asked: "Why do you have all these Europeans write everything? There are plenty of Americans, and young ones too, who can do just as well." And to prove that, he soon introduced me to many of the composers of his generation who, writing for* Modern Music, *became famous as composer-critics, a new departure in America. He brought Sessions, Piston, Harris, to me and soon afterwards Thomson, Bowles, McPhee, Nancarrow,*

[10] Interview, Minna Lederman with Perlis, 17 September 1980, New York City.

Carter. Aaron developed a household interest in the magazine. He seemed to belong to it. He wanted to make it the voice of the American composer. Of course it never was quite that. The international presence remained very strong. But he did his best to give the journal a contemporary, made-in-America quality. In the immediately following years, he met so many people here and abroad that he became a great, vital contact for us. All at once he seemed to know everyone. There was especially Koussevitzky, who proved a tremendous resource not only for Aaron's own advancement but for others of his own period. Aaron could introduce people, and his words, no matter how offhand, were given consideration—though as he recently pointed out to me, Koussevitzky had his own predilections and made his own decisions. Aaron seemed to radiate influence. I never considered this a calculated effect or that, as has sometimes been alleged, he was trying to build a power base. The scene that grew up around him was, more simply, a consequence of his very open personality. He had a very real desire—no, more than that—a need for the companionship of colleagues. His concern for their development was as great as if it were part of his own.

When Aaron traveled through Latin America as a United States ambassador of goodwill, he sent travel letters back to Modern Music. *When he went to Hollywood, he wrote about what that was like. As one of the first serious composers working for radio, he described that process. And when the magazine developed columns, he took on the leading one, "mostly because I wanted to get those scores and records for free." His criticism was always commonsensical, his style precise and matter of fact, and his sermons as brief as possible—a great asset for a magazine whose space was limited. To Aaron, I would always say, "Tell what you're doing." To Roger, "What's on your mind?" And to Virgil, "What's going on in places?" Aaron was very good on a one-to-one basis; he never seemed to enjoy conferences with a lot of people. Things should be done simply, he thought. There were certainly, until even the closing years of the magazine, no conflicts between us. I profited greatly by his ideas and by his worldwide connections, and I think he found it agreeable to have a place where he could set down, with little restraint, in easy prose, his latest thoughts on his latest experiences.*

I've been Aaron's companion many times when he seemed eager to avoid making a fracas. He hated stirring up a fuss over anything. That's how he was, and that's how he remained. He liked things to go along agreeably—anything to avoid a quarrel. Aaron could lose his temper but it's known that he's never done so in public. Virgil seemed to think that Aaron always planned to be cool to avoid controversy, but I didn't see him just that way. Aaron knew what he wanted and what was important to him. He had a self-preserving sense of not wasting himself. His coolness, his apparent imperviousness to insult and injury was deep and instinctive, a mode of self-protection. It kept him going all his life. Situations that might have shattered others seem never to have even affected him. For better or for worse he appeared immune to criticism. From Koussevitzky and Bernstein he might have taken suggestions leading to a better performance of his music; from Menotti, whose theater skills he greatly admired, he might have followed advice about restructuring The Tender Land. *But about his methods of composing, I don't think anyone since the early student days with Boulanger had any great effect on him. Aaron was always confident that his was the right way at least for him and, moreover, that for him things seldom took the wrong turn. Indeed he was not only successful but fortunate. He never put his faith in someone else's promises. His slogan was always do it yourself, yet helpful things outside his control did seem always to happen. He was apparently the right man, at the right time, in the right place.*

Copland's long-held mission has been to fulfill himself as a composer—he wanted, first and last, to compose. Well, that's enough mission for anybody. Then also he had a commitment, a deep, long-lasting one from his early youth, to the specific American situation. Nothing ever persuaded him to deviate from that. His speedy recognition as a leader was not the result of composing the most advanced music. When he first came on the scene there were Varèse and Cowell and other more avant-garde figures already active, many of them getting a hearing at the concerts of the International Composers' Guild. But Copland was what we now call charismatic. And also he had a tremendous curiosity about new music. He would go to more kinds of things than you can imagine. The only other composer anything like that was Elliott Carter in the thirties and early forties. Copland, for three decades, pursued a continuously active interest in what was new, and he took it upon himself to get new music—of course the new music that appealed to him—into public view.

Aaron's speaking was best when brief and to the point, and I for one feel this way about his music, too. The works I prize most are those that show the bare bones, what he himself calls the "hard-bitten" pieces, the Piano Variations, Statements, *and the* Short Symphony, *all written about 1930, and a few of the more daring works of the mid-sixties. Aaron admired those of his colleagues who have written eight, ten, or twelve symphonies, but he himself experimented intensely with smaller and more restricted forms that projected his individual self with great success.* Night Thoughts, *for piano, written as late as 1972, makes an appeal almost as personal and poignant as his early trio,* Vitebsk.

I have known Aaron for a very long time. One forms basic impressions about people that are hard to get rid of. Then one day you wake up and see that there have been changes. Some things about Aaron stayed the same. He was austere in his style of living and simple in his tastes, with little demand for luxury. As he grew older he had greater need for the comforts of home.

The great change that overtook Aaron was entirely natural; it was due to the end of his composing life. He was philosophical about this because, I suspect, he felt he had fulfilled himself. His whole being was centered on writing music, especially at night. A real night owl. One can picture him with the skies dark and the house dark, and only a light in his study, working it out for himself and out of himself. In later years he was projected into public view as a conductor, meeting hundreds of people everywhere. He was charming, he was radiant, he smiled when admirers come up and asked for his autograph. This external life seemed for a time to take the place of everything before. But, more and more, when he came home from out there, he sought tranquillity and rest, no longer to work but to recharge himself. He still liked everything about him to be merry, he had no use for sad stories, and no time to waste on regrets or mistakes. He remained assured and confident. But there was always a modesty about Copland, an attitude of not taking success for granted. Famous the world over, more than comfortably well off, there was still for him a modicum of wonder about it all. Virgil once said to me, "You treat Aaron like a prince." "Well," I said, "he's certainly not imperial. But in his manner, in his way of dealing with the world, yes indeed he is a prince."

During the winter of 1925 my article on Antheil appeared in *Modern Music*, and I wrote a piece for *Musical America* on the value of European study to American composers. In it I made a plea for the establishment of an American National Conservatory.[11] The *Times* printed a lengthy letter I wrote in defense of Mahler, who had been maligned by the critics after Mengelberg conducted his *Second Symphony*[12] in New York. Nadia had put me in touch

[11] Aaron Copland, "What Europe Means to the Aspiring Composer," *Musical America*, XLI:ii (3 January 1925), 25, 27.

[12] Aaron Copland, "Defends the Music of Mahler," *The New York Times* (5 April 1925), Sec. IX, 6.

with Gerald Reynolds, conductor of the Women's University Glee Club in New York, who commissioned me to write two choruses to be performed in the spring. For the first, "The House on the Hill," I chose a text by the American poet Edwin Arlington Robinson, "Children of the Night" of 1897. It is for female voices a cappella and opens with a wordless vocalise divided between two groups of singers. An unusual aspect of the score is the lack of common bar lines; instead, each of the four parts has vertical lines to indicate the stresses of certain words. Its feeling is deliberately simple and meant to reflect the melancholy expression of the abandoned house in the poem: "They are all gone away, the house is shut and still. . . ." The second chorus, "An Immorality," to a text by Ezra Pound from *Lustra* of 1916, is in an entirely different mood. Written for soprano, chorus, and piano, it is complex and lively with snappy, syncopated rhythms. I had incorporated jazz poly-rhythms into *Grohg* and the *Organ Symphony,* but "An Immorality" was my first real jazz piece.[13] It seemed natural for the piano part to be given the difficult rhythms, and I made sure to play it myself at its first performance. When Schirmer in Boston published the choruses in 1926, I wrote to a young composer friend, Israel Citkowitz, "E. C. Schirmer now possesses the signal honor of being the first gentleman to print my music in America. We poor American composers—no conductors and no publishers and no nothing."

My studio was modest and I lived simply, but it did not take long for Mrs. Wertheim's gift to disappear. Some bright soul established the Guggenheim Foundation[14] just when I needed it most. Recommendations on my behalf were sent by Boulanger, Damrosch, Koussevitzky, and the violinist Arthur Hartman to the foundation's adviser, Thomas Whitney Surette.[15] If Mr. Surette did not have much feeling for contemporary music, he admired Nadia greatly and had respect for her judgments. I believe that she was in great part responsible for my receiving the first Guggenheim Fellowship in music. The amount was $2,500 to be used during the academic year 1925-26, and to be spent in whatever way I saw fit. I was delighted when the fellowship was renewed the following year. It meant I did not have to face the difficult problem of how to make a living until 1927.

The competition between the International Composers' Guild (ICG) and the League of Composers was such that a composer could not be allied with both. Since the League had presented my music first in New York, I could have no connection with the ICG. Varèse led his small group of supporters, principally the harpist Carlos Salzedo and American composer Carl Ruggles. These three seemed incongruous to me—Varèse and Salzedo so very French and Ruggles a salty New Englander. Ruggles was suspicious of audiences, fearing popularity might compromise the innovative nature of the group's activities. On the other hand, the League was aiming for larger audiences and more financial support. Claire Reis, executive director, was able to put the League on secure financial footing by gathering support from wealthy music lovers and patrons. Claire had extraordinary organizational ability and a great deal of personal charm. She was genuinely devoted to composers and determined to have the League run primarily by them, but she was smart enough to use outside expertise when needed.

The success of the League for so many years was due in great part to Claire's leadership. When she heard that Stokowski was to conduct two concerts for the ICG in the 1925-26 season, off she went to Boston to get Koussevitzky for the League. The League had commissioned me to compose a chamber orchestra piece. Claire, knowing of my recent association with Koussevitzky, asked him to conduct my newly commissioned work with members of the Boston Symphony in New York in the fall. The Maestro was delighted when I presented him with the idea; he simply repeated what he had already told me—that he was willing to play anything I gave him for the next season. I wrote to Nadia: "At first, I thought of setting part of Rimbaud's 'Saison en Enfer,' but I have changed my mind, and now I think I will write a series of pieces to be called 'Incidental Music for an Imaginary Drama.' I think that is a better idea. I even have a few themes already." These ideas would become my *Music for the Theatre.*

I needed a quiet place out of the city where I could work on the new piece during the summer months. Again, Paul Rosenfeld came to my aid by suggesting the MacDowell Colony in Peterborough, New Hampshire.

In 1906 the American composer and pianist Edward MacDowell had expressed the wish to establish a center where artists in various fields could live and work without interruption, exchanging ideas with one another in a tranquil country setting. Mrs. MacDowell—Marian—also a pianist, had purchased a summer place in Peterborough, New Hampshire, in 1896, where the couple spent their summers. "Hillcrest," as the place was called, seemed a perfect setting for an artist colony. In 1907, a year before the composer's death, Mrs. MacDowell established the Colony, and it was she who was responsible for everything—funding, administration, and maintenance—in order to make her husband's dream a reality. At first, Hillcrest was used as the main building, and studios for housing the artists were modeled after the Log Cabin, built for MacDowell's own use during his lifetime. Marian MacDowell gave her personal attention to every detail. I recall her delivering lunches and leaving them quietly on the porch each day so that work hours would be uninterrupted. Studios were gradually added over the years. A library, residence halls, and Colony Hall were also added, where in the evenings guests were expected to appear for dinner and conversation. Hundreds of acres of beautiful woodlands have been kept undisturbed. The MacDowell Colony offers a unique environment that combines the isolation needed for creative effort with a relaxed atmosphere for exchanging ideas with other artists. Each studio is equipped with just what is needed, but no more than necessary for one's particular art: a cot, an easy chair, a good reading light, and for musicians, always a well-tuned piano. The studios are isolated from each other and differ in architecture; each seems to have sprung up accidentally from whatever had been in its spot previously. There is the Irving Fine cottage (named after a colleague who had stayed at the Colony) and the Monday Music studio. Writers use Veltin cottage and painters love

[13] Ink autograph manuscript at Lincoln Center Library, New York City.

[14] The Guggenheim Foundation was founded by Senator and Mrs. Simon Guggenheim in the memory of their son, John Simon Guggenheim, who died in 1922.

[15] A copy of Damrosch's letter is in Copland's files in the Library of Congress; see also a letter from Koussevitzky to Copland (17 April 1925): "It will be a pleasure to help you gain a scholarship from the Guggenheim Foundation." Two letters from Copland to Hartman are in the Free Library of Philadelphia.

Alexander for its space and light. I no longer recall the name of my first studio, but I can picture it clearly in my mind's eye. (I know that I used Chapman and Phi Beta studios through the years, among others.)

At the Colony in 1925 I met Louis and Jean Starr Untermeyer, Elinor Wylie, William Rose Benet, sculptress Tennessee Anderson (she sculpted a head of me that summer), and composer Henry F. Gilbert from Boston. Gilbert was an unusual man of almost sixty who had written symphonic works incorporating Negro and Indian themes. He was interested in the subject of American music, but he was very much a loner and kept to himself. I shall always remember the amazement on the face of old Henry F. on hearing from me that one of our major symphony orchestras had paid an American composer for the performance rights to his first composition. Gilbert exclaimed, "What? Just like Richard Strauss?"

Another composer at MacDowell that summer was young and very lively and got to know everyone right off. He was just a few years my senior and had an impressive natural musical talent. His name was Roy Harris. There was a freshness and homey quality about Roy at that time. He didn't seem at all like a composer—more like a farmer who had taken it into his head suddenly to become a composer of concert music. Roy had a simple charm and a winning personality when I first knew him. It was fun to have another young composer to talk things over with. When he told me that he needed a teacher, I suggested Boulanger, and a year later Roy was in Paris studying with her.

The atmosphere of tranquillity and seclusion at the MacDowell Colony, without total isolation from other artists, was perfect for me. I stayed at the Colony eight times in all, and later became active on the board of the MacDowell Association, serving as president for several years in the sixties. But as a young composer in 1925, I could not have foreseen that I would receive the MacDowell Colony Medal of Honor in 1961, an award given once a year to an artist of the Colony's choice. Only one thing was on my mind that first summer—a new orchestral work for Koussevitzky to premiere next season.

Certain musical works seem to have careers of their own, independent of those of their authors. For several years after it was written, conductors programmed *Music for the Theatre* more frequently than any other piece of mine. I suspect that this was partly because of the jazz content in several of the movements. It may be difficult to imagine today that the very idea of jazz in a concert hall was piquant in the twenties, but it seems that any piece based on jazz was assured of a mild *succès de scandale*. European composers thought of jazz as an exotic novelty; it was no surprise when Milhaud announced in 1927 that there was not a single young composer in Europe interested in jazz anymore. I was intrigued with jazz rhythms, not for superficial effects, but for use in larger forms, with unconventional harmonies. My aim was to write a work that would be recognizably American within a serious musical idiom. Jazz offered American composers a native product from which to explore rhythm; for whatever the definition of jazz, it must be agreed that it is essentially rhythmic in character. Perhaps jazz was, as Virgil put it, "Copland's one wild oat,"[16] but *Music for the Theatre* and the *Piano Concerto* were characteristic of my musical thinking at the time. And long after the fad of concert jazz faded, the influence of jazz would be felt in the development of poly-rhythms. In a 1927 article, "Jazz Structure and Influence," I addressed these issues, concluding: "It [jazz] may be the substance not only of the American composer's fox trots and Charlestons, but of his lullabies and nocturnes."[17]

Music for the Theatre, composed mostly at the MacDowell Colony, was completed in September 1925 at the Lake Placid summer camp of my former piano teacher, Clarence Adler. Adler had a shack built especially for me up the mountain and named it "The Clouds." He described my visit: "I have listened (at some distance, of course) to Copland in the throes of composition, and it is something to hear! He bangs and hammers at the piano, at the same time singing in shrill, dissonant tones."[18] In New York at the beginning of October, I received a letter inviting me to stay with the Koussevitzkys again for a week before the premiere. "Bring everything you have written in the past months," wrote Koussevitzky. So I arrived in Boston with *Three Dances* (excerpts from *Grohg*) and the new suite.

Music for the Theatre was written with no specific play in mind. It had started with musical ideas that might have been combined as incidental music to a play were the right one at hand. The music seemed to suggest a certain theatrical atmosphere, so I chose the title after developing the ideas into five short movements: The "Prologue" has a certain brashness about it that was typical of my age and the times. It begins rather suddenly with a trumpet solo, followed by a tenderly lyrical passage leading into an allegro mid-section with obvious jazz influence before a return to the lyrical material. (I am told that this resembles the nursery tune "Three Blind Mice," but there was no conscious intention on my part of quoting it.) "Dance," short and jazzy, quotes the familiar popular tune "East Side, West Side;"[19] "Interlude," a kind of song without words, is built on a lyric theme repeated three times with slight changes. "Burlesque," best described by its title, emphasizes another characteristic of the twenties—the love of grotesquerie achieved by a liberal use of harmonic dissonance. It was partly inspired by the popular comedienne Fanny Brice. The "Epilogue" incorporates material from the first and third movements and recaptures the quiet mood of the "Prologue." *Music for the Theatre* is scored for small orchestra and is dedicated to Serge Koussevitzky. The challenging jazz rhythms caused the Maestro even more trouble than the *Organ Symphony*. Koussevitzky really knew nothing about American popular music or jazz—these idioms were not in his Russian bones, so to speak. So it was a matter of familiarizing himself with typically American rhythmic materials. To this end, we spent every evening before the concert in his studio going over the score together.

Koussevitzky decided to program *Music for the Theatre* after Mozart's Overture to *The Magic Flute* and Beethoven's *Fourth Symphony*, and before Wagner's *Prelude and Love-Death*

[16] Virgil Thomson, "Aaron Copland (American Composers VII)," *Modern Music*, IX: 2 (January-February 1932), 67-73.

[17] Aaron Copland, "Jazz Structure and Influence," *Modern Music,* IV:2 (January-February 1927), 9-14.

[18] Clarence Adler, as quoted by M.L.S. (Mary L. Stoltzfus, assoc. ed.), *Musical Courier*, CXXXIV:3 (September 1946), 40.

[19] "The Sidewalks of New York," by Charles B. Lawlor and James W. Blake (New York: Herman Darewski Music Publishing Co., August 1904).

Oct. 6, 1925
135 W. 74th St.
New York City, N.Y.

My dear Mr. Koussevitsky:

Mrs. Reis has asked me to inform you that the League of Composers has accepted my new work for chamber orchestra ("Music for the Theatre") for performance on the 28th of November. I should like to send you the score immediately, but with your permission I shall first have the parts copied, which will take a few weeks. I hope you will have no objections if I come to Boston to hear the rehearsals, and perhaps a day or two before they begin, you will allow me to give you an idea of the work at the piano, as we did last winter with the 'Symphony'!

Since I have mentioned the 'Symphony', I shall take the liberty of pointing out that if you intend to repeat that work, it will be necessary to find another organist, as Mademoiselle Boulanger will not be in America this season. I should be glad to send the organ part to whomever you may select.

Also, I want you to know that I have a new score for large orchestra ("Three Dances") that I am keeping for you and the Boston Symphony. The parts are almost ready, I only await your pleasure in the matter.

I sincerely trust that my new works may not be unworthy to have expended on them the genius of your baton.

With kindest regards to Madame Koussevitsky, I am,

Yours devotedly,
Aaron Copland

Letter to Serge Koussevitsky, 1925

from *Tristan and Isolde*. Boston audiences are brought up not to protest publicly even when greatly shocked in the concert hall. Therefore, the reception of my new piece at its premiere, 20 November 1925, seemed to be of mild surprise and amusement. But the following day, Warren Storey Smith wrote in the *Boston Post*: "*Music for the Theatre* is a sort of super jazz. . . . The conductor exploded a tonal bombshell that left in its wake a mingling of surprise, perplexity, indignation and enthusiasm." On the other hand, the conservative H. T. Parker ended a lengthy review in the *Boston Evening Transcript* that compared me to Gershwin: ". . . a young modernist ready and unashamed with melodic invention; a young American composer neither repressing nor sentimentalizing poetic mood. Wonders are still possible; even Brooklyn may give them birth." And the venerable Philip Hale called me "a young composer of indisputable talent . . . with a great gift of imagination. . . ." Of jazz in the concert hall, Hale asked, "Why should not one movement in a suite be symbolic of American life as it now is?"

The trustees of the Boston Symphony voted their approval for the Maestro to appear in the concert in New York sponsored by the League of Composers. After conducting a full orchestra at Carnegie Hall in the afternoon of 28 November, Koussevitzky led a chamber orchestra made up of Boston Symphony players that evening at Town Hall in an all-modern program. Four Europeans were included—Alexandre Tansman, Prokofiev, Honegger, and Ravel—and one American. The critics in New York were extremely unsympathetic. One commented that Koussevitzky smiled throughout the concert as though he was in on a secret that nobody else knew. Samuel Chotzinoff of the *New York World* described the concert as "One of the League's evening comedies," and he called me "the cherished Scion of the League." But it was Olin Downes of *The Times* who was most scathing: "We do not care if a long time elapses before we listen again to *Music for the Theatre*." A considerable time did elapse before Downes heard the piece again. Seven years later he wrote,

> In 1925 when first heard, this music impressed the writer as ultra modern to the point of affectation. Today he feels that this is music of genuine inspiration and feeling, music composed and not merely invented, that it has a personal color, fancy and, in the best moments, emotion—the work of a young composer finding himself, with something real and not merely derivative to say. . .[20]

Downes even included *Music for the Theatre* in his lecture-recital series of 1934.

This turnaround by a noted critic reminded me early in my career not to take reviews too seriously. I never left a concert hall or read a writeup and felt hurt because I wasn't being understood. I was, on the contrary, rather brazen about it, thinking, "Those dumbbells, they'll see, just give them time." I didn't have any sense of "Oh well, if they think it's awful, it must be awful"—there was none of that. Reviews bothered me only when they upset my parents. After the reception of *Music for the Theatre* in New York, my father, who knew nothing about music, remarked: "After all, these fellows get paid for their opinions. They must know something about music!" But I composed out of real conviction. It never occurred to me to think that everybody was going to love my music right away. I realized I was using a contemporary musical language that most audiences were not accustomed to hearing. And actually, there was a lot of fun in bucking the tide and feeling part of the avant garde out there fighting new battles. That feeling was very much part of the excitement of the times.

Walter Damrosch conducted a concert each season called "Modern Music—Pleasant and Unpleasant." I don't know into which category *Music for the Theatre* fell, but Damrosch included it in his 1926 program. Since Dr. Damrosch had never made any secret of his antipathy to modern music, I was surprised and rather flattered at his conducting this piece; moreover, he invited me to play the piano part. During one rehearsal he stopped the orchestra abruptly on an astringent chord that disturbed him and turning to me asked, "Must that chord be that way?" I stood my ground with all the temerity of youth and firmly replied, "Yes, Dr. Damrosch, that's the way that chord must be."

Braving the wrath of the critical fraternity, Koussevitzky continued to schedule *Music for the Theatre*. He brought it back to New York only a few months after the premiere—this time as a regular part of a Boston Symphony program at Carnegie Hall and the Brooklyn Academy of Music (7 January 1926). Members of the board of directors of the Academy of Music came backstage during intermission to protest the playing of such ultra-modern stuff. "But gentlemen," Koussevitzky said, "Copland is one of your boys. I played it here in Brooklyn to do honor to your city." The representatives from Brooklyn said, "Moreover, we hired the entire Boston Symphony Orchestra, and there were only twenty-four musicians on stage!" "Gentlemen, have patience and you shall be satisfied. The next piece, *Alpine Symphony* by Richard Strauss, uses an orchestra of over a hundred players. They vill all be busy. You shall have your money's worth!" Koussevitzky continued to program my suite—a Paris performance stands out in my mind, because of an incident that involved the well-known French composer Florent Schmitt. It was May 1926 and it was Koussevitzky's first concert in Paris since he had left for Boston. He led an orchestra of French musicians, brought together for the occasion, at the Théâtre National de l'Opéra. I was in Paris, and Koussevitzky invited me to play the piano part. After the concert Schmitt came to me backstage and remarked, "See here, Monsieur Copland, what is the meaning of this? If you Americans begin now to export music instead of merely to import music, where will we poor French composers be?"

In 1933 Koussevitzky introduced *Music for the Theatre* at the Coolidge Auditorium in Washington, marking my debut at the Library of Congress; and in 1938 at Tanglewood, my first piece to be performed at the Berkshire Music Festival. Stokowski conducted the composition in 1932 with the Philadelphia Orchestra. In 1933 Serge Prokofiev wrote from Paris (2 October): "My dear Copland, I received a letter from Moscow, that the performance of your *Music for Theatre* [sic] is announced for this fall. . ." I never heard whether it was played in Russia, but many other performances have taken place through the years, right up to 1989 when the suite was included in a twelve-hour eightieth birthday celebration at Symphony Space in New York City called "Wall-to-Wall Copland."

Several choreographers have found the rhythmic aspects of *Music for the Theatre* appealing.[21] The first recording was made in 1941, conducted by Howard Hanson with the Roch-

[20] Olin Downes, *The New York Times* (26 April 1933), 22.

[21] In 1942 Lincoln Kirstein used the score for *Time Table* by BAllet Theatre, choreographed by Antony Tudor, first presented under the title of *Despedida* by American Ballet Caravan for a South American (cont.)

ester Symphony on the Victor label; Leonard Bernstein recorded it for CBS with the New York Philharmonic in 1965.

I had dreamed of representing American music on the international scene, but had not expected to do so as early as 1927. It was announced that two American works had been chosen to be played at the ISCM Festival in Frankfurt that summer: Henry Gilbert's *The Dance in Place Congo* and *Music for the Theatre.* I played the piano part myself, and it amused me to watch those honest German musicians struggling with jazz rhythms for the first time in their lives! During intermissions at rehearsals the men gathered around the piano to get first-hand advice on how to manage the new American rhythms. Imagine—a young American teaching the Germans anything about music!

Music for the Theatre and my other compositions of this "jazz period" *sounded* American; they could not have been written by a European. That is precisely what I intended at the time, just as I consciously hoped to forward the cause of contemporary American music by my activities and writings. If I was a leader in contemporary music, I was a follower of the modern movement in the other arts. As early as 1916, a group of writers began publishing *The Seven Arts,* a magazine conceived to promote their ideas.[22] Waldo Frank's book of 1919, *Our America,*[23] challenged writers to bring America into the modern art movement. Alfred Stieglitz was the unofficial leader of this group. His gallery was the hang-out for younger artists such as photographer Paul Strand, painters John Marin and Georgia O'Keeffe (later Stieglitz's wife), Waldo Frank and other writers whom I met at Paul Rosenfeld's apartment.[24] They were all aware that music lagged behind the other arts, and they took it for granted that I, as the contemporary composer among them, would do something about the situation. I thought of myself as involved in their movement and instinctively felt part of a "school." I knew that it would take a combined effort if America were to find an artistic voice of its own. In the twenties American composers had few outlets for making themselves known to each other and to the rest of the world. As a start toward alleviating this condition, I wrote a rather bold article for *Modern Music* naming seventeen promising composers between the ages of twenty-three and thirty-three. This may have been daring, but at least it pointed out the fact of our existence. I stated: "In America our new composers have been left to shift for themselves. . . . Perhaps hearing about them may induce someone to let us really *hear* them. . ."[25]

---

tour in 1941; in 1943 the "Prologue" was used by Doris Humphrey and Jerome Weidman for *Decade*; in 1966 *Music for the Theatre* was combined with *Danzón Cubano* for *Lessons in Love* by Peter Darrel, and in 1979 Eliot Feld used the score for his ballet *Scenes for the Theatre.*

[22] *The Seven Arts,* 1-2 (November 1916-October 1917) (New York: The Seven Arts Publishing Company, 1916-17).

[23] Waldo Frank, *Our America* (New York: Boni and Liveright, 1919).

[24] Stieglitz's galleries were considered the most important centers for advanced art in the U.S.: The Little Galleries (also called "291") until 1917; The Intimate Gallery, from 1925 to 1929; and An American Place, from 1929 to 1946.

[25] Aaron Copland, "America's Young Men of Promise," *Modern Music,* III:3 (March-April 1926), 23-20. Copland would write three similar articles at about ten-year intervals: (1936) "America's Young Men–Ten Years Later"; (1949) "The New 'School' of American Composers"; and (1959) "Postscript for the Generation of the Fifties." All repr. in *Copland on Music.*

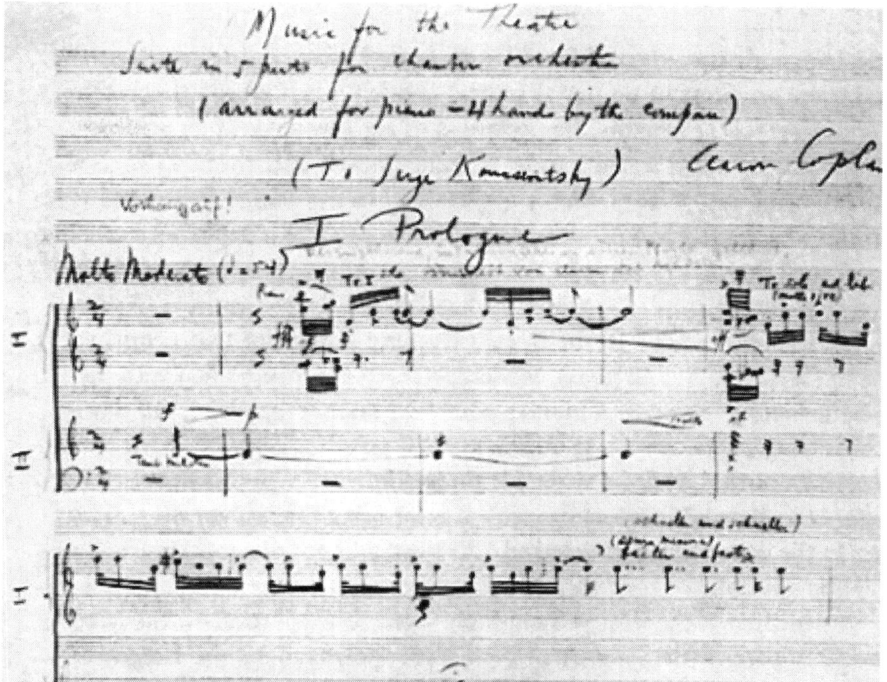

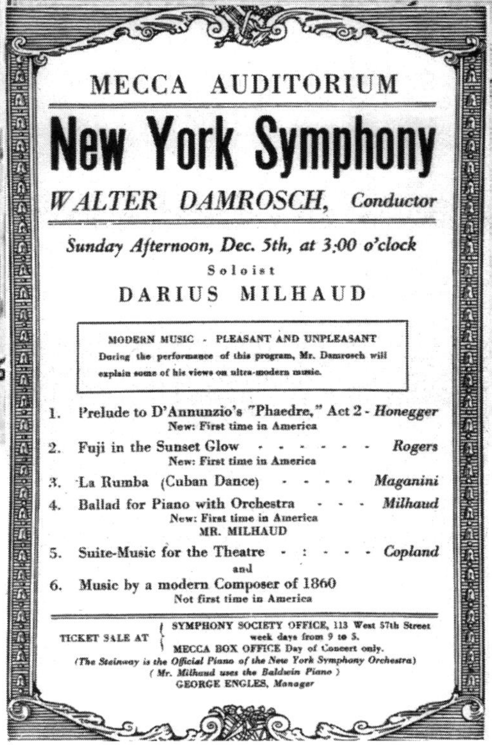

MECCA AUDITORIUM

New York Symphony

WALTER DAMROSCH, Conductor

Sunday Afternoon, Dec. 5th, at 3:00 o'clock

Soloist

DARIUS MILHAUD

MODERN MUSIC - PLEASANT AND UNPLEASANT
During the performance of this program, Mr. Damrosch will explain some of his views on ultra-modern music.

1. Prelude to D'Annunzio's "Phaedre," Act 2 - *Honegger*
New: First time in America
2. Fuji in the Sunset Glow - - - - - - *Rogers*
New: First time in America
3. La Rumba (Cuban Dance) - - - - *Maganini*
4. Ballad for Piano with Orchestra - - - *Milhaud*
New: First time in America
MR. MILHAUD
5. Suite-Music for the Theatre - - - - - *Copland*
and
6. Music by a modern Composer of 1860
Not first time in America

TICKET SALE AT { SYMPHONY SOCIETY OFFICE, 113 West 57th Street week days from 9 to 5. MECCA BOX OFFICE Day of Concert only.

(The Steinway is the Official Piano of the New York Symphony Orchestra)
(Mr. Milhaud uses the Baldwin Piano)
GEORGE ENGLES, *Manager*

Above: Manuscript, first page of the unpublished arrangement for piano four-hands of *Music for the Theatre*

Left: Program of *Music for the Theatre,* 1925

I was convinced that it was important for American composers to hold their own in Europe as well as at home. At that time, recognition abroad was still an important credential. Since Nadia was planning an all-American program to be sponsored by the SMI and Koussevitzky was to conduct *Music for the Theatre,* I decided to return to Europe, so I left with Clurman at the end of March 1926. Once in Paris, we took rooms on our old street, this time chez Mme Simoneau, at 59 Boulevard Pasteur, and renewed old acquaintances: Nadia and her mother, Annette Dieudonné and Marcelle de Manziarly, Virgil Thomson, George Antheil, and Herbert Elwell. Teddy (Theodore) Chanler, Douglas Moore, and Walter Piston were also in Paris, and I met Roger Sessions for the first time that spring at one of Mademoiselle's afternoon teas.

I was uncertain about completing two new pieces for violin and piano for Nadia's concert, so I suggested that the *Rondino* be substituted. I thought that it could be played by the quartet performing Antheil's work. But Antheil did not like the idea, perhaps because he was paying the quartet's expenses, so I was spurred on to finish two new pieces, *Nocturne* and *Ukelele Serenade*, after all. I invited the American violinist, Samuel Dushkin, to play the pieces with me. The program included six premieres. All the young Americans except Antheil were, or had been, Boulanger students. The audience was a distinguished one, since the SMI and Nadia had influential followings in the Parisian art world—even James Joyce made a rare appearance!

Two Pieces for Violin and Piano is about eight minutes in duration. The first piece, *Nocturne,* is slow and in the manner of a blues. It is dedicated to Israel Citkowitz, a promising young composer who was studying with me in New York. The second, *Ukelele Serenade,* dedicated to Samuel Dushkin, is an *allegro vivo.* It begins with quarter tones meant to achieve a blues effect, while arpeggiated chords in the right hand of the piano part simulate a ukulele sound. Later in the piece, the roles are reversed, with pizzicato quadruple violin stoppings representing the ukulele. The bar lines for the two instruments do not necessarily coincide.

A group of composers with the singer Ada T. MacLeish in Boulanger's apartment before a Paris concert of American music, spring 1926 (*left to right*): Herbert Elwell, Copland, MacLeish, Walter Piston, and Virgil Thomson

The American premiere of *Two Pieces* took place at a League concert on 13 February 1927 with works by five other young Americans: Randall Thompson, Teddy Chanler, Evelyn Berkman, Ruth Crawford, and Marc Blitzstein. Nadia promptly sent my new pieces to Schott & Sons. After I returned home, she wrote,

> Strecker takes the two pieces with joy. . . . I will speak with Sam [Dushkin] for some fingering perhaps but of course will not even consider any changes—naturally you will receive proofs (is it the word?). I advise you to write immediately to Willy Strecker in accepting—and perhaps say you are glad to be in his active, living business."

Nadia suggested I submit other works—"Strike the iron while it is hot."

Antheil had gained a reputation as the *enfant terrible* of young American composers. Before Harold and I left Paris, everyone was discussing his *Ballet mécanique,* which was to be premiered on 19 June 1926. In a letter to Israel Citkowitz, I described this unusual event:

> The scene is a beautiful theatre off the Champs-Elysées, filled with an audience of more than 2,000 people among whom one can distinguish James Joyce, Serge Koussevitzky, Ezra Pound, Darius Milhaud, Nadia Boulanger, Marcel Duchamp, Alfred Knopf, Boris de Schloezer etc., etc., each and every one buzzing with the excitement and expectation of hearing for the first time anywhere a program which contained—oh marvel of marvels—your only true rival— George Antheil! who proceeded to outsack the "Sacre" with the aid of a Playola and amplifiers, ventilators, buzzers and other what-not . . . brought forth the usual near-riot so everyone went home content. . . . I am in all honesty bound to repeat my unshakeable conviction—the boy is a genius. Need I add that he has yet to write a work which shows it. If he keeps on exactly as he has started the sum total of all his genius will be exactly nothing. Voila!

When *Ballet mécanique* was given its New York premiere the following April, Antheil invited me to be one of ten pianists on stage. The work created as much of a sensation in New York as it had in Paris.[26]

In 1926 Harold and I left Paris for Zurich to attend the Fourth Annual ISCM Festival, which I was to cover for *Modern Music.*[27] A more adventurous spirit had prevailed at earlier festivals; not only were there few new names, but the music that was performed was not of great interest. Schoenberg's *Wind Quintet* was a failure except with his closest supporters. Anton von Webern, who was present, complained to the critics, "One has no more reason to expect to appreciate this Quintet on a single hearing than to understand Kant after a cursory perusal." Webern's own *Five Orchestral Pieces* was the only work I was really taken with, and it had been

[26] *Ballet mécanique* had its U.S. premiere in Carnegie Hall on 10 April 1927. Composed in 1924 to a scenario by Fernand Léger, it was originally planned for sixteen mechanical pianos and percussion. Reports vary on the instrumentation for the Paris and New York premieres. See George Antheil, *Bad Boy of Music* (Garden City, N.Y.: Doubleday, 1945), 190-96, and Thomson, *Virgil Thomson*, 82.

[27] Aaron Copland, "Playing Safe at Zurich," *Modern Music*, IV:2 (November-December 1926), 28-32.

written in 1913! As usual, the music was either French or German. I found Hindemith's *Concerto for Orchestra* (op. 38) to have "extraordinary vigor and exuberance." We left Zurich with the impression that the music had been secondary; the three-day festival served more as an international meeting place for composers, musicians, and publishers. This in itself was valuable. While in Zurich, I played *Music for the Theatre* on the piano for the Universal Edition representatives with the hope of getting something else in print, but nothing came of it.[28]

Harold and I traveled on to Munich for a week's visit, and Harold told me that he could feel something like Nazism in the air even then, as early as 1926.[29] How we came to find a wonderful little villa for the summer in the Basses Pyrenées I no longer recall, but it was exactly what we wanted. The village of Guéthary is built on the hills that rise from the sea, a half-hour away from Biarritz in one direction, with Spain close by on the other side. I worked steadily on my *Piano Concerto.* We dipped into the sea in front of our Villa Cendrillon whenever relaxation was needed. But by mid-August, Harold was impatient to return to the New York theater scene. I stayed on alone until 1 October and returned to New York with the *Concerto* almost finished and with two short pieces put together from discarded materials, *Blues 1 and 2.*[30]

I moved to 223 West 78th Street, a slightly larger studio. This was hardly the movie version of what a musician's living quarters should be—a large room in an old-fashioned brownstone house on a quiet uptown street, very plainly furnished. A grand piano was set between the two windows and a big easy chair in front of the fireplace. I preferred being alone when composing, but I enjoyed company for the tedious business of copying orchestral parts. Gerald Sykes, a young writer whom I had met in 1925 through Paul Rosenfeld, often came to the studio while I was checking parts for the *Piano Concerto.* Gerald, Harold Clurman, and I became the best of friends. Israel Citkowitz also came over in the evenings. While I sat in the one chair under the only good light, Israel would stretch out on the cot and work on something of his own. After midnight, we would have tea and talk, before he went back out into the wintry nights to his own place.

Roy Harris had gone off to France with his wife and $1,800 given him by Alma Wertheim to subsidize his studies abroad. Roy's letters to me date from the summer of 1925 at MacDowell. They always seemed much like Roy—bigger than life, with a sprawling, open, western feeling. (Roy often teased me about not having been further west than Ithaca.) While I was abroad, Roy wrote asking that I speak to Nadia on his behalf and tell her "I want to study canon and fugue, form and orchestration, learn to play piano, read scores—and if possible conduct. I want to study and learn to speak a language of music." Even before meeting Nadia, Roy was writing instructions that made me suspect he would have

[28] This occasion may account for an arrangement of *Music for the Theatre* for piano four-hands in the Copland collection at the Library of Congress. Unpublished.

[29] See also Clurman, *The Fervent Years* (New York: Alfred A. Knopf, 1950), 13-14.

[30] Later, when a sequence, *Four Blues,* evolved, the original "Blues 1" was removed and renamed "Sentimental Melody, Slow Dance." The original "Blues 2" became "Blues 4." Copland recorded "Sentimental Melody" on a piano roll for the Ampico Company in 1927, and Schott included it in Volume III of an album, *Piano Pieces by Contemporary Composers.* On the cover appeared some of the composers' names—Bartók, Stravinsky, Milhaud, Hindemith, Bornshein, H. K. Schmid, Schulthess, Windsperger, and H. Zilcher. Copland's name did not appear. Evidently, in 1929 he was not as well known as Zilcher.

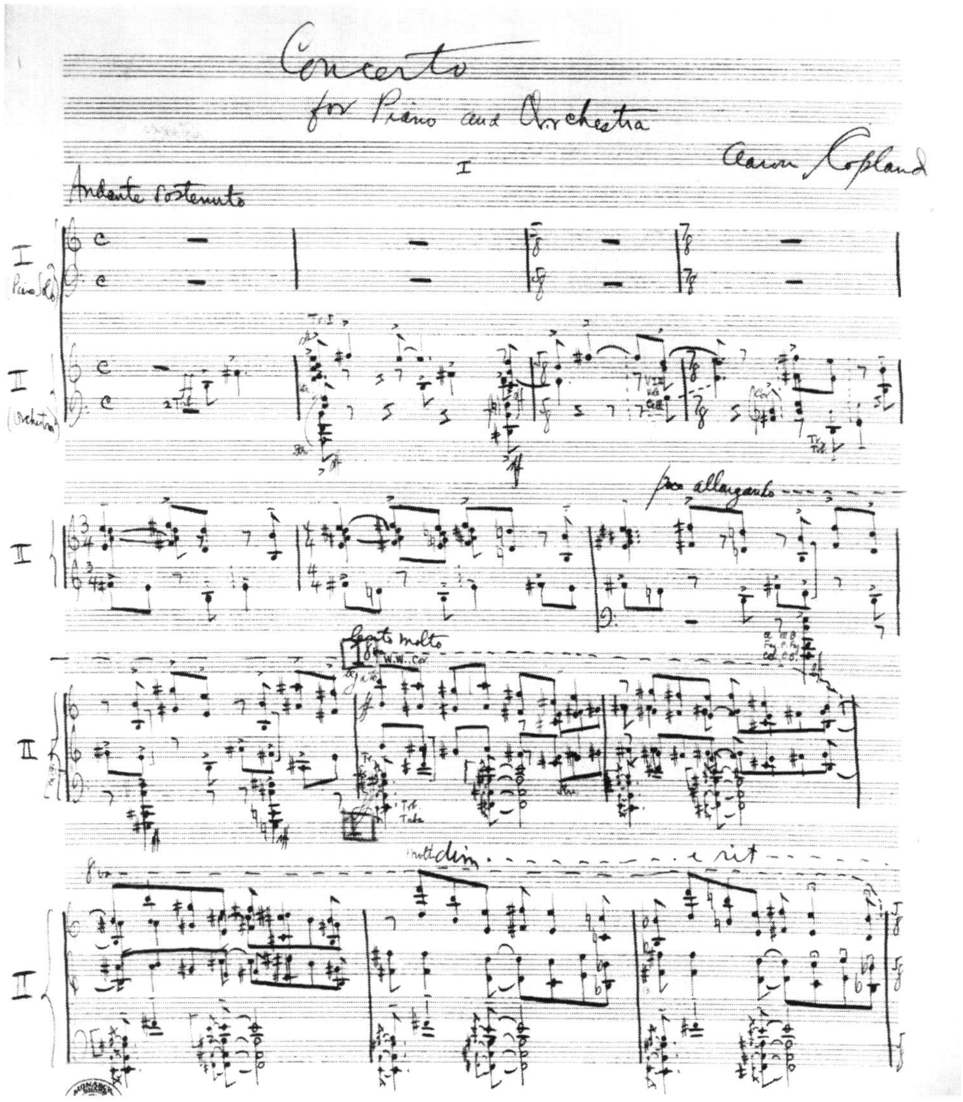

Sketch from the two-piano version of the *Concerto for Piano and Orchestra*

some adjustments to make: "Aaron, will you try to make it clear to Mademoiselle Boulanger that I abominate Ravel and Milhaud and Debussy—and am not moved by Honegger. . . The people out West are looking toward me to make Viking—'yea-saying' music. . . ." About my own music, Roy wrote:

> Am sorry you are writing a piano concerto—I think it is the wrong step—too much of music is lost in personalities—and concertos are largely a matter of personalities—even if you play them yourself—you are hindering the serious development of music.... I wish that you would write a choral symphony.... Jazz is on its way out. Beware for that new piano concerto which so many Copland enthusiasts are waiting for—don't disappoint us with jazz. . . .

The *Piano Concerto* was the last of my works to make explicit use of jazz materials. I have often described myself as a "work-a-year" man—1926 was the year of the *Concerto.* During this period, I was often critically paired with Gershwin. His *Rhapsody in Blue* was a kind of jazz piano concerto, and it was less than two years old when I wrote *Music for the Theatre.* It seems curious that Gershwin and I had so little contact, but the *Rhapsody* had been introduced by Paul Whiteman and his band, a very different milieu than Koussevitzky and the BSO. Gershwin came from Tin Pan Alley and Broadway musicals, while my only connection with the theater was through Clurman—and that meant serious drama. In those days, the lines were more sharply drawn between popular and classical musics. In many ways Gershwin and I had much in common—both from Brooklyn, we had studied with Rubin Goldmark during the same time and were pianists and composers of music that incorporated indigenous American sounds. But even after Damrosch commissioned Gershwin's *Concerto in F* for performance in the same season as Koussevitzky premiered my *Music for the Theatre,* Gershwin and I had no contact. We must have been aware of each other, but until the Hollywood years in the thirties, we moved in very different circles. On one occasion, when we were finally face to face at some party, with the opportunity for conversation, we found nothing to say to each other! I had always enjoyed popular music and admired those who could perform and compose in the lighter vein, but my talents clearly did not lie in that direction. I have no idea today whether Gershwin's *Concerto* of 1925 influenced me toward composing a piano concerto the following year. I doubt it. Koussevitzky had said, "If you write a piano concerto, you can play it yourself," and that temptation was too great to pass up.

I took the score of the *Piano Concerto* to Koussevitzky, he approved it and set to work rehearsing the orchestra on the difficult rhythms and instrumentation. The *Concerto* is scored for large orchestra with alto and soprano saxophones and extra percussion, such as tam-tam, Chinese drums, woodblock, and xylophone. At least I did not have to worry about a pianist; I could play the part myself from memory without practicing it, since it was so fresh in my mind. (Practicing the piano was a musical activity I have always disliked intensely.) The *Concerto* is to be played without interruption, but it is actually written in two contrasting sections, linked together thematically. The first is slow and lyrical; the second fast and rhythmic. Two basic jazz moods are incorporated in each section—the slow blues and the snappy number. The melodic material of the first movement is taken from a traditional blues, one also used by Gershwin at about the same time in his *Prelude No. 2* for piano. The second movement is a modified sonata form, without a recapitulation. A short cadenza sounds like an improvised break, but is not—probably because I was not good at improvisation myself. The rhythms presented in this section were considered extremely difficult. Before the Finale, the first movement material is recalled, followed by a brief Coda. I considered the *Concerto* essentially dramatic in character. As I explained in an interview at the time of the premiere: "The piano is as the main character in a play, carrying on a dialogue with the orchestra and conversing with the other instruments."

My primary aim was to explore new avenues in the area of polyrhythms. I was also experimenting with shifting beats by introducing a variety of highly unorthodox and frequently changing rhythms-7/8, 5/8, 9/8, 1/8, etc., that made the music polymetric—the use of different time signatures one after the other. The challenge was to do these complex vertical and horizontal experiments and still retain a transparent and lucid texture and a feeling of spontaneity and natural flow. If I felt I had gone to the extreme of where jazz could take me, the audiences and critics in Boston all thought I had gone too far. One critic actually accused Koussevitzky of being a malicious foreigner who wanted to show how bad American music was! Another, Penfield Roberts of the *Boston Globe*, wrote (29 January 1927): "No music heard at these concerts in the past 15 years has created so great a sensation. The audience forgot its manners, exchanging scathing verbal comments, and giggled nervously. . . ."

My mother and father had come to Boston for the premiere. I was delighted with Ma when she said that her proudest moment was when I played my *Piano Concerto* in Boston that night. The only criticism that really bothered Pa was the headline in the *Boston Post*: COPLAND'S LATEST IS POOR STUFF. After all, Pa had been a storekeeper long enough to know the meaning of "poor stuff!" In the program notes, I indicated that the *Concerto* was not programmatic; nevertheless, the *Post's* reviewer claimed, "With no effort at all the listener visualizes a jazz dance hall next door to a poultry yard. . . ." Philip Hale, learned arbiter of American mores in music and drama, set the tone of condemnation in his review in the *Herald:* "Copland's *Piano Concerto* shows a shocking lack of taste, of proportion. . .the piano is struck by fingers apparently directed at random." H. T. Parker, the most proper Bostonian of the lot, wrote in the *Evening Transcript* about "the ogre with that terrible Concerto." He published a special editorial to explain his dislike further: "The Copland *Piano Concerto* is a harrowing horror from beginning to end. . . . There is nothing in it that resembles music except that it contains noise. . . ." When complaints reached Parker's desk accusing Messrs. Koussevitzky and Copland of poking fun at America, Parker found himself in the curious position of championing our right to be heard!

With the assistance of Nicolas Slonimsky, then Koussevitzky's assistant, I presented a pre-concert lecture, sponsored by the orchestra, at the Boston Public Library. But familiarizing the audience with the program in advance did not seem to win any admirers. After I left Boston, "Kolya," as we called Slonimsky, with his playful sense of humor (not appreciated by Madame Koussevitzky, who thought him disrespectful) sent me the worst reviews (March 1927): "Enclosed you will find a usual Parkerian grimace at you. . . . You are not forgotten in Boston, and Parker untiringly continues to titillate public minds by mentioning, now and again, your notorious name."

The Boston Symphony gave the first New York performance of the *Piano Concerto* at Carnegie Hall on 3 February 1927. For once, New York was more tolerant than Boston, although Lawrence Gilman in the *Herald Tribune* was the only influential voice in either city

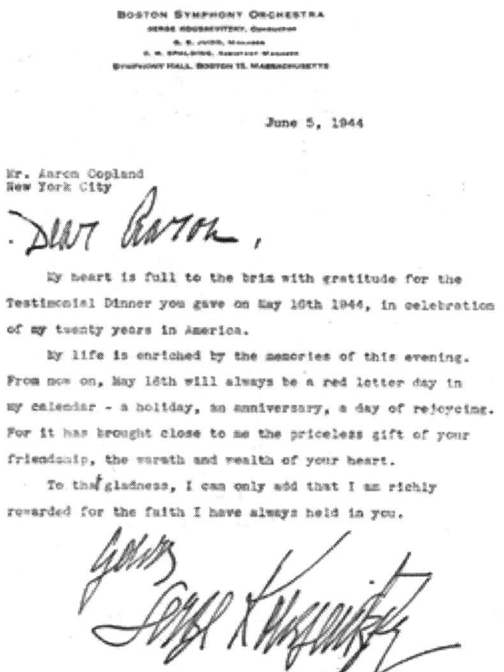

BOSTON SYMPHONY ORCHESTRA

June 5, 1944

Mr. Aaron Copland
New York City

Dear Aaron,

My heart is full to the brim with gratitude for the Testimonial Dinner you gave on May 16th 1944, in celebration of my twenty years in America.

My life is enriched by the memories of this evening. From now on, May 16th will always be a red letter day in my calendar - a holiday, an anniversary, a day of rejoycing. For it has brought close to me the priceless gift of your friendship, the warmth and wealth of your heart.

To that gladness, I can only add that I am richly rewarded for the faith I have always held in you.

Above: Copland and Koussevitsky at Tanglewood at the conclusion of *Quiet City*, 3 August 1941
Right: Letter from Koussevitsky to Copland, 1944
Below: Copland and Koussevitsky at Tanglewood in the forties

to welcome the work "... music of impressive austerity, of true character, music bold in outline and of singular character...." Koussevitzky decided not to take my new piece to Brooklyn (to him, "the provinces"), but the Brooklyn reviewers came to New York. What a pleasant surprise it was to read Edward Cushing in the *Brooklyn Daily Eagle* (6 February 1927): "The Concerto was, all things considered, the most excellent of symphonic jazz expressions, Mr. Copland has quite outdone Mr. Gershwin and Mr. Carpenter.... There is more than jazz in the Concerto...." Alma Wertheim, to whom the *Concerto* is dedicated, threw a gala party after the New York premiere in honor of Madame and Maestro Koussevitzky and me.

The following summer I accepted an invitation to perform the *Piano Concerto* at the Hollywood Bowl, welcoming the opportunity to go west for the first time. There at rehearsals the musicians actually hissed. The conductor, Albert Coates, was distraught: "Boys! Boys, please!" he pleaded, pointing to me at the piano. "He's one of us!" The *Los Angeles Times* reported (21 July 1928): "Bowl stirred up a frenzy... Fans greet sophisticated jazz with derision... catcalls, hisses, laughs and applause follow pianist...." At about the same time, John Kirkpatrick arranged a two-piano version of the *Concerto*. I offered it to the Cos Cob Press, and since they were in a hurry for it, I simply took it for granted that John would like the idea and would get paid what was coming to him; but I miscalculated. John, who was in Paris studying with Boulanger, wrote that I should not have gone ahead without him. I answered (9 April 1929):

> You are absolutely right of course in saying that I had no "right" in arranging for publication without consulting you. Of course if you were a complete stranger to me I shouldn't have done this—but taking a friend's liberty and not expecting you to be fleeced I said go ahead. My mind worked in this fashion: John will want his arrangement published—at best there isn't a large sum of money involved—apparently John doesn't depend on his arrangements for a source of income—ergo, the main thing is to have the arrangement published. It was because of this, that I wrote you in the airy, non-business-like tone I did...the proofs are already finished and I have already corrected them—even before your letters came—so that I must throw myself on your good will and ask that no matter what happens you arrange the matter amicably....

The problem was soon resolved with no further difficulty between us.

A composer sends a piece of music into the world much as a parent sends a child—tending to it for a time until it must go off on its own, and then, to some extent, what happens is out of the creator's hands. After playing the *Concerto* myself in six places in fourteen years (Boston, New York, Hollywood, New York's Stadium Concerts, Mexico, and Chile), the piece was not heard again in this country for sixteen years. During that hiatus it retained its reputation as a shocker, an illusion that was shattered when Leonard Bernstein revived the work with the New York City Symphony at the City Center (21-22 October 1946). Leo Smit was at the keyboard. Juxtaposed with the D Major *Concerto* of Haydn, the *Piano Concerto* seemed anything but shocking, and no one could imagine why audiences in 1927 had walked out on it. After the 1946 revival, the Concerto was called "a relic of Le Jazz hot," "the nostalgic ghost of Paris's left bank," and "the best roar from the roaring twenties."

It recalled a time when anything seemed possible, when we young modernists thought the musical millennium around the corner. Lenny and Leo handled the rhythmic complexities of the *Concerto* with ease. Leo is a far better pianist than I—I had played the work like a composer, while he was a dazzling performer with enormous vitality and yet he kept everything absolutely clean and precise.

Leo played the *Concerto* again in 1953, this time under Charles Munch with the Boston Symphony. When a French pianist, scheduled to do a concerto, canceled at the last moment, Leonard Burkat, then Dr. Munch's assistant, suggested my *Concerto* as a replacement. (Munch had played some of my music in Europe and he liked Leo, who had performed the Alexei Haieff *Concerto* with the BSO the previous year.) So on 16 October 1953 the once notorious "Jazz Concerto" came back home to Boston, where it had been born in 1927. Leo garnered rave reviews, while Munch's conducting was called "rectangular." (After all, one would not expect the jazz rhythms to be in *his* bones any more than Koussevitzky's.) Dr. Munch evidently liked the *Concerto*, and took it to Brooklyn and to Tanglewood in the summer of 1954.

I had not performed it myself in years when Lenny invited me to do it in a concert (9 January 1964) meant to examine the "jazz trend," part of a series of avant-garde orchestra concerts he was presenting at the Philharmonic. My *Concerto* was juxtaposed with more recent experiments by composers Larry Austin, John Cage, Stefan Wolpe, Earle Brown, Morton Feldman, and Pierre Boulez. The modern works were interspersed with standard repertory. How Lenny got away with it, I don't know, since the New York Philharmonic players are not fond of playing modern music. Leonard Burkat, by then head of CBS Masterworks, heard the performance and suggested we record it. I also played the piece under Alfred Wallenstein at one of the "Concerts in the Parks" in the Sheep Meadow in New York (24 August 1965).

The three musicians most closely connected with the Concerto— Lenny, Leo, and me—had a reunion at my eightieth birthday concert at Kennedy Center in Washington. Lenny conducted *Lincoln Portrait*, which I narrated, and Leo played the *Piano Concerto* with the National Symphony Orchestra under my baton. During rehearsal, Lenny came on stage to give advice and assistance, and afterward, Lenny and Leo were full of reminiscences of 1946.

Jazz played a big role in the twenties. But I had been observing the scene around me and sensed it was about to change. Moreover, I realized that jazz might have its best treatment from those who had a talent for improvisation. I sensed its limitations, intended to make a change, and made no secret of the fact. In the Los Angeles *News*, an interviewer reported (20 July 1928):

> Copland to Abandon Jazz in Future Compositions. The young composer of the jazz concerto which has made him internationally famous, and which is to be played at the Hollywood Bowl on Friday night, feels that this composition has exhausted all of the possibilities of the theme for him. His concerto is the culmination of a great many compositions written with a jazz theme; now he will search new fields for inspiration.[31]

[31] Copland continued to point out the limitations of jazz. See "Aaron Copland Finds Flaws in Jazz," *Down Beat,* 25 (1 May 1958), 16, 39-40; and "Modern Music: 'Fresh and Different,'" *The New York Times* Magazine (13 March 1955), 15, 60, 62. The *Times* article was a dialogue with Henry Pleasants, "Modern Music: 'A Dead Art,'" which appeared in the same issue, 14, 57, 59.

INTERLUDE II

When an artist adopts a new style, the reaction is likely to be one of surprise, even anger, as if to say, "How dare you make a sudden change when I have become accustomed to the way you were?" A radical change poses all sorts of questions. What is responsible? What turmoil, what extension into another region of the artistic territory occasioned such a turn in the road? The fact is that abrupt turnarounds are usually not so precipitous or so novel as they seem. With Copland, ideas leading away from a jazz-oriented music to a more abstract style had been in the back of his mind for some time. This new style did not spring suddenly from nowhere—and when it did appear, it incorporated sounds that were unmistakably Copland.

A period of assessment and exploration followed the *Piano Concerto;* the few pieces composed during that time were either experimental or transitional. They functioned as a bridge from the old to the new, very much the way a musical interlude connects familiar passages to new material, preparing the listener for a change. During this transitional period, Copland maintained a rigorous schedule of teaching, writing, lecturing, and promoting concerts. These activities soon established him as the dominant figure in the American contemporary musical world. Several composers—Virgil Thomson, Roger Sessions, and Leo Ornstein—found it either necessary or desirable to remove themselves from New York, but Copland was never comfortable away from the city for long; on the contrary, he preferred to observe and reflect on the active and changing scene around him, an extraordinary one in the years preceding the Wall Street crash of 1929.

Historians have called 1927 a turning point in the development of civilization: national radio networks, underwater tunnels, and international radio-telephone services were established; Lindbergh flew across the Atlantic, affirming the wonder and power of progress and technology. In music, Jerome Kern's *Showboat* was an enormous success on Broadway, Duke Ellington opened to "white only" audiences at the Cotton Club in Harlem, and George Antheil's *Ballet mécanique* shocked an audience in Carnegie Hall. The League of Composers was gaining strength under the effective leadership of Claire Reis; and the Pro-Musica Society, led by E. Robert Schmitz, was arranging for composers Kodály, Bartók, and Ravel to come to America for the first time in 1928.

Since musical performances were virtually nonexistent during summer months, Copland arranged with Minna Lederman to cover two German music festivals for *Modern Music.* Most of the spring and summer of 1927 was spent in Germany. But first a visit to Nadia and other friends in Paris, before traveling with Roy Harris to the ISCM Festival in Frankfurt to hear *Music for the Theatre* performed for an international audience on the Fourth of July. Then on to the Festival of German Chamber Music in Baden-Baden, where Copland met Hanns Eisler and saw Kurt Weill, who was on hand to supervise the premiere of *Mahagonny.* It was Alban Berg's *Lyric Suite* that most impressed Copland at the festival. He wrote, "Berg is now forty-two and it is foolish to continue discussing him merely as a Schoenberg pupil. The similarities between his own style and that of his teacher are only superficial. In reality their natures are opposed. Berg, unlike Schoenberg, is essentially naive, with a warm, emotional, Tristanesque personality. The *Lyric Suite* seems to me to be one of the best works written for string quartet in recent years."[1]

For the remainder of the summer, Copland lived in Königstein, Germany, partly because of a passing acquaintance with members of the wealthy Seligman family in New York who had relatives there, but mostly to be where he could compose without distractions. Königstein was still occupied by the British. Soldiers and military installations were much in evidence, and Copland felt unsettled and uncomfortable there. He composed only one short "Song," later retitled "Poet's Song," to a text by e.e. cummings. Based on a tone row, the work was an early experiment with serialism. It is a difficult piece that reflects the direction of Copland's musical thinking at that time.

Copland was relieved to leave Germany at the end of the summer for a visit to Nadia's country home in Gargenville. Israel Citkowitz and Roy Harris were there (Harris had taken rooms in the small town of Juziers close by). Other Americans were by now flocking

[1] Aaron Copland, "Baden-Baden, 1927," *Modern Music,* V:1 (November-December 1927), 31-34; repr. in *Copland on Music,* 183-88.

to the "Boulangerie," among them Ross Lee Finney, a young composer from Minnesota, who had worked his way to Europe by playing in a shipboard jazz orchestra. Copland's visit to Gargenville that summer was still vivid to Finney: "His presence made such an impact on me! Nadia was to play the organ at Chartres Cathedral and we all traveled together with her by car. Aaron spoke so eloquently about being an American composer and understanding your roots that he made me consider my Midwest background just as valuable as what I was experiencing in France. It was a crucial period for me, and Aaron's influence lasted a very long time."[2]

Copland must have been voicing his relief at being out of the stultifying atmosphere in Germany, but he soon discovered that Gargenville offered its own problems. Citkowitz and Harris, both close to Copland, were not compatible and their constant bickering for Nadia's attentions made Copland feel responsible, since it was he who had sent them to her in the first place. After Copland's return to the States, Israel and Roy confided their troubles and complaints to him, each viewing relationships from his own side of the triangle: Israel's fifteen and seventeen-page letters tightly packed with bitter complaints against Roy's insensitive nature and his wife's impossible behavior; Roy's sprawling messages venting his homesickness for California and his impatience with French rules and restrictions ("Aaron, can't we go together to live in California? Short of that, send me garden seeds for next year from New York. . . I would like to introduce some good melons, sweet corn and potatoes to Juziers farmers from America. . . ."). And Nadia's spidery European script on her ubiquitous black-bordered paper reporting her pupils' progress, asking Aaron's advice and counsel, and causing Aaron to respond (19 December 1927): "Is he [Israel] behaving himself? I often have had visions of him causing you untold trouble and annoyance. Reassure me, please!" Nadia's response: "Now with Israel—he has improved immensely and we must find the money for him—to make it easier—I will not take on the $3.00 for the 2nd lesson a week. I am too glad to bring this little help to a born musician and such a nice boy—" About Roy, she wrote, "great beauties in Roy's symphony—hope you will be pleased—when order will come with, what a musician he can be. . . ."

Aaron wrote regularly to Israel, "knowing how much he needs my moral support," thus making Roy jealous. Both depended on Copland for contacts at home, especially with Koussevitzky, and for programming, teaching, and lecturing about their music. In addition, Citkowitz was helpless about financial matters and depended on Aaron for support. "Last year," wrote Citkowitz in December 1927, "I was so bent on going to Paris that I totally overlooked the means. . . the thought of a job doesn't make me hysterical as it did. . . ." But Israel did not find a job. Alma Wertheim gave $160 toward his support, while Aaron and Nadia continued to look for another patroness, even though Copland's own situation was little short of precarious. Copland sailed from Cherbourg 10 September 1927 (on the R.M.S. Berengaria, second class). When he arrived in New York, the Guggenheim Fellowships had run out, and he had to face the serious problem of how to make a living.

[2] Interview, Ross Lee Finney with Perlis, 20 March 1982, Ann Arbor, Michigan.

When Paul Rosenfeld offered to turn the music courses he had been giving at the New School for Social Research over to Copland, the timing could not have been better. For the next ten years, the New School would provide a modest and dependable source of income. Best of all, Copland could work in the field of music and still have time for composing. The $50 fee paid for each two-hour session one evening a week was a lot of money then; later, when the courses became popular, the New School paid a percentage of the tuitions. The courses were valuable in another way: they provided an opportunity for Copland to observe and evaluate modern music, to consider antecedents and developments, and to view his own music in the context of history, all at a time when he was taking stock of his situation and considering his directions. Every Friday evening, Copland went down to lecture at 465 West 23rd Street (in 1931 the New School moved to 66 West 12th). The lectures proved to be more time-consuming than the young musician had imagined—modern music was the principal subject, most scores were unpublished and unrecorded, and Copland had to play the musical examples himself on the piano.[3] Neither experience nor musical education were required from the sixty-eight people who registered for "The Appreciation of Modern Music" in the fall of 1927. They included a few music teachers and students, businessmen, secretaries, librarians, a playwright (Elmer Rice, then young and unknown), and several others who wrote "no occupation at present" on their applications. The first course ended on 28 December with a concert arranged by Copland of works by Krenek, Stravinsky, Hindemith, Cowell, Ravel, Webern, and Copland.[4]

Lecturing held a challenge similar to that of composing—how to communicate the pleasure and excitement of modern music without being patronizing or jeopardizing quality. The New School classes provided one kind of listener; later (at Harvard, for example) Copland would face different audiences. He wrote to Nadia (16 October 1927):

> My lectures are going brilliantly. I have already played *Oedipus, Créâtion du monde,* Hindemith op. 37, etc. If I weren't a composer it would be very amusing. But as it is, it is even difficult for me to give up several months of the year . . . and it is practically impossible to do any concentrated work on composition unless I devote my entire energies to it.

Israel Citkowitz wrote from Paris: "Your lectures are turning out marvellously and in other words you have again proven that it is impossible for Aaron Copland to make a wrong step—almost as impossible for you to make a wrong one as for me to make a right one. . ." Copland responded by preparing "Lecture IX, The Youngest Generation in America," that included Citkowitz, Antheil, Sessions, Ornstein, and Harris. An undated

[3] Copland's lecture notes are preserved in his files in the Library of Congress.

[4] According to the printed program, the works were: Krenek's *Concerto for Violin and Piano* (Barbara Lull and Copland); Stravinsky's *Serenade for Piano* (Carl Buchman); Hindemith's "Eight Songs from 'Das Marienleben'" (Greta Torpadie and Copland); Cowell's *Aeolian Harp, Advertisement, The Banshee,* and *Antinomy* (Cowell as pianist); and a Group of Pieces for Violin and Piano: Ravel's *Berceuse,* Webern's *Four Pieces,* op. 7, and Copland's *Nocturne and Serenade* (all performed by Barbara Lull and Copland).

memo in Marc Blitzstein's papers describes his friend's teaching: "Copland's lecturing, like his written criticism, is notable for a flat undecorated honesty. He is no felicitous phraser, he has little grace of speech, few quips; and sometimes one stops listening. Almost always something important is missed."[5]

In 1938 when Copland taught general music appreciation instead of modern music, his popular course became the basis for his first book. According to the composer, a gentleman came up to him after a lecture one evening and said, "Mr. Copland, I don't know if you know it or not, but you are talking a book. Next year we'll send a girl down here from McGraw-Hill and she'll take down verbatim what you say." At the end of the following year's series, Copland was presented with the basis of *What to Listen For in Music*. The book has been translated into eleven languages, among them Dutch, Egyptian, German, Italian, Persian, Portuguese, Spanish, and Swedish.[6]

At the close of 1927, Copland's frustration at not composing was mounting, and he wrote to Boulanger in a tone that was a rare departure from his usual "lucky guy" attitude: the score for "As It Fell Upon a Day" sent to Universal in Vienna had been ignored; the violin pieces sent to Strecker made no impression; and the letter Mademoiselle had suggested he send to Mengelberg remained unanswered. But to balance the bad news, he had a commission from Professor Amédée L. Hettich of the Paris Conservatoire for a "vocalise-etude,"[7] and *Music for the Theatre* was being transformed into a German ballet, *Tragödie im Suden, ein Ballet in Fünf Seitze*. (Copland had met Hans Heinsheimer, from Universal's opera department, in Frankfurt during the ISCM Festival; he suggested the ballet version and proceeded to write the scenario himself.) Copland wrote to Boulanger:

> The ballet story is appallingly melodramatic, but the action has been well put to the music, and I have no doubt that the good German opera public will be delighted. The Universal assures me that a production is certain, even possible this season yet. For once, it is pleasant to sit back and watch a formidable organization like Universal do the unpleasant business of finding performances. . . .[8]

The letter ended with: "I've written no new works, helas! When I think that 1927 is coming to a close and that I have produced no work signed 1927, I assure you I have a sinking feeling of the heart. It is as if the entire year were wasted. This won't happen again if I can help it." When Copland realized that commitments for 1928 were already filling his calendar, he announced to the New School that he would not teach until the following fall.

[5] Blitzstein Collection, State Historical Society of Wisconsin, Madison, Wisconsin.

[6] Aaron Copland, *What to Listen for in Music* (New York: McGraw-Hill, 1939) and *Study Guide* (32 pp.), 9th book in course of study of the National Federation of Music Clubs, out-of-print); rev., Introduction William Schuman (McGraw Hill, 1957); Appreciation, Leonard Slatkin (New York: Penguin, 2009); rev. Introduction Schuman, Foreword and Epilogue, Alan Rich (New York: Mentor, 1999).

[7] *Répertoire Modérne de Vocalises-Etudes*, publiées sous la direction de A. L. Hettich, Vol. 8 (Paris:Alphonse Leduc et Cie, 1929). The collection contains over 100 vocalises: no. 1 is by Fauré; no. 71 by Copland. The first volume appeared in 1907.

[8] Heinsheimer's attempts to interest ballet companies failed; the work was never published in this version. Interview, Hans Heinsheimer with Perlis, 21 May 1981, New York City.

Copland kept diaries at various times in his life, primarily when traveling. The only entries of an introspective, personal nature were made between 1927 and 1928. These reflect the more serious side of his personality at that time. Rereading them in 1982, Copland hooted with laughter at their naiveté, but remarked that they still make sense some fifty-four years later:

> DEC. 1927: I have two principles of living which seem apparently, and possibly are actually, contradictory. First: everything is good which makes me act otherwise from my normal self. Second: never do anything which betrays my true nature.
> The first tells me to get drunk, the second tells me that if I get drunk I betray my true nature.
> The ideal would be for my true nature to tell me to leave my normal self. But if it doesn't, should I force it? Thus, the problem.
> (Make a list of examples of the first rule and of the second, thus: the first says to live adventurously, the second to live carefully.
> The first says experience everything, since all experience is good; the second says experience only that which is admirable and good.)
> Tonight it seems to me that I should force myself a little, like one forces a child to take music lessons for the sake of finding any possible latent talent; that is, get drunk twice anyhow if only to prove to myself conclusively that it is not in my true nature to get drunk. (This has other applications!)
> My ever-present fear is that by thinking that I know myself, i.e., my normal self completely, I may circumscribe whatever latent possibilities I may have.
> MAR. 1928: I am anxious above all things to perfect myself. I am bourgeois to the core! This seemingly gratuitous 'perfectionnement' (since I wish it for no reasons of worldly glory or heavenly bliss) comes from an inborn sense of economy, getting the best possible out of my own being. H. is amused when I pass a store and say, "Too bad, they couldn't make it pay." I am anxious to become a more profound person because it supremely satisfies my sense of economy (order) that one being should render the utmost possible profit (good).
> Gide says, "Those who differ from me most attract me most." I might have written that. . . . My imagination takes fire when I am given a glimpse of the workings of a being different from myself. Our differences throw into a stronger light my true self.

According to Gerald Sykes, "Gide was close to Aaron's thinking then. He was reading a great deal and was considerably more introverted than he became later. That's why the music of this period had a distinct feeling of introversion. Aaron lived sparsely, almost monastically, and was as unostentatious and undemanding as anyone I've ever met—not like men who have been spoiled by their wives and are used to living much more sumptuously than Aaron ever thought of doing. Composing and reading were most important to him.[9]

Early in the new year Copland began to compose again. He wrote two short pieces for string quartet: *Lento Molto* was paired with an earlier piece for string quartet, *Rondino*,

[9] Interview, Gerald Sykes with Perlis, 24 October 1980, New York City.

composed in Paris in 1923. *Lento Molto* was not planned as a companion piece to the *Rondino*. Its four short pages of homophonic texture and sustained tranquillity contrast with the earlier work.[10] Since neither piece was long enough to stand on its own, Copland decided to pair them for performance, probably in 1928, if not earlier. Together they have remained as *Two Pieces for String Quartet*. A rescored version for string orchestra was made during the summer of 1928, and Koussevitzky presented them at the end of the year in Boston, where critics and audiences received them as a minor novelty. The two pieces, presumably Copland's only works for quartet, continue to be programmed in both versions.

But Copland wrote another movement for string quartet, probably during the early part of 1928. The undated parts, carefully copied in the composer's hand, were discovered among the composer's manuscripts at the Library of Congress. The score has not come to light. Mentions of a string quartet movement in correspondence to Boulanger and others refer either to this long-forgotten piece or to the *Lento Molto*. Copland to Boulanger (June 1928):

> When I look back at the winter it seems to me that the only real thing accomplished was the fact that I have finished my slow movement for string quartet. I have just made a copy for you because I am most anxious to know what you think of it. Please show it to Roy and to Israel. (I dedicated it to Roy because it was his enthusiasm for the opening phrase which gave me the incentive to finish it.)

Lento Molto is indeed dedicated to Harris. Boulanger responded (23 September 1928): "This piece for string quartet is a masterpiece—so moving, so deep, so simple. . . ." About a month later, Harris wrote to Copland, complaining, "Have not received your string quartet dedicated to a 'budding talent.'" The "new" quartet movement is of approximately six minutes duration, in three parts, with an *assez vite* between slow sections. The piece has been performed and recorded adding a third work by Copland to the string quartet literature.[11]

Soon after Copland met Roger Sessions in 1926, they began to discuss the need for a concert series to implement the League of Composers presentations. These two most promising young American composers of the twenties had been good friends and colleagues for several years. But the original picture of them has been so varnished over by layers of time and events that they are no longer viewed in relation to each other as they once were. Copland and Sessions were to move in such different directions that even they themselves do not recall a time, long ago, when they stood in the same place. But from Sessions' early letters to Copland, the friendship between the two young composers is evident. Sessions' first letter from Paris was written out of enthusiasm for Copland's *Symphony for Organ and Orchestra* and with concern about some of the younger composer's ideas and activities:

Manuscript page of the first violin part of a string quartet movement, rediscovered by Vivian Perlis

> This afternoon I heard Nadia play your symphony, and while I am not in the habit of writing this particular kind of letter I can't refrain from giving you a piece of my mind on the subject. First of all the symphony is magnificent, and I was more impressed than I can tell you. While one does not, as you know perfectly well, get everything from a work on one hearing, I did carry away a big impression—a really big one. It was a revelation and a surprise to me—a revelation in an absolute sense, and a surprise, because the other works of yours which I know did not

[10] Marc Blitzstein admired Copland's *Lento Molto* and arranged it for two pianos. Unpublished manuscript in Blitzstein Collection, Wisconsin Historical Society.

[11] In April 1983 the string quartet movement was played for Copland by the Alexander String Quartet at the composer's home in Peekskill, New York. It was subsequently published and recorded.

lead me to share to the full Nadia's opinion of you—an opinion of which I am sure you must be aware and which I need not enlarge upon.

Sessions continued giving Copland a "piece of my mind" for *Music for the Theatre* and for wasting time on propaganda for other young Americans, including himself. Sessions lightly chastised Copland for thinking of himself as a New York figure rather than an international one. Copland responded, and on behalf of *Modern Music* invited Sessions to write an article. Sessions agreed, "on one condition—that you never ask for another!"[12] He thanked Copland for speaking to Koussevitzky and Henry A. Moe of the Guggenheim Foundation in his behalf. This letter and many others that followed were long, affectionate, worrisome, apologetic, and occasionally contradictory. For example (from 25 February 1929),

> Would he [Copland] forgive the previous letters? Were they still on speaking terms? . . . Barbara tells me always that, to people who don't know me well, I misrepresent myself, and that what I intend as purely ironic and picturesque emphasis is taken seriously. . . I would be the last to advise you seriously not to take an interest in other people's music for I can see that it is so much a part of you—we are quite different in that way.

Sessions admired Copland's article on jazz in *Modern Music* and expressed a desire to hear the *Piano Concerto*. He was very annoyed with "a female relative" in Boston who had sent reviews, implying that Sessions would be pleased to read unfavorable criticism about a rival. Barbara and Roger Sessions expected to be in the States from 15 March to 30 April 1927 and hoped to see as much of Copland as possible. It was in that spring and summer that the composers first discussed starting a concert series. Roger, from Florence on 3 September 1927:

> I think your ideas for the young composers' idea are excellent and subscribe to them heartily. I shall hope to be of some use in practice, if not in theory. . My ideas at first blush would be to have both kinds of concerts—one or two each season, perhaps, of the most ambitious kind, and several of the smaller kind. I agree that "liberal despotism" is the only possible form of government—with the final accent on the despotism rather than on the liberal; and in my capacity as co-despot I gladly pledge cooperation!

Other matters relating to the concerts were mentioned, such as an age limit of thirty-five for composers to be included. "I have some ideas which I think we had better discuss *viva voce* than try to put within the limits of human sized mail. . . ." Both composers agreed in the meantime to look for financial support. Through Minna Lederman, Copland met Mary Senior Churchill, the wife of an architect, Henry Churchill. She was well-to-do in her own right and about Copland's age, interested in the arts and willing to support an adventurous idea. By mail, Copland and Sessions explored titles for the series. As late as 15 March 1928, only five weeks before the first concert, Sessions wrote jokingly, "the

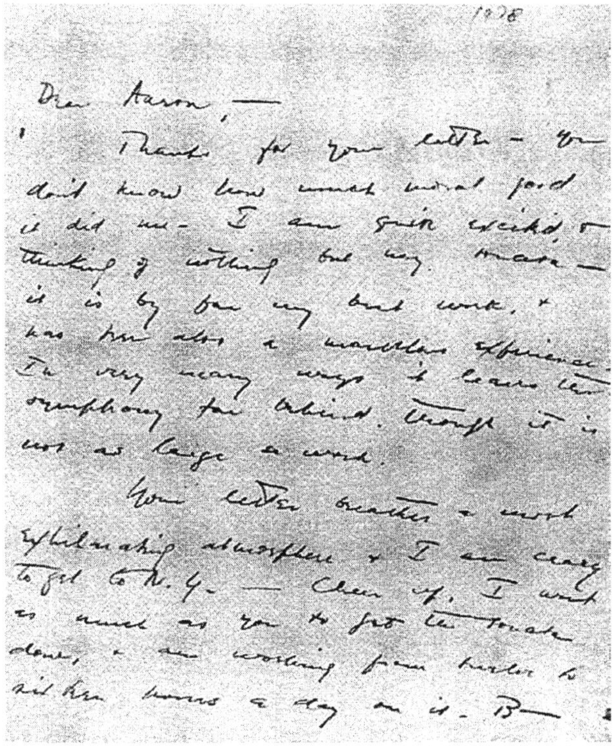

1928

Dear Aaron,—

Thanks for your letter – you don't know how much moral good it did me – I am quite excited & thinking of nothing but my [illegible]— it is by far my best work, & has been also a marvelous experience. In very many ways it leaves the symphony far behind, though it is not as large a work.

Your letter breathes a most exhilarating atmosphere & I am crazy to get to N.Y. — Cheer up, I want as much as you to get the sonata done, & am working from twelve to sixteen hours a day on it. B—

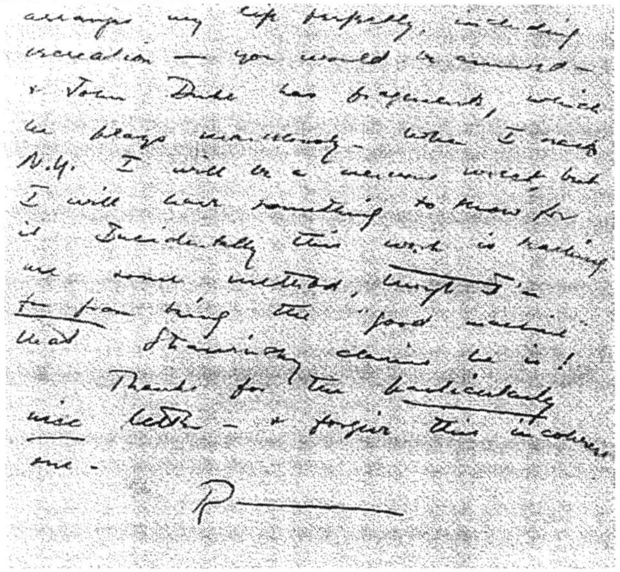

arranges my life perfectly, including recreation — you would be amused— & John Duke has fragments, which he plays marvellously. When I reach N.Y. I will be a nervous wreck but I will have something to show for it. Incidentally this work is teaching me some method, though I'm far from being the "good machine" that Stravinsky claims he is!

Thanks for the particularly nice letter — & forgive this incoherent one —

R—

Letter from Roger Sessions

[12] Sessions sent "An American Evening Abroad" to Minna Lederman for *Modern Music* (November-December 1926), followed by "Ernst Bloch" (November-December 1927) and "On Oedipus Rex" (March-April 1928).

'Enemies of Music'—suggested by a sort of converse of the old Puritan proverb that Hell is paved with good intentions. . . . Please do not gather from this that I approach the problem in a flippant spirit!" They discussed and discarded "Laboratory Concerts," and finally agreed on "The Copland–Sessions Concerts of Contemporary Music." The timing was ironic, for no sooner was the name chosen than Sessions received the Rome Prize and an American Academy in Rome Fellowship. Not only would he be outside New York, he would be out of the country for most of the concerts; therefore, his position would necessarily be as adviser rather than active co-director. In later years, Copland was convinced that Sessions, always conservative and cautious about the use of his name, was sorry he had agreed to its use for the concert series. It is not entirely true, however, that Sessions "did little more than lend my name," as he has claimed.[13] His letters reveal a fuller involvement and influence than that, although they also reflect an increasing sense of concern over his absentee status, and a devotion and admiration for Copland.

Sessions was teaching at Smith College in Northampton, Massachusetts, in the spring of 1928 before returning to Europe. That March he wrote to Copland:

> . . . you must know how much good it does me to see something of you, and to be in touch with you. It has been the chief compensation and a rather "formidable" one, for a dull and disappointing winter in which many lingering illusions over my native country have disappeared. . . . If ever I had any doubts about your future—and I never did have any serious ones— . . . nothing seems surer to me now; and it is more than a comfort to me to feel that way, when my own future seems to me constantly to be hanging in the balance and or worse. Yours is something that I take absolutely for granted, and I have not—for all my doubting nature—had the suspicion of a feeling that I was deceiving myself. Furthermore, you are the only person over here with whom I feel quite myself. . .[14]

As the time for the first Copland–Sessions concert drew near, even Barbara Sessions helped out by writing the prospectus that appeared in the program. She sent it to Copland from Northampton in draft form for changes and corrections. Letters flew back and forth. Sessions wrote (26 March): "You have my O.K. on everything practical . . . the title seems very good. . ." Sessions wrote on 30 March: "I trust your judgment entirely. I'm only sorry [Quincy] Porter is the best I can contribute in the way of composers. . . . As to my playing percussion in V.T.'s [Thomson] work I leave that also to you. Your mild surprise took me a little aback, and I don't know that I want to, so to speak, put such a definite seal of approval on this music without knowing it better. . . ." Sessions went after Theodore Chanler for a piece and Copland wrote to George Antheil. Finally, from Sessions to Copland on 5 April: "Your letter sounds as if you had found this thing more work than you had bargained for—I sincerely hope not. I don't object to M.C. [Churchill] and M.L. [Lederman] helping out, but I do think it is a crime if it seriously upsets you—I only know how one undertakes sometimes to do a thing that grows bigger than one would think. . . ."

The first season featured works by eleven American composers with concerts on 22 April and 6 May 1928 at the Edyth Totten Theatre at 247 West 48th Street (later renamed the President Theatre). Neither Copland nor Sessions was represented with music at the first concert. Copland's only performing duty was the percussion part (in place of Sessions) in Thomson's *Five Phrases from the "Song of Solomon."* Sessions had not been able to complete the piano sonata promised for the opening. Copland, with programs already printed and distributed, reprinted them, substituting Carlos Chávez' *Sonata for Piano* (played by Chávez). Thus, reports on the program for the first Copland–Sessions concert have varied through the years, depending on which of the two printed programs was used as the source of information. Sessions was home in Northampton at the time, working desperately to put the Sonata into playable condition for the second concert of the series. He wrote to Copland: "Don't worry about the Sonata. It isn't finished but I swear to you it will be ready in time—you can count on it absolutely. Also, I like it. . ."

Barbara Sessions wrote to Copland from Northampton after the first concert: "We hated not being there. . . . It certainly looks as if things got a splendid send-off and I should think you and Mrs. Churchill would be more than gratified—we thought of you all to be sure, and we shall have to make up for our disappointment by having a marvelous time when we do come. . ." Sessions' plan was to be in New York from 5 May to 10 May. From Barbara: "Roger wants me to ask you what you intend to do if and when asked to join the League . . . what would we do, Aaron, without your worldly wisdom?—to say nothing of all the other reasons we shall have for missing you far too much, that alone makes me tremble to think of putting an ocean between us. . ." After the first concert, Mary Churchill sent clippings to Northampton, and Sessions responded: "At least we received a good deal of attention. Downes has risen 100 percent or more in my estimation—he alone seems to have realized that the event could be of any importance whatever, and his very timidity is a good sign ... it means, at least, that he is afraid to commit himself too soon. . . Henderson rather surprised me—he seemed next best, in spite of being an old war horse. . ."

Both directors were present at the second concert on 6 May. Copland's *Two Pieces for String Quartet* was performed, and two movements of Sessions' still incomplete *Piano Sonata* were played by John Duke. Duke, who was teaching at Smith, recalls that Sessions brought the music to him almost page by page to learn.

> But as time went on, and it wasn't finished, Roger was in a terrible state about it and finally decided to just have me play the first two movements with an improvised ending to the second movement. I'll never forget the struggle he had. He used to stay up drinking black coffee, and by the time we went to New York, Roger was about all in. We had to change trains in Spring-

[13] See Carol Oja, "The Copland-Sessions Concerts and Their Reception in the Contemporary Press," *Musical Quarterly*, LXV:2 (April 1979), 214. See Oja also for a complete listing of Copland-Sessions Concerts programs, 227-29.

[14] At the close of 1928, Sessions sent Copland an ink score, *Largo* from *Symphony in E Minor*, with the inscription: "For Aaron, Affectionately, Roger. Rome, Dec 4, 1928." Also in Copland's files is Sessions' score for *Chorale Prelude No. 2 for Two Manuals and Pedal*, inscribed: "For Aaron Copland, most cordially, Roger H. Sessions, June 30, 1926." This must have been sent to Copland soon after he and Sessions met in the spring of 1926 in Paris.

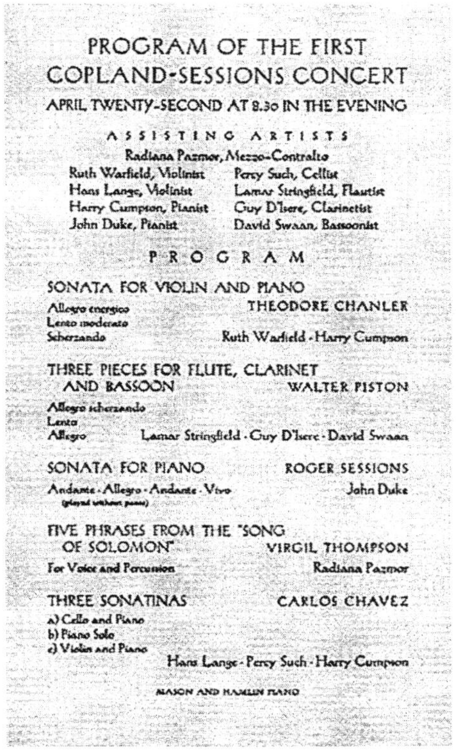

PROGRAM OF THE FIRST
COPLAND-SESSIONS CONCERT
APRIL TWENTY-SECOND AT 8.30 IN THE EVENING

ASSISTING ARTISTS
Radiana Pazmor, Mezzo-Contralto
Ruth Warfield, Violinist — Percy Such, Cellist
Hans Lange, Violinist — Lamar Stringfield, Flautist
Harry Cumpson, Pianist — Guy D'Isere, Clarinetist
John Duke, Pianist — David Swaan, Bassoonist

PROGRAM

SONATA FOR VIOLIN AND PIANO — THEODORE CHANLER
Allegro energico
Lento moderato
Scherzando — Ruth Warfield · Harry Cumpson

THREE PIECES FOR FLUTE, CLARINET AND BASSOON — WALTER PISTON
Allegro scherzando
Lento
Allegro — Lamar Stringfield · Guy D'Isere · David Swaan

SONATA FOR PIANO — ROGER SESSIONS
Andante · Allegro · Andante · Vivo — John Duke
(played without pause)

FIVE PHRASES FROM THE "SONG OF SOLOMON" — VIRGIL THOMPSON
For Voice and Percussion — Radiana Pazmor

THREE SONATINAS — CARLOS CHAVEZ
a) Cello and Piano
b) Piano Solo
c) Violin and Piano
Hans Lange · Percy Such · Harry Cumpson

MASON AND HAMLIN PIANO

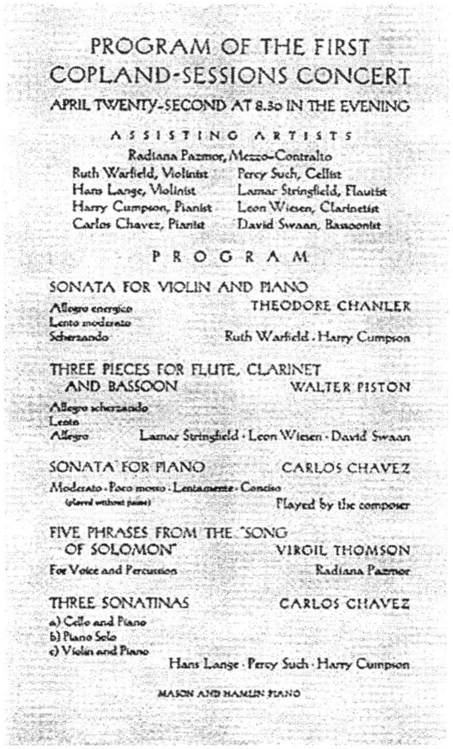

PROGRAM OF THE FIRST
COPLAND-SESSIONS CONCERT
APRIL TWENTY-SECOND AT 8.30 IN THE EVENING

ASSISTING ARTISTS
Radiana Pazmor, Mezzo-Contralto
Ruth Warfield, Violinist — Percy Such, Cellist
Hans Lange, Violinist — Lamar Stringfield, Flautist
Harry Cumpson, Pianist — Leon Wiesen, Clarinetist
Carlos Chavez, Pianist — David Swaan, Bassoonist

PROGRAM

SONATA FOR VIOLIN AND PIANO — THEODORE CHANLER
Allegro energico
Lento moderato
Scherzando — Ruth Warfield · Harry Cumpson

THREE PIECES FOR FLUTE, CLARINET AND BASSOON — WALTER PISTON
Allegro scherzando
Lento
Allegro — Lamar Stringfield · Leon Wiesen · David Swaan

SONATA FOR PIANO — CARLOS CHAVEZ
Moderato · Poco mosso · Lentamente · Conciso
(played without pause) — Played by the composer

FIVE PHRASES FROM THE "SONG OF SOLOMON" — VIRGIL THOMSON
For Voice and Percussion — Radiana Pazmor

THREE SONATINAS — CARLOS CHAVEZ
a) Cello and Piano
b) Piano Solo
c) Violin and Piano
Hans Lange · Percy Such · Harry Cumpson

MASON AND HAMLIN PIANO

Left: Program from the first Copland-Sessions Concert, 22 April 1928, including Sessions' *Piano Sonata*
Right: Replacement program, showing the substitution of Chávez' *Piano Sonata*

field, and he had to lie down on the station seat there. But we made it to New York and I actually played the *Sonata* at the concert. . .[15]

Copland performed in a *Violin and Piano Sonata* by Robert Delaney, a composer favored by Boulanger, and in the Quincy Porter *Quintet*. Richard Buhlig, a well-known pianist who was closely associated with West Coast composers, presented works by Ruth Crawford, Adolph Weiss, and Dane Rudhyar. In writing about the first season, critics pointed out that American composers had not yet found an American sound. Edward Burlingame Hill for *Modern Music* and Paul Rosenfeld both voiced disappointment that despite the "affirm America" movement, the musical works all sounded much like Stravinsky or Schoenberg. Three more seasons of Copland–Sessions Concerts would follow, making a total of ten concerts, eight in New York, and one each in Paris and London. Copland

[15] Interview, John Duke with Richard Miratti for Perlis, 8 December 1982, Northampton, Massachusetts. In the thirties Duke played the entire *Sonata* at a League concert in New York and at a Yaddo Festival concert. An autograph manuscript of Sessions' complete *Piano Sonata* is in John Duke's possession.

took the presentation of them very seriously, as he did his lecturing, although for many years he has enjoyed telling about the lady who came up to him after a Copland–Sessions concert to say, "Mr. Copland, I just love your sessions!"

Roger Sessions[16]

I was enthusiastic about the Copland–Sessions Concerts, but there was nothing I could do because I went to Europe for eight years—three in Florence, three in Rome, and two in Germany. Aaron and I began to move in different directions musically. He wanted to create an American music. I didn't believe in that and don't believe it can be done like that—you create music and if it's genuine and spontaneous music written by an American, why then it is American music. These things have to grow naturally. For me, nationalism is the wrong approach.[17] *Anyway, I don't think it did much good. For any composer I admired in the past, nationalism was not an issue. After all, Bach and Mozart were influenced by Italian music— they didn't think of nationalism.*

If it is written in places that I studied with Nadia Boulanger, it's not true. I knew and saw her often; furthermore, when I first met her I thought I would like to study with her, but I was very young and inexperienced and did not know the rest of Europe then. I came to disapprove of Nadia. She was really a businesswoman, not a disinterested musician at all. Nadia was overworking for her students. People don't realize it, but there were musicians who had nothing to do with Nadia Boulanger. And she had some strange ideas about the U.S. She thought it was a young, inexperienced country that did not know its way around and should have a guardian, and that France should be its guide. I soon discovered there were other countries in the world.

In Rome I met Otto Klemperer who said I must come to Germany. He introduced me to all the musicians. In the second year, Hitler came to power, and the Germans became very anti-Semitic, but Klemperer didn't see it. My wife and I saw it very clearly; furthermore, I knew I met Nazis. Each night I had dinner with British newspaper correspondents, and we knew what was going on, but the Nazis didn't dare bother us for the moment. Later I heard I was being watched. I could and did say whatever I chose and am rather proud of that. I went to Florence, my favorite European city, for the first spring festival. It was clear that Hitler and Mussolini were two quite different things—all the Germans I knew went to Florence to hear the festival. I was asked to pick up Alban Berg at the train when he arrived from Austria, and he was asking me what was going on in Germany!

I don't understand how anyone can say there was jealousy between Aaron and myself How can you be jealous if someone is doing something different than you? If Aaron and I had a dispute, I don't recall it now, so it could not have been very important. I have always liked Aaron very much even though we haven't seen each other often in recent years.

[16] Interview, Roger Sessions with Perlis, 4 May 1983, New York City.

[17] Sessions addressed the issue of nationalism in several publications, among them: "Music and Nationalism," *Modern Music*, IX:1 (November-December 1933), 3-12; "On the American Future," *Modern Music*, XVII: 2 (January-February 1940), 71-75; and *Reflections on the Musical Life in the United States* (New York: W. W. Norton, 1963), 146-53.

American composers may not have sounded independent in 1928 at the Copland–Sessions Concerts, but for the first time they were taking responsibility for presenting their own music. The concerts gave young composers a confidence that would lead to other performances, as well as to the founding of the American Composers Alliance and the American Music Center and to the establishment of American-based publication and recording companies. With their first season successfully accomplished, the co-directors left town—Sessions for Europe and Copland for his first taste of the American West.

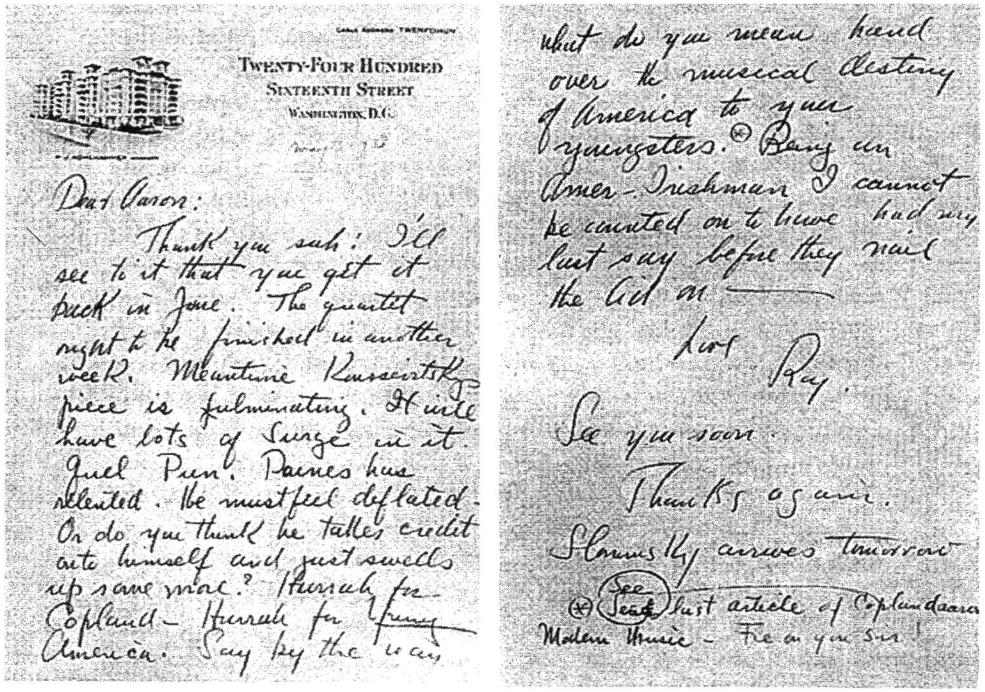

TWENTY-FOUR HUNDRED
SIXTEENTH STREET
WASHINGTON, D.C.

Dear Aaron:

Thank you sah: I'll see to it that you get it back in June. The quartet ought to be finished in another week. Meantime Koussevitzky piece is fulminating. It will have lots of Surge in it. Just Pun! Paines has relented. He must feel deflated. Or do you think he takes credit unto himself and just swells up some more? Hurrah for Copland – Hurrah for Young America. Say by the way what do you mean hand over the musical destiny of America to your youngsters. (*) Being an Amer.-Irishman I cannot be counted on to have had my last say before they nail the lid on ——

Love
Roy.

See you soon.

Thanks again.

Slonimsky arrives tomorrow

(*) See last article of Coplandaaron Modern Music – Fie on you Sir!

Letter from Roy Harris, 1933

MUSIC FOR MUSICIANS
1928 - 1930

I visited Santa Fe, New Mexico, for the first time in the summer of 1928. When in 1977 and 1982 I was invited to participate in the Santa Fe Chamber Music Festival, I could not help but compare the bustling Santa Fe with the sleepy old Spanish town I first saw in 1928. I had heard about Santa Fe from artist and writer friends who told me I could find an inexpensive room with a piano there. Santa Fe proved to be the quiet place I needed before going on to Los Angeles to play my *Piano Concerto* at the Hollywood Bowl. I had in mind to compose two works—a trio and an orchestral piece—and I thought I could make headway on both, since the thematic material was already worked out in my head. I even had fragments of the orchestral piece written down and had played them for Roger before leaving New York. During the past season, my activities and responsibilities had been so demanding that I had not been able to find uninterrupted blocks of time needed for composing. I *had* to give lectures to make a living, I was committed to the Copland–Sessions Concerts and to presenting performances of modern music at the New School,[1] and countless other demands made inroads on my time, such as finding support for Israel Citkowitz in Paris. Santa Fe would provide the privacy I so desperately needed. It seemed strange to be away from Paris at this time of year, and I wrote to Nadia (June 1928):

> I suppose it is time for me to see America a little, and then of course playing at the Bowl is an excellent introduction to the Pacific Coast. Still, I do miss the rue Ballu very much and I feel very much out of what is going on. Perhaps, during the summer you will be able to find a little time to write me. . . .

The quiet time alone in Santa Fe would serve another purpose. I had an important decision to make, indeed a crucial one at this time in my career: whether to take advantage of the tempting offers that were coming my way from abroad, or to stay in New York, furthering the causes of American music while continuing my own work. Carlos Chávez[2] wanted me to come to Mexico to play the *Piano Concerto* with the Orquesta Sinfónica de Mexico in Mexico City, and Roger was urging me to try for the Rome Prize. He pointed out that I could win it and thus have all my time for composing, while at home I had to teach and be dependent on uncertain prizes and commissions. My answer was, "What would happen to our concerts?" But Roger did not consider this sufficient reason not to try for the Rome Prize. Even Israel put in a word for my returning to Europe, writing: "Only some absurd scruples about concerts and duties may keep you in the U.S.A." Nevertheless, sometime during that quiet summer in Santa Fe, my mind was made up. I would stay in New York. I would continue to teach at the New School and to accept lecture engagements. I would direct the Copland–Sessions Concerts. And I would write a major orchestral work for a competition sponsored by RCA Victor that was offering a $25,000 prize to the winner.[3] I wrote to Chávez with apologies and assurances of a long visit to Mexico later and suggested he substitute *Music for the Theatre* for the *Piano Concerto* in his February concert. I wrote to Roger about the Victor competition and my plan to submit a work.

[1] Together with Varèse, Copland arranged a series of six concerts at the New School, beginning with a song recital by Greta Torpadie on 13 January 1928. For 17 December 1928, Copland would produce another "Concert of Modern Music" with works by Chávez, Schoenberg, Szymanowski, Poulenc, Stravinsky, and Ravel.

[2] It is unclear exactly where and when Copland and Chávez met. At a party given for them in the late seventies by Claire Reis in New York, a toast was made to the two old friends, and surrounded by a group of friends and colleagues, they reminisced: "We met in Paris," said Chávez none too certainly. "In Paris? No, in New York—I think!" said Copland. "In '26," offered Chávez. "Really?" said Copland.

[3] *The New York Times* (29 May 1928), 16: "Victor Company Offers $40,000 in 3 Prizes for Native Symphonic and Jazz Compositions. The plan and the rules governing the competition were announced by John Erskine, author . . . at a dinner last night at the Plaza. . . . 'Recognizing a clear division among the ideals of American composers . . . the awards are offered for two distinct classes of compositions. Twenty-five thousand dollars is to be awarded for the best work of symphonic type, in any form which the composer may employ or develop, within the playing scope of the full symphony orchestra.' The closing date is May 27, 1929. The award will be announced on Oct. 3, 1929. . . The Board of Judges . . . will comprise Mme. Olga Samaroff . . . Rudolph Ganz . . . Leopold Stokowski . . . Serge Koussevitsky . . . and Frederick Stock . . . It was said that the prize of $25,000 in the symphony competition is the largest amount yet offered for a single composition. The hope was expressed by speakers that out of the competition would come a great symphonic work which would be truly American in conception."

ORQUESTA SINFONICA MEXICANA

Director, CARLOS CHAVEZ

TEMPORADA 1928-1929

ULTIMO CONCIERTO

EN EL

TEATRO ESPERANZA IRIS

EL

DOMINGO 3

DE FEBRERO DE 1929, A LAS 11 HORAS

PROGRAMA:

J. L. MARISCAL .... SINFONIA
SAINT-SAENS .... CONCIERTO EN SI B. PARA VIOLIN Y PIANO
SOLISTA, SILVESTRE REVUELTAS
AARON COPLAND .... MUSIC FOR THE THEATRE
HONEGGER .... PACIFIC 231

PRECIOS:

Luneta .... $ 2.00
Anfiteatro .... " 2.00
Segundos numerados .... " 1.25
General de Segundos .... " 1.00
Galería numerada .... " 0.75
Galería general .... " 0.50

BOLETOS DE VENTA EN J. F. VELAZQUEZ Y HERMANO, BALDERAS 74; EDITORIAL CULTURA, ARGENTINA, 5. AGENCIA MISRACHI, AV. JUAREZ, 18.

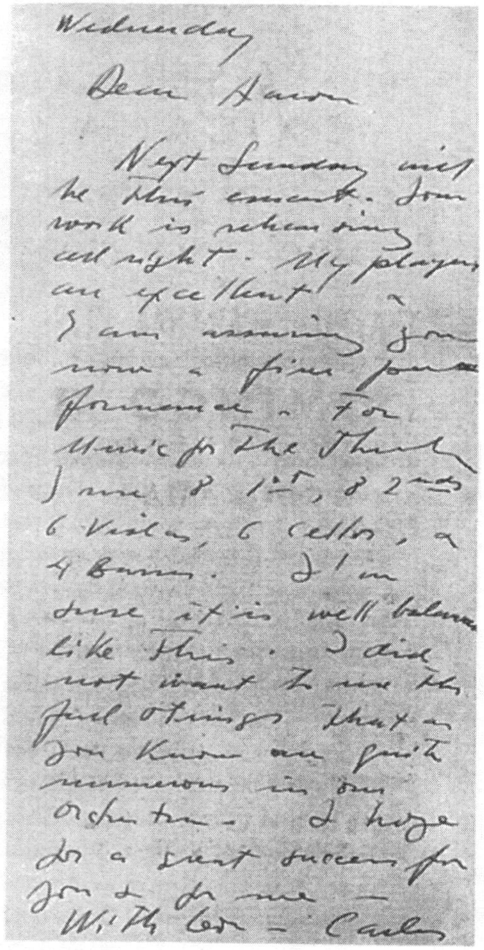
Wednesday

Dear Aaron

Next Sunday will be the concert. Your work is rehearsing all right. My players are excellent and I am assuring you now a fine performance. For Music for the Theatre I use 8 1st, 8 2nd, 6 Violas, 6 Cellos, and 4 Basses. I'm sure it is well balanced like this. I did not want to use the full strings that you know are quite numerous in our orchestra. I hope for a great success for you and for me —

With love — Carlos

Above: Program from Mexico listing Copland's *Music for the Theatre*, and the note from Carlos Chávez written on the reverse. *Left:* Photograph of conductor Albert Coates, actress Norma Shearer, and Copland. Hollywood, 1928

I rested, worked on the *Vocalise*[4] for Professor Hettich in Paris, and practiced for my appearance at the Hollywood Bowl on 20 July. To my amazement, when I stepped off the train in Los Angeles, I was met by manager, president, chairman, photographers, reporters—and two men moving a piano! Someone had cooked up a Hollywood publicity stunt for me to play jazz to the crowds and photographers at the railroad station. I had a heck of a time convincing them that I didn't play jazz, nor was I any good at improvising. I doubt they believed me! I was put up at the Hollywood Plaza Hotel, but had little chance to enjoy the posh surroundings. Not enough rehearsal time had been scheduled for the *Concerto* performance. I wrote to Chávez, "The *Concerto* caused almost a 'scandal'! But it was very amusing to play before the crowd of 17,000 people." After the quiet of Santa Fe, the attention of the press, the radio interviews, and the presence of movie stars was exciting. I was particularly impressed with meeting Charlie Chaplin. After Los Angeles, I spent a week with Henry Cowell in San Francisco. He arranged a reception with members of the New Music Society. They asked to publish "As It Fell Upon a Day" in the *New Music Quarterly* (July 1929), and I invited Henry to send a piece for the next Copland–Sessions Concerts.

After returning East, the remainder of the summer was spent at the MacDowell Colony. Clurman and Gerald Sykes were already there (Sykes had stayed at my place in New York while I was in Santa Fe). I reported to them on the "winning of the West" and got down to concentrated work on the trio and orchestral piece. Long letters from Roger, who was in Juziers for the summer, were added to those from Israel, Roy, and Nadia. At first, Roger sent reports on that lopsided triangle, but as the summer progressed, it seemed that he too became part of the shape of life in Juziers.

One fifteen-page letter from Roger (25 July) ended with a P.S.: "Barbara reminds me that I could have gotten about $30 from Minna L. for an article the size of this letter!" Roger was concerned about Nadia's health. "She drives to Fontainebleau and back each week, and while she is there she leads a life which can't help but be a terrific strain—teaching from 7 A.M. till late in the evening without any let-up, even for lunch—she eats a banana or two at noon apparently. . . . She drives very fast and has a way of sometimes missing a collision by the skin of her teeth. . ." Later that summer, Roger wrote again (19 August): "Nadia is still strange and seems to have something on her mind that she is working herself to death to forget."

Mademoiselle's friends and students seemed to have no idea of what was troubling her. I have read criticism of Boulanger for keeping her personal life private. But this was the French way—it would not have been appropriate for Nadia to confide in her students.[5] Israel described Mademoiselle that summer (11 August 1928): "I'm quite at ease with her

[4] This piece had its first performance in New York in 1935 for a *New Music Quarterly* recording, with Ethel Codd Luening, soprano, Copland, piano. It was arranged for flute for Doriot Anthony Dwyer in 1972 and is published in both versions.

[5] See Léonie Rosenstiel, *Nadia Boulanger,* and reviews of Rosenstiel: Ned Rorem (*The New York Times Book Review,* 23 May 1982, p. 28); Robert Craft (*The New York Review of Books*, XXIX: 9, 27 May 1982, 8-12); Allen Hughes (*The New York Times*, 18 June 1982, C2.

now and our relations are much warmer and closer. She has such a wealth of feelings and sympathy and emotion and understanding. I'm continually amazed and am stricken at such a rare fusion of musicianship, intellect, feeling, intuition, etc. . ." Whatever was disturbing Nadia, she confided this much to me at the end of the summer (23 September 1928):

> Have still one head, two hands and even place for affection—unbelievable, is it not? But so—And I feel quite miserable—hating unfaithfulness over all and with it, lack of courage. But it has to be confessed that after such a year, courage is very low, but very! This preludium played—I declare my shame killed, and everything already better—Now necessary to proceed with order: Terrible not to be able to speak—but you feel, dear Aaron with what an admiration, an affection these awkward words are going to you.

I stayed at the MacDowell Colony as long as possible, working against time to finish the trio, knowing that my return to West 78th Street meant putting it aside again. I returned just in time to deliver the first of my lectures at the New School. This fall, my series was called "Masterworks of Modern Music," each lecture illustrating a subject or a style of music with a major work.[6] Looking back at my lecture notes fills me with renewed wonder and respect for the New School for the opportunity it gave me to explore such topics. These lectures would have been enough to occupy me, but I had several additional commitments: I joined the League of Composers in the fall of 1928, though I was not on the board until 1932, and I was helping to organize the Cos Cob Press, an early effort to assist young American composers to publish music that would not be taken on by established publishers. It was funded by Alma Wertheim. Cos Cob gave composers 50% of music sales, rather than the usual 10%. Alma and Edwin F. Kalmus, the vice-president, depended on my advice and contacts. While it lasted Cos Cob gave a much-needed boost to American music. In 1938 Cos Cob merged with Arrow Music Press, and in 1956 both catalogues were taken over by Boosey & Hawkes. My own music benefited from Cos Cob, in view of the fact that several of my early works were published by it: the *Dance Symphony, First Symphony, Music for the Theatre, Concerto for Piano and Orchestra, Piano Variations,* and *Vitebsk.*

Thanks to Mary Churchill's help, a small office at 1601 Steinway Hall was rented for the Copland–Sessions Concerts. Henry Cowell and Colin McPhee came to New York for the first concert, 30 December, which included Henry's *Seven Paragraphs for String Trio.* McPhee played Nikolai Lopatnikoff's *Sonatina for Piano,* earlier approved by Roger and Nadia in Paris. John Duke performed Bernard Wagenaar's *Sonata for Piano*, and Marc Blitzstein was represented by *Four Songs for Baritone and Piano*, with texts by Whitman. Roger and I both thought George Antheil deserved further hearing, so we were pleased when he sent his *Second String Quartet.* Roger was in Rome, and his promised set of short piano études did not arrive in time for the concert.

[6] The lectures were: The Realism of Moussorgsky's *Boris Godunov*; the Impressionism of Debussy's *Pelléas et Mélisande*; the Post-Romanticism of Mahler's *Das Lied von der Erde*; the Post-Impressionism of Ravel's *Daphnis et Chloé*; the Expressionism of Schoenberg's *Pierrot Lunaire*; the Dynamism of Stravinsky's *Le Sacre du printemps*; the Mysticism of Scriabin's *Prometheus*; the Lyricism of Milhaud's *Créâtion du monde*; the Neo-Classicism of Hindemith's *Das Marienleben*; the Objectivism of Stravinsky's *Oedipus Rex*; and a Summary of Lesser Masterworks.

The reaction of the press was distressing; I would not have been troubled by bad reviews—I had seen enough of those—but for the critics to call the music conservative was a blow to our purpose of presenting stimulating modern music. Olin Downes dismissed the evening as unmemorable: "Music of such poor, weak, and childish character as to afford no justification for public performance. . . ."[7] Antheil's quartet received a particularly poor press and was viewed as an apology for his earlier and scandalous *Ballet mécanique.* Although Roger and I agreed that we should keep the concerts going, we were both becoming more and more concerned about his absentee status. Roger wrote (17 January 1929),

> I have already given the thing—the problem as you state it—a good deal of thought, and have reached certain conclusions—the chief one being that it would be a great mistake to give them up. My 'moral support' as you so kindly put it has I fear not been a too tangible quantity; I hope to improve it . . . and besides, I have reason to believe that press announcements and similar matters may have looked up since you wrote.

Roger was right. The second concert on 24 February stirred up considerably more interest. Included was a rather dissonant *Sonata for Violin and Piano* by the European Alexander Lipsky, three songs by Vladimir Dukelsky (who became better known as the popular song and theater music composer Vernon Duke), and Roy Harris' *Piano Sonata*, played by Harry Cumpson. But it was the final work on the program that woke up the audience—Virgil Thomson's *Capital Capitals.*[8] Composed for male quartet with piano accompaniment and an outrageous text by Gertrude Stein, the work struck the audience as hilariously funny. Virgil directed the proceedings from the piano and accepted "bravos" at the end. He described the occasion vividly in his own autobiography.[9] I conveyed my relief to Roger that the critics at least showed some interest in the music, but the situation engendered by his absence was growing increasingly difficult. Roger wrote (22 March 1929):

> The point is simply that I have no means of knowing the situation in any real sense when I am absolutely ignorant of some of the music that is being played. I have as much confidence in you as I would have in anyone; and yet—in spite of the fact that I myself am wholly responsible for this situation—I am beginning to realize the very great inconveniences as well as the risks involved in my being a completely irresponsible partner. I have to all intents and purposes signed a blank page, and sponsored, as a musician and a composer, something for which I have no responsibility at all; and I have no sure means of knowing, as things are now, whether I would be willing to take that responsibility for the works that are played at the concerts.

Roger was also disturbed by the publicity, which included pictures and biographies of us two directors. "I had understood that we were to keep in the background," he wrote, and suggested we meet for a "good leisurely talk in May or June" to go over our policies and

[7] Olin Downes, "Music: Young Composers Heard," *The New York Times* (31 December 1929), 8.

[8] Thomson's response to a telephone inquiry of 14 October 1982 concerning the title was: "At first, Gertrude's title was *Capitals, Capitals*—two s's, one comma—later, she preferred *Capital Capitals.*" On the concert program of 1929, the title appears as *Capital, Capitals.*

[9] Thomson, *Virgil Thomson*, 136.

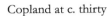

Copland at c. thirty

plans. When I suggested we plan a Copland–Sessions concert in Paris, Roger answered, "Don't you think it is a little premature; that our concerts have not really established themselves sufficiently in America. . . ." Not wanting to abandon the idea, I responded that I would proceed without using our name.

Nadia agreed that a concert of American music in Paris was a good idea. When Mary Churchill offered to pay expenses, I canceled a third Copland–Sessions concert that was tentatively planned for 7 April in New York. I wrote to Nadia (19 April1929) that we had changed our minds and decided to call it "Concert d'oeuvres des jeunes compositeurs americains." I still hoped to include Roger and asked Nadia to urge him to agree that his *Three Choral Preludes* be on the program. I wrote to Nadia (19 April 1929):

> I hope you will be willing to play them. I know how busy you are but is it too much to ask you also to play the piano part in Roy's "Sextette"[10] and in my Trio (the Trio is not difficult). One more word. Be sure that in the last analysis I leave everything in your hands. Whatever you do I'm certain in advance will be right. Unfortunately I can't be in Paris as soon as I had hoped. Because my orchestral piece is not nearly finished I have put off my sailing until May 29 which should bring me to Paris about June 4.

Mary Churchill was in Paris, and I knew she would help Nadia with arrangements. While Mary was in France, I had the use of her country house in Briarcliff Manor, just outside New York. I made a hasty retreat out of the city and went to work.

Looking back at the past season, I realized that the main event for me had been the premiere of *Vitebsk*. The League of Composers had asked for a new work, offering a performance by no less a pianist than Walter Gieseking and two members of the Pro Arte Quartet, violinist Alphonse Onnou and cellist Robert Maas. The score had been finished at the MacDowell Colony in September, but I was still copying parts two weeks before the concert. Gerald Sykes, who lived nearby and worked downtown, would come by at eight in the morning, pick up the parts I made during the night, and deliver them downtown to where the performers were rehearsing.

Based on a Jewish folk song, the trio has often been cited as my only "Jewish" work. But when I was younger, I had set traditional Hebrew melodies for cello and piano,[11] and in the thirties I made arrangements of some Jewish folk songs that were published.[12] In 1926 and 1932 respectively, Roger Sessions and Virgil Thomson wrote about the Jewish elements in my music.[13] It seems to me that my use of Jewish themes was similar to my use of jazz—

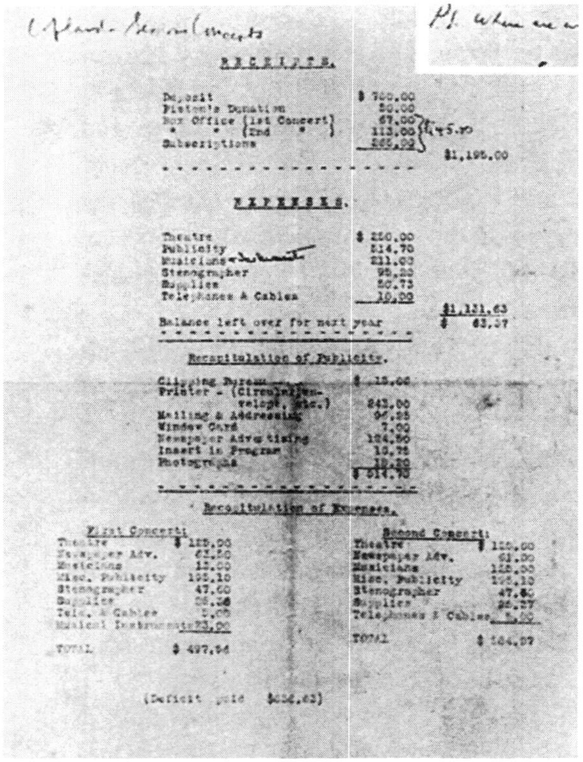

Copland-Sessions Concerts

RECEIPTS.

Deposit	$ 700.00	
Piston's Donation	50.00	
Box Office (1st Concert)	67.00	
" " (2nd ")	113.00	
Subscriptions	265.00	
		$1,195.00

EXPENSES.

Theatre	$ 250.00	
Publicity	514.70	
Musicians	211.00	
Stenographer	95.20	
Supplies	50.73	
Telephones & Cables	10.00	
		$1,131.63
Balance left over for next year		$ 63.37

Recapitulation of Publicity.

Clipping Bureau	$ 15.00
Printer - (Circulars, envelope, etc.)	243.00
Mailing & Addressing	96.25
Window Card	7.00
Newspaper Advertising	124.50
Insert in Program	10.75
Photographs	18.20
	$ 514.70

Recapitulation of Expenses.

First Concert:		Second Concert:	
Theatre	$ 125.00	Theatre	$ 125.00
Newspaper Adv.	62.50	Newspaper Adv.	62.00
Musicians	12.00	Musicians	122.00
Misc. Publicity	195.10	Misc. Publicity	195.10
Stenographer	47.60	Stenographer	47.60
Supplies	25.36	Supplies	25.37
Tele. & Cables	5.00	Telephones & Cables	5.00
Musical Instruments	25.00		
TOTAL	$ 497.96	TOTAL	$ 584.07

(Deficit paid [illegible])

Financial statement for the first two years of the Copland-Sessions Concerts, compiled by Copland

[10] Copland must have been referring to Harris' *Concerto for Piano, Clarinet and String Quartet* of 1927, first performed at a League of Composers concert on 12 February 1928.

[11] Several incomplete short pieces in Copland's juvenilia use traditional Jewish melodies.

[12] "Hora," arranged by Copland, was published in Series I—"Dances of Palestine," *Folk Songs of the New Palestine* (New York: Nigun, 1938). Some other contributors were Dessau, Weill, Milhaud, Toch, Wolpe, Saminsky, Jacobi, and Honegger.

[13] Roger Sessions, "An American Evening Abroad," *Modern Music* (November–December 1926), 34; and Virgil Thomson, "Aaron Copland (American Composers VII)," *b*, IX:2, (January–February 1932), 67-73.

Jewish influences were present in my music, even when I did not refer to them overtly. I have often been asked why I wrote "cowboy" music rather than "Jewish" music. I never thought about these things at the time, but it must have been partly because I grew up in the Eastern European tradition and there was no novelty to it. Every American boy is fascinated with cowboys and Indians, and I was no exception. Also, my mother had grown up in the American West. Many artists (writers in particular) have claimed that they work best out of their own experiences. But for me it was not necessary to have an experience in order to compose about it. I preferred to imagine being on a horse without actually getting on one! In any case, I never gave much thought to including or excluding any kind of influence from my work. It was always a musical stimulus that got me started, as when I heard the folk theme that the Polish-Jewish author S. Ansky used in his play *The Dybbuk*.[14] It appealed to me just as it had to him. Vitebsk, a small Russian village, was the playwright's home; it was there he had heard and transcribed the tune. It seemed an appropriate title for my trio based on the same tune. Years later when I traveled in the Soviet Union, the Russians were amazed that any composer would name a piece of music after the city of *Vitebsk*, a large industrial complex resembling Pittsburgh or Cleveland!

The overall nature of *Vitebsk* is basically a dramatic character study. It is a tripartite, slow–fast–slow form. The introductory opening, a series of major and minor triads struck simultaneously on the piano, is followed by resultant quarter-tone intervals that enhance the Hebraic atmosphere of the piece and set the scene for the appearance of the Jewish melody played by the cello, the instrument that continues to maintain a leading role throughout the section. (The cello's deep tone seemed appropriate for the *molto espressivo* I hoped to achieve.) The fast section is a Chagall-like grotesquerie that reaches a wild climax and interrupts itself in mid-course, causing a dramatic pause. The main theme returns in unison two octaves apart played by violin and cello, punctuated by clangorous chords on the piano. A short coda leads to a quiet ending.

The full title of the trio is *Vitebsk (Study on a Jewish Theme)*, and it was my intention to reflect the harshness and drama of Jewish life in White Russia. So it did not surprise me when the work was described as "hard," "dry," and "dissonant." Performers and audiences have told me that they find *Vitebsk* a strangely moving work. Musically, I knew I had found something that I intended to explore further as soon as I finished the orchestral piece, which would be titled *Symphonic Ode*. *Vitebsk* has been performed frequently (often with me at the piano), and always more successfully than at the premiere, 16 February 1929, at Town Hall where my trio was played after a *Sonata* by Karol Rathaus and before a work by Mario Castelnuovo-Tedesco. The League's audiences knew what to expect—they came to these concerts to hear contemporary music. But, according to Lehman Engel, who was present at the premiere:[15]

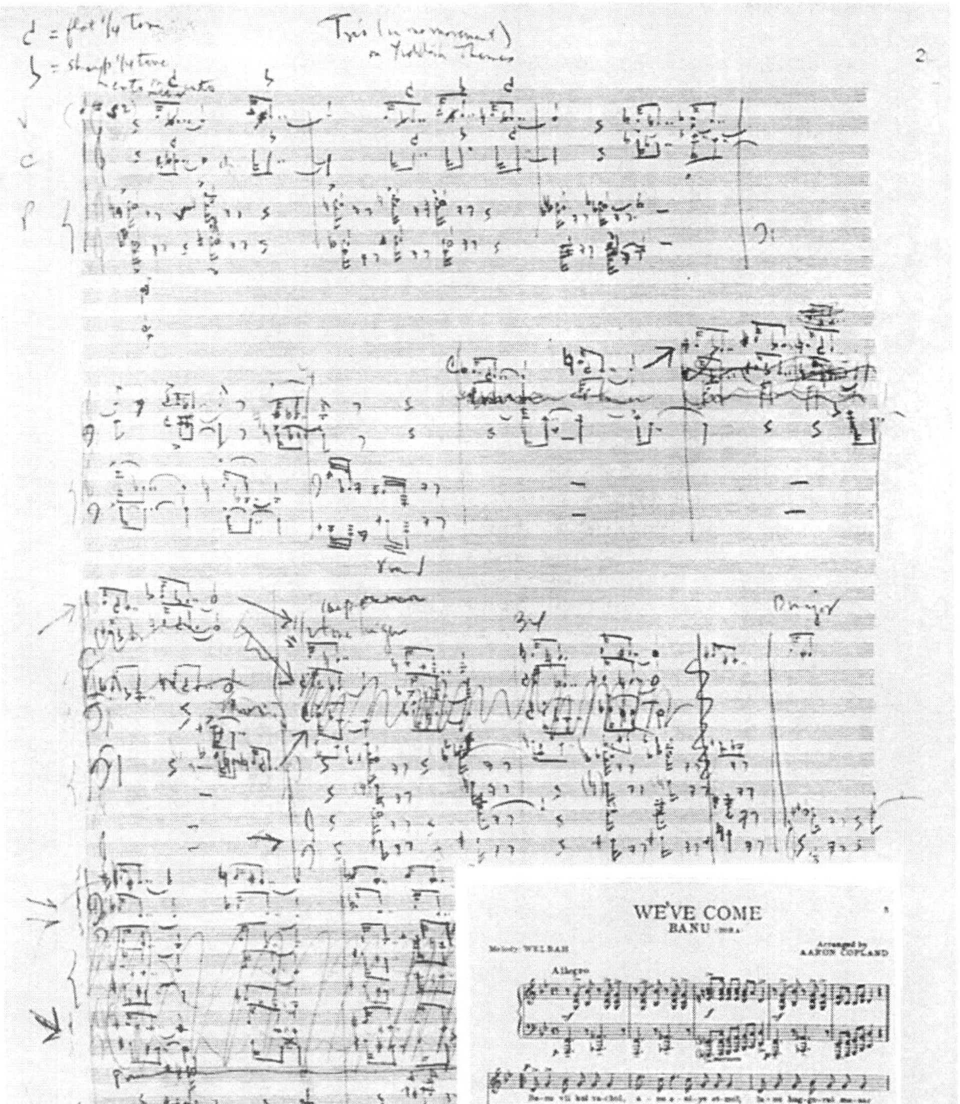

Above: Manuscript page from the sketch score of *Vitebsk*
Right: Published arrangement of a "Hora" by Copland

[14] S. Ansky, pseudonym for Solomon Rappaport (1863-1920), *The Dybbuk*, a play in four acts translated from the Yiddish by Henry G. Alsberg and Winifred Katzin (New York: Liveright, c. 1926).

[15] Interview, Lehman Engel with Perlis, 4 June 1981, New York City. Engel died 29 August 1982.

> It resembled nothing less than a Mack Sennett comedy. The cellist was heavy set (to put it politely), and as he came on stage carrying his large instrument, he knocked over the violinist's stand. While bending over to retrieve the music, he dropped his cello, and it knocked over the violist's stand. There was music all over the floor. Finally, when they were seated and ready to begin, a cello string broke with a loud noise! It was hilarious. For some reason, the nature of the piece and its strange name continued to strike the audience as funny! Laughter was mixed with applause at the end.

This was hardly the reception I had anticipated. I decided to give *Vitebsk* another hearing at the upcoming Paris concert.

A month before my sailing date, I had to face the fact that I would not be able to finish the *Symphonic Ode* in time for the RCA Victor competition. This was to be my first big orchestral piece since the jazz-inspired *Concerto*. I was attempting something different, and the work was not proceeding as quickly as I had anticipated. Does anyone but the composer, I wonder, realize the sheer physical labor involved in writing down all those notes and musical symbols in a way that will eventually translate into sound by a large symphony orchestra in a concert hall? This aspect of composing has little to do with creativity or inspiration, and each composer has his own method of getting the job done. For me it went this way: over a period of time, I made sketches, jotted down fragments, and when the time was right, arranged these fragments into their inevitable order. You must shape the material so that it is logical—just those notes and no others are needed to complete the thought. You eliminate, you revamp. In short, you seek out the inevitable conclusion of what you started by showing it has to go one way and no other. That's what I mean by inevitability. I would make piano sketches and polish and refine them with the appropriate instrumental sounds in my mind along the way. (I would occasionally make jottings for the instrumentation on the piano score.)

A long symphonic work such as the *Ode* naturally presented more problems than a short piece. The *Ode* in its original version was to be scored for a Mahler-like oversized orchestra with eight horns, five trumpets, three trombones, and two tubas. I was not able to finish the orchestral score before leaving for Europe. It would have been a shame not to submit anything to the competition, so I searched my scores for a substitute. Since most of the ballet *Grohg* was unpublished, I found considerable usable material other than *Cortège macabre* and *Dance of the Adolescent* that had been taken from it earlier. By working nights and days for weeks, I extracted three dances from the ballet score, gave it the title *Dance Symphony*, and delivered the score to the competition officials just in time for their end-of-May deadline.

Exhausted, I left Mary Churchill's house. This experience had made me more than ever determined to find more time for composing. The way was suddenly opened by an offer from my well-to-do cousin Percy Uris to support me for a full year with no strings attached! These were lean and hungry years, and although I found it somewhat degrading to accept money this way, I knew that I could not live as a full-time composer by commissions alone. Percy asked me to think it over—but I did not have to consider my answer for long. The judges for the Victor competition decided that none of the works submitted warranted the full $25,000 prize, so they divided it into four awards: $5,000 each to Louis Gruenberg, Ernest Bloch, and myself, with a $10,000 prize to Robert Russell Bennett, who had submitted two compositions. I was more than satisfied to have won the $5,000, which would keep me going for a year, and I asked Percy if his offer could begin a year later, in 1930. Considering his generosity, I am somewhat embarrassed to see now what I wrote then (16 May 1929): "My only objection is that you have no personal conviction about the value of the stuff I turn out, but must take it on hearsay. When a person has a real appreciation of the product I turn out, it is easier for me to accept the wherewithal for turning out that product. . . ." Percy graciously agreed to my proposal. I left Mary Churchill's house knowing that my financial future was secure, and with the anticipation of a rest on shipboard and a reunion with friends in Paris, I felt like a caged animal set free!

In May 1929 Mary wrote that she had met with Nadia in Paris and was terribly impressed with her and all the trouble she was taking for the June concert:

> Boulanger reports to me of 'great complications.' I am sure there have been terrific ones, far beyond my knowledge. I feel hopeful that your presence will dissipate them. Nothing has been said about defraying preliminary expenses. But since I am departing and to forestall any possible needs, I have just deposited $800 in your name at the G.T. Co.

I arrived to find that Nadia had organized everything beautifully. The Salle Chopin was reserved (about 500 seats), and Roy was rehearsing performers for his work. I waited as long as possible for music to arrive from Roger, but finally the program had to be decided without him. Nadia, who had decided not to perform, went all out to make the occasion a gala event by inviting the French musical and social elite and the many Americans studying and visiting Paris that spring. Mary Churchill returned to Paris in time to attend the concert with Minna, Israel, Roy, and Marc Blitzstein. The music was all new to Paris except for Virgil's songs. The reviews were mixed: Virgil got high marks from several critics, including the *International Herald Tribune*, while Roland Petit in *La Revue musicale* praised my pieces. Far more important than individual reactions was the recognition by French critics and an international audience that America had composers ready to be heard in Paris, the artistic capital of the world.

It seemed a good idea to be close to Nadia while working on the *Ode*, so for the summer of 1929, Israel and I took rooms in Juziers chez Mme Blondel. My work was finally going along well. When Roger wrote from Switzerland inviting me to visit and sending train schedules, I had to refuse. On 12 July he suggested we take a trip together ("bring old clothes"), and I responded by suggesting we meet in Paris in September, before my return to the States, to discuss plans for the third Copland–Sessions Concerts. Roger replied, jokingly, "Apparently you will stay in that little mud-hole instead of coming to be near us!"

Koussevitzky had invited me (and several other composers) to present a new symphonic work for the fiftieth anniversary of the Boston Symphony Orchestra in 1931. When I remarked that I intended an expanded instrumentation for this work, he assured me I could have as many brass and percussion players as I wanted—after all, Koussevitzky pointed out, this was to be a special occasion, and he emphasized, "They vill expect, they vill expect!" The Boston Symphony anniversary celebration would be a perfect occasion for the premiere of the *Symphonic Ode.* I had been striving for something grand and dramatic in this work. Composed over a two-year span that was a transitional period for me, the *Ode* is a transitional work—a summing up as well as a looking ahead. Perhaps this was my way of announcing, at about the time of my thirtieth birthday, that I was grown up. The *Ode* resembles me at the time, full of ideas and ideals, introspective and serious, but still showing touches of youthful jazz days, reflections of a Jewish heritage, remnants of Paris (Boulanger's *la grande ligne*), influences of Mahler (the orchestration) and Stravinsky (motor rhythms). Looking ahead, one can hear in the *Ode* the beginnings of a purer, non-programmatic style, an attempt toward an economy of material and transparency of texture that would be taken much further in the next few years in the *Piano Variations,* the *Short Symphony,* and *Statements for Orchestra.* In the *Ode*, a twenty-minute one-movement composition, I was attempting to write a piece of music with an unbroken logic so thoroughly unified that the very last note bears a relation to the first. I used a two-measure blues motif (from my *Nocturne* for violin and piano of 1926) as the musical basis of all five sections. This budding interest in formal structure would become more absorbing in my subsequent works, along with a continuing fascination for polyrhythmic experimentation.

The title *Symphonic Ode* is not meant to imply connection with a literary idea. It is not an ode to anything in particular, but rather a spirit that is to be found in the music itself. When questioned about what this spirit was supposed to be, my response (as quoted in several contemporary newspaper interviews and program notes) was as follows: "What that particular spirit is, is not for me to say. In another connection, André Gide has well expressed my meaning:

> Before explaining my book to others, I wait for them to explain it to me. To wish to explain it first would be to restrain its meaning prematurely, because even if we know what we wish to say we cannot know if we have said only that. And what interests me especially is what I have put into my book without my own knowledge.[16]

The exploration of the unconscious in Gide's writings was one of the influences moving me toward a style in which my music was to stand as pure and absolute, limited in no way by a programmatic or extra-musical connotation.

I wrote an explanation of the complicated meters in the *Ode* on the title page of the sketch-score:

Version for the conductor:	7/8	4/8	9/8	19/8	12/8
to be beat:	3	4	4	4	4

I had even included a short piano piece in 10/6 rhythm.[17] These complicated rhythms and frequently changing tempi caused Koussevitzky and the orchestra players great difficulty. Since most of the rhythms could be beat in 4/4, they could not understand why I had not written them in 4/4! After the first rehearsal, Koussevitzky informed me that the men could not play the *Ode* as written. I laughed at the notion that these were difficult rhythms and told Koussevitzky that there was nothing to it. He replied: "Come up to Boston and take over the rehearsal yourself. For me, the orchestra has been able to play only three bars of the piece in a full hour of rehearsal." I was reluctant to make changes in the score two weeks before the scheduled premiere, so I went to Boston, and Koussevitzky turned a rehearsal over to me. I described the incident in a letter to Israel (29 May 1930):

> I finally heard the 'Ode'! I conducted it myself one morning at a rehearsal in Boston while Koussevitzky listened from the auditorium. I only really heard the slow parts, the fast parts were ruined by being played too slow. The end sounds gloriously. It was a revealing experience. The upshot was that I have for all time given up trying to make music look on paper what it actually sounds like. Applied to the Ode it means that I must completely rewrite the barring of the fast parts throughout. I'm working on it now and have discovered how much easier certain sections might have been written. For example, one part which originally had 13 changes of time-3/4, 7/8, 5/8 etc.—is now entirely 4/4. I never believed it could be done till I tried. So that not a note of the piece will be changed but it will look entirely different on paper. When I think of the loss of time and money (the parts must be completely recopied and recorrected) I could weep. On top of this, I played it at the piano for Hertzka, head of Universal Ed, who happened to be here at Alma's one night, and when he heard it was scored for a Mahlerian orchestra he advised her against publishing it. (Not that she'll take his advice.) "Why you're crazy man," says he, "there are not ten orchestras in all Europe that can supply 18 brass instruments." This darling 'Ode' seems to be having a hard time in a cruel world.

After the rehearsal in Boston, I returned to New York and wrote to Koussevitzky (27 March 1930): "Cher ami, May I suggest that the premiere of the *Symphonic Ode* be postponed to the next season in order that I can revise the notation further." Probably relieved, Koussevitzky agreed, and the journalists had a field day writing about the Copland score that was so modern it could not be played even by the Boston Symphony Orchestra. I was questioned about it constantly. But actually, the changes were minor revisions in notation merely to simplify the parts for the musicians and the conductor. After the *Ode* was finally heard in Boston on 19 February 1932, Koussevitzky conducted it in New York (3 March). Paul Rosenfeld and H. T. Parker of the *Boston Transcript* reviewed it favorably, describing it as "grand," but Lawrence Gilman of *The New York Times*, previously an admirer, was disappointed in a work he characterized as "impotent and unrewarding." Audiences were disturbed by what they considered dissonance. Nonetheless, I have always regarded the *Symphonic Ode* as an important work. I tried hard for something there, and I feel that I succeeded in what I attempted. As was my custom, at the end of the conductor's score (eighty-six ink manuscript pages with Koussevitzky's blue pencil markings) I inscribed the places and dates of completion: "Konigstein, Germany—New York 1927/Santa Fe—Peterboro 1928/Briarcliff Manor—Juziers—NY 1929." The *Symphonic Ode* had not been easy to compose, and it was difficult to perform, particularly at a time when orchestral performers were not trained to play rhythms that have since become standard. Kirkpatrick admired the piece

[16] In the program notes of early performances of the *Symphonic Ode*, the source of this quotation is given as Gide's book, *Preludes*, and the error was reprinted in several newspaper articles and reviews. The correct source is André Gide, *Paludes* (Paris: Gallimard, 1920); the quotation is from the preface page, translated by Copland for his own use.

[17] No score survives. Copland had played this piece for John Kirkpatrick. See Interview, John Kirkpatrick with Perlis, 24 February 1983, New Haven, Connecticut.

and made a two-piano arrangement that we played together several times.[18] John recalls one such occasion:

> Roy Harris invited Aaron and me to play the Ode in my two-piano version. It was about 1935 in Princeton at the Westminster Choir School. I had done an original and a revised version. I was fond of the original which was longer. Somehow, we got our signals crossed, and I started out on the longer version, while Aaron took the shorter one. Of course, we discovered it right away. Aaron, fortunately, could improvise in the style of Copland, but it was a traumatic experience! [19]

After Marc Blitzstein heard us, he commented: "It is strangely richer in the 2 piano transcription than in its original form. . . ." Carlos Chávez conducted the *Ode* on 18 November 1932 during my first visit to Mexico City. I wrote to Koussevitzky about the Mexican orchestra (13 November 1932): "What they lack in technique is made up with love in their Latin-American way. . . . I only realize now on rehearing the *Ode* to what an extent it is inextricably bound up in my mind with you and the Orchestra and that unforgettable week when it was first brought to life. . . ." After the Mexican performance, the *Ode* was not heard again until 1946, when the Juilliard Orchestra took it up under Thor Johnson's direction.

Koussevitzky and I were both disappointed that the *Ode* was so rarely performed. At the time of the Juilliard concert, I contemplated a revision. The opportunity to undertake one came along in 1955, when the Boston Symphony Orchestra and the Koussevitzky Music Foundation offered a commission to honor the seventy-fifth anniversary of the orchestra's founding. Since Koussevitzky had always held the *Symphonic Ode* in high regard, it seemed appropriate to prepare a new version of the work he had introduced twenty-five years earlier. The overall shape and character remained unaltered, but, for practical reasons, the size of the orchestra was reduced and further notation changes were made of the difficult rhythms. (They are still not child's play. At a pre-eightieth birthday celebration in June 1980, when the New York Philharmonic invited me to conduct the *Ode*, some of the players behaved as though they were on vacation, and it came as a surprise to them that Copland's old *Ode* still made them sit up and work!) Changes in the revision were as follows: certain pages that seemed excessively bony were filled out with fuller textures; the opening and closing sections originally written quite high for brass and strings were lowered; completely new measures were substituted only at the start of the 7/4 section leading to the ending; three pages that had been cut from the end of the slow section at the time of the premiere were restored. The revised *Symphonic Ode* is dedicated to the memory of Serge and Natalie Koussevitzky. It was first performed under the baton of Charles Munch in Boston, 3 February 1956. I cannot say that the revised version led to many more performances than the original, and it was not until 1973 that a recording was made by the London Symphony Orchestra, which I conducted.

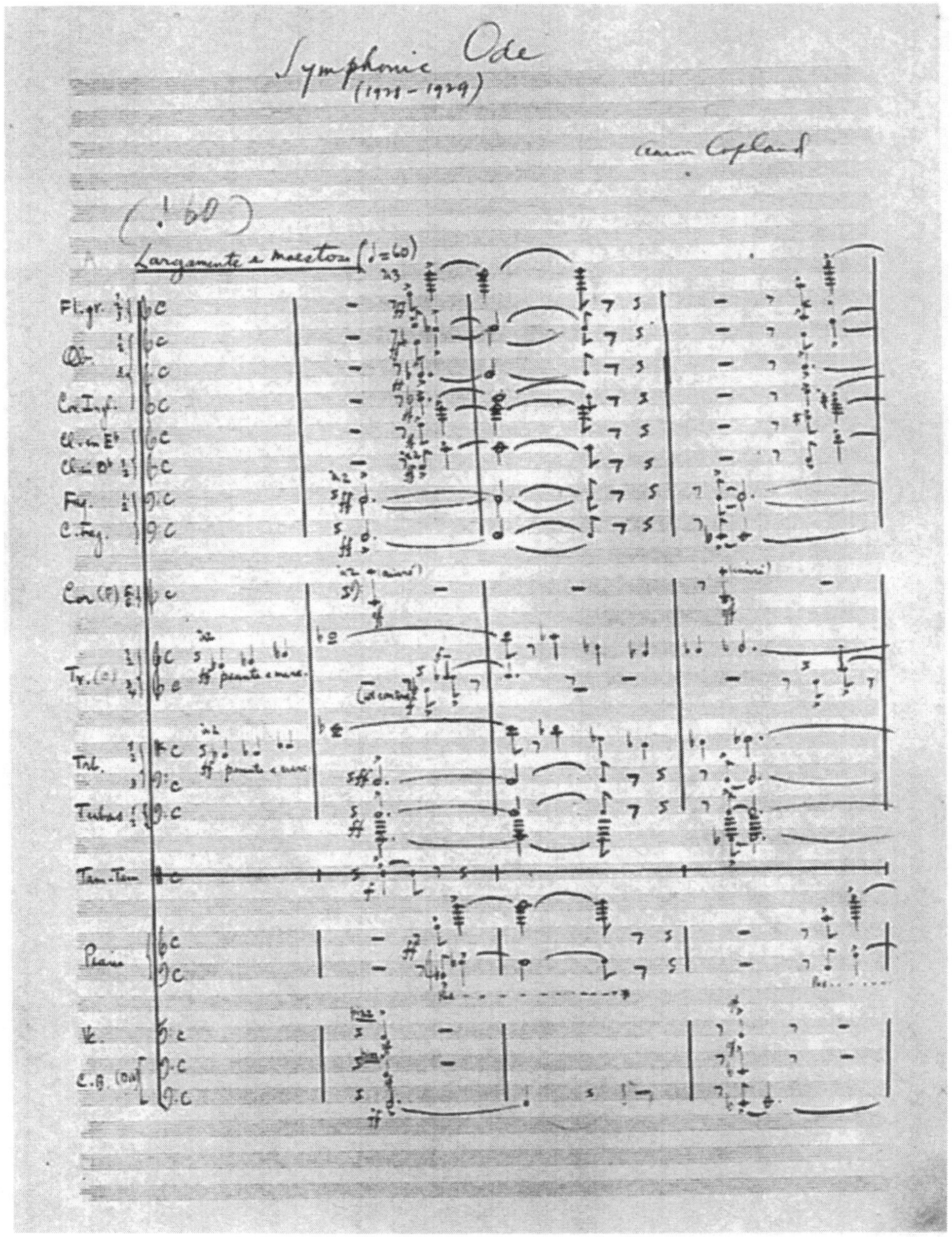

Symphonic Ode

[18] The unpublished manuscript is in John Kirkpatrick's collection, Yale Music Library.

[19] Kirkpatrick interview.

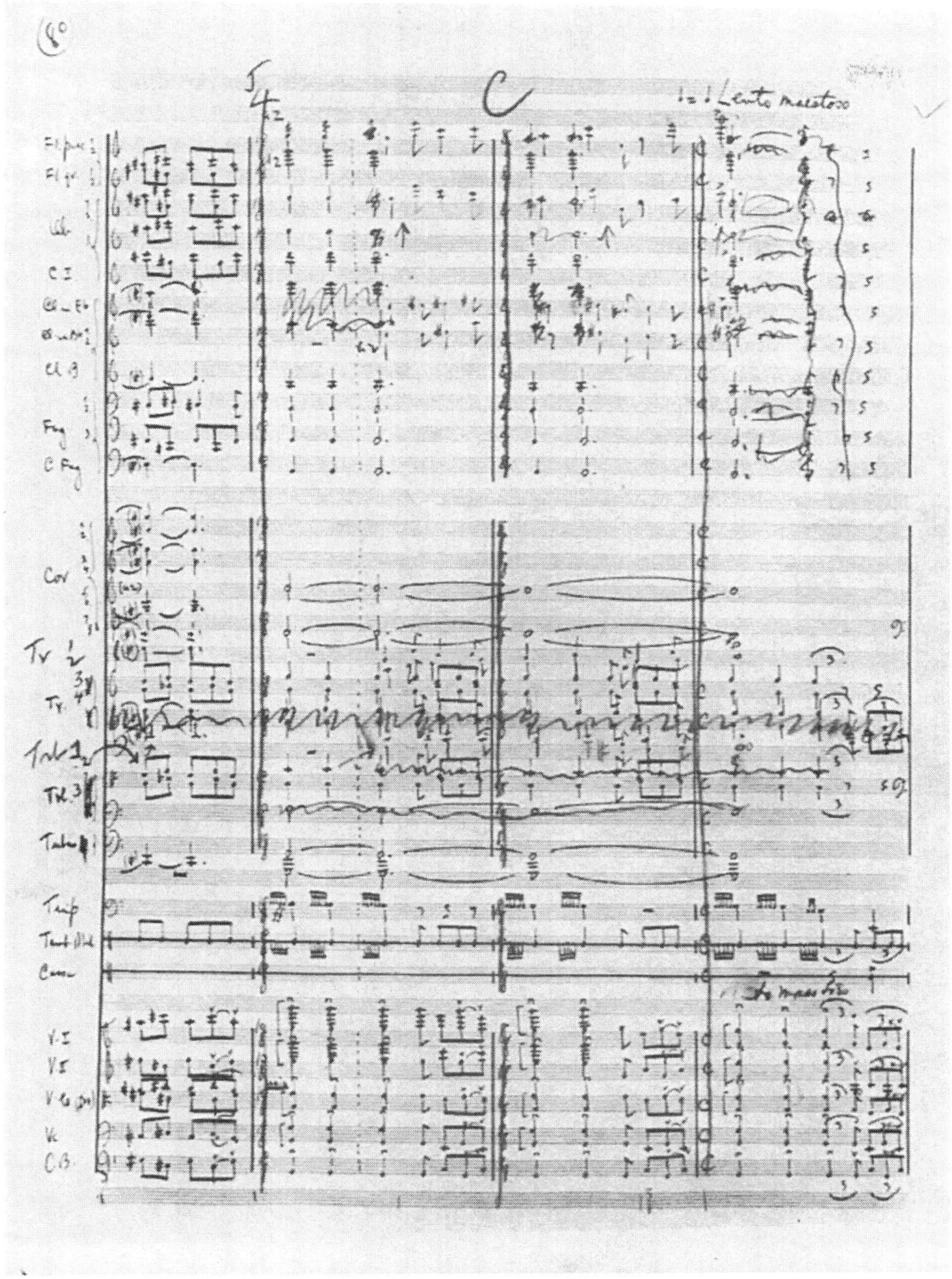

Manuscript page from the revised *Symphonic Ode*

At the end of the summer of 1929, when I was leaving France, one opinion was most important to me. I arrived at my stateroom on the Aquitania and found a letter from Nadia:

> How happy I would be if I could express what your Ode brought me as feeling of greatness, of power, of deepness—but you know my struggles with words &—I am quite miserable! This time more than ever, I have understood who you are, what you come to say, & how you are ready to give it a definite form. The clarity is still more astonishing when one thinks how complex is the language & the work is in my head as if I had heard it many times & carefully studied it. I am so happy. You know what admiration I always have had for you—what confidence—But such a work is however a surprise—& such a moving one. Shall never forget the progression leading to the end, so magnificent—& so many details which now sing in my memory forever I suppose. Why would you ever speak to people—if they love your music, how well they know and love you— Will not try to explain—you know better than myself what I mean—(could you not when orchestrated, send the sketch—I should like so much to speak of the work).

Although it was the height of the Depression when I returned to New York from France that fall, the recent economic disaster did not have an immediate effect on my own situation. I was accustomed to living on very little and owned nothing of value except my piano and scores. Not wanting to pay rent on an apartment while away from the city, I had put my belongings in storage and given up my apartment. My Uris cousins owned real estate, and since there were many apartments empty in New York during the Depression, they offered me one in the Montclair Hotel on Lexington Avenue at 49th Street. Once settled, I resumed my lectures at the New School. Roger wrote from Italy with recommendations and scores for inclusion in the third season of our Copland-Sessions Concerts, scheduled for February, March, and April 1930. Roger's determination to take more responsibility for programming stimulated him to search for new talent among young Europeans and the Americans living in Europe. The Copland-Sessions Concerts are often, and correctly, described as an early attempt to support American composers; however, as I review the programs for the third season, I am struck by the wide range of nationalities represented.

The first concert, on 9 February 1930 at Steinway Concert Hall, featured songs by an eighteen-year-old Italian, Nino Rota, then studying at the Curtis Institute. (Roger was responsible for sending these, which he found "fresh, genuine and musical.") Also included were the young Englishman Jeffrey Mark, Robert Russell Bennett, Vladimir Dukelsky, Robert Delaney, and Henry Brant. Brant was only seventeen years old, recently arrived from Canada, highly recommended by Henry Cowell, and introduced to me by my former piano teacher, Clarence Adler. The second concert, on 16 March, featured "older" composers: Theodore Chanler (*Sonata for Violin and Piano*), Charles Griffes (*Piano Sonata*, played by Jesus Maria Sanromá), Leo Ornstein (*Three Moods, Six Poems, Two Dances,* performed by Ornstein), Chávez (*Sonata* played by Sanromá), and my *Vitebsk* (Clarence Adler as pianist). Roger wrote (11 April): ". . . I am delighted that the concerts are going so well, and am sure the last one will be excellent with Fitelberg & Israel & Roy, it ought to—I don't know Roy's *Quartet,* but I hear excellent things about it . . . & wish I could hear it . . . I am delighted that Bedford is proving itself good for you. . . ." Roger had been responsible for finding

Jerzy Fitelberg's *Second Piano Sonata* and songs by Jean Binet, which were sung by Ethel Codd Luening. Kodaly's Hungarian pupils Pál Kadosa and Istvan Szelanyi gave additional international flavor, as did a work by the Hungarian Imre Weisshaus. The critics praised Roy's *String Quartet,* but in general, the press gave little attention to the series. However, we we had good audiences and a faithful list of subscribers who paid a dollar at each concert for any seat in the house.

The "Bedford" referred to by Roger was the village of Bedford in New York, where I had rented a small house on Hook Road. I left New York City on 1 January 1930 with my lectures finished and the *Ode* orchestration complete. I was most anxious to work on a piano piece that had been in my mind for some time. Gerald Sykes was writing a book and was also in need of a quiet place, so he came to Bedford with me. Only the Copland–Sessions Concerts and the most necessary trips took us from Bedford Village that winter and spring. The Depression was beginning to limit out-of-town lecture recitals. The only one that season was at the Arts Club of Chicago (6 April) on "The Younger Generation of American Composers"—Sessions, Harris, Antheil, Weiss, Thomson, and Copland. That winter in Bedford I became closer to Gerald. I was always close to Clurman, but he was having a love affair during this time and developing a whole new set of friends who believed in him fervently. I wrote to Israel (29 May 1930): "Harold's on his way to being one of the really important critics in America," and continued, "I am totally absorbed with the new piano piece and pleased with my progress. . . . For the moment it is called 'theme and variations.' It's a new form for me and lends itself beautifully to my particular kind of development from a single germ. But it needs time to fully flower and won't be done probably until the end of the summer. . ."

Gerald Sykes[20]

Aaron was driving the first time we went to Bedford. There was a terrible snowstorm, and we came face to face with the Kensico Dam—a very disturbing experience! But we were put straight and went on to Bedford Village. Aaron has often said that he does not like to compose with anyone around, but perhaps this was different because I am a writer, not a musician. I worked upstairs in the house that we rented together, and I knew from past experience in his loft that listening to him compose did not upset me. Aaron was terribly systematic in his preparation for this piano piece. He brought "tons" of music with him and began by playing works from as far back as the fifteenth century, then on to piano pieces by Mozart, Haydn, and others. As time went on, Aaron moved into piano works by Brahms and Schumann. He developed an affection for Liszt, and I recall his admiration for Liszt's enormous technical skill. Meanwhile, he was making notes while familiarizing himself very systematically with a great deal of piano literature. It was an education for me! We discussed the Variations *almost note by note—I think that was the main reason Aaron dedicated it to me. And maybe he also wanted to thank me for my patience. But it wasn't patience at all. Something special was happening. I was seeing Aaron in an inspired moment, and yet he was tranquil and even-tempered, even though he was pressured by time and responsibilities. I lived with the* Piano Variations *for months. It was a wonderful experience—Aaron at his best.*

From the start, my first major piano piece, the *Piano Variations*, had a "rightness." The piece flowed naturally and never seemed to get "stuck" as the *Ode* had, although I worked on it for about two years, off and on. After a concentrated period of composing, I would often find it beneficial to put a piece aside for a while. My critical faculty flowed stronger when I was composing than at other times, and such breaks served to refresh me and to renew my sense of objectivity. Composers vary on this—some like to work all in one fell swoop. My method is slower and perhaps safer, since it leaves less chance of falling too much in love with what one is doing. If a composer's critical instincts are in good shape, the slower approach seems to have more possibility for lasting results.

The *Piano Variations*, eleven minutes in length, consists of twenty variations and a coda. It was not composed in the consecutive order of its finished state. I am told that this is at odds with what I have written about the piece—that each variation is meant to develop organically from the previous one and all contribute to a carefully constructed whole. While this is so, it is also true that I worked on the variations individually, not knowing exactly where or how they would eventually fit together. I cannot explain this contradiction. One fine day when the time was right, the order of the variations fell into place. That time wasnot to come until after we left Bedford Village for Yaddo, the beautiful estate in Saratoga Springs, New York, that had been endowed as an artists' colony, where Gerald, Clurman, and I had been invited to spend the summer of 1930. It was there I derived, from the sixty-two pages of sketches I had carried with me to Yaddo, the seventeen-page score of the *Piano Variations.*

YADDO AND MEXICO
1930 - 1932

Yaddo[1] became so much a part of my life that I often tend to forget how strange the name sounds to those not familiar with it. In fact, the story behind Yaddo is a tragic tale resembling an opera in which all the main characters mysteriously expire before the final curtain. In 1881 a wealthy and handsome young couple, Katrina and Spencer Trask, purchased a five-hundred-acre property for a summer home in Saratoga Springs, a town with a reputation as a very elegant resort. The Trasks restored the original house and grounds. This couple—so idealistic, liberal, and generous in their dedication to the arts—was stalked by tragedy. Their first son died in infancy, and the house at Yaddo burned to the ground. Soon afterward a young daughter, overhearing her parents describe their lives as "shadowed," which she could not pronounce, called the place "Yaddo," and the name stuck. The Trasks built a Gothic-style mansion on the site of the old house and several smaller buildings and beautiful gardens. But tragedy struck again when the daughter and a younger son died. The parents never recovered from this terrible blow: Katrina Trask fell ill and spent the rest of her life as an invalid; Spencer Trask suffered financial reverses in 1909 and was the only person killed in a freak train accident. About ten years before his death, Spencer and Katrina Trask had made plans to endow Yaddo as a retreat for creative artists. Its doors were opened to guests in 1926.

When Clurman met me at the Saratoga railroad station in July 1930, he looked very inhibited, having already received a note from Elizabeth Ames, executive director of Yaddo, requesting that he not monopolize my time! Actually, few rules were imposed on anyone, and we had the privacy necessary for ideal working conditions. When Mrs. Ames had a suggestion or criticism, her custom was to leave a blue note in the appropriate mailbox. Those of us who were at Yaddo during the early years quoted a South American composer who visited Yaddo: "Watch out, or you get blue in the box!" I described my turret studio to Israel: "It is the perfect setting for an outdoor performance of the Tower Scene in *Pelléas*.' I am working extraordinarily well because of it. For the rest, one lives like a wifeless bourgeois—eats well, sleeps in a soft bed, and relaxes in cushioned chairs."

[1]See Rudy Shackelford, "The Yaddo Festivals of American Music, 1932-1952," *Perspectives of New Music, XVII:i* (Fall–Winter 1978), 92-125; and Marjorie Peabody Waite, *Yaddo Yesterday and Today* (Saratoga Springs, New York: The Argus Press, 1933).

Teddy Chanler arrived and I played parts of the *Ode* for him, but I was still keeping the *Variations* to myself. When I wrote to John Kirkpatrick about the piece, calling it "Thematic Variations," he responded, advising me to find a better title. I wrote back, "I should like to call them like Bach did the 'Goldberg Variations'—but thus far haven't been able to think up a good one." Jottings on pencil sketches indicate that I was considering several titles: "Melodic Variations, Twenty Melodic Variations, Thematic Variations, Fantasie on an Original Theme, Variations for Piano, Variations on a Theme, Chaconne, Declamations on a Serious Theme, Theme and Variations." I worked steadily on the piece with only one trip away on 9 August to perform my *Piano Concerto* at Lewisohn Stadium in New York, Albert Coates conducting. (Israel Citkowitz had returned from France, and he met me for a reunion and to attend the concert.) Returning to Yaddo, I roamed the magnificent grounds and began to dream of a festival that might be established there. What had started with the Copland-Sessions Concerts as an attempt to promote the younger generation of composers, I hoped might continue at Yaddo. I always thought of myself as part of a group effort; now it seemed I was to be the ringleader. When I approached Mrs. Ames with the idea for a festival of contemporary American music, she was not unenthusiastic and promised to bring the matter to Yaddo's board of directors.

I did not return to New York until the beginning of November 1930, just in time to begin my lectures. Roger had been visiting his family in Massachusetts all summer and was anxious to discuss our programs for the next Copland-Sessions Concerts. After we met, he sent a letter from shipboard as he left for Europe (29 November 1930): "Our visit was quite perfect in every respect. Among the most important things for me was that I felt that the Copland-Sessions friendship prospered—I am especially happy about that. . ." Two hundred people had enrolled for my New School lectures, and I was teaching Herman Chaloff privately. Figuring my basic expenses at $35 a week, I spent $12 for a room (this fall at the Hotel Lafayette); $15 for food; and $8 for secretarial work—I had to take an extra job that paid $5 for three hours of judging music applicants for the New School. I was also practicing the *Piano Variations* for its premiere on a League of Composers program scheduled for 4 January 1931. The only concert pianist I felt could play the *Variations* at that time was Walter Gieseking, who had participated in the premiere of *Vitebsk*. But he was "not available;" I thought perhaps he had had enough of my modern music. Later, Gieseking wrote from Berlin (22 June 1931):

> During the last week I found time to try out your Variations. This composition is very interesting and most original, but I do not know an audience which would accept such crude dissonances without protesting, except perhaps the League of Composers people in N.Y. and some of the group of the ISCM. I am sorry that I must say that I do not see any possibility of playing your Variations. . . I am sure you will understand that a work of such severity of style is not possible among the normal type of concert-goers.

But I was pleased to be playing the piece myself. The *Variations* filled a special niche as the first of my works where I felt very sure of myself; I knew that if someone else had written a piece using the same materials, it would have evolved quite differently. Moreover, I knew how difficult it would be to explain my intentions to another pianist. On the other hand I was aware that my piano playing did not measure up to concert artist quality. When Virgil Thomson criticized my "hardness of tone," he had justification—my natural attack tends to be hard without that roundness of tone that a concert pianist develops. No doubt I played the *Piano Variations* like the composer I am, although Arthur Berger, my composer-critic friend, admired my playing: "Copland got every ounce of sonority from each tone and it was a good thing too, because there weren't that many tones in the piece!"[2]

The New York premiere critics were negative, including *The Times* and the *Herald Tribune,* where Jerome D. Bohm wrote, "Mr. Copland, always a composer of radical tendencies, has in these variations sardonically thumbed his nose at all of those esthetic attributes which have hitherto been considered essential to the creation of music. . . ." It was not until I played the *Variations* at Yaddo in 1932 that the piece really made an impression. Paul Rosenfeld described the occasion: "No previous performance had revealed its greatness as fully as this at Yaddo, and the power of its contracted, slowly progressive volumes with their flinty, metallic sonorities. . . . One felt its author the composer of the coming decades. . . ."[3] The *Variations* drew a lot of attention because it was new and strange. Arthur Berger wrote: "The *Variations* made an impression in the early thirties that was profound and exciting,"[4] and Marc Blitzstein described the piece as "Lithic."

Among the unusual aspects of the *Piano Variations* are irregular rhythmic patterns within the fundamentally straightforward 4/4 design. The work has been called dissonant, moody, nervous, bare, stark, lonely, concise, precise, and austere. But I was utterly convinced about it, and I was not going to be upset by early unfavorable reactions. In fact I assumed there would be temporary difficulty in having this composition accepted. My family naturally thought it was impractical to write works not easily grasped by an audience. Obviously, it does cut down on the number of potential listeners and even potential performers. But you don't write music thinking, "Is this practical?" If you write something for instruments not readily available, or that is so long people will not want to spend that much time on any one piece—those are practical considerations that might justifiably cross your mind. But I don't think one composes to be practical. That's too sensible. You have to he more adventuresome than that. But you do have to be truly convinced about the value of what you are doing, otherwise there are many reasons for not doing it—minimal financial gain, no favorable criticism in the papers the next morning. You really must be brave, but the bravery is derived from inner conviction. I was absolutely sure that I had put down what I wanted to put down and that it was meaningful to me. It was wise to assume that it was going to take some time before other people would come around to understanding and appreciating it. That has, after all, been the history of much new effort in music.

What kind of music is the *Piano Variations*? It has been said more than once that "Copland doesn't like to talk about his music." I suppose this is as good a time as any to respond to that charge. I admit that I am uneasy with strict technical analysis, just as I have always been disinclined toward rigid methods of composition. I prefer to leave theoretical analysis to those who are experts in theory and analysis. Even then, I feel uncomfortable with strict analysis when it takes the place of discussing relevant matters such as the harmonic structure, rhythmic life, and dynamics of the music. I have occasionally had the experience of not immediately recognizing my own work when it is dissected in this manner! In addition, analysis may be misleading about a composer's intentions, for it can lead to the division of a lifetime of composing into arbitrary style periods. Furthermore, and in a more general sense, my reluctance to discuss musical works stems in part from the realization that our language is woefully inadequate to the task of describing musical experiences.

Having said all this, I will nevertheless take up the challenge and attempt some comments of a musical nature about the *Piano Variations*, one of the few pieces in which I did make use to some extent, but in my own way, of the method invented by Arnold Schoenberg that came to be known as "twelve tone" and from which "serialism" developed. The *Variations* incorporates a four-note motive on which the entire piece is based. Almost every note and chord in the piece relates back to these four notes. The *Variations* cannot be said to have been written according to all the rules of Schoenberg's method—for example, I repeat tones in their original form—but I have no doubt that the construction of the piece shows his influence. At that time we were all influenced by both Stravinsky and Schoenberg to some degree. I never rejected Schoenberg's ideas, even though I was closer to the French way of doing things. I believe that any method which proves itself so forceful an influence on the music of our times must be of considerable interest. In fact, I lectured about serialism at the New School as early as 1928. For me as a composer, the twelve-tone method was a way of thinking about music from a different perspective, somewhat like looking at a picture from a different angle so that you see things you might not have noticed otherwise. It was an aid in freshening the way I wrote at a time when I felt the need of change, and so I view it as an enrichment. It forced me into a different, more fragmented kind of melodic writing that in turn resulted in chords I had rarely used before. Thus my harmonic writing was affected in the *Piano Variations*, and in the works that followed: the *Short Symphony* and *Statements for Orchestra.* These pieces are more dissonant than my earlier works, yet I did not

[2]Interview, Arthur Berger with Perlis, 13 November 1981, Cambridge, Massachusetts.

[3]Paul Rosenfeld, *Discoveries of a Music Critic* (New York: Harcourt, Brace, 1936), 358.

[4]Arthur Berger, *Aaron Copland* (New York: Oxford University Press, 1953. Repr. Westport, Connecticut: Greenwood Press, 1971), 43.

Manuscript page from the *Piano Variations* 1930

give up tonality. If a composer is secure in his judgment, his sense of what is musically valid does not change when he adopts a "new" method. The same judgment is applied to whatever the musical action, no matter what the method may be. Otherwise, one runs a strong risk of merely playing games. As for the traditional theme and variations form, this also I adapted to my own use. The twenty brief variations divide into two sections of ten without episodes or breaks between them, resulting in a sound that flows freely without discernible divisions.

The *Piano Variations* is more serious in intent and feeling than my earlier playful jazz pieces, and it is sharper, more orderly and logical than the declamatory and epic proportions of the *Ode*. Not only was the public perplexed at the direction I took with the *Variations*; some of my friends and colleagues were puzzled, too, and they questioned me about it. To one friend, the poet Lola Ridge, who greatly admired the *Ode*, I wrote (21 April 1931):

> Let me see if I can make more clear what I mean in relation to the Ode and the Variations. To affirm the world is meaningless, unless one also affirms the tragic reality which is at the core of existence. To live on—to develop means, as I see it, to enter always more and more deeply into the very essence of tragic reality. The Ode is an affirmation, of course, with tragic implications. The Variations also affirm, but the reality they affirm is more particularized, it is the reality of our own age and time, while the reality of the Ode is more usual and understandable because it leans more on older and related affirmations with which we are to a degree, already familiar. I don't wish to underestimate the Ode in favor of the Variations but I feel sure that there is a certain essence of contemporary reality which is expressed in the Variations which I was too young to grasp at the writing of the Ode. You will find a certain relation between the Ode and an occasional movement in the grandiose style by Gustav Mahler but it would be much more difficult to relate the Variations to any of the older composers. . . .

Schoenberg was not the sole influence on my work at this time. Frugality and economy were the order of the day; social and economic conditions could not help but affect the music world. Considering these factors, I was fortunate to have the *Variations* published by Cos Cob in 1932.[5] When Martha Graham asked for permission to choreograph the work, I was utterly astonished that anyone would consider this kind of music suitable for dance. The result was *Dithyrambic*. It was my introduction to Martha's unusual and innovative ideas. Her appearances in *Dithyrambic* that season were much talked about and praised, although her choreography was considered as complex and abstruse as my music. If it took some time for audiences and critics to appreciate the *Piano Variations,* concert artists seemed to recognize its worth. As early as 1933, Victor Babin performed the *Variations* at the Eleventh ISCM Festival, and John Kirkpatrick included it in an all-American program at Town Hall in 1936. Through the years, I have had the satisfaction of many performances by wonderful pianists, among them Leonard Bernstein, John Browning, Paul Jacobs, Grant Johannesen,

[5]After publication, John Kirkpatrick wrote to Copland with mostly favorable reactions and Copland responded from Mexico (7 October 1932): ". . . Your remarks about the published *Variations* amused me. You *did* find one mistake—the ties that are missing after Var. 20. But I can't agree about your strictures about the new A flat in meas. 1 of Var. 19 or the E flat in m. 19 of V. 20. That latter E flat is necessary because there has been too much A flat. It comes as a surprise and therefore needs a reiteration in order to really establish it. Therefore to have it twice doesn't in this case, 'spoil the effect.' . . ."

William Kapell, Noel Lee, William Masselos, Robert Miller, Ursula Oppens, Leo Smit, Hilde Somer, and Beveridge Webster.

The idea of transcribing the *Piano Variations* for orchestra was a recurrent one in my mind for some time. A commission from the Louisville Symphony Orchestra gave the incentive to carry out the project. The work was completed on 31 December 1957, and the *Orchestral Variations* was premiered by the Louisville Orchestra with Robert Whitney conducting on 5 March 1958. I wrote the program notes, as I preferred to do when invited. The following is derived from my notes of 1958.

My purpose was not to recreate orchestral sounds reminiscent of the quality of the piano, but rather to re-think the sonorous possibilities of the composition itself in terms of orchestral color. I could not have done this when the *Variations* was new, but with the perspective of twenty-seven years, it was not difficult to orchestrate the piece using the original as a piano sketch with orchestral possibilities. The overall plan remains the same, but the bar lines have been shifted in some instances to facilitate orchestral performance.

The brass, in subdued tones, open the work and the theme is presented in a restrained vein. The quiet feeling persists until Variation VII when the mood becomes bolder. In Variation VIII and IX, singing string tones predominate, and in XI, the oboe is heard in duet with a solo flute. From Variation XII on, the climax builds steadily with an increasing use of brass. Variation XVIII is a Scherzo, with flute and clarinet taking the lead. A section for drums closes the last Variation and leads to a brilliant-sounding Coda.

The *Louisville Courier Journal* carried a review of the *Orchestral Variations* the next day entitled: "New-Old Copland Work Cheered, Also Jeered." Critic William Mootz assessed the audience's reaction as "mostly bewildered." By year's end, Bernstein was conducting the work with the New York Philharmonic at Carnegie Hall. After the performance of 5 December 1958 Howard Taubman of *The New York Times* wrote: "The music has not changed; our capacity to respond has." Taubman admired the *Orchestral Variations*; personally, I am fond of both versions, although neither are performed enough to suit me. Occasionally I hit the jackpot—and the *Piano Variations* and *Orchestral Variations* are included on the same program.

The Depression was affecting the general quality of life in New York. From the carefree twenties, we had plunged into a grim and difficult period. The artist is always the first to suffer, particularly in America, where he does not have the respect enjoyed by creative artists abroad. In the early spring of 1931, I wrote music for a Theatre Guild production, *Miracle at Verdun*, by Hans Chlumberg. Sensing hard times ahead, I planned a long trip to Europe to begin after the final New York Copland–Sessions series. Roger and I had agreed that the time had come to present something unusual. We decided on a film program with music to be played by thirty members of the New York Philharmonic–Symphony Orchestra conducted by Hugh Ross. It took place 15 March 1931 at the Broadhurst Theatre and was considered "arty" and very daring. Included were three films by the young avant-garde photographer Ralph Steiner, one with music by Blitzstein and two with scores by McPhee; films by Cavalcanti and news clips with scores by Milhaud; my *Music for the Theatre*; and

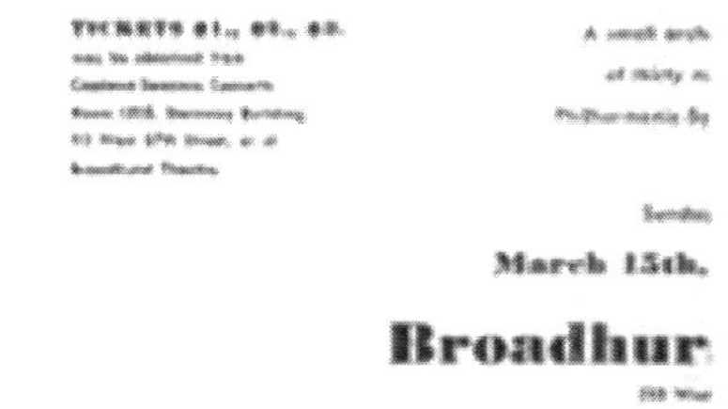

Above: "Music and Films," the program for the Fourth Season of the Copland-Sessions concerts,15 March 1932
Right: Photographer Ralph Steiner with Copland, 1932

Sessions' *Black Maskers*. Roger had sent his music suggesting to me that we use parts of the score: "parts I, V and VIII are best for this performance. . . . I give you carte blanche." A funny thing happened during Steiner's film, *Mechanical Principles*. The film broke, and we had to switch the order of the program on the spot. It must have been handled smoothly, because the papers the following day assumed that *Mechanical Principles* was meant to be given in two parts with the Copland and the Sessions music sandwiched between.

Leopold Stokowski had been promising to schedule the premiere of my *Dance Symphony* since 1930, and he finally did so on 15 April 1931, with the Philadelphia Orchestra at the Academy of Music. It was interesting to hear a work I had composed so long ago—the *Dance Symphony*, derived from my early ballet *Grohg*—given the famous "Stokie" treatment and programmed between his flamboyant orchestral arrangements of Bach and Wagner. The title of the concert reflected the hard times affecting musicians—"Emergency Concert

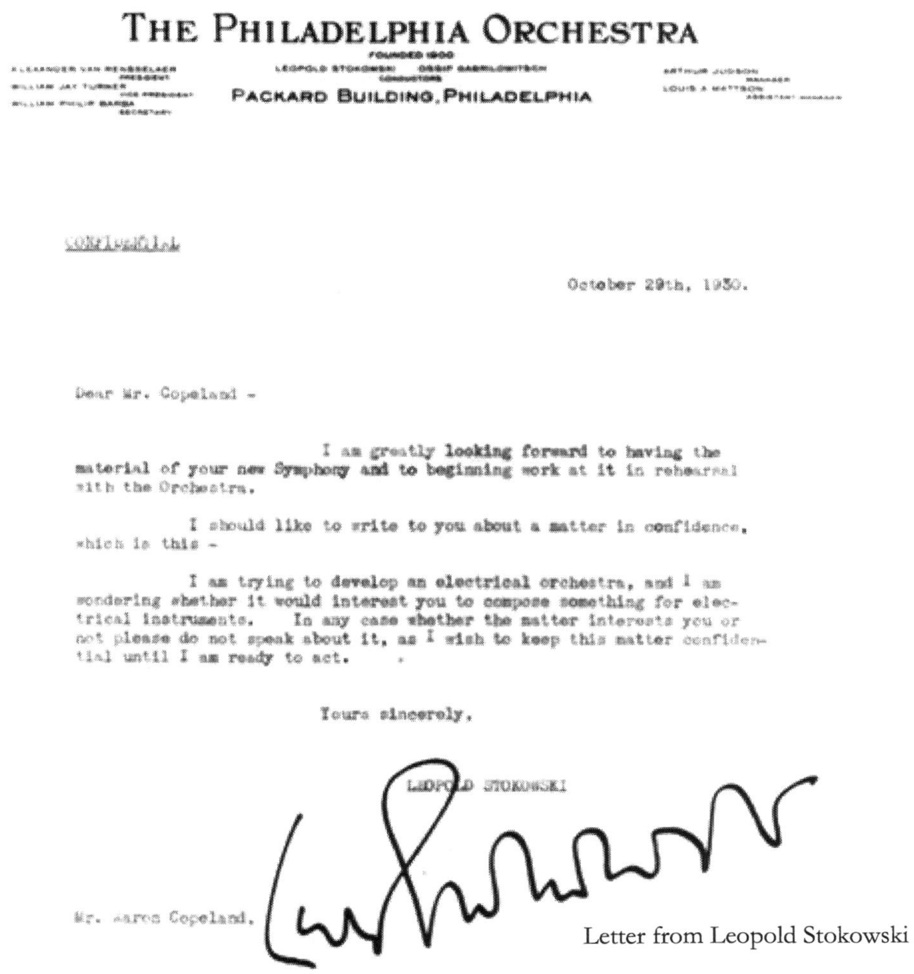

THE PHILADELPHIA ORCHESTRA

PACKARD BUILDING, PHILADELPHIA

CONFIDENTIAL

October 29th, 1930.

Dear Mr. Copeland -

I am greatly looking forward to having the material of your new Symphony and to beginning work at it in rehearsal with the Orchestra.

I should like to write to you about a matter in confidence, which is this -

I am trying to develop an electrical orchestra, and I am wondering whether it would interest you to compose something for electrical instruments. In any case whether the matter interests you or not please do not speak about it, as I wish to keep this matter confidential until I am ready to act.

Yours sincerely,

LEOPOLD STOKOWSKI

Mr. Aaron Copeland.

Letter from Leopold Stokowski

for the Benefit of the Unemployed Musicians of Philadelphia by the Philadelphia Orchestra." From the Benjamin Franklin Hotel after the concert, I expressed critical views of Stokowski's conducting in a lengthy letter to Koussevitzky:

> At any moment you are liable to be shocked by his superficiality of feeling or some detail which is completely out of style with the rest. . . . (the public of course doesn't understand this because everything he does sounds so effective. . . .) He [Stokowski] seems well pleased with the *Dance Symphony* and says he will repeat it at his regular concerts next season. . . . I liked it very much in parts but not as a whole.[6]

Soon after the Philadelphia premiere, I left for Europe, taking with me some sketches for my *Short Symphony*. In Paris I joined up with a new young friend, Paul Frederick Bowles, gifted in both music and literature, who had been studying composition with me. One of his admirers was Gertrude Stein, who called him "Freddy." We planned to visit her before going on to Berlin for May and June. It was because of Paul that I got to spend a weekend visiting Miss Stein and Miss Toklas in their country home near Grenoble. This visit was described in *The Autobiography of Alice B. Toklas*:

> A young man who first made Gertrude Stein's acquaintance by writing engaging letters from America is Paul Frederick Bowles. Gertrude Stein says of him that he is delightful and sensible in summer but neither delightful nor sensible in winter. Aaron Copeland [sic] came to see us with Bowles in the summer and Gertrude Stein liked him immensely. Bowles told Gertrude Stein and it pleased her that Copeland said threateningly to him when as usual in the winter he was neither delightful nor sensible, if you do not work now when you are twenty when you are thirty, nobody will love you.[7]

On Saturday Miss Stein (I have *always* called her *Miss* Stein) gave us a tour of the countryside. When we casually mentioned that we planned to go to the Riviera for the summer or perhaps Tangier, she said, "Ohhh, of course go to Tangier. It is a marvelous place. You must forget the Riviera in summer. That's so awful, so full of Americans." She quite literally talked us into changing our plans, and instead of the Riviera, we headed for Tangier. Tangier was the most exotic place I had ever visited. From there, I wrote to Miss Stein (25 August 1931):

> Tangier is responsible for my not writing sooner. It wasn't easy getting settled. It took a week to find a house and furnish it. We have an African piano which looks like a piano but which sounds like hell! It would sound all right if we could only get a piano tuner who can tune. But they tell me he's not easily found in Morocco. We tried one man who put it more out of tune than it was before he touched it. These are problems you are happily free of, but they make my stay somewhat precarious. Still, if I should have to leave tomorrow, I'd be glad you sent us, because it is lovely to see, and so I have to thank you on that score too. . . .

I had brought only one volume of music to Tangier with me—Mozart's *Quartets and Quintets*—and some music writing paper. But I found the atmosphere not conducive to composing, although I tried to work a little every day. In the evening Paul and I would sit outside a café to watch the local scene. One day, we were invited to lunch at the home of an

[6] For correspondence from Copland to Koussevitzky, see Koussevitzky Collection, the Library of Congress.
[7] Gertrude Stein, *The Autobiography of Alice B. Toklas* (New York: Harcourt, Brace, 1933), 309.

Arab family. I recall that the women disappeared at the sound of a stranger approaching. Only the male members of the family were allowed to be present and we all ate with our hands out of a common bowl. Paul stayed behind in Tangier when I left.

Paul Bowles[8]

In the winter of 1929-30 Henry Cowell gave me a letter of introduction to Aaron, who was living at the Hotel Lexington on the corner of 49th Street. I showed him my music and he agreed to teach me harmony. For counterpoint he thought I should try to go to Paris and study with Boulanger. I was obliged, however, to return to the University of Virginia at the beginning of February. At Easter time Aaron came to Charlottesville, where I proudly introduced him to members of the faculty. In August of that year, thanks to Aaron's intercession, I was invited to Yaddo, where he had a studio in the woods (he was working on the Variations*). During that autumn and winter in New York I had a harmony lesson with him nearly every day. He was due to go to Berlin in the spring, and it was decided that I would accompany him. In March I sailed for Paris. About a fortnight later Aaron arrived. I took him to Gertrude Stein's and she invited him to visit Bilignin later in the year. We stayed only a short time in Paris, being eager to get to Berlin and settle down. Aaron already knew where he was going to live. . . . Edouard Roditi had given me letters for Stephen Spender and Christopher Isherwood, among others. Aaron was less interested than I in exploring the town and leading a social life, but he did consent to having lunch each day with Isherwood, Jean Ross, and Spender at the Cafe des Westens. We saw* Fidelio *at the Kroll-Opera and* Das Rheingold *at the Staats-Oper, and we went to a festival at Bad Pyrmont, where Bartók played. In the summer we returned to Paris, and Aaron went on to Oxford where the ISCM Festival was being held. We met again at Gertrude Stein's in Bilignin. It was Stein who suggested that we try Tangier instead of Villefranche, where friends of Aaron were summering. So, when we had finished our visit at Bilignin, we set out for Morocco. I don't think Aaron really enjoyed being there, but he made the best of it, and even went to Fez. He returned to Berlin about 1 October.*

I saw Aaron in the summer of 1932 when I arrived back in the States. He was engrossed in leading the Young Composers' Group. I remember an unpropitious first meeting with them, after which Aaron shook his head ruefully (grinning nevertheless) remarking on the reluctance of the other young composers to accept me. I returned to Morocco. The next time I was in New York was in the spring of 1935, and Aaron was living in the West Fifties. . . . It was that summer that Aaron, Virgil, George Antheil and I went up to Hartford as hired performers at a party given by the Austins (Chick Austin was the curator of the Wadsworth Atheneum there). The same group, with Marc Blitzstein replacing Antheil, performed at another party in New York, at the house of Mrs. Murray Crane. All this was Virgil's idea; he believed very strongly that music should be paid for. (We all believed it, but he did the campaigning.) In the years that followed, I would see Aaron at parties in Edwin Denby's loft, or at the house of Kirk and Constance Askew. We saw each other often until I came here to live permanently in Morocco.

It seemed that I produced concerts of modern American music wherever I found myself during those years. (It is surprising that I did not attempt one in Tangier!) During the late spring months in Berlin, I stayed in the apartment of a violinist, Max Strub. Within a short time I realized that German audiences knew nothing of American orchestral music beyond a few jazz-inspired pieces, so I arranged a concert of four orchestral works by Americans for the following 9 December, to be sponsored by the ISCM and conducted by Ernest Ansermet. Only one piece was a jazz-inspired work—Louis Gruenberg's *Jazz Suite*. The others were Carl Ruggles' *Portals*, Sessions' *First Symphony*, and my *First Symphony*, which would be the premiere of the new version without organ. Ruggles, a generation older than the rest of us, had worked out an original system of composition. I admired *Portals* and later, in 1965, when I had begun to conduct frequently, I programmed it again in London. I had met Ruggles in New York in the late twenties at the Stieglitz gallery, and when I wrote to ask permission to include *Portals* in the Berlin program, Ruggles responded (9 September 1931): "If you are at the rehearsals, everything will be fine I'm sure. . . ."

Copland with Paul Bowles, 1932

Also in December, the final Copland–Sessions concert took place at the Aeolian Hall in London. It featured American chamber music. It is difficult enough to arrange concerts of contemporary American music under the best of conditions, but when the principal participants are scattered around the globe such an undertaking borders on the impossible. During the planning stages, Bowles was in Tangier and then Paris, Citkowitz in New York, Thomson in Paris, I in Berlin, and the concert in London! Various performers were in other locations. This was Paul Bowles' debut as composer, and he was understandably anxious:

> I didn't receive your letter until ten days or more after you had written it. . . I shall start making the parts, but God knows how right they will be. I wish there were some way of your seeing them before I send them to London. Oh dear, oh dear! I insist on getting them done in time for the rehearsals. In fact I should blow up and die immediately if it could not come off on account of lack of time. . . .

[8] From a memoir sent by Paul Bowles from Tangier, Morocco, 19 March 1979.

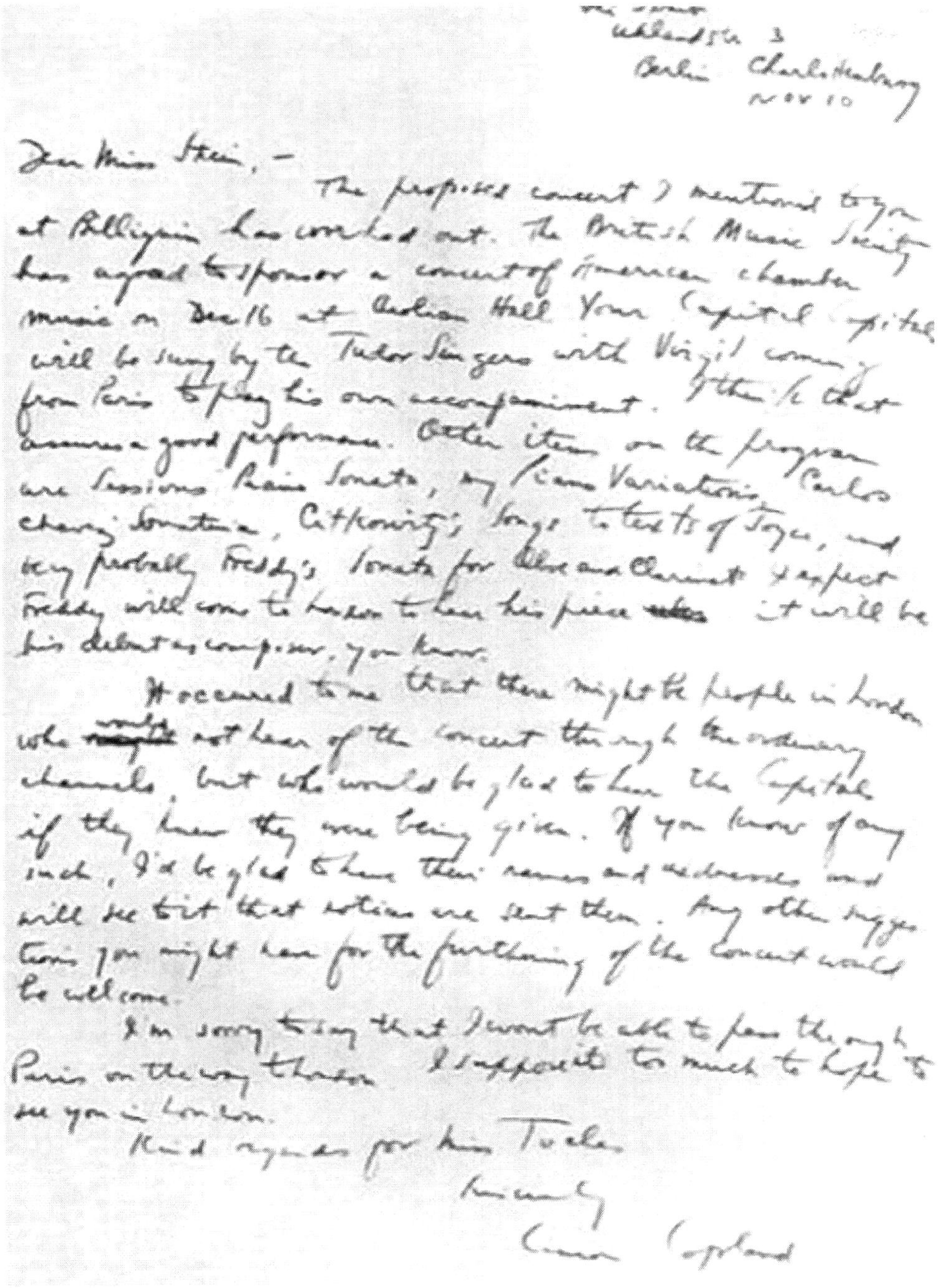
Uhlandstr. 3
Berlin Charlottenburg
Nov 10

Dear Miss Stein, —

The proposed concert I mentioned to you at Bilignin has worked out. The British Music Society has agreed to sponsor a concert of American chamber music on Dec 16 at Aeolian Hall. Your Capital Capitals will be sung by the Tudor Singers with Virgil coming from Paris to play his own accompaniment. I think that assures a good performance. Other items on the program are Sessions' Piano Sonata, my Piano Variations, Carlos Chavez' Sonatina, Citkowitz' Songs to texts of Joyce, and very probably Freddy's Sonata for Oboe and Clarinet. I expect Freddy will come to London to hear his piece — it will be his debut as composer, you know.

It occurred to me that there might be people in London who would not hear of the concert through the ordinary channels, but who would be glad to hear the Capitals if they knew they were being given. If you know of any such, I'd be glad to have their names and addresses and will see that notices are sent them. Any other suggestions you might have for the furthering of the concert would be welcome.

I'm sorry to say that I won't be able to pass through Paris on the way there. I suppose it's too much to hope to see you in London.

Kind regards for Miss Toklas.

Sincerely
Aaron Copland

Letter from Copland to Gertrude Stein, 1931

I answered Paul to bolster his courage, and then wrote to Israel, who had promised me new songs for the concert (18 July 1931):

> Your letter was not calculated to bring joy to the heart of an arranger of festivals! Your old songs would look like rank partisanship. . . I would even he willing to risk that, but I really think you owe it to your "public," to America, to Nadia, to Roger, to me to arrange your life in such a way that it all leads to the production of at least one new oeuvre a year. . . . And remember that all the ideals and ideas we have can best be advanced by tangible examples. There aren't so many of us that we can afford to have you loll by the wayside. . . .

But Israel did not complete his "Blake" songs and sent only one new work to be added to the four "Joyce" songs of the previous year. I wrote to Virgil about *Capital Capitals* (29 October 1931): "Will you come to London to coach the singers . . . and play the piano part at the concert? Say yes— or I'm lost. I'll be there myself and am to play the Chávez *Sonatina* and my *Piano Variations*. . . ." Virgil agreed, and I wrote to Gertrude Stein on 10 November hoping (in vain) that she might attend the concert.

Lest it appear that these concerts of modern music were all glowing successes, let me assure you that this one was not. I no longer recall the details of what went awry, but in a letter written to Virgil later (29 January 1932), I thanked him for being so nice "considering the concert was going about as bad as possible." By the turn of the new year I was in New York, staying in Harold and Stella's apartment at 52 West 58th Street while they were away. Edmund Wilson lived in the building. Clurman was deeply involved with the Group Theatre, which he had started in 1930, and the Stieglitz crowd was still going strong. Several of them lived in the neighborhood, so I saw them often, and by now, Paul Strand, Orson Welles, Mary and Ralph Steiner, William Lescaze, and Carl Van Vechten were also my friends. (After Mary and Ralph divorced in 1933, Mary married Lescaze.) Everyone greeted my arrival home as though I had been away for years, particularly the young composers in town. They often came to my studio in the evening, so when Elie Siegmeister asked if I would be the informal leader of a group of composers to meet every few weeks, it seemed a natural development. The only attempt at organization was to find a name—the Young Composers' Group.

The "regulars" were Arthur Berger, Henry Brant, Israel Citkowitz, Lehman Engel, Vivian Fine, Irwin Heilner, Bernard Herrmann, Jerome Moross, and Elie Siegmeister. They decided on an age limit of twenty-five (except for me, of course). Other than that, there were no rules. We met informally every few weeks during 1932. Visitors came, or were invited when they were in town—Bowles, Chávez, Blitzstein, Antheil, Kirkpatrick, and Thomson. Conversation was very lively, ranging through all aspects of modern music. When things got "hot," I would play the role of peacemaker. Once, I wrote on a postcard announcing the time and place of a meeting—"No polemics!" When Bowles and Virgil were visitors, the regulars were less than friendly toward the expatriates. The Young Composers were interested in the situation of the American composer. Vivian Fine recalls: "There was not a lot of brotherly and sisterly love. We played and severely criticized each other's music."[9] According to Lehman Engel, some of the criticism was unwarranted: "Benny

[9] Interview, Vivian Fine with Frances Harmeyer for Oral History of American Music, Yale, 28 June 1975, Bennington, Vermont.

[Herrmann] always said, 'It stinks!'—no matter what was played. Aaron was the watchdog and took a back seat. He never tried to steer things. I never saw him angry, although heaven knows everyone else was hot-headed at those meetings. We used to tease Aaron—not about his music, but about money. We were students, so naturally we had nothing, but in our eyes, Aaron was a success, yet he always looked for a place to live that was free."[10] Henry Brant wrote a piece called *5 and 10 Cent Store Music*, and the gang all agreed it was his best so far.

Henry Brant[11]

Of the composers at the Young Composers' Group meetings, the most voluble in expressing his views was Bernard Herrmann. The one who brought in the most new music and played it was myself. I had no rivals—I could write faster than anyone else. And Arthur Berger was the critic among us. On one occasion, he, or somebody else perhaps, brought in a clipping from the New York Sun *where the critic was W. J. Henderson. He wrote an article wondering if young people, when they met to talk about music these days, ever pronounced the word "beauty." We decided to satisfy Mr. Henderson and all pronounce "beauty"—and we did so, with expression! There was always a fair amount of excited talk. The entire group was present at the First Yaddo Festival. While there we had meetings in the evening something like the ones at Aaron's apartment. We improvised in the avant-garde styles of the time and did burlesques of some of the new pieces just played. Marc Blitzstein had written a quartet in three slow movements—we did a burlesque of that, four hands, conducted by Bernard Herrmann. From time to time someone would bring in a piece perhaps unknown to all of us—something by Eisler, Ives, or Webern that we'd never seen before. We'd say, "Vivian, play it!" (Vivian was the best sightreader in the group.) Then we would discuss what it was, when the composer wrote it, who else was doing something like it. We really wanted to collect information about new things in music. The idea of writing in the neoclassic Stravinskian manner was something that occurred only to me at that time. I was the first one in the group to do it. Some of the boys criticized it as a pointless conservatism. The views of the group were much more open than later was the case among young composers, and there was much greater curiosity to find out the range of what was going on. Aaron's attitude throughout was one of encouragement.*

I can recall one episode in which Bernard Herrmann, who had the worst handwriting of anyone there, brought in a new piece that was just a scrawl. But he explained it, not hesitating to point out its significant qualities. He spoke in a flippant way about spilling coffee on some of it and so forth, and Aaron said, "Now look, Benny, you've taken the trouble to do it. It's not right for you to be flippant about what you do, because it clearly means a lot to you to do it. And you musn't give others the impression that it shouldn't mean much to them." (These are not Aaron's exact words, but it's the sense of what he said, and in a very friendly way to which offense couldn't possibly be taken.) Aaron introduced music to us also. On one occasion it was Milhaud's The Misfortunes of Orpheus. *Vivian played it, we tried to sing the parts, and Aaron spoke about the harmony, which he said is Milhaud's only, because of its—he used the word—"drugged" quality, which no other composer quite has. Occasionally Aaron would bring in such a piece, usually something he himself happened to be studying. Even though we didn't continue the group for long, it was valued, because this was our only opportunity to get some sort of idea of what was happening.*

[10] Engel interview. See also Berger and Siegmeister interviews.

[11] Interview, Henry Brant with Vincent Plush for Oral History of American Music, Yale, 11 May 1983, Santa Barbara, California.

Brant wrote to me after Arthur Berger published an article about the Young Composers' Group in *Trend*,[12] a magazine that ran from 1932 to 1935 (18 July 1932): "You should get Berger to talk to you about 'vitality and sterility' which have very special implications for him. Moross and Vivian are vital, I am sterile. . ." The group was so often at odds with each other individually that I feared for its survival when I left for Mexico later in 1932. Brant wrote again (22 November 1932): "Let me give you inside and authoritative assurance that the group will hold together, if not because of common sympathies at least on account of common objects for ridicule." Siegmeister and Heilner organized a concert of music by members of the group, to which I was invited as honored guest. But I was in Mexico. Siegmeister wrote (22 December 1932):

> To break the suspense I might as well tell you that the date of our program is Jan. 15—so you'd better cut your Mexican stay short if you want to be in on the fun. The best thing about our bunch is nobody likes anybody else's music— wouldn't touch it with a ten foot pole. Exceptions are me and Irwin—I like both his and my stuff and he says he thinks we're both terrible. We've decided the best thing for the success of the concert is to have the group meet as rarely as possible. It always ends up in a fight or in somebody singing songs they heard in a Harlem speakeasy (not published by Schirmer, or Cos Cob). Two weeks ago the gang got together and Benny showed quite remarkable talents as a "diseuse"—giving Ruth Draper character sketches of the modern composers, from Sibelius through Roger Sessions down to Vivian Fine and Jerry Moross. Then we had a lot of fun going thru those songs in the Ives *114* which he marks, "Though there is no danger of it, I hope these songs will not be sung—at least not in public."

The concert was the climax of the Young Composers' Group. After my return from Mexico, we did not meet again.

Koussevitzky finally conducted the *Symphonic Ode* in the spring of 1932. I wrote to Virgil in Paris (14 March 1932): "I was hoping you could hear my *Ode* which Koussie is doing in New York next week. When he did it in Boston last week the *Transcript* printed your article (but they cut out the tickling duchesses and seducing housemaids line!)."[13] Virgil and I had known each other since our student years in Paris, but now we were more closely in touch because we had a mutual friend in Paul Bowles. Virgil, who had become disenchanted with our former teacher, was urging Bowles to study with Paul Dukas. I received a nine-page letter from Virgil stating his case against Nadia, and ending: "Nadia is not the same as when we were there. . . . I've told you my story and you can give him

[12] Arthur Berger, "The Young Composers' Group," *Trend* (April-May-June 1933.

[13] The line reads: "He [Copland] is not walking with god or talking with men or seducing housemaids or tickling duchesses. He is crying aloud to Israel. And very much as if no one could hear him." Virgil Thomson, "Aaron Copland (American Composers VIII)," *Modern Music*.

[Bowles] any advice you want and he will follow it because he believes in you and I shant say any more about it. I've sent Nadia pupils for years and very little good has come of them, none for European purposes. This is the first time I've done otherwise. I think it's time to change. . . ." I responded:

> You certainly state the case against N.B. well enough and I'm not so blind as to be unaware that there is such a thing. In relation to Paul . . . there is no matter where or how a pupil learns his stuff just so that he learns it. Therefore it makes no difference whether he studies with N.B. or Dukas. But I know absolutely nothing about Dukas as teacher and I do know N.B. can teach counterpoint so I naturally send my friends to N.B. Secondly, it is useless to be a pupil if you are unwilling to enter into a pupil-teacher relationship (Roy was too old to do this and so were you in 1926). I'm all for the teacher influencing the pupil—it doesn't matter what pet ideas the teacher happens to have or what means are employed to drive them home—the pupil should swallow them whole for a time and if he has any guts he'll throw them overboard soon enough. If not, it proves he's just a pupil and it doesn't matter whom he studies with. I know N.B.'s pet ideas and I know the maternal means she employs but I know nothing of Dukas' pet ideas etc. So it boils down to sending pupils to a known quantity. As soon as I feel the disadvantages outweigh the advantages to be gained from being N.B.'s pupil I'll stop sending pupils, but that time hasn't come yet.

Virgil and I continued to disagree about Paul. I worried about his lack of discipline, and Virgil wrote (28 August 1932): "You are shocked because he won't follow the conventional education of a young man of talent. He is frightfully impressed by what you tell him and gets awfully worried because he can't do it." I, in turn, thought that Paul liked to have someone worry about him. I wrote to Virgil (5 December 1933): "And so I play the role of worrier. You encourage him and I'll worry him and together we'll do very well by him." (As it turned out, within a short time Paul got very sick with typhoid and did indeed worry us all.)

This would not be the only time Virgil and I disagreed. We are not much alike in temperament and personality, but we have never had a falling out, even though it has been assumed in the music world that there was terrific competition between us. I doubt either of us would deny this completely, but we could always carry on our friendship and collegial activities—I think because we were honest with each other. We said and wrote what we thought, no holds barred. For instance, in 1931 after Virgil sent me a copy of his *Violin Sonata*, I wrote (5 April): "I think it has lovely things in it, particularly the second movement, but I also think that you are often much too easy with yourself as for instance the too-Handel-like beginning of that 2nd movement and the theme with arpeggio accompaniment of the 4th movement. . . What I like about the piece are those moments of seemingly effortless musicality which are utterly simple and deeply charming. . . ." It was also in 1931 that Minna suggested I invite Virgil to write the article on me for *Modern Music*'s "American Composers" series. I made the request (29 January 1931): "From my standpoint, don't for an instant feel the slightest obligation to do the article on my account. . . . And if you should decide to do it nothing but your honestest judgment would please me. . ." When the piece had appeared, I wrote again (27 January 1932): "Thanks for the article. All my friends thought it very swell. It made me understand your music much better. And it will help me make mine better I hope. . . ." After *What to Listen For in Music* was published in 1938, Virgil wrote to me in not the most complimentary manner. I countered (2 May 1939): "The whole book is a kind of outline of facts. It never occurred to me that anyone would look for an original contribution to musical theory in it. . . The damn thing was never meant for you to read in the first place—" On the other hand, I have always considered Virgil a superb writer and critic. Reviewing his book *The State of Music*, I stated categorically: ". . . the most original book on music that America has produced."[14] Virgil went to live in Paris but kept in touch. I thought he should be in America and said so. I wrote (15 February 1940): "Come home and help instead of sending all that good advice from Paris." Virgil and I have been colleagues through many years. At a dinner at the Plaza Hotel in honor of Virgil's seventy-fifth birthday in November 1971, as part of the entertainment I parodied my *Lincoln Portrait*: "Born in Missouri, raised in Kansas City, and lived in Paris, France, this is what Virgil said: 'I have never known an artist of any kind, who didn't do better work when he got properly paid for it.' And this is what he said: 'Always beware of ex-composers; their one aim in life is to discourage the writing of music!' " I continued, "When standing erect, he is five feet four inches tall, and this is what he said: 'A concert is a meal. It is a feast, a ham sandwich, a chocolate sundae, nourishment to be absorbed with pleasure and digested by unconscious processes.' " And I concluded, "Virgil Thomson, best all-around music critic in the U.S. is everlasting in the memory of those he criticized." Joking aside, Virgil and I have often worked together to give American composers a surer footing in the world of music. Later in our lives, recognition and honors came to both of us, among them membership in the National Institute and Academy of Arts and Letters. In 1956 Virgil agreed to make the presentation to me of their Gold Medal in Music, and I was given the pleasure of presenting him with that prestigious award in 1966.

Virgil Thomson[15]

Minna had tried to get me to write for her when I was going back to France to live there in 1925, and I didn't want to do it. I was giving up all that kind of thing. I'd been writing regularly for Vanity Fair *magazine, and I had been playing the organ professionally, teaching at Harvard, and all that. I said, "Enough of this! My mind has got all of everybody else's music in it." So I went off to be in Paris, where you don't hear music unless you really want to at least it doesn't come to you over the air or around the neighbors and I was walking out on this business of writing. Well, Minna didn't like that idea, so about five years later she asked Aaron to get me to write an article about him. That was my first break back into writing. Minna was shocked when she first saw the piece—she took a strong gulp and then said, "But this is very good!" I used the word "Jewish," you see, and the League of Composers—one hundred percent Jewish—was not accustomed to the word. But I was not bringing up the Jewish question, but the identity. It's as if you couldn't mention to me that my family were Southern Baptists! I used it legitimately, I'm*

[14] Aaron Copland, "Thomson's Musical State," *Modern Music*, XVII:1 (October-November 1939), 63-65.
[15] Thomson interview.

sure, to explain certain psychological traits in Aaron. I thought he was a prophet calling out to Israel. The music has little counterpoint—it's one man speaking with a lone voice. Anyway, Minna had an enormously good editorial sense. She knew a good piece from a not good piece, an interesting piece from a not interesting one. She could even take kids and train them. Minna has a huge place—if anybody wanted to give it to her—in the literacy of the American musical composing group. And in the twenty-two years of her magazine, everybody wrote there. Well, I did this piece on Aaron and it was successful, and I got on with Minna, chiefly by correspondence, of course. After that I would write things for Modern Music *from time to time. I got $25 for each piece.*

Aaron introduced me to his Young Composers' Group when I came back for visits. He had the great gift of being a good colleague, and we became good, loyal colleagues. Some of his friends have tried to provoke quarrels, and maybe mine have, too I don't know. But we weren't having any. Aaron and I were sold on the same general idea, that composers are not rival cheats at some show game on the street. We're all members of the same Fifth Avenue Merchants' Association, and our future and our present depend on being good colleagues.

For the first twenty years of Aaron's career as a composer he carried his American colleagues along with him, because he was successful before anybody else. When he gave concerts, we would be in on it. That included the Copland-Sessions Concerts for which Copland was the charm boy and Sessions was the heavy. Aaron was a strict orchestral and chamber music man and not really as complex a modernist as Sessions, but a good card-carrying modernist nevertheless. He needed support early on and found it from Alma Wertheim and others. He figured out, I think, that he would not make unnecessary enemies. But he never hesitated to make enemies where it could not be done otherwise. Since we were young together, I was aware of some things that could annoy or worry Aaron, but he always went about those matters in a straightforward way by trying to find a solution. And, if you can't find a solution, you live with it. As time went on, Aaron became the patron of American musical youth just like Darius Milhaud in Paris—all the young went through Darius somehow or other. And like that, Aaron looked at everybody, encouraged them if necessary, discouraged them, if necessary. He was valuable as a talent filter for Koussevitzky, and he took it all quite seriously.

I made his musical portrait and when you do that, things turn up. Once you start looking at someone closely, you find things you hadn't expected at all. Aaron turned out to be a long, steady, indefatigable pastoral. And some of the best music he's written is pastoral. I don't see the sidewalks of New York in Aaron as some others do. Aaron, the son of immigrants, adopted the countryside, that first piece, he's the Jewish preacher telling people right and wrong. That's an historical and inherited trait from his family and religious background. Also from Aaron's family is his good sense about business. Whenever it came to the question of a commission by the same person, when Aaron and I would compare notes about how much we were getting or how much to ask, it inevitably turned out that Aaron asked more and got it! But he did it all so gently. I asked him once what he did if he found a publisher charging something he's not supposed to, and he simply answered, "Well, I would just write a letter." Ralph Hawkes from Boosey & Hawkes liked Aaron and saw a good business there and so got him a contract with the London house. It was Aaron who, when I first came back to America in 1940, introduced me to Ralph and recommended that he take me on also. Hawkes tried it. I took him one little choral piece, and he sent me a long, handwritten contract—one of those British contracts—everything pretty in it. Since I couldn't make it out myself, I took it to a young lawyer who wrote Boosey & Hawkes a letter. Ralph didn't answer it. He just sent my music right back, and it never went further. But Aaron had tried; he always did his best to help his fellow composers.

Aaron was involved in the theater personally through Clurman and by musical example through me. I wrote opera, ballet, and film music before he did these things, and I did them in a straightforward manner. There came a time when Aaron needed a simpler approach. He has said and written that I'm one of the few composers who influenced him. The foreign models were Shostakovich and Kurt Weill, and the American model, Virgil Thomson. In the thirties the whole of New York musical and intellectual life was moving into a theory of trade unionism, even occasionally reading Karl Marx. Theater was definitely where things were heading during and after the Depression. And the social content of theater and films was moving away from complexity—any theater audience wants music that is accessible. Didactic modernism gets nowhere with them. It just doesn't communicate in the theater, whether union theater or Broadway capitalist theater or film for great chunks of the population.

Aaron's quite a good conductor—not a star but very competent. Since he stopped writing music, a fact which he deeply regrets but can't do anything about, it's something for him to do. He can travel around the world making money and getting his own music distributed and there's absolutely nothing wrong with it. I've done a bit of it myself. I've never had as many dates as he has, and I don't suppose I'm as dependable a conductor. He's very straightforward about it.

Aaron was the president of young American music, then middle-aged American music, because he had tact, good business sense about colleagues, and loyalty. He conquered Mexico through Chávez, and he inherited England with Benjie's [Benjamin Britten] permission—and Benjie had veto power there. Aaron made good friends all over the world. He was always president of American music of any age or any place he happened to be.

As soon as the dates for the First Festival of Contemporary Music at Yaddo were set for 30 April and 1 May, 1932, I wrote to Virgil and Paul Bowles in Paris and to Roy Harris in California for pieces. Roy answered, "I will write you a work for string quartet and flute—one movement about 12 minutes . . . will be written 'pronto.' . . . Love to you old boy—more power to you, an ancient and tenacious friend. . . ." Bowles sent five songs on his own texts and Virgil a setting of Max Jacob's *Stabat Mater* with string quartet accompaniment (after the festival, I recommended the *Stabat* to Cos Cob for publication). From the Young Composers' Group, I invited Henry Brant and Vivian Fine to submit works and another young composer-pianist, Oscar Levant, whom I had met at an evening at the Gershwins' in New York that past winter. He had played part of an unfinished jazzy piano *Sonatina* for the guests, and I encouraged him to complete it for a premiere at Yaddo.[16] I drew also on the League of Composers and former Boulanger students. In all, eighteen composers were included in three concerts, divided between Saturday morning and evening, and Sunday afternoon.[17] A Conference for Critics and Composers was scheduled for Sunday morning.

[16] Levant felt out of place at Yaddo. He called it a "closed shop" and left before the end of the festival. Oscar Levant, *A Smattering of Ignorance* (Garden City, N.Y.: Country Life Press, 1942), 222-30.

[17] Composers included were Robert Russell Bennett, Nicolai Berezowsky, Paul Bowles, Henry Brant, Carlos Chávez, Israel Citkowitz, Aaron Copland, Vivian Fine, Louis Gruenberg, Roy Harris, Charles Ives, Oscar Levant, Walter Piston, Silvestre Revueltas, Wallingford Riegger, Roger Sessions, and Virgil Thomson. For full programs, see Shackelford, "The Yaddo Festivals . . ." *Perspectives.*

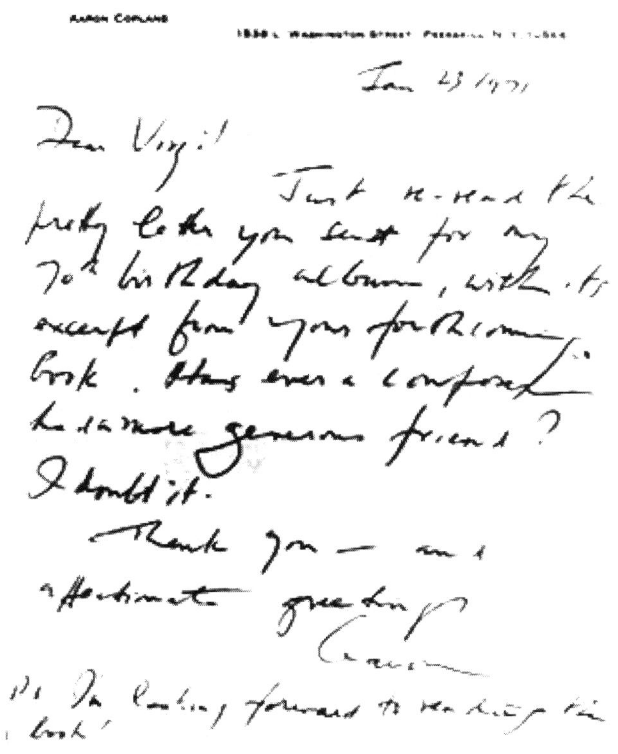
AARON COPLAND

Jan 23/1971

Dear Virgil!

Just re-read the pretty letter you sent for my 70th birthday album, with its excerpt from your forthcoming book. Has ever a composer had a more generous friend? I doubt it.

Thank you — and affectionate greetings

Aaron

PS I'm looking forward to reading the book!

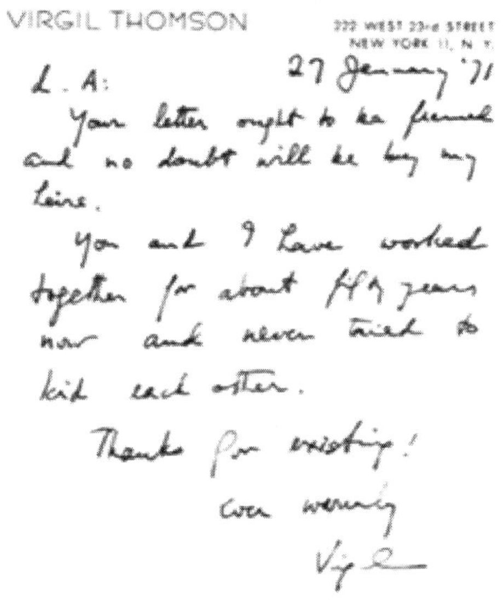
VIRGIL THOMSON

222 WEST 23rd STREET
NEW YORK 11, N. Y.

A. A: 27 January '71

Your letter ought to be framed and no doubt will be by my heirs.

You and I have worked together for about 49 years now and never tried to kill each other.

Thanks for existing!

Ever warmly

Virgil

Above: Letter from Copland to Thomson, 23 January 1971
Right: Response from Thomson to Copland, 27 January 1971

Of all the pieces performed, highest praise went to Roger's *Sonata for Piano* (by now in its complete state), seven songs by Charles Ives, and my *Piano Variations*. George Antheil had been scheduled to perform four piano pieces on Saturday evening. When he canceled at the last moment, I substituted the *Piano Variations*. Perhaps this was a blessing in disguise, for while I was playing, I sensed the music reaching this Yaddo audience in a way that it had not done in New York a year earlier. Both Arthur Berger and Paul Rosenfeld corroborated this in reviews of the festival. Re-reading them, I am reminded that after several requests, I played the *Variations* again on Sunday.

The Ives songs, performed by baritone Hubert Linscott with myself at the piano, were received with great interest—this was the first time a group of professional musicians were paying serious attention to Ives. It was a turning point in the recognition of his music. Arthur Berger was prophetic when he wrote in his review for the *Daily Mirror*: "History is being made in our midst."[18] The Young Composers' Group had "discovered" Ives in the early thirties. Benny Herrmann, Irwin Heilner, and Jerry Moross were particularly enthusiastic, and Ives became an influence on their music. It's true that I was not much interested in Ives until Benny pushed me into looking at *114 Songs*, a volume that Ives had published privately in 1922.[19] When I did investigate, I was amazed. There we were in the twenties searching for a composer from the older generation with an "American sound," and here was Charles Ives composing this incredible music—totally unknown to us! I wrote for permission to include a selection of his songs at Yaddo (7 March 1932) and he sent me a rather curious copy of *114 Songs* (several pages had been cut out or removed, and I never found out why).[20] I chose seven that reflected the incredibly wide variety of style and moods in the collection.[21] I subsequently arranged for these songs to be published by Cos Cob Press—the first commrcial publication of Ives songs

When planning the Second Yaddo Festival I included another Ives song, "Where the Eagle Cannot See," and wrote to John Kirkpatrick (11 September 1933): "Will you have the Ives sonata movement ('Alcotts' from 'Concord') with you (and in your fingers) in case somebody gets sick and we need a substitute?" Our Young Composers' Group had heard John play this at a meeting, and all were impressed. A postcard sent to ives requesting publicity photographs went unanswered; years later, I saw it in the Ives Collection at Yale—scribbled over with characterisic Ives fury against publicity. In 1933 when preparing an article on the *114 Songs* for *Modern Music*,[22] I wrote again to the composer with Sessions wrote from Italy wondering why I would even bother myself with critics in this way. But I decided to go further by expanding my remarks into an article for *Modern Music* in

[18] A.V. B. (Arthur V. Berger), "Yaddo Music Festival," *Daily Mirror* (New York), 3 May 1932, 18.

[19] See interview, Bernard Herrmann with Perlis, Ives Project, Oral History of American Music, Yale, 12 November 1969, New York City. Herrmann died 24 December 1975.

[20] Copland's copy of *114 Songs* was donated to the Ives Collection, Yale Music Library. Ives would occasionally cut pages from copies of *114 Songs* when preparing smaller groups of songs for publication.

[21] The seven Ives songs chosen were "The Indians," "Walking," "Serenity," "Maple Leaves," "The See'r," "Evening," and "Charlie Rutlage."

[22] Aaron Copland, "One Hundred and Fourteen Songs," *Modern Music* XI:4 (May-June 1932), 59-64.

with a list of questions. This time he responded cordially and in great detail.[23] After Yaddo I tried in vain to interest Koussevitzky in performing an Ives orchestral piece. In the forties, the Arrow Music Press, with which I was involved, published some Ives music, and I recall that the composer returned every royalty check for us to use toward publishing other composers' works. As Ives' music gradually emerged, it had an increasingly influential effect on younger composers and eventually on the position of the American composer in the international music scene.

Paul Rosenfeld, who had been an Ives supporter even before Yaddo, admitted that the the rest of the program did not please him. He objected to Yaddo as being a reflection of my own personal taste rather than a representation of the very best American music available. But in practical terms it was absolutely necessary for me to deal primarily with composers who were my friends and colleagues. After all, the music was mostly unpublished and unrecorded, and neither scores nor parts were available. Rosenfeld would publish his criticism in *Discoveries of a Music Critic*,[24] but soon after the festival he wrote them directly to me (15 June 1932):

> ... you must know that I was not very happy about it all until the latter half of the second program . I have come to the conclusion that the best that can be done for all American composers, the weak and the strong, is for the makers of programs to put the strongest foot forward at all times. ... I prefer Ruggles to Berezowsky and Moross to Brant or Fine.... As for Gruenberg: why prefer him to Jerome Kern or Gershwin: they too have works which are short and characteristic in technique and content: I really like Ole Man Ribber. Ornstein's songs seem on a par with Bennett's and one of Rudhyar's moments are worth several of Berezowsky's. As for Cowell and Weiss, I am surprised that you see no reasons for their inclusion in programs which featured Thomson and Blitzstein. Cowell at least makes interesting sounds....

Alfred H. Meyer reviewed the Yaddo Festival for *Modern Music*. He appraised the music, complimented the performers, and commented, "American music need no longer step aside for Europe. . .."[25] Rosenfeld, Berger, Meyer, and Irving Kolodin were the only critics who came to the festival. As chairman of the Sunday conference, "Critics and Composers," it was up to me to express the anger and frustration felt by the composers. I said that the time had arrived for critics to adopt new attitudes, and I accused the critics of neglect and lack of curiosity. I urged my colleagues to join together for their own mutual benefit. "Frankly," I concluded, "under such circumstances I consider daily newspaper criticism a menace, and we would be better off without it!" The following morning, an Associated Press dispatch informed readers of *The New York Times*: "The long-standing feud between composers and critics flared into the open at a conference in Yaddo, the Spencer Trask mansion." I described the blow-up to Virgil, who was in Paris (10 May 1932): "The critics were conspicuous by their absence. I lit into them at a conference. An AP reporter got the story, and thereby stirred a hornets' nest. There is now a case going on of Copland vs the Critics. Since they always treated me with kid gloves they consider it rank ingratitude—biting the hand that fed my reputation." I wrote a response to *The Times*:

> . . . It would be naive to imagine that a conference between critics and composers was arranged at the First Festival of Contemporary Music at Yaddo for the childish purpose of giving composers an opportunity to tell the critics where "to get off at," as the saying goes. On the contrary, our purpose was the thoroughly serious one of considering the relationship between the American composer and the music critics of the daily press and to discover what might be done to make that relationship more vital and more important than it now is. . . . Far from being a "menace" to the composer, he is an absolute necessity. . . .

But *The Times* music critic, Olin Downes, had the last word. "Who," he asked rhetorically, "has created music remotely cognizant of the things that palpitate in such modern American novels as *Arrowsmith* or dramas with such a terrible intensity as *Mourning Becomes Elektra*?" Roger which I asked that the critics attend concerts of the League and the Pan American Association of Composers, and furthermore, that they study scores of new works. "If they knew all this music, and knew it well, they would realize that there is something alive and growing on our own soil which deserves to be championed; for like any new growth, American music needs nurturing. . ." And I pleaded for just one critic "who will concern himself in the creation of an American music to the same degree as Edward Evans in English music, or Henri Prunières in French music. Is that too much to ask?"[26]

It seemed likely that Yaddo would take the place of the Copland–Sessions Concerts, so Roger and I decided to give up our joint effort. Henry Brant coined a phrase at about this time that has become familiar, but that I am not particularly fond of. Henry wrote (2 May 1932): "You are destined to become the 'Dean of American Composers.' The names of your disciples are so far not well established, but such as already exist are even now known as 'Coplandites.' . . . Do you think the late season was so bad for American music? 1. Composers group actually started. 2. Yaddo festival and its notice. 3. Ives began to be noticed."

For the Second Festival of Contemporary American Music at Yaddo in 1933, a Central Music Committee was formed: Richard Donovan, Robert Russell Bennett, Wallingford Riegger, Randall Thompson, and myself as chairman. To further broaden our scope, representatives were chosen in various cities in the East (Piston in Boston, Bernard Rogers in Rochester, Blitzstein in Philadelphia, Carl Engel in Washington); West (Harris in Los Angeles, Cowell in San Francisco); in Europe (Thomson in Paris), and Mexico (Chávez in Mexico City). We hoped to expand this plan further. There were again three concerts—two on Saturday, 30 September; one on Sunday afternoon, 1 October. The Sunday conference with Roger Sessions as chairman featured a discussion between "Interpretive Artists and Composers." A lively session evolved around the social uses of music. Several composers from the original festival were on the program in 1933, while others were being

[23] Correspondence at Ives Collection, Yale Music Library and in Copland's files.

[24] Paul Rosenfeld, *Discoveries of a Music Critic*, 352-60.

[25] Alfred H. Meyer, "Yaddo-A May Festival," *Modern Music*, IX:4 (May-June 1932), 172-76. The performers were Ada MacLeish, Jesus Maria Sanroma, Hubert Linscott, and John Kirkpatrick; Hans Lange Quartet; League of Composers Quartet; and composer-pianists Vivian Fine, Aaron Copland, and Oscar Levant.

[26] Aaron Copland, "The Composer and His Critic," *Modern Music*, IX:4 (May-June 1932), 143-47.

Top: Elizabeth Ames, Copland, and other guests on the porch at Yaddo, 1933
Bottom: Group photograph at Yaddo, 1932
Opposite top: Group photograph at Yaddo, 1932: Copland (*center*) behind Vivian Fine; to the right of Lehman Engel; Roy Harris is left of Engel and Paul Bowles is third from the right.

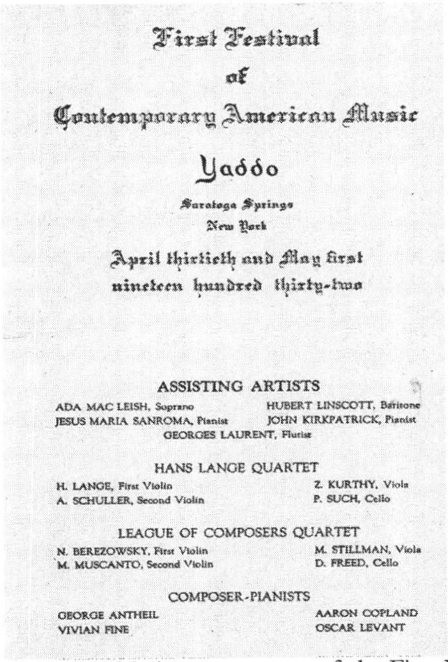

First Festival
of
Contemporary American Music

Yaddo
Saratoga Springs
New York

April thirtieth and May first
nineteen hundred thirty-two

ASSISTING ARTISTS
ADA MAC LEISH, Soprano — HUBERT LINSCOTT, Baritone
JESUS MARIA SANROMA, Pianist — JOHN KIRKPATRICK, Pianist
GEORGES LAURENT, Flutist

HANS LANGE QUARTET
H. LANGE, First Violin — Z. KURTHY, Viola
A. SCHULLER, Second Violin — P. SUCH, Cello

LEAGUE OF COMPOSERS QUARTET
N. BEREZOWSKY, First Violin — M. STILLMAN, Viola
M. MUSCANTO, Second Violin — D. FREED, Cello

COMPOSER-PIANISTS
GEORGE ANTHEIL — AARON COPLAND
VIVIAN FINE — OSCAR LEVANT

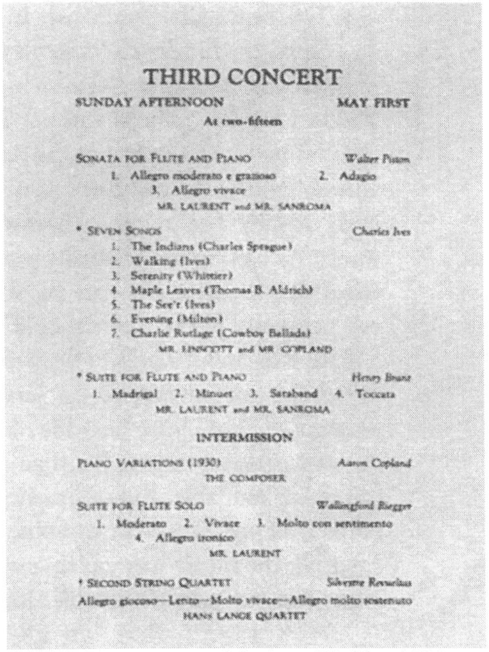

THIRD CONCERT
SUNDAY AFTERNOON — MAY FIRST
At two-fifteen

SONATA FOR FLUTE AND PIANO — Walter Piston
1. Allegro moderato e grazioso 2. Adagio
3. Allegro vivace
MR. LAURENT and MR. SANROMA

* SEVEN SONGS — Charles Ives
1. The Indians (Charles Sprague)
2. Walking (Ives)
3. Serenity (Whittier)
4. Maple Leaves (Thomas B. Aldrich)
5. The See'r (Ives)
6. Evening (Milton)
7. Charlie Rutlage (Cowboy Ballads)
MR. LINSCOTT and MR. COPLAND

* SUITE FOR FLUTE AND PIANO — Henry Brant
1. Madrigal 2. Minuet 3. Saraband 4. Toccata
MR. LAURENT and MR. SANROMA

INTERMISSION

PIANO VARIATIONS (1930) — Aaron Copland
THE COMPOSER

SUITE FOR FLUTE SOLO — Wallingford Riegger
1. Moderato 2. Vivace 3. Molto con sentimento
4. Allegro ironico
MR. LAURENT

* SECOND STRING QUARTET — Silvestre Revueltas
Allegro giocoso—Lento—Molto vivace—Allegro molto sostenuto
HANS LANGE QUARTET

Above left: Announcement of the First Festival of Contemporary Music at Yaddo, 1932
Right: Program of Third Concert

represented for the first time. Nothing of my own was performed.[27] Partly in response to Rosenfeld's criticism, Cowell and Ruggles were now included. George Antheil had canceled in 1932; I wrote again to him in Paris, and finally had a response (7 September 1933) after his return to America: "I should like to play at Yaddo, (1) *The Death of Machines Sonata* (2) Preludes from *100 piano preludes to Femme Cent Tete of Max Ernst's* and (3) *Sonatina 1932*. This ought to be enough if not too much. All three works are related to the '*Death of the Machines' Sonata*. . . . I have dedicated the *Sonatina* to you; Aaron, in admiration of your work, and in appreciation of your friendship."

Randall Thompson reviewed the festival for *Modern Music*: "Gone the nonconformity, gone the hearty satisfaction of smashing everything in sight; gone the passionate conviction, gone the spirit of the Mohawk trail. . ."[28] Well, the festival reflected the times—and the times were calling for a swing away from the experimentalism of the twenties. The Second Yaddo Festival demonstrated the growing need for a simpler, more accessible musical language.

After 1933 I was not to present contemporary American music festivals at Yaddo after all. Following the Second Festival, I proposed that Yaddo be sponsored by the U.S. Section of the ISCM, and I wrote my reasons and suggestions in a lengthy report to Elizabeth Ames, who took the proposal to the Yaddo board of directors. I received a letter from Mrs. Ames (5 May 1934): "It is now very clear to me that it will be impossible for Yaddo to make any decision this spring about when or how the third festival shall be held. . ." The festivals did not resume until 1936, and then it was to present programs combining "old" and "new" music. I was no longer associated with them. In 1940 Yaddo returned to my original idea of all-contemporary American music, but the war then caused a hiatus of six years. The festivals resumed in 1946, 1949, and 1952. The final celebration honored Yaddo's twenty-five years of service to creative artists. When the concert opened with my *Piano Variations* played by John Kirkpatrick, I was in the audience in the Yaddo music room of the mansion where I had played the piece twenty years earlier.

In the spring of 1932 I stayed on at Yaddo to work on the *Short Symphony* and *Statements for Orchestra,* two of my most serious compositions that followed in the style of the *Piano Variations*. I wrote to Kirkpatrick (22 June 1932): "My new work is being upset by the fact that I've started still a newer and am working on the two simultaneously. The newest piece will have 4 or 5 short movements. I have one of these already. . . . Of the other, I have two of the three movements practically done." This, the *Short Symphony*, was written at intervals between 1931 and 1933 in a variety of places from Morocco to Mexico. It is a bare fifteen minutes in length, but as was the case with the *Variations*, those minutes are concentrated in meaning. If I expended a great deal of time and effort on the *Short Symphony,* it was because I was determined to write as perfected a piece as I possibly could.

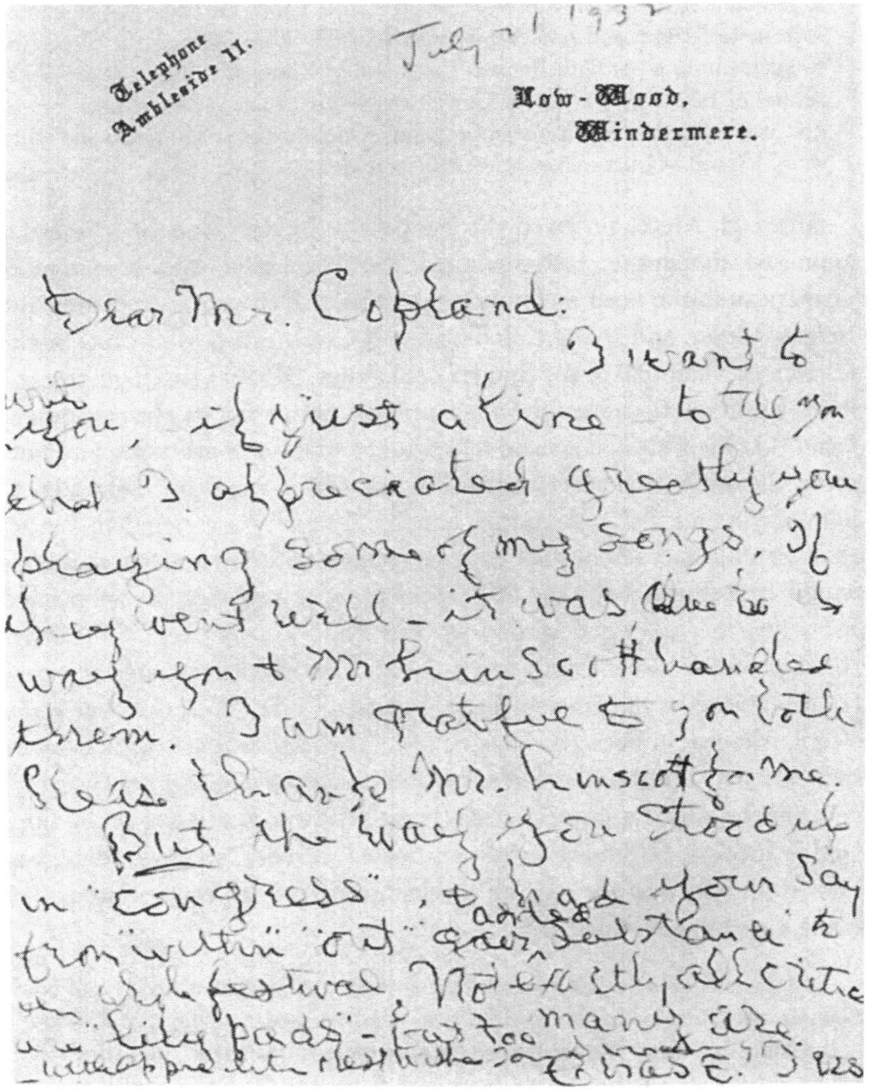
Telephone Ambleside 11.

Low-Wood, Windermere.

July 1 1932

Dear Mr. Copland:

Letter from Charles Ives to Copland (date in Copland's hand)

I had briefly considered naming the piece (at Chávez' suggestion) "The Bounding Line" until another friend (I no longer recall who) wisely advised against it, pointing out that "bounding" seemed more like "boundary" than the "bounce" I had in mind. The *Short Symphony* is actually my *Second Symphony* and is occasionally referred to that way. It is in three movements—fast, slow, fast—to be played without pause. The first movement's main impetus is rhythmic, with a scherzo-like quality. All melodic figures result from a nine-note sequence—a kind of row—from the opening two bars. The second movement,

[27] The composers repeated at Yaddo from 1932 were Israel Citkowitz, Roy Harris, Charles Ives, Walter Piston, and Roger Sessions. Those performed for the first time in 1933 were George Antheil, Theodore Chanler, Henry Cowell, Richard Donovan, Ross Lee Finney, Charles Martin Loeffler, Otto Luening, Quincy Porter, and Carl Ruggles.

[28] Randall Thompson, "The Second Year at Yaddo," *Modern Music*, XI:1 (November-December 1933), 41.

tranquil in feeling, contrasts with the first movement and with the finale, which is again rhythmically intricate, bright in color and free in form. The orchestration includes a heckelphone (baritone oboe), but there are no trombones, and the nature of the music calls for an enlarged chamber orchestra, rather than the full sound of the symphonic ensemble.

The *Short Symphony* has a curious performance history. Both Stokowski and Koussevitzky announced performances, but gave up because of the rhythmic difficulties. Koussevitzky considered the piece for a year and a half. When I asked him, "Is it too difficult?" he responded, "Non, ce n'est pas trop difficile, c'est impossible!" Exactly one week later, Chávez gave the world premiere in Mexico City (23 November 1934) with the Orquesta Sinfónica de Mexico. Carlos sent the program and wrote (1 December 1934):

> . . . We had ten rehearsals . . . the orchestra men were at first skeptical but by the third rehearsal or so they had a real genuine and growing interest. . . . It is impossible to tell you in a few words how much I enjoy the Little Symphony: I already begin to write an essay on it. .. . The way each and every note comes out from the other as the only natural and logic possible one, is simply unprecedented in the whole history of music. . . . There has been very much talk about music in which everything is essential, nothing superfluous, but, as far as I know, exists, yes, the talk about such music, but not the music itself. The Little Symphony is the first realization I know of that, and yet, the human content, the ironic expression, is purely emotional. . .

And I responded (31 December 1934): "How I wish I could have heard it. And what a strange feeling it gives me to think that you have heard a piece of mine which I have not yet heard. . ." The *Short Symphony* is dedicated to Chávez. From the start, he called it the "Little Symphony," and through the years, he never referred to it as anything else.

Partly due to the fact that the piece did not get performed in the States, I prepared the *Sextet*, for clarinet, string quartet, and piano in 1937 while summering in Mexico. The *Sextet* was first performed in New York at Town Hall in 1939 by a Juilliard graduate ensemble. It was announced for the 1941 ISCM Festival and a CBS radio broadcast in connection with it but was abandoned due to the difficulty of the piece and the number of rehearsals required.

The *Short Symphony* itself finally had its U.S. premiere when Leopold Stokowski conducted the NBC Symphony in a broadast from the famous 8-H studio in the RCA Building. Even then Stokowski told me, "It is still a difficult work to perform, and even more to interpret." But it can be done—in 1955 I conducted the Sudwestfunk Orchestra and I wrote to Virgil (24 September),"I'm having a scrumptuous time this week . . .they play 5/8-7/8 in their sleep—and with ten rehearsals in five days the *Short Symphony* sounds like 'Eine Kleine Nachtmusik'!" Leonard Bernstein conducted the first American public performance of the *Short Symphony* in 1957 with the Philharmonic-Symphony Society of New York on a program that included Roy Harris' *Third Symphony*.

I think of the *Short Symphony* as one of my "neglected children" and am perhaps more fond of these works *because* they receive so much less attention. But at least on special occasions they have occasional hearings. For a seventieth birthday celebration, I conducted the *Short Symphony* in an all-Copland program with the New York Philharmonic, and at about the same time, it was finally played by the BSO under Seiji Ozawa. In my eightieth

year I was invited to conduct the *Short Symphony* at Carnegie Hall. Between rehearsals, a violinist came up to me and said, "In my opinion you, Mr. Copland, taught American orchestras to play in 5/4!" I'm sure this is an exaggeration, but even today, with orchestra players capable of complicated rhythms and harmonies, the *Short Symphony* and the *Sextet* are not easy for performers. On a European tour early in 1981, I was scheduled to conduct the *Symphony* in Brussels, and it was canceled for lack of extra rehearsal time; and when the Chamber Music Society of Lincoln Center played the *Sextet* on 31 October and 2 November 1980, *The New York Times* reviewer, Joseph Horowitz, wrote (2 November 1980):

> It is fiendishly difficult to negotiate cleanly . . . however frustrating Mr. Copland's tangle of syncopations, cross-rhythms and shifting meters may seem to the performer, there are no gratuitous difficulties in the *Sextet*. . . One would think that most of the terrors of both versions would have worn off by now for players as well as listeners. One learns to have patience.[29]

I had been promising Chávez a visit to Mexico for several years. The time had come—especially since I was promised an all-Copland program in a series conducted by Chávez at the Conservatorio Nacional de México. I wrote to Chávez (8 August 1932): "You'll be glad to hear that I am studying Spanish and reading a great deal about Mexico, so that I think I can already find my way around the City without a guide! I am spending a quiet summer in New York, working on the same new orchestral piece which I hope to finish in Mexico. And looking forward 'passionement' to my Mexican trip." In my next letter (18 August 1932), I explained my plans. I would drive my car as far as Laredo and take the train to Mexico City, leaving New York 24 August. I wrote: "I am bringing with me a young violinist who is a pupil, companion, secretary and friend. His name is Victor Kraftsov. I'm sure you will like him." (When Victor dropped the last three letters from his name, I no longer recall—it seems to me I always knew him as Victor Kraft!) I had a telegram from Chávez that the all-Copland program—the first ever given anywhere—would take place 2 September. I was determined not to miss such an occasion, so we left New York precipitously and drove to Laredo in eight days, arriving in Mexico City on the morning of the concert.

I wrote "Dear Ma and Pa" letters from Mexico during my five-month visit there just as I had from France eleven years earlier, and the letters covered the same subjects—money, food, and weather: "You can get a regular meal in the swellest American restaurant for 2 pesos (60 cents)." I called Cuernavaca "a Mexican Atlantic City," and sent programs and reviews regularly with my translations, asking Ma and Pa to share them with the family. I wrote home about the attractive small apartment Chávez had found us in Mexico City and described the excitement surrounding the all-Copland concert and the informal and enthusiastic spirit that prevailed. The program, presented by the Conservatorio Nacional de Mexico, at the Teatro de Orientacion, included the following works: *Two Pieces for String Quartet; Piano Variations* (Jesus Durón Ruiz, pianist); "The House on the Hill" and "An Immorality" for chorus directed by Chávez; and *Music for the Theatre* performed by the

[29] Dennis Russell Davies reorchestrated *The Short Symphony* for chamber ensemble and conducted the first performance of his version with the Saint Paul Chamber Orchestra on 17 February 1979 in Minneapolis.

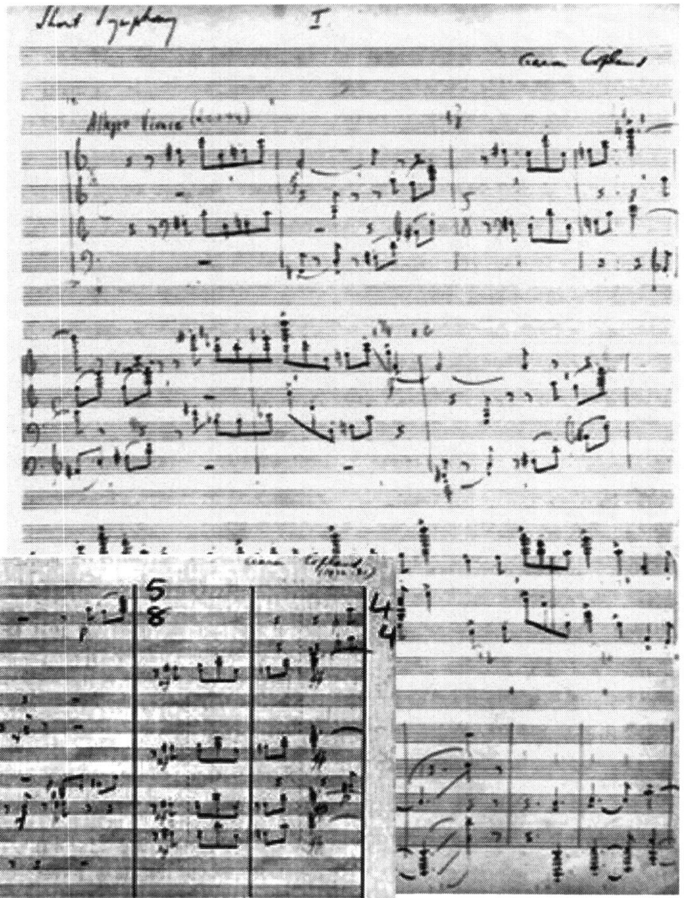

Right: Manuscript page from a four-hand arrangement of the *Short Symphony*

Left: Manuscript page from the orchestral ink score of the *Short Symphony*

conservatory orchestra under Chávez, who spoke about my music from the stage during the intermission. Several of these works were repeated a few weeks later.

Life was quieter for me in Mexico than in New York. The telephone did not ring so often, and I was able to fulfill a commission from the League for a piece to be performed in April. While in Mexico, I composed two *Elegies for Violin and Viola.* (When I decided to use this material in *Statements*, I withdrew the *Elegies* from my list of works.)[30] I spent a great deal of time with Chávez. We had much in common. His dedication to improving conditions for Mexican music was similar to my own efforts in American music. But in Mexico the general educational facilities and music in particular were far behind what we had in the States. Chávez and I admired each other's music, and I was amazed to see where he had come from and how he had taught himself almost everything he knew without formal instruction. Chávez knew what he wanted and was very forceful in getting results; he had the orchestras, although lacking in the kind of technical expertise we had in America, playing more contemporary music than I had ever performed anywhere in a short period of time. I wrote to Virgil (5 December):

> Chávez has complete control of the musical situation here. I wish you knew him personally—he's about as nice a guy as you could hope to meet. They've been playing a lot of stuff here so that I begin to feel as famous as Gershwin. Mexico has turned out even grander that I expected—and I expected pretty grand things. The best is the people—there's nothing remotely like them in Europe. They are really the "people"—nothing in them in striving to be bourgeois. In their overalls and bare feet they are not only poetic but positively "émouvant."

I was beginning to sense something in the Mexican character that was especially sympathetic. When Chávez took me to an unusual night spot called El Salón México, the atmosphere of this dance hall impressed me, and I came away with the germ of a musical idea. I wrote about Mexico to several friends. Gerald Sykes responded that he particularly liked my description of the "silence of the Mexican crowds." But in the concert hall they really let one know how they felt about the music. I could sense approval on 18 November when Chávez conducted the *Symphonic Ode* with the Orquesta Sinfónica in the Teatro Hidalgo. But I recall another occasion when I performed my *Piano Concerto* and some of the listeners took a dislike to it and began to hiss with characteristic Latin vigor. Others in the audience began to shush the hissers with equal vehemence, and between the hissing and the shushing, such a tumult was raised that I looked apprehensively at Chávez for a sign as to whether to stop the performance or go on to the bitter end. "We go on!" muttered Chávez grimly. So we did, and I wondered all the while whether it was the correct thing to take a bow to hisses. At the finish, however, there was sufficient applause to drown the hisses and the bow was definitely indicated.

Our last two months in Mexico were spent in the rural small town of Tlalpam. Before leaving Mexico, Victor wanted to experience swimming in the Pacific, so we had a few

[30] An ink score of *Elegies* dated 1932 includes pencil indications for orchestration and a note from the composer on the first page: "Part I arranged for str orch and used in *Statements* (movt 4-Subjective)." Pencil sketches are also with the composer's manuscripts.

III

Viernes 2 de Septiembre
a las 20.30 horas

2 Piezas para Cuarteto de Cuerda — COPLAND
Cuarteto del Conservatorio
Violin 1o. Higinio Ruvalcaba
Violin 2o. Filiberto Nava
Viola Jesús Mendoza
Violoncello Luis G. Galindo

Variaciones — COPLAND
Piano solo JESUS DURON RUIZ

2 Piezas para Coro y Piano — COPLAND
Upon the hills
An immorality
Coro del Conservatorio
Dirección CARLOS CHAVEZ

INTERMEDIO

Music for the Theatre — COPLAND
Prologue
Dance
Interlude
Burleaque
Epilogue
Orquesta del Conservatorio
Dirección CARLOS CHAVEZ

Top: Program of the first all-Copland concert, Mexico City, conducted by Carlos Chávez. *Above:* Copland visiting a family in Tlalpam, Mexico.
Left: Copland, Mexico, 1932

Copland and Victor Kraft, Mexico, 1932

days' vacation in Acapulco. We then took the train to Laredo to pick up our car. As we crossed the border, I had a sharp pang at leaving Mexico, and I wrote to Chávez from our first stop, San Antonio (2 January 1933): "It took me three years in France to get as close a feeling to the country as I was able to get in these few months in Mexico." Victor and I took turns driving back to New York. We made one-night stops in Houston, Montgomery, Atlanta, Savannah, Charleston, Raleigh, Richmond, and Washington. From Savannah, ten days before arriving home, I wrote to Mary Lescaze (13 January):

> Mexico was a rich time. Outwardly nothing happened and inwardly all was calm. Yet I'm left with the impression of having had an enriching experience. It comes, no doubt, from the nature of the country and the people. Europe now seems conventional to me by comparison. Mexico offers something fresh and pure and wholesome—a quality which is deeply unconventionalized. The source of it is the Indian blood which is so prevalent. I sensed the influence of the Indian background everywhere—even in the landscape. And I must be something of an Indian myself or how else explain the sympathetic chord it awakens in me. Of course I'm going back someday.

INTERLUDE III

Some periods in history are long and stable, with changes so gradual as to be imperceptible; others are short and volatile, with political and economic forces causing sudden shifts that quickly affect the climate. In describing the abrupt change from the twenties to the thirties, George Orwell wrote, "Suddenly we got out of the twilight of the gods into a sort of Boy Scout atmosphere of bare knees and community singing."[1] And Aaron Copland's friend Mary Lescaze recalled, "One morning in 1930 I opened my closet to find everything out of style. I stored away the high- heeled dancing slippers and went out to buy 'sensible' shoes."[2] The glamour of French culture, the exclusivity of the avant-garde, the champagne, formal clothes, and lighthearted parties were replaced by earnest groups discussing serious matters in a charged atmosphere of liberalism and social consciousness: Trotskyism, Marxism, and Stalinism were argued endlessly by the Young Peoples Socialist League and the Young Communist League, and aspects of American culture were written about in The New Republic and The American Mercury. The role of the arts in society was a favorite topic for debate at the Group Theatre, the Young Composers' Group, and the conferences at Yaddo. If a time in history can be located and defined by catch words and phrases, "the masses," "the proletariat," "workers' causes," and "comrade" would henceforth identify the thirties.

In the arts, modernism was "old hat" and realism was "in." "Social Realism became not a style of the period but the style of the period," wrote Tom Wolfe about the art world. "Even the most dedicated Modernists were intimidated. . . . For more than ten years from about 1930 to 1941, the artists themselves, in Europe and America, suspended the Modern movement. . . . Left politics did that for them. . ."[3] Paradoxically, political radicalism produced conservative results in the arts. Social Realism at its worst was propaganda; at best, an art that could be understood and enjoyed by the masses—one that was far from the experimentation and innovation that characterized the twenties. The thirties are con-

Copland was not by nature a political person; he joined neither Socialist nor Communist Party, but for a time in the early thirties he was what might be called a fellow traveler. When questioned about his leftist activities, his answer was simply, "It seemed the thing to do at the time." In fact, so many artists were caught up in the strong wave of sympathy

[1] George Orwell, "Inside the Whale," *The Collected Essays, Journalism and Letters of George Orwell, I: An Age Like This, 1920-1940* (London: Secker & Warburg, 1968), 510.

[2] Interview, Mary Lescaze with Perlis, 25 April 1980, New York City.

[3] Tom Wolfe, *The Painted Word* (New York: Farrar, Straus & Giroux, 1975), 40-41.

for socialism that it *was* the thing to do. The Party slogan, "Communism is twentieth-century Americanism," took full advantage of the "affirm America" movement. In any case, Copland, cautious as he was about politics, was never a loner and would not have found it natural to go underground with those modernists holding to the doctrine of "art for art's sake." Irving Howe, as a young political activist in the thirties, wrote: "Things had gone profoundly wrong. No later discounting of the radicalism of the thirties can wipe away this simple truth. Things had gone wrong not only in America but still more in Europe." Socialism offered a hope of restoring order and improving conditions. Howe also made the point that many politically active artists were from Jewish immigrant families: "Socialism was not merely politics or an idea. It was an encompassing culture, a style of perceiving and judging through which to structure their lives . . . culture could be a high calling. What excited them was the idea of breaking away, of willing a new life. They meant to declare themselves citizens of the world—and if that succeeded, might then become the writers of this country."[4] These ideas were not new to Copland and Clurman. Hadn't they been expressing "cultural politics" for American music and drama since their student years in Paris?

Several influences nudged Copland toward the Left: Mexico and the "people"; the Depression (by now affecting Copland's own family); the Marxist concept of "art for society's sake" espoused by Hanns Eisler and Marc Blitzstein; the lack of an audience for Copland's most recent compositions; and the political idealism of Clurman and the Group Theatre. Considering the repercussions for those who were involved in left-wing activities, it is hardly surprising that Clurman did not deal with his own or the Group's politics in his later published writings. But his letters to Copland at the time were filled with political discussions. After one particularly stimulating visit to the John Reed Club, Clurman wrote (24 May 1932):

> It is clear to me that people like us are the real revolutionaries in America today and that we are revolutionary in our function as artists and leaders. If we perfect our experience in the deepest sense which means relating ourselves as completely as is natural to our temperaments and interest to people around us with the same interests we shall be doing more for the revolutionary change of society . . . than all the theoretical communists in America. . . . The Artist's job today is to fight to be an artist which means to find his kindred, to fight for them too and to relate it to as many still living people as possible . . . and perhaps the Aaron Coplands—because they are as aware of their *world* as well as their art—are in the final analysis the greater artists as well as the greater revolutionaries. . . .

[4] Irving Howe, *A Margin of Hope* (New York: Harcourt Brace Jovanovich, 1982), 11, 9, 59.

Copland was close to the Group Theatre[5] from the time of its formation in the winter of 1930-31 when Clurman, Lee Strasberg, and Cheryl Crawford invited young theater people to meet with them on Friday evenings after showtime for discussions and lectures by the directors and others—among them, Waldo Frank on the relationship of the theater to the American social system and Copland on the uses of modern music in the theater. When the Group ran out of meeting places, Copland offered his Copland–Sessions office at Steinway Hall. Among those who attended regularly were Stella Adler, Morris Carnovsky, John Garfield, Robert Lewis, Sandy Meisner, Clifford Odets, and Franchot Tone. About the Group's beginnings, Clurman wrote:

> . . . one had to divine an approach that might be common to all the members. . . . It was this that added a dimension to the talks and to the whole atmosphere around the Group, that was to become its distinguishing mark, its strength, its impediment, and its wound. . . . For this reason photographers like Paul Strand and Ralph Steiner, a musician like Aaron Copland, an architect like William Lescaze, and many others not directly connected with the theatre found these meetings, and the subsequent development of the group that emerged from them, both stimulating and relevant to their own fields of interest. . . .[6]

Twenty-eight who attended the first winter meetings became the Group Theatre. The following summer the directors found a place in the country, at Brookfield Center, Connecticut, where they all lived and worked together in an atmosphere of high dedication—dissecting, debating, and rehearsing two plays for production in New York. Visitors were welcome to join in the discussions; they included Maxwell Anderson, Copland, Waldo Frank, Gerald Sykes, Paul Strand, and Ralph Steiner. Director Bobby Lewis, then a young actor with the Group, recalls that they were all great talkers, himself included—and Clurman most of all:

> Clurman never tired of talking about the theater! Once Franchot [Tone] despaired of getting a particular play ready in time for performance. I said, "Don't worry. Harold will never stop talking long enough for a production to take place!" But Harold had to define what our theater was. He believed that theater was an idea, not a building or a complex. The Group Theatre's idea was to reflect the life of their times. We practiced a common technique derived from the Stanislavsky system of the Moscow Art Theatre—not a star system, but an ensemble theater. In ten years, twenty-five plays were produced. The Group was an influence all over the world—even felt to this day through their own actions, and subsequently from the Actors Studio which came out of it.[7]

Clurman had always confided his troubles to Copland. Now he had almost more than he could handle: artistic, personal, and financial. Never realistic about money, Clurman loaned what he had to Group members, who were constantly broke, and then turned to Copland for help. From Boston (12 February 1932):

> I want to borrow some money. $150 from you. We got only 1/2 salary last week. We shall get only 1/3 salary this. Can we get out of Boston?—We won't receive any more salary at all till we open the Anderson play—in three weeks. . . If for any of a hundred reasons—"good" or "bad"—you can't lend me this money, don't feel badly about it at all. I shall accept—without a reason and without a doubt. Since all things you do are right to me (Always 100%) I don't feel embarrassed at asking you either—tho I don't like it. And I don't feel sad because money is really a minor trouble to me now.. . . I'm getting all clear within me and strong and am preparing myself for a bunch of real "socks."

Clurman and his co-directors managed to hold the Group together through many "socks." They survived the first two seasons and the second summer at Dover Furnace, New York, but during the third season, the Group was close to bankruptcy. They were saved at the last moment when an arrangement was made to exchange four nights a week of entertainment at Green Mansions, an adult camp in the Adirondacks, for a place to live and work. Copland had helped the Group earlier by introducing them to potential donors (Mary Churchill was one), and he continued to write to benefactors on their behalf; in return, he was named Group Associate. In the summer of 1933, when Copland himself was feeling the pinch of the Depression, a few young actors invited him to stay free of charge in a house on Friends Lake in Chestertown near Green Mansions.

During that summer Clifford Odets and Copland began a lasting friendship. Odets was passionate about music and would frequently turn to it during turbulent periods in his life; he was often at the piano at Green Mansions. According to Bobby Lewis, who was a cellist in his early years, "Sandy Meisner was really a fine pianist, but Cliff was an amateur who thought he was a musician."[8] Odets joined the Communist Party, but Copland preferred to stay closer to Clurman's less keenly focused political idealism. Clurman and the actress Stella Adler, recently married, traveled to Russia together in the spring of 1934 to see the Moscow Art Theatre in action and to meet Stanislavsky. From Clurman to Copland (15 June 1934): "I'd like to go back to the U.S.S.R. next spring! Let's go together!" Clurman was invited to return in 1935, but Copland could not afford to travel there at his own expense. After his return, Clurman wrote impressions of Russia and of the Group (31 July 1934): "They still want automobiles, good parts, cocktails while they are building a revolutionary theatre. They still are Americans who do not understand the element of sacrifice in the making of an integrated world. Russia gave me that picture clearly. . ."

Clurman urged Odets and Copland to collaborate on a play, *The Silent Partner*, described by Odets as "presenting the problems of a symphony, in contrast to . . . less ambitious chamber works. . . ."[9] But the play was dropped after several trials and revisions, before music was written for it. Copland did not work on a play with the Group Theatre until 1938 when he composed incidental music for an experimental drama, *The Quiet City*, by Irwin Shaw. This also was dropped after two dress rehearsals. Clurman wrote, "All that remained of our hard work was a lovely score by Aaron Copland,

[5] For more on the history of the Group Theatre, see Clurman *The Fervent Years* and Margaret Brenman Gibson, *Clifford Odets, American Playwright* (New York, Atheneu

[6] Clurman, *The Fervent Years*, 34.

[7] Interview, Robert Lewis with William Owen for Perlis, 12 May 1981, Irvington, New York.

[8] Lewis interview.

[9] Brenman-Gibson, *Clifford Odets*, 412.

which is not infrequently heard nowadays at orchestral concerts."[10] And Bobby Lewis commented, "This was a good example of Aaron's frugality—he just scooped up all those pages of music and used them later!"[11] Copland maintained friendships with several Group Theatre members for many years—Elia Kazan, Lewis, Odets. He always attended performances in New York, and later, every production Clurman had anything to do with. "I don't remember ever being at a theater without Harold."[12] (In 1980 Copland went to the Harold Clurman Theater for a memorial tribute to his lifelong friend, and as Clurman's associates and friends took the stage to reminisce about him, Copland mused, "Where is Harold? He would enjoy this more than anybody!")

In 1933 even Copland's normally ebullient spirits were low. "This damn Depression!" he wrote to composer Silvestre Revueltas in Mexico. Accepting the invitation to join the League of Composers board in 1932, Copland hoped to implement their programs with music by younger composers, but as he wrote to Chávez (16 December 1933): "It is hard to put new life into the old girl!" Alma Wertheim (now Wiener) turned the Cos Cob Press over to Copland to run for two years on a reduced budget, which allowed for publication of only a few works a year. The fall of the American dollar abroad and the impending threat of Nazism chased composers to the United States, the Europeans running away and the Americans dashing back. No longer was there anyone to study with in Europe. Copland wrote to Chávez: "Everyone is now in New York—Varèse, Antheil, Roy Harris, Sessions, Cowell etc.—but the feeling of camaraderie is not strong. The younger group of composers whom I brought together have even less of an 'esprit de corps.' Last year they were very busy getting famous—this year they are students again, several of them studying with Sessions. . . ." And about conditions at home: "Here in the U.S. we composers have no possibility of directing the musical affairs of the nation—on the contrary, since my return, I have the impression that more and more we are working in a vacuum. There seems to me less than ever a real rapport between the public and the composers and of course that is a very important way of creating an audience, and being in contact with an audience. When one has done that, one can compose with real joy." This increasing discontent with the attitudes toward contemporary music in America opened Copland further to left-wing causes.

The Pierre Degeyter Club (named after the composer of the "Internationale") was a branch of the Workers Music League (the WML, later renamed the American Music League or AML). They were controlled by the Communist-backed International Music Bureau. The Degeyter Club's headquarters were in New York, and there were also branches in Philadelphia and Boston. Under its auspices were choral groups, an orchestra, and a Composers Collective. The Degeyter Club invited Copland to play a recital on 16 March 1934. He asked John Kirkpatrick and a few others to join him. (One work was Kirkpatrick's two-piano arrangement of Copland's *Piano Concerto.*)

[10] Clurman, *The Fervent Years*, 247.

[11] Lewis interview.

[12] Copland to Perlis, December 1976.

Charles Seeger, under the pseudonym of Carl Sands, reviewed the concert in the *Daily Worker*.[13] Copland, in his introductory remarks, had warned the predominantly working-class audience against viewing his compositions from a revolutionary angle. Sands wrote:

> . . . the composer spoke with charming naiveté, claiming that he had not, at the time of their composition, any ideas of that sort in his head. This reviewer held tightly to his seat, waiting for the avalanche to fall, but not one single member of the large audience took him up on the point, which clearly challenges the very basis upon which the club is organized. . . . The issue was all the clearer because the composer's progress from ivory tower to within hailing distance of the proletariat was plainly and graphically told in his music.

What might really have been "naive" was the presentation of such music for an audience, many of whom were hearing their first concert music of any kind. Part way through the difficult *Piano Variations*, several people stomped out. Sands concluded his review: "How about some show there, comrades, of revolutionary discipline, not to speak of courtesy and musical taste?" Undaunted, a few months later on 11 May 1934, Copland presented a symposium with his colleagues Roy Harris, Elie Siegmeister, and Charles Seeger on "The Problems of the Composer in Modern Society."

The Composers Collective[14] was initiated by Jacob Schaefer, Leon Charles, and Henry Cowell after the three had conducted a seminar in the writing of songs for the masses. Although the Collective was under the auspices of the Degeyter Club, the members wanted more independence and a wider membership than the Party-controlled Degeyter Club would allow; they soon made a point of calling themselves the "Composers Collective of New York." There was never a complete break from the parent organization, but friction and disagreements increased during the years of the Collective's existence, from 1931 to 1936.[15] The Degeyter Club was on East 19th Street and the headquarters of the Collective at 47 East 12th; however, the composers usually met Saturday afternoons at 5430 Sixth Avenue in a shabby loft where there was an old upright piano. In a newsletter published by the American Music League, Marc Blitzstein, secretary of the Collective, listed the group's aims:

> the writing of (1) Mass Songs, dealing with immediate social issues . . . to be sung at meetings, on parades, and on picket lines; (2) Choral music for professional as well as non-professional choruses, dealing in a broader way with the social scene. . . . 3) Solo songs, on social themes to be sung at meetings and concentrate the attention on the subjective, private emotions to the exclusion of the realistic social questions. (4) Instrumental music, to carry on the best musical traditions of the past, now threatened by the collapse of bourgeois culture. . .[16]

[13] Carl Sands, "Copeland's [*sic*] Music Recital at Pierre Degeyter Club," in Sands' column The World of Music, *Daily Worker* (New York), 22 March 1934.

[14] See correspondence and notebooks of Marc Blitzstein (Marcus Samuel Blitzstein) and bylaws and minutes of the Executive Committee meetings, State Historical Society of Wisconsin, Madison; David King Dunaway, "Unsung Songs of Protest: The Composers Collective of New York," *New York Folklore*, V: 1 (Summer 1979), 1-19; Barbara Zuck, *A History of Musical Americanism* (Ann Arbor, Michigan: UMI Research Press, 1980); Steven E. Gilbert, " 'In Seventy-Six the Sky Was Red': A Profile of Earl Robinson," lecture delivered to the American Musicological Society, November 1976, Washington, D.C.; and in response to the above, Henry Leland Clarke, "The Composers Collective" (Gilbert and Clarke unpublished).

[15] See Blitzstein Collection.

[16] In *Unison, The Organ of the American Music League*, I:2 (June 1936).

Who belonged to the Composers Collective? In an interview, Charles Seeger answered, "That is what I never say!"[17] A membership list of the Collective is not readily obtainable for several reasons: members have been reluctant to name names; attendance varied from one time to another (for example, Cowell was in at the start and soon out, while Henry Leland Clarke came into the Collective in the late fall of 1934); and several participants took pseudonyms, adding to the confusion. Clarke points out, "It was dangerous to belong to the Collective, and even more dangerous later on to have been connected with it."[18] Clarke took the pseudonym Jonathan Fairbanks, and Elie Siegmeister recalls, "I took the name L. E. Swift, but sometimes I'd forget which name I was using. One time I was listed on a program as Swift conducting the Daily Workers Chorus in an arrangement by Siegmeister!"[19] Marc Blitzstein's minutes from meetings in the spring and summer of 1935 list the Executive Committee of the Collective as Sands, Chair; Swift, Treasurer; Blitzstein, Secretary; and George Maynard.[20] Blitzstein made a distinction between regular members and sympathetic composers; among the latter, "Aaron Copland, who came into a meeting (11 April 1935) for five minutes. . ." Hanns Eisler was the member most strongly affiliated with the Communist Party. He attended meetings of the Collective when he was in New York. According to Clarke, "[Lan] Adomyan was the spearhead of the group and a strong follower of Eisler, but he went off to Spain in the Lincoln Brigade." Jacob Schaefer, older than most of the composers in the Collective, headed a Jewish chorus, the Freiheit Gesang Farein, and a mandolin orchestra. Schaefer was critical of the regulars for writing music too difficult for his workers to sing and play. Earl Robinson said, "We spent an awful lot of time talking about whether pure music, that is, instrumental music, could be useful for our purposes. I said no, and Seeger agreed with me. None of us used folk music at all until he and I started pushing it in 1934 and '35. . ."[21] And Clarke considers that the Collective may have been the start of socially significant folk song in America.

The *Workers Song Book No. 1* (1934) and *Songs of the People* were published by the Workers Music League. Composers included were Carl Sands (Seeger), L. E. Swift (Siegmeister), Jacob Schaefer, Lan Adomyan, Janet Barnes (Jeannette Barnett), Jonathan Fairbanks (Clarke), Copland, Earl Robinson, Hanns Eisler, Stefan Volpe (Wolpe), Karl Vollmer, S. C. Richards (Riegger), A. Davidenko, and George Maynard. *Workers Song Book No. 1* was reviewed by Copland in the *New Masses*. He called it "... the first adequate collection of revolutionary songs for American workers." In assessing the songs, Copland noted, "On the whole, Carl Sands seems to me to have written the best songs. . . These may not be great songs, but they display a directness of attack and a sure technical grasp which is refreshing. . ."[22]

[17] Interview, Charles Seeger with Perlis, Oral History of American Music, Yale, 16 March 1970, Bridgewater, Ct.

.[18] Interviews, Henry Leland Clarke with Perlis, by telephone, 14 May 1982 and 15 September 1983.

[19] Interview, Elie Siegmeister with Perlis, by telephone, 10 November 1982.

[20] In a letter from George Maynard to Vivian Perlis on 10 June 1982: "He [Copland] was a delightful chap, slightly Communized as we all were in those days when we were young and Soviet Russia was idealized."

[21] Interviews, Earl Robinson with Perlis, by telephone, 12 November 1982 and 16 February 1984. (Robinson became famous for his "Ballad for Americans," as sung by Paul Robeson.)

[22] Aaron Copland, "Workers Sing!", *New Masses*, XI: 9 (5 June 1934), 28-29.

Charles Seeger (Sands)[23]

Henry Cowell took me around to this composers' group and I lectured on the dictatorship of the linguistic—making fun, of course, of the dictatorship of the proletariat. I said, "Now, it's all right for you people who are interested in things like that, but what dictates the proletariat? It's language. And they are absolutely in the thrall of language. They may think they can get free of the bosses, and perhaps they will, but the bosses are enthralled with language too. Everybody is. And then if you straighten that out, this theory of yours—Marxism doesn't make sense." Well, they were very nice about it and they said, "Of course, we don't agree with what you said, but what you said is very interesting." In other words, they wanted to get me in! So I joined.

The Composers Collective met every week, wintertime, composing songs for the labor movement. It was Communist-controlled. We had a competition for a May Day song in '34. The words were submitted to a committee first and were published in the old New Masses, *and then a committee was appointed to receive the settings of it. And I was chairman of the meeting which went over the final songs, words and music, so that I spoke last. And of course Aaron Copland won the prize. He wrote a beautiful song. It really was a splendid thing. It was magnificent. We all agreed. We criticized everybody's contribution, and they criticized themselves— true Communist style (as far as I know there was only one real Communist member there, Marc Blitzstein). Henry was out by this time. In California, I think. Also, he wasn't too interested. . . . It came to me, and I criticized my piece. "You know, I'll agree that mine is just about the worst of the whole lot, but I'll put it to you this way," I said to Copland. "Everybody here knows that your song is best. But do you think it will ever be sung on the picket line? And anyway, who would carry a piano into the streets May First or any time?" Well, Aaron was very nice and he said, "No, I don't suppose it ever will be sung in a picket line." He'd made some freak modulations, and some big skips of sevenths in it, had some dissonances, key changes all over the place. "Well," I said, "take mine, for instance. I haven't tried to make a piece of music I admire. I tried to write a piece of music that I think might be sung on the picket line. Do you think there is anybody in New York who couldn't join in with this the second time they hear it?"*

Copland's song "Into the Streets May First!" was set to a poem by Alfred Hayes provided by the Collective. After the contest, the song was published in the *New Masses*[24] and later in the *Workers Songbook No. 2* (1935). An article by Ashley Pettis preceded the music in the magazine: "The *New Masses* feel that the time is ripe for the development of music by the various composers of America for the constantly increasing number of singing workers; a music which is characteristic of them, truly representative of their awakening consciousness and growing power; of their determination and hopes. With this in mind, Alfred Hayes' poem 'Into the Streets May First!' was sent out to the Composers Collective of the Pierre Degeyter Club, New York, as well as to a group comprising some of the most accomplished musicians of America."[25] Pettis listed the contributors: "Lahn Adohmyan,

[23] Seeger interview.

[24] *New Masses*, XI:5 (1 May 1934), 16-17.

[25] Ashley Pettis, "Marching With a Song," *New Masses*, XI:5 (1 May 1934), 5.

Aaron Copland, Isadore Freed, Wallingford Riegger, Carl Sands, Mitya Stillman, L. E. Swift, and one composer who conceals his identity under the nom de plume "XYZ" Pettis discussed each song and gave reasons for the committee's unanimous choice of Copland's. Earl Robinson recalls, "We *agreed*, but we all commiserated over Aaron's song." Pettis wrote as if to prepare his readers: "Its spirit is identical with that of the poem. The unfamiliar, 'experimental' nature of the harmonies which occur occasionally, does not tend to make the unsophisticated singer question. . . Some of the intervals may be somewhat difficult upon a first hearing or singing, but we believe the ear will very readily accustom itself to their sound." Pettis announced that the song would be performed by the Workers Music League at their Second Annual American Workers Music Olympiad (29 April 1934). "The entire ensemble of 800 voices, comprising the revolutionary workers' choruses of New York will participate. . ."

In 1935 Earl Robinson won a competition sponsored by the left-wing Downtown Music School. The prize was free lessons donated by composer Aaron Copland. "Aaron was a wonderful teacher," claimed Robinson. "He never would say how to compose, but when I brought in a jazz-style fugue, he'd play Milhaud's *Création du monde* to demonstrate the use of jazz in concert music. In the summers I went to the Party Camp, Unity Camp. While there in 1936 I composed two songs—'Joe Hill' and 'Old Abe Lincoln,' and I showed them to Aaron. He seemed impressed with the alternation of song and speech in 'Abe,' and with the phrase, 'and these are the words he said.' (Aaron may also have heard my 'Ballad for Americans' in '38 or '39, which includes the same section from Gettysburg Address used by Aaron in *Lincoln Portrait*, and the spoken words, 'Abraham Lincoln said that on November 19, 1863.') When Aaron was composing *Lincoln Portrait*, he said to me, 'Earl, I'm stealing some of your thunder.'"[26]

"Into the Streets May First" as published in *The New Masses,* 1 May 1934

Copland contributed occasional articles and performances to left-wing organizations in the spring of 1935. These articles could hardly be called agitprop. In one, the first issue of *Music Vanguard*, featuring Hanns Eisler on the German workers' music movement, Copland almost seemed to be taking an anti-Party line. He wrote, "The young composer who allies himself with the proletarian movement must do so not with the feeling that he has found an easy solution, but with a full realization of what such a step means, if his work is to be of permanent value to the workers and their cause. . . . But as for myself, I admit to a certain uneasiness of feeling until that 'first symphony,' quintet or proletarian oratorio is forthcoming."[27] A "Gedenkschrift" for Hanns Eisler compiled 17 April 1935 by Seeger included a "Sketch for a Worker's Song" by Copland. Also, in *The American Mercury,* in an issue featuring Emma Goldman on communism in Russia, Copland wrote a straightforward report on a resurgence of activity in American music, with this warning: "It is not even now appreciated that a serious and important type of composer functions among us; nor, as a man, is he properly understood. . . . It cannot be doubted that he occupies little or no place even today in the mind of the public at large."[28] Copland was caught in the dilemma of wanting to reach the "people," but not wanting to use his own music for propaganda. He was not the only composer to face this problem—members of the Collective debated it often, and Henry Cowell and Wallingford Riegger were even less interested than Copland in adapting or changing their music-writing skills and talents to suit Party songs and marches.

The summer of 1934 held an unexpected political experience. When Copland's cousin, Leo Harris, offered him a rent-free cottage on a lake in Minnesota, he accepted, thinking that a period of isolation from the musical, political, and social pressures of New York would be beneficial. Copland and Victor Kraft drove to Lavinia, Minnesota, to the cottage on Lake Bemidji. From there Copland wrote to Roger Sessions that it offered all the advantages of an art colony with none of the disadvantages. He settled down to work on *Statements for Orchestra,* moving ahead steadily to orchestrate five of the projected seven movements. When Victor and Aaron drove into town, they saw Swedes, Germans, radical farmers, tourists, Indians, and lumberjacks coming in and out of Bemidji. One day Victor was amazed to see a little wizened woman selling the *Daily Worker* on a street corner. Then they attended a picnic supper hosted by "red" farmers. Copland wrote to Israel Citkowitz (summer 1934):

[26] Robinson interview.

[27] Aaron Copland, "A Note on Young Composers," *Music Vanguard*, I:1 (March-April 1935), 14-16.

[28] Aaron Copland, "The American Composer Gets a Break," *The American Mercury,* XXXIV:136 (April 1935), 488-92.

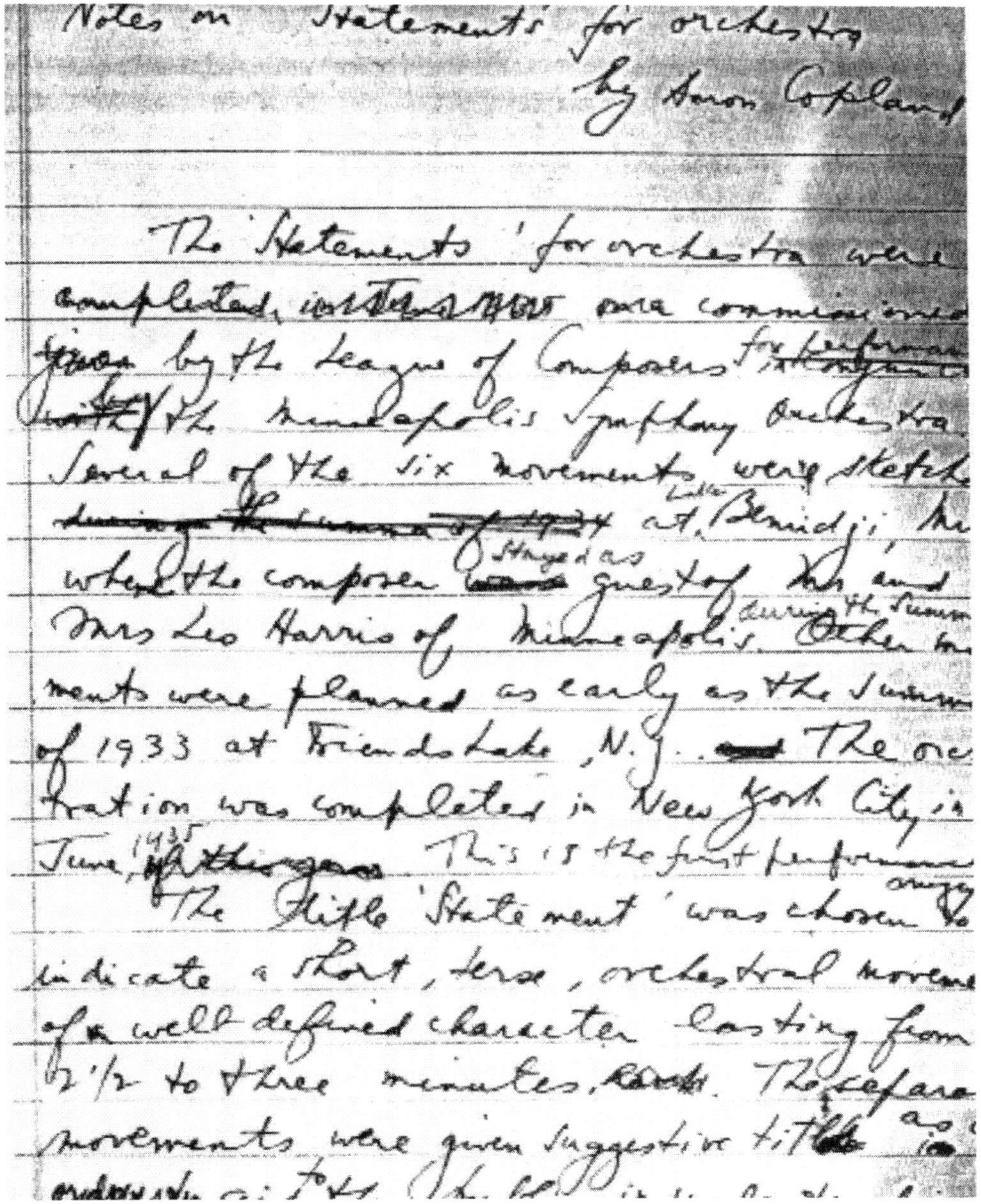
Notes on 'Statements' for orchestra
by Aaron Copland

The 'Statements' for orchestra were completed on a commission given by the League of Composers for performance by the Minneapolis Symphony Orchestra. Several of the six movements were sketched at Lake Bemidji, Minn. where the composer stayed as guest of Mr and Mrs Leo Harris of Minneapolis during the summer. Other movements were planned as early as the summer of 1933 at Friends Lake, N.Y. The orchestration was completed in New York City in June, 1935. This is the first performance.

The title 'Statement' was chosen to indicate a short, terse, orchestral movement of a well defined character lasting from 2 1/2 to three minutes. The separate movements were given suggestive titles as

Aaron Copland's notes on
Statements for Orchestra 1933

> If they were a strange sight to me, I was no less of one to them. It was the first time that many of them had seen an "intellectual!" . . . I wish you could have seen them—the true Third Estate, the very material that makes revolution. What struck me particularly was the fact that there is no "type-communist" among them, such as we see on 4th St. They look like any other of the farmers around here, all of them individuals, clearly etched in my mind. And desperately poor. None can afford more than a 10 cent pamphlet. (With that in mind I appealed to the Group for funds and they sent me a collection of $30 which I presented to the unit here for their literature fund.)

When the farmers asked Copland to talk to the crowd, he at first demurred, but later accepted, making his one and only political speech to farmers in Bemidji, Minnesota.

Copland's political contributions included an occasional benefit performance. On 17 May 1936 at the first Festival of the American Music League, were represented seventeen organizations, among them German, Italian, and Lithuanian choruses, the Fur Workers' Chorus singing in Yiddish, the Freiheit Mandolin Orchestra, along with many individuals. Copland was featured as "one of America's outstanding composers, performing his 'Children's Pieces for Piano.'" [29]

That Copland's music was influenced by the social and political climate cannot be discounted. Convinced that the American people could be reached by good new music, over and over again he asked audiences to open their minds, to "take off the ear muffs," to be less conservative, to give music a chance. He took great pains to teach and to write "what to listen for in music." It was only fair, he considered, that in return the composer meet his audience part way. The challenge was to find a way without sacrificing musical values. Copland wrote, "To compose music of 'socialist realism' has stumped even so naturally gifted a man as Shostakovitch."[30] Never again would Copland attempt to reach a more popular audience with a "workers' song" or for political reasons. When the Popular Front came along in 1935 bringing a wider recognition and appreciation of American folk music, the way was opened for Copland to adopt a simpler, more direct musical style using quotation or simulation of folk tunes in productions outside the concert hall—ballet, theater, radio, and film. Copland was again about to set out in a new direction; as before, the change would not be abrupt or exclusive. For over a year, he worked concurrently on *Statements for Orchestra* and *El Salón México*, the former in his "old" austere style, the latter, the first of the "new" popular works. While he was so occupied at Lake Bemidji, a request came from Ruth Page in Chicago for music for a ballet. Copland wrote to Chávez (15 October 1935): "I almost had two new orchestral works finished when I had to interrupt them to do a ballet to be performed at the Chicago Opera in November. . . ."

[29] As announced in *Unison, The Organ of the American Music League,* I: 2 (June 1936).

[30] Aaron Copland, "1936: America's Young Men—Ten Years Later," *Modern Music.* Repr. in *Copland On Music,* 160.

MUSIC FOR THE PEOPLE

1934 - 1937

Ruth Page was ballet director of the Chicago Grand Opera Company and a well-known dancer and choreographer. When she produced ballets for her own company, the Ruth Page Ballets, she often commissioned music by contemporary composers. Ruth had heard my jazzy *Music for the Theatre,* so she invited me to compose music for a ballet about murder in a nightclub. It was late August 1934; the ballet was scheduled for November. Victor and I drove from Lake Bemidji to Duluth and took a train to Chicago. I discussed the proposal with Ruth and with Nicholas Remisoff, who was to design the staging and costumes. The ballet, *Hear Ye! Hear Ye!,* was to take place in a courtroom, and the plot consisted of three witnesses giving highly divergent accounts of the same nightclub murder; *Hear Ye! Hear Ye!* was a *Rashomon* type of story.[1] Ruth, who was married to a lawyer, wrote the scenario. The idea sounded dramatic, different, and lively. It would be my first experience writing music for a ballet and knowing in advance that it would actually be staged. After a week of discussions, I signed on the dotted line and dashed back to Bemidji to get to work on the ballet, putting *Statements* and *El Salón México* aside for the time being.

Ruth had given me the scenario and "some suggestions to the composer." The cast of characters was as follows: the judge, prosecuting and defense attorneys, six masked jurymen, a crowd of marionettes, twelve chorus girls, a nightclub hostess (Mae West type), her maid, a honeymoon couple, a Negro waiter, a cabaret dancer (Ruth Page), a male dancer, a jealous chorus girl, and a maniac. I was expected to write an overture, several jazz-influenced dances, and various special effects. After five weeks, I returned to Chicago with a working score of forty minutes of music[2]— most of it new, some of it drawn from my earlier ballet *Grohg.* Ruth put me up at her house on Lake Michigan so that we could work closely together. I finished the orchestral score and turned it over to the conductor, Rudolph Ganz, a few weeks before the premiere on 30 November. The day after the opening, the Chicago *Herald* reported: "It was an exciting night at the Opera last night when for the first time a whole evening was devoted to ballet. . . . It was a full house. . . . There was, of course, a great deal of discussion about *Hear Ye! Hear Ye!* the new ballet, which had its premiere. . . ." The program consisted of *La Guiablesse* (music by William Grant Still), danced by Katherine Dunham and an all-black dance group; the premiere of *Hear Ye!*; the premiere of *Gold Standard* (music by Jacques Ibert); and *Iberian Monotone* (to Ravel's *Bolero*), danced by Ruth Page.

Remisoff had designed flashy costumes and vivid effects for *Hear Ye!*[3] During the overture, a movie projector flashed lurid headlines onto a large overhead screen: "RED-HOT JAZZ!" "MURDER!" "GUILTY!" The music incorporated segments of "The Star Spangled Banner," distorted to convey the corruption of legal systems and courts of law. For a bride and groom scene, I prepared a parody of Mendelssohn's "Wedding March." It seemed an effective way to emphasize the cynicism behind the innocence of newlyweds amid white doves and flowers. And for the doves, I composed a flowing flute passage in descending thirds. The ballet ended with the judge going berserk and the opposing lawyers gaily leaving the stage arm-in-arm to the dissonant "Star Spangled Banner." The gala evening was topped off with an elegant supper party thrown by Harold McCormick at the Electric Club, known for its spectacular view of the city. *Hear Ye!* was repeated in Chicago a few weeks later, and Ruth retained it in the repertoire for several seasons. I conducted it myself in New York on 1 and 2 March 1936.

In Chicago the reviews had centered on Ruth Page and the dancers; later, Cecil Michener Smith wrote: "Certainly the music is thoroughly representative of the American scene, and makes no obsequious bows toward any foreign authority."[4] New York criticisms varied. Jerome D. Bohm in the *Herald Tribune*: "The idea is fraught with

[1] Interview, Ruth Page with Perlis, by telephone, 29 November 1982.

[2] A two-piano arrangement was donated to Lincoln Center Library by Ruth Page. In Copland's files are a rough pencil score, a small orchestral one made in 1935, and an incomplete ink score of three cabaret dances. Conductors' scores are at Library of Congress.

[3] For a stage design by Remisoff for *Hear Ye!,* see *Modern Music,* X11:1 (November-December 1934), 18.

[4] Cecil Michener Smith, "Copland's 'Hear Ye! Hear Ye!,'" *Modern Music,* XII: 2 (January-February 1935), 86-89.

possibilities for excitement which are never quite realized; but for those who had never attended one of Minsky's burlesques, there was a suggestively attired and writhing bevy of chorus girls and Miss Page's own costume was perhaps a trifle more immodest than necessity demanded. . . ." And W. J. Henderson in the *Sun*: "The music by Mr. Copland demonstrated again that composer's instinct for the theater. He has made a score which perfectly fits the story and the action. It has a modernist sting in harmony and pungent rhythm, and its incursions into the realm of jazz are made with the certainty of a musician who knows his way about the town." Soon after the Chicago premiere, I wrote to Chávez (31 December 1934): 'It was an experience for me to hear my music with stage action. Now I should like to write an opera, or at any rate, more music for the stage."

I arranged a suite from the ballet that was performed at an all-Copland concert sponsored by the WPA Composers Forum–Laboratory in 1937, but I decided to give it up, drawing from the suite only one section that became Blues No. 2 in my *Four Piano Blues*. I prefer that the original ballet score remain unpublished. The music was really incidental to the dance, and I have discovered that some music is more incidental than other music! Nevertheless, Ruth Page's ballet was important as my first collaborative experience of this kind, and it left me open to other offers for ballets that would be central to my musical life in the next decade. In more practical terms, it was satisfying for me, a slow writer, to produce a successful score in so short a time.

While I was in Chicago I received an interesting letter from Walter Piston (15 November 1934): "What would be your reaction toward the possibility of teaching my composition class at Harvard during the second half-year?" The idea of teaching at Harvard was an impressive one to a fellow who had never gone to college. I wrote to Paul Bowles (8 January 1935): "I think it is very brave of them to have me, don't you?" Little did I realize what enduring benefits would come from teaching at Harvard. Years later I met Douglas Moore for lunch at the Harvard Club in New York. I looked around wistfully, commenting, "I wish I could belong to a place like this!" My friend asked why I didn't join, and I said, "Don't be silly—I never even went to college." "Don't you be silly," responded Douglas. "You taught at Harvard!" Next thing I knew I was signed in as a member of the Harvard Club, and I have used it as my home-away-from-home since I moved to the country.

In February of 1935 I got off the train in Boston and was put up temporarily at Harvard's Eliot House in Cambridge. I wrote to Victor Kraft (3 February 1935): "About 300 boys live here, eat here, etc. Rather exclusive and expensive, and of course very plain. I have nine boys in my class and one girl from Radcliffe." My teaching duties were not demanding—only three hours a week on Tuesdays and Thursdays. I enjoyed the students and was delighted to see Koussevitzky and attend rehearsals of the orchestra. After settling into rooms at 15 Sumner Road, I was able to teach a few private students. One, Mrs. Eda Rapaport, said, "Please make my lessons a little modernistic." While in Cambridge I saw quite a lot of Arthur Berger and got to know a few Harvard music professors—Hugo Leichtentritt and Edward Burlingame Hill, whom I had met earlier at Fontainebleau. And I attended lectures by Alfred North Whitehead on the subject of "Time." When I returned to New York, I had no permanent home, so between leaving Harvard and going to the MacDowell Colony I stayed at Alma Wertheim's apartment on 57th Street and Second Avenue. There I completed the orchestration of *Statements for Orchestra*, dedicating the piece to Mary Churchill. It was used to satisfy a commission from the League of Composers for a new orchestral work to be played by the Minneapolis Symphony under the baton of a young conductor named Eugene Ormandy.

The title, *Statements for Orchestra*, was chosen to indicate terse, short movements of well-defined character lasting only about three minutes. Instead of the original plan for seven short movements, *Statements* was finished with six. Each was given an additional title as an aid to the public in understanding what I had in mind when writing the movements: "Militant" is based on a single theme announced in unison by three flutes, two oboes, bassoon, and strings; "Cryptic" is orchestrated for brass and flute alone, with an occasional use of bass clarinet and bassoon; "Dogmatic" is an allegro in tripartite form, the mid-section quoting from my *Piano Variations*; "Subjective" is the final resting place of *Elegies for Violin and Viola* and is scored for strings without double basses; "Jingo," utilizing the full orchestra, is in rondo form on a chromatic melody with occasional bows to a well-known tune, "The Sidewalks of New York"; and the final section, "Prophetic," is rhapsodic in form and centers on a chorale-like melody sung by the solo trumpet. Occasionally, only four of the six statements are programmed, as in a concert in honor of my seventy-fifth birthday at Alice Tully Hall when Dennis Russell Davies chose to conduct I, IV, V, and VI; at other times, only the first four are played. This strikes me as somewhat ironic, considering that only the last two movements were played for the premiere of *Statements* in Minneapolis—first on an NBC network broadcast on 9 January 1936 and then at a symphony concert on 21 February 1936. My music was again considered "too difficult," although *Statements for Orchestra* is not nearly so demanding for performers as the *Short Symphony*. *Statements* was not heard in its entirety until 1942, when Dimitri Mitropoulos conducted it with the New York Philharmonic.

Of all the reviews, I am most fond of Virgil's, printed in the *Herald Tribune* following the concert of 7 January 1942: "Aaron Copland's six shortish pieces grouped together under the name of 'Statements' are succinct and stylish music. They are clearly written and very, very personal. . . The whole group is a manly bouquet, fresh and sweet and sincere and frank and straightforward. . . . They were admirably played, too, the dryness of Mitropoulos' interpretation suiting to a T that of the Copland musical style." Subsequently, I conducted the work for a recording with the London Symphony Orchestra. To my disappointment, *Statements* remains one of my lesser-known scores.

In the summer of 1935 I was assigned the very same studio at the MacDowell Colony that I had in 1925, and I was struck by the fact that it had been ten years since my first visit. I worked on *El Salón México* and wrote a chorus for the Henry Street Music School where I was teaching part time. They had asked for a work that could be sung by the Girls' Glee Club. The result was "What Do We Plant?," a short and simple setting of a text by Henry Abbey for soprano and alto voices with piano accompaniment. I have always liked the idea of young people singing and playing my music. After all, they grow up and become our audiences. That summer I also composed two piano pieces for a collection Lazare Saminsky and Isadore Freed were editing for Carl Fischer.[5] *Sunday Afternoon Music* and *The Young Pioneers* are again short (two and three pages respectively) and easy to play, while still introducing young ears to the contemporary idiom. The title *The Young Pioneers* has a double meaning, for I had in mind instilling in young piano students the courage to attempt music that is somewhat "modern." After the collection of these piano pieces was played in 1936, Lehman Engel wrote, "Here is real and welcome *Gebrauchsmusik* for America. . . ."[6] My interest in composing for young people escalated to the point where I was considering a suggestion made by Grace Spofford, head of the Henry Street Settlement, that I write an opera for high school students. I wrote to Chávez from the MacDowell Colony (28 August 1935):

> It becomes increasingly difficult to have the sense that there is any public for our music—the public that can afford to pay for concerts is quite simply not interested. . . . In a period of such economic and general social tension music itself seems unimportant—at least to those middle class people who up to now have been our audiences. Is it the same in Mexico? Also, this has personal repercussions. It is no longer easy to be published (the Cos Cob has discontinued publishing for a year already and I don't know when they will resume)—I must make some money in order to live which uses up much valuable time and energy. I mention all these things not to give you the idea that I am discouraged in any essential way, but merely to show you that I have good reasons to feel sympathetic with your own struggles. It is just in such times as these that friends like we are should encourage and sustain each other. . .

Also from the Colony in the summer of 1935, I wrote to Victor Kraft, then working in Chicago: "There are no famous 'names' at MacDowell this summer. It is a good place to work—there's simply nothing else to do!" In midsummer two young composer friends arrived, Nicolas ("Nicky") Slonimsky and David Diamond.

In the fall of 1935 my cousin Percy Uris loaned me a small apartment at the Hotel Lafayette on 9th Street and University Place. After a few months I moved into another Uris building at 1 University Place where Odets was living. I was occupied with producing a special concert series of five evenings, each one devoted entirely to the music of an

[5] *Masters of Our Day*, ed. Lazare Saminsky and Isadore Freed (New York: Carl Fischer, 1943). The album includes pieces by Copland, Cowell, Freed, Hanson, Milhaud, Moore, Sessions, Taylor, Thompson, and Thomson. Copland's two works are also published individually.

[6] Lehman Engel, "New Laboratories and Gebrauchsmusik," *Modern Music*, XIII: 3 (March-April 1936), 53.

Manuscript: first page from the ink score of *El Salón México*

American composer. Included were Harris, Thomson, Sessions, Piston, and myself—what Virgil called "America's up-and-at-'em commando unit."[7] At Mary Lescaze's suggestion, I had written to a patroness, Mrs. Leonard Elmhirst, pointing out that rarely had there been "one-man concerts" of American music, though it was commonplace for painters to hold one-man shows. I explained that the New School was offering their auditorium without a fee, and admission was to be $1 with receipts to be equally divided between the school and the composer of the evening. I asked Mrs. Elmhirst to contribute $1,000 for performers' fees. Once granted, I set to work on programs and arrangements. Since I had been away all summer and the first concert was scheduled for 11 October, my own evening would have to come first. I sent an urgent request to John Kirkpatrick (15 September 1935): "Can you help me out? Mrs. Luening is to do the Song Group on the 11th, but all 3 songs are in storage! Could you bring with you: Old Poem, Pastorale, and Vocalise?"

I counted on John for much more than the scores—in fact, he was the featured performer of the evening, playing my *Piano Variations*, and with me, his two-piano arrangements of the *Symphonic Ode* and *El Salón México*, which was not yet finished in its orchestration. (I had sent John the first part in September, while still working on the orchestration.) One reviewer commented that it was easy to understand why concertgoers would go to *Porgy and Bess* and stay away from a concert like mine "by the hundreds of thousands, which is why Mr. Copland's music is not performed more frequently than it is." Evidently my reputation as a wild-eyed modernist was still secure! On the final concert of 6 December I had planned to play Walter Piston's two-piano arrangement of his *Piano Concerto* with Kirkpatrick. But I wrote to John (7 November 1935): "After due consideration I've decided that the Piston oeuvre is beyond my powers—pianistically speaking. Unless you have any violent objections I plan to invite Miss Gertrude Bonime, who recently played and played well at Virgil's WPA concert to take my place. This hurts me more than it does you." As I looked around at the all-too-familiar small group at these concerts, I knew that I wanted to see a larger and more varied audience for contemporary music.

I was already "experimenting" with a different style of writing in two compositions, *El Salón México* in its finishing stages, and a high school opera. I had no thought of rejecting one kind of music for another—only the feeling that it was time to try something new. *El Salón México* had been "in the works" since my first trip to Mexico in 1932 when I came away from that colorful dance hall in Mexico City with Chávez. I had read about the hall for the first time in a guidebook about tourist entertainment: "Harlem type night-club for the peepul, grand Cuban orchestra, Salón México. Three halls: one for people dressed in your way, one for people dressed in overalls but shod, and one for the barefoot." A sign on a wall of the dance hall read: "Please don't throw lighted cigarette butts on the floor so the ladies don't burn their feet." A guard, stationed at the bottom of the steps leading to the three halls, would nonchalantly frisk you as you started up the stairs to be sure you had checked all your "artillery" at the door and to collect the 1 peso charged for admittance to any of the three halls. When the dance hall closed at 5:00 A.M., it hardly seemed worthwhile to some of the overalled patrons to travel all the way home, so they curled themselves up on chairs around the walls for a quick two-hour snooze before going to a seven o'clock job in the morning.

I realized that it would be foolish for me to attempt to translate some of the more profound sides of Mexico into musical sounds—the ancient civilizations or the revolutionary Mexico of our own time—for that, one really had to know a country well. But my thoughts kept returning to that dance hall. It wasn't so much the music or the dances that attracted me as the spirit of the place. In some inexplicable way, while milling about in those crowded halls, I had felt a live contact with the Mexican "people"—that electric sense one gets sometimes in far-off places, of suddenly knowing the essence of a people—their humanity, their shyness, their dignity and unique charm. I remember quite well that it was at such a moment I conceived the idea of composing a piece about Mexico and naming it *El Salón México*. But to have an idea for a piece of music is far from having the piece itself! I began (as I often did) by collecting musical themes or tunes out of which a composition might eventually emerge. It seemed natural to use popular Mexican melodies for thematic material; after all, Chabrier and Debussy didn't hesitate to help themselves to the melodic riches of Spain. There was no reason I should not use the tunes of the hispanic land on our southern doorstep. My purpose was not merely to quote literally, but to heighten without in any way falsifying the natural simplicity of Mexican tunes.

Frances Toor, a resident American in Mexico City, had published an unpretentious little collection, *Cancionero Mexicano*.[8] I used tunes from that and from an erudite book by Rubén M. Campos, *El Folklore y la Musica Mexicana*.[9] "El Mosco" is the most direct quotation of a complete melody. I also used "El Palo Verde," "La Jesusita," and "La Malacate." If quotation of folk tunes is a sure way for a composer to translate the flavor of a foreign people into musical terms, it also presents a formal problem when used in a symphonic composition. Most composers have found that there is little that can be done with such material except repeat it. In *El Salón México* I decided to use a modified potpourri in which the Mexican themes or fragments and extensions thereof are sometimes inextricably mixed. For example, before the final climax I present the folk tunes simultaneously in their original keys and rhythms. The result is a kind of polytonality that achieves the frenetic whirl I had in mind before the end, when all is resolved with a plain unadorned triad.

I wrote to Chávez about *El Salón México* with some embarrassment (15 October 1932): "I am terribly afraid of what you will say of the 'Salón México'—perhaps

[7] Thomson, *Virgil Thomson*, 254.

[8] Copland's copy, given him by Toor in Mexico City in 1932, is with Copland's manuscripts at the Library of Congress. *Cancionero Mexicano de Mexican Folkways*, ed. by Frances Toor, illustrations by Rufino Tamayo (Mexico: Toor, ca.1931).

[9] Rubén M. Campos, *El Folklore y la Musica Mexicana*, Publicaciones de la secretaria de education publica (Mexico: Talleres graficos de la nacion, 1928).

it is not Mexican at all, and I would feel so foolish. But in America del Norte it may sound Mexican!" And again (28 August 1935): "What it would sound like in Mexico I can't imagine, but everyone here for whom I have played it seems to think it is very gay and amusing." Oddly enough, this composition celebrating Mexico was completed in Bemidji, Minnesota. My Mexican impressions must have been very strong ones! Other projects intervened, so the orchestration was not fully completed until 1936, two years after Bemidji, when I was again in Mexico with Victor. (*El Salón México* is dedicated to Victor Kraft.) To my great relief, when I played it for Chávez in New York, he asked to conduct it after the orchestration was finished. The world premiere was in Mexico City on 27 August 1937, Chávez conducting the Orquesta Sinfónica de Mexico at the Palacio de Bellas Artes. Despite Chávez' enthusiasm, I still felt nervous about what the Mexicans might think of a "gringo" meddling with their native melodies. At the first of the final rehearsals that I attended, an unexpected incident took place that completely reassured me. As I entered the hall the orchestral players, who were in the thick of a Beethoven symphony, suddenly stopped what they were doing and began to applaud vigorously. What they were expressing, I soon realized, was not so much their appreciation of one composer's work, as their pleasure and pride in the fact that a foreign composer had found their own familiar tunes worthy of treatment.

I was moved by that gesture, and the reviews that appeared in the newspapers after the premiere were no less kind. They all seemed to agree that *El Salón México* might well be taken for Mexican music—"as Mexican as the music of Revueltas," which was like saying at that time, "as American as the music of Gershwin." The only typical Mexican percussion instrument I asked for in the score was the gourd. There have been times when no one seemed to know where to find a gourd. One such instance was in London in July 1938 at the sixteenth ISCM Festival with Sir Adrian Boult conducting. Also, I requested that the traditional orchestral E-flat clarinet play with the flavor of a native Mexican instrument. At the first American performance of *El Salón México* on 14 October that same year, the BSO clarinetist Rosario Mazzeo under Koussevitzky's direction handled this wonderfully, as he did on the recording for Victor Records in 1939. *El Salón* was not easy to perform; it presented rhythmic intricacies for the conductor and the players.

The 1938 ISCM concert in London turned out to be an important occasion for me. It was there I first met Benjamin Britten, and it was Ben who introduced and recommended me to Ralph Hawkes of the British publishing firm, Boosey & Hawkes. Mr. Hawkes offered to publish one work, I asked him to take three; we settled on two. Later, I signed permanently with Boosey & Hawkes. I have been very satisfied with this arrangement, though at times I wonder at someone like me, so involved with American music, having a British music publisher! In New York Hans Heinsheimer was working for Boosey, Hawkes, Belwin, Inc. (as it was then named in America). Business was very slow, according to Heinsheimer,[10] so when Ralph Hawkes sent fifty copies of *El Salón México,* Heinsheimer was delighted. He called my piece an "American Bolero" and proceeded to fill orders for scores and rental parts that soon came in from all over. One year after publication in 1938, Boosey put together a list of orchestras that had played *El Salón México*: fourteen American orchestras ranging from the BSO to the Women's Symphony in Chicago; two radio orchestras; and five foreign ensembles. Never in my wildest dreams did I expect this kind of acceptance for the piece![11]

Boosey & Hawkes, wanting to make the most from this unexpected windfall, suggested a piano arrangement. Heinsheimer asked me to recommend someone who could do it quickly and cheaply. I suggested a young musician who had just come to town. According to Heinsheimer: "The young man was also badly in need of money and would therefore do the job for a really miserable fee. This, of course, clinched the deal. We asked Copland to go ahead and order it and after a few days a young Adonis delivered the arrangement, played it brilliantly and convincingly on what was alleged to be a piano ... and left, happily, with his little check. His name is still to be found on the piano version of *El Salón México*. The young man was Leonard Bernstein."[12] Lenny also made a two-piano arrangement.[13] My first meeting with him was on my thirty-seventh birthday, when he was a student at Harvard. We both happened to be at a dance recital by Anna Sokolow in New York. I invited him along with a few friends to the loft afterward for an impromptu party. When Lenny heard *El Salón México* at its first performance by the BSO in 1938, he sensed what I was after and wrote (20 October 1938): "I wish these people could see that a composer is just as serious when he writes a work, even if the piece is not defeatist (that Worker word again) and Weltschmerzy and misanthropic and long. . . ."

El Salón México caught on quickly, and it started the ball rolling toward the popular success and wide audience I had only just begun to think about. Toscanini conducted *El Salón* in a broadcast with the NBC Symphony Orchestra on 14 March 1942.[14] (I was amazed when Walter Toscanini found a piano arrangement of it among his father's papers; he sent me a photocopy in 1961.) Lenny conducted *El Salón* for the New York Philharmonic Young People's Concerts; I particularly recall one such performance on my sixtieth birthday. The score has also been used by several choreographers—among them, Doris Humphrey, José Limón, and most recently Eliot Feld for *La Vida*. *El Salón* was adapted by Johnny Green for a film released in the United States by MGM as *Fiesta* starring Esther Williams and Ricardo Montalban, and in Italy as *La Matadora*. The published piano version of his adaptation is called *Fantasia Mexicana*. *El Salón* was also

[10] Hans Heinsheimer, *Best Regards to Aida* (New York: Alfred A. Knopf, 1968), 170-72, and interview with Perlis, 21 May 1981, New York City.

[11] Copland wrote about *El Salón México* after it was recorded: Aaron Copland: "The Story Behind *El Salón México*," *Victor Record Review*, 1:12 (1939), 4-5.

[12] Heinsheimer, *Best Regards to Aida*, 172.

[13] Kirkpatrick's earlier two-piano version is in his private collection. Bernstein was invited by Boosey & Hawkes to adapt his solo piano arrangemenent for the published two-piano version.

[14] See Robert Charles Marsh, *Toscanini and the Art of Orchestral Performance* (Philadelphia: J. B. Lippincott, 1956), Appendix. This was the only performance of a piece by Copland conducted by Toscanini.

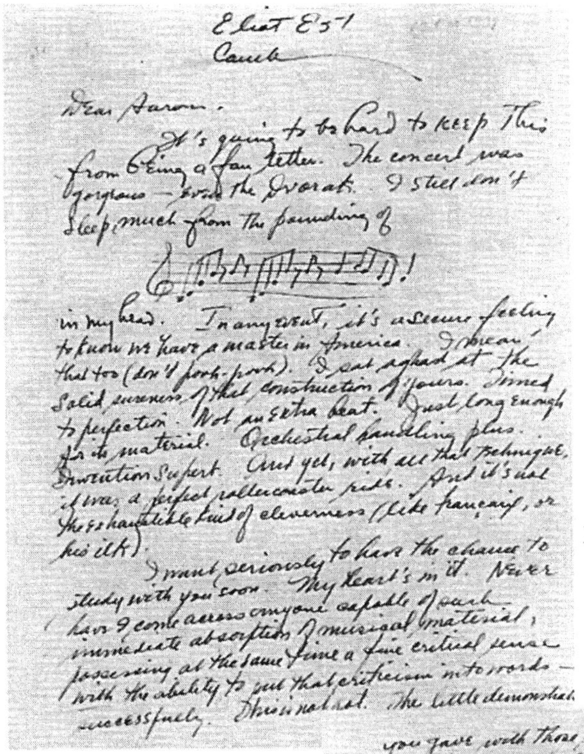
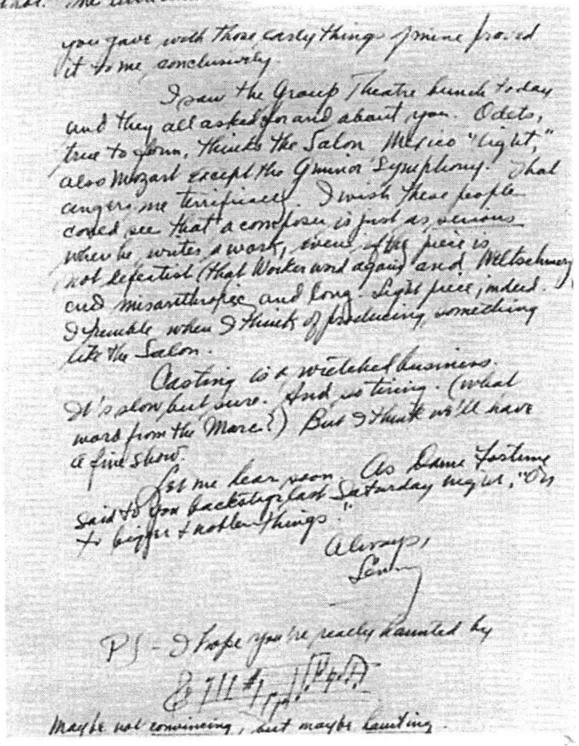

Eliot E-51
Camb

Dear Aaron—

It's going to be hard to keep this from being a fan letter. The concert was gorgeous—even the Dvorak. I still don't sleep much from the pounding of

[musical notation]!

in my head. In any event, it's a secure feeling to know we have a master in America. I mean that too (don't pooh-pooh). I sat aghast at the solid sureness of that construction of yours. Timed to perfection. Not an extra beat. Just long enough for its material. Orchestral handling plus. Invention superb. And yet, with all that technique, it was a perfect roller-coaster ride. And it's not the exhaustible kind of cleverness (like français, or his ilk).

I want seriously to have the chance to study with you soon. My heart's in it. Never have I come across anyone capable of such immediate absorption of musical material, possessing at the same time a fine critical sense with the ability to put that criticism into words—successfully. This is no hot air. The little demonstration you gave with those early things of mine proved it to me, conclusively.

I saw the Group Theatre bunch today and they all asked for and about you. Odets, true to form, thinks the Salon Mexico "light," also Mozart except the G minor Symphony. That angers me terrifically. I wish these people could see that a composer is just as serious when he writes a work, even if the piece is not defeatist (that Worker word again) and Weltschmerz and misanthropic and long. Light piece, indeed. I tremble when I think of producing something like the Salon.

Casting is a wretched business. It's slow but sure. And so tiring. (What word from the Mare?) But I think we'll have a fine show.

Let me hear soon. As Dame Fortune said to you backstage last Saturday night, "On to bigger & nobler things."

Always,
Lenny

PS—I hope you're really haunted by

[musical notation]

Maybe not convincing, but maybe haunting.

Letter from Leonard Bernstein, 1938
(date in Copland's hand)

JAPANESE-AMERICAN MUSIC FESTIVAL
June 22, 1948, Tokyo
· Presented by The Toho Musical Association ·

A. COPLAND　R. HARRIS

コプランドとロイ・ハリス
に就いて
★
クラーレンス・デヴィース

MODERN MUSIC PROGRAM
First Performance in Japan
· 全曲日本初演 ·

1. Orchestra
When Johnny comes marching home .... Roy Harris

2. Violin and Orchestra
Concerto for Violin and Orchestra .... Akira Ifukubè
1. Andante—Allegro
2. Arioso
3. Toccata
TOSHIYA ETO

3. Piano and Orchestra
Concerto No. 1 for Piano and Orchestra .... Fumio Hayasaka
1. Lento
2. Rondo
HIROSHI KAJIWARA

4. Orchestra
El Salon Mexico .... Aaron Copland

TOHO SYMPHONY ORCHESTRA
MASASHI UYEDA
Conducting

Top: The first page of a piano arrangement of *El Salón México* by Arturo Toscanini
Bottom: Program for a Japanese-American Music Festival in Tokyo, 22 June 1948, featuring Copland and Roy Harris, and including *El Salón México*

arranged for concert band by Mark Hindeley in 1972. It was one of my first recorded pieces—in 1939, with the BSO under Koussevitzky for RCA Victor. Lenny included "Saloon" (as we called it) in his conducting debut with the BSO on 8 February 1944.

After hearing the piece played for one of my seventieth birthday celebration concerts, I was still explaining to an interviewer what Lenny seemed to know in 1938. "As I see it, music that is born complex is not inherently better or worse than music that is born simple." But my turn to a simpler style in *El Salón* and other pieces that followed puzzled some of my colleagues. Roger Sessions did not approve of my move to a "popular" style, nor did Arthur Berger. After *El Salón*, I occasionally had the strange sensation of being divided in half—the austere, intellectual modernist on one side; the accessible, popular composer on the other. I have addressed this issue several times in print, and in a letter to Arthur Berger I wrote at some length (16 April 1943):

> . . . for the sake of drawing sharp distinctions you rather overdo the dichotomy between my "severe" and "simple" styles. The inference is that only the severe style is really serious. I don't believe that. What I was trying for in the simpler works was only partly a larger audience; they also gave me a chance to try for a home-spun musical idiom similar to what I was trying for in a more hectic fashion in the earlier jazz works. In other words, it was not only musical functionalism that was in question, but also musical language. . . . I like to think that I have touched off for myself and others a kind of musical naturalness that we have badly needed. . . .

Lehman Engel, as a young conductor of the children's choruses at the Henry Street Settlement Music School, agreed with Grace Spofford, head of the school, that I should compose an opera for children under their auspices. (Lehman had conducted Kurt Weill's *Der Jasager* there before Miss Spofford's tenure.) I agreed and chose my friend, the dance critic and poet Edwin Denby, to write the libretto. I had known Edwin since the twenties in Germany where he had lived and worked as a dancer and writer of opera librettos and dance scenarios. Since his return from Germany, we had seen each other often in New York. My plan was to compose the opera during the summer of 1936 in the quiet town of Tlaxcala, Mexico. Edwin gave me a draft libretto to take along and promised to come to Tlaxcala late in the summer to work with me. I wrote to Koussevitzky from there, "I hope to finish my high school opera here," and to David Diamond (4 July 1936):

> V. and I have gotten lost in the wilds of Mexico. Tlaxcala is a provincial town, very typical and very old. It was all here long before Cortez arrived--and it looks it. We live on top of a hill opposite a 17th century church . . . in a 5 room house, Mexican style, (that is, without any windows!) that costs $14 a month. (It appears we were robbed. It should have been $7!) and we have a cook— Maria. It's all incredibly quiet and picturesque and hopelessly Mexican. No one in the whole town of Tlaxcala talks any English. . . . For the first week I did nothing but hunt for a piano. There was nothing in this town that could boast the name. Then I travelled to Puebla—an hour trip over incredible roads. . . I was getting desperate—for the performance of my Concerto is only 3 weeks off. Today I think I found something that will do—the Padre of the church across the way came to the rescue with a sort of a piano that was discovered in the vestry. Such is life in Mexico.

When I returned to New York in the fall of 1936, *The Second Hurricane* was well under way. I took a quiet room at the Empire Hotel for $8.50 a week and rented a studio in a loft building close by where I would disturb no one with my late night banging. Finally, my belongings came out of storage! The hotel flourishes today where it stood in 1936, but the old building at 115 West 63rd, where my studio was, is the present site of Lincoln Center. You had to go up four steep flights of rickety stairs to get there, passing the other tenants on the way up: the Borinquen Democratic Association, the Comité-Femeninos-Unidos, Flavors by F. W. Kaye & Co. That chocolate scent was so strong, I can smell it now by just thinking about it. I began to have informal gatherings in the loft, serving only beer and pretzels, unless David or Victor shopped and cooked. The first such gathering was in January. About ten composers and a few painters came; Paul Bowles played his new ballet music, and I played some of the opera. I worried that there were not enough seats, but people sat on the cot and on cushions on the floor. The loft went over in a big way. It was a novelty before the time when composers and artists sought out lofts to live and work in. The only way one could get into the place at night was to yell very loud from the street. I would have to run all the way down to open the door. After Victor returned from Paris and Spain as a press photographer, he lived in the loft and set up a darkroom there. We had a few robberies aimed at Victor's photographic equipment. But I chose that hideaway because it was one of the few places in the city where one could make music at any hour of the day or night without jeopardizing the lease. The loft cost $25 a month with no heat (we improvised).

I resumed lectures at the New School (a "music alertness course for intelligent listening") and worked on *The Second Hurricane* whenever I could between other projects. Minna had put me in charge of a column in *Modern Music*, "Scores and Records." It was one of five regular columns; the others were on theater, film, dance, and radio. I considered this a very good deal, since it meant receiving recordings and scores free. It was also a good way to keep in touch with the latest developments. My first article (November—December 1936) began: "Our title, we hope, is prophetic. The time may not be far off when recording companies will issue scores with their records, and publishing firms records with their scores. . . ." Unfortunately, I was overly optimistic, for this prophecy has never been realized. In May—June 1937 I announced the resumption of publication by the Cos Cob Press. One of the scores of interest was Ives' *Washington's Birthday*, the first movement of the *Holidays Symphony* published by Cowell's New Music Orchestra Series. I wrote about this work, composed in 1913, "What unique things Ives was doing during that period! And what a shocking lack of interest to this very day on the part of our major symphonic organizations in this true pioneer musician." In the January–February 1938 issue I covered "Swing" recordings: "the master of them all is still Duke Ellington. . . . Ellington is a composer, by which I mean, he comes nearer to knowing how to make a piece hang together than the others." In March–April 1938 I included newly published pieces by Conlon Nancarrow, the *Toccata* for violin and piano and *Prelude and Blues* for piano: "These short works

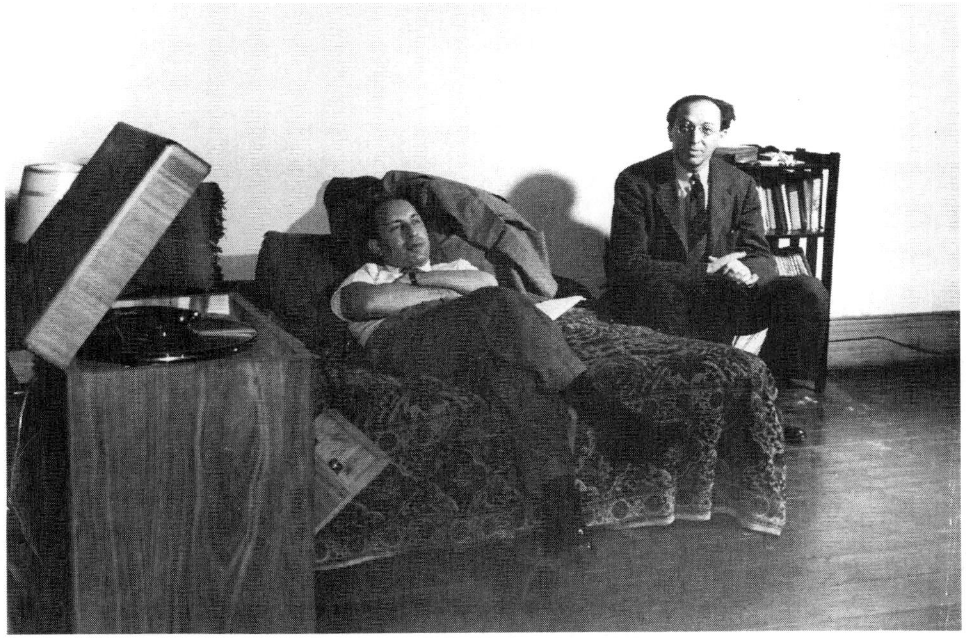

Top: Copland's loft
Bottom: Copland and Clurman in the loft, 1937

show a remarkable surety in an unknown composer, plus a degree of invention and imagination that immediately gives him a place among our talented younger men." The May–June column of "Scores and Records" described two young prizewinners, William Schuman and David Diamond: "Schuman is, so far as I am concerned, the musical find of the year. There is nothing puny or miniature about this young man's talent. If he fails he will fail on a grand scale . . . it seems to me that Schuman is a composer who is going places." I wrote "Scores and Records" for *Modern Music* until the spring of 1939, when I turned it over to Colin McPhee.

Another project of the 1936-37 season was a commission from the Columbia Broadcasting System for an orchestral work to be composed specifically for radio. CBS awarded six such commissions, to Louis Gruenberg, Howard Hanson, Roy Harris, Walter Piston, William Grant Still, and myself. Radio was an exciting new medium—the very idea of reaching so many people with a single performance! I believed that radio was an important new field for the American composer to explore, and I welcomed the chance to compose music that would lend itself to the unique opportunities of radio performance. *Radio Serenade* (as my piece was first called) is in one movement of about twelve minutes' duration in a style designed to bridge the gap between modern composition and the need for a wider public. It was written expressly for a large audience of inexperienced listeners, rather than for the more limited number of sophisticated devotees of the concert hall. Deems Taylor, CBS's Consultant on Music, wrote to give me instructions (28 September 1936): "The instrumentation shall be that of the average radio concert orchestra—that is 37 players. Bear in mind that the string section, playing before the microphone sounds much fuller than it would in a concert hall." CBS even invited the composers to visit the studios for a demonstration of "various effects possible with instruments on the microphone." I decided to use several special effects in the orchestration: a muted trumpet ("felt hat over bell"), other trumpet mutes, a flutist standing at the microphone, bassoons and saxophones for jazz effects, and a vibraphone. To increase audience interest, CBS announced a contest for the best title. (I was to use *Music for Radio* until the winner was announced.)

From January on, work on my high school opera became so all engrossing that I had to put the radio piece aside, but my plan was to orchestrate it immediately after the April opera premiere. In the spring however, I left New York with the score still unfinished. From Mexico I wrote to the authorities for a two-week extension and they agreed. Somehow I got the score and parts to CBS for a broadcast on 25 July 1937 on the program called "Everybody's Music," Howard Barlow conducting. The announcer informed the audience that a prize would be given for the most suitable title. "The prize," he jokingly added, "has no great allure in terms of cash value, although it might someday be a collector's item. Ha ha." The winner was to receive the original score, personally autographed by the composer. Over a thousand suggestions came from the United States and Canada. Davidson Taylor, head of the music section of CBS, sent the titles on to me in Mexico. I responded by telegram: HAVE READ ALL TITLE SUGGESTIONS STOP ASTONISHED AND DELIGHTED BY NUMBER AND VARIETY STOP NO ONE TITLE COMPLETELY SATISFACTORY STOP ACCEPT GLADLY AS IMAGINATIVE SUBTITLE SAGA

OF THE PRAIRIE STOP CLOSE RUNNERS UP PRAIRIE TRAVEL STOP JOURNEY OF THE EARLY PIONEERS STOP AMERICAN PIONEER.

I had used a cowboy tune in the second of the four sections, so the western titles seemed most appropriate. (The piece, of course, had been composed entirely on West 63rd Street in New York City.) A sampling from the titles submitted suggests that a piece of music can evoke a wide variety of associations in the minds of an audience: The Inca's Prayer to the Sun, Machine Age, Spiritual Ecstasy, Sunday at Coney Island, Marconi's World Message, Transatlantic Liner Ascending Ambrose Channel, Subway Traveler, Boy Scout Jamboree, Journey of the British Patrol Across Arabia, Adventures in the Life of a Robot, Futile Search for Order Out of Chaos.

In 1968 when there was no longer live music on radio, *Music for Radio, Saga of the Prairie* was renamed *Prairie Journal.* But somehow the piece has never been called anything but *Music for Radio.* After the winner of the contest was announced in 1937, the lady who had submitted *Saga of the Prairie* was sent my original score as promised. Miss Ruth Leonhardt of Grosse Pointe, Michigan, where are you now?[15]

The premiere of *The Second Hurricane* was scheduled for 21 April 1937, with Lehman Engel conducting. When Sandy Meisner could not serve as director, I took Denby's advice about a young actor-director, Orson Welles, whom Denby called "the most talented person in town." We went to see him, and after I played parts of the score, Orson accepted. The newspapers seemed to enjoy the idea that a dyed-in-the-wool modernist was writing an opera for schoolchildren, so they gave a great deal of attention to every step along the way, particularly the casting. Those kids must have gotten a kick out of seeing their names in the *Times* and *Tribune*! Clearly, we would not present this school opera quietly and skip town if all did not go well. If it was going to be a flop, it would be a big one. The idea of an opera for high school performers appealed to the press, I suppose, for the same reasons it appealed to me. There's a certain excitement in hearing your music sung and played by an enthusiastic group of youngsters that no highly trained organization of grown-up professionals can produce.

Furthermore, it was pleasant to envisage musical contact with an entirely new audience—the youth of America. In a way, *The Second Hurricane* was inspired by them. I had in mind the remarkable growth of school music organizations throughout the country, particularly those in the Middle West, the Far West, and the Southwest. I heard tales of creditable performances with charming fresh voices and good orchestral technique, but with little repertoire to choose from other than arrangements of Gilbert and Sullivan operettas and tenth-rate imitations of Broadway musicals. The Henry Street Settlement supplied the impetus by offering the Grand Street Playhouse and their Music School as proving ground for a production of a work especially designed for high school students.

[15] A search in Grosse Pointe and the Detroit area has failed to locate Ruth Leonhardt. An ink holograph of the score on transparent paper is at the Library of Congress with a memo at the end by Copland: "May-July1937; New York, Hollywood, Mexico." Also at the Library of Congress is a piano sketch, "for study only," and other pencil sketches of the orchestral score (incomplete).

Manuscript page from *The Second Hurricane*

My motives were not all unselfish—the usual run of symphony audiences submitted to new music when it was played at them, but never showed signs of really wanting it. The atmosphere had become deadening. It was anything but conducive to the creation of new works. Yet the composer must compose! A school opera seemed a good momentary solution for one composer, at any rate.

Lehman Engel and I decided on a grown-up chorus from the Henry Street Settlement for the parents' chorus and a student one from Seward High School for the pupils' chorus. Daily rehearsals became part of their curriculum. Lehman got together a professional orchestra to supplement a few teachers from the Henry Street School. The leading parts were cast from the Professional Children's School. When Orson and I went to choose the cast, we were amazed and delighted at the talent and naturalness of the kids. The only difficult casting was the part of Fat—there were no fat boys with bass voices except one, and he had a distinctly Brooklyn accent. Since the opera takes place in the Midwest, the boy had to be replaced. I felt terribly cruel! The part of Jeff, meant for a boy soprano, was not quite right because our Jeff was a little too old, and his voice had changed. But the others seemed perfect. Our only professional adult actor filled the part of the aviator. His name was Joseph Cotten, and he received $10 a performance.

Mary Lescaze began to organize drives for fund raising. She invited prospective donors to her attractive modern town house. At the first of these gatherings, Edwin Denby read a synopsis of the libretto, and I played some of the music. Lehman, who was more outgoing, asked for contributions. Mrs. Leopold Stokowski and Dorothy Norman gave $100 each to match Mary's starter; $875 was collected that day. Since expenses for three performances were figured at $2,250, Mary invited another group—Carl Van Vechten, Constance and Kirk Askew, Lincoln Kirstein, Chávez, and others. Rudy Burckhardt, Denby's Swiss filmmaker friend, showed two films. In one, *145 West 21* (Denby's address), I "acted" the part of a roofer. Denby and the lyricist John Latouche were also in it. It was an amateur production with recorded piano music by Paul Bowles, but it gave everyone a laugh, and more funds were collected. By the beginning of March we had about $1,500 toward the total; the rest was to be made up in ticket sales. I wrote these details to Victor and concluded: "I can think of nothing else but the opera performance. I will always remember this spring as the hurricane season."

Copland and John Latouche as they appeared in Rudy Burckhardt's short film, *142 West 21*

Denby and I had agreed from the start that all stage business was to be simple and natural, and that we would keep before us at all times the premise that this opera was for American youngsters to relate to in their everyday lives and language. Settings, costumes, and orchestration had to be elastic—stretching to accommodate the circumstances and simple enough for young people to put together themselves. It could be performed with two pianos for accompaniment or with an ensemble of thirty, as we had for the premiere. There was to be no curtain and no operatic posturing. Denby explored the problems of creating and choosing a viable opera libretto in an article for *Modern Music*.[16]

Edwin Denby[17]

When Aaron asked me to write the text for an opera, the first thing I wondered about was the costuming—what kind of costumes could students possibly know how to wear on stage? Once we realized that it was best not to have any costumes at all, the story came easily. I read in the daily newspapers accounts of floods and airplane rescues in the Midwest. I added hurricanes for excitement, not realizing that hurricanes do not go inland. The plot was simple as it should be, and was finished in a few days. But when Aaron needed four extra lines of song, it took me ten days to write them! The plot went this way: an aviator comes to the principal of a high school for volunteers to help in flood relief. The principal chooses six pupils, four boys (Butch, Fat, Gip, Lowrie) and two girls (Gwen and Queenie), and off they go in the airplane. It falters and is forced down in a deserted spot near a great river. They unload, and the plane leaves for help. The young people begin to quarrel when they are left to fend for themselves. A small Negro boy, Jefferson Brown [Jeff], appears. He is afraid and lonely. The students fight over the food, while a chorus of parents on stage comment and a chorus of pupils reply. The six students decide to leave in different directions in search of the nearest town. It is then that the hurricane hits hard. They gratefully find each other again and are rescued by a search plane. The moral of the story is stated in the Epilogue:

> *The newspapers made a story out of it like a lot of others.*
> *That's not what we think of, now it's all over.*
> *We got an idea of what life would be like with everybody pulling together,*
> *If each wasn't trying to get ahead of all the rest—*
> *What it's like when you feel you belong together,*
> *With a sort of love making you feel easy.*

[16] Edwin Denby, "A Good Libretto," *Modern Music*, XIII:3 (March-April 1936), 14-21.

[17] Interview, Edwin Denby with Perlis, 6 May 1980, New York City. Denby died 12 July 1983.

We'll remember that feeling even if we six drift apart—
A happy easy feeling, like freedom, real freedom.

We subtitled The Second Hurricane *a "play opera" because of the talking parts. The writing of these came naturally to me, from my experience with German opera. Once the libretto was finished, I stepped out of the picture. I regretted not being around to help Aaron and for the excitement of the premiere, but Rudy Burckhardt and I had an opportunity to go to Haiti, and so we left at the end of February. A few years later I happened to be in Akron, Ohio, when the local high school was putting on a production of* The Second Hurricane. *I could go incognito. It was a real school production with football players in it and lots of enthusiasm and individual touches. Later on in New York, I saw another version by an almost all-black cast at the Museum of Modern Art. They did some very funny parodies of the text. It was totally different from the Ohio production.*

Aaron was eager to do another opera, a grown-up one, and we both promised to think about subjects. I looked into various biographies and historical figures, but nothing seemed right until I was traveling in the Southwest and heard an old-timer, "Arizona Bill," tell a legend of the Southwest. I no longer remember the story, but I was so taken with the subject that I made a libretto based on it. But I had some difficulty getting permission from the storyteller, and then Aaron was not convinced that it was what he wanted. It was put aside, and we never did do another opera together.

The musical challenge with *The Second Hurricane* was to see how simple I could be without losing my musical identity. I wished to be simple to the point of ordinariness. I chose mild and consonant harmonies and easy rhythms. This worked well for the colloquial passages of the libretto where the music approaches operetta, but in the more dramatic moments, it was difficult to make the distinction between grand opera and high school opera. The opera is ninety minutes in duration, in two acts, with seven soloists, three spoken parts, a mixed chorus, and an orchestra using saxophone and a musical saw (or theremin). The music is divided into ten "numbers," with the spoken scenes taking away the necessity for recitative. There is only one motif that is repeated. It appears at the very beginning and again at the end of the opera and typifies the spirit of adventure. For our own work, Denby and I identified each main character with a central motivation or emotion—Fat was "loneliness," Queenie "adolescent love," etc. Jazz elements seemed appropriate for youthful bounce and optimism, and even for jitteriness in a few of the scary scenes.

Denby and I corresponded about the characters from the time I was first writing the music in Tlaxcala. About Queenie, he wrote:

> Queenie ought to have a song that would be musically very sweet and coo-ing. I don't think you need understand the words, but get the feeling of floating in contentment that isn't rationally crystallized, like singing vocalise. It is the tenderest and most intimate personal spot in the piece, the moment that expresses the individual when he or she is sure of his environment. . . . The grace that flows out of a person when he feels sure of contact with everything. It's not an effort and it's not an affirmation. . . . Fat's song is the opposite, being complete loneliness: only I think it should be not ugly just the same, but also attractive. . . .

Denby's depth of understanding and involvement with these fictitious characters helped me enormously. For "Queenie's Song" I wrote a high, long, and sustained melodic line

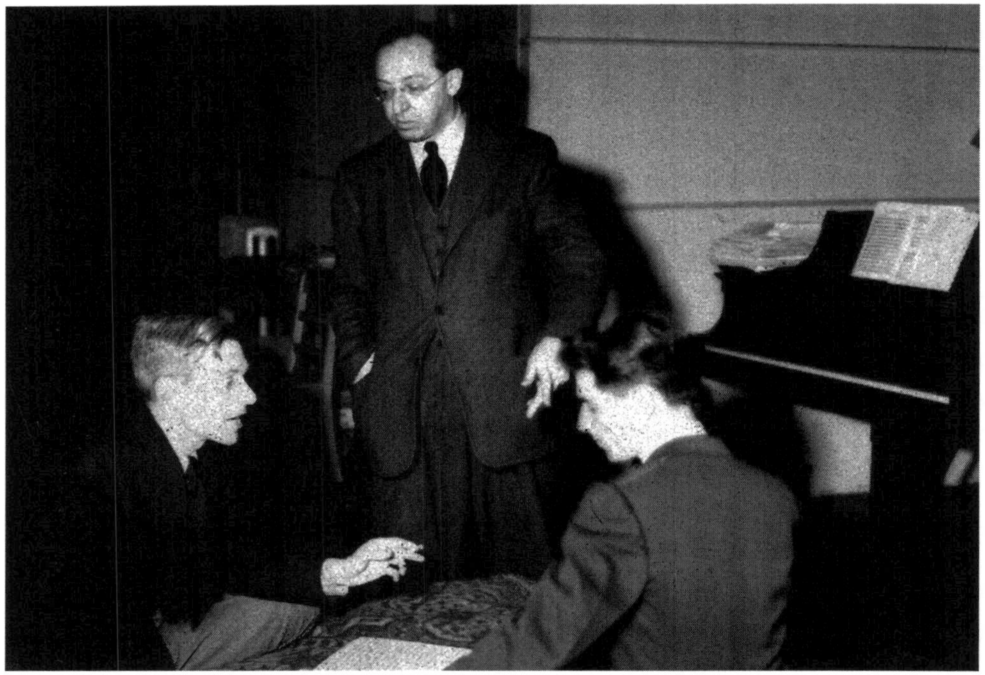

Denby, Copland, and Bernstein studying the score of *The Second Hurricane*

over slowly moving harmonies. (This "aria" has occasionally been used as a solo song; Ethel Luening performed it in a Town Hall recital on 22 March 1937 before the opera premiere.) *Hurricane* was the first work in which I incorporated a North American folk tune—the revolutionary song, "The Capture of Burgoyne." The score of *The Second Hurricane* has been likened to the school of Gebrauchsmusik current in Germany some years earlier, but I felt I had attempted something more ambitious than music "written for use."

Rehearsal schedules and arrangements were complicated. In addition to a cast and orchestra totaling close to 150, Denby had included a ballet pantomime describing what the children imagine rescue work to be like. Orson did not care for this ballet sequence, and it was finally removed from the production. Orson's ideas for staging were original—the two choruses were on stage, and the orchestra was placed on a platform at the rear with the conductor facing the audience. Denby wrote from Haiti: "I wouldn't worry over Orson's part, and I hope his unpunctuality at rehearsals is not bad. He works very hard. You'll see, the best thing to do is to show him you trust him and leave him alone." I took Denby's advice. Orson got busy with staging Marc's *The Cradle Will Rock*, and once the concept for *Hurricane* was set, he left much of the actual work to Hiram Sherman. Virgil was helpful, and Lehman called him "the midwife" of the production. Lehman told me he was amazed at how "cool and relaxed" I was during all this. I asked him why he thought so, and he replied, "Well, you rarely come to rehearsals." The fact was, I had no time for rehearsals—I was frantically finishing the orchestration! But one evening I stepped in to hear the first rehearsal at Henry Street of the Chorus of Parents and the Chorus of Pupils singing together with the orchestra. I wrote to Chávez, "It sounded like Beethoven's Ninth Symphony!" Everyone was so obviously having a good time that it smoothed my frazzled nerves. "If only the audience enjoys themselves half as much," I thought, "all will be well." Edwin wrote: "I don't know how we can resist coming back! Perhaps you'd better save two seats. . . . Don't worry—if one kid is good, the whole thing will work."

The audience for the premiere were mostly adults from what was called the "carriage trade." Due to the organizational efforts of Mary Lescaze, New York's high society found its way down to the Playhouse at 466 Grand Street in a driving rainstorm to see *The Second Hurricane.* Two performances followed, and a CBS radio broadcast (9 May 1937) in which a narrator took the place of the choruses. Following the premiere, Francis D. Perkins wrote in the *Herald Tribune*: "It should prove a very appropriate vehicle for schools throughout the country wishing to present musico-dramatic performances with homegrown talents and without going to great expense for settings and properties. Thus it can be welcomed as a valuable contribution." Some critics called the opera "dull," and others recognized that an opera for high school performers had to be in a musical style suitable for their use. The libretto came in for some adverse criticism, particularly from Europeans and Americans used to hearing only European opera; they found it hard to swallow a plot that we had purposely made simple and natural. But Virgil appreciated what we were after:

> The music is vigorous and noble. The libretto is fresh and is permeated with a great sweetness. Linguistically it is the finest English libretto in some years. . . . Unfortunately the show peters out before the end, the plot falling to pieces at the very moment when our anxiety is greatest about the fate of the characters. . . . Please, Messrs Copland and Denby, do that last part over at greater length and tell us the "real adventure" that you promised us in the beginning. . . . It is nonetheless, of course, a remarkable work.[18]

I had promised to send reviews to Edwin. Some critics called the libretto "innocuous" and "naive," so I wrote reminding him that it takes about fifty years for a musical work to be appreciated. I believed then that Edwin Denby had as good an idea of what a libretto should and should not be as anyone in the country. Edwin responded: "I have to laugh when I think of how when we're eighty the Metropolitan will give it with Martinelli as Gip and Flagstadt as Queenie, and everybody will be completely serious about it. . . . I think you ought to write another opera for grown ups."

In 1938 excerpts of *Hurricane* were presented, sponsored by the *New Masses* with comments by Orson Welles and performances by the Lehman Engel Singers and myself. Productions out of town were not as frequent as we had hoped, but there were a few—in Alaska, California, Ohio, and Tennessee. Paul Hindemith put on parts of *Hurricane* at the Berkshire Music Center's second season of 1941. Leonard Bernstein directed the opera in 1942 at the Peabody Playhouse in Boston. The opera's theme of cooperation was particularly appropriate during the war years, so the Treasury Department sponsored a radio broadcast for the sale of U.S. War Savings Bonds, with the late Alfred Wallenstein conducting a cast from the High School of Music and Art. And in the mid-forties, The Composers Laboratory–Forum in San Francisco produced *The Second Hurricane.*

[18] Virgil Thomson, "In the Theatre," *Modern Music,* XIV:4 (May-June, 1937), 235.

Lenny's television production in 1960 with students from the High School of Music and Art drew fresh attention to *Hurricane.* I was in Russia, but Denby described it to me:

> Lennie's *2nd Hurricane* was an adorable show. . . . the children looked heavenly, sang musically . . . being New Yorkers they also acted like so many little Lennies, no harm at all. . . . Musically it was immeasurably better than any performance ever, and the beautiful freshness of the music is ravishing. Lennie played it for drama, as you would expect, a trifle extra fast and extra slow if one knows the piece, but he gave it a fascinating over-all pace. . . . The spoken text was cut (He wrote and talked the introductory and connecting narration—and sang all the words—inaudibly). . . I don't mind the spoken scenes being cut.

This version was recorded with Lenny conducting and narrating. In 1961 Charles Schwartz invited me to do the narration in a concert version at the Composers' Showcase at the Museum of Modern Art, again with students from Music and Art, Seymour Lipkin conducting. More recently Sarah Caldwell's Opera New England presented the opera at various high schools, drawing on local talent.

The first public school production, Akron, Ohio, 1 and 2 December 1939

C. C. Birchard asked to publish the score soon after the premiere in 1937. This may read like a simple statement, but simple it was not. Various performance requests had to be postponed in 1938 during the publication procedures. Would the cuts from the original be reinstated? Would changes be made in the text—for example, could the word "durn" be allowed in print? What about the ballet? These questions and hundreds of others were discussed and decided by mail between Denby in Haiti, Mr. Birchard in Boston, and me in New York, followed by tedious proofreading of libretto, piano-vocal score, choral and orchestral parts. By late 1938 *The Second Hurricane* was available in published form. The final chorus, "That's the Idea of Freedom," was also released separately by the American Book Company to whom I sold the rights for $50. I was happy to get it, having made only $100 from the opera.

The $500 commission from CBS for the radio piece would not be forthcoming until the goods were delivered, and I would not be ready to do this until summer. A course planned for the New School on "Contemporary Piano Literature" had been abandoned because only two people had signed up for it. (I took this as yet another sign that the public was in no mood for modern music.) I did get $100 from the New School as compensation for all the preparation, and a few fees tided me over—for a lecture on Stravinsky given in Cleveland in February, and for the performance of my *Dance Symphony* by the New York Philharmonic under Artur Rodzinski in a concert sponsored by the League on 11 April. Rodzinski had postponed the performance once already, and when word came that the orchestra did not want to play the piece, I told Claire Reis that I would quit the League in protest if they canceled again. Claire, in her best fighting mood, stormed over to see Rodzinski and told him the League would collapse without me. It was all very unpleasant and spoiled any fun a performance might have been. On top of it, the piece was not played well. It surprised me to hear the reviewers call it "well crafted," since even to me it sounded confused in spots. I was particularly chagrined because Nadia had arrived a few days earlier and was at the performance.

A look at my bank balance persuaded me to cancel a booking on the *Normandie* for the end of April. My idea had been to meet Victor in Paris and travel to Russia with him during the summer. A Russian delegate had promised to get me invited and to find out if I had rubles being held there from the publication of "Into the Streets May First!", but I never heard from him after he left the United States. Also, I wanted to be on hand for the radio broadcast of *The Second Hurricane* announced for 9 May, and for the wedding of my friend Peggy (Rosamond) Rosenbaum in Philadelphia.

Rosamond (Peggy) Bernier[19]

When I first met Aaron, I was at Sarah Lawrence. Some of my friends there were going to Mexico for the holidays, and my father, who was connected with the Philadelphia Orchestra and knew Carlos Chávez, wrote to him to tell him I was coming. So when I arrived in the summer of 1936, Chávez picked me up and invited me to a rehearsal of his Sinfónica de Mexico. *I went, and was very amused at the scene of this orchestra filled with Indian faces—and what were they rehearsing but Aaron's* Piano Concerto! *And Aaron was playing the piano. I sat at rehearsal watching him in absolute delight. He was so pleased with the music and with the orchestra. He was just so happy, bouncing up and down on the piano stool to the jazzy rhythms, and beaming. This orchestra of Chávez's had a very flexible rhythmic sense, but a peculiar nasal quality of sound. I was enchanted to see the composer so clearly enjoying his own music.*

When I went back to Sarah Lawrence, Aaron came out several times to see me; I was in New York City regularly for harp lessons with Carlos Salzedo. Aaron would take me places with him. He took me to my first grown-up party at the Askews (the Askews had a famous salon, Tchelitchew and Dali were regulars), and it seemed to me like the height of glamour. Aaron was amused by this, but he was never taken in by that world. He was comfortable in it, but he had just as much fun at the Automat. I used to go to Aaron's ramshackle loft. It was so dusty that once I saved my pocket money to get it cleaned—he thought that was crazy! And I would go with him like the composer's wife to concerts and pick up programs to be sure he would have them for his archives. I met Edwin Denby through Aaron, and Paul and Jane Bowles, Harold Clurman, Clifford Odets, and all the Group Theatre people. And of course the composers.

When he came into a room, it was literally like a light coming on. I think that everybody else felt that too. Somehow, one was safer with Aaron there—he had a marvelous equilibrium that comforted one. I never intruded in any way on Aaron's personal life, and I knew that anything of that sort would make him uncomfortable. And I never inflicted my own personal life on him. Our relationship was absolutely cloudless. When I was married to Lew Riley, Aaron was already a beloved friend, and he came from New York for the wedding which was in the garden of my father's house in Philadelphia. He knew that I liked "Gip's Song" from The Second Hurricane *very much, so he showed up at the wedding with "Gip's Song" scored, as he said, for "Peggy's harp and Lew's guitar." So we had a Copland work specially written for us.*

In 1941 or '42, Aaron invited me for a weekend at Tanglewood. He seemed terribly proud to have me around, and he showed me off, introducing me to everyone. That's when I met Lenny for the first time. I recall him playing the piano and being Lenny in Aaron's house, and Aaron saying "There's no doubt about that *one!" Lenny had a tremendous feeling for Aaron. He simply adored him.*

I was very fond of Victor Kraft in the early years. He was terribly handsome, but so unsure of himself. In 1941 I was very ill and in hospital here in New York; Victor took care of me when I came out. And Aaron came to visit me in hospital on my birthday with a gift of Gide's essay on Montaigne, signed by Gide, that belonged to him. (Gide meant a lot to that generation of Americans.) Victor was intuitive, affectionate, always taking up lost causes. He was like a character out of a Russian novel. Victor and Aaron were totally different. Victor was very musical. He would be outraged when things weren't right at concerts of Aaron's music and would get terribly angry with Aaron for adapting pieces from his own music instead of writing something new.

We were in South America when Aaron was sent on his first "goodwill tour" in 1941, so we met in Bogota in August. We were together in Havana in December and heard the news about Pearl Harbor on the radio; later we walked on the beach and talked about it. I remember seeing Aaron off occasionally on planes or trains and noticing that he took scores of all kinds of scores to read the way other people took magazines and books.

[19] Interview, Rosamond Bernier with Perlis, 3 February 1983, New York City.

In Paris, just after the war, I went to visit Nadia Boulanger at Aaron's suggestion. It was bitterly cold in her rue Ballu apartment. Absolutely freezing. She was extremely kind to me because of Aaron. Before I left for home, she came by to see me at the Crillon. I wasn't there so she left a goodbye gift. Do you know what she left—a box of Kleenex—the most precious things in Paris then. At that time, when I was with Vogue *magazine, Nadia did an article for me about the young French composers she was championing. Years later, in the early seventies, when Aaron came to conduct in Paris, he and I went together to one of her famous receptions. In the total darkness of the hall downstairs, Aaron reached out automatically and found the light switch—he had been coming there for decades. To Aaron's amusement, the refreshments on offer were as spartan as in his student days. Mademoiselle Boulanger simply did not bother about such things.*

In 1946, also for Vogue, *I asked Minna Lederman for a piece on composers, about John Cage, Aaron, and others. I had Irving Penn photograph Aaron. No matter how much time goes by, we keep in touch. I am always moved by the expression of delight on Aaron's face when he catches sight of me, and his happy, unmistakably Aaron shout of "Peggy!"*

All things considered—especially financial—June 1937 seemed like a good time to accept Clurman's invitation to visit Hollywood to try for a film contract. I had followed George Antheil's column in *Modern Music*, "On the Hollywood Front," with great interest. "Some thing is going on in Hollywood," Antheil wrote. "Composers may remain aloof to it, but only at the peril of being left behind, aesthetically as well as financially."[20] Clurman, who worked for Walter Wanger, was trying to act unofficially as my agent. He talked to Alfred Newman of United Artists, Nat Finston of MGM, and Boros Morros at Paramount on my behalf. Arnold wrote (5 May 1937): "Morros says he knows you have a good reputation, etc. but will you be 'adaptable,' will you adjust yourself, will you realize the *practical* problems! . . . So I say Copland is as practical as Louis B. Mayer, as adaptable as an English diplomat, a regular *mumzer*! (agent's stuff) Alright says B.M. 'How much?—$5,000 for a score and no more than 8 weeks at that price, I tell him. . ."

They asked to see some of my scores at MGM and Clurman went around telling everyone to listen to the broadcast of *Hurricane*. Harold reported (18 May): "I asked Morros immediately if he had heard the broadcast. He had and liked it very much. He is sold on you. . . He feels that you ought to be put on an important picture that needs an impressive score." There was talk among composers of a new art form called "picture music." Schoenberg and Stravinsky had been invited by Morros to do scores for Paramount and Honegger was to compose music for *Joan of Arc* at RKO. Harold urged me to make my presence known in Hollywood soon. Antheil still made me wary; he warned that it was difficult to get a commission for a film score without prior film credits, that Hollywood was a "closed corporation;" and "No one should attempt to come out unless he can write 'piano scores' at the rate of fifteen pages a day. Speed is still one of the main requisities of the film business."[21] But I gathered my courage and decided to go to Hollywood for the month of June. On the train trip out, I was accompanied by Stella Adler's nine-year-old daughter Ellen, whom Harold had asked me to bring along. From the *Santa Fe Chief*, I wrote to Victor back in New York, "It's like traveling with a pet poodle everyone admires."

[20] George Antheil, "Breaking into the Movies" *Modern Music*, XIV:1 (January-February 1937), 82.

When I saw Harold's small house on South Maple Drive, which looked to me like a cross between Brooklyn's Flatbush Avenue and the newer sections of Mexico City, I took a room at the Hollywood Franklin Hotel and rented a small piano. George Antheil and Kurt Weill came by to take me to dinner and Luther Adler invited me to the Brown Derby restaurant, where I was introduced to James Cagney and to Harpo Marx (unrecognizable without the wig). It seemed that everyone was either just going out or just returning from the Brown Derby! Harold took me around to several sets at United Artists and to Paramount to meet His Majesty, Boros Morros, who immediately started calling me "Aaron." I saw Cliff Odets and his wife, Luise Rainer, and the Group people. I wrote to Victor, "They are fed up with Hollywood and yearning for the heat and grime of N.Y." Oscar Levant took me to visit George and Ira Gershwin. I was impressed with the swimming pool and the tennis court in their "backyard" It was hard for me to realize that you could get all that for writing songs and lyrics! I wrote other impressions to Victor (June 1937):

> Hollywood is not nearly as composer-conscious as Antheil's articles would make one think. The whole idea of their wanting "different" music comes solely from Morros' playing around with the idea of Stravinsky, Schoenberg, et al. The conditions of work are very unsatisfactory. Antheil says the cutter can ruin 5 weeks of work by dubbing music indiscriminately. The only thing for sure is there's money here. . .Antheil and his wife have an art gallery and have invited me to do a concert in a series. I will be writing you for music from the loft. Saw Gershwin and spoke with him. He had heard the opera broadcast and asked for a copy. Also said he'd sign my application for membership in ASCAP. . . .

The Group turned out for my concert en masse. Levant played the two-piano arrangement of the *Piano Concerto* with me brilliantly; Jerry Morros took the second piano part in *El Salón México*; and I performed the *Piano Variations*. I left Hollyood for Mexico at the beginning of July without a film contract. Antheil was right about the need for a film credit in order to snap a contract in Hollywood. But how was one to go about that?

In Tlaxcala, the Padre from the church across the way had opened the house for us. I preferred this out-of-the-way place to the suburban living in Hollywood. After *Music for Radio* was finished and sent off to CBS, I went to Mexico City from 13 to 24 July. Elizabeth Sprague Coolidge had invited me to the First Festival of Pan American Chamber Music, where compositions from the Americas (including my *Music for the Theatre*, which I conducted) were presented in six concerts under Chávez' direction. Back in Tlaxcala, I arranged the *Short Symphony* as the *Sextet*. After the world premiere of *El Salón México* on 27 August in Mexico City, Victor headed to Haiti to visit Rudy Burckhardt, and I took a slow train to Vera Cruz, and then a boat to Havana for a few days, before returning to

[21] George Antheil, "On the Hollywood Front," *Modern Music*, XIV:1 (November-December 1936), 47n.

New York. Every restaurant, café, and nightclub in Havana had two orchestras—a rhumba band and a "danzón" sextet. they played alternately, and the music never stopped. The sonority of the danzón was intriguing—predominantly flute that sounded like a clear bright whistle, combined with violin, piano, double bass, muted trumpet, and traps. The music itself is very simple, but it had me fascinated as a lesson in what could be done if the rhythms are amusing and the sonority interesting. I thought at the time that I would someday try a piece based on the Cuban danzón.

Copland in South America, ca. 1937

MUSIC FOR USE

1937 - 1939

Arriving back in New York, I found that three hundred people had signed up for my course, "What to Listen For in Music," and I could look forward to the lectures becoming a book at the close of the series. A few private students still came to me from the Henry Street School. I took my old room back at the Empire Hotel. Victor was away, and Paul Bowles was staying in my loft temporarily. While I was gone, the entire building had been painted bright yellow with red doors and black borders. I went to several rehearsals of Clifford Odets' *Golden Boy,* since this was the only way to see Clurman, and to the opening night and party afterward at Bobby Lewis'. Finally, the Group Theatre had a success!

Roy Harris and Roger Sessions were both in New York that fall, and we were all involved with a composers' committee to support a bill in Congress for a National Fine Arts Department. It seems to me that I spent a great deal of time at meetings—the Fine Arts Bill Executive Committee, the League, Lehman Engel's publishing project that would become Arrow Music Press, and a Composers' Protection Society. Although the Federal Arts Bill was not passed through Congress, our efforts crystallized the aims of composers toward helping themselves, particularly as concerned the collecting of performance fees. The right to a performance fee was established by law, but composers had been cautious about exercising that right for fear it would act as a deterrent to performances. But the time had come for composers of serious music to insist on benefits similar to those made possible by ASCAP for composers of popular music. Thus the American Composers Alliance (ACA) came into being.

Forty-eight composers attended an organizational meeting on 19 December 1937 at the Beethoven Association. I was appointed chairman of the temporary executive committee mandated to draw up aims and objectives. On the committee were Marion Bauer, Roy Harris, Goddard Lieberson, Douglas Moore, Quincy Porter, Wallingford Riegger, Roger Sessions, Elie Siegmeister, Virgil Thomson, and Bernard Wagenaar. Siegmeister presented a list of ideas for discussion; we evolved a program of fifteen points that was presented to a second meeting of the general membership in February 1938. Officers were elected: Copland, president; Lieberson, vice-president; Harrison Kerr, secretary; Henry Gerstle, treasurer. I would serve as president of the ACA for the next seven years, until 1945. There was a sense of excitement and optimism at those first meetings. Our program of aims was sent to newspapers and critics, and we held a drive for membership, resulting in an enrollment of 184 composers. The list included some odd bedfellows—Walter Damrosch and Arnold Schoenberg, Ferde Grofé and Elliott Carter. We announced ourselves in *Modern Music*:

> The Composers Organize. A Proclamation. The American composer of serious music is about to proclaim a new principle for his work as a creative artist. He intends to campaign for the right to make a living by composing. . . The elementary principle that every composer is worth his wage has never been established. . . the American Composers Alliance announces two objectives: first to regularize and collect all fees pertaining to performance of their copyrighted music, in other words, to protect the economic rights of the composer; second, to stimulate interest in the performance of American music, thereby increasing the economic returns.[1]

The ACA was to be considered "the official voice of the American composer." We published a bulletin, a simple brochure that grew as the organization itself gained strength. Our first *ACA Bulletin* of April 1938 listed aims and stated needs: "The composer plays a very minor role in the musical counsels of the nation. WE WISH TO CHANGE THAT! The composer comes last instead of first in the musical scheme of things. WE WISH TO CHANGE THAT!" In 1939 we added a rotating advisory board, and in 1940 chapters were formed in Los Angeles and Chicago. Harrison Kerr was heroic in managing ACA affairs. In the early forties we ran into problems stemming from the necessity to choose between affiliation with ASCAP or BMI. (Until 1938 ASCAP had been the principal collector of performance fees. BMI was founded when radio broadcasting grew, with the function of licensing radio rights and with the idea of breaking the ASCAP monopoly.) As members of ASCAP, Virgil and I of course preferred that ACA connect with them; others, Roger Sessions included, sided with BMI. ASCAP was reluctant to settle an agreement to control the collection of fees for ACA. After three years of discussions between the ACA and ASCAP (not always friendly), a decision was made when BMI offered a contract of $10,000 for ACA radio rights in 1944. We needed the money. Those who held dual membership in ASCAP and ACA were forced to choose one or the other. I resigned as president of ACA, and Otto Luening was elected in 1945. Otto had been learning the "business of music," and as he wrote in his autobiography, "We now became composer-businessmen."[2]

[1] "The Composers Organize. A Proclamation," *Modern Music* XV:2 (January-February 1938), 92-95. See also *ACA Bulletin*, XI:2-4 (December 1963), 25th Anniversary Issue.

[2] Otto Luening, *The Odyssey of an American Composer* (New York: Scribners, 1980), 434.

Since ASCAP and BMI continued to battle through most of the fifties, Otto's increasing awareness of American music in the business world was invaluable to ACA. David Rubin and Roger Goeb followed Harrison Kerr as executive secretaries. Roger set up a library of scores in 1951 at the BMI offices and the Laurel Leaf Award for distinguished service to contemporary American music was established (I was honored to receive it in 1968). By 1953 ACA had a regular radio program on WNYC. When Oliver Daniel became ACA's coordinating manager, he improved the *Bulletin,* initiated concert series at museums in New York City, and established outposts of support for new music all over this country and abroad. He was a founding father of Composers Recordings, Inc. (CRI) in 1954.[3] Oliver made it possible for ACA to change and grow with the times instead of being left behind them. The building of CRI's catalogue and the high quality of its recordings have been influential in promoting American contemporary music. In 1978 the American Composers Orchestra (ACO), the first orchestra devoted entirely to American music, was formed.

By 1938 and 1939 American music.was thriving and growing, but the infant, represented by several groups, the ACA among them, was in need of parental authority. Among those publishing and recording American music were New Music Editions, New Music Quarterly Recordings (led by Luening after Cowell), and the Arrow Music Press, founded in 1938 by Blitzstein, Engel, Thomson, and myself. American music was being published, but no one knew how to distribute it. Luening had discussed the lack of a central library and distribution facility with Quincy Porter and Henry Moe of the Guggenheim Foundation. Together with Thomas Whitney Surette, they founded the Council for the Advancement and Diffusion of American Music. At their suggestion, in March 1939 a group met at my studio to incorporate the American Music Center (AMC). I represented Arrow Music Press and ACA Press and ACA; Howard Hanson, the Eastman School Publications and Recordings; Marion Bauer, the Society for the Publication of American Music; and Porter, Yaddo and the New England Conservatory Recordings. The American Music Center office opened in November 1939 at 37 West 42nd Street in New York City. The idea was for the center to be a nonprofit dealer for distributing published music by American composers at list price. Announcements were sent to newspapers in various cities. Luening served as chairman of AMC boards for twenty years, and Harrison Kerr was again indefatigable as secretary; later Ray Green was just as tireless.[4]

We had a lot of trouble with the publishers at first. They would not believe that we were nonprofit and refused to send us music, either on consignment or on a dealer's discount. Schirmer was particularly resistant, and their influence spread to the other publishers. Eventually, we came to terms. A rental library of orchestral manuscripts was established and composers were invited to place scores in it. The Center, although dependent on funding sources, has grown and prospered. It houses and runs a large and active library of scores, records, and videotapes of all kinds of music, and it is a much-needed clearinghouse for information about every aspect of composition and performance in the United States. After being actively involved with the AMC for many years, I was awarded their "Letter of Distinction" in 1970, and then again in 1975.

I have already told the story of how my lectures, "What to Listen For in Music," became a book. It is true that after the first year's lectures, a gentleman approached me, saying "Mr. Copland, you are speaking a book," but it was up to me to coordinate these materials and prepare them for publication. Also, I had agreed to formulate a study outline to use in conjunction with the book.[5] So in the spring of 1938 I accepted Roy Harris' offer to use his place in Princeton while he was away. When the manuscript was finished, I left for Europe.

It had been seven years since my last trip abroad. I went first to London for the ISCM Festival, where *El Salón México* was performed, and then to Paris. I carried with me two collections of "cowboy" tunes given me before I left New York by Lincoln Kirstein, leading American dance impresario and director of Ballet Caravan. When Lincoln Kirstein asked for a ballet, it was a foregone conclusion that it would be an American subject. Lincoln was attempting to move ballet away from the established Russian traditions and I could not have been more sympathetic with his aims. Still, I was wary of tackling a cowboy theme. Lincoln arranged discussions with Eugene Loring, choreographer for the ballet, and showed me sketches of Jared French's costumes.[6] When I suggested that, as a composer born in Brooklyn, I knew nothing about the Wild West, Lincoln informed me that Loring's scenario for *Billy the Kid* was based on the real life story of William Bonney, a notorious cowboy who had been born in Brooklyn![7] Lincoln was persuasive, and it did not take long to convince me that if I could work with Mexican tunes in *El Salón México*, I might try home-grown ones for a ballet. Thus during the summer of 1938 I found myself writing a cowboy ballet in Paris.

It is a delicate operation to put fresh and unconventional harmonies to well-known melodies without spoiling their naturalness; moreover, for an orchestral score, one must expand, contract, rearrange, and superimpose the bare tunes themselves, giving them something of one's own touch. That is what I tried to do, always keeping in mind my resolve to write plainly—not only because I had become convinced that simplicity was the way out of isolation for the contemporary composer, but because I have never liked music to get

[3] See David Hall, "CRI: A Sonic Showcase for the American Composer," *ACA Bulletin,* XI: 2-4 (December 1963), 21-29.

[4] What was begun in 1939 continues, stimulating performances, commissioning new works, and creating the necessary publicity for the American composer. In 2011 the AMC merged with Meet the Composer, to form a new advocacy and service group, New Music USA.

[5] *Study Guide* for use with Aaron Copland's *What to Listen For in Music.* Ninth book in the course of study prepared by the National Federation of Music Clubs (New York: Whittlesey House. McGraw-Hill, 1939) (out of print).

[6] For reproductions of three Jared French designs for *Billy the Kid,* see *Modern Music* XVI:4 (May-June 1939), 244.

[7] See Walter Noble Burns, *The Saga of Billy the Kid* (Garden City, New York: Doubleday, Page & Company, 1926).

in the way of the thing it is supposedly aiding. If it is a question of expressing the deepest ideas of one's own soul, then you write a symphony. But if you are involved in a stage presentation, the eye is the thing, and music must play a more modest role. There was another reason for being simple in *Billy the Kid.* Our hero, Billy, may have been a complex character from a psychological standpoint but as a stage figure in a ballet, he is a simple figure—a boy bandit who brags that he has killed twenty-one men, "not counting Indians." To use or not to use cowboy songs as the basis for my ballet score was a decision left up to me. So said Lincoln as he slipped two tune books under my arm. I have never been particularly impressed with the musical beauties of the cowboy song as such. The words are usually delightful, and the manner of singing needs no praise from me. But neither the words nor the delivery are of much use in a purely orchestral ballet score, so I was left with the tunes themselves, which, I repeat, are often less than exciting. Nevertheless, I took the songs abroad with me.

While I was in London I received a letter from Elliott Carter (23 June 1938), who was at that time music director for Ballet Caravan, informing me of the instrumentation (an orchestra of about fifty) and enclosing the scenario, several pages of "Notes on Billy the Kid's Character," and suggestions to the composer. Lincoln sent a third collection of tunes to me in Paris. There, in a studio on the rue de Rennes next door to David Diamond, I began to compose *Billy the Kid.* Perhaps there is something different about a cowboy song in Paris. Whatever the reasons might have been, it was not long before I found myself hopelessly involved with "Great Grand-Dad," "Git Along Little Dogies," "The Old Chisholm Trail," "Goodbye, Old Paint," and "The Dying Cowboy." David looked on in wonder as I played "Trouble for the Range Cook." I assured him that I would not use "Home on the Range"—I decided that the line had to be drawn someplace!

Billy the Kid concerns itself with significant moments in the life of this infamous character of the American Southwest, known to the Mexicans as "El Chivato," or simply, "The Keed." The ballet begins and ends on the open prairie. The first scene is a street in a frontier town. Cowboys saunter into town, some arrive on horseback, others on foot with lassoes; some Mexican women do a jambe, which is interrupted by a fight between two drunks. Attracted by the gathering crowd, Billy, a boy of twelve, is seen for the first time, with his mother. The brawl turns ugly, guns are drawn, and in some unaccountable way, Billy's mother is killed. Without an instant's hesitation, in cold fury, Billy draws a knife from a cowhand's sheath and stabs his mother's slayers. His short but famous career has begun. Then, in swift succession we see episodes in Billy's later life—at night, under the stars, in a quiet card game with his outlaw friends; hunted by a posse led by his former friend Pat Garrett; in a gun battle. A celebration takes place when he is captured. Billy makes one of his legendary escapes from prison. Tired and worn out in the desert, Billy rests with his girl. Finally the posse catches up with him.

Eugene Loring[8]

Lincoln gave me The Life and Times of William Bonney *and said, "Read it and try to get a ballet out of it." I had never been west of the Mississippi, but I did an outline, and after Copland got involved, we filled in the action. We decided to use silence whenever Billy kills someone, and the sound of a gun only when Billy himself is killed. We discussed using props, but decided against guns. Each time Billy fires, he does a double pirouette before shooting as though an explosion of fury is going through his body. Billy's victims are always called "Alias" in various characterizations. Since no one knew of a real girlfriend for Billy, we idealized that relationship and treated the Sweetheart as an imaginary character. But the critics, John Martin among them, criticized our use of the Sweetheart's toe shoes among the cowboy boots. We got fond of Billy, although we knew we would finally have to kill him. Aaron composed a march for use at the beginning and end of the ballet to symbolize law and order.*

Billy *was my most successful work; it was a hit from the start and was danced all over South America with great success—in Nicaragua it was called* Billy el Nino. *In our western states, there were still a few old-timers who remembered Billy. One came backstage in San Francisco to tell us that it was all fine, except that Billy really shot left-handed!* Billy the Kid *was the first full-fledged American ballet in style and form as well as content; it was the prototype for the later "western" ballets of De Mille, Robbins, and others that would become American dance classics.*

The premiere of *Billy* was scheduled for October 1938. I went to the MacDowell Colony for the month of September. It was my fourth visit. The first day in the mountain air was always wonderful, and it seemed like unbelievable luxury to have a closet in which to hang my clothes, a shower, and clean sheets in a clean room with no dust anywhere! I was put into Chapman Studio, which I had occupied in 1928, away from the sight and sound of everyone. I enjoyed the ten-minute walk to and from Colony Hall. I reached the very end of the ballet, but then got stuck on the last two minutes. (Perhaps because I knew I would have to begin the drudgery of orchestration as soon as I finished the actual composing.) I stayed in my studio all day, occasionally lighting a fire, eating a basket lunch that arrived on the doorstep daily (except for Sundays when we had midday dinner at the Hall—always chicken and ice cream—exactly the same as in 1925). As a respite from orchestration, which made me feel like an automaton, I worked on a piece for baritone solo and chorus, "Lark," based on a poem by Genevieve Taggard, for the Dessoff Choir commissioned by (and dedicated to) Alma (Wertheim) Wiener who sang in the chorus.[9] (Why the Dessoff Choir did not premiere "Lark" I no longer recall. It did not have a performance until 13 April 1943, when the Collegiate Chorale under Robert Shaw sang the premiere at the Museum of Modern Art in New York.)

[8] Interview, Eugene Loring with Perlis, by telephone, 14 December 1981. Loring died 30 August 1982.

[9] Pencil sketches, typescript of poem, and ink score at Library of Congress. "Lark" was published by E. C. Schirmer, Boston, 1941.

Manuscript, first page of the two-piano score of *Billy the Kid*

A letter was forwarded to me at the Colony from William Schuman, a young composer whom I had met the previous winter. He wrote informing me of the radio broadcast of his *Second Symphony*. I listened and was impressed —with him and with CBS for choosing that kind of American music to present on "Everybody's Music." I wrote to Victor (September 1938): ". . . what I like about it is that it seems to be music that comes from a real urge, which gives it an immediacy of feeling that gets everyone who hears it. If he can build on that, we've got something there." I also received a letter from Lincoln with an encouraging response to the piano score of *Billy*: "I can tell you without an exaggeration that it is the best music we have ever had. . ."

As September wore on at the Colony, the rains came, the river overflowed its banks and flooded the town. There were no papers, no mail, no lights. I left my studio one day and could not return again because streams were flowing across the road. I spent the night on a mattress on the floor in Colony Hall. The next day I tried to reach my studio. The scene was incredible. What one day had been a lovely pine woods now looked like the most desolate war-torn swamp. The road that had taken ten minutes for me to walk took two men with axes two and a half hours to hack their way through. After the hurricane subsided, they found my studio intact and all my stuff safe (including the score for *The Second Hurricane*); but I had to move my music to a new studio to go on working.

The orchestration for *Billy* was finally finished, but I had to make a difficult decision. I wanted to hear Koussevitzky and the BSO rehearse *El Salón México* for the performance of 14 October, but could not afford a hotel. My checking account showed a balance of $6.93! Just then, Koussevitzky wrote, inviting me to stay in his "sanitorium" at 88 Druce Street. I was pleased to be back in Boston—the orchestra was wonderful with my piece, and I enjoyed an evening at Harvard with Lenny Bernstein and his friends, and another at Walter Piston's with Ernst Krenek and Quincy Porter.

Lincoln Kirstein sent a check that made it possible for me to travel to Chicago for the opening of *Billy the Kid*, which was presented by the Ballet Caravan on 6 October 1938, with Eugene Loring in the title role and Marie Jeanne in the part of Billy's Mexican Sweetheart. Michael Kidd was a cowboy in the cast,[10] and I met a young dancer, Jerome Robbins, who also had a minor part. The music was performed on two pianos by Juilliard students Arthur Gold and Walter Hendl, and by them on tour before the New York premiere, which took place at the Martin Beck Theatre, sponsored by the American Lyric Theatre on 24 May 1939, Fritz Kitzinger conducting. Preceding Billy on the program was *Pocahontas*, with music by Elliott Carter. (After Elliott later arranged his *Pocahontas Suite* from the ballet, I sent the score to Koussevitzky with a note [25 September 1939]: "He [Carter] has never been played as yet by any major orchestra, and this is his first important orchestral work. I need not tell you about the quality of the piece as you can see that for yourself." Unfortunately, Koussevitzky was not convinced.)

[10] Michael Kidd is listed in the original cast as Michael Forest. In 1943 he danced the title role in *Billy the Kid,* Ballet Theatre production.

The reviews of the ballet *Billy the Kid* were consistently excellent; to my surprise, even *Time* magazine (5 June 1939) ran a picture and article in their music section. "His music for the 'character-ballet' *Billy the Kid*, much of it based on cowboy songs, was close-knit, percussive, incisive; wasting not a grace note in its evocation of the dapper, New York-born killer who flourished in the Southwest in the '70s and '80s. The choreography of Eugene Loring and the dancing of the Ballet Caravan were no less exciting." I cannot remember another work of mine that was so unanimously well received. *Billy the Kid* was revived by Ballet Caravan in the 1941 season, Gene Loring still in the title role with Alicia Alonso as the Sweetheart; in 1943 by Ballet Theatre with Michael Kidd; and in 1948 at the Metropolitan Opera House with John Kriza and Alicia Alonso. Ballet Theatre took *Billy* on tour to Europe in 1950, but in 1960 the Russians refused it on the grounds that the story glorifies a lawbreaker, In May 1962 *Billy* was presented at the White House at the request of President and Mrs. John F. Kennedy in honor of the visiting president of the Ivory Coast Republic. In 1976, Clive Barnes wrote in *The New York Times,* "With its score still fresh as a wind on the prairies, the ballet maintains its interest and charms . . .[11]

Lincoln Kirstein[12]

The cowboy tunes—yes—I gave them to Aaron and the original idea for the Processional at the beginning of Billy *somehow came from Martha [Graham]. I don't recall much about* Billy *because I don't want to. I didn't like what the ballet became after I agreed to let Ballet Theatre do it. I do care about Aaron though—a saint—the sweetest man I ever knew. He always understood if something didn't work out. Like* Time Table *to his* Music for the Theatre.[13] *Aaron was different about music for the dance than other composers—he took it more seriously and recognized the challenge of translating into sound what one sees on stage.*

In the summer of 1939 I arranged *Billy the Kid* as an orchestral suite, utilizing about two-thirds of the original ballet score. The Suite is in six connected movements, which match the action of the ballet.[14] An introductory prelude, "The Open Prairie," presents a pastoral theme harmonized in open fifths that gives the impression of space and isolation. The second section, "Street in a Frontier Town," is lively and full of action; for western flavor I used quotations from "Great Grand-Dad," "The Old Chisholm Trail," and "Git Along Little Dogies" (but not in traditional harmonies and rhythms), a Mexican dance featuring a theme in 5/8, and "Goodbye, Old Paint" introduced by an unusual 7/8 rhythm. The third

[11] See the Dance Collection, Lincoln Center Library, for a CBS-TV film of *Billy the Kid*, broadcast 8 November 1953, with John Kriza, artists of the Ballet Theatre, Loring as narrator.

[12] Interview, Lincoln Kirstein with Perlis, 11 May 1980, New York City.

[13] *Time Table* choreographed by Anthony Tudor to Copland's *Music for the Theatre* was premiered 27 June 1941 in Rio de Janeiro, Brazil, and revived 13 January 1949 at the City Center in New York. By 1949 *Time Table* was viewed as a pale predecessor of more important ballets.

[14] In the published score, "The Open Prairie" and "Street in a Frontier Town" are the only sections in which titles appear.

The cast of *Billy the Kid* with Erick Hawkins, Eugene Loring, and Lew Christenson, center

section, "Card Game at Night," has a sinister sound achieved by strings built on triads and segments of "Bury Me Not on the Lone Prairie." "Gun Battle." the fourth movement, makes generous use of percussion. The fifth, "Celebration After Billy's Capture," depicts the townspeople rejoicing in the saloon, where an out-of-tune player piano sets the scene. "Billy's Demise," the final section of the *Suite*, makes use of material from the introduction, but with different coloration to convey the idea of a new dawn breaking over the prairie.

The *Suite* is programmatic, but I used musical ideas to tell the story and rhythmic interest to lift the music above a mere collection of folk tunes. For instance, the percussive gunfight is conveyed by rhythmic action instead of simulated gunfire, and the frontier town street scene is a kaleidoscope of tunes, sparked with dissonance and polyrhythms, interrupted by sudden silences. Dance and jazz devices are present, such as the off-beat rhythm of "Great Grand-Dad."

Billy the Kid is one of my most frequently performed works. Lenny recorded it with the RCA Victor Symphony, and other recordings have been made. In addition to the complete ballet score and the *Suite,* "Prairie Night," "Celebration," and "Waltz" are published individually for full and reduced orchestras. ("Waltz" was not included in the Suite.) Philip J. Lang made a band arrangement of "Waltz," and both "Waltz" and "Celebration" have been arranged for violin and piano (edited by Louis Kaufman) and cello and piano (edited by Gregor Piatigorsky). Also published is a piano solo from *Billy* arranged by Lukas Foss, and a collection of excerpts that I took from an early two-piano version of the complete ballet. The music has been used in several films.

When I began to get royalty checks of $40 in 1940 after each performance of *Billy the Kid*, I thought it was amazing. After all, I had been paid a commission by Kirstein to compose it. It seemed like getting money for doing absolutely nothing! It was after *Billy*, when I was almost forty years old, that my mother finally said the money spent on piano lessons for me was not wasted.

An Outdoor Overture owes its existence to the persuasive powers of Alexander Richter, head of the music department of the High School of Music and Art. He had witnessed a performance of *The Second Hurricane* and made up his mind that I was the man to write a work for his school orchestra. I liked the idea of the High School of Music and Art—that gifted students could prepare their careers in the arts at such a school without sacrificing a general education. Richter won me over when he explained that my work would be the opening gun in a campaign the school planned to undertake with the slogan: "American Music for American Youth." I found this so irresistible that I interrupted my orchestration for *Billy the Kid* in the fall of 1938 to write the piece. Mr. Richter suggested a single movement between five and ten minutes in length and optimistic in tone, that would appeal to the adolescent youth of this country. Richter added (13 June 1938): "I am reminded that boards of education throughout this country do not take to ultra-modern composition. It seems to be against the 'institutions of our forefathers,' and what-not. I do not know how you will respond to this hideous reminder, but again I trust your good taste in the matter."

When I played the piano sketch for him, Richter remarked that it seemed to have an open-air quality. Together we hit on the title *An Outdoor Overture.* It is scored for the usual symphony orchestra, but without tuba. "Don't forget the percussion section!" said Mr. Richter. The percussion section was therefore not forgotten.

The premiere performances of *An Outdoor Overture* were conducted by Alexander Richter on 16 and 17 December 1938 with his school orchestra. The piece is dedicated to the High School of Music and Art. The first performance by a "regular" symphony orchestra was given by the Federal Symphony conducted by Alexander Smallens in an all-American concert sponsored by the WPA Composers Forum–Laboratory concerts for the New York World's Fair at Carnegie Hall on 7 May 1939. It included pieces by the Guggenheim award winners in composition, William Schuman and Roy Harris. The World's Fair's symbols of the trylon and perisphere appeared on all the advance leaflets and programs. After the performance, Elliott Carter, writing in *Modern Music,* chastised music critics for not paying attention to it: " 'An Outdoor Overture' . . . contains some of his finest and most personal music. Its opening is as lofty and beautiful as any passage that has been written by a contemporary composer. It is Copland in his 'prophetic' vein which runs through all his works . . . never before . . . has he expressed it so simply and directly."[15] Lenny Bernstein included *An Outdoor Overture* in the debut concert of his New York City Symphony at City Center on 8 October 1945, explaining in a newspaper interview: "A lot of people thought it was kid stuff and refused to play it. I'm very proud of my orchestra—they're young and they're terrific!" In 1954 Cecil Smith wrote in a program note for the London Philharmonic Orchestra: "Youth and freedom and tireless energy are the subject matter of the Overture. This is music without poetising, without introversion. Perhaps it is already a period piece: it is music without a care in the world. Could any composer anywhere have written it after 1938?"

Early in 1939 I provided two scores for plays that never got to Broadway. One was the Mercury Theatre's *Five Kings*; the other, the Group Theatre's *Quiet City*. Orson Welles produced, directed, and starred in *Five Kings*, an adaptation and compilation of three Shakespearean plays—Henry IV, Parts I and II, and Henry V. Burgess Meredith was also featured in the production. Orson gave me a script, and I wrote music where cues were indicated. The orchestra consisted of eight instruments plus organ. I composed "battle" music, fanfares, and even adapted a few French and English traditional tunes.[16] *Five Kings* opened at the Colonial Theatre in Boston at the end of February and closed in Philadelphia in March. An unsigned review in the *Enquirer* stated (2.1 March 1939): "Shakespeare would hardly have recognized himself in this edition and acting." I explained to Virgil in Paris (1 May 1939): "My career in the theatre has been a flop—through no fault of my own I hasten to add. Orson's stock is very low at the moment. Last year's hero arouses very little sympathy."

Undaunted by the failure of *Five Kings,* I accepted Clurman's offer to compose music for Irwin Shaw's *Quiet City*, considered too experimental for outside backers—the Group Theatre had to produce it with their own funds. The play was billed as a "realistic fantasy," a contradiction in terms that only meant the stylistic differences made for difficulties in production. The script was about a young trumpet player who imagined the night thoughts of many different people in a great city and played trumpet to express his emotions and to arouse the consciences of the other characters and of the audience. After reading the play, I composed music that I hoped would evoke the inner distress of the central character. Clurman and Elia Kazan, the director, agreed that *Quiet City* needed a free and imaginative treatment. They and the cast, which included Frances Farmer, struggled valiantly to make the play convincing, but after two tryout performances in April, *Quiet City* was dropped. I arranged orchestral studies from *Five Kings* and *Quiet City*, but dropped the former from my catalogue.

The original version of *Quiet City* called for trumpet, saxophone, clarinet, and piano.[17]In arranging the piece for trumpet and string orchestra, I added an English horn for contrast and to give the trumpeter some breathing spaces. I cannot take credit for what a few reviewers called my affinity to Whitman's "mystic trumpeter" or Ives' persistent soloist in *The Unanswered Question.* My trumpet player was simply an attempt to mirror the troubled main character, David Mellnikoff, of Irwin Shaw's play. In fact, one of my markings for the trumpeter is to play "nervously." But *Quiet City* seems to have become a musical entity, superseding the original reasons for its composition. The work has been called "atmospheric" and "reflective," and David Mellnikoff has long since been forgotten!

The orchestration was completed in late September 1940 in Lenox, Massachusetts; the score is dedicated to Ralph Hawkes of my publishers Boosey & Hawkes. The first performance was by the Saidenberg Little Symphony, on 28 January 1941 at Town Hall,

[15] Elliott Carter, "Once Again Swing; Also 'American Music,'" *Modern Music,* XVI: 2 (January–February 1939), 102-103.

[16] Lincoln Center Library holds the autograph ink score of *Five Kings* with notes by the composer in pencil. The Library of Congress Collection includes original sketches, forty pages of cue sheets, and orchestral parts by copyist (unidentified)—the last bought from Max Marlin 2 September 1965 (Marlin was orchestra director and organist for the production). Cue sheets reveal that recorded music was called for in some places.

[17] The score is at the Library of Congress. Publication of an arrangement using the original instrumentation is available from Boosey & Hawkes, edited by Christopher Brellochs.

conducted by Daniel Saidenberg. The following summer Koussevitzky conducted *Quiet City* at Tanglewood, and again when he was guest conductor for the first time with the New York Philharmonic (19 February 1942). The piece is performed frequently and for some reason is particularly admired by the British. Since it is mostly quiet, it fills a niche in concert programs. When I conducted *Quiet City* with the London Symphony Orchestra soon after my eightieth birthday, it turned out to be anything but a quiet occasion. The elderly heating system in Royal Festival Hall on that cold December evening rattled and thumped so persistently that it was necessary to stop the orchestra and leave the stage. But we played the piece through after intermission, when the noise disappeared as suddenly as it had started.

The World's Fair brought forth an unusual commission—composing music for a puppet show, *From Sorcery to Science*, to be shown at the Hall of Pharmacy. The cast of characters included a Chinese medicine man, an old witch with a head seven feet long and an eye that lit up and popped, a hawk-faced medieval alchemist, an African witch doctor, two modern scientists, a modern druggist, and a modern beautiful girl. The action took place on a large revolving stage. The puppets for this ten-minute show were not your ordinary puppets but twelve-foot-high creations designed and made by the artist and puppeteer Remo Bufano, who had earlier designed the impressive puppets for the operas sponsored by the League of Composers at the Metropolitan—De Falla's *El Retablo de Maese Pedro* and Stravinsky's *Oedipus Rex*. The plot of *From Sorcery to Science*, such as it was, was narrated by a voice familiar from radio. I can hear it now, "This is Lowell Thomas coming to you from the Hall of Pharmacy at the New York World's Fair . . ." The music was to provide atmosphere, background, and continuity. I used two pianos and a wide variety of percussion for the various effects needed—temple blocks, tambourine, cymbals, chimes, tam-tam, gourd, ratchet, maracas. When the show's run was over, I retrieved the music with the idea of someday developing the musical material further, but the score was lost before I could do so. Only recently, a sketch score has turned up at the Music Division of the Lincoln Center Library.[18]

The New Yorker of 3 June 1939 subheaded its music column "Mr. Copland Here, There, and at the Fair." In under two months, *Billy the Kid*, *An Outdoor Overture*, *From Sorcery to Scence*, and music for *The City* were introduced. *The City*, a documentary film, was produced specifically for showing at the World's Fair. It was directed and filmed by Ralph Steiner and Willard Van Dyke, and it was Ralph who brought me into the project. In 1939 the film documentary was a new and exciting concept. Several films on science, medicine, and social problems were shown at the Little Theatre of the Science and Education Building at the Fair. The original idea for *The City* was conceived by Pare Lorentz[19] (already known for *The Plow That*

[18] At Lincoln Center Library: an eleven-page autograph ink score of *From Sorcery to Science* on transparencies with revisions and indications for a fuller instrumentation penciled in, signed and dated "May 4-8 '38"; and instructions, probably by the director or conductor of the production. *From Sorcery to Science* was edited and arranged by Jonathan Sheffer and performed under his direction by the Orchestra EOS in October 2008. It was recorded on *Celluloid Copland.*

[19] The scenario of *The City* was by Henwar Rodakiewicz, the production was supervised by Oscar Serlin, and the music conductor was Max Goberman.

Manuscript page: *From Sorcery to Science*, a puppet show for the 1939 World's Fair

Broke the Plains and *The River*, both with music by Virgil Thomson.) A poetic commentary, written by Lewis Mumford and narrated by Morris Carnovsky, leads the viewer from the scene of a peaceful New England village— "The town was us and we were part of it"—through the blight of industrialism—"Smoke makes prosperity, no matter if you choke on it"—and finally to the new "Green City where children play under trees and the people who laid out this place didn't forget that air and sun was what we need for growing." The American Institute of Planners, a prestigious group of scholars, architects, and city planners, were consultants for *The City*; they were convinced that American cities could and should be decentralized to mirror the spirit of the small town. Steiner and Van Dyke traveled through thirty states filming Americans at work and play. They edited 4,000 feet from the 100,000 feet they shot, for a forty-four-minute film that cost $50,000 to produce. The Carnegie Corporation of New York made a grant toward assisting the production.

Composing music for film is not in itself "easier" than writing concert music except that the form, length, and general tone are set in advance, so the composer does not have to make those initial decisions. After Steiner showed me a rough cut of *The City,* I composed music to fit the five sections.[20] The nature of the visual material called for strongly contrasting musical sections to dramatically underline the differences between country and city life. The film avoided two major pitfalls of documentaries, preachiness and symbolism, and the result was a human intimacy that appealed to all kinds of audiences. I realized when composing music for *The City*, my first film credit, that the composer is in a special position to appreciate what music does for a film because he sees it first without any music. Movie audiences may not consciously realize they are listening to music when they view a film, but it works on their emotions nonetheless. And if the soundtrack breaks down for a moment, the realization of what the music adds becomes acute. While composing for *The City,* I learned the most basic rule: A film is not a concert; the music is meant to help the picture.

The City was premiered on 26 May 1939, and thereafter was open to the public daily for the duration of the World's Fair. The score was praised along with the film in such widely read magazines as *Time, Life*, and *The New York Times Magazine*, as well as in film and music journals. I was fortunate that *The City* was such a good film; in fact, I am told that it has become a classic in the art of the documentary. *The City* started me as a film composer, a direction I would pursue on and off during the next decade. It gave me the credit I needed to approach Hollywood again, and it helped make 1939 the year my name became better known to the American public.

Two offers from CBS that summer influenced my decision to stay close to New York City: one, to introduce and comment on radio broadcasts from Lewisohn Stadium; the other, to compose a short work for the "School of the Air" series. The radio broadcasts were canceled, but the commission brought forth *John Henry*. At a rented cottage in Woodstock, New York, I began to work on *John Henry* by going through the collection of folk tunes put together by Alan Lomax, who was responsible for the radio series and the commission, which carried with it the stipulation that the piece make use of an American folk song. John Henry, as we all know, was a nineteenth-century hero, a black man so strong that hundreds of legends and songs grew up describing his heroic feats. The one I chose is based on the well-known railroad ballad. In it, John Henry pits his strong arms against the speed of a steam pile-driver and wins the contest, but dies in the effort. Knowing my audience was to be a young one, and that young people like their music exciting and not too long, I kept *John Henry* down to less than four minutes and called it "a descriptive fantasy."[21] A clarinet introduces the theme, and to add to the excitement and help achieve the sound of a train and John Henry's hammer, the scoring calls for triangle, anvil, sandpaper blocks, train whistle, and piano, in addition to a chamber orchestra. The material lent itself easily to unorthodox rhythms and harmonies, which I hoped to introduce to young performers and listeners. *John Henry* was broadcast in March 1940, conducted by Howard Barlow and the Columbia Broadcasting Symphony. The original version suited its purpose well enough, but after radio ceased broadcasting live music, I revised the work in 1952 so that it could be performed by high school orchestras as a concert piece.

Most vivid to me about the summer of 1939, which was spent in Woodstock, is Benjamin Britten. Ben and the singer Peter Pears had left England when conditions worsened in Europe—first for Canada and then New York. We had met in England at the ISCM Festival of 1938, and I had spent a weekend at their place, the Old Mill at Snape in Suffolk.[22] The mill and village were as quaint and charming as the address sounded; Britten's studio was in a converted tower of the mill.) We hit it off well together from the start. I had with me the proofs of *The Second Hurricane*. It didn't take much persuasion to get me to play it from start to finish, singing all the parts of principals and chorus in the usual composer fashion. In return, Ben played me the first version of his *Piano Concerto*.[23] Less than a year after this visit, Britten and Pears were on their way to Canada. I wrote, "Dear Benjie, How perfectly extraordinary to think of you here on this side of the water! I can't get used to the idea—but I will."

When I settled on Woodstock for the summer, Ben and Peter decided to take a place close by. Ben and I found we had a great deal in common. We had the distinct feeling of a relationship as composers of the same generation, as well as friends. We played tennis (he always won) and had time for talk and relaxation. Ben was young and very gifted—a delightful person who knew what he wanted to say and said it without fuss or trouble. He was not a hale fellow, but rather quiet, even shy, and quite British. And his music is very direct and British while at the same time very personal. His was a natural and spontaneous gift—Ben was what is called a born musician. His talent was unforced, his training impeccable. He had been a prodigy, so by the time I knew him, he was an accomplished musician.

During that summer in Woodstock we played many things through for each other; Ben was a fine pianist and a great accompanist. Always able to compose what fit his temperament, he

[20] In addition to piano sketches, a typescript of the scenario of *The City,* with cues showing the placement of musical sequences in the film, is at the Library of Congress.

[21] At the Library of Congress: pencil sketch of original version (complete); ink score (bound); and ink score of revised version with parts.

[22] See Aaron Copland, "A Visit to Snape," *Tribute to Benjamin Britten on His Fiftieth Birthday* (London: Faber & Faber, 1963).

[23] Britten's *Concerto for Piano and Orchestra* in D major, op. 13, was composed in 1938 and revised in 1946.

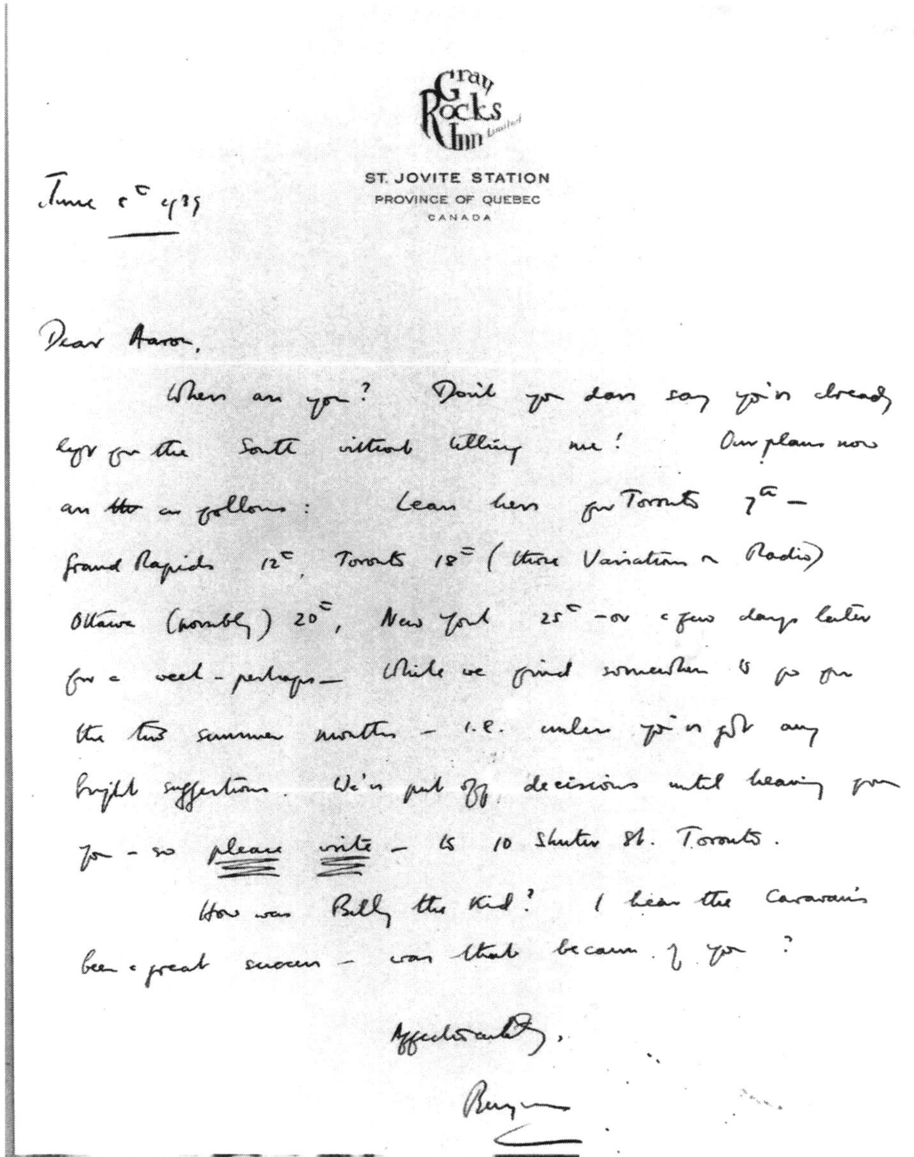
Gray Rocks Inn Limited
ST. JOVITE STATION
PROVINCE OF QUEBEC
CANADA

June 1st 1939

Dear Aaron,

Where are you? Don't you dare say you've already left for the South without telling me! Our plans now are these as follows: Leave here for Toronto 7th — Grand Rapids 12th, Toronto 18th (those Variations on Radio) Ottawa (possibly) 20th, New York 25th — or a few days later for a week — perhaps — while we find somewhere to go for the two summer months — i.e. unless you've got any bright suggestions. We've put off decisions until hearing from you — so please write — to 10 Shuter St. Toronto.

How was Billy the Kid? I hear the Caravan's been a great success — was that because of you?

Affectionately,

Benjy

Above: Letter from Benjamin Britten to Copland, June 1939
Left: Copland and Britten, c. 1950

wrote music in a modern style, yet without danger of upsetting an audience. I thought of him as the voice of England in the contemporary musical scene, and he, in turn, considered me the American spokesman. We had many of the same sympathies, musical and other kinds, and we knew we faced similar problems. Toward the end of August, Ben and Peter left Woodstock. They worried constantly about whether to return to England. I wrote to Ben: "You owe it to England to stay here. After all, anyone can shoot a gun—but how many can write music like you?" Ben had financial problems, so when I went to Hollywood in 1940 and got an agent (Abe Meyer of MCA), I arranged for a film contract for Britten. "If they get you no work in 4 months," I wrote, "the contract is null and void. I think it's safe to sign it. Anyhow, I signed one just like it."

During the three years Ben stayed in America, we saw each other frequently; he and Peter were living on Long Island and we would meet at my loft or attend concerts together. They drove to Tanglewood to see me on the Fourth of July weekend of 1940, and after Ben and Peter returned to England, we kept in touch with each other. In 1945 *Peter Grimes* made Ben famous, and of course Peter Pears sang the title role. It is a great challenge to write opera that really works on stage—very few people are able to do that. Ben's vocal music is very fresh, singable, and effective. He composed many things with Peter's great talent as a singer in mind. After Ben and Peter founded the Aldeburgh Festival, I visited and conducted there and became active in finding support for Aldeburgh in America. It's a great tragedy that Benjie died in 1976 with so much music still in him. I remember him with great fondness, and when I think of him, my thoughts most often go back to the summer of 1939 in Woodstock.

HOLLYWOOD
1939 - 1940

I had been working on a piano piece (the *Sonata*) in Woodstock with no thought of Hollywood. But it seems that *The City* was playing in a movie theater out there and was seen by the producers, who earlier on had not been convinced by my symphonies, opera, and chamber music. Now I finally had a film credit, and I was in! A telegram arrived from Hal Roach, producer, and Lewis Milestone, director, asking me to write the musical score for *Of Mice and Men*, a film version of John Steinbeck's prize-winning play. I flew to the West Coast in October of 1939—my first long plane trip. Why they had waited until the film was completely shot to find their composer, I have no idea. I viewed *Of Mice and Men* twice, but once was enough to know how fortunate I was to have this film offered for my first major movie score. Milestone had translated the fine Steinbeck play into a film that was true to the original, rich in detail, and perhaps even more intense than the play. He captured the poignancy of the simple California ranch hands and enhanced the conception with perfect casting: Lon Chaney, Jr., as the hulking simple-minded Lennie; Burgess Meredith as George, who cares for his childlike buddy with touching dependence; and Betty Field in the only female role. They were directed with rare insight into the characterizations. Here was an American theme, by a great American writer, demanding appropriate music. Obviously, Lewis Milestone, a cousin of Nathan Milstein, was not the ordinary Hollywood director. He was willing to let me do as I saw fit and gave me none of the usual "advice." (He actually added four seconds to the film for the sake of the musical score when I told him it was needed for a particular scene.) Milestone sensed that there were scenes where music should take over to express the emotions of the characters, and others involved with the production wanted a composer who would not follow the formulae for movie music. Not even the music director got in my way.

Once settled, I wrote to Koussevitzky from the apartment rented for me by the studio in the Chateau Elysée on Franklin Avenue (18 October 1939): "Hollywood is an extraordinary place. You must come out here sometime. It's like nothing else in the world. Thank heavens." My arrival did not go unnoticed. *Stage and Screen* of 30 October announced that my appearance on the Hal Roach set was causing something of a stir. "No one has mentioned modern music yet, in conferences. In fact, Copland himself, isn't sure of his approach." Actually, I could not begin to work on any approach until I solved the difficult problem of finding recorded music to use temporarily for the "sneak" previews to which audiences were invited and requested to fill out questionnaires, giving opinions and criticisms of the movie. The producers would go to these previews to see how the movie was being received and to consider changes. During the previews I set to work on the score at a frantic pace. Fortunately I enjoyed working late at night. I liked the studio lot best when it was deserted and seemed to resemble a medieval village or a western ghost town. I had been given a cue sheet marking the parts of the picture for which I was to compose the music, and I had met with Milestone and Roach. They knew my objections to the lush sort of Hollywood music that often had little relationship to the action, emotions, or ideas in a movie. Full-blown symphonic music throughout a film might be fine for a nineteenth-century theme like that of *Wuthering Heights*, but it was not appropriate to the California wheat ranch in *Of Mice and Men*. I discovered that piano music was not suitable either for outdoor scenes, so I tried more natural-sounding instrumentation—solo flute, flutes together, and a guitar for a campfire scene. I insisted on doing the orchestration myself. (Often Hollywood composers turned this job over to arrangers who orchestrated every film they worked on the same way.)

I had a great deal to learn about the technical aspects of filmmaking. Just keeping the music out of the way of the spoken dialogue was not easy—from a composer's point of view, there is always too much talk in movies! I decided to work with a Moviola (making it possible for me to run the film back and forth by myself)—the Moviola was set up next to an upright piano, and I could turn the knob while sitting at the instrument. The Moviola was not the favored way of working on a film in Hollywood then; most composers simply wrote the score to the timings after seeing the film once through. But I was genuinely moved by *Of Mice and Men* and by the inspired performances, and I found that the scenes induced the music if I turned to them while composing.

I made certain decisions: I would not use the leitmotif idea a la Wagner whereby each central character is identified with a theme; I would not quote folk tunes; and I would not underline every piece of the action (I disliked this kind of "mickey-mousing" that composer Max Steiner was so fond of). In certain segments, the music had to reflect the action, at least in a general way. For the big fight scene between Curly and Lennie, I wrote dissonant music by Hollywood standards. I found little difficulty with other dramatic sections where the music could take over: the opening sequence showing George and Lennie running after a train and jumping into a boxcar; the scene where Lennie crushes Curly's hand to the accompaniment of one grinding chord that lasts about twenty seconds; the segment where the old dog is killed; and the ending with about eight minutes worth of continuous music and little dialogue. All these came easily. But the background music was difficult for me. It seemed a strange assignment to write music that is actually meant to be uninteresting. Yet this kind of "neutral" sound is often needed to "warm" the screen or to connect one piece of action to another.

While working on *Of Mice and Men*, I thought of George Antheil's warning about speed-writing. All of a sudden, everyone seemed to be in a frightful hurry—they all sat down to wait for the composer while valuable time passed. I was given about six weeks, but often movie scores were done in much less time. If the shooting of a script would take longer than planned, time would be lopped off the composer's end. I expressed the opinion at the studio that a composer ought to work directly with the picture while it was being filmed. At least when my score was finished there was no cutting. I was told that this was unusual for Hollywood. I had expected problems about the modern-sounding spots, but there were no complaints, even though at the previews with my completed score, the ladies had shown some dissatisfaction with the "raw" and "masculine" aspects of the picture, which my music served to emphasize.

Once the score was finished, I was anxious to hear what the music actually sounded like when put with the film. The players were very experienced, and recording day was wonderful. It seemed pretty fancy to me that we could record more than one sound track and mix them, as in the opening sequence, which begins with outside action and switches to inside a boxcar, showing a hobo playing the Jew's harp. We superimposed the realistic sound of the Jew's harp onto the nonrealistic background of the orchestral music. The orchestra was required to play everything at about the same dynamic level, since the sound adjustments were not made until the time of dubbing with the film. Every composer dreads the dubbing room. The awful thing that happens there, from the composer's standpoint, is that the music starts to disappear. The score that was so clear and satisfying when recorded gets further away the minute anyone on the screen opens his mouth! It is a moment for great self-control. In a position to ruin everything was not a musician, but a sound engineer. I made some mild objections, but I was asked, "Haven't you heard of the union?" Moreover, the particular sound man assigned to *Of Mice and Men* was overly sensitive to criticism, and so it was difficult to give any. Whenever I would say something, it was too late—the spot was already dubbed! Another problem that affected the composer and could give him grave discomfort was that there was not a way yet invented to predetermine sound levels in the theaters. Adjustments would be left up to each theater manager. It seemed to me utterly ridiculous to take so much pain about proper levels for the music and dialogue and then leave it all up to chance in the theaters.

My overall experience with *Of Mice and Men* was a good one. I was satisfied that the score enhanced the movie, making it more intense and more meaningful. To some in Hollywood my music was strange, lean, and dissonant; to others it spoke with a new incisiveness and clarity. I was an outsider to Hollywood, but I did not condescend to compose film music; I worked hard at it. Perhaps this is why I was accepted. And I genuinely liked some things about the film industry, particularly that music was made to be used on a daily basis, and that composers were actually needed there. Also, the accent was entirely on the living composer. But I was puzzled at why film composers were so isolated from the rest of the music world! In 1939 there were four major figures—Erich Korngold, Max Steiner, Alfred Newman, and Herbert Stothart—and these men were not known outside of Hollywood.

The premiere of *Of Mice and Men* on the West Coast on 22 December 1939 was an all-out glamorous Hollywood opening night. I stayed in California just long enough to attend. Another picture was offered to me right away, but I turned it down because it was not a very good one. My agent was absolutely shocked! Several people were surprised to see me back in New York. There seemed to be an idea that once one went to Hollywood, he was lost forever to the rest of the music world! But I could enjoy going back and forth to California occasionally without moving there. It was such a nice change from New York—the weather was beautiful, and the pay was good. Furthermore, film music was a very live subject as a new art form and open for serious discussion. Back in New York, I lectured about it at the Museum of Modern Art and wrote a few articles about my first Hollywood experience.[1]

If some were surprised at my prompt return from Hollywood, others were relieved. The affairs of the League and of ACA had piled up while I was away. I continued to give lectures in and out of town, although I was no longer teaching regularly at the New School. Discussions were under way toward a new book. Finally I was experiencing some modest financial success, and I was able to buy a typewriter and have repairs made on my car. But it was not a happy time. With the threat of impending war, the atmosphere was one of nervousness and insecurity—everyone was worrying about friends and relatives abroad and those at home who might have to go into the service. I wrote to Ben Britten, "I find it hard as hell to go on putting down notes on paper as if nothing were happening." Composers as well as writers and artists were drawn to patriotic and nostalgic themes, and the American public, fearing violence to come, was comforted by works like Thornton Wilder's *Our Town,* which looked back at an America of simple, homespun values that seemed to have been lost. When Sol Lesser, the Hollywood producer, asked me to compose the musical score for the screen version of the play about life in the small town of Grover's Corners, New Hampshire, U.S.A., I welcomed the opportunity. For one thing, I admired Wilder's play; for another, I was irritated that film music had become so pat, so conventionalized, when the medium was still so young. *Our Town* was the perfect vehicle for putting to the test opinions I had voiced in the press—that film music should follow the organic structure of a story, and that the music must be appropriate to the nature of that story. *Our Town* could not have been further from *Of Mice and Men* in subject, setting, characters, and feeling. Here was my chance to show that a composer, within a short period of time, could write different-sounding scores, each appropriate to the film it accompanied. Finally, the fact that Wilder had written most of *Our Town* at the MacDowell Colony, and that Grover's Corners was

[1] Aaron Copland, "Second Thoughts on Hollywood," *Modern Music,* XVII:3 (March-April 1940), 141-47; and Aaron Copland, "The Aims of Music for Films," *The New York Times* (10 March 1940), Sec.2, 7.

patterned after Peterborough, New Hampshire, was too much for me to resist. I flew to Hollywood on a sleeper plane. It took all night and I felt like a hero.

Thornton Wilder worked closely with Sol Lesser on the film scenario. As a play, *Our Town* had certain technical features that were "filmic": flashbacks, a narrator, and fast scene changes. But the subject matter and the treatment were not ones that would normally be expected in a Hollywood movie. The play is essentially plotless in the usual sense of the term (it was frequently called quasi-documentary), it is innocent of romantic intrigue, and deals entirely with unassuming, everyday people in simple settings, with virtually no scenery. For the film version, Wilder and Lesser were counting on the music to translate the transcendental aspects of the story. As with *Of Mice and Men*, most of *Our Town* was filmed before my arrival in Hollywood. In New York after reading the play, I wrote some musical themes and later marveled that they seemed so right when put with the picture. Lesser asked if I would use popular tunes in the score. But I felt that the songs of the period of *Our Town*, numbers like "Down on the Farm" and "Give My Regards to Broadway," were inappropriate to the spirit of the film; moreover, considering the eternal, universal qualities of the story, direct quotes would have pinned the period down too specifically. But I used harmonies suggestive of church hymns associated with small New England towns of the early twentieth century.

In practical terms I worked in much the same way as I had on *Of Mice and Men*, first viewing the film several times with Sam Wood, the director, and then using a moviola placed next to a piano while composing the music. Again I was moved by the beauty of the film. The poignancy of the play was intact, and there was a haunting quality that made it all very touching. *Our Town* dared to be simple and at times very funny; it challenged me to meet its high standards. The performances were exceptional—Martha Scott as Emily and Frank Craven as the narrator recreated their roles from the stage production; other leading roles were taken by William Holden, Fay Bainter, Beulah Bondi, and Guy Kibbee. This was not an ordinary motion picture. The camera itself seemed to become animate, and the characters spoke directly to it. Once the narrator actually placed his hand before the camera lens to stop a sequence and introduce the next.

My job was to create the atmosphere of a typical New Hampshire town and to reflect the shifts from the real to the fantasy world. Because of the nostalgic nature of the story, most of the music had to be in slow tempo. I was mystified as to how to get some variety into it and wrote to Victor, "I'd give my shirt for one decent 'allegro.'" Percussion instruments and all but a few brass were omitted. I relied on strings, woodwinds, and the combination of flutes and clarinets for lyric effects. Since *Our Town* was devoid of violence, dissonance and jazz rhythms were avoided. In the open countryside scenes, I tried for clean and clear sounds and in general used straightforward harmonies and rhythms that would project the serenity and sense of security of the play. The most difficult problems came when scoring the graveyard scene where Emily joins the ranks of the dead. It was not meant to be morbid or depressing, so any hint of funereal music would have been out of place. In keeping with the metaphysical mood, I used choral sequences with unusual harmonies, hoping that their unconformity would suggest something of the preternatural quality of the scene.

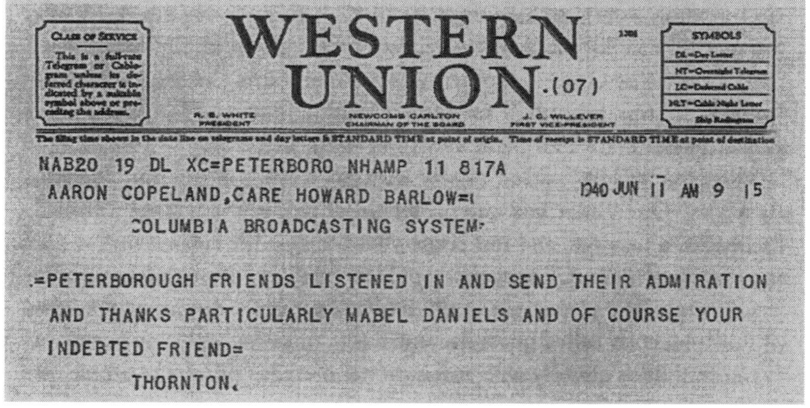

WESTERN UNION (07)

NAB20 19 DL XC=PETERBORO NHAMP 11 817A
AARON COPELAND,CARE HOWARD BARLOW=
1940 JUN 11 AM 9 15
COLUMBIA BROADCASTING SYSTEM=

=PETERBOROUGH FRIENDS LISTENED IN AND SEND THEIR ADMIRATION AND THANKS PARTICULARLY MABEL DANIELS AND OF COURSE YOUR INDEBTED FRIEND=
THORNTON.

Top: Manuscript: sketch of the "Dog Scene" from *Of Mice and Men*
Bottom: Congratulatory telegram from Thornton Wilder to Copland (Mabel Daniels was a composer living in Peterborough)

Sol Lesser gave me an office with a view at United Artists' lot, but I worked with my back to the window, since the view was of huge gas tanks, hardly conducive to recalling the rural charms of New England. In four weeks I wrote a score of over forty-three minutes—two weeks less than it took to compose *Of Mice and Men.* Being mostly slow, the music did not take as long to write. Any composer will tell you that it does not take as long to write one half-note as it does to write four eighths.

Our Town had its Hollywood preview at Grauman's Chinese Theater on 9 May 1940. Lawrence Morton wrote, "Hollywood is to be congratulated, Roach and Lesser highly praised for acquiring Copland's services . . . he has a passion for the expression of the American spirit in music. It is not only new in Hollywood but to all of musical America."[2] The world premiere took place in Boston on 24 May, named "Our Town Day" by the mayor. The New York opening was held at Radio City Music Hall on 13 June, where the film shared the bill with the Music Hall Grand Organ, the March of Time, the Music Hall Symphony, and the Rockettes. Critics were unanimous in praise and in agreement that the picture was even more deeply moving than the play. Bosley Crowther of *The New York Times* wrote (14 June 1940):

> We hesitate to employ superlatives, but of *Our Town* the least we can say is that it captures on film the simple beauties and truths of humble folks as very few pictures ever do; it is rich and ennobling in its plain philosophy—and it gives one a passionate desire to enjoy the fullness of life even in these good old days of today.

I lost no time in arranging about ten minutes of music from the film score for a suite that was broadcast a few days before the film opening in New York by the CBS Orchestra under Howard Barlow's direction. (I was the regular commentator for the program.) After the film premiere, I took some time to prepare a more careful version of an *Our Town Suite* that was introduced at a Boston Pops concert on 7 May 1944 by Leonard Bernstein, to whom the piece is dedicated. I conducted the London Symphony Orchestra for a recording, and I arranged excerpts for piano that are published and have been performed by several pianists, among them Andor Foldes and Leo Smit.[3]

[2] Lawrence Morton, "About Aaron," *Ron Wagner's Script*, 15 June 1940, 18-19.

[3] When Carl Van Vechten set up a George Gershwin Memorial Collection at Fisk University Library in Nashville, Tennessee, and asked for a manuscript, Copland donated the score of the piano pieces from *Our Town.* The original piano score of the orchestral suite was donated to the Motion Picture and Television Museum in Hollywood. In Copland's files in the Library of Congress is an unpublished arrangement of "Story of Our Town" for violin and piano, signed and dated "1940."

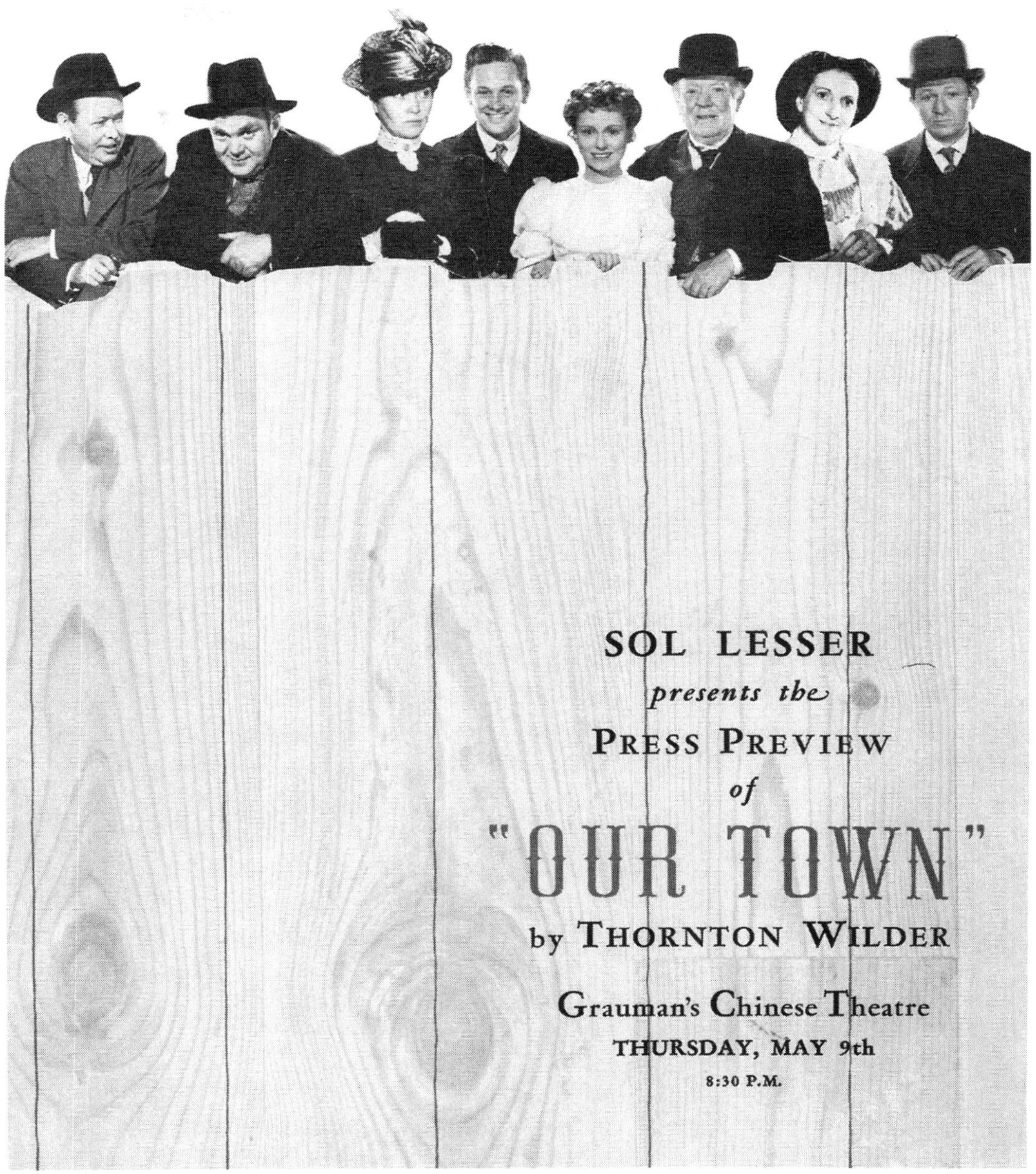

Publicity release for *Our Town*

INTERLUDE IV

It was a long way from Hollywood to Tanglewood, but to Copland in the summer of 1940, Lenox, Massachusetts, looked like Grover's Corners, U.S.A. Copland felt far more comfortable in the Berkshires than in California. By this time he was more often described as "the Dean of American Composers" than "that wild young modernist," and since he had always looked more like a teacher or a businessman than a brooding genius, he did not have to change his style of dress, cut his hair, or shave off a beard. Nevertheless, Copland's casual and breezy manner always invited informality. It was not unusual to hear a friendly, "Hi Aaron," called from across a street in New York City by a total stranger. It would have been difficult to imagine such freedom with Paul Hindemith, the other composer invited by Koussevitzky to teach during the first season of the Berkshire Music Center.

Koussevitzky had often talked to Copland of his plan:

> . . . a Center where the greatest living composers would teach the art of composition, the greatest virtuosi the art of performance, and the greatest conductors the mystery of conducting orchestras and choruses . . . such an elite would result in a creation of new and great values in art . . . and in the education and training of a new generation of American artists.[1]

Koussevitzky had been nurturing this dream since his youth in Russia. When the Boston Symphony replaced the New York Philharmonic after the first two seasons of the Berkshire Music Festival, Koussevitzky lost no time in convincing his trustees that a Music Center was necessary and important. Only three concerts were held during the summer of 1936 in an open field under a tent in Stockbridge. In 1937 the 210-acre Tanglewood estate was donated to the trustees of the orchestra by the Tappan family, and again the festival was made up of three concerts. When a typical Berkshire rainstorm almost drowned out a performance of the *Ride of the Valkyries,* a funding drive was begun on the spot. By 1938, the "Shed" designed by Eliel Saarinen was built and the concerts increased to six. Copland's *Music for the Theatre* was one of the works performed that season. On a beautiful site overlooking the lake, the Shed continues to be the principal facility for the Berkshire Music Festival, or "Tanglewood," as the largest and most famous of American summer music festivals is generally called.[2] In 1939 and 1940 the festivals included nine concerts each season. At the opening ceremony of the Berkshire Music Center (BMC) on 8 July 1940, a chorus sang Randall Thompson's newly composed "Alleluia," which has become a tradition at each summer's opening. Koussevitzky, affectionately called "The Doctor" by everyone, gave a speech in which he reminded the peaceful gathering that at that very moment similarly beautiful landscapes in Europe were being destroyed by war. "If ever there was a time to speak of music, it is now in the New World."

There was at least one member of that audience who needed no reminders about the European war situation. Paul Hindemith wrote to his wife, Gertrud, still unable to leave Europe, that the Berkshires brought to mind North Switzerland. Hindemith, in America since the previous February, had endured a difficult winter of teaching in Buffalo, where neither the weather nor the students were satisfactory; moreover, he was concerned about Gertrud's safety. Hindemith's music, performed frequently worldwide during those years, had been banned in Nazi Germany since 1934. In 1937-38 the composer traveled to America primarily to attend a concert in Washington of his works sponsored by Elizabeth Sprague Coolidge. When he returned to Germany, he found conditions had worsened, so he and his wife moved to Switzerland, and then he came on to America. Tanglewood was a godsend after Buffalo, especially since Hindemith had no idea until midsummer where he would go next.[3] The two composition teachers at Tanglewood had little in common;

[1] From Koussevitzky's statement to the trustees of the Boston Symphony Orchestra, 1939. Quoted in "A Tanglewood Dream," 25th Anniversary Album, ed. Daniel Selznick, 1965.

[2] For collections relating to Tanglewood, see Lenox Library Association, Tanglewood minutes from 1934 to 1944, Lenox, Massachusetts; Stockbridge Library, papers of George Edman, first clerk of the Berkshire Music Festival, Stockbridge, Massachusetts; and Boston Symphony Orchestra, inactive and active records of the Berkshire Music Center and the administrative files of Tanglewood, Symphony Hall, Boston, Massachusetts. The above cited in Susan Kaufman, "Archival Resources for the Arts in Berkshire County, Massachusetts," 30 April 1983, unpublished research paper, Spaulding Library, New England Conservatory of Music, Boston, Massachusetts. See also Koussevitzky Collection, Music Division, Library of Congress. For histories of Tanglewood, see James R. Holland, *Tanglewood* (Barre, Massachusetts: Barre Publishers, 1973), H. Kupferberg, *Tanglewood* (New York: McGraw Hill, 1976), Moses Smith, *Koussevitzky* (New York: Allen, Towne & Heath, 1941), 274-95 and Andrew L. Pincus, *Scenes from Tanglewood* (Boston: Northestern University Press, 1989; and *Tanglewood and the Clash Between Tradition and Change* (Boston: Northeastern University Press, 1998).

[3] This information and other background material about Hindemith from Luther Noss, former Dean Emeritus and Curator of the Paul Hindemith Collection, Yale.

Hindemith did not take the American composer seriously, and Copland, while admiring Hindemith's musical talent and craftsmanship, considered the German a "deep-dyed academician." Perhaps Koussevitzky had chosen two such different personalities with an eye toward exposing students to a broad range of musical styles and methods. More likely he was pleased to have both the most famous German composer and the best-known American at his new school. Furthermore Koussevitzky knew that he could depend on Aaron to keep the peace.

Koussevitzky planned the Music Center with two divisions: an Institute of Advanced Study, to include the composers and their students, Dr. Herbert Graf's "opera dramatics" program, and Koussevitzky's conducting students; and the Academy, or Department of Music and Culture, for more general students to sing in the chorus and perform in the orchestra.[4] The first season, Olin Downes gave a lecture series on "Music and Integrity," and Abram Chasins discoursed on "Ornamentation." Archibald T. Davison of Harvard, Randall Thompson, the director at Curtis, and Howard Abell of the Milton Academy all lectured. Hindemith wrote to Gertrud in Switzerland (14 July 1940):

> I am living in two very nice and quiet rented rooms in the home of Mr. Driscoll, pastor of the Congregational Church in Lenox . . . Tanglewood is a blend of Donaueschingen, Ankara, and the Berlin Hochschule, and everything going on here seems to be good. I am naturally a very 'famous' teacher here and the students have already spread rumors about all of the surprising things I am doing with them. . . .[5]

Thirteen composition students had been accepted by Koussevitzky, who with Copland's help had reviewed scores and applications during the previous spring. Requests to study with one or the other composer were honored; otherwise students were arbitrarily assigned. On arrival, Hindemith was given his list of students: John Colman, Norman Dello Joio, Lukas Foss, John Klein, Harold Shapero, Robert Strassburg, and Charles Naginski. Colman had studied briefly with Hindemith in Berlin. He had received some encouragement, but also advice that he seek a conservatory education. Colman applied from his second year at Juilliard to study with Hindemith at Tanglewood, but Hindemith refused to have him in his class. In an interview Colman said, "My feelings were hurt badly by Hindemith's behavior. But Copland said, 'I'll teach you,' and although I did not particularly want to study with Copland, wasn't that nice of him!"[6]

Hindemith met with his six students daily; in addition he taught two evening classes a week to the Academy. Hindemith wrote to Herbert Fromm, a former student from Buffalo, with whom he had become friendly (15 July 1940):

[4] The chorus and orchestra performed Bach's *B Minor Mass* conducted by Koussevitzky on 15 August, and the orchestra played Hindemith's *Concerto for Strings and Wind Choirs*, Copland's *Music for the Theatre*, and Stravinsky's *Histoire du soldat*.

[5] Quotations from Hindemith's letters to Gertrud Hindemith and to Herbert Fromm, courtesy Hindemith Collection, Yale.

[6] Interview, John Colman with Caitriona Bolster, Oral History of American Music, Hindemith Project, Yale, 21 November 1976, New York City.

> The students (at least, the so-called composers) are awful. There was some conflict at first since they all came with large scores and wanted recognition, and they showed no love for me. They did not like at all to have to start small and hated the idea of having to sing what they had written. But when I made them work for hours at the blackboard on strict counterpoint exercises and they saw that none of them was able to solve even the simplest ones, they became pliable, relented and are now quite good and mannerly. . .

In the years to follow, Hindemith would teach many American composition students with varying results and influence.[7] But two qualities were obvious from the start—Hindemith was an absolutely extraordinary musician with a powerful and difficult personality.

Harold Shapero[8]

I wanted to study with Hindemith because he wrote fast and I wanted to get the secret of how to do that. I was always getting stuck. But it didn't rub off on me. The first shocking thing was that I was not going to be allowed to hear any of my compositions that summer. He would not look at our compositions or allow them to be played. Instead, we had exercises in two-voice counterpoint. Hindemith was more interested in what we could do on the spot right then and there that summer. Also, we were assigned an instrument to be learned, one quite the opposite of what we ordinarily played. I was a pianist, so I took the trumpet. Hindemith demanded a lot of work. I would come back to my room—Tanglewood was not very organized that first year—I had five jumping musician roommates in one room at the Cranwell School, including Lenny Bernstein, Arthur Winograd cellist, Raphael Hillyer violist, and a clarinetist. I was trying to compose in this mess. (And I drove them crazy with my trumpet.) I complained to Hindemith and he said, "You can go to the woods." I had the stupidity or nastiness to say, "Well, the bugs get all over your music paper." Hindemith considered this disrespectful. He went to Copland and complained about this fresh student. So immediately we had a confrontation. Years later Copland remembered the way Hindemith came running to him, saying, "That young man Shapero is impossible," and then two seconds later me coming in, screaming, "That Hindemith, he's a monster." That's how it started, but it finished up a lot better.

The main thing about Hindemith as a teacher in those days was his energy. He met us five days a week for five hours every morning with a little time off for a swim. That degree of involvement was staggering when you consider he had already been writing his own music each morning before he started with us. To me, he resembled an electric motor, a little dynamo. Short, compact, with very strong muscles. And he sort of churned and left a wake. He swam that way too. He was a powerhouse personality. As a teacher he did some interesting things with us. But he would really put us down. All of us. He would think nothing of telling us we were terrible, we had no technique, and so forth. We may not have had much, true, but we weren't absolute zeros! At first he was martinet-like but he did sort of mellow, or else we got used to him. His procedure was to sit at the piano with each member of the class who brought a piece in. He'd put the piece up with a page of blank music paper to the right. He had a pencil which was one of those push-button types. When he wanted to go fast, he didn't even have to bother to turn the pencil. He could just squeeze

[7] For interviews with other Hindemith students, see Oral History of American Music, Hindemith Project, Yale.

[8] Interviews, Harold Shapero with Bolster, Oral History of American Music, Hindemith Project, Yale, 24 April 1976, and with Perlis, 9 October 1980, Natick, Massachusettts.

it—bang, bang, bang as though he was a human musical typewriter. He'd look at your piece, scan it with his eye quickly and have you play it if you insisted, but he didn't need that. He'd immediately make judgments: "This is pretty . . . this isn't a bad way to go, this is a wrong modulation." And then he'd rewrite your piece for you while you were waiting—just like having your pants pressed! Pure Hindemith just by changing an interval here and rhythms there. It was always better of course. You realized you were being dominated, yet the process of watching him write at that speed with technical strength and coherence was awesome. "Well, you know," he said, when I told him I was impressed, "it's taken me a long time to come to the point where there's no time lost between my head, elbow, and arm." In other words, his mind and pencil.

From having started off wrong, he took a shine to me and to Lukas Foss, and invited us to visit him for private instruction after the Tanglewood semester. So I came breathless into the house in Lenox, and there was a big sheet of orchestral paper on his desk that had a motive on it with a big fermata. I said, "That's an interesting motive." "Yes, it looks pretty good," replied Hindemith. Then we went with the paper to the park in Lenox with a bunch of manuscript paper and he said, "Okay, fill the page with melodies. I'll be back." I didn't know what to do. So I filled the page full of Hindemith-like melodies to please him. He came back in a couple of hours, looked quickly, and said, "That's not it. Keep writing. Write melodies, okay?" We went on this way for two or three days, all morning and all afternoon on the park bench. I didn't have the vaguest idea of what he was after! In desperation, in the middle of these things I was trying to write Hindemith-style, I finally put down a melody from a little woodwind trio I had written as a freshman at Harvard. That day when he came by, he came right to that tune and said, "That's it. You finally found it, build on it." All I could think was, "Thank goodness, it's over. I don't have to sit here any more!" He was very pleasant, and by that time, we all thought he was lovable! In the meantime, while I was on that park bench, he had written the entire first movement of his E-flat Symphony.

Copland met with his students individually—not in class as Hindemith did—and he held orchestration classes a few times a week. His students were Josef Alexander, Harold Brown, Donald Fuller, Charles Jones, Robert Palmer, John Verrall, and John Colman (after Hindemith refused him). Copland delivered four lectures to the Academy that summer: Berlioz; Musical Form; American Music; and Debussy, Schoenberg, and Stravinsky. Compared with Hindemith, Copland was supportive, but Robert Palmer makes this point:

> It is important to remember that Aaron was as sharp a critic as I've ever come across. He could put his finger on trouble spots, but without tearing a work down. He didn't always like what was brought to him, but if he liked a work, you could be sure that he did. What was remarkable about Aaron as a teacher was this combination of giving the necessary criticism without ruining a young composer's confidence.[9]

Copland thought that students could learn a great deal from hearing their pieces played and that it was wasteful not to take advantage of the performers who were right at hand. (After regular classes ended, Copland got together with composers and performers who had stayed on at Tanglewood, and they read through works not played earlier. "But don't tell Hindemith!" warned Copland.) Hindemith wrote to Gertrud: "Copland wants to have his students' works performed and always speaks of them as finished composers, while I consider mine to be raw beginners in need of appropriate training. Koussevitzky is completely on my side and happily agrees with my decision to forbid anything by my students to be performed." This is a rather surprising statement, since it has been thought that Koussevitzky did not agree with Hindemith's teaching methods.[10] But nothing in Hindemith's correspondence indicates problems between the two. In fact, late in August Hindemith wrote to Gertrud: "He has offered me no less than the Directorship of the entire school, but I am not particularly attracted by that. . . ."

Koussevitzky's conducting students were Leonard Bernstein, Lukas Foss, Richard Bales, and Thor Johnson. Each received a scholarship of $50. Copland saw as much of Bernstein as the frantic pace of the six-week term allowed. Harold Shapero soon became Copland's close friend, and Lukas Foss, who had searched Copland out at the Empire Hotel in 1937 when Foss was only fifteen, also knew Copland well by the summer of 1940. Foss would run to Aaron whenever Hindemith threw him out of class after saying, "Write in any style you want, but write in my style while you study with me. At least you'll have my world, then eventually maybe you'll have your own." And Foss finally thought that Hindemith was right and went on to study with him at Yale. In an interview, Foss talked about Hindemith and Copland: "They got along because Copland never doesn't get along. But I think Aaron had a hard time. Because Hindemith would say things like 'Why should my pupils study orchestration with you? If anybody knows orchestration, it's me!' That kind of thing, which no American would say. And Aaron would answer mildly, 'Well, it just happens to be something I like to teach.'"[11]

In midsummer one of Hindemith's composition students, Charles Naginski, drowned. Because of Hindemith's reputation as a taskmaster, the tragic incident caused speculation about whether Naginski had taken his own life. Hindemith wrote to Gertrud (6 August):

> I have one less student—he was drowned night before last. He would go in the lake every morning with the class but he could not swim and so just paddled around a little. In spite of that, he went alone last Sunday afternoon to a nearby lake to bathe. When he did not return the police dragged the lake and found him dead. He was 31 years old and somewhat neurotic. Perhaps I could have straightened him out in time (he wanted to come to Yale to study); he was not overly talented but could have been quite good. The school was rather upset over the incident. [12]

[9] Interview, Robert Palmer with Perlis by telephone, 12 May 1983.

[10] See Howard Boatwright, "Paul Hindemith as a Teacher," *Musical Quarterly*, L:3 (July 1964), 282. Boatwright states, "His [Hindemith] ideas of what ought to be accomplished at a summer school such as Tanglewood did not coincide with those of Koussevitzky." Boatwright recalls, "Hindemith once told his class at Yale. . . that Copland complained to him about the morale of his [Hindemith's] composition students." Hindemith tells this story in *A Composer's World*, deleting Copland's name: "Once I had a discussion on this subject with a well-known composer. He said, 'I think your system of teaching composers is all wrong. It discourages young people." Paul Hindemith, *A Composer's World* (Gloucester, Massachusetts: Peter Smith, 1969), 215.

[11] Interview, Lukas Foss with Bolster, Oral History of American Music, Hindemith Project, Yale, 11 November 1976, New York City.

[12] Nicolas Slonimsky recounts the incident in *Music Since 1900*, 486: "Charles Naginski, 31-year-old Egyptian-born American-Jewish composer of brilliant eclectic gifts, drowns in the Housatonic River by accident, or more likely, by design." The following September (1940) Naginski's *Sinfonietta* was performed at Yaddo.

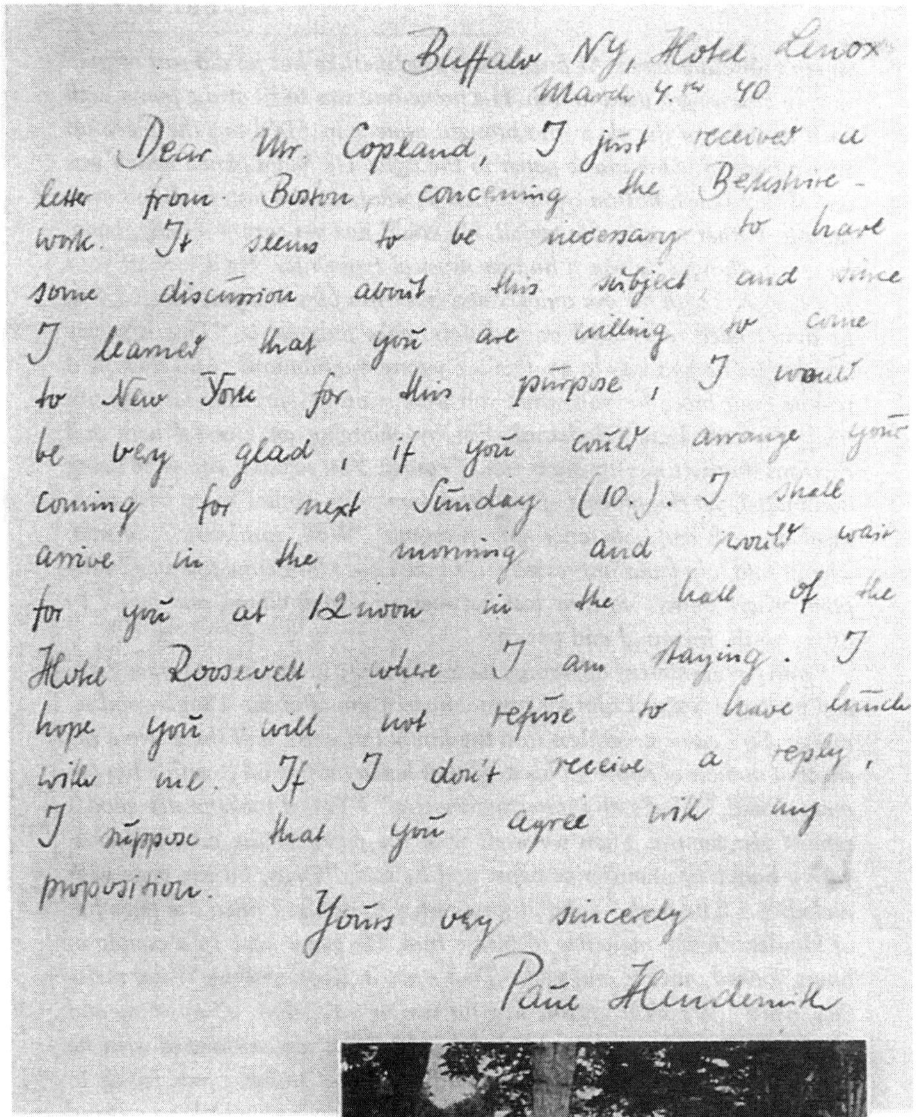

Buffalo NY, Hotel Lenox
March 4th 40

Dear Mr. Copland, I just received a letter from Boston concerning the Berkshire-work. It seems to be necessary to have some discussion about this subject and since I learned that you are willing to come to New York for this purpose, I would be very glad, if you could arrange your coming for next Sunday (10.). I shall arrive in the morning and would wait for you at 12 noon in the hall of the Hotel Roosevelt where I am staying. I hope you will not refuse to have lunch with me. If I don't receive a reply, I suppose that you agree with my proposition.

Yours very sincerely

Paul Hindemith

Above: Letter from Paul Hindemith, 1940
Right: Copland, Margaret Grant, Hindemith, and friend at Tanglewood, summer 1940

Harold Shapero recalls composition class the next morning as silent and deadly. "After about two hours went by, the tension got extreme. And Hindemith suddenly burst out and said, 'They say I killed him.' Nobody could reply to that. Hindemith wasn't unsympathetic. He tried to figure out what he'd done and if it could have been his fault. He did talk about it. And then we let it lie, and that was the end of it."

Although Naginski's death cast a shadow on the BMC's first season, the Festival Concerts during the final three weeks were a diversion. Each performance attracted from between eight to ten thousand people. Eleanor Roosevelt was one of the famous guests at a Tanglewood concert that summer, and even Toscanini made an unannounced visit. The major American work conducted by Koussevitzky was Roy Harris' *Third Symphony*. Hindemith's symphony *Mathis der Maler* was given a great deal of attention. Hindemith found Tanglewood so attractive that he stayed in Lenox for a few weeks after the season to work on his symphony before going to New Haven to begin a new life as Professor of Music at Yale.

Copland also remained to work on the *Quiet City* suite and to compose an organ piece commissioned by H. W. Gray, the English publishers. (Gray had invited several American composers to write short organ works for a series: Frederick Jacobi, Douglas Moore, Piston, Sessions, Leo Sowerby, and Bernard Wagenaar.) Copland composed a four-page piece first called *Improvisation*, in three sections, the outer ones quiet with polytonal harmonies, enclosing a contrasting midsection. The title was changed to *Episode*. It was played first by William Strickland in March 1941, soon after publication.[13] Hindemith and Copland were both sufficiently impressed with the BMC's first season to agree to return the next season. Copland shared Koussevitzky's elation and enthusiasm at having so many superb musicians and students together in one place. The Center was Koussevitzky's pride and joy until his death in 1951, and for Copland, a very special place to return to year after year for twenty-one memorable summers over a span of twenty-five years.

At the close of the summer of 1940, Harold Clurman, always philosophical on special occasions, wrote to his friend:

> The thirties had a certain drive—the Depression and the realistic mood . . . ten years of the Group. . . . What has happened? All around me I notice a new thing. People are not talking so many generalities. They are not driving forward with a vague hope or a collective optimism: they are asking themselves—Who am I? What am I? Where do I belong?. . in a word, taking stock. . . . The period of the 1940s will be one of reaction. Don't you think all this will show itself in music too somehow? What is happening to your own work? Or don't you have too conscious a sense of it? I know you have always been able to work without theory or too much consciousness. Still . . .

The fact is that Copland composed little after his return to New York in the fall of 1940. The atmosphere, so filled with uncertainty and turmoil, was not conducive to writing music. Victor, who had been working as a photographer's assistant during the summer

[13] Alfred Publishing Company, Inc., holds the copyright for *Episode*. An incomplete score at the Library of Congress bears the following inscription on the title page: "Episode/Improvisation/Piece for Organ."

months, was waiting to be called into the service; Blitzstein was already in uniform; and Copland worried about Nadia—would she make it safely out of Europe in time?

Bela Bartók refused to allow his music to be broadcast in Nazi countries, causing furor in his native Hungary, and Copland joined with others in forming an American Music League to support his brave gesture. But otherwise Copland had no outlet for his patriotic feelings. Socialist activities had slowed down after the WPA's Federal Music Project came into being, under which artists were paid for performing civic duties. The war years would be difficult ones for composers. Few in the service could work in the field of music; those at home had to choose between creating patriotic works or composing in isolation. Roger Sessions, who disliked overt nationalism in art, addressed the issue again in an article called "American Music and the Crisis" in which he stated, "The composer is faced by the impossibility of finding his public within himself."[14]

Copland wrote to the Department of State offering his services. While waiting for an answer, he immersed himself in organizational activities— the League, the Arrow Music Press, the ACA, the American Music Center. His fortieth birthday was celebrated quietly with his family. Copland, usually casual and philosophical about birthdays, was less so about this one. David Diamond wrote to him (19 November 1940): "I am sorry my birthday greetings upset you. Really, Aaron, I only meant it in all sincerity. . . . Just the same I hope you have forty more and I never forget one."

The time seemed right for considering a suggestion from Whittlesey House for a second book, so Copland began to organize and collect materials. In *What to Listen For in Music*, his target had been the general listening audience; but for his next book, he wanted to tackle the problems of contemporary music. The result was *Our New Music*, published in the fall of 1941, a year after Copland began to assemble articles written previously for *Modern Music* and other journals.

Our New Music was not meant to be a dictionary of modern music or a prediction of who the most promising young composers of the future would be; rather, it was intended as a guide to mainstream developments in contemporary music. Copland began by tracing the roots of modernism in the nineteenth century, giving emphasis to Moussorgsky as a pivotal figure. Two main sections followed: one on European composers, the other on Americans. Of Schoenberg and the twelve-tone system, Copland wrote: "Already it begins to sound surprisingly dated. . . . It creates a certain monotony of effect that severely limits its variety of expression. . . But for a long time to come it is likely to be of interest principally to specialists and connoisseurs rather than to the generality of music lovers. . . ." (Later, Copland would admit that the twelve-tone movement "took a position no one could have foreseen—that is one of vital importance after World War II.") Included in the European section were early and later Stravinsky, Bartók, Ravel and Roussel, Satie and Les Six, and

[14] Roger Sessions, "American Music and the Crisis," *Modern Music*, XVIII:4 (May-June 1941), 211-17.

Top: Copland, Koussevitsky, and Bernstein at the closing ceremonies of the Berkshire Music Center, 1941
Middle: Copland and Lukas Foss, summer, late forties
Bottom: Copland and Bernstein, Tanglewood, summer 1940

Milhaud. In the American chapter, Copland examined six contemporaries: Ives, Harris, Sessions, Piston, Thomson, and Blitzstein. Chávez was given a full chapter, and Copland himself was represented by the reprinting of an autobiographical sketch, "Composer from Brooklyn," which had first appeared in 1938 in the *Magazine of Art.* Concluding chapters reviewed the role of the media—radio, film, and phonograph music. About the change to a new decade, Copland wrote:

> The decade 1930-1940 marked the end of the experimental phase of contemporary music. For almost forty years, music had passed through a series of revolutionary crises, as a result of which all the stultifying rules of harmony, rhythmic phrase, and melodic construction had been broken down. By 1930, composers everywhere began to sense the necessity for consolidating the gains made for their art. . . .

Copland believed that the pendulum had swung into a period in which "the more revolutionary twenties were normalized, one of new simplicity that has left certain of our musical elite with a sense of being let down."

Olin Downes' review in *The New York Times* (19 October 1941) praised *Our New Music* for "brilliant and admirable pages," but criticized Copland for claiming that modern music was ready for the mainstream of musical listening. Copland responded: "My book is not a plea for any kind of musical modernism. It is quite simply a statement of my picture of what modern music is and how it got that way." Downes followed Copland's letter with a second article (30 November), setting off a heated debate. Theodore Chanler's review of *Our New Music* in *Modern Music* was entitled, "The New Romanticism,"[15] and Virgil Thomson reviewed *Our New Music* for the *Herald Tribune* as a "Fireside Chat from the President of American Music." Thomson praised the book:

> What gives it its unique quality among books about modern music, is its gentlemanly, its humane tone. . . . There are bitter books and pugnacious books and log-rolling books and joke books about that subject. Practically nowhere else is there a book on modern music at once so enlightened and so sweetly frank as Mr. Copland's.

Thomson explained that Copland was not all sweetness—

> He grants to each of his friends and enemies no more or no less than what is fair. His friends and his enemies both may well be grateful for his having placed them in the line-up at all and for not having hogged the center place himself.

Certain remarks in "Composer from Brooklyn" were viewed as a retreat from Copland's long-standing support of modern music. For example:

> During these years I began to feel an increasing dissatisfaction with the relations of the music-loving public and the living composer. The old 'special' public of the modern music concerts had fallen away, and the conventional concert public continued apathetic or indifferent to anything but the established classics. It seemed to me that we composers were in danger of working in a vacuum. . . My most recent works, in their separate ways, embody this tendency toward an imposed simplicity.

[15] Theodore Chanler, "The New Romanticism," *Modern Music*, XIX: (November-December 1941), 65-67.

Copland did not intend his remarks as a rebuttal of former works, but they were frequently taken as such; moreover, publication in book form gave them emphasis. When preparing a later revised version of *Our New Music*, Copland was relieved to have an opportunity to clarify his position. In *The New Music: 1900-1960,* published in 1968, he wrote:

> I have learned, to my discomfiture, that the writing of an autobiographical sketch in mid-career is fraught with peril. Commentators, pleased to be able to quote literally, are convinced that they have pinned the composer down for all time. Thus, the final two paragraphs of my brief memoir have done me considerable harm. The mention of "an imposed simplicity" was taken to mean that I had renounced my more complex and "difficult" music, turned my back on the cultivated audience that understands a sophisticated musical language, and henceforth would write music solely for the "masses." Quoted and requoted, these remarks of mine emphasized a point of view which, although apposite at the time of writing—the end of the '30s—seem to me to constitute an oversimplification of my aims and intentions, especially when applied to a consideration of my subsequent work and of my work as a whole. . . .[16]

The revision also gave Copland the chance to retract his statements on Schoenberg and the Viennese school and to bring up to date the composers who had continued to produce works since *Our New Music.* In the revised version, the section on the media, which had become outdated, was replaced with accounts of musical developments since World War II such as chance operations and electronics. *Our New Music* and *The New Music* are still informative; moreover, they have value as biographical sources on Copland, providing insights and perspectives on his career and the changes in his thinking. If one examines both versions of the book side by side, certain Copland traits are constant; among them: an openness in admitting errors, a gracefulness in correcting them, and a loyal and steady support of modern music as a substantial and worthwhile body of artistic works deserving attention by audiences of all times. Copland's writings on music express vividly and with a sense of immediacy what it meant to be a composer in America during the earlier years of this century.

Copland made his living from writings and lectures during the winter of 1940-41. His carefully kept financial accounts show several fees in 1940 of about $100 each for lecture recitals in Allentown, Pittsburgh, and Philadelphia, at the Town Hall in New York, and at Dartmouth and Colby colleges. Royalties of a few hundred dollars were received from Ballet Caravan for *Billy the Kid*, and over $400 from McGraw-Hill (parent company of Whittlesey House) for *What to Listen For in Music*, and a $250 advance for "Book II." Modest royalties were trickling in from Boosey & Hawkes. The major musical event of the season was the premiere of *Quiet City* in January in New York and Koussevitzky's conducting of it in Boston on 18 April 1941.

In April a response arrived from the State Department designating Copland a member of the President's Advisory Committee on Music. "The Committee is to advise the Depart-

[16] Aaron Copland, *The New Music: 1900-1960*, 161.

ment of State through the Division of Cultural Relations regarding musical interchange American republics and the coordination of activities in this country which concern inter-American music." When Copland wrote to Clurman that he expected to be sent to South America on a goodwill tour, Clurman replied, "I am impressed! You are coming into your proper field now: diplomacy!" Knowing that Tanglewood, followed by the South American trip, would soon take his full time, Copland again needed a quiet place where he could compose without interruption. He chose Cuba. Only Victor was told of his whereabouts. After checking into the Royal Palm Hotel in Havana, Copland went to work, and returned at the end of May with *Our New Music* ready for the publisher and the *Piano Sonata* almost finished. It was time to pack up for Tanglewood.

One evening early in June 1941 Copland carried two suitcases down the four flights to his car parked outside the loft. When he returned after going back up for the rest of his luggage, the two valises were gone. One was filled with personal belongings; the other with music. Copland went directly to the 20th Precinct police station to report the theft. A reward was offered, and the Department of Sanitation was asked to be on the lookout for odd sheets of music paper. (Copland's fear was that whoever had forced open the window of his car might be so disgusted at finding nothing but papers in one suitcase that he would throw it away.) The newspapers covered the story and even interviewed Mrs. Harris Copland about her son's loss— "His little mother hoped the thief would not destroy the manuscripts, believing them the works of 'just an ordinary' musician." Victor (still waiting to hear from his draft board) volunteered to go around to the neighborhood junk dealers and ragpickers. Before leaving for Lenox, Copland listed his loss for the Great American Insurance Company: "Collected themes for Billy and The City in binding, Sorcery to Science—pencil, Piano Sonata—two movements in ink, 10 pages on thin paper, The Elegies—broad paper, proofs of the Lark; pr rubbers, 4 toothbrushes, Yardley's, "The Critical Composer," mms blank, date-book, article: "Composers Without a Halo," flannel pants, 1 suit, sweaters, some gloves, shoes."

The thief was apprehended. A postcard from Victor to Aaron sent to Stockbridge on 10 June reported: "He's admitted sole guilt, but having a hell of a time getting stuff back. Everything's been dispersed. So far, 3 pr pants and a few other things. . . ." The music manuscripts were not recovered. This was a painful loss, particularly the notebooks of musical ideas collected over several years and the *Piano Sonata*, whose reconstruction had to be undertaken immediately while still fresh in the composer's mind. John Kirkpatrick, for whom Copland had played the *Sonata*, wrote out what themes he could recall and sent them on 7 July 1941.

Copland had rented a very pleasant house in Stockbridge. (He liked it so much that he arranged to rent it again in 1942.) When Bernstein heard about the house, he wrote: "There's a great problem concerning quarters. . . . Is it really impossible to live in your house? You don't work anyway during those six weeks. And think of the fun! We're all feeling rather anti-dormitory. . . ." Copland rejected this idea, recalling the noise and excitement of the students at Cranwell the previous summer, but Bernstein was often at his house in 1941 and guests came every weekend. Rosamond Bernier recalls, "Copland would whisper to me, 'There are *guests* in the house!' as if to say that there were *mice* in the kitchen!"

Again in 1941 Hindemith and Copland divided the duties of the composition department; Olin Downes returned to lecture on early music and to lead public rehearsal discussions on Saturday mornings, supplemented by guests Howard Hanson (who came up to lecture when his *"Romantic" Symphony* [no. 2] was scheduled for performance with the BSO), Putnam Aldrich, and Carleton Sprague Smith. Boris Goldovsky joined Dr. Herbert Graf in the opera program; Gregor Piatigorsky and Jesus Maria Sanromá were on hand to teach chamber music; and Hugh Ross and G. Wallace Woodworth ran the chorus. A new addition on the scene was the Theater Concert Hall, again designed by Saarinen, with funds donated by Mrs. Mary Curtis Bok. The Doctor's assistant, as in 1940, was Stanley Chapple, and his conducting students were Bernstein, Foss, Thor Johnson, Walter Hendl, Richard Korn, and Robert Whitney. An excellent student orchestra was made up of the best of more than 700 applicants from all over the country. The composition students numbered sixteen. This year it was Harold Shapero who was barred from Hindemith's class, even though he had just won the Rome Prize. Shapero wrote to Copland (16 June 1941):

> Hindy doesn't think I ought to be in his class this summer. It is my extremely embarrassing task to ask you if you still have any room, and are prepared or willing to soak up Hindemith's outcasts, particularly me. . . .Enclosed find a postcard which I hope will make your task easier. Ever since Lenny told me that you get about 75 letters a day, I've considered it a crime to inflict mail upon you.

Copland took Shapero into his group, which was made up of the Mexican-Indian Blas Galindo (sent by Chávez), the Canadian Barbara Pentland, the Hawaiian Dai-Keong Lee, as well as Sam Morgenstern, Gardner Read, Robert Ward, and Arnold Chaitman. In Hindemith's group were Lukas Foss, Norman Dello Joio, John Klein, Herbert Fromm, and newcomers Montague Cantor, Paul Gelrud, and Ulysses Kay.

Copland gave each student a private lesson of an hour and a half and taught two advanced orchestration classes a week. In addition to analyzing major works to be performed in the festival, Copland taught orchestration of contemporary radio and movie music. Gardner Read recalled, "Copland gave us a passage in *Of Mice and Men*, told us to score it in our own style and then showed us his score." In summing up the benefits of the summer's study, Read wrote, "Copland and I were at sword's point for some days because he called me a romanticist. . . . But it did make me question whether or not my music was a bit too lush, too complex, for contemporaneous expression. It made me sure that if I were standing my own ground, it was with reason. . . ."[17] Hindemith again taught his students in class for over four hours every day. He introduced American students to early music, reading from Zarlino and other theorists in class, and though there were no scores or early instruments at Tanglewood, he would appear at chamber music classes with pages he had copied out himself the previous winter from the Yale Music Library.

[17] Gardner Read, "Tanglewood: Investment in Musical Futures," *The Music News*, XXXII: 20 (18 December 1941), 6-7, 22.

During the Music Festival of 1941, proceeds from one concert were designated for British War Relief and for a collection of BSO recordings to be shipped to American musicians in the service. Compositions by American composers were included on Koussevitzky's programs: Samuel Barber's *Violin Concerto* and Copland's *Quiet City*, which was paired with Hindemith's *Concerto for Violoncello and Orchestra*, Piatigorsky as soloist. Olin Downes lectured on the contemporary pieces at the Saturday morning rehearsal. He stated that, in his opinion, "Copland was at his best in the poetic mood of *Quiet City*." Audience and critics were enthusiastic. Immediately following the closing ceremonies of the Music Center, Copland left Tanglewood for Mexico to begin a four-month tour of South America for the State Department—to include Ecuador, Peru, Chile, Argentina, Uruguay, Brazil, and Cuba.

Accepting the plaudits of the audience after a performance of Hindemith's *Cello Concerto* are *(left)* Gregor Piatigorsky, *(center)* Serge Koussevitzky, and *(right)* Paul Hindemith; Tanglewood, Sunday, 3 May 1941

THE EARLY WAR YEARS

1941 - 1942

South America as a whole does not exist. As I was to discover on my first tour in 1941, it is a collection of separate countries, each with different traditions, at different stages of musical development, and with practically no musical contact with each other. Only as I traveled from country to country did I realize that you must be willing to split the continent up in your mind. Also, one could not go south of the border with a critical attitude and the expectation that the level of performance and education would parallel that of North America. Both North and South had experienced a colonial past and had formerly looked to Europe for artistic leadership and inspiration. During the war years the need to reaffirm national characteristics accelerated. The United States government, as part of an effort to improve inter-American relationships, placed leading Americanists in government agencies to promote Pan-Americanism. Carleton Sprague Smith coordinated musical activities for Nelson Rockefeller's Committee of Inter-American Affairs.[1] Rockefeller was only twenty-five. He was determined to set up an ideal model of what inter-cultural relations should be. I had been preceded in Latin America by Kirstein's Ballet Caravan, by Toscanini and the NBC Orchestra, and by a quintet of woodwind performer-composers that included David Van Vactor, Alvin Etler, John Barrows, Adolph Weiss, and Robert McBride. Rockefeller's committee seemed more interested in American composers than in virtuoso performers, as was the case later on. When it became clear that a cultural mission to South American countries by a composer who could speak directly with native composers would be useful, I was chosen by the Committee for Inter-American Artistic and Intellectual Relations, an agency set up by the Coordinator of Inter-American Affairs. On the committee was Henry Allen Moe, secretary of the Guggenheim Foundation. Dr. Moe arranged for a grant of $3,100 to cover my four-month tour. He instructed me (14 August 1941):

> I want you, please, to come back with a list of composers and musical scholars who in your judgment based on your own knowledge are first-rate and who ought to be given funds to come to the United States for sound music purposes. Among such persons is, in my mind, [Heitor] Villa–Lobos of Brazil; if he is interested in coming to the U.S. please ask him when and for how long and what he would want to do here. . . In Latin America there has been adopted the word 'goodwillings.' We want no part in 'goodwillings.' We want to assist hard and serious professional work . . . .

[1] Gilbert Chase was Latin American Music Specialist at the Library of Congress, 1940-43, and Charles Seeger was chief of the Music Division of the Pan American Union.

During the summer I wrote to Carleton Sprague Smith to inform him of the lectures I could give in Spanish and the music I wanted to play and conduct. Carleton made the appropriate contacts in each country. I was expected to send detailed reports describing and assessing individual composers, administrators, educational facilities, government attitudes to music, and so forth. Toward this purpose, I made entries in a diary upon leaving each city. Fortunately I kept this diary, and from its seventy-eight pages I can reconstruct the highlights of my journey:

20–28 AUGUST: Meetings with three Mexican composers of the younger generation: Salvador Contreras, Pablo Moncayo, Daniel Ayala. With Blas Galindo they form a group known as "Los Cuatro." Of this group Galindo would seem to be the most gifted. Certainly his technique is the most advanced of the four. All these composers write music very much in the style of the Mexican School, founded by Chávez and Revueltas. Thus far, in their early thirties, the Four have not exceeded their older confreres. They are limited in their use of form which tends always to be sectionally constructed and in types of melodic material which tend always toward the Mexican popular tune. Their forte is orchestration, learned mostly by performing under Chávez in the Orquesta Sinfónica de México. I know Galindo well from Tanglewood where he has just last summer been my student. I visited with musicologists who were mainly Spanish refugees and with Rodolfo Halffter, a refugee Spanish composer. Everywhere I travel the composers are playing their music and showing me their scores. . . .

29 AUGUST: Guatemala City overnight, then Cristobal and Bogota, Colombia. The attitude of creative musicians in Colombia is pessimistic. The request I heard most often was "send us more records!" I was invited to give two radio programs on the National Radio: for the first, I read a page of greeting in Spanish and played recordings of *El Salón México* and *Music for the Theatre*; on the second, I presented works by three Americans—Harris, Piston, and Bowles. Several Colombian composers gathered at the radio station, and following the broadcast, I played some of my own piano pieces, and we talked until the early morning hours. In Quito, Ecuador, I spent a few days before traveling on to Peru. There, I discovered that previous reports were true—no orchestras, no conservatory, and no teachers. "Send us composers," they pleaded, "to teach harmony, counterpoint, and composition in Spanish." .. .

7 SEPTEMBER: Lima, Peru. I was met by the city's outstanding musical personalities. Preceding me had been successful performances of *Billy the Kid* by Ballet Caravan, and the film version was being shown in local movie houses. The Orquesta Sinfónica Nacional invited me to

conduct *Billy* on 10 September. The players left much to be desired technically, but they were lively and enthusiastic. I heard the usual pessimistic story of musical life from the composers. I am spending time with André Sas,[2] a Belgian who has lived in Peru for the past twenty years.

15 SEPTEMBER: Santiago, Chile. I was met by their foremost musical figure, Domingo Santa Cruz, who acted as my host and explained the workings of the Fine Arts Faculty, the official center of all musical life in Chile, of which he is dean. Composers here are highly organized, perhaps because they are not only isolated from the general public, but also from the rest of the Continent, being on the West Coast. Their musical compositions reflect this group tendency. I found Chilean composers definitely behind the times with the romantic and chromatic music they write, and always rather more complex than necessary. Although the music is meticulously written and sensitively handled, all the music seems to have a rather derivative air. Santa Cruz is probably as good a composer as one can find on the West Coast of S.A., and the only young composer-conductor I can recommend for study in the U.S. is twenty-two-year-old Juan Orrego[-Salas], pupil of Santa Cruz. I have been invited to a farewell party by the Chilean composers at the Faculty of Fine Arts. I plan to play my new *Piano Sonata* for the first time. Have been invited to return for a week in October to conduct the orchestra, to lecture, and to preside over a jury to distribute prizes among Chilean composers. Have accepted. . . .

26 SEPTEMBER: Buenos Aires, Argentina. There is a young composer here who is generally looked upon as the "white hope" of Argentine music. He is now twenty-five and is certainly the first candidate for a trip to the States from any standpoint. Alberto Ginastera would profit by contacts outside Argentina. He is looked upon with favor by all groups here, is presentable, modest almost to the timid degree, and will, no doubt, someday be an outstanding figure in Argentine music. Certainly he is far ahead of any of the young men of his age here. The only composer I have met in South America who is using the twelve-tone system is Juan Carlos Paz who seems more like the typical figure of a composer in our modern music movement—serious, learned, literary, and somewhat heroic. One would like to see what his music was before he adopted the twelve-tone system about six years ago . . . an interesting figure, worth watching. . . . I lectured to about 200 people for an organization, La Nueva Musica, headed by Paz.

10 OCTOBER: A night boat to Montevideo. As everywhere, I was treated cordially by the Embassy officials and dignitaries from the local government. The Instituto Interamericano de Musicologia is based in Montevideo, headed by Francisco Curt Lange. I am scheduled to address this group on the subject of modern music in the U.S. There is to be a formal reception and concert including Harris' *Trio* which I will play with local musicians, Sessions' two chorale preludes, and a few of my own works. Two of the lectures which I had prepared in advance in Spanish are very much in demand—"The Influence of Jazz" and "Music for Films." American movies are very popular down here. They know *Of Mice and Men*, so my film lecture, punctuated with visual illustrations, has been particularly well-received. South Americans are very sociable; receptions are held after each concert and lecture. I have met Andres Segovia and the talented young composer Hector Tosar. The nearest parallel I can think of to Tosar is Shostakovitch. Tosar's music has the same easy appeal, and the same dash.... The Colon Orchestra, under Juan José Castro, played *An Outdoor Overture*, and for once, I am satisfied with both the orchestra and the conducting—but the audience was small.[3] At a party afterward, I was delighted to see my old friend, Nicolas Slonimsky, who is travelling around South America collecting materials for a book.[4] In José Maria Castro, brother of Juan José, I found a composer with a fresh style and personality added to an excellent technique. None of the usual Gallicisms or nostalgia or "effect" music so current down here. I should very much like to have him come to New York, and he says he wishes to come. Paz planned a concert of All North American chamber music sponsored by La Nueva Musica for 21 October with works by Sessions, Harris, Gerald Strang, Cowell and me. It was this concert at which my *Piano Sonata* had its public premiere. The impression was favorable. . . .

24 OCTOBER: Return to Santiago to serve as judge for a contest of Chilean composers. In my absence, a concert had been arranged for 5 November at which I conducted the Orquesta Sinfónica de Chile. The program included *An Outdoor Overture, Quiet City, El Salón México,* and the *Piano Concerto* for which I was soloist. . .

5 NOVEMBER: Return to Buenos Aires and on to Rio de Janeiro. I have tried to hear as much native music as possible in each country; in Rio, it is the samba band. Brazil's outstanding musical personality, Heitor Villa-Lobos, takes care that I hear the real thing. Villa-Lobos is an independent type. He picks me up in his car and we drive into the mountains around Rio to see the sights. When he heard that I was interested in native music he took me to an "Escola de Samba" up in one of the famous "morros" of Rio.[5] I was struck by the rhythmic similarity to what I had heard in Cuba, but the melodic line is savage and more gutteral than any I have heard anywhere, with no harmony at all—only rhythm and melody. The music was overpowering in the small room where it was performed. Villa-Lobos is rather touchy about coming to America. He is firm on one point—he wishes to come purely as an artist—to be in no way connected with official or governmental authority. I let that pass and explained that a short trip would prepare the way for a real concert tour of imposing proportions later. Finally, he said laughing, "One would think that Copland came here just to get me to come to the U.S.!" His music has one outstanding quality—abundance. He is a kind of de Falla of Brazil in his best works, and a kind of Respighi of Brazil at other times. The works are likely as not to be loosely thrown together in an inextricable melange of authentic Brazilian atmosphere plus a full quota of modern French methods of composition. At times it is enormously picturesque. Free of prejudices, full of rhythmic and figured formulas, sometimes cheap and vulgar, sometimes astonishingly original, and full of temperament—a temperament that is profoundly Brazilian. In Brazilian music folklore informs everything. It is unusually rich—with Negro, Indian, Portuguese, and possibly Spanish influences. Combined with the Brazilian temperament, their music has more "face" than other groups of composers in South America.

[2] Sas wrote after Copland returned to the States (2. February 1942): "Just as you have to practice your Spanish, I must rehearse my English . . . it was a very great pleasure to meet you in Lima, where I am living almost as an anchor in a desert. The bad is that you came and disappeared just as a comet. I remember your piano Sonata that you played unfinished here.. . ."

[3] This report to Dr. Moe had direct results. By the end of the year Juan José Castro was in New York. Copland alerted Claire Reis to the idea of the League paying more attention to South American music. "An Evening for Juan José Castro" was held 7 December 1941 at the Museum of Modern Art.

[4] Nicolas Slonimsky, *Music of Latin America* (New York: Thomas Y. Crowell, 1945).

[5] "Escola de Samba" in the "morros" refers to a popular kind of social club located in the hills above Rio.

8 DECEMBER: Havana, Cuba. Lectures at the Lyceum on modern American composers and meetings with local composers. Gilberto Valdes has his own radio orchestra for which he composes music based on Cuban motifs. He should be the George Gershwin of Cuba, but he lacks both technique and the faculty of self-criticism. José Ardevol is an intelligent musician whose work deserves to be better known up north. Serious music in Cuba has suffered a severe blow with the deaths of its leading figures—Amadeo Roldán in 1939 and Alejandro Garcia Caturla in 1940. In a concert of Cuban and American works, I again played my *Piano Sonata.* I have been away four months. The Japanese attacked Pearl Harbor yesterday. It seems strange to be in Cuba with the United States at war. I am grateful to find American friends, Rosamond and Lew Riley, who are in Havana at this time. . . .

9 DECEMBER: Some thoughts en route to New York: South America is in the process of becoming. You can only be interested in these countries if you are interested in growing things. The countries that have developed most rapidly are those with the richest folklore—México and Brazil; whereas, the most interesting thing about Chile is its musical set-up—the Faculty for Fine Arts which is run by and for composers and artists. Argentina's musical creativity is underestimated in North America—composers are better off than we thought. Everywhere, French influence is predominant. Composers work under great difficulties with no opportunity to publish, few orchestras, little contact with live audiences, few radio performances, and little government support (except for Chile). I marvel that there is any creative work done at all, and I am impressed by the good that one energetic man can accomplish—such as Chávez in Mexico, Santa Cruz in Chile and Villa-Lobos in Brazil. It seems remarkable that we have not thought much of South America before! My general recommendations to the Committee for Inter-American Relations are as follows: supply more records for radio stations, and more published music to music centers; establish a distribution center in both North and South America; assist in the publication of South American works; publish a magazine in both languages.

Décimo Ciclo de Cultura Musical

EXTRA

MARTES 21
DE OCTUBRE
A LAS 21.30

El TEATRO DEL PUEBLO, presenta:

AUDICION XXVIII

LA NUEVA MUSICA

(Antología de las tendencias actuales)

CONSAGRADA A LA MODERNA MUSICA NORTEAMERICANA

y en honor de los maestros

Aaron Coplan y Nicolás Sloninsky

Intervienen: Anita Sujovolsky (violín) - Hilde Heinitz de Weil (viola) - Sofía Knoll (piano) - Aarón Copland (piano) - Nicolás Sloninsky (piano) - Esteban Eitler (flauta) - Francisco Heltay (violín) - German Weil (violoncelo)

TEATRO DEL PUEBLO
BUENOS AIRES

MINISTERIO DA EDUCAÇÃO E SAÚDE
UNIVERSIDADE DO BRASIL
ESCOLA NACIONAL DE MÚSICA

18.º Concêrto Oficial
Ultimo da Série de 1941

TERÇA-FEIRA, 25 DE NOVEMBRO
ÁS 21 HORAS

MUSICA MODERNA NORTE-AMERICANA
em homenagem ao eminente compositor

AARON COPLAND

Com a colaboração de:

CRISTINA MARISTANY
ALDA BORGERTH
OSCAR BORGERTH
EDMUNDO BLOIS
IBERÊ GOMES GROSSO
MOACYR LISERRA
ANTÃO SOARES
ARNALDO ESTRELLA
FRANCISCO MIGNONE

CONCIERTO
DE
OBRAS CONTEMPORANEAS
NORTEAMERICANAS Y CUBANAS

Presentación de
AARON COPLAND
Compositor, Director y Pianista

ORQUESTA DE CAMARA DE LA HABANA
Dirección: J. ARDEVOL

Con la colaboración de César Pérez Sentenat y Rafael Morales, pianistas; Alberto Bolet, violinista, y Alberto Roldán, violoncelista.

LYCEUM
Calzada y 8, VEDADO
JUEVES, 11 DE DICIEMBRE 1941,
5.30 P. M.

Top: Program from Buenos Aires, 21 October 1942
Middle: Program featuring the world premiere of the *Piano Sonata,* Brazil, 25 November 1942
Bottom right: Program from Cuba, 11 December 1942

Copland and Chávez at the piano with (left to right): Domingo Santa Cruz (Chile), Alberto Ginastera (Argentina), and Juan B. Plaza, (Venezuela), Caracas, 1957

I made my reports to the Committee and to the Guggenheim Foundation, and wrote an article, "The Composers of South America," in which I concluded: "From now on, whatever other result the world crisis may bring, it is a safe bet that musical relations with our southern neighbors will be different."[6] I am told that my 1941 expedition opened the way for many Latin American musicians to make contact with the world of concert music. For me, it was the beginning of friendships and associations that would continue through many years. I realized that such an experience enlarges one's field of vision. It made me feel concern for the provincialism that seemed to be typical of the music scene in New York, where there was a small circle of composers encouraging each other. The tendency to lean back and depend upon that small-circle encouragement seemed to me a lessening rather than an enlarging of one's capacities. While in Rio I wrote to Nadia (24 November 1941):

> It was so nice to receive your birthday note—so far from home. I was delighted. . . . My trip through South America has been fascinating. It has been like discovering a new continent. . . . You are well known here. . . . I also had time to complete my *Piano Sonata* which I am anxious for you to hear. . . .

An additional advantage of the South American trip had been the opportunity to test out the *Sonata* before braving it in New York. I felt able to write to Cliff Odets from Rio that I would play "his *Sonata*" for him soon after my return.

When I originally agreed to compose the *Piano Sonata*, I had asked Odets (2 January 1939): "Is a dedication and a presentation of the manuscript worth $500 to you? It would take me about 2 months to write, I think." Cliff agreed and promptly sent half the commission. One robbery, several interruptions, and almost three years later, the *Sonata* was ready. I have always been grateful to Odets for stimulating me to compose the second of my three major piano works; moreover, he never showed any impatience about delays as the months turned into years. Cliff invited friends and colleagues to his apartment for a first hearing. Clurman and Diamond were in California, but Denby and Blitzstein were present. I never knew how much Cliff really understood about music, but I do know that he felt it deeply. Whatever he thought about the *Sonata*, not an easy work to absorb from a first hearing, he never expressed anything but praise, and after that evening in late December 1941, he wrote to Clurman, "There is a bread-like truth about the *Sonata*." Under an exclusive arrangement with Boosey & Hawkes whereby my compositions were published soon after completion, the *Piano Sonata* appeared in print in 1942. Copies were sent to pianists and teachers. The reactions were favorable. John Kirkpatrick and his wife Hope Miller, a singer, had been performing recitals at various college campuses in the Midwest and the East at which the *Sonata* had been included. "It stands up awfully well with repeated playings," John wrote to me. "Has any pianist trotted out the *Sonata* in public in New York yet?" I had intended to play the premiere myself at a Town Hall Music Forum in February, but I responded that I would be pleased to have John beat me to it. His answer

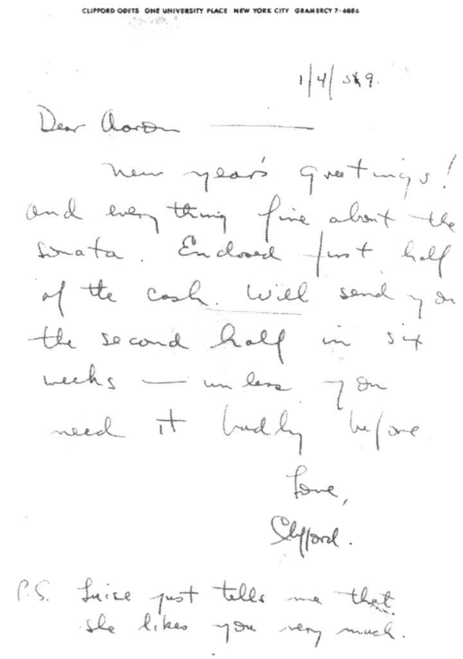

CLIFFORD ODETS ONE UNIVERSITY PLACE NEW YORK CITY GRAMERCY 7-6086

1/4/39.

Dear Aaron ——

New year's greetings! And everything fine about the sonata. Enclosed just half of the cash. Will send you the second half in six weeks — unless you need it badly before

Love,

Clifford.

P.S. Luise just tells me that she likes you very much.

Above: Letter from Clifford Odets, 1939
Right: Program including the New York premiere of the *Piano Sonata* performed by John Kirkpatrick

[6] Aaron Copland, "The Composers of South America," *Modern Music*, XIX: 2 (January-February 1942), 75-82.

in return was: "Your card with its revelations of your plans of Feb. 17 makes me almost regret our own plans, but the gracious way you put it gives me rather a trusted feeling of responsibility. I'll do my best by you. Would you like to accept a box to decorate? It'll be like old times, back in the twenties—first performances of Copland and Harris, things of Ruggles and Ives, and 'classics.'"[7]

I always connect the *Piano Sonata* with my old teacher, Rubin Goldmark. He thought of sonata form as music's highest goal. It was what a composer aimed for, even more than the fugue. One thinks of the sonata as dramatic—a kind of play being acted out with plenty of time for self- expression. It seems to me that my *Piano Sonata* follows that idea. It is a serious piece that requires careful and repeated study. There is considerable dissonance in it, yet the work is predominantly consonant. Not as spare and bony as the *Piano Variations*, the themes in the *Sonata* are fuller and the chords more protracted than in the earlier piece. But every note was carefully chosen and none included for ornamental reasons. The *Sonata* lies somewhere between the *Variations* and *Our Town*. Its three movements follow a slow, fast, slow sequence and are separate in character, but with subtle relationships between them, so that each seems to grow from the preceding. The first movement is a regular sonata allegro form with two themes, a development section characterized by disjunct rhythms and a playful mood, and a clear recapitulation in which the opening idea is dramatically restated. The second movement scherzo is rhythmically American—I never would have thought of those rhythms if I had not been familiar with jazz. This has to do with a dependence on the eighth note as the basic rhythmic element—very demanding for the pianist because the rhythmic units shift through 5/8, 6/8, 3/4, and 7/8. Leo Smit has reminded me that the instructions in my score for the scherzo read "mezzo piano, delicate and restless." According to Leo, "That's hard to do—even when you're nervous!"[8] The third movement of the *Sonata* is free in form and further from the classic sonata than the previous movements. The British music historian, Wilfrid Mellers, whose writings about American music I have long admired, pointed to the final movement of the *Piano Sonata* as "the essential Copland . . . its relinquishment of the time sense . . . is a phenomenon of quite profound spiritual and cultural implication."[9] Mellers' allusion to a sense of "immobility" in the *Sonata* seems to say in prose what I had in mind when composing the music. The *Sonata* does not end with the usual flash of virtuosic passages: instead, it is rather grand and massive.

John and Hope Kirkpatrick's recital of January 1943, which featured the New York premiere of the *Piano Sonata*, included works by Bach, Purcell, Harris, Beethoven, and Ives. Virgil reviewed the recital in the *Herald Tribune* (10 January 1943): "Superb piano playing. Mr. Kirkpatrick is interesting no matter what he plays." About the *Sonata*: "I was afraid for one whole movement that this piece was not going to get anywhere, and I was still a bit nervous during the second. Happily it got to going along in the finale and became very grand indeed." Reviews were mixed, as I had grown to expect for my more difficult pieces, but Kirkpatrick continued to perform the *Sonat*a and Lenny took to it as though it was his own. When in February 1943 I was called back to Hollywood, the Town Hall Music Forum featuring my music took place without me— "Copland Misses His Own Party," captioned one review. Lenny played the *Sonata* not once, but twice. The second time was unplanned and came after the Forum. Denby reported to me: "Lenny spoke, and then Virgil—brilliant, of course, but in fits . . . and Lenny played the *Sonata* again, this time to absolute perfection. Minna was there and Bill DeKooning with Elaine. . ." Virgil represented the critics, Israel Citkowitz sat in for me, David Saidenberg and Lenny were the "Interpretive Artists," and Odets represented a "Layman's Viewpoint." Clifford wrote to me that very night: "I would not be your true friend if I did not tell you here how beautiful the *Sonata* sounded on a third and fourth hearing. It has real nobility and so it impressed many varied persons. Modern music aside, in the romantic style I clasp your hand and embrace you!" I responded (10 February 1943): "I'm glad the *Sonata* improves with hearing. I have an inside feeling that I've written something decent there and I continue to have it despite some sourpuss criticisms!"

Judging from the pianists who have performed the *Sonata* through the years, it seems that my feelings were not unfounded. Lenny continued to play the *Sonata*, even in Japan, and Leo Smit, as "a young pianist on his way up," studied and played it in 1945. From then on Leo was closely associated with my piano music.[10] In 1945 Ingolf Dahl introduced the *Sonata* on the West Coast, and in 1948 Andor Foldes played it in Sweden. Also in the forties, I had a letter from the twenty-four-year-old pianist William Kapell (3 January 1946):

> I began intensive work on the *Sonata* once more . . . because all along in my mind was the idea of playing it in Carnegie Hall this season. However, after two weeks I can see that this work needs exactly as much maturing and ripening and mellowing as a Chopin Sonata or a Beethoven Sonata, and I am not willing to take the risk of doing it less than the full justice it deserves. Because, to my mind, this towering work is the one truly great piano composition to come from our country. I adore it, and my great wish was to play it this year. . . . I am going to practice it so that it, and it alone, can be my choice of a great American work when I play in Europe next August. This is a promise I have made to myself. And next year, with your approval of my conception of your work, I will play the *Sonata* in New York. . . . I have just heard Leo Smit's recording of the *Sonata*. It is superb. He understands every bar, and the last movement is very moving and powerful in his conception. He is fortunate to have had the benefit of being with you so much. I hope that is a pleasure you'll allow me to enjoy some day. Because, you have a way of playing your own music that is quite unique.

Other pianists who have played the *Piano Sonata* come to mind: Easley Blackwood, Leon Fleisher, Robert Helps, John Kozar, Noel Lee, Radu Lupu, William Masselos, and Robert Miller. To my surprise, the choreographer Doris Humphrey chose the *Piano Sonata* for one of her most successful dances, *Day on Earth*, created for the José Limón Company in

[7] See John Kirkpatrick, "Aaron Copland's Piano Sonata," *Modern Music*, XIX:4 (April-May 1942), 246-50.

[8] Interview, Leo Smit with Perlis, 29 January 1981, New York City.

[9] Wilfrid Mellers, *Music in a New Found Land* (New York: Stonehill Publishing Company, 1964), 81-101. Mellers and Copland corresponded from 1942 on, after Copland read Mellers' article, "Language and Function in American Music," *Scrutiny*, X (1942), 346-57.

[10] See *Aaron Copland, The Complete Music for Solo Piano*, performed by Leo Smit, produced by CBS Masterworks in 1979, released in honor of Copland's eightieth birthday.

1947.[11] Since I could not attend the premiere in Boston, Doris and the dancers came to New York and danced it privately for my approval. I was proud to be part of this beautiful work. As John Martin wrote in *The New York Times* (4 January 1948):

> It is amazing what Miss Humphrey has found in Mr. Copland's *Piano Sonata.* It is difficult music, spare and sinewy, with phrases that use all kinds of rhythmic irregularities to get themselves shaped in their own design. Beneath its surface the choreographer has seen its hardy sweetness, its earth quality, its stalwart, unsentimental statement of beauty. The inherent intricacies of the score have been illuminated by choreographic phrasing that is far less simple than it appears. One is never aware of difficulty, of possible divergence of purpose in score and choreography; it is all one in substance and texture, as if, indeed, the composer had written for this special end.

Leonard Bernstein[12]

The Piano Sonata *is my favorite piece of Aaron's. I adore it. I recorded it for RCA, and they let it drop. But it's been recently reissued. I always thought that the way Aaron played his own music was ideal. Whenever I've heard anybody else play his music, no matter how wonderful—Leo Smit, Noel Lee, even when Willy Kapell played the* Sonata *before he died—I was never really happy with it. But that's a personal thing. Aaron's music just always seemed so natural for me to play or conduct—as though I could have composed it myself, so to speak. (The first piece that I felt I couldn't have composed was the* Piano Fantasy.*) But Aaron's playing, I adored. It was bangy, but that's the way you had to play it. And it was delicate. Delicate is one of his modes, and harsh was another one; he's a great dualist, you know, Aaron, almost in a Manichaean way. He saw everything in terms of good and evil, light and dark, in a dualistic fashion. I think that's because he was always in the middle. So there's something about seeing the world in this dualistic way, and choosing the middle course between the two, in other words, not becoming a biased person in any way. I don't mean bigoted, I mean biased. I don't mean to do any dime-store psychiatry, but when I say "in the middle," I mean able to see both sides. But not in a Hamlet-like way, in which seeing both sides causes you torture inside. It's not that. It's that there's total good, there's total evil, and Aaron walks a true path of plainness.*

That's one of his biggest words—plain. It's plain. That applies to a lot of music of his, as you know, and he used the word above his own music a lot. Sometimes I'd bring him a piece of mine, and he'd say, "I wish it were plainer, it's too chromatic," or, "There are too many notes in that chord," or, "It should be spaced more plainly." It's not Aaron to be either ecstatic or in the depths of despair, or anger, or fear, or guilt, or dancing in the streets, or making a fool of himself by celebrating. I mean, you can't quite picture Aaron in a Mardi Gras parade, can you? Can you imagine Aaron wearing a ring, a jeweled cufflink? It's unheard of! Or wearing some kind of natty leisure suit? Plain, plain, plain! It goes with Appalachian Spring *and* Our Town, *which I think of as a self-portrait of Aaron. No conspicuous consumption. He wasn't miserly, just pinch-penny. It was part of his plainness, it was part of thrift. One of those Puritan virtues like being fair—you're thrifty. It was not easy for Aaron when he was young to be a social success. But if you make those feelings positive as he tended to do, instead of living in dejection with them as negative feelings, the way was to adopt the route of plainness. And make a virtue of that, which then could be, and was, and is, attractive in a very special way.*

Aaron was the most moderate man I've ever known. I'll give you an example of what I mean. I came to New York once, and we met for breakfast. Aaron ate either in the Empire or in the Horn Hardart across the street. But I seem to associate this with an Empire Hotel dining room. Aaron didn't seem his usual bubbly self. I've had a lot of breakfasts with him. He'd take The New York Times, *and open it—he'd read the headline first and then, "Who died?" This was a very cheerful look at the obituaries, and then he felt caught up. It was always in a kind of giggly way, that kind of Aaron we know. But that one breakfast, he was not saying anything and not reacting to what he was reading. I said, "Is something the matter?" And he said, "Well, I have a headache. It's nothing, it'll go away." I found out later that day, or maybe it was the next day, that his father had died the night before. Talk about moderation! And all I could get out of him was, "Well, I have a headache." I think that is a key story about Aaron Copland. It has to do with being a "sober citizen," a "judge-nose," as a friend used to call him, who, at one point wrote "Into the Streets May First!" and lived to regret it and never wrote anything else like that. At Tanglewood, when we had composers' forums every Monday night at the Lenox Public Library, Aaron was the moderator, and he was a perfect moderator. Seeing both sides. But he had very conclusive opinions of his own. It's just that he was always ready to admit the possibility that there was a question about the opinion he held. Only once have I seen Aaron angry. But that is not to say he did not have inner passions. They seemed to go into his music, a rare combination of spontaneity and care.*

I never forget a Copland birthday. Two of the most important events of my life happened on 14 November—the first in 1937 when Aaron and I met for the first time. Actually it begins before that. When I was a student at Harvard, Arthur Berger introduced me to Aaron's Piano Variations *by taking me in to Briggs & Briggs, our music store, where they had little booths where you could listen to things, and he said, "I think you ought to hear this." It was Aaron playing his* Variations *on that old Columbia record. I went crazy about this piece. Enter David Prall, my great philosophy professor, who was a music fan. David bought me the sheet music because I couldn't afford it, and he also bought himself a little piano, so that I could play it for him. I wrote a paper in my aesthetics course, which I took with David, on the* Variations. *There's a third person involved in the beginning, and that was a graduate student, who was the librarian of Eliot House, and his name was I. Bernard Cohen. I.B. has been the head of the History of Science Department at Harvard for years. He became a very good friend of mine—why, I don't know, because I was this little junior and he was a fancy graduate student, who knew more about Isaac Newton and everything else than anyone in the world. He had a great love for music and poetry. One evening we found ourselves in Jordan Hall in Boston, attending the out-of-town debut of a dancer called Anna Sokolow, then married to composer Alex North, who wrote all the music for her dancing and was playing in the wings. We became real fans of this girl, who was then completely unknown. When we went back for autographs, she was terribly moved, and said, "Oh, you must come to my debut in New York," which was on 14 November 1937.*

In those days for me to go to New York was a whole business. I didn't have the money or the time—I was a provincial Bostonian, Harvard Schmarvard, it wasn't so many years since I had discovered there was such a thing as a world of music and concerts, things you could go to, and that people could buy a ticket and go to hear Rachmaninoff play a recital in Symphony Hall. (How amazing. I mean, to think

[11] See the Dance Collection, Lincoln Center Library for two films of *Day on Earth*: one, filmed in 1959 by Helen Priest Rogers at Connecticut College, as part of the Film Notation Project, with José Limón and others; another, filmed in 1972 by Dwight Godwin at the Juilliard School for the Jerome Robbins Film Archive, performed by members of the Juilliard Dance Ensemble.

[12] Bernstein interview.

how provincial, and how restricted I was in the ghetto created by my father.) I.B. called a friend of his in New York named Muriel Rukeyser, the poetess. (In those days we said "poetess.")—the poet, and a very good one, too. He arranged with her to procure tickets, because she was going to the Sokolow debut. I saved up, and we took the train and went to New York, and found ourselves sitting in the first row of the first balcony at the Guild Theatre. We were old hands, we had seen this in Boston, we were the experts on Anna Sokolow. For everybody else in the front row of that balcony it was news, and so I guess we were looked at with some sort of bemused interest by the others, because we seemed to know so much about Anna's repertoire. I think Muriel was sitting on my left, and I.B. to her left, and on my right sat this unknown person, with buck teeth and a giggle and a big nose, of a charm not to be described, and when I was introduced to him, and found that it was Aaron Copland next to whom I was sitting, I could have been blown away—I was blown away. Because I had become a lover, a fanatic lover, of the Piano Variations, *and in fact I had learned them and spoiled many a party by playing them when people'd say, "Oh, come on, Lenny, play something." I could empty the room, guaranteed, in two minutes by playing this wonderful piece I had just learned by Aaron Copland, whom I pictured as a sort of patriarch, Moses or Walt Whitman–like figure, with a beard, because that's what the music says. It's hard as nails, as Moses was hard as nails, with his tablets and prophesying and shattering those two tablets of the Law, and then trying again. I had this kind of connection in my mind between Moses and Aaron. And so I was shocked to meet this young-looking, smiling, giggling fellow, whose birthday it happened to be.*

Aaron was giving a party for himself at his loft. He invited everybody in that row, comprising all sorts of people like Muriel Rukeyser, Virgil Thomson, Paul Bowles, and Edwin Denby, poets and literary people, musicians, Rudy Burckhardt the photographer, and of course Victor Kraft. He invited all of us in the row to attend this party. It was my real introduction to New York and to the elite sort of artistic community. It was there that, in conversation, Aaron discovered I was his great fan and that I knew the Piano Variations. *He said, "You do? A junior at Harvard knows. . ." "Yeah." So he said, "I dare you to play it." And I said, "Well, it'll ruin your party, but. . ." He said, "Not this party." So I played it, and they were all—he particularly drop-jawed. And it did not empty the room. I was then learning the Ravel* Concerto *too, so I played some of that, and I remember distinctly Paul Bowles, sprawled out on some sort of studio-bed that everybody was sitting on, saying in that rather perfumed drawl of his, "Oh, Lenny, ne Ravelons plus (Let's not Ravel any more)."*

He was very witty. I don't remember anything more, except I thought Aaron Copland was about the most sensational human being I'd ever come across, and with the passage of many decades, I haven't changed my line. The only trouble is I don't see him enough anymore, because he doesn't go out much, and I don't go out much—I mean that would be an expedition. But I do miss him. I do miss him very much, and I miss his music. We had a personal relationship, of course, that was very strong. He had to come to Boston for something soon after that, and so he came and he stayed in the guest quarters of Eliot House where I lived, and we went to the performance of Saloon, *as we used to call it—"Play the old* Saloon." *Whenever he came to Boston, we saw each other, and the times I came to New York, we always saw each other. We'd take walks in the park, and—I mean, he was a friend. And, after all, he was almost two decades older than I was.*

I graduated from school in '39. I went to New York to look for a job. Didn't find one. Ran out of money. Couldn't pay for a meal. Adolph Green had sublet an apartment on East 9th Street, which had a Steinway grand in it of all things, and he said if I would chip in with him, we could have it for the summer. So I did. Aaron set up a visit with Davidson Taylor at CBS for me, and he couldn't have been

Copland and Bernstein, 1941

nicer and kinder, but he said, "We just don't have a job at the present time." Aaron called some other people. None of them worked out. I got to the end of that unbearable hot summer in that dirty 9th Street apartment, full of roaches—but there was that Steinway. I remember working on "Lamentation" there.[13] *Whatever I wrote, I showed Aaron. And that's the closest I ever came to studying composition with anyone. But Aaron's criticism was as good as years of composition study as far as I was concerned. He wouldn't go into great detail, but he would say, "That note is not fresh, because you've just used it here," or, "All this whole section sounds like warmed-over Scriabin, out! Throw it away, but this is good. Work on that." So it was stylistic more than anything else, with some formal commentary, but he never talked about my sense of harmony or counterpoint or any of the things that I suppose a composition teacher would have done.*

When he made a four-hand arrangement of Billy the Kid, *I remember playing it with him, which is how I learned the piece, really. I think that was the first time anybody had played it with him. I felt most honored about that. He'd just finished it. I had a similar experience with* Rodeo *later on at Jacob's Pillow, when he had to play it for Agnes de Mille the first time. There was a party after a performance for the cast backstage, or something like that, while we were playing* Rodeo *for Agnes, and the people backstage were furious because we were ruining their party with all the noise. (Agnes recalls it somewhat differently in her book.) I wrote about sixteen bars of* Rodeo *for Aaron where he needed a jazzy barroom piano sequence in one of the tunes.*

[13] "Lamentation," movement III of "Jeremiah," *Symphony No. 1.*

I finished the summer of '39 with no job, and went back home in defeat with $4 left in my pocket. There I was, twenty-one, a Harvard graduate, and nowhere to go, nothing to do. Aaron had a house in Woodstock that summer, and he invited me to come up in my loneliness and despair. So I went there for a few days to study some scores and get them into my head. I remember sitting on the train to Woodstock with these scores in front of me, trying to memorize them for an upcoming conducting audition with [Fritz] Reiner in Philadelphia and saying, "Oh, my God, this is terrible."

I arrived in Woodstock, and there was Aaron in his house, with two or three cats to which I'm allergic. It was hay fever season, too, around the beginning of September. All the pollens of Woodstock were out, but these two or three cats—I became so ill with these running eyes and sneezing and swollen—I could barely see the notes of the score I was trying to prepare, and it was in this condition I arrived in Philadelphia for my audition with Reiner. I was accepted at Curtis. My father gave me $40 a month to live on, barely enough to pay my room rent at one of these boardinghouses they had for Curtis students. Also Mitropoulos sent me money. My God, the generosity of that man! Every once in a while he'd just send me a check from Minneapolis. It was that year I got $25 for doing Saloon *for piano for Aaron. Then I made the two-piano arrangement, and I think I got $50 for that, or maybe another $25. And then that summer, Koussie opened Tanglewood, and that was—maah!—such an explosion in my life.*

Tanglewood was wonderful. I came in as a student, and Aaron came in as head of the composition department, but we both became very close to Koussevitzky. Aaron and I were close anyway, and that's what that first summer at Tanglewood seems to be about—meeting Koussevitzky, becoming insanely close like his son. He adored Aaron, Aaron adored him, and that summer for me was about them. It was a marvelous summer. Hindemith was one of these guys who just loved music and poured out some that was great, some that was terrible, and some that was everyday. It was always recognizably Hindemith, with masterpieces every once in a while. But Aaron was the exact opposite. Music streams out of him and, God knows, there is fluidity and prolificity, but he is a maniac for "la note choisie," as he always put it. You have to find "the note that costs," I remember him saying after he first came back from Hollywood where he had been paid, for the first time, a substantial amount to write music for a commercial purpose. We were playing Of Mice and Men, *a score I fell in love with, and I said, "Oh, I love that F sharp in the bass," or whatever it was. And he said, "That's the note that costs." It was a variation on Nadia's "la note choisie."*

Aaron and I have Tanglewood in common ("Tangleberg" or "Tangle-foot," as we jokingly called it). Aaron had a charming house in Stockbridge in 1941 and the same one in '42 where younger composers and performers were almost always welcome. I saw composers come from all over the world to study with Aaron. He used to talk to me about conducting at Tanglewood and would ask me things and say, "I really can't ask Koussie to give me lessons!" Aaron developed his own sort of grinning style, and it was good and got better. Only for one piece, I think it was Appalachian Spring, *did Aaron really come to me for advice.*

In New York, I often saw Aaron with Clurman. The fact that he and Harold Clurman were roommates in Paris amazed me. It is one of the most incredible facts about Aaron Copland. And they loved each other so! When I talked to Harold about Aaron, his face would light up. But can you imagine two less likely roommates?

I worried and complained terrifically during the early forties and always took my troubles to Aaron, who would tell me to "stop whining." He seemed to have such complete confidence in me that he didn't show a bit of surprise when on Sunday, 14 November 1943, I made a dramatic success by filling in for the ailing Bruno Walter and conducting the New York Philharmonic. All Aaron's predictions came true. And on his birthday.

I conducted Aaron's Third Symphony *in Prague in 1947. The* Symphony *has become an American monument—like the Washington Monument or the Lincoln Memorial. I particularly love the third movement. In 1947, I wrote to Aaron that the last movement needed a cut, and Aaron adopted that cut. His use of* Fanfare *in the* Symphony *is a matter of musical economics and that's Aaron's thrift again. (*Fanfare *has become the world's leading hit tune.) Some of the* Symphony*'s last movement is just gorgeous—those high, fleeting, hovering things. And there's a tune there, "Because I'm Leaving Cheyenne, [Goodbye, Old Paint,]" that should be the Tanglewood hymn with words written to it to be sung every year at the closing ceremonies.*

I have conducted at many a Copland event, most recently for several eightieth-birthday celebrations. Conducting Lincoln *with Aaron himself as narrator had a special poignancy and appropriateness. You know, Aaron always had some kind of identification in his mind between plainness and Abraham Lincoln.*

Americans on the home front were gathering their resources. I wrote to Archibald MacLeish, Chief Librarian of Congress, who was serving as Assistant Director of War Information, to offer my services, and he referred me to Harold Spivacke, Chief of the Music Division, serving also as Music Chairman for the Army and Navy. But Spivacke responded, "I really cannot advise you about the possibility of getting into the army at the present moment. . . ." Therefore I was delighted to receive a letter from Andre Kostelanetz suggesting I compose a patriotic work: a musical portrait of a great American. He put teeth into the proposal by offering to commission such a piece and to play it extensively. Andre explained (18 December 1941):

> Next summer I am conducting a number of concerts with major symphony orchestras. The first part of each program will consist of standard symphonic repertoire, and the second part of the program will be devoted entirely to three new works by American composers. These three works have a correlated idea in that they are to represent a musical portrait gallery of great Americans. . . . Some of the personalities which occur to me are George Washington, Paul Revere, Walt Whitman, Robert Fulton, Henry Ford, Babe Ruth. . . . In addition to approaching you on this matter I am writing to Virgil Thomson and Jerome Kern.

My first choice was Whitman, but when Kern chose Mark Twain, Kostelanetz requested that I pick a statesman rather than another literary figure. Lincoln was a favorite during the war years.[14] Furthermore, I recalled that my old teacher, Rubin Goldmark, had composed an orchestral threnody in 1918, "Requiem Suggested by Lincoln's Gettysburg Address."

Lincoln seemed inevitable. When Virgil and I discussed our choices, he amiably (and wisely) pointed out that no composer could hope to match in musical terms the stature of so eminent a figure as Abraham Lincoln. Virgil, who had been making musical portraits

[14] See Charles C. Alexander, *Here the Country Lies* (Bloomington, Indiana: Indiana University Press, 1980), 194: "The favorite American historical personage in the Front years was Abraham Lincoln. The . . .Lincoln vogue dated from the 'twenties, when John Drinkwater's Broadway dramatization of Lincoln's life, Stephen Vincent Benet's epic poem 'John Brown's Body,' and Carl Sandburg's two volumes on Lincoln had all made the Civil War leader the personification of the innate, democratic goodness of America."

of famous people for years, chose two living subjects: Fiorello LaGuardia and Dorothy Thompson. I had no great love for musical portraiture, and I was skeptical about expressing patriotism in music—it is difficult to achieve without becoming maudlin or bombastic, or both. I was hoping to avoid these pitfalls by using Lincoln's own words. After reading through his speeches and writings, I was able to choose a few excerpts that were particularly apposite to America's situation in 1942. I avoided the temptation to quote only well- known passages, permitting myself the luxury of only one from a world-famous speech. The order and arrangement of selections are my own. The first sketches of *Lincoln Portrait* were ready in February 1942, and the entire work completed by mid-April, the orchestration following a few weeks later. The musical material is original with the exception of two songs: Foster's popular "Camptown Races" and a ballad first published in 1840 under the title "The Pesky Sarpent," but better known as "Springfield Mountain." In neither case is the treatment literal; the tunes are used freely as in *Billy the Kid.*

Lincoln Portrait is a thirteen-minute work for speaker and full orchestra, divided roughly into three sections. In the opening, I hoped to suggest something of the mysterious sense of fatality that surrounds Lincoln's personality, and near the end of the first section, something of his gentleness and simplicity of spirit. I was after the most universal aspects of Lincoln's character, not physical resemblance. The challenge was to compose something simple, yet interesting enough to fit Lincoln—I kept finding myself back at the C-major triad! The first section opens with a somber sound of violins and violas playing a dotted figure that turns into a melodic phrase by the eighth bar; the second subject is a transformed version of "Springfield Mountain." This section ends with a trumpet solo, leading without pause into an unexpected allegro for full orchestra. The second section is an attempt to sketch in the background of the colorful times in which Lincoln lived. Sleigh bells suggest a horse and carriage of nineteenth-century New England, and the lively tune that sounds like a folk song is derived in part from "Camptown Races." In the conclusion, my purpose was to draw a simple but impressive frame around the words of Lincoln himself—in my opinion among the best this nation has ever heard to express patriotism and humanity. The quotations from Lincoln's writings and speeches are bound together by narrative passages, simple enough to mirror the dignity of Lincoln's words. For example, "That is what he said, that is what Lincoln said." And, "He was born in Kentucky, raised in Indiana, and lived in Illinois. And this is what he said. . ." The background music in the final section, while thematically related to the orchestral introduction, is more modest and unobtrusive, so as not to intrude on the narration. But after Lincoln's final ". . shall not perish from this earth," the orchestra blazes out in triple forte with a strong and positive C-major statement of the first theme.

After Kostelanetz received the finished score, he wrote (19 April 1942): "I cannot tell you how happy I am about the *Lincoln Portrait.* You have written a magnificent work which I believe, aside from its wonderful musical value, will convey a great message to the American public. I want to thank you again for dedicating it to me." Andre asked only that his exclusive performance rights be extended to spring 1943. As he wrote in his autobiography: "Nineteen forty-two was probably the year when morale was lowest. . . . That spring seemed a good time for the *Lincoln Portrait.*"[15] *Time* magazine reported,

> Three composers went to work on a job usually reserved for painters. The results, four works for symphony orchestra: Copland's *Lincoln Portrait*, Kern's *Portrait for Orchestra (Mark Twain)*, Thomson's brassy *Mayor LaGuardia Waltzes* and *Canons for Dorothy Thompson.* Kostelanetz commissioned the works for performance during the summer concert rounds he will make with his diminutive wife, coloratura Lily Pons. Next week, three of the portraits will have their premieres in Cincinnati.

The premiere took place on 14 May with the Cincinnati Symphony Orchestra, William Adams as speaker. Goddard Lieberson covered the concert the following day for the *New York Herald Tribune*:

> . . . Mr. Kostelanetz was able to get from the composers what he wanted, music for large masses of people. And, in the vernacular, he hit the jackpot. . . . I want to record that I have not seen so excited an audience for some years as was this Cincinnati one upon the completion of Copland's *Lincoln.*

Kostelanetz conducted the piece in several cities; audiences seemed to be moved and critics were kind. "Kosty" had a noncommercial recording made in Toronto with a speaker whose British accent sounded odd for *Lincoln.* I wrote to Ben Britten (16 June 1942): "Reports say that audiences get all excited by it. Moral: you can't go wrong with the Gettysburg Address to end a piece (Why not try Magna Carta?). I hope to hear a live performance in July." In Hollywood Clurman went with Odets and Eisler to hear *Lincoln* performed with Edward G. Robinson narrating—the actor who always played a tough guy in the movies! Harold wrote (15 August 1942):

> Odets said he was proud of you, Eisler said, 'a good job.' . . . The audience was held. I was held, as nearly always with your music. . . . I wanted to hear it again, was sorry it ended so soon and had a feeling that the audience desired more. I would have wished it more ample in dimension and duration.

In Washington the Fourth of July concert of 1942 featured *Lincoln Portrait* and was given on a barge in the Potomac with the Lincoln Memorial in the background. Carl Sandburg agreed to narrate. When it was over and there was no applause at all, Carl said to Andre, "We were a flop." But Kostelanetz soon realized the audience had been moved beyond applause, and he reminded Sandburg that Lincoln himself had heard no applause after delivering his Gettysburg Address. When the concert was repeated in Washington on 15 July, I was in the audience for my first "live" hearing of *Lincoln Portrait.* As Andre mounted the open-air podium not 500 feet from the Lincoln Memorial, he recognized Mrs. Franklin D. Roosevelt, senators, congressmen, and members of the cabinet in the audience. It was seven months after Pearl Harbor; the country was in grave danger. After the concert Andre told me that he felt Lincoln's words "with a terrible new clarity," and we both knew that the audience felt it also.

[15] Andre Kostelanetz, *Echoes: Memoirs of Andre Kostelanetz* (New York: Harcourt Brace Jovanovich, 1981), 101.

The first radio broadcast of *Lincoln* took place on Andre's regular CBS Sunday afternoon program, 16 August, again with Sandburg as speaker. I was invited to say a few words of introduction. Sandburg, always a great popular success, added a dimension to the work, being Lincoln's biographer and a famous American poet in his own right. A fine recording was made of *Lincoln* with Kostelanetz and Sandburg that went out of circulation (as did two other early versions featuring Melvyn Douglas and Kenneth Spencer as narrators). Kosty enjoyed telling Sandburg stories. There are two lovely ones about the poet's guest appearances as speaker in the work when he was getting quite old. About to do *Lincoln* again, Kostelanetz invited Sandburg, thinking, "Oh well, if he doesn't read the speaker's part too well, everybody will understand. After all, he is such a distinguished gentleman, and he fits the role." So he invited the poet, and somewhat to his surprise, Sandburg accepted. At the morning rehearsal, during the section of the piece before the speaker stands up to narrate, Sandburg complained about feeling chilly, so someone miraculously found a blanket and put it over him. The rehearsal resumed, and everything proceeded smoothly. On the evening of the concert, Kostelanetz asked his advisers, "Do you think we ought to give him the blanket? He is liable to feel chilly again." "Well," they said, "the audience will understand. After all, he is such an old man, nobody will mind, so let's give him the blanket." They spread it over him and the concert began. During the orchestral introduction the speaker is seated onstage for ten minutes. Kostelanetz was conducting, and the time came for Sandburg to get up. But when the conductor motioned to him, there Sandburg was, fast asleep under the blanket! Kosty, in a stage whisper, called, "Carl, Carl," and the old boy, obviously confused, staggered to his feet, looked around as if to say "Where am I?" Fortunately he recovered his senses just in time to pronounce the opening line: "Fellow Citizens! We cannot escape history."

On another occasion, twenty years after the first memorable Washington concert, Kostelanetz wanted Sandburg for *Lincoln* again—this time for the opening of the Lincoln Center Promenade Concerts of 1962. He went to North Carolina to make the request in person. Sandburg was evasive and would not make a commitment. Finally when it was time to leave, Andre asked Carl's wife, Paula, why Sandburg was reluctant. It seems that the poet did not want to appear in public wearing glasses! Eventually it was worked out: since the concert was being televised, Carl could use the new invention, the Teleprompter, without his glasses. The audience knew nothing about it; in fact, they and the critics marveled at the poet's extraordinary memory. But Sandburg had been warned about the strong television lights, so he closed his eyes during the introduction, this time on purpose. Poor Andre was panic-stricken, thinking Sandburg had fallen asleep again! But all went beautifully.

Koussevitzky conducted *Lincoln Portrait* with the BSO, with Will Geer as narrator. The program on 3 April 1943 also featured the first performance of Schuman's *A Free Song* for chorus and orchestra. John Burk, BSO press and program annotator, sent reviews of *Lincoln* to me in Hollywood. I wrote to thank him (23 April): "The advantage of having so large a batch at one time is that they all cancel each other out. The nicest report you sent was that of the Doctor's enthusiasm." Elliott Carter heard the BSO performance and wrote (1 May): "Koussevitzky did not catch the subdued power and mystery at the beginning, and the scherzo was too brilliant because of K's nervous beat. Geer was a bit too folksy. . . ."

One performance of *Lincoln* I remember vividly was in Caracas, Venezuela in 1957. The concert was held in an enormous outdoor stadium with a capacity of I don't know how many thousands of people. I was conducting, and the speaker in the *Portrait* was a Venezuelan actress, Juana Sujo. She was a fiery young thing, and very impressive at the rehearsals. Just five minutes before the concert was to begin, there was an announcement backstage that the local dictator was about to arrive for the concert. This amazed everybody because, as I was told, he had always been afraid of appearing in public for fear that someone might take a shot at him. He walked into the stadium with a group of ten or twelve henchmen. They were all seated in the first row. He was much hated, particularly by my soloist, the fiery actress, and she was out to get him, so to speak. When she got to the end of the piece, which was also the end of the concert, she recited with great emphasis the lines: "Government of the people—Por el pueblo y Para el pueblo"—the whole audience of about 6,000 people stood up and started screaming and yelling and applauding. They told me that nine months later that particular dictator was out of power, deposed! I was given credit for starting that revolution.

A not-so-happy occasion in the history of *Lincoln Portrait* was "the Busbey incident." This refers to the banning of my piece for performance at the Eisenhower inauguration. It was scheduled for the Inaugural Concert at Constitution Hall in January 1953, but Representative Fred E. Busbey, Republican of Illinois, objected on the grounds that I had allegedly associated with Communist front groups. Strange as it seems today that such a work could come under suspicion, during the McCarthy period these allegations were not unusual. Busbey said, "There are many patriotic composers available without the long record of questionable affiliations of Copland. The Republican Party would have been ridiculed from one end of the United States to the other if Copland's music had been played at the inaugural of a President elected to fight communism, among other things." Claire Reis was so furious, she fired off a telegram on behalf of the League of Composers. "No American composer, living or dead, has done more for American music and the growth of the reputation of American culture throughout the civilized world than Aaron Copland. To bar from the Inaugural Concert his music, and especially music about Abraham Lincoln, will be the worst kind of blunder and will hold us up as a nation to universal ridicule." But the Inaugural Committee stood by its decision.

When Richard Nixon was Vice President, he attended a concert of my music and during intermission, expressed enthusiasm for *Lincoln* to Mrs. Paul Hume, wife of the well-known critic. He said he had once been asked to narrate it, but hadn't wanted to appear to be aping Lincoln. Nixon explained that he was sorry he hadn't ever heard the piece earlier. Mrs. Hume responded, "Well, you might have, except for a change of plans" (she was, of course, referring to the Busbey incident). Nixon quickly changed the subject. A decade or so after the Busbey incident, the United States Information Agency chose to distribute *Lincoln Portrait* with the narration translated into Arabic, Bengali, Burmese, Cambodian, Chinese, Greek, Hindu, Hungarian, Indonesian, Latvian, Lithuanian, Polish, Portuguese, Spanish, Turkish, Ukrainian, Urdu, and Vietnamese. Times change.

Top: Carl Sandburg narrating *Lincoln Portrait*
Middle: Adlai Stevenson narrating, Copland conducting a rehearsal for a performance of *Lincoln Portrait* at Lewisohn Stadium, 12 July 1964
Bottom: Narration by Coretta Scott King, Copland conducting

Lincoln Portrait was not intended as a strictly musical work. It is for a large audience and special occasions. *Lincoln* was a piece "made for use"—in this case, Kostelanetz' wartime programs. I never expected it to be performed frequently, but my publisher tells me *Lincoln Portrait* is played even more often than *Appalachian Spring*. During the Bicentennial, when Lenny went on a national and international tour with the New York Philharmonic, William Warfield narrated *Lincoln* in English, German, and French for the appropriate audiences. It was amusing to hear: "*Citoyens, nous n'echapperons pas a l'histoire . . . c'est ce qu'il disait, Abraham Lincoln.*" I had never thought of narrating *Lincoln* myself, nor did anyone else until Bill Schuman put together a Copland festival at Juilliard in 1960 and invited me to speak the part. On the occasion of my eightieth birthday at the all-Copland gala at the Kennedy Center, I found myself at the podium again, Lenny conducting. President and Mrs. Carter appeared in their box for the first time in public since Carter's defeat in the election a few weeks earlier. Rosalynn Carter had once spoken the narration, and she was particularly anxious to hear *Lincoln* that evening. When they appeared in the presidential box, a full house stood to cheer them, and my closest friends and relatives sat with President and Mrs. Carter as I spoke Lincoln's words about the country and the presidency. It was a poignant moment.

After the first recordings, others featured Hollywood actors as narrators: Henry Fonda, with myself conducting the London Symphony Orchestra; Charlton Heston, Maurice Abravanel with the Utah Symphony; Gregory Peck, Zubin Mehta and the Los Angeles Philharmonic. These actors adopt understated approaches compared to Sandburg's earlier spunky rendition. Adlai Stevenson's convictions and his stature as U.S. Representative to the United Nations gave his performances and the recording (with Eugene Ormandy and the Philadelphia Orchestra) a special appropriateness.[16]

Two activities became habitual whenever I returned from an extended trip out of New York: first, an appraisal of my financial situation; next, a visit with Claire Reis, who would bring me up to date with everything that was going on. Since it was December, the end of the year, I added up my income for 1941. The "most successful American composer" at age forty-one had earned a total of $4,557.61, made up of small royalty amounts from Boosey, Arrow, Birchard, McGraw-Hill, Ballet Caravan, and Columbia Recordings (for $.48 and $.80). Other fees were culled from occasional lectures, writing and teaching—the mainstay, the Berkshire Music Center's $1,000 for the previous summer. I cer-

[16] Among the many who have narrated *Lincoln Portrait* are: Walter Abel, William Adams, Marian Anderson, Edward Arnold, Leonard Bernstein, Kingman Brewster, Myron Bush, Jorge del Campo, Rosalynn Carter, Jerome P. Cavanaugh, William Conrad, Aaron Copland, Walter Cronkite, Melvyn Douglas, Hugh Downs, Dan Evans, Jose Ferrer, Henry Fonda, Seamus Forde, Barry Foster, Will Geer, Arthur Godfrey, Robert Goheen, Lorne Green, June Havoc, Roland Hayes, Edward Heath, Charlton Heston, Jacob Javits, James Earl Jones, Edward Kennedy, Otto Kerner, Eartha Kitt, Canada Lee, Max Lerner, John V. Lindsay, Eugene McCarthy, Raymond Massey, Adolph Menjou, Burgess Meredith, Zero Mostel, Frank D. O'Connor, Fess Parker, Gregory Peck, Walter Pidgeon, Thomas Pulaski, Claude Rains, Basil Rathbone, Edward G. Robinson, Eleanor Roosevelt, Robert Ryan, Luis Salazar, Carl Sandburg, Willie Stargell, Adlai Stevenson, Kenneth Spencer, Juana Sujo, John Charles Thomas, Franchot Tone, Charles Del Vecchio, Sam Wanamaker, William Warfield, and Andre Watts.

tainly had plenty of reason for being "pinch-penny." It was uncomfortable and unnerving to live from one small amount to the next, particularly in wartime when regular sources might become nonexistent at any moment. I was sorely tempted to accept a teaching position (with pension guaranteed) offered me at Brooklyn College, but just at that moment, I received the commission of $1,000 for *Lincoln* from Kostelanetz.

Minutes of the Executive Committee of the League and letters from Claire had trailed me around South America, so I knew that my first obligation was to host the tea in honor of Juan José Castro and to speak informally about my experiences in South America (16 December 1941). Next, Claire let me know (painlessly, over tea in her lovely sitting room) that it was up to me to choose and locate film segments for an event to be held at the Museum of Modern Art on 8 February 1942, billed as "Hollywood Fiction Pictures with Distinguished Musical Scores by Americans and Europeans—Running Comment by Aaron Copland." (It seems that no one at the museum knew anything about the subject.) I chose segments from the following: *The General Died at Dawn*, music by Werner Janssen; *Once in a Blue Moon*, Antheil; *Juarez*, Erich Korngold; *So Ends Our Night*, Louis Gruenberg; *Ladies in Retirement*, Ernst Toch; *Citizen Kane*, Bernard Herrmann; and *Of Mice and Men*. We distributed a questionnaire and a summary of the technical and expressive problems involved in composing music for motion pictures and had a lively discussion after the "concert."

During this period, the League and many other groups were concerned with Russian War Relief. At the request of the Union of Soviet Composers, letters and telegrams were exchanged and music was sent to Russia, but nothing was heard from the Russian group after their country went to war with Germany. We began to hear a great deal of Russian music—Shostakovich was the biggest hero. Interviews with the Russian composer in Moscow about works written while Leningrad was under siege were printed in *The New York Times*. They greatly interested the American people and affected attitudes among composers. Shostakovich said, "I consider every artist who isolates himself from the world as doomed. . . . I think an artist should serve the greatest number of people. I always try to make myself as widely understood as possible, and if I don't succeed I consider it's my own fault. . . I'm writing about the man in the street . . ." Dmitri Kabalevsky also became a familiar name. In fact, Kabalevsky seemed to be performed more than any American composer that season.

Statements for Orchestra was finally performed in its entirety by the New York Philharmonic, Mitropoulos conducting (7 January 1942). But as I wrote to Robert Palmer (25 January 1942): "The big success of the winter has been Bill Schuman's *Third Symphony*. . . ." I had felt for some time that here was "a big talent." Bill was typical of young American music of the time—left of center, but more tonal and less experimental than the generation that came of age in the twenties. Schuman's work reflects his personality—full of drive and conviction, not lacking in emotional content, with a love of the grandiose and a wonderful eloquence.

William Schuman[17]

One evening, about a year after Frankie and I were married in 1936, we were invited to a party at the studio of Harry Cumpson, a pianist who was playing new music. I met Aaron for the first time there, and I recall hearing a recording of The Second Hurricane *that evening. We began to see each other at ACA meetings and other musical events around town, and then Aaron was on the jury (which included Harris, Riegger, and Sessions) for a contest sponsored by the Musicians' Committee to Aid Spanish Democracy for which the prize was a performance and other rewards. My* Second Symphony *won, and Aaron came to the concert. The WPA orchestra was made up of people who, for the most part, had never played in a symphony orchestra before. They were there because they needed work—not because they could play the music. But Aaron realized what was happening, and he listened to the symphony again when it was selected for broadcast on CBS. (In those days, when you were performed over the radio on a Sunday afternoon, there would be reviews the next day across the entire United States. People paid attention to those radio orchestras.) A few months later, a postcard came from Aaron. To show how long ago that was—it was a penny postcard. On it, he wrote simply: "Please send the score of your symphony to Serge Koussevitzky, 88 Druce Street, Brookline, Mass." So I did, and some weeks later, a letter came saying Koussevitzky would perform the work and wanted to meet me when he was next in New York. Tickets were left at the Carnegie Hall box office, and after the concert, Aaron and Roy Harris took Frankie and me backstage. In bringing my music to Koussevitzky's attention, Aaron once again gave a young composer an incredible boost.*

In 1938 Aaron wrote a few sentences about my music in Modern Music, *an important endorsement, using the power of his pen as another way of helping a young composer. Aaron is ten years my senior, which doesn't mean anything now, but it was a big difference then—Aaron was already established, and I was just beginning. He was always wonderfully generous with his time when I took him scores, although I was not his pupil in the formal sense. Once when I was very much the neophyte, I showed him fifteen or twenty measures of music for a ballet (later abandoned), and he said: "Well, when you have some music, I really want to see it. It looks like a good beginning." Aaron was always tactful.*

As a teacher, Aaron was extraordinary. There have been great teachers—Hindemith, for example. But he taught his pupils how to be little Hindemiths—no mean trick. Copland would look at your music and try to understand what you were after. He didn't want to turn you into another Aaron Copland. He would sit down at the piano, read through a score, and make comments. When he questioned something, it was in a manner that might make you want to question it yourself. Everything he said was helpful in making a younger composer realize the potential of a particular work. On the other hand, Aaron could be strongly critical. And he could become angry if he felt that a composer, through influence, had attained some position that he did not deserve. Because of his agreeable disposition, Aaron is never thought of as being exacting, and this does him an injustice.

From the late thirties on, Aaron came to our home at least a few times a year, I visited his loft often, and Frankie and I drove up to Tanglewood several times. We stayed with him on our first visit in 1941. I was

[17] The Schuman material is derived from: interviews with Perlis on 2 June 1983 and 29 December 1983 at Greenwich, Connecticut, and New York City; the program book for the Kennedy Center Honors of 7 December 1979; and an address delivered on the occasion of the dedication of the Copland School of Music, Queens College, 29 April 1981. It was edited by William Schuman. For extensive oral and video interviews with Schuman, see the Oral History of American Music, Yale.

composing my Fourth Symphony, *and I brought the score with me to show to Aaron. About the second movement, he said: "I want to question the ending." Because he questioned it, I saw some things that I could criticize myself. So I changed it, and the ending worked very well. In the late fall and winter of 1942, we gave Aaron our house in Larchmont for a month or more, where he finished his* Piano Sonata.

Through Aaron I became involved with the League of Composers, and I was even on the board for a short time. I thought it a doctrinaire organization, and whereas Aaron was not dictatorial, the satellites around him, especially the boys writing for Modern Music, *were. The magazine was important through the distinction of its major contributors. Aaron was powerful there also, but he didn't seek power. His power came because not only was he one of the leading composers, but a natural leader. Aaron's use of power was constructive—he would take things in which he saw merit and promote them.*

One evening in his loft, Aaron played a recording of Lincoln Portrait *for me. I was very moved by it. After I heard it several times "live," I decided that for me, the popular nature of* Lincoln *took it out of the class of his other works, which repaid with additional hearings. I wrote to Aaron, who was then in Hollywood, "The best time for* Lincoln *is the first." His response was: "If it's played only on Lincoln's birthday I'll be happy enough." Many years and many performances later, Aaron accepted my invitation to narrate* Lincoln *for a special benefit concert at Juilliard. It was the nineteenth of February 1960, and the first time Aaron ever spoke the part. We had marked an "x" on the floor where he was to stand, but when the time came, he forgot to stand on that spot. Consequently, he was out of range of the microphone. But he projected a Lincolnesque aura, so he got away with it.*

The year I became president of Juilliard, 1945, we talked about a teaching position for Aaron. We discussed it a lot. One day we took a long walk, and I remember precisely what he said: "You know, I just can't get myself to take a job. I've never had a regular job, and that's what's bothering me." Aaron came very close that time. Actually, he accepted, and then changed his mind. He just didn't feel right about it.

In 1955 for the fiftieth anniversary of Juilliard, we commissioned Aaron to compose a new composition for the festival of American music. The result was the Piano Fantasy, *the third of Aaron's major piano works. It was not finished until 1957, but was well worth the wait. For his sixtieth birthday, we planned an all-Copland week at Juilliard. We showed the film,* The City, *Aaron gave a public lecture, and many of his compositions were performed, among them,* In the Beginning, Nonet, *and scenes from the opera* The Tender Land. *Aaron is a composer with an extraordinarily high percentage of successful works. If his catalogue is not the largest in quantity, it is prodigious in quality. And each work bears his stamp, yet each is special unto itself.*

I was to change my thinking about Lincoln Portrait; *in it, the Copland added dimension to Lincoln's compassionate utterances. In compositions such as* Rodeo *and* Billy the Kid, *the Copland sound transforms traditional American folk material into the most sophisticated art by discerning potentialities in simple music that could only be perceived by an artist of extraordinary imagination. What an amazing musical world Aaron makes out of songs like "Bury Me Not on the Lone Prairie" and "Sis Joe." Aaron is, of course, no mere populist. His compositions include music of the most esoteric complexities. To the uninitiated it could almost seem as though there were two separate composers at work. Not so, for the same Copland sound that informs the popular music is, in its unique way, heard in the master*works *he has created in every medium.*

William Schuman (*seated far right*) meeting with composers in Virgil Thomson's apartment at the Chelsea Hotel: Copland (*standing center*) and (*left to right*) Samuel Barber, Thomson, and Gian Carlo Menotti

Aaron has earned the highest regard from his peers. He is the object of our affection and esteem because we recognize his preeminence. Contrary to the ancient wisdom that holds, "two vinegar salesmen can't be friends," composers of serious art music do have a spirit of camaraderie, and nowhere is the letter and spirit of this communal concern so apparent as in the person of Aaron. The core of our appreciation is, of course, for the astonishing scope and diversity of his music. What he has given us is that Copland sound—the unmistakably distinctive personal utterance. In its most popular vein, it can be perceived as national. By now it is hard to imagine anyone who has not been stirred by the noble sound of Fanfare for the Common Man. *We've all heard it countless times both in the original and in dilution from legions of imitators. But no second-hand user can ever supplant the master, because the true Copland sound is not a mark of identification that can be divorced from the context in which it is heard.*

There have been stretches of time when Aaron and I, because of heavy professional commitments, have not seen each other. But I cannot think of a single occasion or decision in my composer's life that I did not report to Aaron and benefit from his encouragement and friendship. We worked together on more committees and boards than I can even begin to name here, and we have had the satisfaction in our lifetimes of seeing this country change from one that imported virtually all its performing artists and exported all its students, to one that exports the greatest performers all over the world and imports students to study here.

Aaron's birthdays were celebrated with gatherings of distinguished colleagues and friends. My role in each of these events was master of ceremonies. Aaron and I shared these occasions so often that a standard

repartee developed. I might say: "Introducing Aaron is my favorite pursuit—not highly remunerative work, but steady." Aaron would get up and say, "I'm a lucky guy."

There were other public gatherings that gave me the opportunity to speak seriously and thereby to return a little where I had received so much. It was, after all, in large measure through Aaron that we had the first emergence of a truly indigenous American art music. A whole school of composers came into being in this country while Aaron was at the center as teacher, composer, and critic. If Aaron can say, as he has, that music is "one of the glories of mankind," then we can say, and we do, that Aaron is one of the glories of music.

In the spring of 1942 Bill Schuman invited me to Sarah Lawrence College, where he had been teaching since 1935, to hear his students perform my two choral pieces; I made an occasional visit to Ben Britten and Peter Pears, safely out of Europe and living in Brooklyn; and I took a quick trip to Boston to see Lenny's production of *Hurricane.* But mostly, I stayed home composing. I had to finish a composition commissioned by Hugh Ross, conductor of the Schola Cantorum, to honor the first conductor of the Schola, Kurt Schindler, who had been responsible for bringing to light many unknown and forgotten folk songs.

I chose a "dance-song" from Schindler's final publication, *Folk Music and Poetry of Spain and Portugal.* "Las Agachadas" (no. 202) is a song from Burgos in northern Spain. The words of my song are those in Schindler's book. I had seen and heard groups in South America sing such pieces, and I hoped to give "Las Agachadas" a realistic native feeling. It is written for two groups of singers—solo group and an eight-part mixed chorus. I gave up the idea of instruments when I realized that the larger group could represent a village band, simulating an accompaniment by singing a thrumming refrain. The solo group is instructed to sing "with the freedom of a peasant style."

The Schindler Memorial Concert took place at Carnegie Hall on 25 March 1942. The dancer Paul Draper interpreted some of the "dance-songs," and the Schola Cantorum performed the commissioned pieces. These were by Bernard Wagenaar, Juan José Castro, Chávez, Cowell, Pedro Sanjuán, Deems Taylor, and myself.

One day in April Agnes de Mille phoned. She had an idea for a ballet that she wanted me to hear about.[18] Franz Allers, musical director of the Ballet Russe de Monte Carlo, took me to her studio. When she started to tell me about it being a cowboy ballet, I immediately said, "Oh no! I've already composed one of those. I don't want to do another cowboy ballet! Can't you write a script about Ellis Island?" But Agnes countered with, "This is going to be different." And then she got up and loped around her studio, showing me some of the steps she was going to use. "Well," I said, "I'll go home and think about it." I came to the conclusion that since de Mille was a very different person from Eugene Loring, it was bound to be a very different ballet. Loring was interested in legendary figures and grandiose effects, while Agnes was after something lighter and more bouncy. So I telephoned her and said, "I'll do it."

[18] See Agnes de Mille, *Dance to the Piper* (Boston: Little, Brown, 1951), 271-302, and *Speak to Me, Dance with Me* (Boston: Little, Brown, 1973), 337.

She sent me a scenario titled simply: "American Ballet by Agnes de Mille." It began: "This is the story of the Taming of a Shrew cowboy style. It is not an epic, or the story of pioneer conquest. It builds no empires. It is a pastorale, a lyric joke . . . the quieter and gentler and simpler the style the better. There are never more than a very few people on the stage at a time . . . one must be always conscious of the enormous land on which these people live and of their proud loneliness. . ." The story was simple—about a cowgirl infatuated with the head wrangler on a ranch. She dresses and acts like a man, hoping to impress him. Agnes also sent a "time-plot" mapping out sequences to the minute. This is a sample of what I had to work with: "Hoe-Down, 4 minutes. Introduction-16-24 measures—girl appears. Pause and silence for about 4 counts while she faces boy. Dance begins on walk—hit a fiddle tune hard. Verse and chorus with brass yells and whoops. Vamps in-between, long tacet toward close for tap cadenza, 8 measures of frenzy. Kiss, tacet or pianissimo. Finale windup—the beginning of the tune again, curtain comes down as the big promenade starts."

The finished ballet did not deviate from Agnes' original script. Agnes sent suggestions for tunes—one with a good "riding rhythm," one called "Ground Hog," and another for the waltz she had heard in Virgil's film, *The Plow That Broke the Plains.*[19] I enjoyed composing the waltz and welcomed "Buckaroo" and "Hoe-Down" as opportunities for some lively rhythmic sections. Agnes was to rehearse the Ballet Russe in July, so she needed the music as soon as possible. By the time I left for Tanglewood in late May of 1942, I had much of *Rodeo* in my head and had only to write it all down.

Agnes de Mille[20]

The title became Rodeo *when [Sol] Hurok wanted something short for advertising, so "The Courting at Burnt Ranch" became a subtitle. It was subsequently dropped altogether. The Ballet Russe had no idea who I was; although it was fourteen years after my first public appearance, I had no reputation, nothing. But it was wartime, and they wanted an American ballet on an American theme by an American. I said, "That would be nice in this country." They didn't know what that meant—nightclubs, probably. I didn't like most of the Ballet Russe pieces, I thought them pretentious. When I made my suggestions for a cowboy ballet, the company manager complained to his colleagues in Russian that I would probably ruin the Ballet Russe.[21] Martha Graham advised me, "You be arrogant. If you are not rude, they won't respect you." So I dug in my heels and said I wanted the best American composer for the music, Aaron Copland. Aaron had done* Billy, *and it was strikingly new and very good. Even earlier than* Billy, *I had been working on cowboy-style dances and had performed them in London. I went for my interviews to Ballet Russe in clothes borrowed from my sister. After [Sergei] Denham hired me, Florine Stettheimer was suggested for the scenery, but I*

[19] The tune in Copland's "Saturday Night Waltz" from *Rodeo* is a version of "Old Paint." It was used earlier by Thomson in the film, *The Plow That Broke the Plains,* and in the suite derived from the film, section three, "Cattle."

[20] Interview, Agnes de Mille with Perlis, 25 June 1980, New York City.

[21] Sergei J. Denham was director of the Ballet Russe de Monte Carlo, Inc.

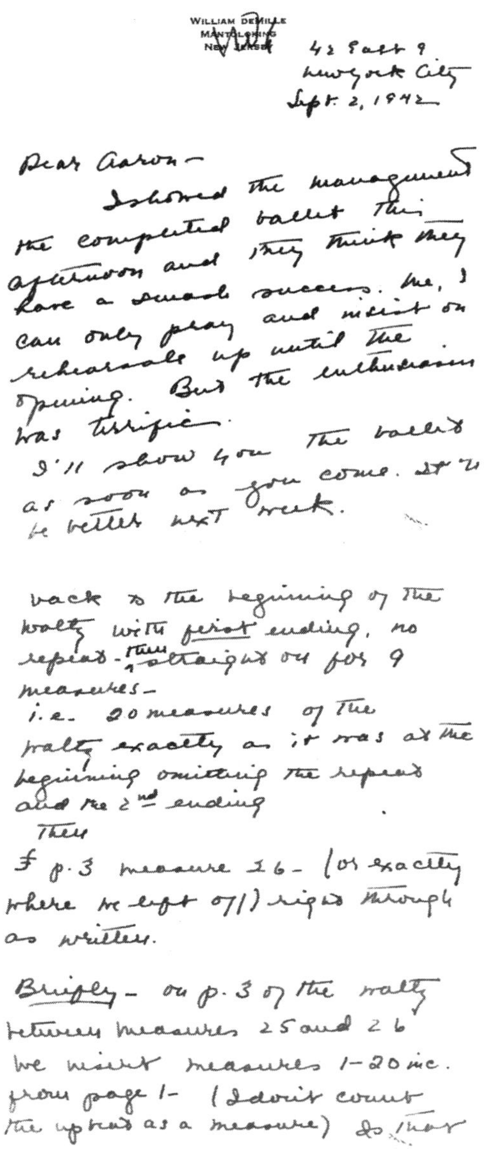

William DeMille
Mantoloking
New Jersey

43 East 9
New York City
Sept. 2, 1942

Dear Aaron—
I showed the management the completed ballet this afternoon and they think they have a smash success. We, I can only pray and insist on rehearsals up until the opening. But the enthusiasm was terrific.
I'll show you the ballet as soon as you come. It'll be better next week.

back to the beginning of the waltz with first ending, no repeat—then straight on for 9 measures—
i.e. 20 measures of the waltz exactly as it was at the beginning omitting the repeat and the 2nd ending
Then
from p. 3 measure 16—(or exactly where we left off) right through as written.

Briefly—on p. 3 of the waltz between measures 25 and 26 we insert measures 1–20 inc. from page 1—(I don't count the upbeat as a measure) Is that

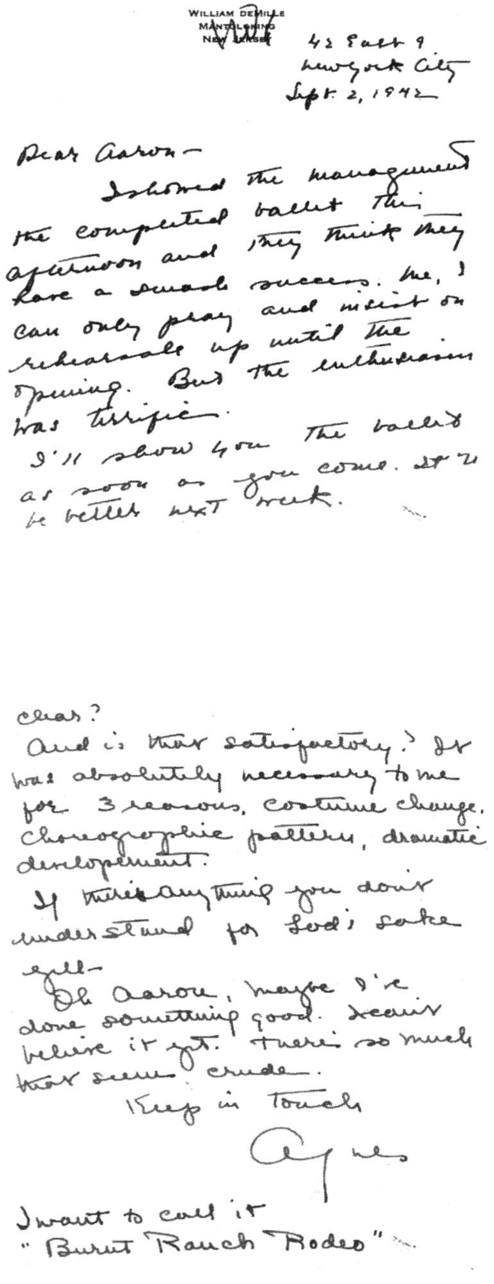

William DeMille
Mantoloking
New Jersey

43 East 9
New York City
Sept. 2, 1942

Dear Aaron—
I showed the management the completed ballet this afternoon and they think they have a smash success. We, I can only pray and insist on rehearsals up until the opening. But the enthusiasm was terrific.
I'll show you the ballet as soon as you come. It'll be better next week.

clear?
And is that satisfactory? It was absolutely necessary to me for 3 reasons. Costume change, choreographic pattern, dramatic development.
If there's anything you don't understand for God's sake yell—
Oh Aaron, maybe I've done something good. I can't believe it yet. There's so much that seems crude.
Keep in Touch
Agnes

I want to call it "Burnt Ranch Rodeo".

Letter from Agnes de Mille about *Rodeo*

didn't want her, so the young unknown Oliver Smith was asked to make some sketches for Rodeo. *They were brilliant. I said, "Make some more." They weren't so brilliant. He had hit on it the first time. "There's one proviso," I said to Denham and associates, "I dance the lead at the opening night in New York." At that they just fainted. "Take it or leave it," I said. They took it, giving me $500 for the ballet for five months' work. (Later, I got $12.50 and then $8.50 royalties. It was a sliding scale, you see—downward.)*

Aaron finished the score and played it for me up at Jacob's Pillow in Lee, Massachusetts, where I was working for a few weeks with Ted Shawn and Ruth St. Denis when the new theater opened. Aaron was teaching at Tanglewood, and he called when the score was ready and came over with a young friend. I didn't know who he was. They came after an evening's performance, and I told Shawn and the company that I was going to do a new ballet for Ballet Russe, and wouldn't they like to hear the score? While Aaron and his friend were at the piano, I looked around and realized there was nobody there to hear him. Not a soul but my mother and me! I thought, "This is very odd." But Aaron said, "I have got to do it and go. It's getting late." So we started. I got more and more excited and finally I was just screaming, yelling and dancing. He'd written the music on transparent paper that kept slipping, and during the waltz it fell to the ground. The boy with Aaron kept pushing the music back in place. Aaron said to him, "Could you play the treble part? I can't play it." This boy played wonderfully. I said in the waltz part, "Aaron, this section is pretty dull." He giggled, and said, "I think it is, too. I'll do something about it." The friend said, "You'd better!" I remember thinking, "Of all the impudence! To talk to the Maestro like that!" The boy was Leonard Bernstein.

At the end I was yelling and dancing and heard rustlings behind the scenery. I followed the whisperings and went up a stairway, opened a door, and there was Shawn and the entire company in a long line. "For God's sakes," I said, "I asked you to come down. Weren't you interested?" And Ted Shawn said, "Agnes, it's because of music like that that we are having war." "You're joking," I said. And he looked at me and said, "No." And I looked around at the company and asked, "He's making fun of me, isn't he?" The cast said, "Oh no." And all of them dead serious. Shawn said, "I find this the reverse of music. It is a step backwards." I said, "Well, they are downstairs, can they have a drink or something to eat? What shall I do—tell them they've caused a war and reversed civilization?" Shawn said, "I repudiate their music. But I welcome them as human beings." With that he threw open the door, and Aaron and Lenny came in and sat on the floor, giggling and whispering together—in a rather naughty manner, but they had felt very put out by this extraordinary ostracism. I think Shawn must have been just plain jealous of my opportunity to do this ballet. After all, he'd never been asked by Ballet Russe.

As planned, I appeared to rehearse Rodeo *in New York in July, but I got more and more nervous and angry with the Ballet Russe management because they didn't schedule rehearsal time. And this dance needed extra work, since the classically trained Russian dancers weren't used to this kind of dance at all. They found my American folk-dance formations unnatural, and the emphasis on comedy and acting was difficult for them to come to terms with. It didn't seem possible that we would open that fall after all. I wrote to Aaron in exasperation, and I wrote an angry and threatening letter to Denham. Well, finally, we got under way. I'd have to talk to the girls about gestures they knew nothing about: "Do you know what a corset is? Do you know what you wore under it? Do you know what the bones are and what they stick into? And how you have to stretch to get it comfortable? You girls haven't got an inch of flesh—no breasts, no hips, no nothing, so you don't know what these girls in* Rodeo *had to do in order to settle themselves before they were armed for a battle to get a man."*

Rodeo *has to be performed by very fine actors with real sincerity. If it's done just for easy laughs and quick effects it's cheap as hell and just slides by and doesn't mean a thing. When I was onstage, it mattered to me. That girl was fighting for her happiness. I used to stand there with real tears pouring down my face—I couldn't get the man I wanted and I didn't think I'd ever have any man. You can't imagine some of the letters people have had the idiocy to write me—one said that Women's Lib should take action against this ballet! Well, in 1895 or 1900 a woman had to have a man or she was considered an outcast and became the family drudge.*

During rehearsals I realized we needed a little more music in one spot. Aaron was still at Tanglewood; for some reason I couldn't phone him, and you couldn't send a wire because of the war. It had to be an emergency— you couldn't wire and say, "Must have four bars of music." And so I had to write, and Aaron refused. I didn't like it at the time, but he was right; it would have distorted the form. So I put in a tacet.

Aaron and I didn't do any further work on the score again after he played it for me at Jacob's Pillow, and he didn't see Rodeo *until a few days before our opening in New York. The cast was scared to death. That opening night—16 October 1942—I gave the performance of my life. I got twenty-two curtain calls. A telegram came afterwards from the Theatre Guild asking me to come talk to them about their new musical show,* Green Grow the Lilacs, *with words and music by Rodgers and Hammerstein. (When it opened it had the title* Oklahoma!) *As for* Rodeo, *the business manager of Ballet Russe soon realized that this strange American ballet was their meal ticket; there were seventy-nine performances in 1942 and 1943 alone! When I was traveling with the company in* Rodeo *they gave me $3 a day expense money, total, to live on. I turned in my Pullman ticket and sat up in coaches with the soldiers, who were all over the place by that time. It was rough going. I carried my clothes in a straw basket so I wouldn't have to pay porters. Out west I stayed with families, but in San Francisco I remember a disreputable place I shouldn't have gone near, as a young woman.* Rodeo *has stayed in the ballet repertory. In 1976, a year after I had a severe stroke, I supervised the ballet for the Joffrey company from a wheelchair, and it was a major success.*

In the fifties I asked Aaron to compose another ballet for me using sea chanties, but he said he didn't want to repeat himself. Then in the seventies we met at the Harvard Club, and I asked him again for music for a ballet, but he said, "Agnes, I don't think I'm ever going to compose anything else. I'm having such a good time conducting." And I said, "Aaron, that's too bad because there are lots of good conductors and there will be more. There's only one of you as a composer. One. And it's you we need." He asked, "Have you ever conducted?" I looked at him and said, "You know, Aaron, I've been asked a lot of damned fool questions in my life, but this tops them all."

One of the works I particularly enjoy conducting is *Rodeo*. After Franz Allers led it in 1942, the Ballet Russe invited me to take the podium at the Metropolitan Opera House in 1948. Years later in 1976, I conducted the American Ballet Theatre production. I am told that *Rodeo* is one of the most popular of all American ballets. Inevitably it was compared with *Billy the Kid.* The New York critics, John Martin and Irving Kolodin, praised *Rodeo.* Kolodin in the *Sun* wrote:

> The Ballet Russe de Monte Carlo awoke to find itself with a genuine American ballet today, and is it surprised! . . . Many curtain calls for Miss de Mille, the performers, Mr. Copland and a believable amount of vocal enthusiasm from the large audience. However, Mr. Copland's bow, a mixture of a lope and a curtsy, seemed also to have been choreographed by Miss de Mille. . .

Agnes de Mille in the premiere of *Rodeo*

Audiences and critics cheered the ballet when the company went on tour. In Chicago Claudia Cassidy wrote in the *Daily Tribune* (26 December 1942): "*Rodeo* is a smash hit. What Miss de Mille has turned out in this brilliant skirmish with Americana is a shining little masterpiece." Cassidy praised Kermit Love's costumes and Oliver Smith's settings as well as my score: "Not the least of its wisdoms is asking the orchestra to put down its instruments and clap rhythmic hands in the square dance scene."

It is particularly gratifying that *Rodeo* has withstood the test of time. A revival in 1972 by the American Ballet Theatre with Christine Sarry in the leading role was described by Anna Kisselgoff in *The New York Times* (7 January): "*Rodeo* looks new rather than dated. Its interweaving of real and stylized folk steps, unforced humor and unpretentious atmosphere have the mark of virtuosity as well as obvious charm." Personally, I never think of *Rodeo* without Agnes. She gave depth to the role, while still being hilariously funny. It was the de Mille choreography that made *Rodeo* a blend of serious ballet and musical comedy, and the work catapulted Agnes into a fabulous career, one that would change the entire look of the American musical theater.

It seemed fitting to extract an orchestral suite from the ballet—*Four Dance Episodes from Rodeo* was published in 1943. It omits only five minutes of music from the complete ballet, and like the original score, the suite calls for slightly enlarged orchestral forces. The piano takes an important role, as is often the case in my scores. The first section, "Buckaroo Holiday," is the most complex of the four. Included are variations on two folk tunes, "If He Be a Buckaroo by His Trade" and "Sis Joe." I used a rhythmic device to achieve a lilting effect that, together with some unprepared key changes, make for a comic touch, further emphasized by the use of a trombone solo in introducing the "Buckaroo" folk song. Extended pauses further exaggerate the syncopation. "Sis Joe" also undergoes rhythmic transformation before both tunes blend in a canonic treatment for full orchestra. "Corral Nocturne" is characterized by woodwind solos in 5/4 time. I was striving here for a sense of the isolation felt by the heroine. In "Saturday Night Waltz," the third episode, country fiddlers are heard tuning up, followed by hints of the tune "Old Paint." The tempo is a slow 3/4 with the accompaniment of 6/8 as a cross rhythm. The final movement, "Hoe-Down," is the best known and most frequently performed of the four episodes.[22] Two square dance tunes are included: "Bonyparte"[23] and a few measures of "McLeod's Reel" played in folk fiddle style. Pizzicato strings and xylophone add a comic effect to "Bonyparte," and the music winds down like a clock before the tune returns for the last time. Arthur Berger has described "Hoe-Down" (along with *El Salón México*) as "virtually photographic."[24] *Four Dance Episodes from Rodeo* was first performed by the Boston "Pops" under Arthur Fiedler on 28 May 1943.

Tanglewood in the summer of 1942 was different from the two previous seasons. The Center began as usual with a ceremony followed by tea in the garden. Viewing the peaceful scene, few would guess the bitter battle fought by Koussevitzky to make possible the opening of the Music Center that year. With wartime gasoline shortages, the Berkshire Music Festival had been canceled. But to close the school as well was not possible—at least to Koussevitzky. When his board of trustees stood firm against him, the Maestro threatened to pay for running the Center himself. The Koussevitzky Music Foundation was incorporated in memory of Madame Natalie Koussevitzky, who had died early in 1942. With the Maestro's own funds and contributions from several individuals, the Berkshire Music Center summer of 1942 was saved. A large student orchestra, divided into "first" and "second" groups, worked daily with Koussevitzky and his assistants. To the amazement of all, a series of public concerts was announced in place of the BSO Festival concerts. (Lenny Bernstein and Lukas Foss worked with the second orchestra along with three other specially chosen conducting students, Frederick Fennell, Walter Hendl, and Robert Zeller.) There were many chamber music concerts, Olin Downes' lectures, and a production of Nicolai's *Merry Wives of Windsor* by the opera department. I taught a course in twentieth-century music, and the Composers' Forums were initiated at the Lenox Library and patterned on the popular Town Hall Forums of the Air. We discussed topics such as "What About Opera?", "Government Support of the Arts," "Music Education for Non-Professionals," "Nationalism," and so forth. The subjects seemed new and fresh then, and we even thought they were solvable. But I have seen the same topics up for discussion year after year.

Koussevitzky had another major disappointment before the opening of the BMC in 1942—Stravinsky, who had agreed to teach, canceled. However, Koussevitzky was fortunate in engaging the noted Czech composer Bohuslav Martinu in his place. Among my student composers were Pablo Moncayo, Allen Sapp, Blas Galindo, Harold Gramatges, Barbara Pentland, and Romeo Cascarino. Martinu's list included Alan Hovhaness, Owen Reed, Spencer Hoffman, Frank Amey, and John Cowell. Once the Center opened, it was a great effort for me to finish *Rodeo*, but I had promised Agnes to have the score ready before the end of the summer. I worked too hard, yet as I wrote to Ben Britten, who had returned to England in June: "It's wonderful being back—so relaxing and peaceful. I'm doing a frothy ballet for the Monte Carlo people on the usual wildwest subject—full of square dances and Scotch tunes and the like. . . ."

Koussevitzky conducted the "first" student orchestra on 12 August in a program that included Howard Hanson's *Third Symphony* to an enthusiastic audience. But it was the concert of 14 August that caused a sensation. The entire day was billed as a Russian War Relief Benefit. Lukas conducted the "second" orchestra in *Billy the Kid* in the afternoon. A supper intermission followed, and in the evening, Koussevitzky conducted the "first" orchestra in the American premiere of Shostakovich's *Seventh Symphony*. This work, composed during the siege of Leningrad, had elicited enormous public interest and much advance speculation in the press as to who would be given permission to conduct the first American performance. Toscanini was granted the first radio broadcast, and Koussevitzky was given permission for the premiere public performance. It was Koussevitzky's courage and skill in proceeding with his student orchestra instead of with the BSO that amazed everyone. But he knew just what he was doing—Koussevitzky was out to show his board of trustees and the world of music what could be accomplished at the Music Center. What better way than by presenting this much-discussed new symphony by the controversial Dmitri Shostakovich? Excitement grew as dignitaries, ambassadors, and newspaper critics arrived in Lenox. We all invited guests—mine were Marc Blitzstein, Robert Palmer, and David Diamond. The reviews for Koussevitzky and the orchestra were unanimous in praise, but divided on Shostakovich—the composer Koussevitzky considered as great as Beethoven. Following the concert, Olin Downes wrote in *The New York Times*:

[22] "Hoe-Down" is also published in a string orchestra version, for solo piano, and for violin and piano. The complete ballet is available for solo piano. "Hoe-Down" and "Saturday Night Waltz" have been arranged for two-pianos by Arthur Gold and Robert Fizdale.

[23] "Bonyparte," a Kentucky variant of the tune "Bonyparte's Retreat Across the Rocky Mountains," was taken by Copland from John and Alan Lomax, *Our Singing Country* (New York: MacMillan, 1941), 54-55.

[24] Berger, *Aaron Copland*, 57.

In a neighboring box sat Princess Juliana of the Netherlands. The occasion was brilliant and imposing, like the finale of the symphony, which at the close of a highly dramatic interpretation, received an ovation, which lasted for a good ten minutes, of a shouting, cheering audience which rose to its feet as it extended this homage to the distant composer, to the land and the cause which his symphony symbolized, and to the conductor and the student orchestra, which had carried out his wishes with a spirit and technical proficiency that elicited the highest praise. . . . Aside from the question of the actual value of the score, the performance tonight could be summarized in terms of unsparing praise of all that Koussevitzky and his American boys and girls did in proclaiming Shostakovich's message. Not a point in the score was missed. . .the conductor more than vindicated his vivid comprehension of the symphony, the prowess of the young players whom he had assembled and drilled, in the short space of five weeks, for a really heroic task.[25]

The closing ceremony of the Berkshire Music Center in 1942 was conducted in an atmosphere of apprehension. The future of the school was in danger, and we all knew it. Worse, we recognized that many of the talented young artists we saw that day were facing futures far different from what Dr. Koussevitzky's Music Center had prepared them for. Within a year's time Koussevitzky had lost his wife and his great dream. The school and the festivals became war casualties in spite of the successes of 1942; neither would resume in full force until 1946.

A brief return to New York convinced me to make a change from the Hotel Empire to a place in the country. I rented a small cottage, Dellbrook Farm, from Mary and Bill Lescaze for $30 a month, caretaker included. Located in Oakland, New Jersey, it was not far from New York. I set to work reviewing my film scores; it struck me that a suite might successfully mirror in musical terms the wide range of American scenes in the three films for which I had written music, *The City, Of Mice and Men,* and *Our Town.* The result was *Music for Movies*, a suite in five movements for small orchestra. None of the music was transcribed literally from the films. The greatest modifications come in the opening and closing sections. All were reorchestrated from full orchestra to small ensemble. "New England Countryside" is based largely on the title music of *The City*; "Barley Wagons" originally accompanied an outdoor landscape in *Of Mice and Men*; "Sunday Traffic," also derived from *The City,* serves the purpose of a scherzo in the suite; "The Story of Grover's Corners" was developed from *Our Town*—it was a kind of theme song in the film; and "Threshing Machines" was compiled from several dramatic scenes in Steinbeck's story. *Music for Movies* is dedicated to Darius Milhaud, whom I considered a pioneer in the field of film music. The first performance was at the Town Hall Forum concert of 17 February 1943.

Claire Reis had invited several composers to write pieces for the League's twentieth anniversary, to be celebrated at a concert sponsored by Town Hall on 9 December 1942. I felt that Claire and the League deserved a big vote of thanks from composers, and I was pleased to be included. Also, her request gave me the incentive needed to put to paper some musical ideas that had been in my mind since my earlier trips to Cuba. *Danzón Cubano* was composed for two pianos in the fall of 1942 while I was staying at Dellbrook Farm. It is based on Cuban dance rhythms, particularly the danzón, a stately dance, quite different from the rhumba, congo, and tango, and one that fulfills a function rather similar to that of the waltz in our own music, providing contrast to some of the more animated dances. The special charm of the danzón is a certain naive sophistication. Its mood alternates between passages of rhythmic precision and a kind of nonsentimental sweetness under a nonchalant guise. Its success depends on being executed with precise rhythmic articulation. *Danzón Cubano*, six minutes in length in two contrasting sections, makes use of four simple Cuban dances—simple from a melodic standpoint, but with polyrhythms and the syncopated beat typical of the Cuban danzón. I did not attempt to reproduce an authentic Cuban sound, but felt free to add my own touches of displaced accents and unexpected silent beats. In fact, I arranged one of the tunes in the traditional "blues rhythm," giving the final product something of an inter-American flavor. At the premiere, the work was called *Birthday Piece (On Cuban Themes).* As commentator for the program, I explained to the audience that *Danzón Cubano* was "a genuine tourist souvenir."

Lenny played the premiere of *Danzón* with me. This was not the usual League of Composers audience, but a subscription concert of the Town Hall Endowments Series. It seemed that everything, including *Danzón Cubano*, was too "moderne" for them—until the final piece by Louis Gruenberg, which incorporates the familiar "Man on the Flying Trapeze." Claire and I agreed that it was a good thing Schoenberg's contribution had not been ready in time to be included.

Danzón Cubano was soon picked up by duo piano teams wanting to expand their repertoires, and it is often paired with *El Salón México*. I was pleased when requests for the music came from Mexico and Latin America. In the forties Leo Smit made an arrangement of *Danzón* for solo piano; I prepared an orchestral version in 1946, taking full advantage of the Cuban rhythms to make use of an interesting battery of percussion. It has become better known than the original two-piano version. The Baltimore Symphony under Reginald Stewart gave the premiere of the orchestral version on 17 February 1946, and Lenny conducted it soon afterward with the BSO as well as for its New York premiere with the Rochester Philharmonic at a Gershwin Memorial concert on 16 March. The choreographer Eliot Feld used my music for a dance also called *Danzón Cubano*, pairing it with another of his works, *La Vida*, to my *El Salón México*. Feld and I participated in a "Dance in America" television program at which we discussed various aspects of the choreographer's relationship to music. Eliot asked me why my *El Salón* is longer than *Danzón Cubano*, and I replied jokingly that it was probably because I had spent so much more time in México than in Cuba. In a more serious mood, Feld remarked that he related to certain jazz phrases and to the reconciliation of the classical traditions with the present day in my music.

Eugene Goossens, conductor of the Cincinnati Symphony Orchestra, had written to me at the end of August about an idea he wanted to put into action for the 1942-43 concert season. During World War I he had asked British composers for a fanfare to begin each orchestral concert. It had been so successful that he thought to repeat the procedure in World War II

[25] See Olin Downes, "Shostakovich Seventh Receives First U.S. Concert Performance," *The New York Times* (15 August 1942), 12.

with American composers.[26] Goossens wrote: "It is my idea to make these fanfares stirring and significant contributions to the war effort, so I suggest you give your fanfare a title, as for instance, 'A Fanfare for Soldiers, or for Airmen or Sailors.' I am asking this favour in a spirit of friendly comradeship, and I ask you to do it for the cause we all have at heart. . . ." As with *Lincoln Portrait*, I was gratified to participate in a patriotic activity. Goossens, a composer himself, suggested the instrumentation of brass and percussion and a length of about two minutes. He intended to open the concert season in October with my fanfare, so I had no time to lose. I composed an introduction for the percussion, followed by the theme announced by trumpets, and then expanding to include groups of brass. The challenge was to compose a traditional fanfare, direct and powerful, yet with a contemporary sound. To this end, I used bichordal harmonies that added "bite" to the brass and some irregular rhythms. The music was not terribly difficult to compose, but working slowly as was my custom, I did not have the fanfare ready to send to Goossens until November. I had some difficulty with the title. The piece has been *Fanfare for the Common Man* for so long that it is surprising to see on my sketches that other titles were considered: *Fanfare for a Solemn Ceremony, for the Day of Victory, for Our Heroes, for the Rebirth of Lidice, for the Spirit of Democracy, for the Paratroops, for Four Freedoms*. . . . After I decided on *Fanfare for the Common Man* and sent the score to Goossens, I think he was rather puzzled by the title. He wrote, "Its title is as original as its music, and I think it is so telling that it deserves a special occasion for its performance. If it is agreeable to you, we will premiere it 12 March 1943 at income tax time. . . ."

I was all for honoring the common man at income tax time. Since that occasion, *Fanfare* has been played by many and varied ensembles, ranging from the U.S. Air Force Band to high school groups who transpose the piece because their trumpets cannot quite manage the high C. A band arrangement of *Fanfare* has been made, but the instrumentation often is adapted to particular needs—in 1983, Notre Dame's band performed the piece with one hundred clarinets! *Fanfare* was played at the ground-breaking ceremony for Lincoln Center with President Eisenhower in attendance and for the Nixon presidential inauguration. It was used to introduce the "Omnibus" television series in the fifties, for the Olympics, and by John Curry, who skated to *Fanfare* at the 13th Winter Olympiad. *Fanfare* is often played at events that have to do with outer space. Recently it was used to announce the television celebration of the Centennial of the Brooklyn Bridge. To my amazement, several "popular" musicians also have taken up *Fanfare*. Woody Herman asked to arrange it in something called "boogaloo style." I must admit that my initial response was, "What's that?" The popular Emerson, Lake, and Palmer group made two versions of *Fanfare*—one was so similar to my own that I wondered why they wanted to do it at all. After that, Keith Emerson felt more comfortable about showing me his more original version. They took *Fanfare* on tour, as did Mick Jagger with a version by the Rolling Stones. While I have listened with interest to these arrangements, I confess that I prefer *Fanfare* in the original version and as I used it later in the final movement of my *Third Symphony*. At the the time I composed *Fanfare for the Common Man* I was becoming anxious about my financial situation, since *Danzón Cubano* and *Fanfare* were both contributions to causes I wanted to support. Little did I think in the fall of 1942 that these works, composed for particular occasions, would be used so frequently.

Copland correcting proofs of *Dánzon Cubano* for the League of Composers' 20th Anniversary Concert

To mark the twentieth anniversary of the League of Composers, *Modern Music*'s first issue of 1943 was to be a special edition titled "Two Decades in Review." Minna invited me to prepare an article summing up the period.[27] I wrote about the recognition of the American composer at home and abroad, and about the composer's entry into the world of business in order to take responsibility for his own affairs. I pointed to the startling differences resulting from radio broadcasting and phonograph recording. Finally, I chastised critics and historians for "the lack of serious, critical, full-length studies of compositions by American composers." (No one had followed Paul Rosenfeld's early lead; nothing similar to *An Hour with American Music* had been published since 1929.)[28] In conclusion, I wrote: "It is true that nobody wants to write 'modern music' any more. Yet the modern movement has been historically sound and musically fruitful. . . it was an exciting time for musical ideas and works. We can consider ourselves lucky if we produce as vital a progeny in the next twenty years."

[26] Titles of fanfares by other composers commissioned by Goossens: *Fanfare for the American Soldier*, Felix Borowski; *Fanfare for Paratroopers*, Paul Creston; *Fanfare de la Liberté*, Darius Milhaud; *Fanfare for American Heroes*, William Grant Still; *Fanfare for the Fighting French*, Walter Piston; *Fanfare to the Forces of Our Latin American Allies*, Henry Cowell; *Fanfare for Russia*, Deems Taylor; *Fanfare for France*, Virgil Thomson; *Fanfare for Freedom*, Morton Gould; *Fanfare for Airmen*, Bernard Wagenaar; *Fanfare for the Medical Corps*, Anis Fuleihan; and *Fanfare for Poland*, Harl McDonald. *Fanfare for the Common Man* was published in *Ten Fanfares by Ten Composers for Brass and Percussion* (New York: Boosey & Hawkes, 1944).

[27] Aaron Copland, "From the '20's to the '40's and Beyond," *Modern Music*, XX: (January-February 1943), 78-82.

[28] Paul Rosenfeld, *An Hour With American Music* (Philadelphia: J. B. Lippincott Company, 1929).

Left: Sketch page of *Fanfare for the Common Man* with early provisional titles
Right: Manuscript, first page of the ink score of *Fanfare for the Common Man*

INTERLUDE V

When President Franklin D. Roosevelt changed from The New Deal to a wartime economy, the Great Depression was over. People moved off the bread lines into the factories. World War II was a war of just causes, and patriotism ran high: It was not long before patriotism and prosperity went hand in hand. A feeling of exhilaration and excitement filled the air as the country began to have a new look. Suddenly, all sorts of people were in uniform, feeling special: young men in active service (the few not in uniform lived in a state of shame); older men in the Civil Defense to conduct air raids and blackouts; women in the WACS or Nurses Corps; and even the youngest "Victory Girls," who baked cookies with rationed sugar for servicemen—all were in uniform.

From 1941 to 1945, war was a national preoccupation and a unifying force stronger than any the country had ever experienced. Everyone wanted to do his share for the war effort; the result was a communal solidarity that has been compared to the days of the American frontier.[1] The Depression and the war have been viewed by social scientists and educators as "rich opportunities to help create a true collective democracy in the United States."[2] Across the nation, families grew Victory Gardens and bought war bonds, and in the evenings, everyone gathered around the radio for the latest war news. When President Roosevelt's Fireside Chats were broadcast from the White House, the sound of his voice was so inspiring that it is still recalled by those who heard it so many years ago.

At first, there was an air of unreality about the war, given the fact that the economy was booming and the country itself seemed in no physical danger. Many Americans felt guilty to be living so well while there was killing and destruction abroad, their natural humane impulses in conflict with feelings of satisfaction in punishing the Germans and Japanese. In his excellent book *Culture as History*, Warren I. Susman describes the change in the psyche of the American people after the "Age of Insecurity" of the Depression: "An age of shame and fear had passed into history; it was somehow to be followed by an age that frankly thought of itself as an age of anxiety. . . ."[3] As the war dragged on, and the bloodshed and killing escalated, patriotic activity was the most effective means of dealing with the rising waves of uncertainty that threatened to destroy morale. Recognizing this, the Office of War Information devised radio programs, posters, and slogans ("The War Against Fascism"; "Loose Lips Sink Ships") to make the people feel that what they did or said really counted.

The sudden production boost that catapulted farmers, factory workers, and businessmen into prosperity did nothing to help creative artists: art galleries, subsidized concerts, theaters, and publications devoted to the arts folded, and recording companies and instrument makers struggled to survive. Some did so by adapting to war-related needs: The Steinway Company, for example, kept their factory open by making coffins for the State Department.[4] The public had little appetite for productions of ballet, opera, and symphonic music. Literary critic and historian Edmund Wilson wrote in his memoirs:

> I felt pleasant when I went to the opera, and sat in my excellent seat downfront before the performance began. I thought, this is probably all wrong—is there an element of sadism in my satisfaction: to sit peaceful, well fed, and secure. . . when the performance began, I realized that it was impossible to enjoy the masterpieces of musical art in the teeth of what was happening in Europe.[5]

If the immediate effect of the war on the arts was little short of disastrous, in the long run, the displacement of European artists would result in profound changes. Within a few years in the late thirties and early forties, the best of Europe's creative talent landed on American shores, causing a dramatic shift in the focus of world culture. Many of the greatest artistic figures of the century left Europe, their lives totally disrupted in midcareer. Those who came early were able to bring families and belongings along; others stayed in Europe too long and had to flee quickly, leaving everything behind. Conductors, opera singers, performers, and composers—Paul Hindemith, Stefan Wolpe, Darius Milhaud, Kurt Weill—all came. Some were Jewish, others were married to Jews, and still others were connected with activities considered subversive by the Nazis. Many chose to wait out the war in Pacific Palisades, California, an area reminiscent of the Riviera. There one could find Stravinsky, Schoenberg, Otto Klemperer, Nadia Boulanger, Heinrich Mann, and Bertolt Brecht. When the war was over, leaving much of Europe in ruin, most of these artists stayed on. Whether America gained or lost from such a strong dose of Europeanization, and what the effects were on individual creative figures, are matters yet to be fully explored by historians.[6]

[1] See Louis Worth, *Community Life in a Democracy*, ed. Florence C. Bingham (Chicago: National Congress of Parents and Teachers, 1942).

[2] Warren I. Susman, "Culture and Commitment," in *Culture as History* (New York: Pantheon Books, 1984), 201.

[3] Susman, *Culture as History*, 209.

[4] See interviews, Henry and John Steinway, Steinway Project, Oral History of American Music, Yale.

[5] Edmund Wilson, *The Forties* (New York: Farrar Straus Giroux, 1983), 43.

[6] For a prototypical study of the émigré composer, see the Hindemith Project, Oral History of American Music. See also Dorothy Crawford, *A Windfall of Musicians* (New Haven: Yale University Press, 2010).

Few artists, whether native or émigré, were able to pursue their chosen careers as they had prior to the war. Literature and drama took a backseat to *Life* magazine, the fine arts to Bill Mauldin's "Up Front" cartoons, and concert music to Kate Smith's ubiquitous "God Bless America." The contemporary arts, struggling in the best of times, barely survived. It was particularly difficult for those concerned with so esoteric an activity as modern music to find a connection to the war effort. Composers competed vigorously for the few commissions offered for patriotic works, and promoters tried to convince the public that contemporary music could stimulate free debate, thereby promoting democracy.

One series of concerts, the Town Hall Music Forum, declared in its brochure: "It becomes more important than ever before to encourage the writing, the hearing, and the discussion of new music, for a major part of our battle is to prove that the democracies are not decadent. We believe this can best be shown through a display of the vitality of that all important segment of democratic society—the free artist." A major event of the 1943 season was "An Aaron Copland Evening," featuring a concert followed by a forum, in which the audience was encouraged to "fire away with bouquets or brickbats" at the composer.[7]

Other musical organizations adapted themselves to the war as best they could. The League of Composers offered to make a survey of the abilities and skills of composers of draft age for the Army and Navy Recreation Commission in Washington, and they sponsored a program by composers already in the service. Claire Reis, the indomitable executive director of the League, formed a committee to produce two seasons of "Wartime Concerts for Soldiers and Sailors" on the mall in New York's Central Park and in Prospect Park in Brooklyn. A benefit for Russian War Relief was organized, and, at Mrs. Reis' urging, Copland wrote to Prokofiev requesting new works by Russian composers (a response was not received). The League commissioned a series of eighteen short works on wartime subjects, which Artur Rodzinski, conductor of the New York Philharmonic, agreed to play as a patriotic gesture at the opening of each program. Many of the commissioned composers derived their pieces from personal experiences; for example, *The Anxious Bugler* by John Alden Carpenter and *In Memoriam—The Colored Soldiers Who Died for Democracy* by William Grant Still. One of the most poignant was Bohuslav Martinů's *Memorial to Lidice,* in honor of the Czechoslovakian town destroyed by the Germans. Even Charles Ives, who had not composed for many years, made his contribution by arranging his World War I song "He Is There" for chorus as "War Song March: They Are There."[8]

The League's publication, *Modern Music,* featured war-related articles, such as Sessions' "Artists and This War" (1942) and Milhaud's "Music and Politics" (1944). One column, "By Cable to *Modern Music* from Moscow," included information about Russian composers and activities, with a great deal of space devoted to Kabalevsky, Miaskovsky, Shostakovich, and Prokofiev. Editor Minna Lederman printed correspondence from servicemen regularly. Most reviews were of patriotic music, such as William Schuman's "A Free Song," Copland's *Lincoln Portrait,* and Roy Harris' *Fifth Symphony* (dedicated to the U.S.S.R.). She wrote to Copland (22 September 1944), "News from Europe is all people want right now. It makes all the difference between being successful or just visibly fading out."

Popular culture, always a barometer of the mood of a people, followed the usual pattern in wartime, adding patriotic songs to the ubiquitous love ballads and nonsense tunes. Irving Berlin's "This Is the Army" came closest in popularity to World War I's "Over There." The airwaves reverberated with the Andrews Sisters' renditions of "The Boogie Woogie Bugle Boy of Company B," "Don't Give Up the Ship," and "The White Cliffs of Dover." Performers were enormously popular and very much in demand. Many were sponsored by the U.S.O. and often went to the camps and hospitals under dangerous and uncomfortable conditions. Some, such as bandleader Glenn Miller, never returned.

Movies were a tremendous influence on the lives of Americans at home and a major source of entertainment for the armed forces. As in other fields, the rise of Hitler brought some of the best talent in films to America. It is interesting to note that none of the refugee filmmakers made films opposing Nazism. In a book about Hollywood in the forties, Otto Friedrich cites fear of retaliation as one reason. He explains further:

> Hollywood as a whole made movies for profit and it earned about one-third of its income from abroad. The studios did not want to offend anyone, neither Fascists or anti-Fascists. . . . Hollywood's political timidity toward Naziism was also a consequence, however, of its feelings about Jewishness and anti-Semitism.. . . Anti-Semitism in America in 1940 was widespread and strong.[9]

Hollywood continued along its glamorous way, convinced that the film studios were doing their patriotic duty by boosting the spirits of the American people. Producers looked for material with a patriotic or uplifting message, such as *Commandos Strike at Dawn,* featuring Paul Muni (music by Louis Gruenberg), or *Mission to Moscow* (music by Max Steiner). Semidocumentaries, such as *Siege of Leningrad* and *Moscow Strikes Back,* exploited pro-Russian sentiments by using film shot by Soviet cameramen and with music by Russian composers. The Office of War Information, responsible for authorizing scripts, was effective in spreading propaganda for the New Deal. When Russia was an ally, liberal writers such as Lillian Hellman were wooed and encouraged as avidly as they were castigated when Russia became the enemy. According to film critic Pauline Kael:

> A lot of movies were very condescending to Europeans and Asiatics. There were films like *Bataan* with Robert Taylor screaming epithets about the Japs. . . .We had stereotypes of a shocking nature. . . . In contrast, there was *The Grand Illusion*, one of the great war films of

[7] The program for "An Aaron Copland Evening" (17 February 1943) included *Divertimento for String Orchestra* (Mozart), *Music for the Theatre, Piano Sonata* (first U.S. performance), *Music for Movies* (premiere). Performers were the Saidenberg Little Symphony, Daniel Saidenberg, conductor, Copland, pianist.

[8] Other composers represented were Henry Cowell, Douglas Moore, Nicolai Berezowsky, Norman Della Joio, Howard Hanson, Roy Harris, Bernard Herrmann, Werner Josten, Darius Milhaud, Walter Piston, Quincy Porter, Bernard Rogers, and Roger Sessions. See Claire R. Reis, *Composers Conductors and Critics* (New York: Oxford University Press, 1955; Detroit Reprints in Music, 1974) 163-66.

[9] Otto Friedrich, *The City of Nets* (New York: Harper & Row, 1986), 46-47.

all times. . . In *The White Cliffs of Dover* the people know that the war is coming home because two little German children are already warlike. *The Clock* was a popular movie. It featured Judy Garland and Robert Walker as two kids who meet in New York. He's a soldier who has to leave in a couple of days. They meet, fall in love and are separated. . . .That was the kind of thing people could love.[10]

Hollywood is an example of America's schizophrenia in the 1930s and 1940s: while the country was struggling to survive the Great Depression, followed by a life-threatening war, Hollywood was in its halcyon days.[11] For musicians, it was the one place "real" money could be made, sometimes for doing very little. As for composers, they were paid whether they were working or not. For example, composer (former jazz pianist) Mel Powell went to Hollywood after studying at Yale University with Paul Hindemith and trying to eke out a living as a "serious" composer. Powell was astounded to spend his first six weeks waiting to be called to the studio, while checks of five hundred dollars arrived regularly each week. According to Powell, "I thought at the time—boy, this is it—the way for the composer in America!"[12] Before Powell could go to Hollywood, he had to get a film credit, and as Copland had done before him with *The City*, Powell accepted Willard Van Dyke's offer to compose music for documentaries. Not knowing anything about film scoring, Powell went to see Copland. "I remember Aaron telling me, 'Never write a woodwind solo for film—it sounds as though it is crawling on the top of the screen. The warm body of strings will get in nobody's way.' "

Some of the finest performers from Europe could be found playing all kinds of things in the movie studios. Powell was hired by the most powerful studio, MGM (Metro-Goldwyn-Mayer). On the payroll were twenty full-time composers, among them André Previn and Adolph Weiss, and many virtuoso performers. Powell's first experience was typical of music in the Hollywood studios at the time. As pianist for a "Tom and Jerry" cartoon, he was to play a glissando after counting sixty-eight measures of rest:

> I had never been on a sound stage before. I arrived at the studio a little nervous. I was handed earphones, and over the earphones a voice counted the measures for me. You might say I was over-informed about that glissando! When we got to measure fifty the earphones warned me to get ready, and at sixty reminded me that we had eight measures to go. I played the finest white-note gliss you'd ever want to hear just as Tom the Cat ran up the clock to catch Jerry the mouse—and I finished just right. The conductor beamed at me as though I had just played a remarkable performance of the Emperor Concerto! And that was it for a few weeks. When André [Previn] came in and heard what I had done, he said, "You don't mean you use your fingers to play a glissando?" And he handed me a rubber comb saying, "From now on, use this. You don't want to hurt your fingers." (André always had a perfectly balanced outlook and sense of humor about what was going on.) I wondered about all the magazines around the studios and learned that they were for the musicians, who spent lots of time sitting around. You could be accompanying Judy Garland in "Over the Rainbow" for a while, and then wait an hour or two before having anything else to do. These same musicians also played in the splendid Monday "Evenings on the Roof" concerts. Often one heard passages from *Pierrot Lunaire* or some other serious work being practiced over in the corner. Cushy as it was, after a few months, I became disenchanted and returned east.

Copland knew very well the price paid by those who chose to work in Hollywood: in exchange for financial security, they endured almost complete isolation from the established concert-music circles. Once a musician became part of the entertainment business, it was virtually impossible to change the image. Mel Powell and André Previn are rare exceptions. Previn has described the situation as "a peculiarly American attitude. Here, one is not allowed to have worked in the commercial media. In Europe everybody does, and nobody even blinks. The irony now is there's a whole generation that doesn't know I've ever done anything except stand in front of a symphony orchestra!"[13]

Copland and Virgil Thomson had reputations for composing excellent film scores, but they were saved from being labeled "film composers" by not staying in Hollywood too long. In retaliation for the patronizing attitudes of concert composers, film composers became a tight group, a "closed shop," as Copland described them. They were convinced that their highly developed craft was understood only by colleagues in the film community, with few exceptions—Copland among them, probably because he did not patronize film composition. Some highly admired film composers (Bernard Herrmann, Alex North, David Raksin, Miklos Rozsa, Bronislaw Kaper, Elmer Bernstein, and Leonard Rosenman) also wrote concert music, but they were rarely encountered on concert programs, and almost never on the East Coast. Nevertheless, Copland believed that the best film composers were those who had gone through traditional channels of study, those who, like Rosenman and North, had yearned to compose symphonies, chamber music, and opera.

When Alex North asked Copland for advice about his music in 1945, Copland responded (11 October 1945), "Sounds to me as if you have a case of 'stage fright.' I'd be glad to see the Clar. work and offer friendly advice, however. Maybe all you need is to face the Muse squarely, look her in the eye, and conquer." Later, North wrote to Copland (10 November 1957), "Someday I will tell you why I have worked like mad out here these past five years, writing scores in three weeks, sacrificing my yen to write 'absolute'–I never knew when the axe would fall." In 1956, Copland included North, along with Herrmann, Rosenman, and Gail Kubik, on a list of composers he most admired in Hollywood. Copland knew what it took to compose a successful score for a major film. He thought that a composer like North, who had a special talent for film composition and could write a score like *Death of a Salesman*, had little reason to be apologetic.

The estrangement between film composers and concert composers is part of a larger picture in American music. A division has separated concert and popular music since Colonial times. These attitudes, strengthened in the nineteenth century and continued in

[10] Pauline Kael in Studs Terkel, *The Good War* (New York: Pantheon Books, 1984), 123.
[11] See Clayton R. Koppes and Gregory D. Black, *Hollywood Goes to War* (New York: the Free Press, 1987).
[12] Mel Powell interview with Vincent Plush, Oral History of American Music, Yale. 13 May, 1983, Van Nuys, California.

[13] See Steve Metcalf, "Previn, the maestro looks back at Hollywood roots." in *The Berkshire Eagle*, Sunday, 19 June 1988, E.6.

the twentieth, include a suspicion of money-making in connection with the arts and the belief that in order to create, an artist must suffer. Film composers were not suffering. Films were part of the world of entertainment, a world that had little to do with what the public viewed as art music.

Copland had deplored the narrow views of some of his colleagues from the time of his first Hollywood film, *Of Mice and Men*. He recommended that the Composers News-Record of the League of Composers carry a report in each issue, "Film Scores in Progress," and he devoted entire sessions to film music in his lectures at home and abroad. Copland praised the work of Herrmann and Rozsa, comparing them with the "old-fashioned" Hollywood writers Tiomkin, Newman, and Steiner:

> Take his [Herrmann] orchestral approach. *The Magnificent Ambersons* had a sleigh ride accompanied by eight celestas only—an unheard of combination, unobtainable outside Hollywood. The title music for *Hangover Square* was scored for piano solo instead of the usual full orchestra, and *Anna and the King of Siam* called for winds and brass without strings. The other composers in Hollywood watch what Herrmann does—and with reason, for he is one of the few men who has been able to introduce a few new ideas in the Hollywood musical scene. Miklos Rozsa is generally considered to be in a class with Newman and Steiner—that is, much sought-after by producers. His film scores for *The Lost Weekend* and *The Killers* were much appreciated. He has made liberal use of the so-called echo-chamber, which gives a macabre, unearthly effect. But such effects are quickly overdone. . . . I like more the music he wrote for the beginning of *The Killers*—stark and dramatic, in an idiom which takes full advantage of modern musical resources.[14]

Copland was in his forties during the war, too old for the draft. He accepted commissions for patriotic works and continued to serve on the Advisory Committee on Music and the Pan-American Union in Washington. He corresponded with Harold Spivacke (chief of the music division of the Library of Congress and music chairman of the joint Army and Navy Committee on Welfare and Recreation), requesting more active war service.[15] The War Department occasionally sent Copland to army camps and colleges to present lectures, such as "Music in America at War."[16] But for the most part, he felt disconnected from the war effort. When Abe Meyer, Copland's Hollywood agent, wrote about Samuel Goldwyn's plan to produce a lavish and costly pro-Russian film, Copland was immediately interested. Patriotism was not Copland's sole motivation; it had been three years since *Our Town*, and he needed the money. He had rejected several scripts, judging them too frivolous for the times, but when he heard that the intellectual and liberal-minded playwright Lillian Hellman was responsible for writing Goldwyn's new film, *The North Star*, and that the Office of War Information had reviewed the script, pronouncing it "a magnificent job of humanizing the plain people of Russia," Copland was convinced that this was what he had been waiting for. A contract was negotiated, and he left for Hollywood in February 1943.

There was something about Los Angeles that seemed closer to the war than New York. It had become a big metropolis filled with defense plants and shipyards, and it was very much alive and thronging with people, many in uniform, at all hours of the day and night. Bands of young Mexicans wearing zoot suits roamed the city. During the time Copland was in Los Angeles, the atmosphere became increasingly uneasy, culminating in the zoot suit riots of June 1943. The large Japanese population in Los Angeles contributed to the tension, and Copland would find that Hollywood had become clannish with the arrival of the Europeans: The German-Jewish group stayed to themselves; the British formed their own emigré colony; and the American moviemakers viewed them all as outsiders. But when Copland first arrived in Los Angeles, it was so different from New York that he found it exhilarating. Copland rented a piano, a small house to put it in (on Hollowell Plaza Drive), and got down to work on the score for *The North Star*.

[14] See Copland's lecture notes on film music at the Library of Congress.

[15] See the correspondence between Copland and Harold Spivacke and G. Howland Shaw, Assistant Secretary of State at the Library of Congress.

[16] See Copland's lecture notes at the Library of Congress.

Publicity release for *The North Star*

THE WAR YEARS

1943 - 1945

The North Star was a Samuel Goldwyn production that cost more than 3 million dollars and was more than a year in preparation. The original screenplay was by Lillian Hellman, author of *The Little Foxes* and *Watch on the Rhine*, plays I had seen and admired. *The North Star* was about a Russian agricultural community before and after the Nazi invasions. Goldwyn assembled an impressive cast and staff for what was the most costly production of his career. Lewis Milestone, with whom I had worked on *Of Mice and Men*, was director; Ira Gershwin wrote lyrics for several songs and choruses, and a noted Russian, David Lichine, was engaged as choreographer. The cast included Anne Baxter, Dana Andrews, Walter Huston, Ann Harding, Walter Brennan, Jane Withers, Erich von Stroheim, Farley Granger, and Dean Jagger, and the publicity releases boasted "A Company of One Thousand."

An exact replica of a Russian airplane cockpit was constructed, and a complete Russian village of twenty buildings was built on the back lot of the studio where once had stood an English village for *Wuthering Heights*, and at another time, the tropical town for *Hurricane*. The buildings included thatched-roof cottages, a school, a hospital, an assembly hall, a radio station, and a railroad station, complete with a freight train and ten cars built from specifications of a Russian railroad system. These were not mere shells of buildings but ones with interiors and hundreds of authentic props. Irving Sindler, a veteran property man on the staff, was famous for having his name appear on a prop in every picture he ever worked on: In *The North Star* it was etched on the side of a sewing machine that was shown being rescued from a burning village by a peasant housewife.

Everyone on the set kidded about the livestock—pigs, horses, cattle, chicken, and sheep increased in quantity as the picture progressed. Sixty pigs were born on the village set. The dogs came from the Los Angeles pound. They had never had it so good! Later they were adopted by employees and members of the cast. One mongrel became famous for disappearing. When Mr. Goldwyn offered a large reward of five hundred dollars, the public interpreted it as the kindhearted gesture of an animal lover; in fact, Goldwyn would have faced a large loss if retakes had had to be made with a different dog (I was told that the dog, "Dada," had cost Goldwyn four dollars at the local pound).

I was brought out to Hollywood quite early for this film and saw some of it being shot. It was a soft life with nothing much to do, yet I was on salary the whole time. I remember being present at the shooting of a scene when the "evil" Germans—it was action during the war and the Russians were the good guys and the Germans the bad ones—were burning the village, which was portrayed much like an American town with people at work, women at home, and children at play. The peasants were all brilliant, and the kids were all beautiful and very smart. On that particular day when I was watching the shooting, the Germans were burning down the whole village. It was fascinating to watch because the soldiers would run in carrying their torches on fire and would touch the straw roofs of these simple peasant houses, producing lots of flames. But hidden behind the cameras, right behind me, was the fire department, ready to put out the flames the instant they stopped turning the cameras! It looked so very realistic in the film, and you said to yourself, Oh my Lord, those awful Germans are burning down a whole village!

The North Star provided unusual scope for the musical score. I wrote to Nadia Boulanger (23 April 1943), "The film I am doing calls for a great variety of music—songs, choruses, orchestral interludes, etc. It is like having a new toy to play with. But in Hollywood, one never can foretell the result. In my case I am learning a lot—excellent preparation for operatic writing!" There were decisions to make, principally questions of style. Since the picture took place in Russia, how authentically "Russian" ought the music to be? (Shostakovich might have faced the same problem had he been asked to supply a score for a movie set in the United States.) When I saw that the actors were Americans performing without even attempting Russian accents, I decided to use a musical style that would suggest, rather than emphasize, the Russian flavor. This was not an unfamiliar challenge: I had adapted Mexican folk material in *El Salón México*, and American cowboy tunes for *Billy the Kid* and *Rodeo*. By using the same technique with Russian folk songs, I developed fragments of a few carefully chosen tunes until they became very much my own, while still retaining a sense of their Russian derivation. (I had found a book of old Russian folk songs in the library before leaving New York.) Several sequences called for Russian-sounding music, but only in four instances did I make direct use of actual Soviet material.[1] To my mind, the

[1] Copland derived his Russian tunes from *Russische Volkslieder* (Leipzig: J. H. Zimmermann). From Copland's conducting score in his files: "Going to School" was from Zimmermann, No. 2, which he arranged for two accordians; "Song of the Fatherland" was composed by I. Dunayevsky, transcribed by Copland, lyrics adapted by I. Gershwin; "Younger Generation" and "Collective Loading Time Song" were adapted from traditional Russian melodies; "Death of a Little Boy" and "Scorched Earth" were composed by Copland.

most effective was "Song of the Fatherland," sung by the children at the end of the school term, a kind of Russian "My Country 'Tis of Thee." I also used the "Internationale," but the orchestral setting was my own. During the advance screenings, some of the Russians brought over by Goldwyn told him that my music wasn't Russian enough. After the film was released, I was amused to hear from Lillian Hellman that the Russians liked the film and the score, but some of them complained that the "Ukrainian" tunes came from the wrong part of the U.S.S.R.!

I composed three songs with lyrics by Ira Gershwin: "No Village Like Mine," sung by the young people who are interrupted by the falling of Nazi bombs on the village; "Younger Generation"; and "Song of the Guerrillas."[2] Lillian Hellman wrote to me after a quick trip to the West Coast when we did not get to see each other: "What music I heard and what Ira sang for me, seemed fine, and I am grateful to you." Ira Gershwin also wrote lyrics for a choral piece I composed (it was played on a "March of Time" broadcast dedicated to Russia). I made arrangements for balalaikas, worked on a ballet interpolation for Lichine, and had my first chance at a bang-up battle sequence. Finally, the time came to compose music for the titles and credits. I wrote to my friend Victor Kraft back in New York (9 September 1943), "The title music is pastoral-like, with a heavy middle part when the Foreword comes on about those awful Germans. Everyone is shocked because there is no fanfare for Goldwyn's credit, but even I couldn't solve the problem of a fanfare in a pastorale."

Except for the title music, which was conducted by a musician from Warner Brothers, I conducted the score myself. It gave me more control of the results. It stands to reason that the composer who has already worked through the material has a better chance of accuracy than someone who comes in to conduct the music cold. I heard the recorded dialogue through earphones while the picture flashed before my eyes. Timings are inserted throughout film scores to help with the synchronizing, and important musical cues are indicated in the rough cut so the conductor can know exactly where he is.[3] We recorded for four days, and the musicians in the orchestra seemed unusually pleased with the material they were given to play. I wrote again to Victor: "Now I spend most of my time in the Purgatory Room—dubbing to you. They are doing all they can for me but oh what a heartpain it gives one to hear the music played at those inhuman levels. Well, the fact is a movie is not a concert with pictures, but pictures with some offstage noises. Still I come off pretty well."

I spent very little time in my small house in L.A., until I got a traffic summons and could not drive. I have never learned my way around a kitchen, so I found a fellow who was serving lunch at the studio to make my dinner every evening I stayed home. I was much relieved not to have to go out to restaurants. Once in a while, I had dinner with friends—Jerry Moross, Ingolf Dahl, and even Stravinsky invited me to their places. I saw quite a lot of Lawrence Morton, instigator of the Monday Evening Concerts, and of the Group Theatre people. Bobby Lewis took me to the movies and kidded me about "watching" with my eyes closed (I had to admit that I really went to hear the music).[4] I got a kick out of seeing some movie stars off the set: Farley Granger was friendly; Ruth Ford invited me to a cocktail party; and I met Groucho Marx at a modern music concert one evening. Groucho heard my *Piano Sonata* played at the concert, and at intermission, he expressed surprise at the advanced idiom of the piece. "Well," I said, "you see, I have a split personality." And Groucho shot back, "It's okay, Copland—as long as you split it with Sam Goldwyn."

Many distinguished personalities were living in Hollywood at the time of *The North Star*—Schoenberg, Stravinsky, Toch, and others—but, strangely enough, they didn't make a

[2] "Younger Generation," "Song of the Guerrillas," and "No Village Like Mine" were published individually as sheet music for voice and piano by Chappell & Co., Inc. (no longer available) and in piano-vocal and choral SATB, arranged by Frederick Fay Swift, by Boosey & Hawkes.

[3] A score copy with autograph corrections by Copland is at the Music Division, The New York Public Library at Lincoln Center, donated by Elliott Carter.

[4] Interview, Robert Lewis with William Owen for Perlis, 12. May 1981, Irvington, New York.

culture. The musical life seemed provincial, with no signs of improvement on the horizon. I depended a great deal on letters from friends at home to keep in touch with what was going on in the music world and for news about performances of my compositions: *Fanfare for the Common Man* was premiered in New York by George Szell and the Cincinnati Symphony (14 March 1943) while I was in Los Angeles, and *Four Dance Episodes from Rodeo* by Alexander Smallens with the New York Philharmonic (22 June); Artur Rodzinski conducted the *Suite from Billy the Kid* for a radio broadcast; and Lenny Bernstein played my *Piano Sonata* at the Composers Laboratory-Forum in New York. I was to have been on the panel, and virtually everyone I knew commented about my absence and about Lenny's performance. Lenny wrote about it himself, adding that he had just finished composing a piece, *Dedication to Aaron Copland.*[5] Also, he had attended the premiere of my choral piece *Lark* (13 April 1943), and commented, "It has a lovely sound, and it was fairly well sung, except that Bob Shaw missed the whole point—the 'spurtive ascension' in the music. You know what I mean. But as good as a piece without its essential quality can sound, that sounded good. It's kind of foolproof, you know."

Otto Luening reported about the founding of the American Music Center (21 March 1943): ". . . missed your judgment, strength and wisdom. . . . I suppose your particular brand of nuthouse equals this in its own way." David Diamond filled me in on what was going on with the New York crowd:

> Janie [Bowles] was very peculiar the other night. Nothing pleased her. Paul [Bowles] was very obtuse and Arthur [Berger] was all musicology and proverbs. Esther [Berger] was cagey. Everyone keeps saying, why doesn't Aaron write a symphony when he's capable of getting such wonderful ideas down . . . make lots of money, come back and write a wonderful large orchestra work and show people that you can pull it off.

David was not the only colleague concerned about my possible defection to Hollywood. I could read the relief behind Elliott Carter's lines: "It is good news that you are writing a violin sonata. . . ." Even Lenny expressed it: "I had a long fight with Kirk and Constance Askew about whether you could hold out to the Hollywood glamour. They were skeptical. I was, of course, loyally adamant." I responded (6 March 1943): "Of course you were right. Hollywood glamour couldn't get me in a million years." I knew that William Faulkner had written his best work, *Light in August*, after a stretch in Hollywood. I knew what my friends did not—that I was composing during the waiting-around periods on the film production, that I was collecting ideas for a ballet for Martha Graham and for a large work, either a piano concerto or a symphony. I mentioned the concerto idea to Hans Heinsheimer, who was then with my publishers, Boosey & Hawkes in New York. Heinsheimer mentioned it to Rodzinski, who wrote to me immediately (3 March 1943):

> Here is my offer: I never heard you play the piano, but I guess if your concerto will be difficult, then you certainly must be a good pianist to do justice to it. If you are a pianist only for domestic use, then your concerto wouldn't be technically too difficult. In both cases, I will be more than delighted to present you with the New York Philharmonic next season, providing this will be the American premiere.

[5] The unpublished Bernstein score is in the Copland collection at the Library of Congress.

AROUND THE STUDIO

Mr. Goldwyn confers with his production staff.The producer attends to various details, from approving the preliminary sketches and advising on direction and cuts, through to the cutting of the background music.

Lewis Milestone, Samuel Goldwyn, Anne Baxter

James Wong Howe, Percy Ferguson, Mr. Goldwyn,

Ann Harding, Dean Jagger, Amy Carter, Miss Baxter, Mr. Milestone, and Mr. Goldwyn.

Messrs. Goldwyn, Milestone and Jagger, and Misses Carter and Harding.

Photographs made on the set during production of *The North Star* for use in a publicity release

Rodzinski then jumped the gun by announcing to the newspapers that I would premiere a new piano concerto with him, thus creating some misunderstandings when I gave up the idea of composing another piano concerto after all.[6]

With Lenny's urging, Victor Kraft decided to join me in Hollywood. "He'd be so much happier there," wrote Lenny, "and you would be so much happier. So why not?" It's true that Victor was not happy in the loft we used for work space on Sixty-third Street. Victor complained: "The Femininos are a fire hazard. The street gets more and more slummy and full of wayward kids." Victor was working with photographer Margaret Bourke-White, and when she came to Hollywood to do publicity photos for *The North Star*, Victor came and stayed from April to June. Later that summer, Lenny Bernstein was appointed assistant conductor of the New York Philharmonic, and he wrote this amazing news to me immediately on Philharmonic stationery, adding, "I have so much news for you—won't you please hurry home? The score must be done by now. . . . Come back!"

The recording of the film score was finished during the first week of September. I was pleased at the prospect of going on to different things. I wrote to Bill [William] Schuman (22 September 1943):

> I feel like a general exiled to Syria, and any news from headquarters is manna to the expatriate. I hope you like the picture when you see it. There is more than an hour's worth of music and you can actually hear about half of it, which is pretty good as pictures go. After seven and a half months on it, I am in a mood to doubt whether any picture is worth that much time. On the way home, I am stopping off in Harris country—Denver and Colorado Springs to make lectures on the South Americans. Never been in that part of the USA. Unfortunately the patriarch Himself [Roy Harris] will be in the east just as I get there.

I left Los Angeles for Denver to deliver lectures at two army camps, at the Phipps Museum, then the Art Institute in Colorado Springs, and at the University of Colorado at Boulder. Victor had gone to Mexico and was urging me to join him, but the Hollywood job had taken longer than expected and I was anxious to get back to New York. After I returned, I wrote to Ira Gershwin about our songs from *The North Star*, and he responded (22 November 1943): "I'm sorry to hear the songs aren't being played on the air. . . . It may be as in the case of Harburg and Kern's *And Russia Is Her Name* that songs from *North Star* would be considered controversial by the advertising agencies, which, frequently, control the policy of music on their programs." He promised to write to the publishers, however, and signed the letter "Your lyric writer, Ira."

The North Star was released in October 1943, just before Russia became an enemy instead of an ally. Except for *The Daily Worker*, most of the reviews were unfavorable. For the most part, it was taken as propaganda, and as *The Journal American* reviewer commented, "not even good propaganda." It must have been a great disappointment to Goldwyn. Some re-

[6] Hans Heinsheimer, representing the newly formed Boosey & Hawkes Artists' Bureau, wrote to Copland (26 May 1943) to arrange a contract between Copland and the New York Philharmonic for the world premiere of a Copland piano concerto to be played by the composer on 10 February 1944, with a provision for cancellation. A letter requesting the cancellation (unsigned carbon, 12 October 1943) from Boosey & Hawkes to Bruno Zirato of the Philharmonic is in the Copland collection at the Library of Congress.

Lillian Hellman

May 30, 1943

Mr. Aaron Copland
c/o Samuel Goldwyn
1041 N. Formosa Avenue
Hollywood, Calif.

Dear Aaron:

I am sorry not to have seen you when I was on the coast. I had a miserable week, and people who didn't see me are lucky.

I only wanted to say here that what music I heard, and what Ira sang for me, seemed fine and I am grateful to you.

My warm regards,

Lillian

viewers cited the fact that the familiar stars constituted a barrier to acceptance of the film as Russian; and it was inevitable that comparisons were made with the great Russian films. Lillian told me that when she visited the U.S.S.R., she found that Soviet officials viewed *The North Star* "as a great joke." She wrote, "But outside of Moscow there were simple peasants glad to find themselves so noble on the U.S. screen." I was somewhat surprised to receive an Academy Award nomination for the musical score, and *Variety* carried a favorable notice (5 January 1944):

> Further indication of the advancing maturity of film music can be seen in Aaron Copeland's [sic] score for the recently released Sam Goldwyn-RKO story of the Russian people, *North Star*. In this score, Copland duplicated his successes in *Of Mice and Men* and *Our Town*. The music based on Russian themes is so authentic as to be capable of deceiving even the experts into thinking them genuine.

Some years later, Lillian wrote to tell me that *The North Star* was being released for television: "It has been butchered, with any favorable remarks about the Russians deleted and turning them from the heroes to the villains of the movie. This travesty now goes by the name *Armored Attack*."

I had carried sketches for a violin and piano piece with me to California. During the frequent periods when I had to wait for the studio to move ahead on *The North Star*, I played through the piano parts of violin sonatas from various periods. My idea was for the piano to complement the violin rather than merely accompany it; thus the title: *Sonata for Violin and Piano*. But the piece is usually referred to as *Violin Sonata*. I had just completed it when I heard that a friend had died while on active duty in the South Pacific. *The Sonata for Violin and Piano* is dedicated to Lt. Larry H. Dunham (1910-1943).[7]

For whatever reasons, at that time I had little desire to compose a dissonant or virtuosic work, or one that incorporated folk materials. Nevertheless, certain qualities of the American folk tune had become part of my natural style of composing, and they are echoed in the *Sonata*. It is composed in the usual three movements, with the last two to be played without pause. The first movement, based on an eight-note phrase with the interval of a fourth prominent, alternates in mood between a tender lyricism and a more rapidly paced section. Changes in the timing occur throughout; in fact, the strong feeling of contrasting moods in the composition is achieved mainly through rhythmic changes. The second movement, in a simple ABA form with two-part counterpoint between the instruments, is calm and bare in outline. The scherzo-like third movement is characterized by irregular rhythms and a strong penetrating melody. The *Sonata* ends with a short coda that refers back to the theme of the opening movement.[8]

I asked Louis Kaufman, a violinist friend in Hollywood, to check the violin part and to play through the piece with me, and from Hollywood I sent the *Sonata* to David Diamond (a violinist himself). David responded (29 October 1943):

> Got back from Rochester last night and found the violin part to your *Sonata*. Thanks, and I'm already practicing and refingering. Kaufman's fingering is certainly very special. I'm doing it my way—as all violinists should: individual ways.

David and I played through the *Sonata* for friends at my loft, before the first public performance, which took place at a concert of contemporary American and English music presented by Boosey & Hawkes at Times Hall (17 January 1944). Ruth Posselt was the violinist, I the pianist. The music critic of *The New York Times*, Olin Downes, called my piece "poor and characterless." The rest of the concert, with works by Quincy Porter, Benjamin Britten, and Eugene Goossens, fared little better. Downes wrote of ". . . one dismaying thing, namely the persistence of its rearward vision, and the absence, as it impressed the writer, of any consciousness of a new age or a changing order." Virgil Thomson's review in the *Herald Tribune* was more favorable about my *Sonata*: "I suspect it is one of its author's most satisfying pieces. . . . It has a quality at once of calm elevation and of buoyancy that is characteristic of Copland and irresistibly touching."

[7] At the Library of Congress: pencil copy of the first two movements; first pencil sketch; ink score (36 pages); score for "Lento" movement, and violin part.

[8] Copland's description of the *Violin Sonata* is derived from his early program notes.

Louis Kaufman sent me some very nice reviews after the West Coast premiere of the *Violin Sonata* (May 1944). I wrote (2 June): "I was delighted to know that it had gone over so well. I feel certain your fiddling had a lot to do with it." We played the *Sonata* together at Kaufman's Town Hall recital in New York (14 March 1945), and in 1948 we recorded it for the Concert Hall Label. (I turned to Kaufman later when I needed help with bowings and fingering for the violin and piano arrangements of "Hoe-Down" from *Rodeo* and "Waltz" from *Billy the Kid*.) The *Sonata* has made an occasional appearance on violin and piano programs, and more recently, it has been heard in arrangements for other instruments. Almost forty years after I composed the *Violin Sonata*, a young clarinetist, Timothy Paradise, came to see me for permission to play an arrangement of the *Violin Sonata* for his instrument. I never would have believed that such an arrangement would be so successful! I particularly admired the way the grace notes at the end of the piece sounded. Another young clarinet player, Michael Webster (son of my old friend, pianist Beveridge Webster) helped prepare the clarinet version for publication. Paradise had set the *Sonata* a whole step lower; Webster took it down another full step (the published clarinet arrangement is a major third below the original). In the late seventies, bassist Gary Karr paid me a visit to play a version of the *Violin Sonata* for double bass. Gary took the violin part down a whole octave in appropriate places, and in the second movement, he used harmonics that worked like a charm for his instrument.

Harold Clurman left for Hollywood in the fall of 1943 just as I returned to New York, to my room at the Empire Hotel and to my loft, which Clurman described as "that dismal sanctuary on Sixty-third Street." Clurman wrote: "My apartment is pretty and theatrical in Stella's taste [actress Stella Adler, Clurman's wife]—not monastic as in yours. Why, my beloved friend of all time, must every one of your permanent residences have a hangover of Washington Ave. in Brooklyn?" My rent at the Empire Hotel had gone up from $8.50 a month to $3.25 a week, and although I usually rented the loft to a friend (Leo Smit or Edwin Denby) when I went away, I was beginning to yearn for a place of my own in the country. I even began to look with the help of my friends Mary and Bill Lescaze (Bill was an architect and knew his way around the real estate scene). But I put it off and answered Clurman: "If I continue to live simply, I can get by with the money from *The North Star* plus fees for a few lectures, leaving me free to spend most of my time composing."

My teaching assignments included five lectures as the Horatio Appleton Lamb lecturer at Harvard in the spring of 1944.[9] I enjoyed Cambridge and returned to New York only for a meeting at the Blue Ribbon restaurant, called by Margaret Grant, secretary of the Koussevitzky Music Foundation, to discuss arrangements for a testimonial dinner to honor Koussevitzky's twentieth year as conductor of the Boston Symphony. What began as a gesture by composers to show appreciation for Koussevitzky's devotion to American music grew to include organizations and institutions, performers, critics, patrons, and friends—even the Russian Embassy! The event took place at the Plaza Hotel (16 May 1944). I acted as

[9] Copland's lectures in 1943-1944 included Mt. Holyoke College (2 December 1943) and the University of Chicago (April 1944).

host, and there were many tributes and toasts. The original purpose of the evening was kept in mind—the program listed all of the American works performed under Koussevitzky's leadership. It was a reminder that he had championed not only recognized talents but many lesser-known composers.[10]

Victor Kraft had returned to the States while I was teaching at Harvard, and since he knew his way around Mexico, we drove down there together for the summer and early fall of 1944. I had read a book by an American who had spent eight months in the tiny town of Tepoztlán in 1927 and did an anthropological study of the place. No American had lived there since. Although only a few hours from Mexico City, Tepoztlán was definitely off the main road and pretty much the way it had been in Cortez' time. It is 5,500 feet up amidst extraordinary mountains. The Indians there are full-blooded Aztecs, and the older folks still spoke the Aztec language in preference to Spanish. They were not friendly to strangers. I wrote to Bill Schuman, "Being the only gringo makes one feel very conspicuous—a simple walk through town turns one into a symbol and puts the whole civilized structure on trial. I try to be a worthy representative— but it's a strain." There were no newspapers, radios, or telephones, and no traffic because the streets were unpaved. Victor and I had the only livable house in the village. It was charming in the simple Mexican patio style. It had a separate studio with a piano of sorts (borrowed from a wealthy American who lived in Cuernavaca, the nearest city), and the whole place came complete with cook and gardener. Nights were dark, since there was no electricity. I wrote to Arthur Berger (8 September 1944):

> Twice a week a kind of public dance takes place in the open-air market. Instead of doing jarabes and huapangos, I am amazed to see the people attempting a kind of Tepoztlán version of a fox trot. The nearest movie house is fifteen miles away, but obviously its effect has been felt. The whole thing is hardly conducive to inspiring a "Salón Tepozteco."

Nothing ever happened in Tepoztlán, so when a special messenger arrived with a letter for the gringo, it caused a lot of excitement. The letter, mailed from Brooklyn a week earlier, was from my sister Laurine, telling me of our mother's death. It was upsetting being so far from home at a time like that! I wrote to Lenny (26 July): "The trip turned out to be a sad one. Five days after I left, my mother died suddenly, and I didn't get the news in time to attend the funeral. I was relieved to know that the end came so painlessly—but I've been left with a depressed feeling nonetheless." I wrote to Koussevitzky (7 September): "The first part of the summer left me distressed because of the news of my mother's death in July. It is an experience that time alone can help to adjust. . . . I am hard at work on the symphony I plan to do for you." Eventually, letters were delivered to me in Tepoztlán from my friends. Harold Clurman advised, "Read Sholem Aleichem to understand yourself better, your Mom and Pop or at least my Mom and Pop." I heard from Nadia: "My thoughts are all going to your Mother, who must have been so proud of her son—and in her memory, I kiss you tenderly . . . as when you were a little boy." And Lenny wrote (16 August), "I wish I could be with you now that your Mother has died. . . . I wonder what really goes on in your insides now. And what of your Father? You must be very worried about him." I was worried about Pop. His memory was going, and after Mother died, he became much worse. Lillian Coombs—the same Lil who had been with the family all these many years—was taking care of Pop, and she and Laurine kept me informed. Lil wrote (30 August):

> He was in pretty bad shape on the 21st so he had to be sent away. I am home all tired out. . . . I know how you feel—we all feel the same way. So you all have to be brave and take the situation as it comes . . . the Missus would want you all to keep in touch with each other just as before she kept you all together. The boss may be here for quite a while. Yours always, Lilly.

The reality of Mother's death came home to me sharply only after I returned to New York. As Nadia wrote in her annual birthday letter, "This year, for the first time, your Mother will not be there." Pop's health continued to deteriorate, and when I returned home, I met with my family to make arrangements for his care. Pop never recovered and died six months after Mother (2 February 1945). (My brother Leon stayed on in the house on President Street in Brooklyn and Ralph managed the property.)

While in Tepoztlán, I felt so far away from everything and everybody that I suddenly wished I was sitting in the middle of Times Square! However, working conditions were good and I was determined to make headway on the commission I had been given by the Koussevitzky Music Foundation. But first, I had to take a few weeks to compose a radio piece promised to Paul Whiteman, Director of Music for the Blue Network (a division of the American Broadcasting System). The commission would help pay for the summer.

Copland in Tepoztlán, Mexico, 1944

[10] Lesser known American composers performed by Koussevitsky included Mabel Daniels, Arcady Dubensky, Henry Eichheim, Blair Fairchild, and Alexander Steinert. For a complete list, see Aaron Copland, "Serge Koussevitzky and the American Composer," *Musical Quarterly*, XXX:3 (July 1944), 261-64. At the testimonial dinner Randall Thompson's "Alleluia" and Schuman's "Holiday Song" were performed by the Collegiate Chorale under Robert Shaw. Howard Hanson and Copland made tributes; Koussevitzky responded.

The "Blue" had a newly established "creative music fund" from which it paid commissions for "streamlined works, or symphonettes," to be performed by the Whiteman Orchestra on the Philco Radio Hour. Commissions went to Stravinsky, Bernstein, Roy Harris, Richard Rodgers, Morton Gould, Peter De Rose, Erich Korngold, Victor Young, Ferde Grofe, and me. The agreement was for the network to retain first broadcast rights and exclusive performance rights for a year; accrued royalties would go to the "Blue" until the sum originally advanced was returned to the fund. The works were to be performed one each week, beginning July 1944.

My piece, *Letter From Home*, had been sketched in Cambridge the previous spring. While completing it in Mexico, I wrote to Arthur Berger, "It's very sentimental, with five saxophones that are sometimes five clarinets and sometimes four flutes—but it modulates!" (The original version for radio orchestra included alternatives to the saxophone, since I knew that five sax players would not always be available.)[11] The title of my seven-minute piece was not meant to be taken too literally—I meant only to convey the emotion that might naturally be awakened in the recipient by reading a letter from home. I sent the score off to Paul Whiteman and a copy to my publishers. Hans Heinsheimer responded, "Whiteman intends to conduct your piece himself (is that a threat or a promise?)." After the broadcast (18 October 1944), Heinsheimer wrote:

> Despite the shortcomings of the performance, it is a lovely piece. Poor Whiteman was over his head. . . He said in *The New York Times* that in order not to bother anyone with these pieces, he plays them at midnight when nobody listens in. . . . He never removed his cigar during rehearsals and never took his nose out of the score for an instant.

Whiteman made a recording, which I heard when I got home. It was much too fast from beginning to end. Nevertheless, I was grateful to Whiteman for commissioning the piece.

Letter From Home was given its first public performance by the Cleveland Orchestra under George Szell (27 February and I March 1947) with an expanded and revised orchestration.[12] I was not able to attend, so Heinsheimer again reported: "It seemed a little hurried—more the letter of a German PW to mutter." In 1962, I revised the instrumentation again, providing a slightly shortened version, with an orchestral setting suitable for about twenty-five instruments.[13]

I had long been an admirer of Martha Graham's work. She, in turn, must have felt a certain affinity for my music, since as early as 1931 she had used my *Piano Variations* for a solo dance composition—*Dithyrambic*. Surely only an artist with an understanding of my work could have visualized dance material in so rhythmically complex and thematically

[11] The autograph score of the original version is in the Paul Whiteman Collection at Williams College. A recording of the radio broadcast is also in the Whiteman Collection. Pencil sketches and a piano reduction with instructions for instrumentation are in the Copland collection at the Library of Congress..

[12] Szell used 3 flutes, piccolo, 2 oboes, English horn, 2 clarinets, bass clarinet, 2 bassoons, 2 contrabassoons, 4 horns, 3 trumpets, 3 trombones, 1 tuba, timpani, percussion, harp, and strings.

[13] The instrumentation of the 1962 revised version of *Letter From Home* was performed at Copland's eighty-fifth birthday concert at Avery Fisher Hall, the New York Philharmonic, Zubin Mehta conductor (14 November 1985). *Letter From Home* is also published in an arrangement for school orchestra (with piano conductor).

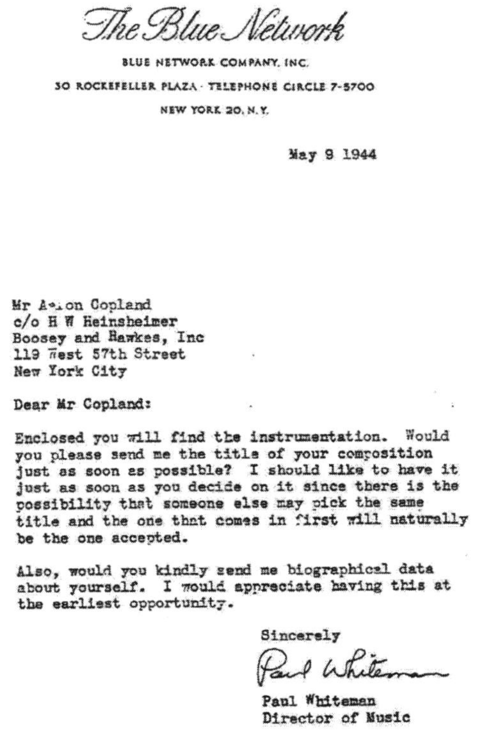
The Blue Network
BLUE NETWORK COMPANY, INC.
30 ROCKEFELLER PLAZA · TELEPHONE CIRCLE 7-5700
NEW YORK 20, N.Y.

May 9 1944

Mr Aaron Copland
c/o H W Heinsheimer
Boosey and Hawkes, Inc
119 West 57th Street
New York City

Dear Mr Copland:

Enclosed you will find the instrumentation. Would you please send me the title of your composition just as soon as possible? I should like to have it just as soon as you decide on it since there is the possibility that someone else may pick the same title and the one that comes in first will naturally be the one accepted.

Also, would you kindly send me biographical data about yourself. I would appreciate having this at the earliest opportunity.

Sincerely

Paul Whiteman

Paul Whiteman
Director of Music

abstruse a composition.[14] From then on, we had hoped to collaborate on a stage work. In 1941, Martha asked whether I would compose music for a ballet on a Medea subject, but the script seemed rather severe to me, so I declined the offer.[15] Then, in 1942, Martha's partner, Erick Hawkins, introduced Elizabeth Sprague Coolidge to Martha's work. Aware of Mrs. Coolidge's interest in contemporary music, Hawkins suggested she commission original scores for three new Graham ballets.[16] The commissioning of new music for modern dance was most unusual at that time, but Mrs. Coolidge, with typical energy, translated her enthusiasm into action by inviting Martha to create the ballets for the 1943 program of the fall festival sponsored annually by the Coolidge Foundation. Each commission was for five hundred dollars, an amount Mrs. Coolidge thought appropriate for little-known composers. Erick

[14] *Dithyrambic* was a ten-minute solo, danced by Graham, 6 December 1931. It received positive reviews by audiences and critics.

[15] After Copland turned down the script, *Daughter of Colchis*, Graham sent it to Carlos Chávez, who composed a score Graham considered incompatible with the script. (Chávez eventually composed music for a Graham ballet with a different script, *Dark Meadow*.)

[16] For a thorough description of the commissioning of the ballet, see Wayne Shirley, "Ballet for Martha, the Commissioning of *Appalachian Spring*," *Performing Arts Annual* 1987 (Library of Congress), 102-23.

Hawkins (backed up by Harold Spivacke) convinced Mrs. Coolidge that Martha's dances ought to have music by established composers. They suggested that commissions be offered to Heitor Villa-Lobos and myself. Ostensibly because Villa-Lobos was so far away, Mrs. Coolidge suggested Paul Hindemith; Martha countered with Carlos Chávez, and the decision was made for Chávez.[17] Mrs. Coolidge need not have been concerned about the amount of the commission—as far as I was concerned, five hundred dollars was not a small amount in those days.

Since I had met Mrs. Coolidge in Mexico in 1938, she wrote to me directly (23 July 1942): "Although I may be a little premature in writing to you before Dr. Spivacke addresses you officially, I am allowing myself the pleasure of asking you . . ." and I responded (31 July), "I have been an admirer of Miss Graham's work for many years and I have more than once hoped that we might collaborate. It particularly pleases me that you should make this possible."[18] I heard from Martha (7 November): "I think I am the most fortunate dancer anywhere to have you and Chávez. I cannot believe it as yet . . ." Mrs. Coolidge told Martha that the working out of the ballet could be in our hands. She asked only that the score be about one-half hour long and ". . . for an ensemble of not more than ten or twelve instruments at the outside . . . a small orchestra with one instrument of each kind, both wind and strings with piano."

Martha hoped that I could complete the score by July 1943 so she could create the dance during the summer for performance in October. But when I left for Hollywood in February to work on *The North Star*, the script Martha had promised by Christmas had not yet arrived. She wrote

> (7 October 1943): "The ballet has to do with roots in so far as people can express them, without telling an actual story."
>
> Once the music comes I never look at the script. It is only to make a working base for the composer and myself. Now it exists in words, in literary terms only and it has to come alive in a more plastic medium which music is to me. So please feel free to let the music take its own life and urge.

The first script arrived in the early spring with a working title, *House of Victory*. It included biblical quotations, an Indian girl, and references to the Civil War.[19] The script began: "This is a legend of American living. It is like the bone structure, the inner frame that holds together a people." Although the script was to change considerably as the ballet developed, it was already possible to recognize the essence of Martha's ideas. I had misgivings about the spoken word and the Civil War episode, but only when Martha asked me my opinion did I say so. I liked the idea in general, and I told Harold Spivacke, 'I think I have my first theme."

[17] See Erick Hawkins to Elizabeth Sprague Coolidge (16 June 1942), Hawkins and Coolidge Collections, the Library of Congress.

[19] Two Graham scripts are in Copland's files at the Library of Congress: the rejected *Daughter of Colchis* and *House of Victory* (later *Appalachian Spring*). The script Copland presented to Mrs. Coolidge is in the Coolidge Collection, the Library of Congress. It is untitled and bears the inscription "Name?".

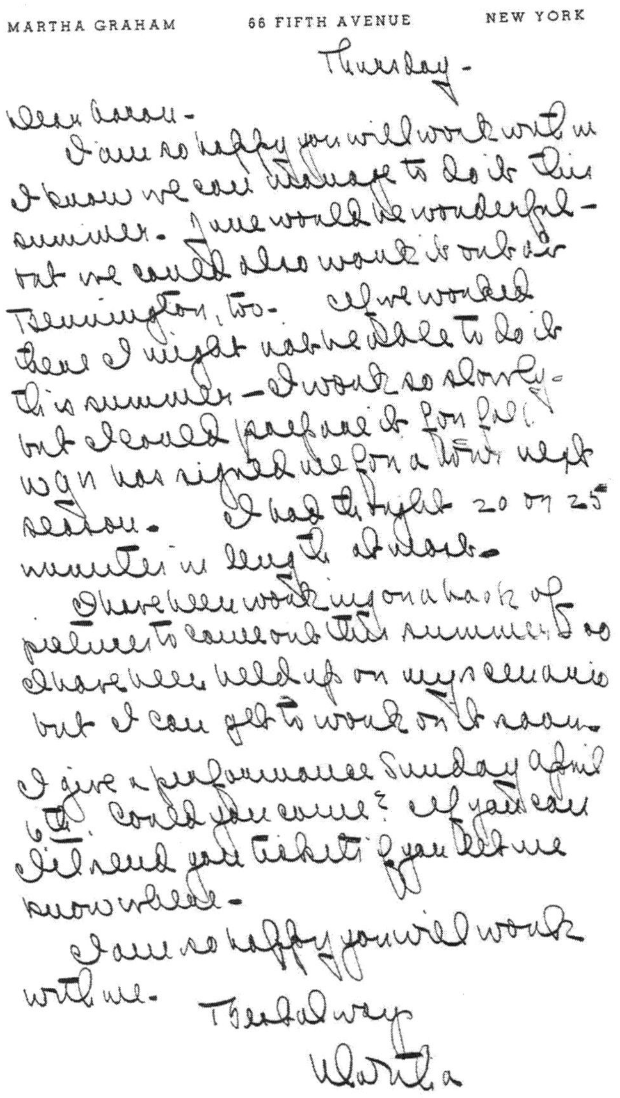
MARTHA GRAHAM 66 FIFTH AVENUE NEW YORK

Thursday-

Dear Aaron-

I am so happy you will work with me. I know we can manage to do it this summer. June would be wonderful - but we could also work it out at Bennington, too. If we worked there I might not be able to do it this summer - I work so slowly - but I could prepare it for fall. [illegible] has signed me for a tour next season. I had thought 20 or 25 minutes in length at most.

I have been working on a book of pictures to come out this summer so I have been held up on my scenario but I can get to work on it soon.

I give a performance Sunday April 6th. Could you come? If you can I'll send you tickets if you let me know where.

I am so happy you will work with me.

Thine always

Martha

When composing for the dance, I found it best not to know the choreography in advance. Finding the musical ideas to suit the feeling and the spirit comes first. Then, when the composer has a general idea of what the dance is about and appropriate timings for the sequences, it becomes possible to set the musial ideas on paper. I was pleased to hear from Martha ((22 July):

Martha's ballet (eventually to be called *Appalachian Spring*) concerned a pioneer celebration in spring around a newly-built farmhouse in the Pennsylvania hills in the early part of the last century. The principal characters are a bride and her young farmer husband. After Martha gave me this bare outline, I knew certain crucial things—that it had to do with the pioneer American spirit, with youth and spring, with optimism and hope. I thought about that in combination with the special quality of Martha's own personality, her talents as a dancer, what she gave off, and the basic simplicity of her art. Nobody else seems anything like Martha, and she's unquestionably very American. There's something prim and restrained, a strong quality about her, that one tends to think of as American. Her dance style is seemingly, but only seemingly, simple and extremely direct. Martha carries a certain theatrical atmosphere around with her always, and she communicates that to her dancers.

I found the Shaker song "Simple Gifts" in a collection of Shaker tunes published in 1940.[20] The song had previously been unknown to the general public. It is sometimes known as "The Gift to Be Simple" or by the first line of text, " 'Tis the Gift to Be Simple." I no longer recall who led me to this songbook, but I felt that "Simple Gifts," which expressed the unity of the Shaker spirit, was ideal for Martha's scenario and for the kind of austere movements associated with her choreography.[21] "Simple Gifts" was originally meant to be used for dancing. I read that the dance would have been in "a lively tempo, with single files of brethren and sisters two or three abreast proceeding with utmost precision around the meeting room. In the center of the room would be a small group singing the dance song over and over until everyone was both exhilarated and exhausted." Lest this seem very scholarly, my research evidently was not very thorough, since I did not realize that there never have been Shaker settlements in rural Pennsylvania![22]

For practical reasons, Harold Spivacke was urging me to stay close to the instrumentation Chávez was using for his commissioned ballet: string quartet, four woodwinds, and double bass. My original plan called for double string quartet and piano, but I decided to add a double bass and three woodwinds. I wrote to Spivacke, "That adds up to thirteen men, which is one more than your original letter called for."

I had only about one-third of the music written by midsummer for what was to be an October premiere, and Chávez' situation was even worse than mine. By the end of August, after many frantic letters, telephone calls, and telegrams between all concerned, there was no choice but to postpone the program for a full year, until the fall of 1944. I went to see Martha and played her what I had written so far, and she was enthusiastic. Chávez continued to delay during the winter months: When he finally sent some music to Martha, it was

[20] The book of Shaker songs was compiled by Edward Deming Andrews. Elder Joseph Brackett, Jr., composed "Simple Gifts" in 1848 for dancing during Shaker worship. See Edward Deming Andrews, *The Gift to Be Simple: Songs, Dances and Rituals of the American Shakers* (New York: J. J. Augustin, 1940; New York: Dover Publications, 1962).

[21] In the script Graham sent to Copland (and in Mrs. Coolidge's script at the Library), she described a segment of the leading dancer's role, then called "The Daughter": "She begins to dance in some simple way something like a song, any kind of song."

[22] See Roger L. Hall, *The Story of "Simple Gifts"* (Holland, Michigan: The World of Shaker, 1987).

so far from what she had expected that she wrote to Spivacke in concern over how to proceed.[23] Victor Kraft, who had stayed in Mexico, had seen Chávez and wrote: "It would be a great loss to Martha and Spivacke to lose his score. Chávez feels good music can't be done the way shoes are made to order." But Spivacke thought he had no choice but to suspend the commission. It was then given to Paul Hindemith.

Martha and I continued to correspond about various aspects of the ballet (she was either on tour or teaching at Bennington College). By the beginning of 1944, I wrote, "It is quite safe to go ahead; set the date, and I will send completed piano sketch. The orchestration is a mere detail. With me it always comes last." I completed the piano score in the spring of 1944 while teaching at Harvard, and the orchestration during a very hot July in my New York loft and at Helen and Elliott Carter's Fire Island dining-room table. I asked a young pianist friend, Leo Smit, to help me make some piano records so Martha would know my tempi. I played through the score on a rather doubtful-looking (and sounding) instrument at the Nola Studios. It cost twenty-six dollars for two sets of records: one for Martha and one for the Library of Congress.[24] When I left for Mexico, I asked Leo to make sure the recordings were sent out.

I have often thought about what a wild chance a choreographer takes by agreeing to work with music not heard in advance. Martha once described it to me as "that dreadful moment when you hear the music for the first time." So I waited anxiously while at Tepoztlán to hear her reactions and I was immensely relieved when she wrote (5 August):

> The music is so knit and of a completeness that it takes you in very strong hands and leads you into its own world. . . . I also know that the gift to be simple will stay with people and give them great joy. I hope I can do well with it, Aaron. I hope you will be here before the performance so that we can check with you. I do not have any idea as yet so we must get together on that.

My plan was to fly to Washington directly from Mexico, arriving 26 October. I wrote to Spivacke (26 September 1944), "My budget will stand $4 or $5 a day for a room—but the main thing is to put me where 'everybody' will be. Half the fun of going to festivals is bumping into people in your hotel lobby." I stayed at the Hotel Raleigh for $4.50 per night. I no longer recall whether I met anyone in the lobby. What I do remember is the pleasure of seeing my music actually danced to—I had seen nothing at all before the dress rehearsal! To my initial surprise, some music composed for one kind of action had been used to accompany something else. For example, music originally conceived for children at play was used for the Revivalist's dance. But that kind of decision is the choreographer's, and it doesn't bother me a bit, especially when it works.

The first thing I said to Martha when I saw her in Washington was, "What have you called the ballet?" She replied, "*Appalachian Spring*." "What a pretty title. Where did you

[23] The *Daughter of Colchis* script finally settled with Samuel Barber. It became one of Graham's most successful ballets, *Cave of the Heart*.

[24] The recordings are at the Recorded Sound Reference Center, the Library of Congress. (A tape duplicate available to the public is missing the ending.)

get it?" I asked, and Martha said, "Well, actually it's from a line in a poem by Hart Crane." I asked, "Does the poem itself have anything to do with your ballet?" "No," said Martha, "I just liked the title and used it."[25] My title had always been *Ballet for Martha*, and it became the subtitle of *Appalachian Spring*. The music had always been connected in my mind with Martha's extraordinary stature as an artist and as a human being, and with the American quality of her personality.

Martha Graham[26]

The first time I met Aaron Copland was at a concert in which I heard Aaron's Piano Variations. *After the performance when I was introduced to Aaron, I asked might I choreograph to it. He threw his head back and laughed that wonderful laugh of his and said, "Very well, but I don't know what on earth you'll be able to do with it." Years later when I commissioned a work from Aaron, I drove him to near desperation: I could not decide on a title and the day of the first rehearsal I noticed he had written on the title page, "Ballet for Martha." Finally I shared with Aaron the title,* Appalachian Spring, *and he laughed and sighed, "At last!"* Appalachian Spring *has been one of the pleasures of my life—a kind of keystone and I treasure every note of it and the experience I had to be able to choreograph to it.*

I have been amused that people so often have come up to me to say, "When I listen to that ballet of yours, I can just feel spring and see the Appalachians." But when I wrote the music, I had no idea what Martha was going to call it! Even after people learn that I didn't know the ballet title when I wrote the music, they still tell me they see the Appalachians and feel spring. Well, I'm willing, if they are! The only problem I have ever had with the title is the pronunciation. After always saying Appalachian with the third syllable accented, I was told, when traveling in West Virginia in 1972, that it's supposed to be pronounced with a flat a. So, I'd been pronouncing it wrong all those years!

At the time of the Washington premiere, no one thought of me as a conductor, least of all myself! Louis Horst, Martha's music director, conducted, and I sat in the audience close to Mrs. Coolidge. Nothing quite matches the excitement of a first performance for a composer. The audience reaction to *Appalachian Spring* was terrific and so was mine. Martha was extraordinary. I have seen (and conducted) performances with other fine dancers in the leading roles, but I just don't think of *Appalachian Spring* without Martha as the Bride and Erick Hawkins as the Husband.

[25] The early scripts approximated a dramatization of "The Dance," a poem by Hart Crane. For further explanation, see Interlude VI.

[26] Martha Graham sent the material quoted here to Perlis 22 November 1988.

Erick Hawkins[27]

Something in my bones said if you are going to try to invent any new aspect of dance movement you have to have contemporaneous new expression in the music. Lincoln Kirstein was deeply committed to getting some American feeling into ballet. When he got Aaron to do the music for Billy the Kid, *I recognized its virtues right away (I was born in Colorado, and so the idea of using a cowboy as a subject seemed perfectly natural). I danced in Aaron's* Billy the Kid *in 1938 with Lincoln Kirstein's Ballet Caravan. Lincoln took Ballet Caravan to Bennington College School of the Dance, headed by Martha Graham. I was already an admirer of Graham's work. I knew that Balanchine was never going to get into the American swim and that I would never find my way with him, so I went to take Martha Graham's course at her Fifth Avenue studio. Her group was working on* American Document. *To my surprise, Martha put me into the dance, making changes in the choreography. Within one month, I became Martha Graham's partner and the group's first male dancer (the following year Merce Cunningham became the second). I was also one of the few ballet dancers ever to work with Martha.*

American Document *heralded a narrative dance style, one that led the group in a new direction. After appearing with Martha and Merce in* El Penitente *and* Every Soul Is a Circus, *I did less and less with Ballet Caravan. I loved what Martha was doing. She had become convinced that it was important to relate more directly to her audiences. For the next twelve years, I worked as Martha's principal dancer, and also as teacher, manager, publicist, and fundraiser.*

I approached people for money for the Martha Graham Company, not because I liked doing so but because without it, the Company could not afford sets and costumes. I felt that Martha's art deserved better scores than her musical director Louis Horst could regularly supply, and ones that used instruments other than two pianos. When I heard that Elizabeth Sprague Coolidge had a foundation at the Library of Congress, I wrote and encouraged her to see Martha dance, and then asked her to commission composers for new works, Copland among them.[28] *Once Mrs. Coolidge decided to do the Copland-Hindemith-Chávez dances at the Library on her music series, she agreed to give Isamu [Noguchi] five thousand dollars to do a whole new proscenium for the stage and for the designs. I was responsible for all the financial reports right down to the fifty dollars for the rocking chair!*

I feel responsible for Isamu's work with Martha on Appalachian Spring. *Having such a great artist as Noguchi was a real breakthrough and satisfied three terribly important elements of the dance—the movement, the music, and the scenery. Dancing in Noguchi sets, you felt you were in a world that the great sculptor had created, a whole new world, one that was not on a stage.*

There's no question that one reason Appalachian Spring *took hold was the charm of Aaron's music. It has a simplicity of texture; there are no highly contrapuntal sections to divert the listener from the dance. In Martha's earliest works, she chose either a completed musical score or had a new work in hand before*

[27] Interview, Erick Hawkins with Perlis, 19 December 1985, New York City.

[28] Martha Graham's fee for the choreography was covered by a Guggenheim Fellowship. Costs for the costumes were $425 and for curtains, $150. See Hawkins correspondence, the Library of Congress.

The original cast of *Appalachian Spring* (left to right): May O'Donnell, Martha Graham, the Followers, and Erick Hawkins

The entire original cast (left to right): Martha Graham, Erick Hawkins, May O'Donnell, Merce Cunningham, and the Four Followers

creating the dance. With Appalachian Spring, *she wrote the scenario and worked out some of the dance without the music, sending Aaron the timings for the sections and general ideas for each segment. But it all really came together after Aaron sent the music. Fortunately for all of us, it was wonderful.*

One day when Aaron was working on the score, I went up to see him at the Empire Hotel. He mentioned possibly using a second piano as well as the strings, woodwinds, and the single piano. I was appalled and said, "Aaron, you simply can't get two pianos in that pit!" And I remember when we danced the piece at the National Theatre in New York, you could barely get by the one piano. When we went on tour, we had a terrible time because we took with us the four strings, the woodwinds, and the pianist but had to pick up four additional strings on the road and rehearse them every afternoon. Sol Hurok lost money, and we lost money.

The original people in Appalachian Spring *were very special, and some of the movement in the dance was naturally ours. Martha, as a beautiful creator, could take things we would try out and suggest and make them into her own choreography. I did everything with Martha in those days—from renaming the group "The Martha Graham Company" to projecting a scheme for a nonprofit corporation to sponsors. I wrote to Koussevitzky and others for support of that idea. I believed in it. We all had such wonderful hope. It was a time when we all thought that American art was going to blossom and continue to blossom.*

The premiere of *Appalachian Spring* was the climax of a festival to honor Elizabeth Sprague Coolidge on her eightieth birthday. As it turned out, the delay that had caused everyone so much difficulty gave time for Mrs. Coolidge to recover from a serious illness. The evening of dance followed three days of The Tenth Festival of Chamber Music at the Library of Congress (30 October 1944). There in the front row of the Coolidge Auditorium was Mrs. Coolidge in her customary seat, an unusually interested spectator. The program opened with *Imagined Wing*, music by Milhaud[29] followed by *Mirror Before Me* (later called *Herodiade*), music by Hindemith; and after intermission, the small stage was transformed with a set by Isamu Noguchi for *Appalachian Spring.*[30] The farmyard was suggested by a simple fence rail and the house by a peaked entrance and one wall. The Revivalist's pulpit was a stump and his acolytes sat on a bare bench. The rocking chair for the Pioneer Woman was only a suggestion of a chair. Even when the script was in its early stages, Martha had envisioned "a new town, someplace where the first fence has just gone up . . . the framework of a doorway, the platform of a porch, a Shaker rocking chair with its exquisite bonelike simplicity, and a small fence that should signify what a fence means in a new country."

The program was repeated the following evening and recorded.[31] In addition to Martha and Erick Hawkins, the original cast of *Appalachian Spring* included Merce Cunningham, who describes how the role of the Preacher came into being:

[29] For the third ballet, Graham used Milhaud's *Jeux de Printemps*. Reports from the dancers confirm that *Imagined Wing* was put together at the last minute and was not successful.

[30] See interview, Isamu Noguchi with Tobi Tobias, Dance Collection, The New York Public Library at Lincoln Center, January-February 1979. Noguchi had previously designed sets for Graham in a similar style for *American Frontier*.

Graham said, as I remember it, "I don't know whether you are a preacher, a farmer or the devil" (I think there were four categories and don't remember the last). She shortly said, "Why don't you work on it?" She left the room and I began to try out movements with the pianist obligingly playing short sequences over and over. I worked that afternoon and part of the next, and later on the second afternoon asked Graham to come and see what I had made. "I don't know if this is what you want," I said. I did the dance, and afterward Graham said, "Oh, it's fine. Now I know what to do with the rest of the piece."[32]

May O'Donnell took the part of the Pioneer Woman; and Nina Fonaroff, Marjorie Mazia, Yuriko [Kikuchi], and Pearl Lang were the Followers. Yuriko, at a rehearsal of a performance I conducted, said (June 1982): "This was my first artistic role. I had not heard of the Shakers, and Martha told me who they were and described the austerity of their lives." Pearl Lang and May O'Donnell also described their experiences with *Appalachian Spring* in interviews.

Pearl Lang[33]

I first danced in Appalachian Spring *as one of the four Followers. The dancers were not involved in the early stages of a work—that was Martha's time with the composer and with Louis Horst. In the process of choreographing a work like* Appalachian Spring, *Martha would say things that would enhance the imagination of the dancer and that were important to hear—not only what she said but how she said it—not only what is danced but how it's danced at the time of the creation of the work. In the midst of rehearsals, Martha would say, "You know there was an innocent kind of religion there, and they had a kind of ecstatic wildness—that Shaker bursting out to the point where something issues out of the body, and it's a movement." I remember in one section, Martha saying, "Do it as though you're shouting 'I've got Jesus by the foot!'"—it had to have that kind of ecstatic religious commitment. Aaron's music fired us to do so much more than we had ever anticipated. That's the great thing about Aaron's music for dance—it drives the choreographer. It drives the dancer.*

I was dancing in Agnes de Mille's Carousel *during rehearsals for* Appalachian Spring. *(De Mille had borrowed me from Martha, and that enabled me to pay rent and eat. Before that, Merce Cunningham and I were working at Schrafft's—he was behind the soda fountain and I was carrying trays.) I would get on a sleeper after the evening performance of* Carousel *in New York and at 9 A.M. be on the floor at the Library of Congress in Washington for rehearsal until four. Then I would catch The Senator back to New York and do a performance. And this went on for two solid weeks!*

It was extremely painful for Martha to turn over roles she had created for herself to someone else. The first role of hers I danced was El Penitente*: and then I learned the Bride in* Appalachian Spring. *I*

[31] The recording of the second Washington performance is at the Recorded Sound Reference Center, the Library of Congress.

[32] Cunningham sent this description to Perlis, 9 April 1989.

[33] Interview, Pearl Lang with Perlis, 19 December 1985, New York City.

Martha Graham and Erick Hawkins in the premiere performance of *Appalachian Spring*, 30 October 1944

danced the role on and off for several years. (In 1955 I left the company officially but have come back every other year as a guest soloist.) How does one perform a very famous role after a famous dancer has done it? As one of the Followers, I had been onstage all through the work, and I had been able to see exactly what Martha did every night. I was there when she was creating the work, so I knew the style of the piece—where the energies were, and the punctuations. When Appalachian Spring *is done now, it is different. The difficulty is that people who are dancing it have never seen Martha do it, and films just about tell you which foot you start on, and where you are on the stage and not always that, because the element of space, the third dimension, and the attacks are distorted.*

One evening when Aaron was conducting in 1975, I found myself onstage with Rudolf Nureyev—I didn't even know he was going to dance the Preacher! Appalachian Spring *is choreographed almost like an opera—the soloists all have arias. The Husband and the Bride, of course, have to dance a great deal together; the Followers and the Preacher have to dance together, but the Bride has nothing to do with the Preacher (except there's a little Sunday walk where we shake hands, but you don't need to rehearse to do that). Between Nureyev and Cunningham there's a world of difference. The Preacher is an enchanting role and most male dancers want to do it. I think Nureyev heard the rhythm as very Russian. Neither in the choreography or in the manner of dancing is it Russian—it was only Russian when Nureyev did it. When Merce did it, or Bertram Ross, or Mark Ryder, who was the second dancer in the Preacher role, it was very American in style. It has humor, and Nureyev, always cast as a tragic figure in Martha's other pieces, wanted to do this as a lark—and it is a lark, but it's very difficult technically.*

Appalachian Spring *is a joyous piece and that's unusual for Martha's repertory. Without* a tragic *moment in it—there is only the hint of one—the allegro toward the end of the Bride's solo where she rolls down the stairs, there is an anticipation of a storm, of something dissonant in her life. The Preacher's part had much more darkness in it originally the way Merce did it—a lot of the movement—the arm stretched down from on high directly following the square dance. I always thought it meant you would roast in hell if you continued to dance!*

I don't think there is another dance that has sustained year after year after year as Appalachian Spring *has. It's a classic—a national treasure. I was there from the very beginning, so it is half a lifetime that I have lived with this work, and I am still always moved by it. Aaron's music seems to peel away all extraneous sounds that might interfere with the spine of the thing— which Noguchi did with the sets and Martha with the choreography. But then to keep the spine glistening takes a tremendous amount of work.*

I was born in Illinois outside of Chicago and the feeling of space there was and still is a very important thing to me. Since coming to New York, I had never gotten over not being able to see the horizon—the inner person can't move out. The idea of space is like fuel to a dancer. Aaron has given sound to this space. There's a reason why Russian dancers and American dancers are the best in the world—because we have the concept of space in the land. American dancers trained in the west know space differently, jump higher, than dancers who are trained in urban areas. Not too many dancers who were trained in New York City become soloists. Isadora Duncan was a westerner; Martha grew up on the West Coast, as did Merce and May [O'Donnell]. Erick and I are midwesterners.

It may seem to people who are not dancers that it's easier to dance to the rhythmic sections in Appalachian Spring, *but perhaps the more creative movement comes in the sustained and quiet sections. The movement then takes on its own focus. You are not dancing concomitantly to a beat. This is particularly true in* Appalachian Spring.

At the time of Aaron's seventy-fifth birthday, I was privileged to be invited to choreograph one of his works for a concert at Alice Tully Hall,[34] *and when he had his eightieth, one of the celebrations was a "Wall-to-Wall Copland" day at Symphony Space. I read a letter to him from the stage. Here's a part of it that I did not get to say:*

> *I am very grateful for the opportunity to at last say something to Aaron Copland, because dancers are usually seen and not heard. What are dancers' tools? Essentially, a usually obstinate and resistant body, a restless soul, and time, of which there is never enough, energy less than enough, and space that is so increasingly being annihilated and for which the dancer has an insatiable need. Aaron seems to supply what dancers don't have. We thank Aaron for the wide use of time that his music provides, for the energy his music ignites in us, and for the limitless space that we hear in his sound. With Aaron's music, one leaps not across the stage, but across the land. And above all, we thank him for the wonder of that defiant innocence and affirmation that sings in his music about America.*

[34] See discussion of Copland's seventy-fifth birthday celebrations.

May O'Donnell[35]

I was a good strong American western girl studying dance in Los Angeles, and someone watching the class said, "You should go to New York City and work with a person called Martha Graham." So I came to New York, looked in the telephone book and found Martha's name and the address on Ninth Street. Martha taught where she lived—it was the Depression and nobody had any money. She took me in her class in the spring of 1932.

My first adventure in dance with Martha was Primitive Mysteries, *which is one of the most difficult dances imaginable. I survived that and I stayed with Martha until 1938. When Erick first came into the group and he and Martha got together, I had been with Martha six years and wanted to try some things of my own. I loved Martha and worked well with her, but she was beginning to get some younger dancers in, and it was a practical time for me to leave. After five years in San Francisco, the war came along, and all activity stopped, so I came back to New York. One day when I was getting settled, the phone rang, and it was Erick asking me to come back to dance with the Graham Company. I agreed, but as a guest artist, because I had started to develop my own dance vocabulary and needed to continue with my own work. I stayed as guest artist from 1944 to 1950. I had a sense of what Martha's style was and she seemed to need me as a foil—being larger and taller and as a sustaining power against her exuberance.*

At the studio, there was tension growing between Erick and Merce, and Martha was getting more involved with Erick—she was very much in love with him—and he used that sometimes to obtain the authority to run things. I didn't like getting into their personal situations, but I liked the work. The next thing I knew I was at Bennington. Martha had started Appalachian Spring *during the winter, so the rest of the cast knew their parts before I did. The stylization was already set when I went into it. My part, the Pioneer Woman, was like an integral thread that held the whole thing together in a delicate way. I was the prevailing spirit, and it was a right part for me. I could work with Martha and try different things, asking her if it worked. I tried to do my part like an early American primitive—an archaic quality actually. Martha could trust me to feel the style of it.*

Appalachian Spring *opens with a sense of horizon. We each take our places almost like characters in a play. My first movement was to sit. I could just take time to sit quietly, but I could never turn to see where that seat was! I didn't have a solo, but I might run through the others, blessing each of the girls, or stand behind Martha, or look out over the bright future as though watching the generations, or send Erick on his way with a kind of maternal gesture—always that kind of benign, hopeful, devotional thing. The transitions would be filled out with me reminding everybody that there was hope, there was a new land, fresh possibilities. It was a free part in a peculiar kind of a way. Martha never said, "May, make your arm go this way or that." She would instill me with that kind of brightness and devotion that comes out of a land you love and out of a culture you love—Martha never talked quite like that, but if you felt it and you did it, and it was convincing, she would love it too, and then she didn't mind what you did. She worked in a more definite way with the rest of the group, because they were a stylized whole and had to have a precision and a concentrated kind of control.*

[35] Interview, May O'Donnell with Perlis, 19 December 1985, New York City.

Martha didn't talk to me about the music. She never, as far as I know, worked with her dancers and composers together. And I never saw Aaron during the time we were working things out. It was one of the most successful of collaborations between Aaron and Martha, and a turning point for Martha, coming between her symbolic works and her Greek pieces. It was the peak of Erick and Martha's feelings for each other, and while Merce was still with the group. Appalachian Spring *has a gentleness and sweetness about it that you don't expect from Martha. It was not easy for Martha to be that simple. It was a one-of-a-kind dance for her. The audience was so surprised to see Martha doing that kind of a piece, and they loved it.* Appalachian Spring *is a dance people can relate to—most people cannot imagine being Clytemnestra, but everyone can imagine being a bride!*

Appalachian Spring came in for the highest praise from reviewers. The dance critic of *The New York Times* concluded (5 November 1944), "It is, as the saying goes, a natural." I was quite amazed when my music won so many awards and became so popular. I must admit I'm influenced by public opinion! When you are working on a piece, you don't think it might have use past the immediate purpose for its composition, and you certainly don't consider its lasting power: You are so relieved just to have it finished for the premiere! Of course, I was delighted to receive a Pulitzer Prize for *Appalachian Spring*. It was announced on the front page of *The New York Times* (8 May 1945), under the big news: THE WAR IN

"All the News That's Fit to Print"

The New York Times.

LATE CITY EDITION

NEW YORK, TUESDAY, MAY 8, 1945. THREE CENTS

THE WAR IN EUROPE IS ENDED! SURRENDER IS UNCONDITIONAL; V-E WILL BE PROCLAIMED TODAY; OUR TROOPS ON OKINAWA GAIN

...ND-WIDE DRIVE

...ines Reach Village a... e From Naha and ...my Lines Advance

...IORE SHIPS SUNK

...ch Planes Again Hit ...pan's Life Line— ...yushu Bombed

Pulitzer Awards For 1944 Revealed

The Pulitzer Prize awards announced yesterday by the trustees of Columbia University included: For a distinguished novel, to "A Bell for Adano," by John Hersey; for an original American play of the current season, to "Harvey," by Mary Chase.

Among the newspaper awards were those to Hal Boyle, Associated Press war reporter, for distinguished correspondence; to James B. Reston of The New York Times for his reporting of the Dumbarton Oaks Security Conference; to Joe Rosenthal, Associated Press photographer, for his photograph of marines raising the American flag at Iwo and to The Detroit Free Press for "distinguished and meritorious public service" in its investigation of legislative corruption at Lansing, Mich.

Aaron Copland received the prize in music for his ballet "Appalachian Spring." The award for biography went to Russel Blaine Nye for his "George Bancroft: Brahmin Rebel."

Further details of the awards will be found on Page 18.

GERMANY SURRENDERS: NEW YORKERS MASSED UNDER SYMBOL OF LIBERTY

GERMANS CAPITULATE ON ALL FRONTS

American, Russian and French Generals Accept Surrender in Eisenhower Headquarters, a Reims School

REICH CHIEF OF STAFF ASKS FOR MERCY

Doenitz Orders All Military Forces of Germany To Drop Arms—Troops in Norway Give Up —Churchill and Truman on Radio Today

By EDWARD KENNEDY
Associated Press Correspondent

REIMS, France, May 7—Germany surrendered unconditionally to the Western Allies and the Soviet Union at 2:41 A. M. French time today. (This was at 8:41 P. M., Eastern Wartime Sunday.)

Announcement of the 1944 Pulitzer Prize winners on the front page of *The New York Times* the day the war ended (Copland's name appeared on page16)

EUROPE IS ENDED! A happy day all around. Louis Biancolli from the *New York World-Telegram* viewed the prize as a sign that American ballet had come of age. He wrote: "... the Brooklyn boy who made top concert billing is one of America's most versatile writers. The man's mark is as much on the dance as on the symphony, not to mention the screen.... Ballet is giving rise to a whole new school of serious American music."

Martha took *Appalachian Spring* on a tour sponsored by Sol Hurok during the winter months. It included Boston, Cincinnati, and Cleveland, before the New York premiere (14 May 1945)[36] The National Theatre run was for seven performances. Martha wrote to me (1 May 1945):

> It is a beautiful piece, Aaron. I have reworked it, particularly the points you spoke about, the variations, principally the last one of Erick's, the solo, certain points of my solo and May O'Donnell's.... I've also worked on the costumes. It's been a joy to do so.

Edwin Denby, dance critic of the *New York Herald Tribune*, wrote (15 May 1945):

> *Appalachian Spring* has a mysterious coolness and freshness, and it is no glorification by condescending cityfolk of our rude and simple past; it is, despite occasional awkwardness, a credible and astonishing evocation of that real time and place. To show us our country ancestors and our inherited mores as real is a feat of genius no one else who has touched the pioneer subject in ballet has been able to accomplish. The company, and quite particularly Mr. Cunningham in a thrilling passage, were excellent.... Mr. Copland's score is a marvel of lyricism, of freshness and strength; and with thirteen instruments he seemed to have a full orchestra playing.

A few weeks after the Pulitzer was announced, The Music Critics Circle of New York voted its annual awards: to Walter Piston's *Symphony No. 2* for symphonic music, and to *Appalachian Spring* in the category of dramatic composition. Winning an award from the music critics was the biggest surprise of all—after having been lambasted by those gentlemen so frequently through the years! Virgil wrote in the *Tribune* (2 June 1945):

> Aaron Copland's *Appalachian Spring* received the award for dramatic music with only two dissenting votes. One of these went to Jerome Moross' ballet, *Frankie and Johnnie*, the other to Arnold Schoenberg's *Ode to Napoleon*. Personally I have no quarrel with the outcome. I voted for the Copland piece myself because, though the *Ode to Napoleon* contains musical writing of far higher methodological sophistication, I consider Copland's ballet to have a greater degree of specific expressivity.

Appalachian Spring was hailed as a breakthrough for Martha, who had been recognized as one of the most gifted of modern dancers and choreographers, but with appeal only to those "in the know," and who, until this ballet, had not had a popular success. Its enormous popularity was partially due to the lyric and joyous quality of the dance. *Appalachian Spring* was Martha's last work about America and the American spirit, and it came at a time when she was at the height of her artistic powers. We composers respected not only her achievements as a dancer and choreographer but the fact that since 1934 she had used nothing but original music, most of it American. As Virgil pointed out, Martha had reached a place musically toward which she had been heading for some time:

> Miss Graham has given us in the past music by reputable living composers ... but none of this has ever been strong or memorable.... The Copland and Hindemith scores are another line of musical country, I assure you, higher and more commanding and incredibly more adequate both to the support of a choreographic line and to the evocation of their stated subjects. .. Miss Graham's work has long leaned toward the introspective and the psychologically lurid. Copland, in *Appalachian Spring*, has, by the inflexibility of his pastoral landscape mood, kept her away from the violence of solitary meditation and drawn her toward awareness of persons and the sweetness of manners ... she turns out to be, as one has long suspected, not only an expressive dancer but a great actress, one of the very great among living actresses, in fact.[37]

Appalachian Spring had a great deal to do with bringing my name before a larger public, particularly after the Pulitzer Prize. However, it was Martha's admiration for the music that held the most meaning for me. She wrote (14 September 1945): "You are quite the sensation of the music world and other worlds, too. I am happy over your acclaim. It is certainly your year, Aaron. If I could sing, I would sing. With deep gratitude for working with me and letting me dance your piece."

When I told Martha I wanted to arrange an orchestral suite from the ballet score, she readily agreed. The *Appalachian Spring Suite* is a condensed version of the ballet, retaining all essential features but omitting those sections in which the interest is primarily choreographic (the largest cut was the Minister's dance). The *Suite* follows a sectional arrangement of eight sequences and is scored for an orchestra of modest proportions. I wrote to Harold Spivacke (May 1945): "I recently finished a version of the ballet for normal-sized orchestra (about twenty minutes long) and it will be premiered next October by Rodzinski and the Philharmonic. .. I think we can all congratulate ourselves on a happy ending."

In addition to the New York Philharmonic's premiere, the *Suite* was performed in the first Boston Symphony Orchestra concerts of the season conducted by Koussevitzky (6 October 1945). After Lenny conducted it in London in 1946, he wrote (23 June 1946), "... my one comfort these days is studying it. I manage somehow to borrow some of that fantastic stability of yours, that deep serenity. It is really amazing how the clouds lift with that last page." Lenny made his Italian debut conducting *Appalachian Spring* (16 May 1948) and wrote about the audience: "It was a wild success.... I love the one that wonders what a *Bolletto per Marta* is, and the one that says it reminds him of American movies." Even Virgil Thomson, who did not conduct very often, conducted *Appalachian Spring* in Barcelona in 1954. In June 1946, I had a letter from Mrs. Coolidge: "I am so pleased to read that the Tanglewood program of July 27th includes an orchestral version of 'our' ballet. I am glad to say that I expect to be present at this performance and it would give me a great deal of pleasure if you could use one of my tickets and sit with me during this program as you did during the original performance in Washington two years ago."

[36] In New York, *Appalachian Spring* was programmed with *Salem Shore*, music by Paul Nordhoff, and *Death and Entrances*, music by Hunter Johnson.

[37] Virgil Thomson, "Two Ballets," *New York Herald Tribune*, 20 May 1945, reprinted in *The Art of Judging Music* (New York Alfred A. Knopf, 1948), 161-64.

The first recording of *Appalachian Spring Suite* was made under Koussevitzky's direction for Victor in 1945. Evidently, I felt uneasy about cuts that had to be made to suit the demands for a broadcast in 1946 (less than for Victor's set of six 78 rpm records), for I wrote to Koussevitzky (26 February 1946), "I am a little nervous. Cutting is always a dangerous business;" and again (27 October), "The cuts are made. . .the big cut is slightly different than the one we discussed." In 1954, Eugene Ormandy invited Martha Graham and the dance company to perform the ballet in Philadelphia, accompanied by the Philadelphia Symphony Orchestra, for which I orchestrated the sections previously excluded from the *Suite*. Ormandy promised to record the complete ballet for Columbia, and I felt something had to be done to make the seventh recorded version of *Appalachian Spring* different from the others. I knew that the Philadelphia's legendary strings would not hurt such a recording! Another top conductor who performed *Appalachian Spring* was Pierre Monteux with the San Francisco Symphony, but he made an unauthorized cut and did what seemed to me an uneven interpretation.[38]

For some time in the late sixties, my friend Lawrence Morton in Los Angeles had been urging me to prepare a concert version using the original scoring. I thought that once the listening public had become used to the large version, the thirteen-instrument one would sound "skinny," so I was hesitant about making it available. Lawrence said, "You are wrong, you are wrong! The thirteen-instrument version has a different atmosphere, it's more personal, it's more modest, more tender, closer to what the ballet was originally about." And he added, "You come out to California and conduct it and you will see for yourself if I am right or not." So I went and conducted it at a concert in honor of my seventieth birthday at the Los Angeles County Museum of Art, and as everybody seemed very enthusiastic,[39]

[38] For correspondence about the Monteux recording, see the Copland collection in the Library of Congress.

[39] The first performance of the thirteen-instrument version was at the Leo S. BingTheater (14 November 1970); first European performance was at Queen Elizabeth Hall, London, with the English Chamber Orchestra, Lawrence Foster conducting (13 October 1971).

I decided to publish it and am very glad I did. Often people (particularly the English) tell me they like the thirteen-instrument version better than the full orchestra because it seems more intimate and more touching. I, myself, am glad to have both arrangements available. In time, I have come to think that the original instrumentation has a clarity and is closer to my original conception than the more opulent orchestrated version. *Appalachian Spring* in the original orchestration is recorded by Dennis Russell Davies and the St. Paul Chamber Orchestra.

I have conducted several recordings of *Appalachian Spring* myself: with the BSO for R.C.A., about the time of my sixtieth birthday; with the London Symphony Orchestra for Columbia Records; and with the St. Paul Chamber Orchestra for Columbia's "Meet the Composer" series (the thirteen-instrument version for which I reinstated the episode that had originally preceded the final variations of "Simple Gifts"; it added a variety necessary when omitting the full orchestra dynamics).[40] I have conducted all of my own compositions as well as works by other composers, but *Appalachian Spring* is the one I know best from a conducting point of view. I have often admonished orchestras, professional and otherwise, not to get too sweet or too sentimental with it, and I have reminded performers that *Appalachian Spring* should be played cooler than Tchaikovsky and lighter and happier than Stravinsky's *Sacre du Printemps*. My own favorite place in the whole piece is toward the end, where I have marked "misterioso." I would tell string players that we don't want to know where the up and down bows are.[41] They must have a special sustained quality there—kind of organlike in sound, with each entry like an Amen.

[40] The 1974 Columbia Records release of *Appalachian Spring Suite*, original thirteen-instrument version, conducted by Copland, includes a rehearsal recording. A tape of this document, an early demonstration of Copland's conducting language and style, is at the Recorded Sound Reference Center, in the Library of Congress.

[41] Copland's comments here are taken from the 1974 rehearsal recording, see note 39.

INTERLUDE VI

Forty-one years after the historic premiere of *Appalachian Spring*, Martha Graham and Aaron Copland attended a performance of their ballet together: Graham was ninety-one, Copland eighty-four. It was 21 April 1985. Composer and choreographer sat quietly in the wings at the New York City Center as dancers from the Martha Graham Dance Company in various costumes milled about, stretching or rehearsing a few steps. Occasionally, dancers leaped on or offstage on either side of the elderly pair. Graham and Copland hardly spoke, yet each seemed intensely aware of the other's presence. As the familiar opening music of *Appalachian Spring* was heard and the dancers took their places one by one onstage, everyone backstage—dancers, guests, stagehands—felt the significance of the moment.[1]

Difficult as the birth of *Appalachian Spring* had been, it was blessed with success from the premiere on. Those connected with the original production went on to extraordinarily successful careers: Erick Hawkins, Merce Cunningham, May O'Donnell, and Pearl Lang as solo dancers and choreographers with their own companies; Isamu Noguchi as one of the most celebrated visual artists of the century; and Copland as a great American composer.[2] Some ballets take time to work into the repertory, others disappear soon after the first season, yet others are vehicles for one dancer only. *Appalachian Spring* is the rare example of a dance that has continued to speak to performers and audiences through the decades.

In 1944, with World War II at its grimmest and the world in turmoil, people yearned for the kind of pastoral landscape and innocent love that Martha Graham's most lyrical ballet offered. *Appalachian Spring* affirmed traditional American values that were being dramatically challenged by Nazism. Audiences knew immediately what the country was fighting for when they saw *Appalachian Spring*, even though it had no explicit patriotic theme. However, the real test of this ballet's success has been in its power to reaffirm established ideals through so many years of chaotic change and rapidly shifting mores. Even in today's turbulent, confused, and unloving age, *Appalachian Spring*'s sensitivity and integrity reach out to audiences. It has gone beyond the world of dance, where it is considered a classic, to become an American symbol: Mention Aaron Copland, Martha Graham, or Appalachian Spring anywhere in the world, and America comes immediately to mind.

Every work of art derives from a complex set of circumstances. In addition to the patriotic climate in the contemporary arts that was engendered by the war, the determinants for *Appalachian Spring* included Erick Hawkins' desire to promote Martha Graham and her company; Harold Spivacke's determination to expand performing arts at the Library of Congress; and the personal and professional lives of those involved at the time of the ballet's creation.

Appalachian Spring was the culmination of Martha Graham's "Americana" period, one which began with American Frontier and continued with American Document and Letter to the World. Graham's desire to create an American "look" in dance paralleled other activities in the arts in the thirties and forties: photographer Alfred Steiglitz and the

Martha Graham and Copland at the Kennedy Center Honors, December 1979

[1] The leading roles were danced by Yuriko Kimura, Bride; Tim Wengerd, Husband; Janet Eilber, Pioneering Woman; Larry White, Preacher. Stanley Sussman, conductor.

[2] The other two Followers, Marjorie Mazur and Nina Fonoroff, also have had long and successful careers; Jean Rosenthal became a leading theatrical lighting designer, and Edythe Gilfond, a highly acclaimed costume designer.

"affirm America" movement; Harold Clurman and the Group Theatre; Lincoln Kirstein and Ballet Caravan; and Copland's own patriotic works.[3] Sculptor Noguchi said, "Appalachian Spring was in a sense influenced by Shaker furniture, but it is also the culmination of Martha's interest in American themes and in the puritan American tradition."[4] American writers William Carlos Williams and Emily Dickinson were sources for Graham's creative ideas. One poet admired by both Graham and Copland was Hart Crane (Copland had known Crane in the twenties; when the poet died, Copland sketched a page in his notebook with the heading "Elegy for Hart Crane," 1932). It was Crane's American epic *The Bridge*[5] with its mixture of nationalism, pantheism, and symbolism that was the basis for the script Graham devised for the Coolidge commission. Graham was drawn to a section of *The Bridge* called "The Dance." There she found the line "O Appalachian Spring!" The stanza of Crane's poem ending with this line does not refer to springtime in the Appalachian Mountains, but to the uninhibited joyful leap of a mountain spring:

> I took the portage climb, then chose
> A further valley-shed; I could not stop.
> Feet nozzled watr'y webs of upper flows;
> One white veil gusted from the very top.
> O Appalachian Spring!

Martha Graham did not correct the impression that the title of her ballet *Appalachian Spring* refers to the Appalachians in springtime. Perhaps she interpreted Crane's "O Appalachian Spring!" as a general salute to springtime. In any case, in 1975 she gave this description to dance critic Anna Kisselgoff of The New York Times:

> It's spring. There is a house that has not been completed. The bare posts are up. The fence has not been completed. Only a marriage has been celebrated. It is essentially the coming of new life. It has to do with growing things. Spring is the loveliest and the saddest time of the year.

An evocative title can become inextricably connected with a work in the public mind, although it may mean far less to a composer or choreographer, who frequently decide on titles after works are created. Difficult as it is today to think of *Appalachian Spring* as anything but that, the piece had earlier working titles: Graham's *House of Victory* and *Eden Valley*; and Copland's *Ballet for Martha* (or *Martha's Ballet* as on the first rough sketches of the score).[6] He has often stated: "I was fully aware of her very special personality and it affected my writing of the piece. In my own mind it was a 'Ballet for Martha.' Very much so."

[3] For more about the "affirm America" movement, the Group Theatre, and other American influences, see Interlude III.
[4] Interview, Isamu Noguchi with Tobi Tobias.
[5] Hart Crane, *The Collected Poems of Hart Crane* (New York: Liveright, 1933). See 19-23 for "The Dance," a part of the long poem *The Bridge*. The stanza ending with "O Appalachian Spring" appears on p. 20.
[6] See Coolidge Collection, the Library of Congress, for manuscripts: bound ink score with dedication "To Elizabeth Sprague Coolidge" (Copland wrote simply "Ballet" on the first of 84 pages); first rough sketches and 84 miscellaneous pages showing various instrumentations, cues from Graham's scenario, such as "Fear of the Night" and "Day of Wrath," and dates "5 Ju 43, 20 Ju 43" (p. 47 shows the theme and 5 variations with the title "Shaker Melody: 'It's the gift to be simple'"). See also ink score for piano (copies in the Copland collection at the Library of Congress and at Boosey & Hawkes). The piano score differs considerably from the instrumental versions, particularly in the variations section.

While the influences on the creation of Appalachian Spring included Graham's interests in American roots and identity, the ballet's enduring qualities stem more from a kind of poetic universality than from specifics of a time and place. Although American in spirit, the ballet is first and foremost a love story, and audiences relate to it, as they tend to with a beautifully told love story. Martha Graham and Erick Hawkins' personal relationship was at its most passionate during the time *Appalachian Spring* was created; their love affair strongly affected the subject and form of the ballet. Martha Graham created the Bride for herself, and the role of the Husband for Hawkins. The energy of the dance is concentrated on these two, and the lovers' scenes hold a kind of stillness, a fragility, that separates them from the action going on around them. It was Graham's great genius to retain the intensity of the relationship while idealizing and abstracting the Bride and Husband just enough so that they reach beyond themselves to express the springtime of the nation as well as the springtime in their own lives.

It was Copland's good fortune to find himself with key people at important junctures in his career—Boulanger when he went to study abroad, Koussevitzky just as he returned to the States, and then Martha Graham. Perhaps it was partly luck (as Copland frequently claimed) that brought these two creative figures together to create one single gem of a dance, but what Copland modestly credits to happenstance had a great deal to do with his highly developed sense of selectivity. Copland recognized Graham's genius and knew he wanted to work with her (other dance commissions had been discreetly refused). Typical of Copland was his confidence once a decision was made: No matter how many convoluted letters and complex scripts Martha Graham sent (and there were many), Copland never doubted for a moment what she was doing or worried about changes and delays.

Aaron Copland's temperament was a perfect foil for Martha Graham and the ballet she created in 1944. Although warm, witty, and sociable, Copland was also detached, wry, and objective. Essentially a very private person, he did not make overt gestures, either in person or in his music. He did not intrude on others, nor does his music intrude or impose itself on the scene in collaborative works. The result for *Appalachian Spring* was music with a quiet glow, a Puritan restraint, and the tenderness of young love.

Copland seemed to intuit the vocabulary of dancers as he did filmmakers—not their words but their gestures. There is a similarity between the sequence of actions and their formalization in dance and film that match the cumulative effect of musical phrases in composition. Copland understood precisely what Graham meant when she told him that the written script would have little resemblance to the final product; he knew very well that a collaboration between dance and music was not tied to verbal language.

It is interesting to note how closely some of the dance movements in *Appalachian Spring* match the music. One example is when the four Followers mimic the staccato pattern of sixteenth notes in Copland's score. Graham has them do so unconventionally—by squatting on their toes—and she has them do so for dramatic reasons—to project the idea that they are, in fact, Followers, not free agents. A choreographic analysis of Appalachian Spring shows similar instances where Graham chose specific steps and phrases that connect closely to the rhythmic elements in Copland's score,[7] and other segments where the dance has a great deal of freedom from the music. The choices for Graham had to do with a combination of visual image and dramatic integrity.

One of Copland's great accomplishments is that much of his music, so perfectly matched to dance and film, can exist independent of its original purpose. After all, Appalachian Spring is known best as a symphonic suite. Because Copland's work, no matter how specific the purpose, was stimulated by musical ideas, it would be possible for his Appalachian Spring music to be used for one scenario or another, or to stand on its own as a purely musical composition. The "illusion of space," described by dancers such as Pearl Lang, was accomplished in specific musical ways: wide-open intervals and octaves; light instrumentation (primarily winds and strings) to achieve the "transparent" texture; and a minimizing of intricate chromaticism, difficult polyrhythms, and complicated polymeters.

Graham and Copland were not to collaborate again after *Appalachian Spring*. The choreographer went on to work with other outstanding American composers, among them Samuel Barber and William Schuman, with whom she had more direct contact than she had had with Copland (he had been in either California or Mexico while Graham was choreographing *Appalachian Spring*). When in 1974 Martha Graham asked Copland to provide a score for a ballet based on Hawthorne's *The Scarlet Letter*, Copland had virtually stopped composing, and he had no choice but to refuse. The score for *The Scarlet Letter* was composed by Hunter Johnson, and the dance was premiered in 1975 during the fiftieth anniversary of the Martha Graham Dance Company, a year that also marked Graham's sixtieth anniversary as a performer, the beginning of the Bicentennial celebrations, and Copland's seventy-fifth birthday.

Martha Graham and Copland at the New York City Center, 1965

[7] See Marta Robertson, "Aaron Copland's *Appalachian Spring*: Music and Dance Interactions," presentation at the Sonneck Society Annual Meeting (14 April 1988).

If Copland could not compose a new piece for that landmark season, he could accept Martha Graham's invitation to conduct *Appalachian Spring* for the Company's "Gala," which featured works on American themes (16 December 1975). Although Copland's conducting career had become very active, this was the first time he conducted the ballet version of *Appalachian Spring*; in fact, it was his first conducting of any dance since Ruth Page's *Hear Ye! Hear Ye!* of 1934. Copland shared the 1975 program with Stanley Sussman, a "regular" Graham conductor.[8] Copland told Anna Kisselgoff of *The New York Times*, when asked how he felt about conducting his own Pulitzer Prize score— "Nervous!" The great Russian star Rudolf Nureyev had requested the Preacher role in *Appalachian Spring*. On the afternoon of the performance, Copland arrived for rehearsal at the Mark Hellinger Theater. All went smoothly until the moment arrived for the Preacher's dance. Nureyev had taken his position on a small platform at the rear of the stage. At the appropriate time in the score, Copland launched into the music and Nureyev came forward, but instead of beginning the dance as expected, he stopped the performance and continued walking forward, not halting until he was directly in front of the conductor. Copland looked up in surprise—he had no idea what would come next. "Maestro," said the great Russian dancer, "may I ask for four beats in order to position myself before I begin the dance?" Copland, visibly relieved, said, "Why, of course," and he wrote the cue in his score so that Nureyev would have time to come center stage and position himself—Russian ballet style.[9]

In the spring of 1982, Copland conducted *Appalachian Spring* for the Graham Company for the last time. When he arrived at the New York City Center for dress rehearsal, he was greeted by Pearl Lang, ballet mistress for the season's performances of *Appalachian Spring*. As conductor Stanley Sussman turned the podium over to Copland, the orchestra members welcomed the composer warmly, and the dancers stood poised to begin. Copland opened his score and picked up his baton. Soon it was clear something was amiss: Copland had conducted the Suite so often that some of his tempi were too slow for the dancers. Copland conferred with Sussman, who advised that certain tempi, such as in the duet, go faster, and similarly, in the theme and variations.[10] Another difficulty was that the placement of instruments in the ballet orchestra is different from the concert orchestra, with basses and cellos separated instead of on the same side. But there was a more serious problem: Some of Copland's conducting score did not match the orchestra parts or the action onstage.

After rehearsal, Copland stepped down to confer with Sussman. Sussman said to Copland, "I hope you don't mind my telling Aaron Copland how to conduct certain tempi in Appalachian Spring!" And Copland replied kindly, "I have been conducting it a certain way for twenty-five years, and I'm sure I can make some changes for this performance."

[8] The program opened with *Fanfare for the Common Man*, conducted by Copland, followed by a Martha Graham talk and dances: *Diversion of Angels*, music by Norman Dello Joio; *Letter to the World*, music by Hunter Johnson; and *Appalachian Spring*.

[9] Anecdote recounted to Perlis by David Walker, who was at the rehearsal. Also in the cast were Yuriko Kimura, Bride; Ross Parkes, Husband, and Janet Eilber, Pioneering Woman.

[10] Stanley Sussman met Copland during the summer of 1959 when he was a student in Leon Kirchner's composition class at Tanglewood. In addition to an active conducting career (principally for the dance), Sussman continued to compose.

If the ballet conveys the impression of simplicity, it is deceiving. The work is not easy for the dancers or the musicians. Several versions exist, each with a different score.[11] At the 1982 rehearsal, only Sussman's score matched the current Graham Company production,[12] and it contained eighteen years of markings reflecting cast changes and other variables. Conducting scores in general can become highly personalized; Sussman's for *Appalachian Spring*, with its overlaying of cues, tempo markings, and assorted directions, would have been difficult for Copland to use at any time, no less the afternoon of the performance! The solution was for David Walker (Copland's assistant), who was present at the rehearsal, to mark changes in red pencil into Copland's score during the few hours between rehearsal and performance. None of this was in any way apparent to the audience, who applauded the composer at the beginning and end of the ballet. To the amazement of those at the rehearsal, all went smoothly.

In October 1987, Martha Graham invited two great Russian stars to dance in Appalachian Spring for her Company's "Gala": Rudolf Nureyev in the Revivalist role; Mikhail Baryshnikov in that of the Husband (Teresa Capucilli was the Bride). After rehearsal, Nureyev said, "Please don't ask me about Copland's music. I can say only I definitely love it."[13] And Baryshnikov said, "*Appalachian Spring* is about passion and possession."[14] In the evening, the audience, having waited patiently for the stars to appear, broke into cheers as each of the great Russian dancers came onstage, drowning out some of Copland's most tender music. Nevertheless, by any measure, this performance conducted by Stanley Sussman must be considered a dramatic moment in the rich history of *Appalachian Spring*. For those present who knew that Copland was seriously ill, it was a moving, if bittersweet, experience[15] as they recalled the many times Copland had taken his bows onstage with Martha Graham or greeted her backstage after a performance of *Appalachian Spring*. The last time he had done so was in the spring of 1986. Martha Graham took her old friend's hand and said, "Aaron, life has been wonderful to us, hasn't it?" Copland responded simply, "Martha, it certainly has." Some things never change.

Martha Graham Company Gala, Ocober 1987: Rudolf Nureyev, Revivalist; Mikhail Baryshnikov, husband; Teresa Capucilli, bride.

[11] Scores include (1) ballet for thirteen instruments (the original score as conducted by Louis Horst in 1944 is in the Martha Graham Company archive and is marked by various conductors for later productions); (2) original ballet with augmented orchestra (varied as needed by the Graham Company) see note 12; (3) original ballet for full orchestra (arranged by Copland in 1954 at the request of Eugene Ormandy and Martha Graham); (4) *Appalachian Spring Suite* for full orchestra (premiere by New York Philharmonic with Artur Rodzinsky in 1944); (5) *Suite* for original thirteen instruments arranged by Copland in 1970; (6) *Variations on Shaker Melody* for youth orchestra, band, solo piano, piano four-hands. Performance scores published by Boosey & Hawkes are numbers 1, 3, 4, 5, and 6. A new score of above number 3, full ballet for full orchestra, is planned for publication in 2013.

[12] An example is the ten measures at the start of the Bride's solo that do not appear in other scores. The Graham Company used the original thirteen-instrument score and parts with augmented strings (woodwinds and piano remain as they were). According to Sussman, the orchestra was usually about thirty in number.

[13] Nureyev spoke briefly to Perlis following the rehearsal.

[14] See Anna Kisselgoff, "Dance View," *The New York Times*, 18 October 1987, C 26, 40.

[15] David Walker and Vivian Perlis attended the dress rehearsal; Perlis and composer Ron Caltabiano (Copland's assistant from 1985 to 1989) were present for the performance.

ACROSS THE AMERICAS
1945 - 1949

A commission for a major work to be played by the Boston Symphony had been offered to me by Koussevitzky in March 1944. It would be my prime concern for two years following *Appalachian Spring.* But it was still wartime, and one could not in good conscience refuse requests of a patriotic nature. I tried to refuse when Eugene Goossens asked me to contribute to an unusual project he cooked up for the Golden Jubilee of the Cincinnati Symphony in 1945, but Goossens would not take no for an answer. His idea was for ten composers to write a variation on a theme by Goossens. He pointed out that the entire work would be dedicated to the men in the armed services. Goossens ignored my refusal, sent his theme along, and wrote, "I hope when you see the theme and realize that I don't need your minute-and-a-quarter variation until the beginning of October, you may perhaps find a free minute here and there to relax and pen something in your inimitable fashion. It is unthinkable that you should not be in our ultra-select group of composers." (The contributors in the order of performance were Paul Creston, myself, Deems Taylor, Howard Hanson, William Schuman, Walter Piston, Roy Harris, Anis Fuleihan, Bernard Rogers, and Ernest Bloch.) Along with his sixteen-measure "Jubilee" theme, Goossens sent instructions that my variation be "spirited in feeling and in A major."

Variations on a Theme by Goossens was performed in its entirety by the Cincinnati Symphony on 23 and 24 March 1945. Then it disappeared from the scene. Recently, someone in Cincinnati got the idea of performing my variation again. My publishers searched out the score, and the thirteen-page variation was performed and recorded by the current conductor of the Cincinnati Pops Orchestra, Erich Kunzel (14 September 1986).[1] *Jubilee* is about three minutes in duration and similar in style to *Fanfare for the Common Man.* Another war-related commission came from the Office of War Information. I had been in touch with them because Lenny Bernstein wanted me to help plan two concerts of American music in Paris, and he needed help in contacting officials in France. Understandably, the French had other matters on their minds in the spring of 1945. The plan fell through, but the OWI put their Overseas Motion Picture Bureau in touch with me about composing a score for a film concerning life in a small New England town. It would be for distribution abroad and to the armed services. Instead of Paris in the spring, I went to Bernardsville, New Jersey, where I rented a small cottage, "Claremont," on the estate of a wealthy gentleman concert pianist who was away. Victor Kraft returned from Mexico and came along with me. I told very few people where I was going, with the idea of having some uninterrupted composing time. The cottage was ideal for my needs. I could get into New York easily by train to work on the film score, and use the rest of my time to meet various deadlines. I arranged the *Appalachian Spring Suite*, made an arrangement for violin and piano of "Hoe-Down" from *Rodeo,* and completed the slow movement of the symphony for Koussevitzky.

The film score, *The Cummington Story*, was composed during one week in June, with the orchestration and recording finished a month later.[2] A piano was moved into the projection room at the OWI office in New York, and I was given a print of the film with the narration. The fifteen-minute documentary, one of a series called "The American Scene," was for distribution to servicemen and twenty-two foreign countries during the war. It was essentially a plea against intolerance. The story concerns a group of refugees from Eastern European countries, their arrival at a hostel in the town of Cummington, Massachusetts, the difficulties they encountered with the townspeople, and the final acceptance by both sides. The closing words by the minister of the church sum up the message: "Strangeness between people breaks down when they live and work and meet together with people as neighbors."

The Cummington Story was shot in Cummington (not far from Pittsfield) because the town actually had a program for refugees, with a house on Main Street that was available for ten or twelve refugees at a time. The townspeople were pleased to cooperate in what was considered "psychological warfare." Included are scenes of the town hall, the church, the *Cummington Press,* the former home of poet William Cullen Bryant, and the surrounding

[1] Copy of the ink score of Goossens' *Jubilee Variations* was found by Sylvia Goldstein of Boosey & Hawkes in 1986 among Goossens' papers in London, which are privately owned. The 1987 recording by Telarc of Copland's variation by the Cincinnati Pops Orchestra with Kunzel conducting includes *Lincoln Portrait,* narration by Katharine Hepburn.

[2] Rough sketches for *The Cummington Story* score in Copland's files cite:"Begun June 12; composition finished June 28/ orchestration-1945 June 19/ Recorded July 24." The original score consists of fourteen sections.

countryside. I have seen the film recently and still find it straightforward and rather touching. Having been made on a very limited budget, it has a simplicity that is appealing.[3]

The narrator in *The Cummington Story* takes the part of the minister of the town. Except for his voice, there is no sound but the musical score, which is continuous but for one silent segment—when the town's "old stove league at the general store" gives the silent treatment to Joseph, the newcomer. For the segment that shows Anna, the refugee woman, singing her child to sleep on their first night in Cummington, I used an unaccompanied Polish lullaby. In another section, the refugees perform part of a Mozart trio. During most of the film, the music, scored for full orchestra, takes over as the camera shows outdoor scenes. The main theme is related to the Polish lullaby, and a second theme consists of an ascending and descending figure. For the country fair scene, with horseracing and ox-cartpulling contests, I used a phrase with offbeat rhythms that repeats over and over again.

After the film score was recorded, I retrieved my music and placed it in my files. (In 1962, while looking for something to satisfy a commission for a short piano piece, I salvaged the main theme of *The Cummington Story* and arranged it as a short piano piece, *In Evening Air.* [4])

The OWI liked the film score and asked whether I would cooperate on another matter. Could they put the Radio Program Bureau in touch with me? I agreed, and to my surprise, I heard from Roy Harris, who had just become chief of the music section. Roy wrote, "The OWI is making a democratic survey of the opinions of our leading musicians concerning American music. That means you! Send me a list of ten composers you consider most worthy to represent American culture to European nations." I explained that it was a difficult task because such a list would vary according to the purposes for which works were chosen. But finally, I sent the following:

> For a broad radio audience I would prescribe RR Bennett or M. Gould rather than a R. Sessions, altho from a purely cultural standpoint I think the latter more significant. But the significance would only be apparent to an elite public. Well, anyhow, for the purposes of a poll, here are ten names: Barber, Diamond, Gershwin, Harris, Ives, Piston, Schuman, Sessions, V. Thomson, R. Thompson.

While in Bernardsville in the summer of 1945, I felt my *Third Symphony* finally taking shape. I had been working on various sections whenever I could find time during the past few years. My colleagues had been urging me to compose a major orchestral work (especially when I went to Hollywood). Elliott Carter, David Diamond, and Arthur Berger reminded me about it whenever they had the opportunity. A note from Sam Barber sent from Italy was typical (16 September 1944): "I hope you will knuckle down to a good symphony. We deserve it of you, and your career is all set for it. *Forza!*" They had no way of knowing that I had been working on such a composition for some time. I did not want to announce my intentions until I was clear in my own mind what the piece would become (at one time, it looked more like a piano concerto than a symphony). The commission from Koussevitzky stimulated me to focus my ideas and arrange the material I had collected into some semblance of order.

Copland (*left*) visiting Samuel Barber (*middle*) and Gian Carlo Menotti (*right*) in Mt. Kisco, New York, summer 1945.

A forty-minute symphony is very different from a short work for a specific purpose. It has to be planned very carefully and be given enough time to evolve. I had put the first movement of my *Third Symphony* together in Mexico during the summer of 1944, and the second in the summer of 1945. David Diamond came out to Bernardsville for a few days in July, and we showed each other what we had of our symphonies. David was composing a great deal, and his work was becoming more and more classical in style. He was working on his *Fourth Symphony* at that time, and I kidded him, saying if he was not careful he'd turn into the Glazunov of American music. David was horrified. After he returned home, he wrote about my symphony: "Can't tell you how impressed I am by the two mvts. . . As elusive as the opening theme is, it sticks pretty easily with me." A few other friends came out to visit—Marc Blitzstein, Leo Smit, and Lenny, who was full of plans for his New York City Symphony Orchestra. For the most part, I kept to myself and left the cottage only when I had to work on *The Cummington Story* in New York,

[3] The credits read: "United Films/ The American Scene; A Series #14/ *The Cummington Story*/ Music Composed by Aaron Copland." No other credits are cited. The script was written by Howard Smith Southgate, produced by Frank Beckwith, and directed by Helen Grayson. Larry Madison was director of photography. See Richard Dyer MacCann, *The People's Films* (New York: Hastings House, 1973), 143-54, and Richard Meran Barsam, Nonfiction Film (New York: E.P. Dutton, 1973), 217. Barsam writes: "Viewing these films, a foreign audience would get these impressions: America is a country of small towns, quiet churchgoing citizens, and lazy leisure-time activities. . . . *The Cummington Story* (1945), a beautiful and moving evocation of the American Dream captures all that is best in a small New England town, and, by implication, the country." Barsam's Appendix (p. 301) lists the film as twenty minutes in length and gives the producer, editor, and narrator as Sidney Meyers for the USIS. Prints at the Museum of Modern Art, New York, and at the Library of Congress.

[4] For *In Evening Air*, see Interlude IV.

and once to see Sam Barber and Gian Carlo Menotti at their home, "Capricorn," in Mt. Kisco. By September, I was able to announce to Irving Fine, "I'm the proud father—or mother—or both—of a second movement. Lots of notes—and only eight minutes of music—such are scherzi! It's not very original—*mais ca marche du commencement jusqu'au fin*—which is a help." Having two movements finished gave me the courage to continue, but the completion seemed years off.

When I had to give up the Bernardsville cottage in the fall of 1945, Victor found another rental on Limestone Road in Ridgefield, Connecticut. Again, I told almost no one where I could be found. I felt in self-exile, but it was essential if I was to finish the symphony. By April I had a third movement to show for it. With Tanglewood reopening in the summer of 1946, and an October date set for the premiere, I headed to the MacDowell Colony for the month of June to work on the last movement.

It was my first visit to the Colony since 1938. I found a nice studio with a fireplace waiting for me (the studio David Diamond had occupied in 1935). Musicians in residence were Esther and Harold Shapero and Mabel Daniels. "Sonny" Shapero played jazz in the evenings, and I loved listening to him improvise. When I showed him the completed movements of my *Third Symphony*, he thought I should make some changes (I didn't).[5] Sonny was a severe critic—he listed only about thirty objections, so I figured it must be a marvel of a piece! While I was at the Colony, Victor returned to New York and wrote that he hated the job he had just taken with *Harper's Bazaar*. I responded, "Your letters always sound as if they were written while seated on a volcano. . . . Why not give yourself two years of apprenticeship and if nothing happens by then to make you happier, you can start to complain and I'll listen." I urged Victor to be in touch with a psychoanalyst—someone I had heard recommended highly—and eventually he took my advice.

I left the Colony reluctantly, knowing how limited my composing time would be once I got to Tanglewood. I received a letter from my agent, Abe Meyer, who said that Sam Goldwyn was willing to pay twelve thousand dollars for a picture if I would go right out to Hollywood. Of course, I had to turn it down, along with an offer to teach at UCLA—or no symphony! I worked whenever I could during the summer, and I played parts of various movements for everyone who came to visit. Paul Moor has reminded me, "You played the *Third Symphony* and explained that it was the first time you had used thirty-second notes. I was flabbergasted when you turned to me and said, 'React!' I didn't know how to react, but you were tactful and went on to explain various things in the score."[6]

[5] See interview, Harold Shapero with Perlis, 9 October 1980, Natick, Massachusetts: "I loved the first and second themes, but I didn't like one theme and told him that he ought to take it out: 'That's awful. All this other stuff's so pure and that heavy thing comes in.' Aaron sort of smiled. What amazed me was when the *Symphony* got completed, that theme, which I still don't like in the first movement, comes in in a minimal form in the third movement, and it's very interesting. I didn't like it or think it was necessary at the time, but it was necessary. Aaron knew it and left it there. I don't remember his ever changing anything for anybody."

[6] See also interview, Paul Moor with Perlis, 1 June 1980, Peekskill, New York.

The title page and manuscript: first page of the piano sketch of the *Third Symphony*

Copland with Marc Blitzstein in Bernardsville, New Jersey, 1945

To get a piece finished, it helps to have a definite date by which time you must be finished. In the case of the *Third Symphony,* I knew from the start that the original 1945 date might be unrealistic, but now, it had to be completed for the opening of the 1946 BSO season. After Tanglewood, I stayed on in the Berkshires to work on the orchestration. It was a mad dash! The finishing touches were put on the score just before rehearsals were to start for the premiere, 18 October 1946. It was two years since I had started working on the piece in Mexico.

This commission meant a great deal to me, above and beyond the money: The work would receive its world premiere by Koussevitzky with the BSO, an organization I greatly admired, and the score was to be dedicated to Madame Natalie Koussevitzky, who had died in 1942. I knew the kind of thing Koussevitzky liked to conduct and what he wanted from me for the occasion. I was determined that this piece be a major work. To be sure, I was influenced by the circumstances of the commission, but the conditions for the writing of such a piece had been in place for some time. The Koussevitzky Foundation made no demands of me, other than to suggest that the premiere take place in 1945, and that the manuscript eventually be deposited with the archive of the Koussevitzky Music Foundation at the Library of Congress.[7]

[7] The orchestral score is in the Koussevitzky Foundation Collection, the Library of Congress, with the dedication: "To the memory of my dear friend/ Natalie Koussevitzky/ *Third Symphony*/ Composed by Aaron Copland/ Commissioned by the Koussevitzky Music Foundation." On the last page (255) Copland inscribed the date of completion: "Sept 19, 1946."

In the program book for the first performance, I pointed out that the writing of a symphony inevitably brings with it the question of what it is meant to express. As I wrote at the time, if I forced myself, I could invent an ideological basis for the *Third Symphony.* But if I did, I'd be bluffing—or at any rate, adding something *ex post facto*, something that might or might not be true but that played no role at the moment of creation.[8]

The *Third Symphony,* my longest orchestral work (about forty minutes in duration), is scored for a big orchestra. It was composed in the general form of an arch, in which the central portion, that is the second-movement scherzo, is the most animated, and the final movement is an extended coda, presenting a broadened version of the opening material. Both the first and third themes in the first movement are referred to again in later movements. The second movement stays close to the normal symphonic procedure of a usual scherzo, while the third is freest of all in formal structure, built up sectionally with its various sections intended to emerge one from the other in continuous flow, somewhat in the manner of a closely knit series of variations. Some of the writing in the third movement is for very high strings and piccolo, with no brass except single horn and trumpet. It leads directly into the final and longest of the movements: The fourth is closest to a customary sonata-allegro form, although the recapitulation is replaced by an extended coda, presenting many ideas from the work, including the opening theme.[9]

One aspect of the *Third Symphony* ought to be pointed out: it contains no folk or popular material. Any reference to either folk material or jazz in this work was purely unconscious.[10] However, I do borrow from myself by using *Fanfare for the Common Man* in an expanded and reshaped form in the final movement. I used this opportunity to carry the *Fanfare* material further and to satisfy my desire to give the *Third Symphony* an affirmative tone. After all, it was a wartime piece—or more accurately, an end-of-war piece—intended to reflect the euphoric spirit of the country at the time. It is an ambitious score, often compared to Mahler and to Shostakovich and sometimes Prokofiev, particularly the second movement. As a longtime admirer of Mahler, some of my music may show his influence in a general way, but I was not aware of being directly influenced by other composers when writing the work.

I went up to Boston before the premiere and played the score for Koussevitzky in the evenings on the piano at his home. I never had the feeling that this was necessary, only helpful in familiarizing him with the rhythms. Koussevitzky had a Russian point of view; he would feel things differently than a native American. Some of the parts that I thought were expressive of a certain American simplicity, Koussevitzky would tend to "lean on."

[8] Copland's analysis of the *Third Symphony* here is derived from his program notes for the first performance.

[9] At the Library of Congress: miscellaneous rough sketches not in order; a rough pencil sketch with many datings and other markings; a separate folder marked "Movt IV" with detailed indications for "last movt plan;" pages of corrections; piano ink-sketch copy; bound ink-orchestral score copy with large markings in blue crayon (perhaps Koussevitzky's conducting score).

[10] Copland discounts what seems to be quotation of the cowboy tune, "So long, Old Paint."

But he certainly could whip up a storm! I always remember that he gave a very effective version of the final movement.

The premiere was set for the Friday afternoon subscription audience. The reception and reviews were generally favorable. The *Third Symphony* was hailed as a major American symphony along the lines of Roy Harris' *Third Symphony.* A few weeks after the Boston premiere, Koussevitzky conducted my *Third Symphony* at the Brooklyn Academy of Music and at Carnegie Hall in New York, and the critics agreed that it was a "big" work. *Time Magazine* quoted Koussevitzky as he came offstage: "There is no doubt about it—this is the greatest American symphony. It goes from the heart to the heart." [11] The review was mixed, however, accusing me of stealing from others as well as myself, and of being "too popular to be a great composer." Virgil Thomson wrote a long and thoughtful piece for the *Herald Tribune,* which was essentially laudatory but not devoid of negative criticism. In part, here is what Virgil wrote:

> What is a mature artist? It is any free-lance worker who has practiced his profession long enough to know on inspecting his finished work whether it really says most of what he has meant to say and who is willing for his work to mean forever what it does in plain language really say. Any composer who crawls thus naked out on a limb has written great music. Shooting him down will not wipe out that fact. It will merely prevent his doing it again. I should like Copland to do it again.[12]

It took time for my friends and colleagues to decide how they felt about the *Third Symphony.* Arthur Berger wrote an article about it in an all-Copland issue of *Tempo* magazine in 1948[13] and included a long section dealing with it in his book about my music (1953).[14] Arthur's view was that it represented both a summing up and a step forward in terms of the technical demands of a large orchestral work. Irving Fine wrote, "I am not entirely in sympathy with the symphony's popularist tendencies, but you would not expect otherwise from me." Later on, Irving admitted, "It does get better on hearing it a third time, and I think it will make its way surely. It has some of the noblest music you have ever written, which means some of the most inspired music of our generation." When I complained to Lawrence Morton that some of my colleagues were calling the *Third Symphony* "too triumphant" and were urging cuts, Lawrence responded in his typically laconic fashion, "Since most of the persuaders have themselves never known any triumph as composers, how would they have any way of knowing whether a compositional statement was 'too triumphant'?"[15]

[11] "Copland's Third," *Time* magazine (28 October 1946), 55.

[12] Virgil Thomson, "Copland as Great Man," *New York Herald Tribune*, 24 November 1946, 6.

[13] Arthur Berger, "The Third Symphony of Aaron Copland," *Tempo* no. 9 (Autumn 1948), 20-27.

[14] Arthur Berger, *Aaron Copland* (New York: Oxford University Press, 1953; reprinted Westport, Connecticut: Greenwood Press, 1980).

[15] For a summation of Copland's *Third Symphony*, including the cut in the final movement, see William Malloch, "Copland's Triumph," *Opus* (February 1988), 22-25.

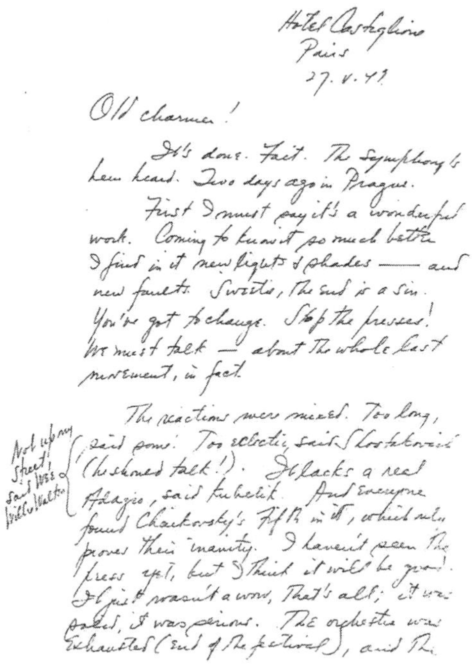

Hotel Castiglione
Paris
27.V.47

Old charmer!

It's done. Fact. The Symphony's been heard. Two days ago in Prague.

First I must say it's a wonderful work. Coming to know it so much better I find in it new lights & shades — and new faults. Sweetie, the end is a sin. You've got to change. Stop the presses! We must talk — about the whole last movement, in fact.

The reactions were mixed. Too long, said some. Too eclectic, said Shostakovich (he showed talk!). It lacks a real Adagio, said Kubelik. And everyone found Tchaikovsky's Fifth in it, which only proves their inanity. I haven't seen the press yet, but I think it will be good. It just wasn't a wow, that's all; it was solid, it was serious. The orchestra was exhausted (end of the festival), and the

Not up my street! said Wee Willie Walter

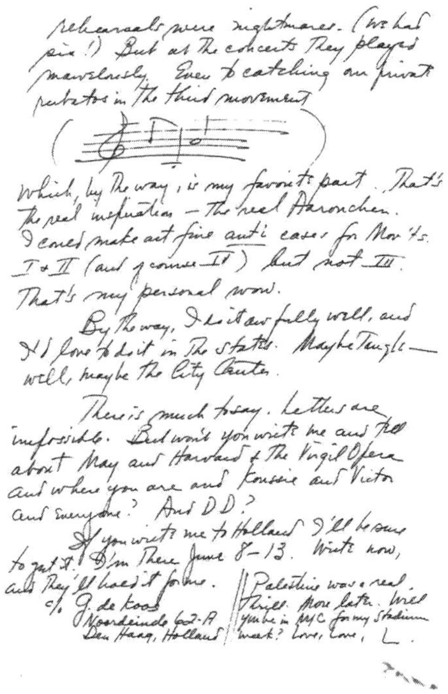

rehearsals were nightmares. (We had six!) But at the concerts they played marvelously. Even to catching our private rubatos in the third movement

which, by the way, is my favorite part. That's the real inspiration — the real Aaronchen. I could make out fine anti cases for Mov'ts. I & II (and of course IV) but not III. That's my personal wow.

By the way, I do it awfully well, and I'd love to do it in the States. Maybe Tangle — well, maybe the City Center.

There is much to say. Letters are impossible. But won't you write me and tell about May and Harvard & the Virgil Opera and where you are and Koussie and Victor and everyone? And DD?

If you write me to Holland I'll be sure to get it. I'm there June 8–13. Write now, and they'll hold it for me.
c/o G. de Koos
Noordeinde 60?-A
Den Haag, Holland

Palestine was a real thrill. More later. Will you be in NYC for my Stadium week? Love, love, L.

Letter from
Leonard Bernstein to
Copland, 27 May 1947

The *Third Symphony* has come to be viewed as something of an anomaly, standing between my abstract works and the more accessible ballet and film music. The fourth-movement finale is perhaps the clearest example of this fusion of styles. I, myself, have thought of this piece as being closest in feeling to the *Symphonic Ode*, at least in intention: a full orchestral work for the concert hall that makes a serious statement. Personally, I am satisfied that my *Third Symphony* stands for what I wanted to say at the time. The musical ideas that came to me (or that I chose) were appropriate for the particular purpose of the work.

The conductor who has always understood my music almost intuitively is Leonard Bernstein: His conducting of the *Third Symphony* is closest to what I had in mind when composing the piece. Despite misgivings about some passages, particularly the ending, Lenny conducted the *Third Symphony* in Prague only months after the world premiere. In 1948, after conducting it in Israel, Lenny seemed more positive about the piece (8 November): "The *Symphony* seems to be a success! . . . After the fourth performance it has begun to sound, and quite magnificent at that. It's really a fantastic piece! I must confess I have made a sizable cut near the end and believe me it makes a whale of a difference."[16] At the time, I thought it was pretty nervy of Lenny to take it on himself to make a cut. Being a careful and slow worker, I rarely felt it necessary to revise a composition after it was finished, and even more rarely after it was published. In the case of the *Third Symphony*, however, I came to agree with Lenny and several others about the advisability of shortening the ending. It's interesting to note that with a cut of eight measures, the difference was apparent and was commented on when Lenny conducted this new version with the BSO at Tanglewood in 1952.[17] When he conducted the New York Philharmonic for a television broadcast of my *Symphony*'s fourth movement, I said jokingly from the stage to The Young People's Concerts audience, "Maestro Bernstein conducts the music as if he wrote it. But I just want to make one thing clear. He didn't write it, I did!"

When Chávez invited me to Mexico to conduct the *Symphony* in June 1947, Koussevitzky advised against it. I decided to try it out, however, since at least it would be across the border! (I was also scheduled to conduct *Appalachian Spring Suite* and *Two Pieces for String Orchestra.*) For weeks before leaving for Mexico, I stood in front of a mirror in my studio and flailed my arms around and snapped my fingers. I really got cold feet when I arrived in Mexico City and saw my name staring at me from posters all over town! I was revived by telegrams announcing that I had won the BSO Merit Award and the Music Critic's Circle Award of 1946-1947 for the *Third Symphony.* As rehearsals proceeded, I gained confidence. I was not sure the orchestra would learn the work, but I certainly did! I wrote to Lenny (4 June 1947): "My main trouble is giving cues for entrances. Kouss said to me before I left, 'If you ruin MY Symphony I vill keel you.'"

[16] For Bernstein on the *Third Symphony*, see interview, Bernstein with Perlis.

[17] The pages showing the cut for the final version are in Copland's files in the Library of Congress.

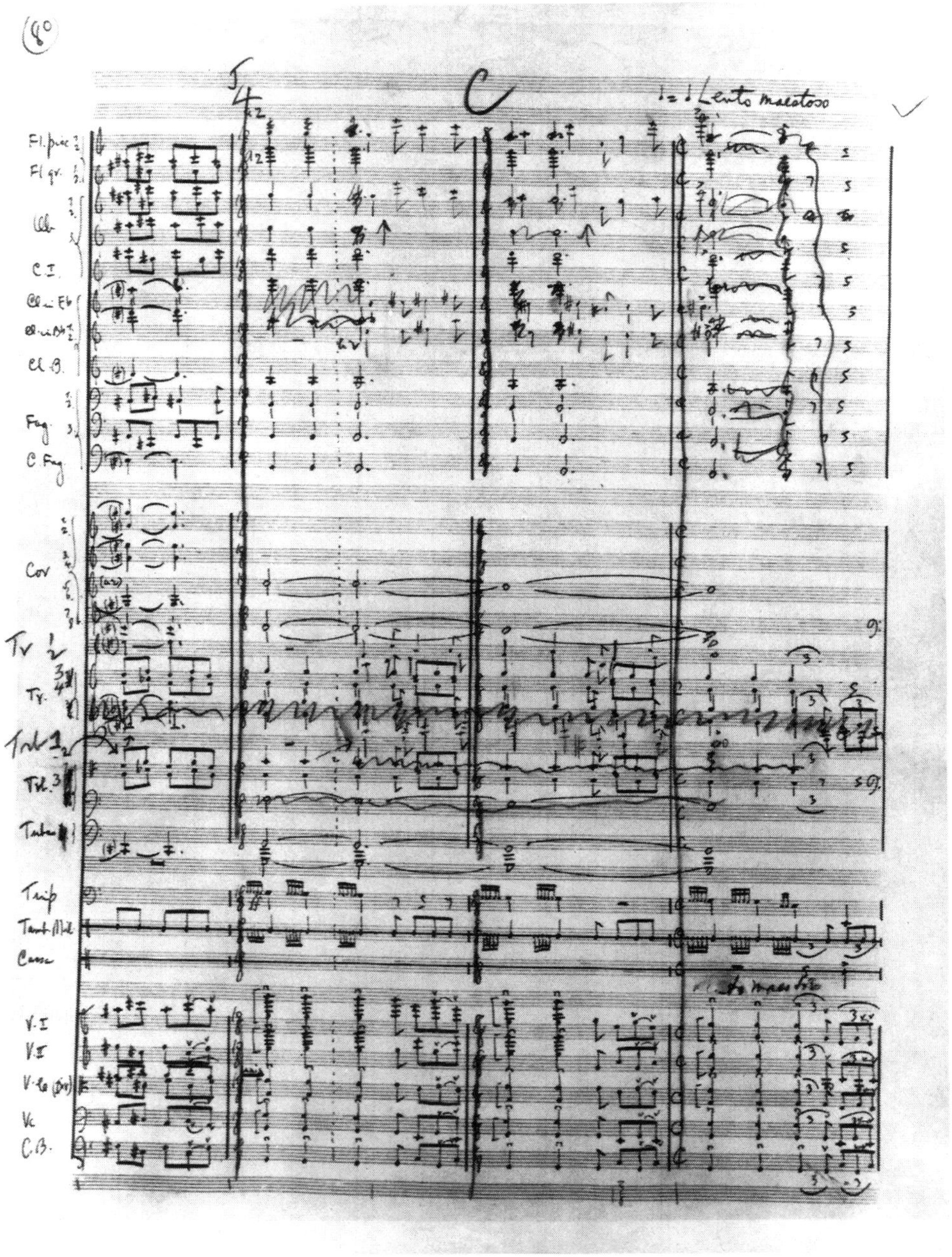

Manuscript page from the fourth movement of Copland's conducting score for the *Third Symphony* showing the beginning of the cut suggested by Bernstein

As much as I enjoyed working with the Sinfonica musicians, I found the Mexican audiences icy toward modern music, and I had very little idea of what, if anything, they got from the *Third Symphony*. Helen and Elliott Carter happened to be in Mexico at the time. They remember going with me to rent my tuxedo. The jackets were all several sizes too big for me, with the sleeves hanging down over my hands! After the concert, I had some fun showing them the "Salón México" dance hall. Helen Carter still recalls how they frisked Elliott and me before allowing us into the hall, to make sure we had no guns![18]

The *Third Symphony* has been performed and recorded by many different orchestras and conductors. George Szell wrote to me while I was on the State Department tour of Latin America in 1947 (16 September 1947): "I have studied the work during the summer and got rather close to it and hope to be able to give a satisfactory performance. Needless to say, I shall be glad to have you sit in at the rehearsals and help me with your suggestions and criticisms." So I went to Cleveland, and later Szell conducted the *Third Symphony* in New York and for a radio broadcast (21 December 1947). Antal Dorati made the first recording with the Minneapolis Symphony, and I have conducted two recordings myself, both with English orchestras.[19] Lenny continued to program the *Third Symphony,* particularly for special birthdays.[20] His conducting of it in 1985 left me marveling at how he had that tough New York Philharmonic playing like angels—well, there's only one Lenny Bernstein![21]

It was brave of me to accept a commission for a choral work to be premiered at a Symposium on Music Criticism at Harvard in May 1947, never having composed anything of length for chorus. If I was going to have the work ready in time, I had to get away from New York. Verna and Irving Fine lived in Cambridge, and Verna's mother, Florence Rudnick, had a comfortable apartment in Boston, which she left in the winter months. Verna arranged for me to use Mrs. Rudnick's place while she was in Florida from February through April 1946, and they agreed "not to tell a soul." I wrote to Verna, "I plan to use the BSO as an address, and to be mysterious about my real whereabouts. It's come to this! A nice simple guy like me."

The Department of Music at Harvard suggested that I use a Hebrew text for the choral piece, but I opted for part of the King James Version of the Bible (Genesis 1:1; 2:7) con-

[18] Helen Carter also described to Perlis the visit to rent the tuxedo and the dance-hall experience (August 1988).

[19] Copland made recordings of the *Third Symphony* with the London Symphony Orchestra and the Philharmonia Orchestra.

[20] Bernstein conducted the New York Philharmonic in a weekend of subscription concerts for Copland's seventy-fifth birthday, with Roy Harris' *Third Symphony* and David Diamond's *Violin Concerto* No. 3 (premiere); for the eightieth and eighty-fifth birthdays, Bernstein conducted Copland's *Third Symphony* with the Tanglewood Music Center orchestra; also for the eighty-fifth, the New York Philharmonic, with the Harris and Schuman *Third Symphonies.*

[21] As is Bernstein's preference, the 1985 concerts were recorded live and the Copland *Third Symphony* was released with *Quiet City* in a digital recording by Deutsche Grammophon.

Manuscript, first page of the pre-final score of *In the Beginning*

cerned with the seven days of creation. My plan was to use a mezzo-soprano soloist and mixed chorus a capella to tell the oft-told story in a gentle narrative style using the biblical phrase "And the next day . . ." to round off each section. I was uncertain about how it would proceed until I got to the third day of creation—only then did I feel that my idea would work.

In The Beginning is dedicated to Nadia Boulanger. I have been told that its duration of thirteen and one-half minutes is long for an a capella work. It does not incorporate folk music or jazz materials, but jazz rhythms are used in various sections, particularly for the verse "And let there be light in the firmament of the heavens. . . ." A cadenza-like passage for the singer and a final coda force all the voices to the top of their range, bringing the work to a climax that I hoped would depict the text—"And man became living soul"—in musical terms. Because the solo part is difficult and exacting and there are some quick harmonic changes for the chorus, I included an optional piano part as an aid to the singers when the piece was published. Organ has occasionally been substituted for piano.

I finished the score just in time for the rehearsals at the end of April 1947.[22] A prestigious group gathered in Sanders Theatre for the Harvard Symposium[23] to hear commissioned chamber music works on the first day; the three new choral works the second day (Hindemith, Malipiero, and Copland); and new dances by Martha Graham on the third.[24] The choral concert took place in Memorial Hall, Robert Shaw conducting, Nell Tangemen soloist (Shaw also conducted the New York premiere at Carnegie Hall). All agreed Shaw had done an expert job, and *In The Beginning* was given a cordial reception by the critics.

Of all the times I, myself, conducted *In The Beginning*, one stands out as most memorable: in Israel during the Passover week concerts at the Ein Gev Music Festival, with the Tel-Aviv vocal ensemble and soprano Naomi Zurin (21 April 1951). A stage had been built for the performers, but the audience, comprised of outstanding artists as well as members of the surrounding kibbutzim, sat in the open air. It was not that the performance itself was so much better than others, but the setting and the experience of conducting my work in Israel gave the occasion a special quality.

The last time I conducted *In The Beginning* was at Brown University as part of the 1980 commencement proceedings, at which I received an honorary degree. The students put on a concert of my vocal music, and I was moved by their dedication and enthusiasm. They were not musicians, but their obvious excitement and pleasure at having me in their midst heightened my enjoyment, although at first they were tense and afraid to look at me. I realized that these young people might never again have the experience of working with a living composer. The Brown University chorus was made up of a varied group—from delicate young girls to the captain of the football team, who happened to be the head of the chorus. I told him to "get tough" and "don't be sentimental!" Conducting a student group is a very different experience from conducting a top-flight professional chorus. You feel as though you are all in something special together. The Brown group was well trained, yet I could enjoy hearing their sound change as I worked with them. I try never to be patronizing to nonprofessionals, and I like to make them feel more comfortable by getting a laugh once in a while. On this particular occasion, I told the Brown students, "Creation was quite a stunt, so make it grand— don't be pathetic about it. What happened after creation is an entirely different story!"

A catalogue of a composer's published works gives only part of the picture. In addition, there are projects that are abandoned and others that are considered but not accepted for one reason or another. A production that took time and effort without coming to fruition was *Tragic Ground*, a musical planned by choreographer Agnes de Mille and stage designer Oliver Smith. Their idea was a musical play based on Erskine Caldwell's novel *Tobacco Road*; when the rights could not be secured, Caldwell's *Tragic Ground* was substituted. Lynn Riggs was to write the script, I the music. We did several songs together, among them "I Bought Me a Cat" (an arrangement of an Arkansas folk song) and an original ballad, "Alone at Night."[25] The script for *Tragic Ground* was turned down by various producers, until finally, Agnes wrote (22 November 1946): "Dear Fellow Grounders, There is not enough humor in the story. We are at a deadlock. The project is abandoned."[26]

I considered various film scripts carefully before I turned them down: a feature film with John Wayne; an MGM adaptation of Ketti Fring's book *God's Front Porch*; and Samuel Goldwyn's *Earth and High Heaven*,[27] featuring Koussevitzky and the BSO playing music I composed. An offer I had considered was from the famous Billy Rose, who invited Stravinsky, Schuman, and me to compose pieces for a big show he was putting on in 1945. I figured I could ask Billy Rose for $2,500 plus $1,000 advance against royalties. But Billy wrote (18 April 1944):

> Frankly, I didn't know that modern composing came so high. The terms you outline are several times as expensive as they would be had I asked Kern, Rodgers or Cole Porter . . . if the theatre is that fat I haven't discovered it.

Another "might-have-been" in 1946 was an offer from Woody Herman, made through Goddard Lieberson (Goddard was a representative of CBS then, before becoming president of Columbia Records). Goddard wrote (5 August 1946), "Woody wants a piece. Something Copland, not Woody Herman, for his band. Woody does not want any strings. He suggests a contract along the exact lines of our deal with Stravinsky." At about the same time, I was approached to compose a clarinet concerto. It would have to be one or the other. The request for the concerto was from Benny Goodman, and I accepted it.

[22] See Copland's files for ink score with corrections in red pencil dated "April 5, 1947." See also the Library of Congress for pencil manuscript with directions for mezzo-soprano: "in a story-telling manner," "freely and naive (in a gentle and narrative manner) like reading of a familiar oft-told story," and ink manuscript dated "April 1, 1947."

[23] Participants in the symposium included E. M. Forster, Roger Sessions, Archibald T. Davison, Alfred Frankenstein, Olga Samaroff, Virgil Thomson, Otto Kinkeldey, Olin Downes, and Paul Henry Lang.

[24] The Graham Company performed *Dark Meadow*, music by Chávez, and *Night Journey*, music by Schuman.

[25] During a visit in 1983, Copland's friend Paul Moor played and sang "Alone at Night" from memory; in 1984, he transcribed the song and sent it to Copland. No other manuscript exists.

[26] Materials relating to *Tragic Ground* are in Copland's files. Copland drew on some of them later when preparing his arrangements of *Old American Songs* and when composing his opera *The Tender Land*.

[27] See Abe Meyer correspondence in Copland's files about *Earth and High Heaven*.

I asked Benny whether he could send some of his recordings, and he responded, "I'm looking forward in anticipation to the piece. I do think it would be easier for you to get the two sextet albums from your record dealer or even a phone call to Goddard Lieberson may get quick results as they are recorded for Columbia. . . ." I listened to the recordings, made some notes and took them with me on a four-month tour of Latin America. I hoped to compose some of the concerto during that time.

I did a brash thing in the summer of 1947: I fell in love with a house in the Palisades area and rented it for three years, just before leaving for Latin America. I had been wanting a place of my own for so long that I was afraid to let this one go. I rationalized that at least I would have a proper home to return to from my travels. My loft in New York had been robbed again: Victor lost expensive photographic equipment and his violin, while I lost only some clothes and a few days in leaving for Mexico. We did as the police advised—put bars on the windows, padlocks on the door, and riveted the skylight down, but the time had come for a change.

In 1946, I had visited friends, the pianists Robert Fizdale and Arthur Gold, in a house they had rented in Sneden's Landing.[28] I had been impressed with the fact that it was close to the city but gave the feeling of being way out in the country—the tiny village on the Hudson with one general store was a pocket between Palisades State Park and the next state park. I started looking in that area, never dreaming I would find something right away! The house I found at Sneden's Landing was a rambling white Colonial, rather unusual in that it had been built in three installments. The earliest part dated from pre-Revolutionary times and had been a one-room house belonging to Molly and William Sneden, whose ferryboat crossed from Sneden's Landing to Dobbs Ferry. In fact, the story goes that George Washington used the boat during the Revolutionary War. The original house had been added to twice. Wide lawns led down to the Hudson River, and lovely old trees, a grapevine, and flower beds added to the natural setting. My studio was to be situated on the side of the house where there were no neighbors to be concerned about (I was always sensitive about that—it was one of the reasons I wanted to be out of the city). For some reason, perhaps to do with the ferryboat, the Sneden's Landing house was called the "Ding Dong House." I wrote to Victor from South America: "That name will have to go!"

Victor was in charge of moving our things from the loft while I was away (Leo Smit was moving in), and getting the house in order. He wrote to me in Rio to say, "I have hired us a housekeeper, and we have a kitten named 'Quetzel.' Truman Capote drove out to Sneden's Landing with me one day—Truman really loved it." I responded in a more practical vein: "Have you bought dishes? What will we have to eat out of?"

My 1947 tour of South America stemmed from the belief many of us in the arts had in those days—that the history of twentieth-century music was going to be written from both North and South America. In hindsight, perhaps we were naive. I was chairman of a committee called The U.S. Group for Latin American Music, which sponsored cooperative programs between this country and three Latin American countries—Argentina, Brazil, and Uruguay. The committee included two experts on Latin American culture, Gilbert Chase and Carleton Sprague Smith, and composers Paul Bowles and Henry Cowell. The executive director, Erminie Kahn, somehow convinced a tractor company to sponsor a competition to select young composers for scholarships to the Berkshire Music Center. Considering that I was about to leave on a four-month tour of Latin America sponsored by the State Department, the committee asked me to keep an eye out for talented young composers and to make recommendations for the Tanglewood scholarships.

[28] See interview, Robert Fizdale with William Owen for Perlis, 15 February 1982, New York City.

Copland in front of the State Department in Washington before his 1947 tour of Latin America

The tour was to include not only the big cities of Montevideo, Buenos Aires, Rio de Janeiro, Sao Paulo, and Porto Alegre but smaller places where no one had ever seen an American composer and where any composer of symphonic music was a rare bird. In all these places, our government had cooperated with local persons to maintain cultural centers for the teaching of English and the spreading of comprehensive ideas about our civilization, in order to expand the picture of the United States beyond what could be obtained from the Hollywood movies that were seen everywhere. I was to deliver twenty-eight lectures before sixteen different organizations, nineteen radio talks, and five concerts at which I either played and/or conducted.

I landed in Rio de Janeiro on 19 August 1947. It was quite a jump from Tanglewood—in space, in language, in musical atmosphere. The only thing in common with the Berkshires was the housing shortage. Nothing had been arranged in advance. I had to stay in a dingy airport hotel until the beginning of September when Eleazar de Carvalho found me an apartment. I prepared lectures and made the usual dull rounds of embassy receptions. Finally settled into the apartment on top of a mountain overlooking the Rio harbor, I wrote to Verna and Irving Fine: "The view is superb but the piano stinks! Well, you can't have everything! I feel as though I am living in the country but can walk down to the city in ten minutes. The streets are always full of people—no one ever seemed to want to go home!" The city was as beautiful as I remembered. A friendly, democratic feeling was in the air and this came across because of the lack of color lines. It was endlessly amusing to sit at a sidewalk cafe and watch the passing scene.

With Carvalho back in Rio, the Berkshire Music Center and American composers were not entirely unknown. His first concert with the Orquestra Sinfonica Brasileira after his return was devoted to an all-American program—my *Third Symphony*, Bill Schuman's *Symphony for Strings*, and Peter Mennin's *Folk Overture*. This was a brave gesture, since the public had heard comparatively little contemporary music of any kind. Musical conditions reminded me of what we had had at home some thirty or forty years earlier. Opera was the big social event in Rio, and the mere carrying through of a full symphonic season was quite an achievement. I was somewhat disappointed in the Orquestra. My *Third Symphony* was performed three times, but it didn't improve much.

I stayed for eight weeks in Rio de Janeiro, which gave me time to deliver a series of twelve lectures, "Panorama of American Composers." This was essentially the course I had presented at Tanglewood during the summer: The first two were delivered in English before the Ministry of Education and the Brazilian Press Association; and the others were translated and read in Spanish at the Instituto Brasil-Estados Unidos. I took part in a chamber-music concert (15 October), playing *Vitebsk* and the *Violin Sonata*. The audience was small but sympathetic. In general, there was a very restricted group interested in new music—only the opera stars seemed to draw the crowds.

A German composer named [Hans Joachim] Koellreutter had all the talented young pupils in Rio. Somewhat like Ardevol in Cuba, he was the leader of the new generation, which published a magazine, *Musica Viva*, had radio programs, and held seminars. It was a curious situation, in which Brazilians were being brought up by a typical German twelve-toner. I attended a concert of works by his pupils, and both master and pupils made a singularly humorless impression. I knew that Koellreutter could not harm gifted young people, but he certainly encouraged a lot of dullards to imagine they were composers! Along with the *Musica Viva* tenets went many pious pronouncements about the "Muse of Music" and the social role of music. It was all very German and rather jejune.

Before my arrival, I had received very lively letters from Villa-Lobos, which would begin with "I've got atomic news!" or some equally colorful phrase. Villa-Lobos was only slightly less ebullient in Brazil. I was relieved to see him so friendly, because I had not seen him since a concert of his music I had organized for the League of Composers a few years earlier, which had not been a success. Not having had access to many of his printed scores, I had settled for music that was not the best Villa-Lobos, and after the program at the Museum of Modern Art (February 1945), I was conscience-stricken. I had often scolded the League's board about programs I thought were not carefully chosen, but no one scolded me, not even Villa-Lobos when he heard about it. In Rio, Villa-Lobos took me to visit his school, which trained music teachers, and he showed me his studio, where copyists and engravers were all working on his manuscripts. We searched for local music up in the hills together, but it was difficult to find a real samba—the Broadway version had exerted a baleful influence on Rio's samba composers. Camargo Guarnieri suddenly turned up from Sao Paulo, and we made plans for my Sao Paulo visit. Guarnieri seemed against most things Brazilian.

One very embarrassing thing happened in Rio: The critics put on a lunch inviting twenty of the most important people, but they had neglected to tell me where it was to be, so I missed the whole thing! Pictures were taken, with my chair empty. I felt as though I had to explain myself to all of Rio. However, I then left in a blaze of glory when the Academy of Music, headed by Villa-Lobos, gave an *homenaje* with speeches and music in my honor.

I arrived in Sao Paulo for a four-day visit (16 October). They were organized to the hilt for my arrival. It began with a reception at the airport with representatives of the governor, the Ministry of Culture, the Musicians Sindicato, the Uniao Cultural, the consul general and, of course, Guarnieri. I was informed by the U.S. consul that I must leave my card for the governor and that caused a moment of consternation—I didn't have a printed card (I never have had one). More receptions and lunches than I could count took place. I gave a lecture on film music in Spanish for an audience of four hundred, made radio appearances, and played the *Piano Variations* at a morning concert in the opera house, which was full at 10 a.m.! Also on the program was Guarnieri's *Second String Quartet*, which struck me as a good playable work, if nothing surprising. The middle movement has definite Gershwin touches, which Guarnieri assured me were "pure Brazilian." Before leaving town, I made an official visit to the local conservatory, and it was like walking into the middle of the nineteenth century. An all-girl chorus sang, and somebody played my *Cat and Mouse*.

My next stop was Porto Alegre in the south of the country, a clean and compact little city that seemed to be peopled mostly by blond Germans. It reminded me of Guatemala City or Baden-Baden. I visited the local Belas Artes school and met the composers. My lecture in the Teatro Sao Pedro with 169 in the audience was rather lost in a place seating 1,000. I flew to Buenos Aires for a few days preparatory to returning for two weeks in November. The city looked larger and more imposing than in 1941. Switching from the little Portuguese I knew to proper Spanish was very confusing. I had dinner with the Ginasteras and afterward we all went to José Maria Castro's bookshop, where I found composers I had met in 1941—everyone seemed genuinely glad to see me again. I was impressed all over again with how sweet a person Ginastera was.

By the end of October, I was in Montevideo, Uruguay, an overnight boat ride from Buenos Aires. I conducted the Sodre Orchestra, considered the best in South America next to the Colon in Buenos Aires. The concert (1947) included my *Lincoln Portrait.* I also conducted *Appalachian Spring* and *Outdoor Overture*, and Hector Tosar played his *Piano Concertino* (led by a local conductor). The concert was obviously a huge success, and everyone seemed to think I was a good conductor.[29] Tosar said I was influenced by Lenny Bernstein and that my left hand was like Bruno Walter! The second *homenaje* of the trip was made by composers who looked much older than I had remembered them.

The two weeks in Buenos Aires were the busiest of all: Ginastera had planned several activities with the Liga de Compositores, including an entire concert of my music by Argentine musicians. Ginastera made a simple, sincere, and touching introductory speech to a packed house—I apparently had a "public" there. The Sociedad Hebraica gave a reception followed by a lecture on film music, also to a full auditorium. I was surprised to see my 1945 documentary, *The Cummington Story*, shown there in a Spanish version. I enjoyed meeting young composers at a series of lectures on American music at the Instituto Cultural Argentino Norteamericano. Arrangements had been made for me to conduct an all-Copland program with the Colon Orchestra, which in Buenos Aires terms is like the Philharmonic at Carnegie Hall. I suggested including something by Ginastera but was informed that, for political reasons, it would not be possible. The Colon was a first-rate orchestra, and I felt that it would be a real testing ground as to whether I could venture the same kind of program in the States. At rehearsal, however, the orchestra seemed rather less good than I expected. They were not very smart about rhythms. I conducted the entire concert in their enormous opera house—the same program as in Montevideo, with the addition after intermission of the *Third Symphony.* The house, as large as the Metropolitan Opera, was full. The ambassador and his wife attended, and at the reception afterward, I was afraid I might have to shake hands with Mrs. Peron, but it seemed she never went to musical affairs. I wrote to Verna and Irving Fine, saying, "With Mexico that makes three orchestras I've handled since June. Bernstein better look out."

Publicity had been distributed about the Tanglewood scholarships, but the only composer I felt deserved one was Sergio de Castro. He played works for me that showed a clear logical mind, and at times, real inspiration. He reminded me of Israel Citkowitz—the same type of childlike innocence and purity of spirit. I also spent some time with Julian Bautista, a Spanish refugee composer whose music was expertly done but with no originality whatever. I always felt like commiserating with composers such as Bautista; they come so close to having everything it takes, and then their music adds up to nothing.

On my forty-seventh birthday, some of the composers suddenly produced a birthday cake after supper; the Fines sent a wire; and Victor called from New York. When he told me that "The house on the Hudson looks swell," it made me want to go right home. I still

[29] For a description of the 1947 performance of *Lincoln Portrait*, see 145.

Copland in Recife with Brazilian musicians, November 1947

had to travel up the north coast of Brazil, however. It was in those smaller places that I met and heard some real Brazilian samba composers. Bahia, one of the oldest towns in Brazil, is charming and colorful, and claimed to have preserved the real samba. I discovered that it is not the rhythmic element that gives the samba interest. The bottom rhythm is always the same; it is the freshness of melodic line, plus the cross accents, plus the highly amusing sound of the carioca words that make them indigenous and very hard to sing, copy, or remember. I was told they must be simplified for ordinary Carnaval use, and I don't wonder. In Bahia, I heard an instrument called the birimbau. No one seemed able to tell me its origins. I'd never heard anything like the sound that several birimbau players make—a sweetly jangled tinkle.

I flew to Recife (21 November) and was taken directly to the radio station for a broadcast. People there seemed in awe of me, even the newspapermen! I was honored by a full evening's demonstration of Recifian popular arts. Most interesting was a dance, the frevo, which is no cinch: You dance it alone in a deliberately restricted space to music deriving from street marches, similar to our New Orleans jazz. For my benefit, an army band of twenty-eight men was rounded up to play frevos on an exceedingly hot night, and they played with deadpan faces—on army rations and army pay. I thought how easy it would be to make an orchestral piece out of the frevo—or easier still—a band piece. Recife at Carnaval time is said to outrival Rio, and from my brief twelve-hour visit there, I could well believe it. I heard some drumming that was phenomenal. Gradually, I was able to distinguish a basic 4/4 rhythm, but what they packed into it!

My next stops were Fortaleza and Belem. I gave lectures to full auditoriums but felt that the reactions were provincial. I was getting anxious to return home, and I wrote to Victor from Belem, which is almost at the equator and very hot: "Please!! Hang out my overcoat at the loft so it won't smell of mothballs. Bring it with you to Washington." (After returning to Rio, flying to Puerto Rico, and landing in Miami, a State Department employee escorted me to Washington to report on the trip.)

I received a great deal of attention as a cultural ambassador. The South Americans really went for that kind of thing in a big way. I had more receptions in my honor in those few months than in years at home, but I did not meet as many new composers this trip as in 1941. I was hard put to make recommendations of Brazilian and Uruguayan artists for Tanglewood, but Argentina was developing more rapidly. The daily diary I kept helped me in making my reports to the State Department,[30] and was useful for an article I sent to *The New York Times*,[31] for lectures at Tanglewood the following summer,[32] and in retelling the adventure for this book.

Once back in the States, what I really wanted to do was stay put and enjoy my new home, but I had only one week before going to Cleveland, because I had promised Szell I would attend the rehearsals of the *Third Symphony*, and then on to Boston for an MTNA (Music Teachers National Association) conference to make a report to the Committee for Latin American Music. Nevertheless, I marveled at all the space in the house at Sneden's Landing. What a wonderful feeling it was to be roosted at last! Victor caught me up on things: Lenny had conducted *Statements* while I was away; *Billy the Kid* had been danced several times; and my book *What to Listen for in Music* had been published in German. I was amused no end to imagine me telling the Germans anything about what to listen for in music!

Soon after my return, I met with my publishers. Hans Heinsheimer, whom I had known since 1928, had been in charge of my music at Boosey & Hawkes for several years.[33] He had an assistant who was also familiar with my catalogue—Arnold Broido. Sylvia Goldstein began working for Boosey in 1940. Soon she knew all about my music, and for many years she was in charge of contracts, permissions, and many other matters.[34] In the changing world of music publishing, Sylvia has been the steady and indispensable link with my publishers. In the early days, publishers took on more management and publicity duties for their composers: new scores were distributed to performers, conductors, and colleagues; and the Boosey & Hawkes publication *Tempo* reached a wide audience in the music world. Ralph Hawkes, who had become my friend as well as my publisher, recommended a "cutting service" in England, and since 1946, the pale-green clippings from Durrant's Press Cuttings arrived at my house continuously. In 1948, when Heinsheimer left Boosey (I believe he once told me they let him go because he was writing a book), a young lady named Betty Bean, who had been working on a library of American music for the Soviet-American committee, took Heinsheimer's place as director of serious music. I had seen Betty Bean briefly in Rio in September; once home, there was a great deal of work to do to catch her up with my affairs.

I was involved with several organizations that now required my time and attention, among them the Composers' Forum, the Soviet-American Music Council, and the League of Composers. I always went to see Claire Reis after a trip. She brought me up to date on the news in the music world, particularly the League of Composers. Most unfortunately, *Modern Music* finally was forced to cease publication. The National Composers' Committee of the League, of which I was chairman, agreed on the need for a newsletter. In February 1947, the first issue of *The Composers News-Record* was distributed, with Everett Helm as editor. This was in no way intended as a replacement for *Modern Music*. As I explained in a front-page note, "We want to establish contact with composers in our own country and between ourselves and composers living in the rest of the world. Europe is gradually coming to life again, musical centers in South America are stirring."

The loss of *Modern Music* was a serious blow to the League's prestige, and by 1947-1948 the board was rife with internal friction and personal differences. During the war, Claire had done her best to keep the League alive, but the freshness of spirit and enthusiasm that had characterized the organization's early years had faded. At one time, I even suggested to Claire that we change the League's name to give it a new start, but that idea was voted down by the board. Claire had been the strength of the League of Composers since its inception in 1923. After her husband's sudden death in 1947, she felt the need to resign and she wrote this to me in confidence with the hope that we might find some new direction before her resignation became known. I wondered how the League could exist without Claire! We composers owed her an enormous debt of gratitude.

On a personal level, Claire and Arthur Reis' friendship had meant a great deal to me. I was away when Arthur died, but when I returned, I was determined to do as much as I could to help Claire during the difficult period following Arthur's death. When Claire's resignation became official (1948), I accepted the position of director of the League of

[30] See travel diary #3 for 1947 Latin American tour. Also pertaining to the tour, in Copland's files in the Library of Congress are scripts, lecture notes, drafts and final typescripts, bills and receipts for expenses, fan mail, invitations, calling cards, and programs. See also Donald Fuller, "A Symphonist Goes to Folk Sources," *Musical America*, LXVIII:3 (February 1948), 29, 256.

[31] Copland, "Composer's Report on Music in South America," *The New York Times*, 21 December 1947, X 9.

[32] The diary formed the basis of the 1948 lecture course "Music of Latin America." See also Tanglewood Newsletter (1948).

[33] See interview, Hans Heinsheimer with Perlis, 21 May 1981, New York City.

[34] See Copland's files in the Library of Congress for Boosey & Hawkes correspondence.

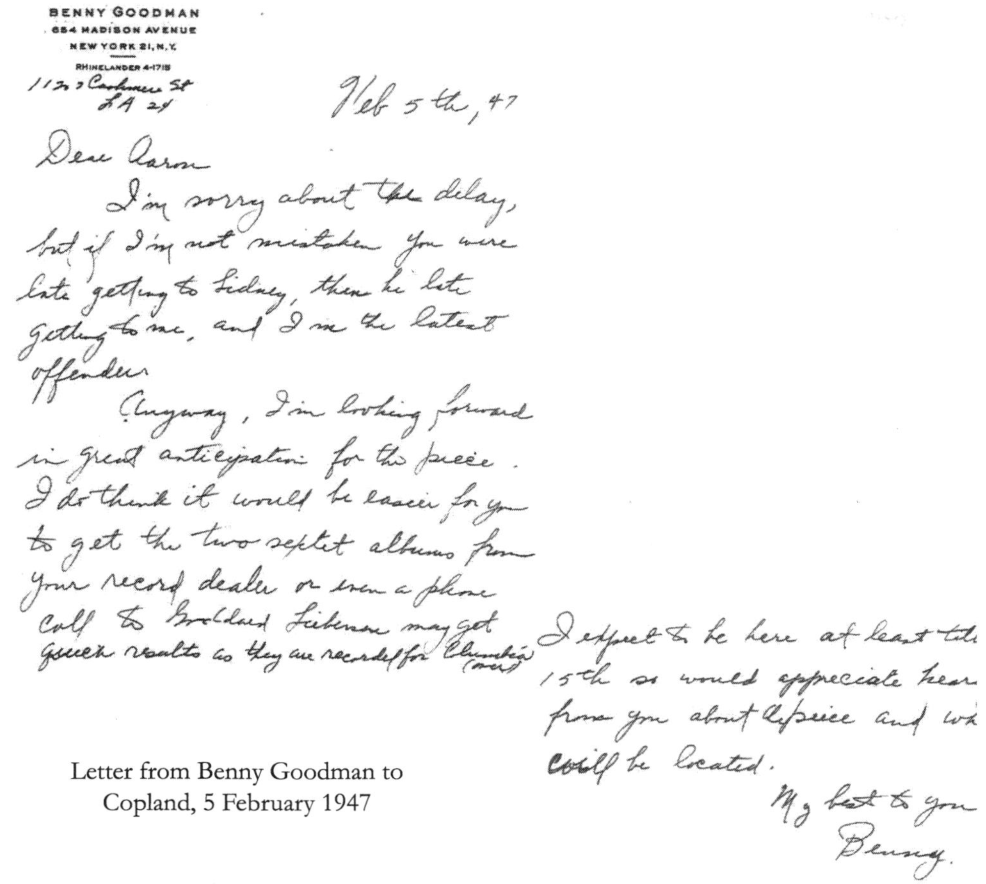

BENNY GOODMAN
684 MADISON AVENUE
NEW YORK 21, N.Y.
RHINELANDER 4-1715

[illegible] St
LA 24

Feb 5th, 47

Dear Aaron

I'm sorry about the delay, but if I'm not mistaken you were late getting to Sidney, then he late getting to me, and I'm the latest offender.

Anyway, I'm looking forward in great anticipation for the piece. I do think it would be easier for you to get the two septet albums from your record dealer or even a phone call to Goddard Lieberson may get quick results as they are recorded for Columbia (over)

I expect to be here at least till 15th so would appreciate hear from you about the piece and wh could be located.

My best to you
Benny.

Letter from Benny Goodman to Copland, 5 February 1947

Composers with the idea of supervising a restructuring of the organization (I held the position until 1951). It was important to act quickly so as not to lose our membership and past support: A notice went out announcing the changes and the events planned for the 1948-1949 season, the League's twenty- fifth anniversary.[35]

Sacks of mail had accumulated while I was away! I have always answered correspondence myself. At times, Victor helped me (as David Walker did later), but even so, I always dictated responses. The most important mail had been coming from Hollywood: Abe Meyer, my agent at MCA, kept me informed about film projects, and now he had a "hot" prospect.

[35] Richard Franko Goldman became executive director; and various committee chairmen completed the board. An office was secured at Steinway Hall and concert manager David Rubin and assistant Claire Rosenstein were drawn into the organization. A concert to honor Edwin Franko Goldman took place as planned.

I was willing to listen. The house at Sneden's Landing was a big expense compared to the Empire Hotel and the loft, and if I wanted to eventually build or buy a place, I would have to increase my income.[36] Hollywood was the only way for me to do that.

I had composed the first movement of the *Clarinet Concerto* for Benny Goodman while traveling in Latin America, and from Rio, I had written to Victor (4 October 1947), saying, "I badly need a fast theme for part 2. The usual thing. I used the 'pas de deux' theme for part 1, and I think it will make everyone weep." I had hoped to finish the piece soon after returning to Sneden's Landing, but what Abe Meyer was offering in Hollywood was too good to turn down: a film script adapted from John Steinbeck's 1938 novel *The Red Pony.* I admired Steinbeck, and after reading the book, I knew this was a film for me. A contract was negotiated with Republic Pictures, which called for ten weeks of work at $1,500 a week for less than one hour of music, which I was to compose, orchestrate, and also conduct. I rationalized about the *Clarinet Concerto*: since I had not been able to find a theme for the second movement, it would be a good idea to put it aside temporarily.

I left for the San Fernando Valley at the beginning of February 1948 to work on *The Red Pony.* Lewis Milestone (with whom I had worked on *Of Mice and Men* and *The North Star*) was producer and director for *The Red Pony.* The cast included Myrna Loy, Robert Mitchum, Louis Calhern, Shepperd Strudwick, and Peter Miles. Steinbeck's well-known tale is a series of vignettes concerning a ten-year-old boy and his life on a California ranch. It is not a typical Western with gunmen and Indians. There is a minimum of action of a dramatic or startling kind. The story gets its warmth and sensitive quality from the character studies of the boy Tom, his grandfather, the cowhand Billy Buck, and Tom's parents, the Tiflins. The kind of emotions that Steinbeck evokes in his story are basically musical ones, since they deal with the unexpressed feelings of daily living.

In directing *The Red Pony*, Milestone left plenty of room for musical treatment, which made the writing of the score a gratifying task. The principal restriction of most movie scores is having to write in small two- or three-minute forms. *The Red Pony* offered larger opportunities, such as a six-minute sequence describing a fight with a vulture, for which I composed dissonant music with complicated rhythms. This was more readily accepted for enhancing a dramatic situation in a film than it would have been in the concert hall. Much of the story called for simple harmonies and clear melodies and, of course, some of the inevitable steady rhythmic accompaniment to simulate cowboys on horseback. Searching through my notebooks of musical ideas, I came across "kids' music" written for the unproduced musical *Tragic Ground.* It was ideal for *The Red Pony.*

I always found that relating music to a picture was a stimulus rather than a restriction. It set the imagination going. But I had to be moved by what I saw on the screen, and I was never moved when a film had too much sheen or when the style was overly dramatic. *The*

[36] Copland's income in 1947 was $17,473—up slightly from 1946.

Above: Publicity release for *The Red Pony*
Right: Copland on the set of *The Red Pony* with Peter Miles, who played the role of Tom

Red Pony had none of that. It was not a pathbreaker or an epic type of film, but it was moving in a quiet way. My aim was to compose music that would not obtrude and that would reflect what I saw. It was a challenge to think up instrumental colors to suit a particular situation: when the pony is being operated on and the little boy winces painfully, I used three bass clarinets to match the dramatic situation; and for Tom and his school friends, I came up with the instrumentation of toy trumpet and tuba. The only problem I had with *The Red Pony* was that it was shot on the same ranch that was used for *Of Mice and Men.* Now I ask you: If you had to look at the same landscape every day, could you think up different music?

I did not like what I heard from Harold Clurman about the political situation building up in Hollywood as a result of the Cold War, but I was totally removed from all that in the San Fernando Valley, and my schedule was very concentrated and demanding. I had to come up with fifty-two minutes of orchestrated music in eight weeks and be ready to record it during the last two weeks of my contract. All of my efforts were directed toward that purpose, so I had no direct contact with any of the red-baiting that Clurman had written me about before I went out to California (25 October 1947):

> Of course none of this is funny, but how can one not laugh? On the Hanns E. [Eisler] case—please let me use your name for a protest from musicians.[37] Even Stravinsky says he will sign a protest if it goes to the authorities . . . but not to the press. Lenny says he will sign every protest—public and private—and says all the composers, conductors, etc. will follow suit—especially if Aaron signs.

I agreed to lend my name for the Eisler benefit. While I was working on *The Red Pony*, I heard from Harold again (17 February 1948): "How do you like Hollywood in these sour days?" Later (March), he wrote, "I'm glad that you're for Wallace . . . the [Eisler] benefit 'tho too long, went off well. Good reviews by D. D. [Diamond] and V. T. [Thomson] but poor Eisler is still in a jam. Olin Downes is trying to get Toscanini to get Eisler a visa."

The Red Pony was not a commercially successful film. The critics admired certain aspects, one being the musical score, but since the film was not widely distributed, the music was rarely heard. When Efrem Kurtz, newly appointed conductor of the Houston Symphony Orchestra, asked whether I would accept a commission for a work to be premiered by his orchestra, I suggested a suite to be drawn from the film. In reshaping the score, I recast much of the musical material to achieve continuity for concert purposes, although all the music in the twenty-four-minute suite may be heard in the film.[38] It breaks down into six sections: "Morning on the Ranch"; "The Gift"; "Dream March and Circus Music"; "Walk to the Bunkhouse"; "Grandfather's Story"; and "Happy Ending." Although some of the melodies in *The Red Pony* may sound rather folklike, except for a tinge of "So long, Old Paint," they are actually mine. *The Red Pony Suite* is dedicated to my friend Erik Johns, and was premiered by Kurtz with the Houston Symphony (30 October 1948).[39]

When *The Red Pony Suite* was about to be recorded, I wrote to John Steinbeck asking for a commentary to be used with the music. He responded (17 July 1964):

> The music for *The Red Pony* is very beautiful. I wish the picture could have been as good. Except for the music, I am not unpleased that this film, to the best of my knowledge, is still held as hostage in a bank vault. I am glad that the suite is not a captive—your suggestion that I write some kind of commentary for the music also pleases me very much and I would like very much to do it. I would also be happy to narrate it on tape, at least for you to decide whether I can do it well enough. However, you are holding the baton on this.

[37] Composer and political activist Hanns Eisler (brother of communist Gerhart Eisler) was active in the Composers' Collective in the thirties.

[38] Bernard Herrmann conducted the LSO in the first performance in England, a BBC broadcast in 1956. For materials relating to *The Red Pony,* see the Library of Congress: film "open score," pencil with cues written in, such as "He let him die" and "dissolve to stable," measures numbered in red pencil, dated "Jan 29–March 26, 1948"; ink score for *Suite from the Red Pony* ("Childrens' " crossed out on title page). For onionskin masters of conductor's score and parts, see Brigham Young University, Republic Pictures Collection.

[39] Andor Foldes wrote to Copland asking permission to make a piano arrangement from *The Red Pony,* but it was never realized. A band suite was arranged by Copland from the last four movements of the orchestral version. The first performance was by the U.S. Navy Band, Anthony A. Mitchell conducting at the Midwest Band Clinic, Chicago (December 1968).

However, when I suggested that the version with his commentary be for children, Steinbeck balked. He explained (September 22):

> This is an old theme with me. The reason I have never written books for children is not because of the children but because of the so-called adults who choose what books may be printed for children. Children have nearly always understood my work—and yours. It is only critics and sophisticates who do not. . . . Children have always understood the little book *The Red Pony.* They have been saddened by it, as I was when it happened to me, but they have not been destroyed by it. . . . When you wrote this suite, being an artist and therefore automatically truthful, you let the sombre come into your music to balance the gaiety and to give it proportion and significance. And children surely understand that as they understand form, being instructed by heartbeat and morning and night. In your original music, I remember that you had a passage which covered an owl's sweep down on a rabbit and you had a fantastic passage during the fight of Jody with the buzzard, which was of course man's defiance of death. Children think a great deal about death, much more than adults do, for to the idcentric child his own death is the death of the world. . . . What I am trying to say, I guess, is that if you want a children's version, you must get someone else to write it for you. Surely you may use my notes as you wish, but sometime I would hope that you will let a group of children hear a "children's version" and soon after hear mine, and judge for yourself, their reaction. . . Sorry to be so vehement, but this is one of my strong feelings.

After Steinbeck's letter, I gave up the idea of a narration, but I did call *The Red Pony* "a suite for children," since the music and action were intended to come from a child's point of view.[40]

My first spring at Sneden's Landing was glorious. Instead of getting back to work on the *Clarinet Concerto,* I relaxed and used the remaining time before Tanglewood to put together *Four Piano Blues.* I composed one new "Blues," which, when put together with three others written at various times, formed the suite.[41] None of the pieces is very difficult. Each is dedicated to a pianist with some special connection to my piano music: Leo Smit, Andor Foldes, William Kapell, and John Kirkpatrick. The order of *Four Blues* does not follow the order of composition.[42] The first performance was by Leo Smit in a League of Composers concert in New York (13 March 1950).

I finally finished the *Clarinet Concerto* after the 1948 Tanglewood season. It is about sixteen and one-half minutes long and dedicated to Benny Goodman. Goodman had commissioned a work by Bartók in 1938 and from Hindemith in 1947, the same year he approached me. I never would have thought of composing a clarinet concerto if Benny had not asked me for one. I can't play a single note on the instrument! Other than my arrangement of the *Short Symphony* as the *Sextet,* in which clarinet is one of the featured instruments, the only experience I had with clarinet writing was orchestral parts. I had long been an admirer of

[40] For a television presentation, narrations were arranged by Katherine Rosen (18 March 1973).

[41] Ink transparencies are at the Library of Congress. A cover page indicates in pencil a tentative title—"In the American Grain/Pieces for Piano." Pencil sketches include *Three Blues.* One page contains the title *Five Sentimental Melodies* (1926), and sketch pages for "III" are dated in two places: "22 Jan 47" and "4 Jan 48."

[42] *Blues No. 1* (1947) is dedicated to Leo Smit; *Blues No. 2* (1934), to Andor Foldes; *Blues No. 3* (1948), to William Kapell; *Blues No. 4* (1926), to John Kirkpatrick.

Manuscript page of the original coda of the *Clarinet Concerto*; changes suggested by Goodman written in pencil. The memo at the top reads: "1st version—later revised—of Coda of *Clarinet Concerto* (too difficult for Benny Goodman)."

Benny Goodman, and I thought that writing a concerto with him in mind would give me a fresh point of view. We did not work together while I was composing the piece, but after it was finished and sent off, Benny wrote to thank me and to say: "With a little editing, I know we will have a good piece." When we played it through together, he had clarinetist David Oppenheim around for moral support. I had written the last page too high, so it had to come down a step. Benny made a few other suggestions—one concerned a high note in the cadenza (I knew Benny could reach that high because I had listened to his recordings). He explained that although he could comfortably reach that high when playing jazz for an audience, he might not be able to if he had to read it from a score or for a recording. Therefore, we changed it.[43]

The first movement of the *Clarinet Concerto* is a languid song form composed in 3/4 time, rather unusual for me, but the theme seemed to call for it. The second movement, a free rondo form, is a contrast in style—stark, severe, and jazzy. The movements are connected by a cadenza, which gives the soloist considerable opportunity to demonstrate his prowess, while at the same time introduces fragments of the melodic material to be heard in the second movement. The cadenza is written fairly close to the way I wanted it, but it is free within reason—after all, it and the movement that follows are in the jazz idiom. It is not ad lib as in cadenzas of many traditional concertos; I always felt that there was enough room for interpretation even when everything is written out. Some of the second movement material represents an unconscious fusion of elements obviously related to North and South American popular music: Charleston rhythms, boogie woogie, and Brazilian folk tunes. The instrumentation being clarinet with strings, harp, and piano, I did not have a large battery of percussion to achieve jazzy effects, so I used slapping basses and whacking harp sounds to simulate them. The *Clarinet Concerto* ends with a fairly elaborate coda in C major that finishes off with a clarinet glissando—or "smear" in jazz lingo.

I assumed that Benny would schedule a performance soon after the work was finished, but almost a year later, he wrote (14 February 1949), "I'm terribly disappointed about not being able to perform the concerto May 10th but obviously with my present state of affairs I would be silly to take on such an important job at this time. [Goodman had a virus infection and was also changing management.] I am anxious to play the concerto in public and I will put in a lot of hard work with Ingolf Dahl in L.A.; meanwhile I'll keep in touch with you until we find the opportune time to perform it." I made a tape recording of the score for two pianos and sent it off to Benny. The premiere of the *Clarinet Concerto* finally took place 6 November 1950, Fritz Reiner conducting the NBC Symphony of the Air from the NBC studios.

[43] The first version of the "coda" cadenza is at the Library of Congress, with a memo by Copland: "too difficult for Benny Goodman." Faint pencil jottings are on a second version, which became the published version. See also pencil score of 57 pages showing first movement (almost complete) and second with changes and deletions, dated "Dec 1945/Feb 1946." Also a rough pencil sketch score is dated "Feb 20 46/Aug" with the first-movement title "Pas de deux." This score is paginated 58-87, with some pages blank and others of solo clarinet writing.

[44] Interview, Benny Goodman with Perlis (telephone), 24 March 1984.

Benny Goodman[44]

I made no demands on what Copland should write. He had completely free rein, except that I should have a two-year exclusivity on playing the work. I paid two thousand dollars and that's real money. At that time, there were not too many American composers to pick from people of such terrific status—as Hindemith and Bartók. I recall that Aaron came to listen when I was recording with Bartók. Copland had a great reputation also. I didn't choose him because some of his works were jazz-inspired. In my mind, the Clarinet Concerto *was related to the ballet because of the 3/4 time in the first movement. We never had much trouble except for a little fracas about the spot before the cadenza where he had written a repetition of some phrase. I was a little sticky about leaving it out—it was when the viola was the echo to give the clarinet a cue. But I think Aaron finally did leave it out. The work is difficult for the players, especially the rhythms. We were fortunate to get Fritz Reiner to do the premiere. Aaron and I played the concerto quite a few times with him conducting, and we made two recordings.*

Our first recording was for Columbia with the Columbia String Orchestra, but it's the second recording we made in the sixties that's the best. Once when I was in Rome at the American Academy in the fifties, I played Aaron's concerto with a friend of his at the piano. The kid surprised me by knowing how to play jazz! [Harold Shapero].[45] *A lot of clarinetists have played Copland's* Clarinet Concerto *by now, all the best ones, and all over the world. Of the concertos I commissioned, the Copland is performed most. It's a very popular piece. Aaron and I did it out of town, but not in New York until 1960 at Carnegie Hall [17 November]. That was something! We played it with the Cleveland Orchestra [1968], and in L.A. in the seventies. I've always felt good about that commission and about playing the* Clarinet Concerto *with Aaron conducting.*

Lenny Bernstein had wanted to conduct the premiere of the *Clarinet Concerto* at Tanglewood, and he wrote from Israel, where he was conducting the Israel Philharmonic (21 May 1951): "I fought with Kouss valiantly over the *Clarinet Concerto*, to no avail. Benny and Tanglewood don't mix in his mind. By the way, here in Israel, BG means Ben-Gurion." At about the same time, Koussevitzky telephoned me to suggest I arrange the first movement for full orchestra and call it "Elegy." And he told me he wanted it for BSO performances in December 1950. I agreed at first, but then after sober reflection, I had to write my feelings to him (29 August):

> Dear Sergei Alexandrovitch: Ever since our telephone conversation about the *Clarinet Concerto* arrangement the thought has been growing in my mind that I made a mistake. You can understand how easy it would be for me to make such a mistake: my natural desire to please you and the thought of the wonderful interpretation you could give such a piece and the suddenness of your definite proposal and your persuasiveness on the telephone. . . . I am convinced that it takes away from the integrity of the concerto as I originally conceived it, and I am basically

[45] See interview, Harold Shapero with Perlis: "It was terrific. He played his head off. I remember telling Benny when he got to the interlude, 'You're supposed to swing it. It's written for you, you know.' So he said, 'Yeah? You think so?' Benny was very resistant to criticism of any kind. He did loosen it up. When we got done with the performance, he said, 'Okay, kid, now tell me how to play jazz.'

Benny Goodman and Copland at rehearsal of the *Clarinet Concerto* with the Los Angeles Philharmonic, c. 1970

> unwilling to do that—at least until the work has had a chance through several seasons to make its own way as a complete concerto. . . . I know this decision will not make you happy, but try to see it from my point of view, and you will realize that it makes me even less happy.

The concert premiere of the *Clarinet Concerto* (Reiner's was a radio broadcast) was by the Philadelphia Orchestra, Ormandy conducting, Ralph McLane as soloist (28 November 1950). Early reviews were not overwhelmingly enthusiastic; in fact, one might call them lukewarm. The piece was described as "lightweight." Virgil wrote in the *Herald Tribune*, "It sounds as if some essential explanation were lacking, as if a ballet or a film belonging to it had been left out." The fate of a piece of music is a curious thing—so much depends on the first reception. But with the *Clarinet Concerto,* after a somewhat inauspicious send-off, it has become one of my most frequently performed works and a standard for clarinetists. Gervase de Peyer has performed and recorded it, as well as other outstanding soloists, like Harold Wright, Stanley Drucker, Richard Stoltzman, and David Glazer. I always thought that it would help if a player had some knowledge of jazz, yet when jazz clarinetist Johnny Dankworth attempted the *Clarinet Concerto* in concert, he ran into difficulty. It was the recordings Benny and I made that garnered the good notices and really launched the *Clarinet Concerto.* I was pleased when we had the chance to do a second recording—the first had been one of my earliest as conductor, and I was concerned that I had conducted the first movement too slowly.

During a year abroad in 1951, I conducted the *Clarinet Concerto* in London, Rome, and Trieste. European orchestras enjoyed the novelty and audiences appeared genuinely welcoming. Gradually, the piece grew in popularity, so that when Lenny Bernstein took the New York Philharmonic to Japan for eleven concerts as part of Expo 70, it was the only American composition on the schedule. The Philharmonic received an overwhelming reception in Japan—in Osaka and Tokyo—where, according to *The New York Times* (10 Sept 1970):

> Leonard Bernstein tossed his baton to the crowd in exultation. The audience of 2,400 brought the orchestra's first-chair clarinetist Stanley Drucker back for four curtain calls. . . . After eight minutes of applause, he [Bernstein] motioned for silence and declared in Japanese: "We are delighted, very happy."

When we were planning the second recording, Benny played the *Clarinet Concerto* for Yale clarinetist Keith Wilson and asked his advice. Years later, I was in New Haven to conduct, and Vivian Perlis took me to Wilson's master class at Yale (1980).[46] They had all studied my piece and had no trouble "swinging," where swinging was called for. The students asked questions and took my picture, while I put on my "Mt. Rushmore" look. One young clarinetist asked whether I would compose another clarinet concerto for them, and I answered laughingly, "I wish I could!"

I had made a clarinet and piano version for rehearsals with Benny, which has been used occasionally for concerts, something I had not foreseen. When I heard it, I thought it stood up well, so the clarinet and piano arrangement was published. I am told that the clarinet glissando at the end is much more difficult without the orchestra to back up the soloist.

My friend, pianist Bob Fizdale, told Jerome Robbins that the recording of the *Clarinet Concerto* was out, and when Jerry heard it, he asked me whether he could use it for a ballet. I admired Jerry's work and told him to go ahead. The ballet is called *The Pied Piper*, and Jerry said he did in the dance what he heard in my music.[47] The Piper is the clarinetist and he wanders around on stage, and then parks himself on a high stool. At the end of the ballet, a large group of dancers participate in a kind of conga line behind the Piper. I am told that once, when the ballet was performed on tour, a clarinetist simply refused to be onstage, and George Balanchine had to go up and pantomime the part while the clarinetist played it from the pit!

The Pied Piper had its world premiere at the New York City Center (4 December 1951).[48] It was well received in New York, Washington, and even in Paris in 1952. Genet's (Janet Flanner) "Letter from Paris" in *The New Yorker* included the following in her review of a dance program (31 May 1952):

> In the end, it was *Pied Piper*, here titled *Le Joueur de Flute*, with Jerome Robbins' choreography and dancing and Aaron Copland's brilliant, lyric, jazzed music, that really took the cake. After the final curtain, the packed house broke into a rare pandemonium of laughter, applause, and bravos.

[46] The class session was taped, see miscellaneous tapes, Oral History of American Music, Yale.

[47] Interview, Jerome Robbins with Perlis, 10 August 1981, New York City.

[48] The principal dancers were Jerome Robbins, Diana Adams, Nicholas Magallanes, Jiliana, Roy Tobias, Melissa Hayden, Herbert Bliss, and Tanaquil LeClerq.

I had not intended to return to Hollywood soon after *The Red Pony*, but when I heard through my agent, Abe Meyer, that producer-director William Wyler of Paramount Pictures was looking for a composer for *The Heiress*, I could not help but be interested. The film script was based on a stage play by Ruth and Augustus Goetz, which had been derived from the nineteenth-century novel *Washington Square* by Henry James. I had read the novel and seen the play on Broadway, starring Wendy Hiller in the principal role. The cast of the film included Olivia de Havilland, Sir Ralph Richardson, Montgomery Clift, and Miriam Hopkins. The plot is about a plain young heiress who, after falling in love with a handsome and ambitious young man, agrees to marry him against the wishes of her father, who suspects that the gentleman is after his daughter's inheritance.

Since the drama is more concerned with the psychological relationships between the characters than with external action, I felt that the music might be an important element. Abe Meyer sent me the film script with a note (14 May 1948):

> After you have read the script, Wyler would like you to write him your ideas about the treatment of the music. While I believe that he has great confidence and respect for your musical judgment, I got the feeling that there was a slight question in his mind as to how your music, which is predominantly modern, could be fit into a period picture.

After giving considerable thought to the type of musical score I envisioned for *The Heiress*, I wrote to Wyler:

> In my opinion, the picture does not call for a great deal of music, but what it includes, ought to really count. It should contribute to the tone and style of the picture. My fear is that a conventionally written score would bathe the work in the usual romantic atmosphere. What I would try for would be the recreation in musical terms of the special atmosphere inherent in the James original. That atmosphere—as I see it—would produce a music of a certain discretion and refinement in the expression of sentiments.[49]

I saw certain similarities in *The Heiress* to what I had encountered when composing the score for *Our Town*, where it was necessary to recreate the feeling of life in a typical New Hampshire town around 1900. My method then had been not merely to confine myself to the harmonies and melodies of the period but to make use of every resource in order to suggest the essence of a particular time and place. I hoped to do the same for *The Heiress.*

Wyler responded favorably to my ideas and comments (19 June 1948):

> Naturally, I would not be so mechanical in my thinking as to throw out any music which postdates the technique and development of music up to 1850. I, too, want to take advantage of the growth in music during the past hundred years and create the feeling and emotion of the past through proper use of modern musical resources.

[49] See Copland's files in the Library of Congress for pencil draft of Copland's letter to Wyler.

PARAMOUNT PICTURES INC.
WEST COAST STUDIOS
5451 MARATHON STREET — HOLLYWOOD 38, CALIF.
TELEPHONE HOLLYWOOD 2411 — CABLE ADDRESS "FAMFILM"

June 19, 1948

Dear Mr. Copland:

Thank you for your letter of May 29th. Of course, I am "still interested" in having you compose the score for THE HEIRESS. Please do not let the fact of my not having answered more promptly mislead you as to that. I start shooting Monday, June 21st, and as you can imagine, the past few weeks have been very rushed for me.

Our present schedule indicates that we will finish shooting by Labor Day, and allowing a reasonable time for editing, I should say the picture should be ready for scoring by the last week in September. Once I know definitely, I shall let you know.

I agree with what you say abou the "conventionally written score" and feel that a special Jamesian tone of discretion and refinement is necessary for THE HEIRESS. Naturally, I would not be so mechanical in my thinking as to throw out any music which postdates the technique and development of music up to 1850. I, too, want to take advantage of the growth in music during the past hundred years and create the feeling and emotion of the past through proper use of modern musical resources.

As for the arrangements between you and Paramount, I have spoken to Mr. Louis Lipstone, the head of the Music Department here at the Studio, and he informs me that he will contact your agent at MCA. As you know, I do not have any hand in settling the terms, or drawing up the contract, but the proper people will, I am sure, get to work on that immediately.

Meanwhile, I am enclosing a copy of the final screenplay for your use. Please let me know if you have specific suggestions for any scenes regarding music. You may have some thoughts which I ought to bear in mind while shooting, such as allowing enough time for music, etc.

I really am looking forward to our association in the Fall, and I hope that if you have any questions or suggestions you will keep in touch with me.

Kindest regards.

Sincerely,

William Wyler

WW:es

Mr. Aaron Copland
Palisades
Rockland County, New York

Copland and William Wyler, Hollywood, 1948

By mid-July 1948, a contract had been signed, and the final script arrived while I was teaching at Tanglewood. Along with it, Wyler sent along a song, "Plaisir d'Amour," by the eighteenth-century composer Giovanni Martini,[50] which was to be sung by the male lead character, Morris Townsend. Wyler wrote (24 July):

> I feel that it is a charming song and comes off very well in the scene as shot. I believe you can use this song to advantage in the score, not literally, but possibly as thematic material for the scoring of the love scenes, the scene of the jilt, and the final sequence between Catherine and Morris.

Before turning a film over to the music department, Wyler liked to hold sneak previews without music. Depending on the reactions, he made changes and did retakes. *The Heiress* fell behind schedule, and therefore, I did not have to leave for Hollywood until mid-November. The first thing I did, of course, was see the picture. The initial viewing by the composer is a solemn moment—after all, he will have to live with the film for at least several weeks. The solemnity is emphasized by the exclusive audience that usually views the picture with the composer: producer, director, musical director of the studio, picture editor, music cutter; in fact, everyone involved. It is difficult for the composer to view the photoplay coldly, and there is an understandable compulsion to like everything. What a relief it was to see that *The Heiress* was really very good!

The film was still not finished, which meant that I could collect ideas and start composing without feeling rushed. After a few weeks, I was given half the picture to score. I wrote Victor, who was taking care of my affairs back in Sneden's Landing (14 November 1948), "I am to try for a Dec. 26th recording date if possible—looks like a hectic Christmas for me." I worked from a script with timings and cues for the musical sequences. These were indicated by titles derived from the plot ("Cherry Red Dress," "Early Morning Visitor," "Morris Suggests Love," and so forth.)[51] I saw no reason not to use whatever period music I could to strengthen the score (mazurkas, polkas, and waltzes), with the idea of weaving them into original music composed in nineteenth-century style.[52] My plan was to give each principal character a musical motive, leitmotiv style, to be developed as the drama unfolds; these themes were to be introduced in a "Prelude" during the opening titles.

I was not finding composing for *The Heiress* as easy as I had hoped. For one thing, there were no outdoor scenes, which would have given me the opportunity to compose music with a wide instrumental range, as in *The Red Pony*. Also, I'd never before written a really grown-up love scene (*Our Town* had a boy and girl affair and *The North Star* a young kind of kiss), but in *The Heiress*, I had to figure out what to do when the lovers embrace à la Tristan and Isolde. It seems that nobody has invented a new way to compose love music! I was surrounded by popular songwriters at the studio who were turning the tune "Plaisir d'Amour" into a pop song for general propaganda. I saw very little of William Wyler, but more of his assistant, Lester Konig. The secretaries at the studio tended to address me as "Dr. Copland," in spite of my protests. Everyone on the set said that, although *The Heiress* was a wonderful film, it would make no money because it was a serious and mature drama.

By mid-December, I had only about eight minutes of music ready to record. It was a mad scramble to finish by the end of the month. I could not judge the finished product because I'd never heard the music played in sequence from start to finish, but I sensed that the score had some good spots along with the ones that sounded movie-like. Wyler seemed very pleased with what he heard on the recording stage, but he wanted to try the film at one of those little neighborhood theaters where people don't know they are going to see a new picture.

Copland working on the film score for *The Heiress*

[50] Martini (1741-1816) was the pen name for Johann Schwartzendorf. "Plaisir d'Amour" was composed by Martini and Jean Florian.

[51] See Copland's files for photocopies of two-piano score with markings toward the orchestration by Copland, orchestrator Nathan Van Cleave. It includes the following sections: "Prelude;" "Cherry Red Dress;" "Virginia Reel," featuring "Galop de Bravura by Jules Schulhoff;" "Mazurka No. 1," incorporating "Gaetana" and "First Love Mazurka" by E. Ketterer, arranged by Van Cleave and George Parrish; "Polka No. 1," using "Coquette Polka" by Charles D'Albert; "Gavotte" by F. Joseph Gossec, arranged by Copland; "Waltz No. 2," using "Queen of the Flowers" by Ketterer; "Fortune Hunting," based on the folk song "Ching-a-Ring Chaw," arranged by Copland; "Dream Gavotte," composed by Gossec, arranged by Copland; "Early Morning Visitor"; "Morris Suggests Love," using "Plaisir d'Amour," arranged by Copland. Additional cues: "Proposal," "Catherine's Engagement," "The Appointment," "The Departure," "Paris," "Reunion with Morris—Parts I and II," "A Plan to Elope—Parts I and II," "Anticipation," "Love Not Consoled," "A Defeated Catherine," "new Intro: To Love," "Doctor's Examination," "A Sick Doctor," "Intro: A Sick Doctor," "A New Catherine," "Washington Square," "Five Years Later," "Morris Returns," "Morris Unmasked," "Catherine's Triumph," "The Bolted Door," "Cast," "Three Irish Reels (Fiddlin Silas, Miss McCloud's Reel, The Pioneer)," "My Love Loves Me," adapted from "Plaisir d'Amour." See Library of Congress for bound scrapbook engraved with gold lettering: "Presented to LC by Paramount Pictures Corp., Hollywood, Ca.," dated 30 November 1948; also: Wyler's revision dated 20 January 1949; timings; script.

[52] Copland wrote his own mazurka, waltz, and polka. The polka was played by hand organ.

There is a scene in the film where the young lovers, who are disapproved of by the girl's father, decide to go off and get married right there and then. It's close to midnight and the young man leaves to get ready and promises to return soon. A carriage is heard approaching and she goes out to greet it. To her disappointment, it passes. After this happens several times, and it is getting quite late, she finally has to admit to herself that he is not going to return—she's been jilted. The situation was ideal for a composer because nobody is saying much, so there is little conversation to get in your way. She is all excited—"he is coming, he is coming!"—and I had written a very romantic kind of music, expressing her emotions. Well, when they took the film out for the sneak preview and that scene was played, at the moment Olivia de Havilland realizes that her bridegroom is not in the passing carriage, the audience burst into laughter! Wyler came up to me after the film ended and said, "Copland, you've got to do something about that scene, because if the audience laughs at her then, they'll never take her seriously, and we won't have a picture! We might as well go home and forget the whole thing." I protested, "But how can I stop an audience from laughing?" He said, "I don't care how you do it, but do something to stop them from laughing."

I began to wonder whether I could stop an audience from laughing. It was certainly worth a try. So I threw out the music I had written and substituted a completely different kind, much more dissonant than you normally hear in a motion-picture theater. Fortunately, I had taken my notebook with musical ideas along to Hollywood, and I found something I thought I could use for that crucial scene when Catherine is jilted by her lover. (It was, of all things, a variation originally composed for my *Piano Variations* of 1929. It had not fit into the *Variations* at the time, but it worked well when adapted for the film.) They brought in an entire orchestra—at considerable expense—to record about three minutes of the new music. Then they took the film out for another showing, played the same scene, and there wasn't a sound in the house! I'm sure the audience didn't even know they were listening to music, except for the few musical ones who were there, but it worked on them anyway. It created the kind of tension Wyler had intended for that scene. Clearly nothing could be considered funny with that dissonant, rather unpleasant-sounding music going on!

Wyler had relied on the camera and the music to take over in several segments where dialogue was abandoned altogether. During those silent close-ups, I found that the use of a ground or passacaglia bass could generate a feeling of continuity and inevitability, as well as provide the necessary dissonance when combined with other music. For example, when Catherine realizes her fiance has abandoned her, she cries out to her aunt, "Morris must love me for all those who have not." The dialogue stops, the two women sit silently, and the music takes over. I used a theme heard during Catherine and Morris' love scene over a pedal in the basses. Late in the film, when the embittered Catherine confronts her ailing father, I made use of the instrumentation of three bass clarinets, which had worked well in *The Red Pony*.

When recording *The Heiress*, I saw no reason not to make use of "Hollywood tricks." In fact, I was interested in trying out techniques that were not customarily used on the concert stage. One was called "sweetening"—a technique Benny Herrmann had used in several

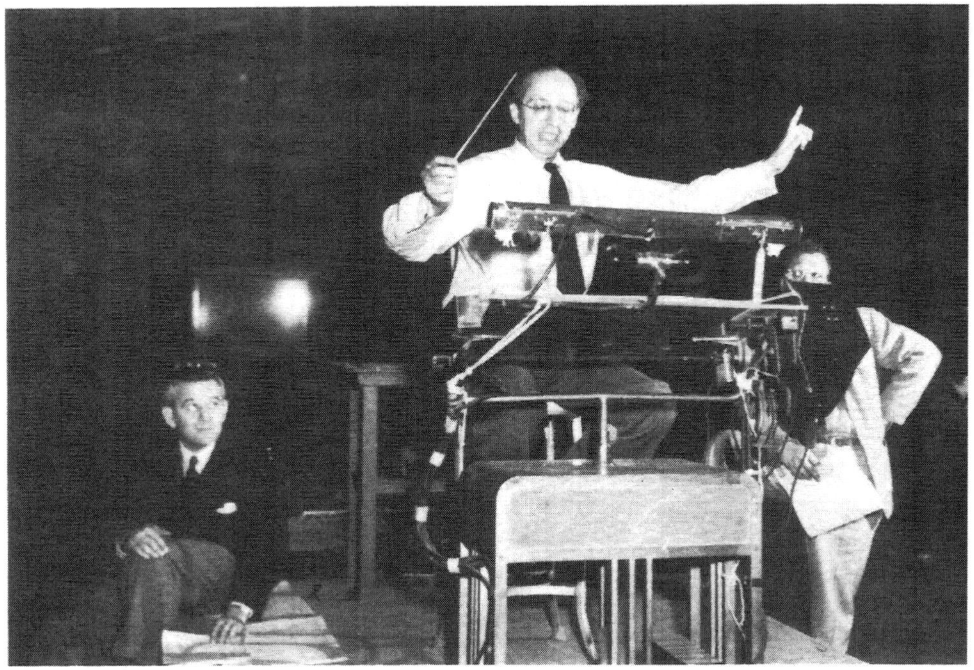

Copland conducting the studio orchestra during a recording session of music for *The Heiress*. William Wyler is seated at the left

films. The music is recorded first with full orchestra, and then it is recorded again using only the strings. When both are used together, the string sound is considerably altered. I found this effective for the end of *The Heiress* when the dramatic situation called for an intense sound.

I had not objected to using the song "Plaisir d'Amour" in the film, and I even adapted it in my own style after it was heard in its original form.[53] I balked, however, when I was asked to ditch my title music and make an arrangement of the tune instead. I had the right to refuse, but it seems that the producers had the right to ask someone else to arrange the title music. After the score had been completely finished and recorded and I had returned to New York, I learned that "Plaisir d'Amour" had been inserted into my title music![54] All I could do was to issue a statement to the press disclaiming responsibility for that part of

[53] See Copland's files, "curiosity" folder, for correspondence from Joseph C. Keeley, editor, *The American Legion Magazine*, questioning why Copland, rather than Martini, was credited with the music in *The Heiress*. See also responses by Mort Nathanson, Copland, and Louis Lipstone.

[54] See score (photocopy) in Copland's files for two versions of the "Prelude": Copland's original, dated "30 Nov 1948"; and one marked in pencil, "after my departure from Hollywood," with Copland's name crossed out and dated "22 January 1949." In fact, the version arranged after Copland left Hollywood segues to bar 26 of the original version, so both were used.

The first page of Copland's original version of the title music for *The Heiress*, with suggested instrumentation penciled in by the composer

The first page of the title music for *The Heiress* as changed by the studio (after forty-one measures, the film score returns to measure twenty-six of Copland's original version)

the score. It was a disagreeable incident that marred an otherwise satisfying collaboration. I had invited Lawrence Morton to be present at the recording sessions, and after he heard what happened, he wrote to me about my original title music: "It is not pretty, perhaps, as is its substitute, but it is certainly much more relevant to the film that Wyler produced."

The world premiere of *The Heiress* took place at Radio City Music Hall in New York City (6 October 1949). Dimitri Tiomkin, Max Steiner, and I were nominated for an Academy Award in 1950. When I won, I was told that it was the only instance of a score winning an Oscar after having been shorn of its overture, the part of a score that usually makes the strongest impact. I heard from Ingolf Dahl from Los Angeles (24 March 1950):

> At last Oscar has found a worthy home—congratulations! We are terribly happy about the fact that sometimes (all too rarely) Hollywood shows good sense. Etta and I were fully determined to walk down Hollywood Boulevard with picket signs in case Tiomkin had received the award! This gives me also an opportunity to tell you how deeply impressed I was with *The Heiress* music. The main title, of which I was forewarned, was a scandal.

While in Hollywood for *The Heiress*, I rented a small house in Los Angeles. I saw Lawrence Morton and Ingolf Dahl frequently, and other colleagues occasionally: Poulenc, when he came to visit in December; Roy Harris, who was on the scene part of the time; and Stravinsky, who invited me to his home for dinner one evening. I did a few lectures at UCLA. Alfred Wallenstein asked me to attend rehearsals and the performance of my *Third Symphony* by the Los Angeles Philharmonic, and I even did some conducting myself. The studio musicians were so bored playing movie scores, they had formed an orchestra for their playing pleasure and invited me to conduct *Appalachian Spring* and *Statements*.

When I needed some secretarial assistance, I asked a young dancer, Erik Johns, whom I had first met in New York, to help me out. We became friends and enjoyed exploring California together when I was not working on the picture. Between finishing the recording, the dubbing, and the next preview, we drove to San Diego, where we spent New Year's Eve and had a few days' vacation in Ensenada, Mexico. Erik traveled back east with me on The Super Chief at the beginning of 1949.

I never worked in Hollywood after *The Heiress*—perhaps they gave me the cold shoulder because of my critical statement to the press after my title music was changed. Also, I may have been on the boycott lists as the Cold War escalated. I did have a few offers, among them one from William Wyler, who was very anxious to have me do the score for *The Big Country*, but I was not able to fit it into my schedule. In the fifties and sixties, Hollywood productions became more commercial and less artistic, and I was outspoken about the movie studios not bringing in fresh blood from the outside.

I have often been questioned about whether I liked writing movie music, the implication being that it was possibly degrading for a composer of symphonies to trifle with a commercial product. "Would you do it anyhow, even if it paid less well?" asked one interviewer. My answer was that I would, and moreover, that I thought most composers would, principally because film music constitutes a musical medium with a fascination all its own. At the time I was composing for films, I believed that it was a new form of dramatic music, related to opera, ballet, and theater music, and that it should be explored for its own unique possibilities. From Hollywood, when I was working on *The Heiress*, I wrote an article for *The New York Times* stating my position: "Someday the term 'movie music' will clearly define a specific musical genre and will not have, as it does nowadays, a pejorative meaning."[55]

[55] Copland, "Tip to Moviegoers: Take Off Those Ear-Muffs," *The New York Times Magazine*, 6 November 1949, 28-32. See also Frederick W. Sternfeld, "Copland as Film Composer," *Musical Quarterly*, XXXVII:2 (April 1951), 161-75.

INTERLUDE VII

The summers at Tanglewood from 1946 to Koussevitzky's death in 1951 made a lasting impression on those fortunate enough to have been there. Many people have had the experience of a brief period of time (perhaps college or the war) of such intensity and concentration as to affect an entire lifetime. The Koussevitzky years at Tanglewood held that quality—from the youngest musician to the most senior faculty, everyone had the sense of something wonderful happening all the time. Koussevitzky's vitality, idealism, and dedication were contagious. Composer Jacob Druckman said about his student years at Tanglewood: "It was exciting, exhilarating, glamorous to be in the same place every day with the likes of Koussevitzky, Aaron, Lenny, Lukas—everyone you saw was someone you had heard about and admired. It was a young musician's dream come true."[1]

For Copland, it was the three years he spent in Paris as a young man in the twenties that proved to have the most powerful influence on his life; after Paris, the Koussevitzky summers at Tanglewood were most memorable. In Paris, Copland had come into contact with the two major influences on his musical life—Boulanger and Koussevitzky. At Tanglewood, Copland's relationship with Koussevitzky matured. Other close friendships, as well as many contacts in the music world, were made and strengthened by Copland at Tanglewood in the forties. Moreover, it was the only place Koussevitzky, Copland, and Bernstein had the opportunity to be together over an extended time.

The Berkshire Music Center, which had opened in 1940, was officially closed after the 1942 season because of the war, but Serge Koussevitzky, its founder and director, had been determined to keep Tanglewood alive.[2] When the Boston Symphony Orchestra board voted not to allocate funds, Koussevitzky arranged for "minifestivals" to be supported by the Koussevitzky Music Foundation, which had been established in 1942 in memory of Koussevitzky's wife, Natalie.[3] The reopening of Tanglewood in 1946 signaled the rebirth of the arts in America. A summer festival of such magnitude as Tanglewood was unique outside of Europe. For several years, until other organizations followed suit, Tanglewood had little competition for the best students and players.[4]

Koussevitzky welcomed students and faculty, and Randall Thompson's "Alleluia" rang out again in the Theater-Concert Hall: Tanglewood was back in full swing. Four hundred students were enrolled, many on the newly enacted GI Bill of Rights.[5] Koussevitzky invited musicians he considered most talented in his or her field to become part of the Tanglewood "family." Many had been on the faculty in 1942; most would return in future years.[6] Copland's popularity and his stature as the leader of American composers made him the perfect choice as Koussevitzky's assistant. With Copland in charge, Koussevitzky knew he could count on things running smoothly.

When Copland saw the cottage near Pittsfield that had been chosen for him before the summer of 1946, he decided to stay at Heaton Hall, a hotel in Stockbridge, where he worried about not having a piano, and about paying for his room by the day, with extra for visitors (Victor Kraft and Paul Moor both visited that summer). In August, Copland moved into a charming converted stable and arranged for a piano to be delivered. At the end of the following season, Copland found the barn in Richmond that would become his Tanglewood home. It belonged to Mrs. Ralph Hooker (later, the Gettys family, then the Birts). The barn had an artistic history: Alexander Calder had lived there and built some of his sculptures and mobiles in that space. It was still very "barny" and informal, and the surrounding meadows assured Copland the privacy he needed for composing.

In 1946, members of the student orchestra played Copland's *Sextet*, and the BSO performed *Appalachian Spring* under Koussevitzky. The big event of the season, however, was the American premiere of Benjamin Britten's *Peter Grimes*.[7] Copland invited Britten to come

[1] See video interview, Jacob Druckman with Vivian Perlis, 16 July 1985, New York City. Segments of this interview can be seen on the documentary television production *Aaron Copland: A Self Portrait,* directed by Allan Miller, produced by Ruth Leon, and Vivian Perlis (1985).
[2] For Copland at Tanglewood from 1940 through 1942, see Interlude IV. For a history of Tanglewood, see Herbert Kupferberg. *Tanglewood* (New York: McGraw Hill, 1976).
[3] During the war, the trustees of the Boston Symphony Orchestra and the Berkshire Music Festival board argued over control of Tanglewood; the Orchestra won. See Koussevitzky Collection, the Library of Congress. In 1944, the festival consisted of a two-weekend, four-concert Mozart Festival with thirty members of the BSO, Dorothy Maynor soloist; in 1945, a three-weekend Bach and Mozart Festival with forty orchestra members, duo-pianists Abram Chasins and Constance Keene, pianists Alexander Brailowky, Alexander Borovsky, Robert Casadesus, and Lukas Foss.

[4] See Copland's files at the Library of Congress for complete lists of students and faculty of the composition department from 1940-1965, with Copland's comments on his students, and lists of programs and activities. See Koussevitzky Collection, the Library of Congress, and the Music Center files at Tanglewood for bound yearly reports.
[5] Tuition in 1946 was $120 (up $20 since 1942).
[6] Regulars at Tanglewood included Tod Perry (assistant to Boston Symphony manager George E. Judd and Koussevitzky's executive secretary, succeeding Margaret Grant), Leonard Burkat (librarian), Robert Shaw and Hugh Ross (choral music), Gregor Piatigorsky (chamber music with Ralph Berkowitz, accompanist), Irving Fine (harmonic analysis), and Olin Downes (lecturer on music criticism). Faculty for individual instrumental teaching were members of the BSO. Copland said, "Titles didn't mean too much. Everybody took care of his own classes and his own work."
[7] Professional singers in the production were William Home, Joseph Laderoute, Florence Manning, Frances Yeend. Two students, Mildred Miller and Phyllis Smith (later Curtin) soon made impressive

Left to right: Copland, Bernstein, and Koussevitzky, summer 1947

from England, and then worried about what he would think of a student performance. With Bernstein conducting and several professionals to bolster the students, *Peter Grimes* was such a success that the following season Koussevitzky gave Boris Goldovsky a free hand to build a special opera program. Many leaders in the operatic world started their careers during the sixteen years Goldovsky led the opera program at Tanglewood, among them Sarah Caldwell.

Leonard Bernstein and Eleazar de Carvalho were Koussevitzky's conducting assistants (Carvalho was the thirty-two-year-old Brazilian recommended by Villa-Lobos). Bernstein was conducting in London and did not arrive in Lenox until a week into the season. He wrote to Copland (23 June 1946):

> Don't let Kouss think bad thinks about me because I'm staying. He must know how much I want to get back to the Boiks. And I'm scared Kouss will take away some of the summer chores I really want to do—like the Festival concerts. Don't let him. It's on your head! Keep Tanglewood safe for Bernstein!

Copland was to share the composition program with the European composer Bohuslav Martinů, but soon after Martinů's arrival, he fell off the porch of a Tanglewood building

professional careers. *Peter Grimes*, commissioned by the Koussevitzky Music Foundation, had had its world premiere in London in 1945. (According to Leonard Burkat, Koussevitzky referred to Britten's opera as "Peter und Grimes.") Britten and stage director Eric Crozier came to assist director Max Graf at Tanglewood. Graf withdrew close to performance time to go to Hollywood, and Koussevitzky never invited him back. Graf's assistant, Boris Goldovsky, became director. Among Goldovsky's many successes at Tanglewood was the first American performance of Mozart's *Idomeneo, Re Di Greta* (1947). See Boris Goldovsky, *My Road to Opera* (Boston: Houghton Mifflin Company, 1979).

in Great Barrington. Irving Fine taught Martinů's students until Copland found a replacement in Nikolai Lopatnikoff.[8] Copland's students were Jacob Avshalomov, James Beale, Edmund Haines, Ned Rorem, Leonard Meyer, and several South Americans Copland had met during his 1941 Latin American tour.[9] The presence of many foreign students added an international flavor to the atmosphere. Among the Latin Americans were Julián Orbón and Alberto Ginastera. Orbón, who had met Copland earlier in Cuba, described how the Latin American composers would get together to play their music at Tanglewood: [10]

> We would invite Aaron, who was like a father figure of Latin American composers, and he would comment, "Oh, you Latin people—you are something!" One day I was riding in Copland's car together with Hector Tosar and Ginastera. Copland said, "My God, I have to drive very carefully, because I have with me the hope of Latin American music!" And Ginastera said, "Well—and the reality of North American music!"

Alberto Ginastera[11]

When I first became aware of modern music, I heard Copland's Music for the Theatre. *I was a very good friend of an Argentine conductor who knew Copland, Juan José Castro, and he introduced the work to me. After that, Copland came several times to Argentina. The first date was 1941, at the time of the world premiere of his* Piano Sonata *in Buenos Aires. I was writing the ballet* Estancia *and I played it for him. I was applying for a Guggenheim Fellowship, and Aaron was one who spoke for me. We exchanged letters, and in 1942 I obtained the Fellowship, but I could not come until the war was finished. Toward the end of 1945 I arrived in New York, and I met Copland often at concerts. He introduced me to many people, and especially Mrs. Claire Reis, head of the League of Composers. One time at a party, I was in conversation with other people speaking English, and I was looking very diligent. Copland said, "I never saw anyone like Ginastera, who can arrange his face like somebody who understands everything, and I know that he doesn't understand anything at all!"*

Copland obtained the scholarship for me to go to Tanglewood. My main reason was to study the problems of education and music institutions, and this was very useful for me, because in Argentina I created the first music school of professional level and the first chair of musicology. Copland instructed me where to go to investigate. He told me that one very great experience would be Tanglewood. Just that year of 1946 was a very remarkable year, because there were Latin American composers who became well known, and there was also Bernstein and Lukas Foss. It was one of the years you never forget. And then I attended Copland's classes, because I was very much interested in the teaching of composition. It can be said that I was a pupil

[8] The Martinů-Lopatnikoff students were Sarah Cunningham, Earl George, George Hurst, Louis Lane, Hugh Mullins, Grace Schneck, Howard Shanet, and Vladimir Ussachevsky.
[9] In addition to Orbón and Ginastera, Latin Americans at Tanglewood in 1946 included Roque Cordero (Panama), Jeanette Herzog (Argentina), Claudio Spies (Chile), Juan Orrego-Salas (Chile), and Hector Tosar (Uruguay).
[10] Interview, Julián Orbón with William Owen for Perlis, 1 July 1981, New York City.
[11] Interview, Alberto Ginastera (Aurora Ginastera translating) with William Owen for Perlis, 23 November 1981, New York City.

Copland in front of his summer home; the barn studio in Richmond, Massachusetts, *below*, 1949

of Copland. His spirit is very open and generous. Every time he could help us in trying to open a certain door, he always did it. These powerful communications were due also to the fact that he spoke Spanish.

At Tanglewood, Koussevitzky was like the Czar. We were very much impressed each time we saw him, especially when he wore a cape with red silk inside. Koussevitzky was like a star in the firmament to us.

Copland and I were on the jury of a competition in Caracas in 1957. By chance, it was the same people that had been at Tanglewood in 1946, only Tosar was missing. One day, they took a picture of all of us. It was like the famous group of Les Six, when one was missing, Auric. We took a picture of Tosar and put it on our photograph.

In my country, I have been the equivalent of what Copland is in this country. There is a parallel: our love for humanity and for our countries. What Copland did could be bigger because it is a much bigger country. I always say that I am a composer thanks to the United States. When I was thrown out of Argentina in 1952, I was in a very bad situation. But when I returned, I had a group of private pupils, and I also made music for pictures and had a radio program of contemporary music. It was for the last hour of the night. I played many records of the music of Copland.

I have a great admiration for Copland's Piano Variations. *Twenty or twenty-five years ago, it was a work that the public did not understand; now, it is a classic work of the twentieth century. I believe it is very interesting to compare a work in piano form and then arranged for orchestra. I always would have students make their versions and then compare them with Copland's own* Orchestral Variations.

Copland has created American music in the same way Stravinsky did Russian music, or Falla Spanish, or Bartók Hungarian, because he's an artist with a great personality. The following generations have had a great influence from Copland—some have made international music—but, at the same time, lost the American character that is in Copland's music.

Copland is a man full of realism and optimism. I never saw him without a smile. The other day, we saw each other when Queens College named the music school for him. The newspaper had a picture the next day of the two of us, and my look is full of much emotion, but Copland has a big smile—as always—just as the first time I saw him in the forties.

Following the successful 1946 season, applications flooded in for 1947. The word was out that the Berkshires was the place to be if you were a young performer or conductor on the way to a professional career. The faculty and administration was essentially unchanged from the previous summer.[12] Arthur Honegger was the European composer invited to share the composition department with Copland. He no sooner arrived from war-torn Paris than he suffered a serious heart attack. Copland again had to find a replacement. This time he asked Samuel Barber, who came to Tanglewood to take Honegger's students for the remainder of the season.[13] Copland taught eight of the sixteen composition students: Sidney Cox,

[12] Administration: Copland, Perry, Burkat; Chapple was dean of students with Berkowitz assisting; Koussevitzky's conducting assistants were Bernstein, Carvalho, Burgin, and Chapple; Primrose headed the chamber music program while Piatigorsky was on leave; Ross and Shaw supervised choral conducting and singing; Fine, harmonic analysis; Herford and Wolff, solfège.
[13] Barber's students were Gordon Playman, Daniel Pinkham, Leon Ricklis, Ruth Wylie, Jack Fitzer, Samuel Beversdof, Jean Miller, and Howard Shanet.

The 1957 reunion of Copland with the Latin Americans who had been at Tanglewood in 1946: Chilean Juan Orrego-Salas, Spaniard Julián Orbón, Panamanian Roque Cordero, Mexican Blas Galindo, Cuban Harold Gramatges, Uruguayen Hector Tosar (represented by his drawing), Puerto Rican Hector Campos Parsi, Venezuelan Antonio Esteves, and Argentinian Alberto Ginastera

William Flanagan, Jan Novak, Knut Nystedt, Carlos Riesco, Ned Rorem, Russell Smith, and Douglas Townsend. Copland, together with Bernstein and Fine, taught a course in American music, one of the first of its kind,[14] and he coached student composers in presenting their works once a week.

Koussevitzky directed the Festival and the Music Center with great energy and dedication. His pride in Tanglewood led to such statements as "Our student orchestra is one of the best orchestras in the country, as good as Cleveland or Cincinnati," and students were stimulated to play better than they thought they could. When prominent visitors praised Tanglewood as "an American Salzburg," Koussevitzky asked, "Why a Salzburg? Why not Tanglewood, U.S.A.?" The Director's passionate belief that everyone should be involved with music had lasting influence on Copland. To achieve his goal, Koussevitzky organized the Center into five departments, the fifth being for amateurs.[15] He incorporated public forums at the Lenox Library into the curriculum, usually planned and moderated by Copland. The forums gave amateurs and audiences the opportunity to discuss topics such as "What relevance does popular music have in today's world of serious music?" and "What is the place of women in music?" Leonard Burkat attended a forum in which BSO manager George Judd, Stanley Chapple, and Richard Burgin discussed "What opportunities exist for the professional artist in his career under present conditions?" Judd's remarks about "selling" music prompted Koussevitzky to pronounce furiously, "An artist is not a sack of potatoes!"[16]

Koussevitzky also believed that composers should be able to conduct. Copland had a turn, but Koussevitzky was not complimentary and very soon he urged Copland to forget conducting and concentrate on composing. Irving Fine, Harold Shapero (and later, Peter Mennin) were expected to take turns directing the student orchestra. For years, Fine told his favorite Koussevitzky story and it has been repeated by others ever since: Fine was conducting Brahms' *Variations on a Theme by Haydn*, and the performance was unsteady and uneven. Koussevitzky was listening in the wings. When Irving Fine walked off after taking his bows, Koussevitzky called to him: "Fine! Fine! It was awful!"

One of Koussevitzky's ideas, carried out each summer until his death, was to conduct the BSO at a Festival concert in a major work by a young American composer. In 1947, it was Copland's *Third Symphony*, played in a season featuring all the Beethoven symphonies. Koussevitzky managed what no conductor had done before: to attract large audiences with outstanding performances of standard repertoire, while including enough contemporary music to make programs interesting and varied. However, Koussevitzky's affection for contemporary music did little to endear him to the BSO's board of trustees (as Koussevitzky called them, "Trusties"). Finances always being a problem, Koussevitzky constantly had to justify himself and to compromise on expenditures.[17]

The amount of music performed during the short school session was unbelievable: In the forty-two days of the 1947 session, sixty-one concerts were given, of which forty-one were by the students. With so many performances taking place in such a short time, it was necessary to have a library of scores and parts on the grounds. Space was cleared at the Main House, and Irving Fine recommended to Copland a young assistant librarian from the Boston Public Library.

Leonard Burkat[18]

Irving suggested me to Aaron, then Aaron to Tod [Thomas D. J.] Perry, who was executive secretary, and Tod got approval from Koussevitzky. I began in 1946, with a six-week leave to work for the Berkshire Music Center for fifty dollars a week plus a fifty-dollar housing allowance. That sounded awfully good to me. I lived with my wife and young child in a cottage down a dirt road around the lake. (Koussevitzky was

[14] Each of the three faculty lectured once a week for five weeks, ending with a panel discussion. See Copland's files in the Library of Congress for course outline.
[15] The five departments of the Center were: I. Conducting (orchestral, choral and operatic); II. Orchestra and Chamber Music (including song repertoire); III. Composition; IV. Opera; V. Ensemble Playing and Choral Singing (including the Festival Chorus, Madrigal Group, and Small Choir).

[16] In Copland's files at the Library of Congress, there is a manila folder, "Tanglewood Forums," with a typewritten list of topics through 1956 and handwritten outlines of each forum Copland moderated.
[17] In 1947, total operating expenses were $24,548 for the Music Center; $137,780 for the Festival; $62,786 for building and maintenance; and $17,036 for cafeteria expenditures.
[18] Interview, Leonard Burkat with Perlis, 11 May 1986, Danbury, Connecticut.

Copland, Koussevitzky, and Arthur Honegger at Tanglewood, 1947

always complaining that my car was dusty!) When I was invited back for the 1947 season, the library in Boston did not give me leave, so I quit my job to return to Tanglewood for the summer.

The library there took up much of the first floor of the old house, and Aaron's studio was right above it. I was tested by Aaron. He would ask what I thought about Mahler's symphonies, when they were hardly known at all, and about a Schumann symphony, I remember, and he was surprised when he found that I really knew the scores. Later, when Stravinsky's Agon *first came out and we were looking it over, Copland said, "Everybody who wants to compose from now on will have to know this score."*

Koussevitzky was our lord and our master. This was his place. He had thought it up—invented it—and brought it into existence. He made it exactly what he wanted it to be—a kind of meeting place for people he considered to have the best musical minds and the greatest musical skills and the highest artistic aspirations. He threw them all together with very broad instructions, saying to us, "Do something! Here are all these young people. Make them think and work the way you do, and maybe even live the way you do." For

Koussevitzky, it was important to live on an elevated plane and to conduct everyday affairs with the same seriousness of purpose that went into conducting a concert. He was an elevated personage of the kind that there were very few of then—and there are many fewer now. This was the Koussevitzky ethic with which Aaron fit so well. As for the rest of us, if we were not capable of at least aspiring to do the things Koussevitzky wanted done, we just didn't belong there. The effect that he had on the students, on us, and on the musical life of this country is inestimable.

I quickly got involved in doing more than running the library, and acquired a variety of responsibilities at Tanglewood and in Boston. After Koussevitzky died, Judd fired me a couple of times, but [Charles] Munch and Harry Cabot, the president of the trustees, rehired me. Judd soon retired, Tod moved up into his job of general manager, and I became artistic administrator of the orchestra and principal administrative officer of the Music Center. Without Koussevitzky's advocacy, the trustees were unsure that they wanted to spend the money needed to keep the school alive, and I helped get it over that crisis.

That kind of thing could not be Aaron's burden, but he was responsible for a great deal, more than anyone ever knew, especially in the early years. Many of Koussevitzky's composer discoveries were people whom Aaron brought to his attention. Aaron never claimed any great credit for it. It was just what he did when he thought the music deserved it; that's all. It became obvious that Koussevitzky relied on Aaron and Lenny a great deal, and more on Aaron because of his age and experience. Aaron didn't want to be involved in too much operating detail himself, but he wanted people around who could be trusted to take care of it. He would not have stood for careless work, and he knew who deserved his confidence.

As administrator of the Music Center until 1963, when I left to take a job with CBS, I consulted with Aaron on many aspects of its operation. When Paul Fromm offered to support the study and performance of new music at Tanglewood, Aaron, Irving, and I discussed the possibilities and came up with the idea of attaching a group of chamber-music players to the composition department, and these Fromm Fellows of 1957 were the very first "new-music group."

Aaron looked and acted then much as he does now, except that he was firmer of step. His voice was the same. He could always say very serious things in a light way, and he always had that little, amused chuckle. He was kind and gentle—a person as lacking in cruelty, or even harshness, as one might ever encounter in the current musical world.

As programs and activities expanded, new facilities were added to the campus: a student-orchestra rehearsal stage; a cafeteria where the old lunch bus stood; and the Nathaniel Hawthorne "little Red House" used for classroom space, and as an historical site for visitors. Tanglewood's grounds have always been open to the public, and it was Koussevitzky's idea that college students conduct guided tours. It has become a time-honored tradition for children of Tanglewood regulars to lead the tours. Tod Perry (manager of the orchestra from 1954 to 1979 and connected with Tanglewood since 1940) explained: "It is a kind of nepotism, I suppose, although certainly not exclusive. There's quite an alumni of Tanglewood guides— the Bernstein and Silverstein kids, our own, and also people such as Dan Gustin and Harry Kraut."[19] As audiences grew, so did traffic and the constant need for expanded

[19] Interview, Tod Perry with Perlis, 4 August 1987, West Stockbridge, Massachusetts.

Above: Copland with students of the Berkshire Music Center on the lawn at Tanglewood

Right: Copland at the piano surrounded by fellows of the Music Center, 1948

parking facilities and tourist accommodations. As Copland said, "It was a tough job to find rooms for visitors, even for those of us who were Tanglewood 'regulars.' In all the years I spent in the Berkshires, I never felt that the permanent residents of Stockbridge and Lenox ever got used to the influx of so many strangers every summer."

Everyone was much too busy at the beginning of the season to celebrate the Fourth of July, so the Music Center's official holiday was Koussevitzky's birthday (26 July). Everything would come to a halt and a gigantic cake would appear. Each year, faculty and students outdid themselves to surprise Koussevitzky with an original musical program: A conducting student presented "Also Sprach Koussevitzky:" Lenny produced his famous "Koussevitzky Blues" (with the refrain, "Come the Revolution and we'll all wear capes!"); and in 1947, Bernstein conducted a new work, "Fanfare for Bima" (using the tune Koussevitzky

whistled to call his cocker spaniel).[20] In addition to Koussevitzky's birthday, the opening ceremonies and the closing parties at the Curtis Hotel for the faculty were the special occasions. Afterward, Copland would stay on in his Richmond barn to compose and to enjoy a more peaceful time in the Berkshires.

At the end of the 1947 season, Koussevitzky married Olga Naumova, his late wife Natalie's niece, who had lived with the Koussevitzkys and acted as their secretary for eighteen years. Olga, with her quiet and soft- spoken manner, drew composers to her, and several counted her a close friend, among them Bernstein and Copland. In an interview a year before her death, Olga Koussevitzky said, "One of Serge's first pupils was Bernstein—young, enthusiastic. And Aaron. Very much at Serge's side. Aaron was always his closest advisor and friend. It was a very wonderful and warm relationship."[21]

Among Copland's composition students when the Music Center reopened in 1946 was the young Ned Rorem; Rorem returned to study with Copland in the summer of 1947.

Ned Rorem[22]

The first of his music I ever heard was Quiet City *in 1940, and it bowled me over. Except for Chicago composers, Sowerby and Carpenter mainly, the notion of American music hadn't quite taken with me. Now here suddenly was Aaron Copland's gem, at once so French—like all I adored—with its succinct expressivity, yet so unFrench with its open-faced goodwill. So I tried to find as many of Copland's records as possible, although except for* El Salón México, *there wasn't much available.*

We first met when I was nineteen and a student at Curtis. I used to go up to New York each month to seek various modes of art and fun unavailable in Philadelphia. I knocked on Lenny Bernstein's door (I didn't know you were supposed to phone people first), and we hit it off. He had Copland's Sonata *on his piano, and played it for me, and again I was bowled over, despite—with its almost mean angular aggressivity—its difference from* Quiet City. *So Lenny picked up the phone and made a date for me to visit Aaron. That would have been February of 1943.*

I went next day to the West Sixty-third Street studio, which I recall as a single narrow room as long as the block and compartmentalized by shelves heavy with air-checks and acetates of his various scores. Aaron was affable, immediate, attentive, with that wonderful American laugh; in the four-plus decades since that day, I've seen him behave with the same unaffected frankness not only with other young unknowns but with countesses and Koussevitzkys. He played me a tape (only it wasn't called a tape then) of Of Mice and Men, *of which I was especially touched by the super-simple D-minor moment for solo string, illustrating the death of Candy's dog. I played him a juvenile trio, my* Opus Minus One, *which I still have in a drawer somewhere. We talked about whether tunes came easily, and gossiped about Mexico and Chicago. That was that.*

[20] For descriptions of other Koussevitzky birthday presentations at Tanglewood, see interviews: Leonard Burkat, Lukas Foss and Howard Shanet.

[21] Interview, Olga Koussevitzky with Perlis, Oral History of American Music, Yale University, 31 May 1977, New York City.

[22] Interview, Ned Rorem with Perlis, 20 January 1987, New Haven, Connecticut. Revised by Rorem, August 1988.

Ned Rorem and Copland, 1946

When I moved to New York the following year, Aaron was a regular fixture at new music concerts, and always surrounded. A few times he came to dine on West Eleventh Street, where I lived with Morris Golde; once with our mutual friend, the painter Alvin Ross, who did both our portraits. But it wasn't until 1946 that I really grew to know him.

In the summer of 1946, I got a scholarship to Tanglewood and became one of Aaron's six students. We bunked in one huge stable in a Great Barrington girls' school along with Martinů's six students and Martinů himself, who took a fall and had to be replaced by Lopatnikoff The twelve student composers had two lessons a week with their respective maestros, plus two group sessions, plus access to rehearsals. It was the happiest summer of my life. Aaron lived near Pittsfield and invited me to dine once or twice, and to see Fiesta, *an Esther Williams movie that used* El Salón México *as background music. He also offered me scotch and sodas (he was never a drinker, but I was) that quite went to my head: Aaron was my teacher, after all. "Don't tell anyone," said he, "because one can't make a habit of inviting students out." But what did he really think of me?*

I was always a lone wolf and never became one of Aaron's regular flock, any more than I became one of Virgil's, except that I worked as a copyist for Virgil, so I knew him better. Aaron had an entourage, so did Virgil; you belonged to one or the other, like Avignon and Rome, take it or leave it. I left it. Or rather, I dipped my toe in both streams.

Virgil's "Americanness" predates Aaron's. Virgil's use of Protestant hymns and, as he calls them, "darn fool ditties" dates from the twenties. Aaron's use came later. One may prefer Aaron's art to Virgil's, but give Virgil full credit: Aaron knew a good thing when he saw it. Although he's had wider influence, he'd not be what he is without Virgil's ground-breaking excursions. Virgil invented his own folk music (a little as Poulenc and Ravel did) and left it rough hewn, while Aaron took actual folk music and revamped it into sheer Copland.

I gleaned less out of the one-to-one meetings we had at Tanglewood than from the classes. The class in orchestration was most canny. Aaron had us score the same passage—five or six measures—from a piece of his. We did this, each in our own corner for an hour, then regathered to compare results against the original. Very instructive. Appalachian Spring *had just been published, and we all carried our own little score around like holy writ, the way the Latin-Americans carried around the Falla* Harpsichord Concert *and the French students* Pelléas. *But Aaron, sly fox, had us orchestrating sections of* Statements, *which we couldn't possibly have known beforehand. Sometimes he would invite outsiders. For example, Britten came to talk about* Peter Grimes, *and Harold Shapero analyzed his* Classical Symphony. *We had classes in movie music, and one in modern vocal music. Aaron had yet to write the* Dickinson songs, *and didn't feel himself a song composer.*

He was more interested in other composers than any composer I've known. That was the season he imported youngish geniuses from all over South America and listened patiently to every note of every one, then commented in a very general way. He was less a pedagogue than an advisor—a sort of musical protocol expert. I remember Marc Blitzstein saying about Aaron that he would sit and listen to these kids play this damn music and let it go clear to the end of the piece without stopping—he was so patient!

The next summer, I went back to recapture Paradise. You never quite can, can you? And yet I did. By then, I had already published a few songs and had a firmer ego than the year before. I remember saying to Aaron during the class, "You did this last year. "And he said, laughing, "Oh, I know, yes, but don't tell anybody." I returned to Tanglewood for a few days in 1948 when Hugh Ross introduced my Sappho Madrigals. *Then I stayed away until 1959 when I stopped by for lunch with Aaron and Harold Clurman. In the shade of the shed, I shed a tear, and haven't been back since.*

I have never been able to squeeze a compliment out of Aaron. He was always willing to write recommendations, always willing to socialize, but my music was nothing he would include on programs. Perhaps I lacked a musical identity (except in the few dozen songs from the mid-forties, which are inimitable) until I started thinking bigger and writing symphonies. What I learned from Aaron wasn't what he taught me per se. Rather, it was through observing how he did what. Aaron stressed simplicity: Remove, remove, remove what isn't needed. That stuck. The leanness! particularly in his instrumentation, which he, himself, termed "transparent," and taught me the French word dépouillé. *Stripped bare. It's the opposite of German, every note's there and you hear it. The* dépouillement *was certainly something he got from Paris, from Boulanger—but he was not seduced, as I was, by so-called Impressionism. Our respective Frenchnesses were at opposite ends of the scale, and that, I think, put him off.*

Aaron brought leanness to America, which set the tone for our musical language throughout the war. Thanks largely to Aaron, American music came into its own. But by 1949 there started to be a give and take between the United States and Europe. Europe woke up where she had left off in 1932, like Sleeping Beauty—or Sleeping Ugly—and revived all that Schoenbergian madness, now perpetrated ironically not through the Germans but through Pierre Boulez, who was a most persuasive number. The sense of diatonic economy instilled in us by Copland was swept away in a trice and everyone started writing fat Teutonic music again. It was as though our country, while smug in its sense of military superiority, was still too green to imagine itself as culturally autonomous; the danger over, we reverted to Mother Europe.

In 1949, when I was living in Paris, Shirley Gabis (now Perle) and I invited a half-dozen people over for Boulez to play his Second Sonata, *and Aaron came. At least one of us left the room in the middle,* so discombobulating was the performance, but Aaron stuck it out with a grin. On the one hand, he was aroused by the nostalgia of his own Parisian past when everyone tried to épater le bourgeois; on the other hand, Boulez was appealing and sharp as a razor and Aaron would have liked to be taken seriously by the younger man and his bunch. Artists, even the greatest, once they achieve maxiumum fame, are no longer interested in their peers' reaction so much as in that of the new generation. Who knows what Boulez thought of Aaron's music? The French have always condescended to other cultures. Except for Gershwin, names like Copland or Harris or Sessions were merely names when I first dwelt in France, and are still (pace Carter and Cage) merely names there. Anyway, that same day, Aaron sat down and played his Variations, no doubt to prove he was just as hairy as Boulez, but the effect was one of terrific force and form, and yes, inspiration, thrown at the hostile chaos of the enfant terrible.

I came back briefly to New York in 1952 and visited Aaron in one of his sublets (this one was deep in the south Village). Patricia Neway was there, rehearsing The Dickinson Songs. I was terribly interested (and, as a songster myself, maybe a bit jealous) that Aaron kept the verses intact without repeating words not repeated in context, and at how sumptuously, even bluesily, melodic the songs were despite the jaggedly disjunct vocal line. He had already written the Piano Quartet, his first leap into the tone-row bandwagon. But here now again was the crystalline (his word) master, clear as mountain dew.

During the fifties, we saw each other less often, since I lived in Europe for that decade. But whenever he was in Paris, I invited him chez Marie Laure de Noailles, where I lived, or chez Marie-Blanche de Polignac, who "received" on Sunday evenings. I can still see him in these two extraordinarily beautiful houses, amidst the fragile Proustian society, Renoirs all over the walls, breast of guinea hen all over the table, the dizzy scent of Lanvin perfume pervading the salons, and Aaron so down to earth with his famous contagious giggle, so plain, so—dare I say it?—Jewish, and at the same time cowboyish. For it's notable, maybe even something to be proud of, that the first truly important American composer is a Jew, yet a Jew who never, as Lenny did, wrote Jewish music. Except for Vitebsk. Always at these functions, he was duly impressed but anxious to get to the sonic core of the situation, meet whatever musicians might be there, or listen to Poulenc, or Jacques Fevrier, or maybe Georges Auric playing four-hands with the hostess. Mostly, though, he was probably unexcited by the tone, anxious for something more current, more vital.

One of Aaron's letters takes me to task because in my first book, The Paris Diary, I wrote disobligingly about Boulanger. He wrote me that he simply would not endorse a book that was so vindictive about someone he had always loved and needed. (That slap did me good, and reversed many an exhibitionist stance.) I saw Aaron angry another time—in Rome in 1954. I was sitting with him at a concert, and somebody played a piano sonata of Georges Auric that went on and on and on. And when it was over, Aaron was just beside himself with impatience and annoyance and said, "What a hell of a piece!" Meaning in a very negative way. He got up and whirled out into the lobby and was very offended.

As Aaron's fame swelled during the sixties and seventies, his influence waned. In January of 1966 when he went to Salt Lake City, where I was teaching, to conduct the Utah Symphony, I told the university that, sure, I'd invite him to give a talk if they would cancel all classes and guarantee a full house. There was a full house, all right, but strictly of faculty and townspeople.

The honors that accrue to Aaron evermore vastly appear so often to be simply praiseworthy, a touch standoffish, treating the man like a saint. Now, to be a saint, you must once have been a sinner, and I feel that it diminishes Aaron to avoid discussion of his various temptations. We all recall his friendly reticence, his hunger for gossip, although he himself was not given, as Virgil was, to gossip. Aaron never said nasty things to others, but I've seen him cool to people who wanted something from him or who were too clinging. People like to talk about how friendly Aaron was. He was easy enough to talk to, but in fact, he knew exactly how friendly to be, and he knew who he was. People who know who they are, are intimidating, because most people don't. I think it's to belittle Aaron to infer that he was a man without temperament. People are inclined to sanctify him, as though he had no temperament or sexual urges at all! I have seen Aaron elated, especially when a new piece was being played (you never get blase about that first performance). I've seen him struck dumb by the beauty of a passing human being. I've seen him depressed, dark, near tears about the plight of an arrogant friend we both loved; but he never actually talked about his personal life, except elusively. His rapport with Victor Kraft was ambiguous, and, in any case, pretty much deromanticized by the time I knew them both. It's not my place here to speculate on later loves—his generation, even including Auden, was circumspect. Indeed, Aaron is the most circumspect famous person I have ever known, considering how much he encouraged others to let down their hair.

I am thrilled to discover how cyclic our world becomes if you live long enough. In just the past two or three years, I've heard any number of scores by young men and women in their twenties, scores that do more than emulate the wide-open spaces of Aaron's most beloved works—they actually sound—in timbre, tune, and hue—like steals from the master. Always admired by the masses, he's becoming readmired by fickle youth.

Nevertheless, I asked three members of this youth recently, "Is there any composer whose next work you just can't wait to hear?" They had to stop and think. They were not agog as we once were about how the Clarinet Concerto was going to sound, how the new Nonet was going to sound, or how Inscape would be received. These were events. Aaron Copland wasn't the only one, but he was the chief one whose new works we were all avid to hear. I don't think it was because we were specifically younger. It's that the whole world was younger; there were fewer composers around; the repertory of American works was slimmer, so any new addition was a thrill. Aaron was the king and in a sense still is. There hasn't been another man since then from whom all young composers await each new endeavor with bated breath, and whose endeavor usually doesn't disappoint.

In 1948 (the spring after Ned Rorem's second Tanglewood summer), it was announced that the French conductor Charles Munch, who had made his American debut in Boston in 1946, would become music director of the Boston Symphony after Koussevitzky's retirement in 1949. Several tributes were made to Koussevitzky marking the occasion.[23] Although Munch would not take over until the fall of 1949—and even then, Koussevitzky had no intention of retiring from Tanglewood—from the time of the announcement of

[23] When a gold watch was presented to Koussevitzky in Carnegie Hall at the end of the orchestra's spring tour (16 April 1949), he addressed the audience: "I know that all of you have not liked the new music I have played. But it was necessary to play it, for the good of the art and of the young new artists, the composers." A work had been commissioned from Copland for chorus and orchestra with text by Walt Whitman, but Copland could not compose it in time, and he wrote his apologies to Koussevitzky. A dinner was held at Symphony Hall with the orchestra players as guests; the program featured a "Cantata" composed by six Tanglewood alumni living in Boston. The dedication on the score reads: "For Serge Koussevitzky. 'In grato Jubilo, an Occasional Cantata' by Irving Fine, Daniel Pinkham, Gardner Read, Alan Sapp, Herbert Fromm [Paul Fromm's brother], Lukas Foss. The text by David McCord. Musical offering from the Boston Chapter of the Tanglewood Alumni Association composed for Dr.

Above: Copland and Darius Milhaud at Tanglewood, 1948

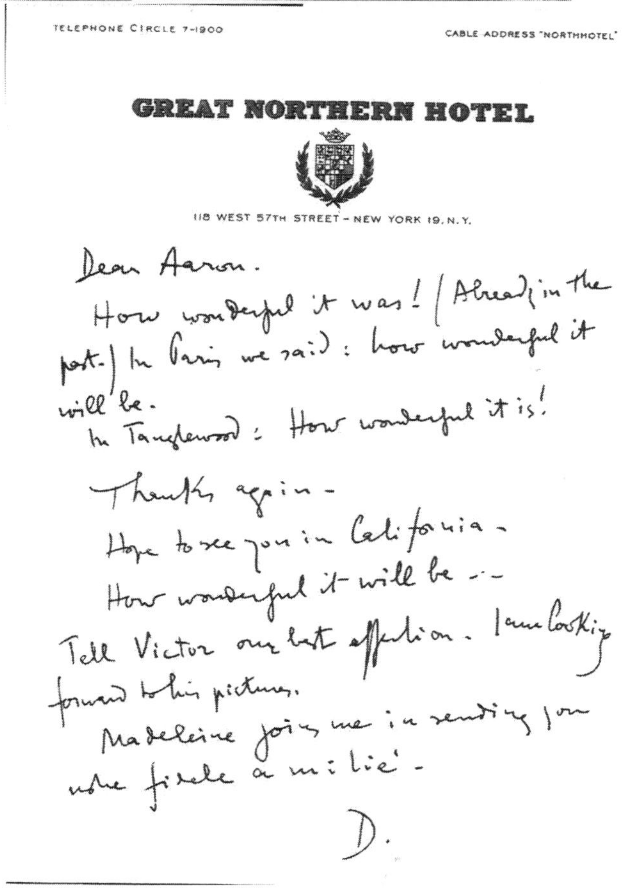

TELEPHONE CIRCLE 7-1900 CABLE ADDRESS "NORTHHOTEL"

GREAT NORTHERN HOTEL

118 WEST 57TH STREET - NEW YORK 19, N.Y.

Dear Aaron.

How wonderful it was! (Already in the past.) In Paris we said: how wonderful it will be.

In Tanglewood: How wonderful it is!

Thanks again -

Hope to see you in California -

How wonderful it will be --

Tell Victor our best affection. I am looking forward to his pictures.

Madeleine joins me in sending you notre fidele amitié -

D.

Right: Letter from Darius Milhaud to Copland, fall, 1948 (undated)

Munch's appointment, Koussevitzky felt that his position was threatened. Those involved with the administration of the Festival and Music Center were aware of the internal politics in 1948 and 1949, but for the public and the student body of the Center, activities proceeded as energetically as usual,[24] and the faculty remained essentially unchanged.[25]

Irving Fine and Copland planned the 1948 lecture course, which dealt with very old and very new music (Julius Herford presented the "old"; Copland the "new"). A new series, "Aspects of Music," was initiated and taught twice a week by various faculty members. Copland again moderated the public forums. Darius Milhaud was visiting composer. He wrote to Copland (27 May 1948), "You are a real darling, and it is nice that you can send a car to fetch the old wheelchaired composer and bring me to Tanglewood." Before Milhaud's arrival, Copland read his autobiography[26] and wrote to Victor, "What a happy childhood he's had, maybe that's why he's so nice now." Milhaud and Copland taught the regular composition students,[27] and a third group from other areas of concentration was taught by either Fine or Foss. Copland taught seven students in 1948. During the summer, he heard a piece by a young violin student. Later on, Copland said, "It became clear to me during those years [1948 and 1949] that one of the students at Tanglewood, Jacob (he was then called "Jack") Druckman, was a very talented fellow."

Jacob Druckman[28]

I had always thought of myself as a composer, but in my late teens I thought I would make my living as a violinist playing in symphony orchestras to support the composing habit. I spent the summer of 1948 at Tanglewood as an orchestral violinist and ended up hating it. I also felt that nobody was paying any attention to the music I was writing. After that first summer at Tanglewood, I turned my back on music and spent most of the year working as a commercial artist. Then, just on a fluke, as a kind of last chance, I sent some scores to Aaron, and he accepted me as a student and gave me a scholarship to study composition

Koussevitzky and performed for the first time at the Testimonial Dinner in his honor upon the completion of his 25th season as conductor of the Boston Symphony Orchestra, Symphony Hall, 2 May." Phyllis Curtin was soprano soloist. Leonard Burkat organized the creation and performance of this work. A copy of the "Cantata" is in Verna Fine's collection of Irving Fine's papers. For Koussevitzky's response at the banquet, see Koussevitzky Collection, the Library of Congress. The League of Composers gave a banquet at the Waldorf-Astoria, New York (20 May 1949). Claire Reis put together an album of composers' letters for presentation to Koussevitzky. Copland was host, Schuman spoke, and Koussevitzky conducted the Tanglewood Alumni String Orchestra. See Copland's files in the Library of Congress for list of invitees, the invitation, speech texts, program, and letters. See also Koussevitzky Collection, the Library of Congress, for correspondence between Reis and Koussevitzky, typescript of Schuman talk, Blitzstein about excerpts from *Regina* (sung at the dinner), and seating list.

[24] See Koussevitzky Collection, the Library of Congress.

[25] Ralph Berkowitz became Koussevitzky's executive assistant; Sarah Caldwell joined Goldovsky's staff as opera coach.

[26] Darius Milhaud, *Notes sans musique* (Paris: Renée Juilliard, 1949).

[27] In 1948, Milhaud's students were Olga Gratch, Robert Kurka, Hector Tosar, John Freeman, Bruce Howden, Lester Trimble, Arthur Frackenpohl, and Eugene Kurtz. Copland's students were Sidney Cox, Edward Lewis, Charles Strouse, Pia Sebastiani, William Flanagan, Robert Nagel, Herbert Brün, and Edino Krieger.

[28] See video interview, Jacob Druckman with Perlis, July 1985, New York City.

at Tanglewood. (Aaron had heard my first string quartet during the summer of 1948.) The whole path of events changed after that.

Aaron was a huge presence at Tanglewood. It was, in those years, one of the most glamorous places ever. In the middle of it was Aaron, not only as the important American composer at the time but also as the person reaching out to other composers. When I first went to study with him, I thought of Copland as representing a kind of neoclassic Americana. My own natural inclinations had very little to do with Americana, and I worried that he would be unsympathetic to other kinds of music. I remember in an early lesson my bristling when he said, "How come you always use intervals like minor thirds and major sevenths? Why don't you ever use a perfect fifth?" And I thought, This is the Americana bit rising up. But that was not the case at all. He was very erudite and his tastes were catholic. He could criticize twelve-tone composers and had a genuine interest in composers of all kinds of music, as well as those working closer to his own style. Aaron had a wonderful eye and ear for the shape of a piece. He could very quickly recognize the original premise of a work and just as quickly put his finger on spots that didn't live up to the promise of the opening. Copland was really the most amazing teacher.

By the time I met Aaron, he was already a totally establishment person, and to the young and revolutionary, it could have rubbed the wrong way. I think I was suspect of him a little bit, but I'm not sure whether that was a result of deep conviction or just simply a product of my youth. Aaron's influence on my music was not direct: I don't think my music ever sounds like Aaron Copland's music. The influence was more as an example, particularly in the kind of citizen that he was in the world of music—shouldering of responsibility and not being out for his own personal glory and gain. He felt as though the advancement of the art was his responsibility, and this was a wonderful influence on many of us. Aaron was the kind of person who goes out and creates something that was not there, who invents festivals, invents occasions, invents ways to help young composers. This is the kind of citizenship I am talking about, the encouragement and vision that he had.

Through the intervening years since Tanglewood, I have seen Copland only occasionally. I would visit him and show him what I was up to. He was supportive in the sense of being interested in what I was doing and treating me as though I was a real composer, which was even more necessary for me than the opening of doors. But later, I would hear from people that he mentioned my name and recommended me in various places. I felt very close to Copland, but our relationship has always been one of a certain distance, a certain respect. It took me a long time to bring myself to call him Aaron; in fact, it was not until I joined the Koussevitzky Music Foundation board and found myself sitting elbow to elbow with him that I did.

Aaron's was an enormous personality. It may be a new idea in the history of the arts that we need a personality, that we need an identity, that we need to be able to recognize a composer upon hearing the first few measures of the music, but it is a mysterious thing when it happens. It's that magic that we talk about as charisma. We don't know how it happens but it is wonderful when it does. There are so many composers around that are good, but Aaron's voice is distinctly his. His works have already entered into the mainstream of the repertoire and certainly will continue to be performed. They are beyond the question of this year's fashion.

In 1949, the famous French composer Olivier Messiaen joined the faculty.[29] Copland heard from Milhaud: "I miss the Tanglewood atmosphere very much and specially you and Vic and Lenny and Fine and Lukas and of course Dr. K., the magician of this music land. Now you must take a little time for me and write about Olivier the Messiah." Messiaen made a strong impression on the young composers at Tanglewood.[30] They seemed to find his mysticism a refreshing change from the current twelve-tone vogue. Copland's composition students were Martin Boykan, Joseph Harnell, Edward Lewis, Lee Pockriss, Gerald Kechley, Mark Bucci, and Samuel Adler.

When Irving Fine suggested that the 1949 lecture series be "a retrospective survey of the wild and wooly twenties," Copland agreed, making the comment, "It seems funny that it's all history now." Two events are remembered most vividly by those at Tanglewood in 1949: one, the State Department movie being made for distribution abroad that disrupted the regular curriculum[31] and put Koussevitzky on the warpath; the other, the accident that took place on the Richmond Road when Copland ran into a cow. Almost forty years later (24 July 1987), during lunch at Copland's home, talk was about Copland hitting the cow, and he declared excitedly, "Just a moment! You have it all wrong! It was the cow who walked in front of my car!" The story has been retold through the years by several people, among them Arthur Berger[32] and Verna Fine, who were both on the scene when it happened.

Verna Fine[33]

At the end of each Tanglewood season, Koussevitzky would give a dinner party on Sunday night at the Curtis Hotel in Lenox for the faculty and their wives. It was always very nice but sad—similar to the last days of summer camp. The most memorable of those occasions was in 1949. Aaron, Irving, and I were driving home to nearby Richmond, where we were sharing a house for the summer. Aaron was driving, I was sitting in the middle, and Irving was to my right. In a car behind us were Arthur and Esther Berger, who were staying with us those last two weeks. It was a very foggy night, so we were going very slowly. Suddenly, there was this huge cow standing smack in the middle of the road. Aaron slammed on the brakes, but it was too late. I let out a great scream, and then we all got out of the car. The poor cow was beyond help. Arthur almost fainted; I lost my voice for three days; but Aaron and Irving were cucumber-cool. Aaron's Studebaker was badly damaged—undrivable, in fact—so we drove on to the house in the Bergers' car, called the police, and returned to the scene of the "crime."

The police, who were extremely hostile, actually wanted to put Aaron in jail! They took him to Pittsfield, and Irving, as a Massachusetts resident, put up bail. We tried to explain the accident to the police, but they

[29] See Kousscvitzky Collection for letter from Messiaen (19 February 1949) agreeing to an interpreter, $1,000 fee and $360 expenses.

[30] In 1949, Messiaen's students were Easley Blackwood, Harry Freedman, Sidney Palmer, Irving Mopper, Jean Catoire, Jack Fitzer, Lockrem Johnson, Carlos Riesco, Robert Turner, and Herman Berlinski.

[31] The International Motion Picture Division (MPO), Hamilton McFadden, chief of the Department of State, arranged with George Judd and Koussevitzky for a film for foreign distribution. It was directed by Larry Madison. Included are segments of Koussevitzky conducting the BSO and the Festival Chorus in a commissioned work by Randall Thompson, and Copland conducting the Department II (student) orchestra.

[32] Interview, Arthur Berger with Perlis, 13 November 1981, Cambridge, Massachusetts.

[33] Interview, Verna Fine with Perlis, 8 November 1987, New York City.

Copland teaching a class at Tanglewood, c. 1949

wouldn't listen: "We will talk only to the perpetrator of the crime," they declared. Aaron finally got out and returned home with Irving, who "sprang" him at about 2 A.M. The next morning, the news was broadcast on the radio, and the local paper ran the headline COPLAND KILLS COW!

Irving and I had known Aaron since the winter of 1943-1944, when he came to the Harvard University music department to teach composition, replacing Walter Piston, who was on sabbatical. Irving was a faculty instructor. One night, he invited Aaron to our apartment for dinner. It was love at first sight, just as if we had known him all our lives. Aaron was an informal sort of person, and he felt entirely comfortable with Irving, who was, as Aaron often said, very simpatico. Let's face it—at that time, Harvard was a pretty stuffy place! Aaron became like an older brother to Irving. They were both soft-spoken, and they loved to talk about music—I never remember them talking much about anything else. They both gave the impression of being calm and unruffled. They also had in common the fact that they were good listeners, and they listened closely to each other. For years, Irving and Aaron had long-distance conversations once or twice a week. Aaron used to say, "Irving, I can count on one hand the people who call me just out of friendship, who aren't after a letter of recommendation for something or other. In fact, maybe I can count them on one finger—you."

Harold Shapero, Lukas Foss, and Irving—the three musketeers, as we used to call them—were all in the Boston area in 1944. Harold wasn't married yet; Lukas was living in a tiny studio; and although Aaron had a beautiful sublet on Memorial Drive facing the Charles River, it was our apartment in Cambridge where we all got together, and where I did the cooking.

I first saw Aaron conduct that same year. He was invited to do Outdoor Overture with the Boston Pops, and on the podium he looked like a modern dancer. We sat there laughing hysterically. Afterward, the good-natured Aaron made fun of himself: "If I can see the first deskmen, then I can't see the percussion! And if I see the percussion, I can't see the score!" Aaron's conducting improved later when he did more of it (and when he got better eyeglasses).

Aaron was writing Appalachian Spring, and he showed us the sketches and played some of it for us. He invited us to Washington for the world premiere. We stayed at the same hotel as Aaron and went to all the fancy parties with him in a chauffered limousine. The premiere was a sensational success. When Koussevitzky was to conduct the Appalachian Spring Suite, he had some problems with the rhythms and asked Irving to re-bar some sections. But Irving refused at Aaron's request and eventually "Koussie" struggled through those difficult rhythms.

Irving, unlike many of Aaron's composer colleagues, was never critical of his lighter music, because he felt that Aaron maintained the same integrity as in his serious pieces. Irving thought Aaron had discovered something special and often said he wished he could do something similar.

Aaron suggested to Koussevitzky in 1946 that Irving be brought to Tanglewood to teach harmonic analysis. Because Irving was in the academic world, Aaron often turned to him for teaching and organizational ideas. They did a lot of co-lecturing. Both were good administrators. If truth be known, the courtship in the fifties of Paul Fromm and his support of contemporary music at Tanglewood all germinated over the dinner table when we lived together in the early Tanglewood years. The original Brandeis University Creative Arts Festival was planned the same way. Irving had joined the Brandeis faculty in 1950; after Koussevitzky died in 1951, Irving and Aaron got the idea of putting on a festival at Brandeis in June 1952 as a Koussevitzky memorial, one that would also honor the initial graduating class of the newly founded Brandeis University.[34]

In the summer of 1946, we didn't live near Aaron, but the next summer, we found a little cabin behind a guest home in Richmond owned by a Reverend Cutler. I made lunches for everyone and took them over to the Tanglewood grounds. Aaron rented a suite with a separate entrance near Reverend Cutler's, and every night we had elegant dinners together prepared by Mrs. Cutler. At the end of the summer, Aaron arranged to rent the Gettys' barn the next summer, and in 1948, we all had our meals together at the spacious Kelley mansion, which we rented for the summer. I got two helpers, one to take care of our new baby, the other to help in the kitchen. I ran a "restaurant" every night with typed menus.

In the summer of 1949, Aaron couldn't get the Gettys' barn, but the Kelley mansion had been remodeled and was even larger and more beautiful. Aaron rented a suite in one wing, Lukas took another, and Irving and I and our young daughter had the main part of the house. Three pianos were moved in, one for each composer. Lenny often came for dinner, and we had other musicians as guests—Walter Piston, Harold Shapero, and Arthur Berger among them. Once the actor Farley Granger, an old friend of Aaron's, appeared for dinner. Victor Kraft was around a lot. He was moody but charming and handsome and helpful, always working on Aaron's car and taking delightful pictures. I often did Irving's secretarial work, and I also typed for Aaron. He was a pleasure to work for. In 1950 and 1951, we all rented separate places, but we still ate dinner together several times a week.

[34] See Abram L. Sachar, "A Host at Last," *Atlantic Monthly Book Press* (XIII, 1976), 145-49.

Copland with Irving Fine (*right*), a student, and Professor Erwin Brodky (*left*) at Brandeis University, c. 1951

At Tanglewood, I got to know Aaron's family. I went up to Laurine at a concert in 1947 and said, "Oh, you don't know how lucky you are. How I would love Aaron for my brother!" She looked at me in amazement. I don't think they ever came to terms with how great a man had come from their family. Still, Laurine was charming and beautiful. She and her husband, Charlie Marcus, and Aaron's brother Ralph and his wife, Dorothy, came up regularly every summer to hear Aaron's music. Ralph was very quiet. I noted with surprise that neither Laurine nor Ralph looked at all like Aaron.

After Koussevitzky died, Tanglewood could never be the same. It was my impression that Aaron and Irving lost some of the enthusiasm they had had for the place in the "Koussie" days.

Later on, when Aaron traveled all over the world as a conductor, he always brought back gifts—a Yemenite necklace from Israel for me, books for Irving, and toys for our three daughters. We never saw the thrifty side of Aaron that everyone talks about. As recently as 1980, when Aaron and I traveled back from Washington together after his eightieth birthday concert, he insisted on paying my air fare.

Irving died suddenly of a heart attack on August 23, 1962, in Boston. Aaron flew up for the funeral. A few weeks later, he telephoned to tell me that Lenny planned to conduct the New York Philharmonic in the Adagio movement from Irving's Notturno for Strings and Harp *(4, 5, 6, and 9 October 1962). Aaron said he would like to escort me to the opening concert. These were the first subscription concerts of the Philharmonic in its new hall at Lincoln Center. Little did I know what Lenny had planned! Before the performance, a microphone dropped from the ceiling and Lenny gave a moving tribute to Irving. I was overwhelmed, and Aaron squeezed my hand and comforted me.*

The official gala opening of Lincoln Center's new hall had taken place a week or so earlier, when Aaron's Connotations *was given its premiere. Instead of attending with Irving as planned, I had sadly watched it on television at home. When I saw Aaron, he told me the famous Jackie Kennedy story to cheer me up. I asked Aaron what the First Lady said when they went off-camera backstage before the TV camera caught her backing away from that infamous, sweaty Bernstein kiss. Aaron is no mimic, but he managed a passable imitation of Jackie's high-pitched, breathy voice:*

> *I opened the door for her leading into the TV viewing room and she said, "Oh, Mr. Copland." We took a few more steps and she said again, "Oh, Mr. Copland." At about the fourth "Oh, Mr. Copland," we arrived backstage. What do you think she meant, Verna?*

I replied, "Aaron, it's obvious; she hated your piece!"

Aaron called me often after Irving died, and when I was in New York, we would meet for dinner at the Harvard Club or go to a concert together. When I moved out of the Boston area and came to New York, we saw each other often at Peekskill as well as in the city. I was always included in important celebrations or when Aaron would receive an honor.

One night several years ago at dinner, Aaron confided, "I don't feel comfortable with the twelve-tone system, but I don't want to keep repeating myself. And remember, Verna, I don't have a Robert Craft. Stravinsky was lucky that he had a young guy around showing him Webern, bringing him music with which he wasn't familiar. I don't have anybody coming to me all the time to show me the new things." I was impressed with Aaron's honesty.

There were a lot of important people in our lives. Many were Irving's friends, who "dropped" me after he died. Yet I couldn't have predicted that Aaron would have stayed so close. He was wonderful to me, and I

Victor Kraft, c. 1949

have felt devoted to him all these years. It was good to know that Aaron liked me for myself, not just because I was Irving's wife. Aaron was not only a great composer; he was a great human being. What a combination!

In 1950, French composer Jacques Ibert shared the composition program with Copland,[35] who wrote to Victor (6 July):

> Ibert has arrived. The barn is okay. I lead a life of lonely grandeur in Richmond. I eat at Fines three times a week and scrounge the others. De Sabata is coming in spite of Kouss, not because of him.[36] The fireworks can be expected that week. . . Kouss doesn't look very well. He is amazingly insecure about the future of himself as director. . . . Lenny due 19th. *Salón Méx* for student orch.

Copland's brother Ralph wrote (20 July): "Another summer has rolled around and we are again 'Tanglewood conscious.' The ladies have put the burden of finding accommodations on you." Copland invited his family for their annual visit to Tanglewood when *El Salón México* was being performed. Also scheduled were student performances of the *Violin Sonata* and *Sextet* (the latter was studied under Foss but considered too difficult to perform given the allotted rehearsal time).

Copland reported at the August faculty meeting that he was well satisfied with the composition program. He lectured on the music of Roger Sessions in a series called "Music: Pro and Con," in which modern works were presented by students, and speakers were asked to attack or defend each work.[37] The Tanglewood Festival celebrated the two hundredth anniversary of Bach, and the popular "Tanglewood on Parade" featured Eleanor Roosevelt narrating Prokofiev's *Peter and the Wolf*. Ralph Berkowitz went to coach Mrs. Roosevelt at Hyde Park. Leonard Burkat recalls her first rehearsal with the orchestra: "Mrs. Roosevelt's voice and accent were so strange that halfway through, Koussevitzky turned to the concertmaster, Richard Burgin, and asked incredulously in Russian, 'Doesn't she speak English?' Nevertheless, the performance was a great success, and Mrs. Roosevelt donated her fee to the Music Center and to the Wiltwyck School for Boys ($1,250 to each).

Bernstein was away for part of the 1950 season, leaving Richard Burgin, Carvalho, Foss, and Howard Shanet as Koussevitzky's assistants.

Above: Copland at a rehearsal at Tanglewood; (*right and below*): Copland practicing in the Theater-Concert Hall

[35] Considered for visiting composer had been Malipiero, Poulenc, Walton, Ibert, Kodaly, Dallapiccola, and Boulanger (Boulez' name came up every year; he never accepted). Boulanger refused and Walton cabled Copland (6 January): SORRY IMPOSSIBLE WRITING. Ibert's students were F. Cook, Stanley Kregs, Kaljo Raid, Charles Schwartz, Forrest Suycott, Raymond Wilding-White, Robert Cantrick. Copland's students were Georgia Akst, Martin Boykan, Theodore Snyder, Gerald Kechley, Henrich Gandelman, Joseph Harnell, and Jacob Druckman.

[36] Koussevitzky was disturbed when the board of the Symphony invited Victor De Sabata as guest conductor without consulting him. See Koussevitzky Collection, the Library of Congress.

[37] Copland's talk on Sessions can be found in Copland's files of lecture notes, # 3. Other lectures on various subjects were given by Peter Gradenwitz, Arthur Mendel, Hans David, Lukas Foss, Julius Herford and Irving Fine.

Howard Shanet[38]

My presence at Tanglewood came about through Copland. I telephoned him at a mutual friend's suggestion, and I went on at length about how much I wanted to go to Tanglewood. It suddenly occurred to me that I hadn't made it clear to Aaron that I meant in conducting! Here I was talking to America's best-known composer, and I couldn't make myself say that I didn't mean to study with him at all! When Aaron said, "My class is filled, but you may get into Martinů's group," I thought I had better go along. I dug out whatever scores I had and sent them along with an application. To my surprise, I was accepted as a composer to study with Martinů, and returned the next year in Honegger's class.

One of my jobs was to organize the student composers' concerts. On one occasion, I had to conduct a quintet because no one else would take it on. Afterward, Aaron came up and said, "Why didn't you tell me you were a conductor?" I said, "That's what I have been trying to do all this time!" Aaron offered to tell Koussevitzky about me.

Koussevitzky was an idealistic man who was accustomed to having his own way. That means there was a pragmatic side to Koussevitzky, and Aaron had to live with both sides. For someone to remain in Aaron's capacity of running Tanglewood without infuriating Koussevitzky, he had to be a special kind of personality. A consummate administrator. Aaron always had to maintain a diplomatic stance. I don't think any of us ever witnessed Aaron in a disagreement with Koussevitzky; they always seemed on superb terms. Nevertheless, Aaron's own personality was strong. He could be firm without being abrasive. These same qualities made him a good teacher of composition. He could make his own opinions known, yet accept each student's different style. He would not impose his own ideas.

There were two things about Tanglewood that concerned Koussevitzky most: one, that he should be separated from the place at all, ever; the other, that a kind of vulgarization was creeping in. There was already talk of bus lines, advertising, pop music. When we were in Hollywood on tour, representatives of the cultural community there offered Koussevitzky the chance to have a West Coast Tanglewood. He was tempted, but it was unthinkable for him to leave his Tanglewood. He thought of it as his own child, which could not be replaced with another. He even addressed those of us who worked with him as "Kinder" perhaps because he did not have children of his own, he was always warmly interested in young people. Koussevitzky called me "Hovardt"; Seymour Lipkin was "Lipushka"; and Lenny was "Lenushka."

In the summer of 1952, I was a junior faculty member at the Music Center. At a staff meeting, I spoke my mind about what I viewed as an abandonment of certain of Koussevitzky's ideals. Maybe I said too much. It was not Aaron's style to speak out. He doesn't work by making a hassle, and maybe he didn't see it my way. I was young and brash. I asked for a leave and after that, I didn't return to the Tanglewood faculty, although I remained on good terms with my colleagues there and went to visit once in a while.

Following the 1950 season, Koussevitzky wrote a letter to the Boston Symphony trustees (18 November 1950): "I ask that you protect Tanglewood from influences foreign to its initial ideal. I ask the Trustees as long as I am living and able to carry on the responsibility of Tanglewood, to entrust me with the full, undivided artistic authority as Director of the

[38] Interview, Howard Shanet with Perlis.

BMC and the Festival." The board agreed, without knowing that Koussevitzky would not live long enough to direct his beloved Tanglewood through another season. He became seriously ill in Phoenix, Arizona, where he and Olga were staying after his conducting tour. After he returned to Boston and it was clear he would not recover, the Fines wrote to Copland in Italy (30 May 1951), but the letter did not arrive in time. Therefore, Copland had a terrible shock when he heard the news from his cook the morning after Koussevitzky's death (4 June 1951). A service for Koussevitzky was held in Boston at the Protestant Episcopal Church of the Advent on 7 June; the funeral was the following day in Lenox at the Church on the Hill. Copland sent a telegram to Olga Koussevitzky, who wired back, "Thank you, dear Aaron, awaiting your return." Copland decided he could best honor Koussevitzky by carrying out a commitment to produce a Koussevitzky Music Foundation concert in Rome (11 June).

Knowing Irving Fine was at home completing arrangements for the upcoming season, Copland wrote (15 June), "If I were after a job of course I would drop everything here and dash home. But I'm not." Copland advanced his return date by a few days, arriving in time to face opening the Music Center without Koussevitzky (24 June 1951). The trustees had decided not to appoint a new director. They released the following announcement:

> We propose to create a Faculty Board which would assume powers of leadership for the 1951 season. This board, composed of Aaron Copland (who was nominated chairman), Leonard Bernstein, Hugh Ross, Gregor Piatigorsky, Boris Goldovsky, Richard Burgin, and William Kroll, met on six occasions for consideration of the school's work-in-progress as well as with an eye toward the Center's future.

The opening exercises of 1951 were of a commemorative nature (1 July). Copland and Bernstein spoke. The following is part of Copland's talk:

> We sense our loss more than anyone else can. I was a friend of Dr. Koussevitzky for about twenty-eight years. It seems to me that his spirit is so clearly among us that it would he impossible for us not to carry on our work in the meaning of that spirit. I think that above all things Dr. Koussevitzky would have wanted us to talk about the future of our school rather than about the past and about the possible accomplishments of our school rather than his past accomplishments. It was his vital personality which inspired all of us to carry out the plan born in his mind. In this spirit, at this moment I want you all to rise for a moment of silence in memory of Dr. Koussevitzky.[39]

A memorial concert was presented with representatives of all the departments of the Center; every year since then, a Koussevitzky Memorial Concert has been included in the Festival, usually conducted by Bernstein.

Copland settled into his barn in Richmond and got to work. Bernstein, who was to have been on leave, changed his plans and took charge of the conducting classes. Foss, Burgin, Carvalho, Lipkin, and Shanet were all on hand, and along with the other regular faculty

[39] For Copland's opening addresses in full, see the Berkshire Music Center yearly reports.

members, they did their best to make things seem normal. Luigi Dallapiccola arrived as visiting guest composer,[40] and William Kroll came to assist Piatigorsky with the chamber music program. The students studied and played Copland's *Vitebsk* and *Statements for Orchestra*, conducted by Copland.

Charles Munch, as music director, was not greatly involved with the Center and seemed willing to have those who had administered it continue to do so. As Tod Perry pointed out:

> Aaron's role took on major importance and was even more essential. I was always interested in the Music Center and continued active in it, and Leonard Burkat, of course, who became administrator in 1954 when I succeeded Judd as manager of the orchestra. Leonard was helpful to Munch since he spoke French.[41]

In the years immediately following Koussevitzky's death, those who had been chosen by Koussevitzky as his Tanglewood "family" kept the Music Center running smoothly, despite periods of serious financial difficulties. Nevertheless, Koussevitzky's death marked the end of an era.[42] One of his greatest achievements had been the founding of Tanglewood and the Berkshire Music Center. With the burgeoning of summer festivals throughout the country, there is still nothing like Tanglewood. Although many changes have taken place through the years, the basic aims and spirit as conceived by its founder have remained constant. Tanglewood is still Koussevitzky's dream come true. His sense of mission, old-fashioned as the word may seem, has never completely faded. Moreover, Tanglewood's unchanging beauty seems to imbue the place with a presence of its own, a grandeur that presides over the many and varied activities on its sweeping lawns and beneath the towering trees. When David Del Tredici returned in 1986 to hear one of his works performed during the Contemporary Music Festival, he gazed out over the distant views and commented in amazement, "I haven't been here for over twenty years, and it looks exactly the same—not even a leaf is out of place."

Serge Koussevitzky (1874-1951)

[40] Dallapiccola's students were James Francis Brown, Pierre Mercure, Raymond Wilding-White, Robert Pitton, Arnold Freed, Julia Perry, and Mimi Sandbank. Copland's students were Noel Farrand, Robert Parris, Bryan Dority, Norman Grossman, and Charles Schwartz.

[41] See interview with Tod Perry.

[42] For recordings of Koussevitzky's voice and for Copland about Koussevitzky, see Recorded Sound Research Center of the Library of Congress and Oral History of American Music, Yale.

AROUND THE WORLD
1949 - 1953

Europe was coming alive again in the world of the arts. I could hardly believe it had been twelve years since I had been abroad! I planned a trip for May and June of 1949. Erik Johns traveled with me to England, France, Italy, and Belgium.[1] Our first stop was London, where I visited old friends Ben Britten and Peter Pears. I wrote in my diary, "Benjie's charm is still potent and derives from a combination of severity and boyishness." After Michael Tippett came to call at our hotel, I wrote, "He is charming with a very un-English warmth at first sight. He has a sort of British Roy Harris personality." Juan Orrego-Salas was in London, and we met for lunch. He had just come from the Palermo Festival, and I was interested in hearing about the struggle between "progressive" Italian musicians and the twelve-toners. Of the people I met for the first time, I was most interested in composer-critic Wilfrid Mellers: "I am impressed with this pixie-like individual who seemed to know more about American music than anyone I have met in a long time."

Erik and I drove into the countryside one day to have tea with Leslie Boosey of Boosey & Hawkes. I lectured in Birmingham and visited Cambridge, returning to London to attend a rehearsal of *In the Beginning* for a broadcast by the BBC, and for receptions in my honor by the English Speaking Union and the British Council. Many composers attended, even William Walton and Constant Lambert. Erik saw to it that we visited the museums and theaters. Of most interest to me was *The Heiress*, with Peggy Ashcroft in the leading role.

Paris seemed more hectic than I had remembered, yet wonderfully the same. I took my first walk on the boulevard St. Germain to the Café Flore and felt nostalgic in a nice way. On the first night, I went for dinner (to the restaurant David Diamond and I used to enjoy in the thirties) with younger composers Charles Strouse, Bill Flanagan, and Gary [Gerhard] Samuel. We talked about Nadia, and the following day, I met all the new Boulangerie when I went to see her on the rue Ballu.[2] Nadia had returned from the States, where she spent the war years—first in California, then Boston. I always had my scores sent to her as they appeared, and I continued to send promising students to study with her. Each year, Nadia counted on my advice in choosing the annual composer awards of the Lili Boulanger Fund. It struck me that Nadia had become rather set in her ways. She remained rigidly aloof from the current excitement about serialism, claiming that such music failed to move her. She would not open herself to students using the method. (Nadia never addressed the issue with me, but it must have been shocking for her when both Stravinsky and I began to use serialism.) During my 1949 visit, Nadia had scheduled a concert by Leo Preger, and I was hard put to see what she was so enthused about, but we had a joyful reunion. We went together to the Champs Elysées Theater and to visit Poulenc in his charming apartment. Before I left Paris, Nadia invited twelve guests for a formal dinner in my honor, among them François Valéry and my old friend Marcelle de Manziarly.

Pierre Boulez was the topic of conversation wherever music people got together in Paris. I met him for the first time when John Cage took him along to a party given by Gary Samuel. Noel Lee played some of Boulez' new music, and the evening had a French intellectual atmosphere quite different from New York gatherings. Boulez was cordial and invited me to a soirée at his apartment later in the week. I described the evening in my diary:

> Cage and Merce Cunningham were there. Typical artists garret apt. Boulez impressive. Young man of twenty-four. He played parts of a piano sonata— seemingly unplayable. Pupil of Leibowitz and Messiaen. He has learnt much from both. Piece rhythmically schemed on a non-melodic twelve-tone row basis. I said in mock despair, "But must we start a revolution all over again?" "Mais oui," says Boulez, "sans pitié." It adds up to a new way of organizing music, such as the fugue must once have been. If one listens for melodies, one is lost. There are patterns of sound, some monotony, but also much conviction, particularly when Boulez himself plays it. How another pianist might do it is hard to say, and public reaction impossible to predict. Anyhow it's new, and therefore exciting. Boulez turns his back on the Satie line, adores Webern. The French are obviously unpredictable.

I saw Boulez on another occasion in Paris—when he played parts of his *Sonata* for some of the Boulangerie. They were quite obviously disapproving. I found myself in the odd position of defending Boulez after he left the gathering! It occurred to me that the

[1] See travel diary no.4 in the Library of Congress.
[2] Composers of the "new" Boulangerie were Noel Lee, Bob Middleton, Lawrence Rosenthal, Sarah Cunningham, and Thea Musgrave.

Boulangerie had its limitations. they seemed to have a conservative-modern attitude, much influenced by the Messiaen-Leibowitz axis. Of the young Boulangerie, Noel Lee impressed me most—he was charming and obviously gifted.

My friend Peggy Bernier was in Paris! She put on a swanky reception in my honor to which *le tout* Paris came—Poulenc, Auric, Messiaen, Nadia, the Vicomtesse de Noailles (27 October 1949). I wrote, "Messiaen seemed very self-concentrated and looked somewhat seedy, but poetic. Auric was friendly and Poulenc amusing." Peggy told some scandalous tales about composer Florent Schmitt, intending (with some success) to shock Nadia. Messiaen invited me to visit him in the organ loft at the Trinité during a regular noon church service. I went and was shocked to hear him improvise everything from the "Devil" in the bass to what sounded like Radio City Hall harmonies in the treble. I couldn't understand how the church allowed it!

A visit to the Boosey & Hawkes office in Paris proved disappointing—they had very few of my pieces available. I found the same story when we got to Rome. There was only one performance of my music in Paris when I was there—Franz Waxman conducting *Lincoln Portrait* (1 June). The audience was so meager that he canceled a second scheduled performance.

Since Sir Adrian Boult was conducting my *Third Symphony* in London (3 June), I returned for the occasion. Boult was at first disturbed by various difficulties in the piece, but the broadcast performance went well. I wrote my impressions: "Boult was not 'fired' by hearing the music and his conducting took on a *pompier* quality. But he tried hard, which is something." We had a minor tragedy when Erik lost his passport in London. I had to leave him there to work it out. He made it back to Paris in time for a formal reception at the ambassador's home, where neither of us knew a single soul. Later, we had dinner with Paul Bowles, Bob Fizdale, and Arthur Gold. Bowles was bored with Paris, having become interested only in Africa. He thought I was going to be upset with him because he had abandoned music for writing novels. When he saw that I was not, he invited me to lunch with Alice Toklas and for a visit to the Stein–Toklas apartment to see the paintings.

Upon our arrival in Rome, we were met by composer Alexei Haieff, who showed us around and took us to the American Academy.[3] During the next few days, there were the usual receptions and sightseeing. I was interviewed on the radio and somehow managed to reply in Italian after some heavy coaching. We left Rome for Florence, which seemed nice and small-townish compared to everywhere else we had been. I spent some time with Luigi Dallapiccola, and wrote, "He is a lively character, a milder version of the young Villa-Lobos. Same vivacity and sharp tongue. I should think Florence would be too small for him. Am anxious to know his music better." I also saw Newell Jenkins, who was conducting some of my works, and he told me, "The Italians don't really care a fig about knowing American music, and are completely unaware of it, except for Gershwin."

After a few days in Venice, we traveled to Nice and then on to Brussels, where I played the *Piano Variations* and *Four Piano Blues* for a radio broadcast. When we returned to London for the trip home at the end of June, Erik was so enamored of Europe that he stayed on, while I got back just in time for the 1949 Tanglewood season.

I stayed on in the Richmond barn when Tanglewood was over, to work on a piece commissioned by The National Broadcasting Company for the first anniversary of the "Universal Declaration of Human Rights" of the United Nations. (The Declaration had been adopted and proclaimed by the General Assembly, 10 December 1948.) The short piece for orchestra and speaking voice was to be performed at Carnegie Hall (10 December 1949). It was not difficult to compose, for the words, which were drawn from the United Nations charter, were in themselves inspiring:

> We, the peoples of the United Nations, determined to save succeeding generations from the scourge of war, which twice in our lifetime has brought untold sorrow to mankind, and to reaffirm faith in fundamental human rights, in the dignity and worth of the human person, in the equal rights of men and women of all nations large and small, and to promote social progress and better standards of life in larger freedom, have resolved to combine our efforts to accomplish these aims.

Preamble is a patriotic work of under six minutes duration. It was originally conceived as a hymn, which explains why the tempo is slow and stately. An introductory fanfare for brass is taken up by other instruments of the orchestra. The principal melody is announced quietly by violas and a muted horn. *Preamble* has occasionally been likened to *Lincoln Portrait* because of the narration, but the musical style is quite different. It is a more formal work and without the inclusion of any folk song material. (The only similarity is the C-major climax at the finale of both works.)

Formal invitations went out from the Secretariat of the United Nations for the special event, which also included the premiere of *United Nations March* by Shostakovich and the finale of Beethoven's *Ninth Symphony*.

Performers were The Collegiate Chorale and the Boston Symphony Orchestra, conducted by Bernstein. Sir Laurence Olivier read the narration in *Preamble*. The audience included U.N. delegates, who were addressed by General Carlos P. Romulo, president of the U.N.; Mrs. Roosevelt, who had played a vital role in drafting the Declaration of Human Rights; and Trygve Lie, Secretary General of the United Nations. Prior to the concert, a forum was held on the topic "Freedom of Information." The entire program was televised by NBC and broadcast coast to coast the following day. *Preamble* was heard again on the ninth birthday of the United Nations, conducted by Charles Munch with the Symphony of the Air. The program was the first public concert ever held in the General Assembly Hall, which held 2,500. Another memorable performance was when Duke Ellington spoke the narration in a concert of all-American works during the French-American Festival at Philharmonic Hall, Lincoln Center (30 July 1965).

After the specific occasion for which *Preamble* was composed, I revised the accompaniment so that it can be played by orchestra alone (with a similar version for band and another for pipe or Hammond organ.)[4] The title was changed to *Preamble for a Special Occasion*. The

[3] See interview, Alexei Haieff with Perlis, 8 October 1984, New York City.

[4] For preparation of the organ arrangement, Carl Weinrich assisted Copland with the registrations.

orchestra and band arrangements are used occasionally, sometimes with a different narration, such as during the Bicentennial, when James Stewart read the Preamble to the Constitution to the accompaniment (15 January 1976). The organists have been most inventive in their use of *Preamble* for various degree programs and as a recessional.

I had been sketching ideas for my *Quartet for Piano and Strings* for several months but only began to work on it in earnest during my sixth visit to the MacDowell Colony in June 1950. After a slow start, I made real headway on the first movement. There were few distractions at the Colony—Lukas Foss and Vittorio Rieti were in residence but both were deeply engrossed in their own projects. I spent most evenings reading at the Colony library or in my own room. I wrote to Claire Reis, "I am intrigued with a biography of P. T. Barnum and surprised nobody's done a musical comedy on his life!" The social highlight of my month was a visit with Mrs. MacDowell. She was still sharp as a whistle at age ninety-two. The realization that she hadn't started the Colony until she was fifty made me feel quite young and energetic about starting something new as I approached my fiftieth birthday.

From the MacDowell Colony I went to Tanglewood and worked furiously on the second and third movements of the quartet when the season was over. The work had been commissioned by Mrs. Elizabeth Sprague Coolidge to commemorate the twenty-fifth anniversary of the Coolidge Foundation and was to be premiered by the New York Quartet during the Eleventh Festival of Chamber Music at the Library of Congress.[5] I wrote to Irving Fine (22 September), "I played the first movement for Schneider and he didn't turn a hair." And again I wrote (19 October), "I should be done with the *Piano Quartet* tomorrow, Oy—what a relief!" I inscribed "To Elizabeth Sprague Coolidge"on the title page and at the end of the forty-three page score: "October 20, 1950, Sneden's Landing, N.Y." The premiere was 29 October, a mere nine days later!

I was well aware that serial composition was the dominant method of composition during the years following the war.[6] Among young composers, it was considered the "new" music. I cannot say that I admired much of what I heard—so often it seemed that individuality was sacrificed to the method. Boulez effectively demonstrated that the method could be retained without the German esthetic. It was twenty years since I had composed the *Piano Variations*, in which I had explored certain possibilities of serial composition and adapted the method to my own use. I was interested in trying it again with the hope that it would freshen and enrich my technique. The *Piano Quartet* seemed like an ideal opportunity: I explored a more abstract and esoteric idiom with chamber music than I could with other types of music.

Composing with all twelve notes of the chromatic scale can give one a feeling of freedom in the formulation of melodic and harmonic ideas. In addition to the fact that there are more notes to work with, taking a different perspective produces material you might not come up with if you were not thinking twelve-tone-wise. It's like looking at a picture from a different point of view. It was not the contrapuntal possibilities that interested me in serialism, but the opportunity it gave to hear chords in a different way. My use of the twelve-tone method in the *Piano Quartet* did not adhere strictly to the rules, particularly as regards repetition of the row. I sketched various rows and chose to use an eleven-note one that would lend itself to development and flexibility.[7] Portions of the row are employed in several places (and in various alterations) motivically, in contrast to the usual practice of the composers of the Second Viennese School. Also, the feeling of tonality or of tonal center is rarely missing.

In the first movement, *Adagio serio*, which has been described as "fugal," the row is announced in an outright manner at the start of the piece by the violin. The second theme, announced by the cello, is a retrograde form of the row. The second movement, *Allegro giusto*, longest of the three movements, is a fast-moving scherzo with jazz-derived rhythms. In some passages, all of the instruments play high in the treble of their registers (the violin has harmonics and pizzicati); in other sections, there are big leaps between the voices. The third movement, *Non troppo lento*, is in a simpler mood. It is in five flats, and is the only movement with a key signature. The form is episodic, with sections loosely based on the original theme. Its beginning resembles the first movement in that it opens with strings alone. In place of the traditional contrasting second theme, I used two motives derived from the series. Toward the end of the *Quartet*, ten notes of the series are presented in a figure of descending whole-tone scales in parallel major sixths. The piano writing is at times far above the treble staff and characterized by wide leaps. In two places, I ask the pianist to use "a glassy tone" and the strings to play "impassively and somewhat draggingly." The *Piano Quartet* ends quietly, *pp morendo*.[8]

The *Quartet* was intended for the cultivated listener. Most audiences find the work puzzling, some find it moving, others find it puzzling and moving. The audience for the premiere was of the puzzled variety.[9] However, they at least seemed to enjoy the ending of the *Allegro*. Critic Lawrence Morton caught the idea of what I was after: "It [the final movement] dwells in regions of immobility, impassivity, and quietude, except for a few impassioned outbursts." Other critics debated whether the *Quartet* was a breakthrough to a new style or a return to the old one of the *Piano Variations*. In any case, they were less than delighted. Olin Downes wrote in *The New York Times* (1 November 1950), "It is Copland on one of his most intellectual jags, and we submit that it is neither beauty nor convincing art." Arthur Berger speculated that I was trying to reconcile the two camps of Schoenberg and Stravinsky, formerly considered irreconcilable. I was certainly not consciously attempting

[5] The members of the New York String Quartet were Alexander Schneider, violin; Milton Katims, viola; Hermann Busch, violoncello; and Mieczyslaw Horszowski, piano.
[6] For Copland on serialism, see Edward T. Cone, "Conversation with Aaron Copland," *Perspectives of New Music*, vol 6, no. 2 (Spring-Summer 1968), 57-72.

[7] See sketches of the *Quartet for Piano and Strings*, Copland Collection, the Library of Congress. Also: ink score, 43 pp. signed at end: "Oct 20, 1950/Sneden's Landing, N.Y."; miscellaneous sketches and complete pencil sketch.
[8] Copland's analysis here was written for the program notes of the Ojai Festival, May 1951.
[9] See Recorded Sound Research Center, the Library of Congress, for interview by Pierson Underwood with Copland the day following the premiere of the *Piano Quartet* during the Eleventh Coolidge Festival.

Manuscript page showing twelve-tone series, inversions, and chords for the *Piano Quartet*

any such thing. But Arthur was right on the mark when he said I was developing certain principles of serial treatment with which I had already come to grips.[10]

I had had very little direct contact with Arnold Schoenberg, but I had respect for him and interest in his ideas. It was ironic that in 1949, just as I was using the twelve-tone method

[10] Arthur Berger, *Aaron Copland* (New York: Oxford University Press, 1953), 83-85, and David Joseph Conte, "Aaron Copland's Piano Quartet—an Analysis," Master of Fine Arts thesis, Cornell University.

invented by him, a statement appeared in the *Herald Tribune* by Schoenberg, accusing me of making "malicious remarks" about him![11] Schoenberg attacked me ". . . for giving students advice to use 'simple' intervals and to study the masters. . . . It will certainly take a generation of sincere teaching until this damage can be repaired. . . ." Schoenberg proceeded to compare me with Stalin! I wrote a response to the newspaper (25 September 1949), after which Schoenberg made a rather grudging apology: "If my words could be understood as an attempt to involve Mr. Copland in a political affair, I am ready to apologize—this was not my intention." Finally, the affair was settled amicably: I wrote to Schoenberg directly (13 February) and he responded (21 February 1950), "I am always ready to live in peace."

The first New York performance of my *Piano Quartet* was at a League of Composers all-Copland retrospective at the Museum of Modern Art, marking the end of my chairmanship of the League (5 November 1951).[12] Lawrence Morton, director of the Ojai Festival in California and an active promoter of contemporary music in the Los Angeles area, programmed the first West Coast performance (6 May 1951) and several others.[13] I used to joke with Lawrence (somewhat wistfully) that were it not for him, my *Piano Quartet* might not have been heard at all!

Lenny Bernstein did not hear the *Quartet* until some time later, when he received the recording on which it was paired with the *Clarinet Concerto*. He wrote from Cuernavaca, Mexico:

> I rejoice particularly in the scherzo, because I think it is the longest sustained piece of continuity you have written in a long time, and it is really continuous, yes really, and it goes and goes in a remarkably convincing way. I feel rather close to the tonal way in which you are handling tone-rows (I'tve done it too, here and there); and I find that this movement is a real triumph. The last movement is beautiful, too, in a way which has already become awfully familiar to Coplandites, so that it is not such a thrill as the second. And the first is lovely, but I never did go for you and fugues, especially here where the opening is so reminiscent of the third Hindemith Quartet. Imagine, Hindemith? Who'tda thunk it? But it makes a fine piece, especially for records, because you want to hear it again and again (of course, with two or three mambos in between): And I still think you are a marvelous composer.

Twenty-five years after the premiere, I was back in Washington at the Library of Congress (23 and 24 October 1975) as pianist in the *Piano Quartet* with the Juilliard Quartet. In 1978, when I was composer-in-residence at the Cabrillo Festival, the *Quartet* was performed with Dennis Russell Davies at the piano, and the next day a critic wrote, "What has happened to the smiling, dignified gentleman we'tve been seeing around town the last few days? These are the strange harmonies of youth on the prod, defying convention."

[11] Virgil Thomson, "Music in Review," *New York Herald Tribune*, 11 September 1949, V 5.
[12] The League of Composers program in honor of Copland featured the Juilliard and New York quartets, the Schola Cantorum, with Hugh Ross conducting and soloists Sara Carter, Winifred Cecil, Katharine Hansel, Julius Baker, Leonid Hambro, and David Oppenheim. The program included "As It Fell Upon a Day," *Sextet*, Seven Songs from *Twelve Poems of Emily Dickinson*, *Piano Quartet*, and *In The Beginning*. Program notes were by Arthur Berger.
[13] Other programs in which Morton programmed the *Piano Quartet*: 1956-1957 season: American Chamber Players with Ingolf Dahl; 1978 Monday Evening Concerts, the Sequoia Quartet with Charles Fierro.

Left: Copland and Minna Lederman at his fiftieth birthday party, 5 November 1950

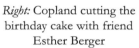

Right: Copland cutting the birthday cake with friend Esther Berger

Left to right: Composers Leon Kirchner, Copland, John Lessard, and Harold Shapero at Copland's home in Sneden's Landing, New York, 1950

Composers meeting at Copland's home, Sneden's Landing, New York, 1949 (*left to right standing*): Gerhard Samuel, Donald Fuller, Arthur Berger, Jerome Moross; (*seated*): Leon Kirchner, Copland, Israel Citkowitz, David Diamond, and Elliott Carter

The premiere performances of the *Piano Quartet* had kicked off the celebrations in honor of my fiftieth birthday. If I had to have a fiftieth birthday, the benefits in terms of performances and articles in the magazines and newspapers outweighed my reluctance to face the fact that I had reached the century's halfway mark.[14] A gala black-tie party was given by Alma Morgenthau on the evening of 14 November after a League concert in my honor, just when the entire East Coast was being buffeted by violent hurricane rainstorms. Traveling was hazardous, and I almost missed my own party! We were without electricity and heat at Sneden's for four days. I missed only one birthday celebration—in Philadelphia, where Ormandy was conducting the *Clarinet Concerto*, but when it was repeated in New York, I managed to get through the flooded streets and highways into the city (28 November 1950). The performance was good enough, but I had to conclude that Ormandy had little feeling for jazz style. Weather notwithstanding, I delivered several out-of-town lectures,[15] returning home to find forty-five birthday telegrams and cards to acknowledge.

[14] Olin Downes, "Copland at 50" *The New York Times*, 29 October 1950, X 7; "Trailblazer from Brooklyn," *Time Magazine* (20 November), 50-52; Robert Sabin, "Aaron Copland Reaches the Half Century Mark," *Musical America* LXX.13 (15 November 1950).

[15] Lectures in late fall 1950 included Toronto Conservatory, Canadian Broadcasting Corporation, Brandeis University, and the New England Conservatory.

I attempted to sum up the previous decade in an article for *The New York Times*, entitled "The New 'school' of American Composers."[16] I pointed to the fact that young composers of the forties had grown up with an American, rather than a European, influence, instead of what my generation had—the other way around. Composers were only now beginning to look to Europe again. I put myself on the line (as I had at the end of the twenties and thirties) by naming those representatives of the new generation I considered most promising. They were: Robert Palmer, Alexei Haieff, Harold Shapero, Lukas Foss, Leonard Bernstein, William Bergsma, and John Cage.

The Twelve Poems of Emily Dickinson was composed mostly at Sneden's Landing at various times, from March 1949 to March 1950. I wrote a few songs before turning to the *Piano Quartet,* for which I had a deadline. When the *Quartet* was finished, I returned to vocal writing. My friends kidded me about carrying books by and about Emily Dickinson around Sneden's Landing for months.[17] The house and grounds were old-fashioned and romantic and somehow just right for the nineteenth-century New England poet with her love of nature. I played some of the songs for Lukas and Irving during the summer of 1949 at Tanglewood. By the end of the year, I was finally up to number eleven, and I felt myself bogged down. As a break, I arranged five American folk songs. I wrote to Irving, "No one else may like them, but Hawkes [publisher] is delighted! The Dickinson cycle is done except for a fast song in the middle (why didn't you tell me fast songs are hard to write!)."

I had never thought of myself as a vocal composer. As a student, I had composed several songs for voice and piano, but my music really developed from essentially instrumental techniques. I had not composed for voice and piano since 1928. I am not sure why—perhaps because I did not come into contact with suitable texts. I read quite a lot of poetry but rarely found a poem with sympathetic subject matter and language not too complex that I felt was appropriate for setting to music. I had always liked the poetic prose of Gerard Manley Hopkins and at one time had the idea for a song cycle to Hopkins't poetry—a male singer intoning the poem without accompaniment and with interludes that would be purely instrumental. I even had a title ready: *Readings from Hopkins.* After abandoning that idea, I thought about setting some American poetry, perhaps influenced subconsciously by the songs of Charles Ives. I thought of Walt Whitman, especially the poem "Come, Heavenly Death," but gave that up because the poem's own rhythm seemed to defy musical setting. Then, while looking through an anthology, I came upon a poem by Emily Dickinson that appealed to me. There was something about her personality and use of language that was fresh, precise, utterly unique—and very American.

Emily Dickinson, born 1830 in New England, was a recluse after the age of twenty-three. After she died in 1886, it was discovered that she had written hundreds of poems, of

[16] Copland, "The New 'school' of American Composers," *The New York Times Magazine*, 14 March 1949, 18, 51-52; reprinted in *Copland on Music*, 164-74.

[17] In Copland's library there was a copy of Emily Dickinson *Poems, First & Second Series*, edited by Mabel Loomis Todd and T. W. Higginson (Cleveland: The Living Library, The World Publishing Company, 1948). This is a reissue of the publication of the 1890s. Other of Copland's sources (Bianchi/Hampson primarily) were not among his books. In her thesis for a Master's degree, "Strange Company," from New York University (1988), 39, n.19, Helen Didriksen discussed Copland's text sources for the *Songs*.

which only seven were published during her lifetime, and those anonymously. I once went to visit the Dickinson house in Amherst, Massachusetts, and actually walked upstairs to see what she saw out of that window—she wouldn't come down, and even had her meals up there. I was surprised to see that from her window one could see the main crossroads of the town, and I remember thinking that the view must have given her some idea of what was going on in the outside world.[18]

Originally, I had no intention of composing a song cycle using Emily Dickinson's poems. I fell in love with one poem, "The Chariot." Its first lines absolutely threw me: "Because I could not stop for Death, he kindly stopped for me; the carriage held but just ourselves and immortality." The idea of this completely unknown girl in Massachusetts seeing herself riding off into immortality with death himself seemed like such an incredible idea! I was very struck with that, especially since it turned out to be true. After I set that poem, I continued reading Emily Dickinson. The more I read, the more her vulnerability and loneliness touched me. The poems seemed the work of a sensitive yet independent soul. I found another poem to set, then one more, and yet another. They accumulated gradually, and when I had perhaps more than six, I began to think about how I would order them. But when I had twelve, they all seemed to run to their right places.[19]

The poems themselves gave me my direction, one that I hoped would be appropriate to Miss Dickinson's lyrical expressive language. Her poetry, written in isolation, was folklike, with irregular meters and stanzas and many unconventional devices.[20] The songs center about no single theme, but they treat subject matter particularly close to Miss Dickinson: nature, death, life, eternity. It was my hope, nearly a century after these remarkable poems were conceived, to create a musical counterpart to Emily Dickinson's unique personality.

Titles for the songs derive from the first line of each poem, except for "The Chariot." This poem, the first I started with, became the last in the cycle. The song I finished first was "The World Feels Dusty." Each song is meant to be complete in itself and can be sung separately or in smaller groupings, but I prefer them to be sung as a cycle. They seem to have a cumulative effect. Although the songs are commonly referred to as a "cycle," only two are related musically—the seventh and twelfth. When thinking about a title for the group of songs, I kept in mind that it was Emily Dickinson and her poems that should be in the forefront. Looking at my sketches, I am reminded of the various titles I considered:

[18] For Emily Dickinson, see Richard B. Sewall, ed., *Emily Dickinson: A Collection of Critical Essays* (Englewood Cliffs: Prentice Hall, Inc., 1963).

[19] Pencil sketches at the Library of Congress indicate various alternate orderings of the songs.

[20] The first edition by Mabel Loomis Todd and Thomas Wentworth Higginson (1890) attempted to correct the unconventional aspects of Emily Dickinson's poetry. *The Dickinson Songs* predated a more reliable variorum edition by Thomas H. Johnson (1955). Copland used an edition by Martha Dickinson Bianchi and Alfred Leete Hampson (1914-1930), which did not change Dickinson's intentions as much as Todd and Wentworth; however, scholars maintain that it also contained errors and misreadings. In a symposium in Columbus, Ohio (5 May 1988), Dickinson scholar Daniel R. Barnes pointed out that Copland made minor changes in Dickinson's texts (for example, in "The Chariot," a stanza is missing and a line is changed).

Emily's World, Amherst Days, Dickinson Cycle, Toward Eternity. I finally settled on *Twelve Poems of Emily Dickinson.* However, the work is most often referred to as *The Dickinson Songs.* [21]

The Twelve Poems of Emily Dickinson constitutes my longest work for solo voice, having a performance time of approximately twenty-eight minutes. The songs were composed for a medium-high voice and require a singer with a rather wide range. I gave a great deal of thought as to how my essentially instrumental style of writing could be adapted for vocal purposes. Since I was accustomed to composing for piano, it was the vocal lines that were my real challenge. I followed the natural inflection of the words of the poems, particularly when they were conversational. There is a certain amount of what is called "word painting"—an occasional birdcall, flutterings, and grace notes in the introduction to the first song, "Nature, the Gentlest Mother," the bugle-like melody for the voice in "There Came a Wind Like a Bugle," and so forth. In a few instances, the meaning of a line led me to use a melisma. The harmony is basically diatonic, with some chromaticism and polytonality, and much of the piano writing is contrapuntal.[22]

Ives, Mahler, and Fauré have been mentioned as influences on *The Dickinson Songs*, particularly the romantic fifth song, "Heart, We Will Forget Him," which has been likened to Mahler. Miss Dickinson's poems are preoccupied with death, as is so much of Mahler's work. But as important to my work as these three composers have been, I see no direct influence. Perhaps I am too close to the picture; it is certainly possible that they were part of my working apparatus. *The Dickinson Songs* (and the *Piano Quartet* in the same year) stem more from other impulses and influences. I have always had an aversion to repeating myself. In retrospect, I must have felt subconsciously that I had gone as far as I could with the full-fledged style presented in *Appalachian Spring* and with full-scale conventional symphonic work as in the *Third Symphony.*

In May 1950, when *The Twelve Poems of Emily Dickinson* was finished, I "premiered" it for a group of composer friends who had been meeting informally on Sunday evenings to listen to and discuss new music at the home of Alma Morgenthau. I wrote to Leo Smit, "They seemed to 'go over' as a cycle. Think of it—twenty-eight minutes' worth of songs!"

The next task was to find the right voice for the first performance—a singer with the appropriate range (a traditional soprano would have to change keys or at least transpose certain passages),[23] an above-average security of rhythm, and an enthusiasm for contemporary music. Douglas Moore, who arranged the Sixth Annual Festival of Contemporary American Music at Columbia University, at which *The Dickinson Songs* would be sung for the first time, asked Virgil Thomson for suggestions. Virgil mentioned Alice Howland, and since both Moore and Thomson thought she was wonderful, I agreed to the choice. They were right—she was wonderful. The premiere took place at Columbia's McMillin Theater (18 May 1950). The program opened with songs by John Edmunds and Howard Swanson. My songs followed the intermission.

[21] See Copland, the Library of Congress: other poems considered and rejected, among them "A Bird Came Down the Walk" and "Only a Shrine, but Mine;" five different prefinal versions of the piano introduction to the first song; pencil sketches; ink transparencies dated "April 10, 1949" with a list of the final ordering of the *Songs* and another showing their order of composition; a bound copy of the holograph of *Eight Poems.*

[22] For musical analysis, see Robert Michael Daugherty, doctoral dissertation, part I, Ohio State University (1980).

[23] Copland worked out transpositions for the traditional soprano voice. See Copland to Leo Smit (13 October 1960): " #3 up minor third; # 4 up minor second; # 7 up major second; # to up minor third; # 11 up major second; #12 up minor second."

Alice Howland[24]

I was singing contemporary music and Virgil Thomson knew my work, so it must have been how Copland heard about me. I sang Ives songs and that might have influenced Copland, too. But I don't think he ever heard me sing before he gave me the music for The Dickinson Songs. *I took the score home to study and got together with Aaron a few times to rehearse. It all seemed very compatible. We just hit it off right away and had no difficulty at all. The songs have some unusual leaps and intervals, but compared to some of the composers I sang—Ives, Krenek, and Schoenberg—*The Dickinson Songs *were not so difficult.*

I did not know the poetry of Emily Dickinson before the Copland songs. It was my introduction to her, and I liked them very much. When Aaron set them, he avoided anything too sweet or melancholy, which could have been easy to do. They have a kind of naive quality that he captured. I think if Aaron had written more songs, he would have had more experience about singers—they are taught to choose only songs that show their voices off best. Of his twelve Dickinson songs, a singer would have a few that fit best, a different few for each singer. I think that is why they have not been performed as a cycle more often. For my voice, the best songs were "Heart We Will Forget Him," "The Chariot," and "Going to Heaven!"

The premiere was a special event. After all, Copland was already an established composer. The piano parts are strong, but he was thoughtful about not covering my voice. It was a wonderful experience singing the songs with him playing! We had no trouble at all, and we were well satisfied with the performance. But The Dickinson Songs *were not a popular success from the first, and no one seemed very eager to hear them again right away. I soon retired from concerts and went on to teaching. I never had the opportunity to sing Copland's* Dickinson Songs *again.*

The critical reception in the newspapers the next day was not overly enthusiastic.[25] Even my admirers admitted to being disappointed. I wrote to Verna and Irving Fine, saying, "I s'pose you heard my songs were done and got a panning in the press. Never occurred to me that they were that hard to hear—but taken all of a piece, apparently they are. I dedicated the nicest song to you. So there!" (Each song is dedicated to a composer friend in the following order: David Diamond, Elliott Carter, Ingolf Dahl, Alexei Haieff, Marcelle de Manziarly, Juan Orrego-Salas, Irving Fine, Harold Shapero, Camargo Guarnieri, Alberto Ginastera, Lukas Foss, and Arthur Berger.)[26]

[24] Interview, Alice Howland with Perlis, 6 December 1988, New York City.

[25] Ross Parmenter, "Columbia Begins Sixth Music Fete," *The New York Times*, 19 May 1950, 31.

[26] No specific reasons have been discovered for Copland's choices concerning the dedications. When asked, he said, "At the time, something about each song felt right for each person." The dedicatees themselves had no further information when questioned by Didriksen.

Perhaps it was because of the fact that these songs were composed as "art" songs that they were not readily accepted. They are not folk in style and contain no extramusical associations or quotations. Virgil Thomson, expert vocal writer that he is, criticized my "cruelty" to the singer, while admiring "the wide melodic skips, which are in themselves highly effective in a declamatory sense and strikingly expressive." Virgil had caught the fact that I meant for the range to be rather extreme. A few of my composer friends admired the songs right away, even in print. William Flanagan wrote:

> Probably the most important single contribution toward an American song literature that we have to date. Above all, Copland's songs really sing, and in their singing they set standards of accomplishment and stylistic integration that American composers of songs will find difficult to ignore in the future.[27]

Henry Cowell praised the songs,[28] as did Irving Fine.[29] It was not until *The Dickinson Songs* were around for a while, however, that they were more fully admired by others. I sent them to Irving before they were published, and with my permission, he played them for Koussevitzky, who (according to Irving) liked only certain ones—"Dear March" and some of the slow ones. Irving wrote me that Koussevitzky did not think that the music fit the words for "Going to Heaven!." But he wouldn't let Irving take the music home and insisted on keeping the score to study them better.

Personally, I always felt very well satisfied with *The Dickinson Songs*. I am often asked which are my favorites: I am particularly fond of "The Chariot"; "Going to Heaven!" is so different that it's fun to play and to sing for an audience; I like "Sleep Is Supposed to Be" a lot, and "Dear March" as it breezes along. Encouraged, I could fall in love with all of them!

Two years after the premiere, when I accompanied Patricia Neway at Town Hall, the audience and critics responded more warmly than they had when the songs were first heard. In 1954, Pat Neway and I made a short concert tour on which *The Dickinson Songs* were included, and we drew crowded houses in Detroit. In the middle of the night on the sleeper to Pittsburgh, Pat woke me to whisper that she had lost her voice. She continued on to New York in a dejected state, while I frantically telephoned Washington, D.C., for Katherine Hansel to fill the breach. She did, dear girl, by meeting me in Pittsburgh and singing *The Dickinson Songs* without time to even rehearse them. All went off well.

I always thought of *The Dickinson Songs* as being sung by a female, but when a recording by a male singer was sent to me from England, the singing was so musical and with such excellent diction, I liked it, even though it did seem strange to hear a man singing those words. After all, they were written by a woman from a woman's point of view.[30]

[27] William Flanagan, "American Songs: A Thin Crop," *Musical America*, LXXI I: 2 (February 1952), 23, 130. Sec also Flanagan liner notes for Columbia Records.
[28] Henry Cowell, "Current Chronicle," *Musical Quarterly*, XXXVI (July 1950), 453.
[29] Irving Fine, "Solo Songs," *Notes*, XI (December 1953), 159-60.
[30] Robert Tear and Philip Ledger recorded the *Songs* for Argo. Other recordings were Adele Addison with Copland, re-released on Columbia Records with *Old American Songs* by William Warfield; also for Columbia, Martha Lipton (as a mezzo, she found it necessary to transcribe some of the songs); Mildred Miller for Columbia Records.

I began orchestrating *The Dickinson Songs* in 1958, hoping they might have a wider hearing. I found that only eight of the twelve were suitable.[31] The orchestration calls for thirty-nine players (or a thirty-two member ensemble with a reduced string section). I didn't finish the orchestration until 1970, just in time for the songs to be premiered for a seventieth birthday concert at the Metropolitan Museum of Art in New York by the Juilliard Orchestra, Michael Tilson Thomas conducting, Gwendolyn Killebrew as soloist.

Several fine singers have been drawn to *The Dickinson Songs:* [32] one was Adele Addison, with whom I made a recording. A television film[33] was made with Phyllis Curtin. Phyllis and I enjoyed performing *The Dickinson Songs* together in the sixties and seventies.

Phyllis Curtin[34]

I was Phyllis Jane Smith in 1946 when I first met Aaron Copland at the Berkshire Music Center. It was my first summer at Tanglewood, and my big moment came when I took the part of one of the two nieces in Britten's Peter Grimes, *which was given its American premiere that summer. Tanglewood is the closest thing I have to a musical alma mater, and Aaron was, of course, always on the scene. He gave me* The Dickinson Songs *in Boston when he was Charles Eliot Norton Lecturer at Harvard in 1951-1952. From time to time I looked at them, but I really couldn't sing them. I didn't have enough character and presence in the middle of my voice to make those songs do what I felt they had to do. About every five years or so, I'td take them out to see if I had grown to the point where I could sing them.*

One time I saw Aaron during that ten-year period, and he said, "Do you ever sing my songs?" I replied, "No, I never do, but it's not because I don't like them, it's that I can't sing them." He asked, "Why don't you transpose them?" I almost fainted, because most composers I knew were offended if you even suggested such a thing. That was such a nice easy free thing for Aaron to say. But I answered, "Well, I think because I like the keys they're in. It's just the right speech for those songs." It was about fifteen years after I first saw The Dickinson Songs *that I sang them. By that time, my voice had grown and developed and they really fit beautifully.*

The first thing those songs did for me was very interesting. I had never liked Emily Dickinson. I used to read her and get very exasperated. I didn't like her personality—I thought she was unnecessarily quirky and coy. But as soon as I could sing Aaron's songs, I began to understand Emily Dickinson! It is my conviction, after having sung these songs hundreds of times, that nobody has ever understood her as Aaron does. If anybody ever sent Emily Dickinson's "Letter to the World," it's Aaron Copland. It was Aaron who found the musical voice for Emily Dickinson, and the times when I sang them best, I had the feeling that she was speaking.

[31] The eight orchestrated songs are "Nature," "Wind Like a Bugle," "The World Feels Dusty," "Heart We Will Forget Him," "Dear March, Come In," "Sleep Is Supposed to Be," "Going to Heaven!," and "The Chariot." The setting is for flute (piccolo), oboe, two clarinets, bassoon, horn, trumpet, trombone, harp, and strings.
[32] Other singers associated with *The Dickinson Songs* are Nell Tangeman, Martha Lipton, and Meriel Dickinson.
[33] Allan Miller, producer, "Lincoln Center Presents," WNET Channel 13, New York City, 1964.
[34] Interview, Phyllis Curtin with Perlis, 5 August 1986, Lenox, Massachusetts.

Above: Manuscript, first page of the voice and orchestra version of "Going to Heaven!" from *The Twelve Poems of Emily Dickinson*

Left: Phyllis Curtin and Copland taking a bow after a performance of *The Dickinson Songs* at Tanglewood, 1972

I sang Aaron's Dickinson Songs *often with him at the piano. I never felt anything but delight when we did them together. Aaron never varied much from the score. Sometimes he played klinkers or sometimes with less grace and smoothness than other times, but I never once felt uncomfortable. It was always real. Together, we might move a little faster in one performance than another, depending on several things—our disposition, our nerve, or how much Aaron had practiced. If he wasn't in finger, things would change a little in the performance. I would accommodate to that. But you don't think about those things, you feel them. I liked singing with Aaron at the piano. I have always preferred strong pianists. I don't care much for the ones who shy back and don't live with the music.*

There were funny little interpretative things once in a while. I remember the first time we ever rehearsed The Dickinson Songs *together; when we got to "Going to Heaven!," he stopped me and said, "Phyllis, but that's so strong!" I said, "That's just how looking at the music makes me feel. And you dedicated this piece to Lukas Foss, and that's how Lukas' rhythms always make me feel." Aaron said, "Oh, that's interesting." We did it again and it was fine with him. Just his asking me about it probably made me think slightly differently. I sang a wrong note in the first song and he pointed that out to me, saying, "Do it again." I did, and he said, "I kinda like it that way. Sometimes I find my best music on other people's pianos."* Of *course, from then on, I sang his note. But it was a sweet little exchange.*

I never had a single bad review of any kind for me or for the music in all the times I sang The Dickinson Songs. *I usually did them as the second half of a recital. I don't know that I think of them as cyclical, but I think of them as all part of Emily's life, as part of her personality, as part of her living in New England, so that they progress one to the other, but not in a story form. Only occasionally did I split* The Songs *up, singing perhaps three. I did that once on a program when Helmut Schmidt went to the White House, and one of the songs was "There Came a Wind Like a Bugle. "A fierce July thunderstorm came up soon after I started! When I sang the entire cycle once at Marlboro, Blanche Moyse said, "This is the American* Winterreise." *I agree—it is a major song cycle of this century— no question about it. And it is so marvelously American. To my thinking,* The Twelve Poems of Emily Dickinson *is Aaron's major work.*

I don't find difficult leaps in the vocal writing. Maybe that was part of waiting until I felt really right for it, but once it happened, there again it seems to me one of the geniuses of this piece that I don't even think of it as having intervals. I think of it as having words, words such as "the world feels dusty"—nobody ever set the word dusty in that way. There are similar things all the way through that to me are the shape of words, so I can't even tell you what intervals are in it anymore. "Sleep Is Supposed to Be" really worries a lot of students. Well, here is Emily's whole idea about all those people when she was in her teens, those who were standing up and declaring for Jesus. That's what those intervals are to me. They are part of a wonderful New England sermon. It is the pattern of Emily's remarkable speech that Aaron understood absolutely.

I feel about Aaron's orchestrated version of eight of the songs as I do about Alban Berg's Seven Early Songs. *I couldn't wait to sing those with orchestra, and some of it is very lovely. But there is more color with the piano than there is with the orchestra, and that's exactly how I feel about Aaron's* Dickinson Songs. *I think they were hatched in his mind with piano, and that's what does it best, which is not to say that he didn't do a brilliant job of orchestrating. Perhaps if a singer learns them first with the orchestra, she might not feel the same way at all. Once, I did* The Songs *with orchestra at Tanglewood, Aaron* conducting *(1972), and we had to wait while the orchestra rehearsed Charles Wuorinen's* Violin Concerto. *It was so loud I thought I would lose my mind. I finally said to Aaron, "I can't sit here and wait. I don't think I'll be able to hear when it gets to be my turn." Aaron kind of giggled and said, "This is the first time I have ever felt like a nineteenth-century composer."*

During the winter of 1950, I took a break from *The Dickinson Songs* with the hope of recharging my inspiration. I set a group of American folk songs, calling them *Old American Songs.* The five songs in the set are drawn from completely different sources. "The Boatmen's Dance," a minstrel show tune by Daniel Decatur Emmett, composer of "Dixie," is from the Harris Collection at Brown University. I composed the accompaniment in imitation of minstrel banjo playing. "The Dodger," a satirical political song, was found in the John and Alan Lomax book, *Our Singing Country*. It dates from the presidential campaign of 1884, when Grover Cleveland defeated James G. Blaine. "Long Time Ago" is a sentimental ballad, also from the Harris Collection.[35] "Simple Gifts" is the Shaker song used in *Appalachian Spring*, arranged in a style closer to the original, with a direct and straightforward melodic line and simple hymnlike harmonies. The last of the five songs, "I Bought Me a Cat," is a children's nonsense song resembling "Old MacDonald's Farm." I learned it from the playwright Lynn Riggs, who had sung it as a boy in Oklahoma (we had hoped to use the song in the ill-fated *Tragic Ground* theater project). The accompaniment imitates barnyard sounds in the choices of harmony and figurations. Paul Moor has reminded me that I used to sing "I Bought Me a Cat" for friends, and that I always clapped my hands twice before the last line of each stanza—"and my cat says fiddle-eye-fee."[36]

I sang the songs for Peter Pears and Ben Britten when they came to visit, promising to send them on to England when I finished them. Peter told me, "I like them very much indeed—we shall do them first at Aldeburgh June 17, then Amsterdam June 30th; then again here in July; probably Edinburgh Festival September 3rd, & in London in October—So you see! They will, as singers say, prove a most useful addition to my repertoire! I am still a little inclined to make the cat say 'fiddle my fee!'" Peter and Ben did the premiere performance of *Old American Songs I* (17 June 1950) at the Aldeburgh Festival and made the first recording.[37] The following winter, the baritone William Warfield and I gave the American premiere at Town Hall (28 January 1951). Warfield's ability to sing in a variety of styles, and his warmth and sense of humor was an ideal combination for these folk songs. Warfield could be gentle and lyric one moment, playful and humorous the next. We made a recording of *Old American Songs I* together with the Columbia Symphony Orchestra for Columbia Records; it was paired with the *Clarinet Concerto*, and reissued in 1980.

[35] "Long Time Ago" was an anonymous blackface tune. The words were adapted by George Pope in 1837 and set to music by Charles Edward Horn.
[36] See Paul Moor to Perlis, 29 December 1984, Peekskill, New York: "Aaron set 'I Bought Me a Cat' with Agnes de Mille's *Tragic Ground* in mind. His clapping obviously was connected in his mind with what he had expected the dancers to do in the show. The surprise came with the very last stanza when Aaron clapped three times, accenting the last clap to heighten the effect. I've always wished some singer would interpolate the hand claps."
[37] The Pears/Britten recording was reissued by EMI in 1980.

William Warfield and Copland during the recording of *Old American Songs I*, 1955

I always enjoyed playing or conducting the songs with Warfield. I have heard other singers treat these songs in a more formal lieder style. Recently, a baritone performed "Simple Gifts" on a television show and there was nothing at all "simple" about it! But Warfield always brought genuine warmth to the songs.

Everyone seemed to enjoy singing and hearing *Old American Songs* I so much that I decided to arrange a second set in 1952. *Old American Songs II* also includes five songs from diverse sources: "The Little Horses," a children's lullaby from the South based on a version from Lomax's Folk Song USA.; "Zion's Walls," a revivalist song (originally meant for Tragic Ground and later used in my opera), with original words and music credited to John G. McCurry; "The Golden Willow Tree," a variant of a well-known Anglo-American ballad often called "The Golden Vanity," which I heard on a Library of Congress recording for banjo and voice; "At the River," the 1865 hymn tune everybody knows and loves by Reverend Robert Lowry, and "Ching-a-Ring Chaw," a minstrel song from the Harris Collection at Brown University. I had to change the existing text of "Ching-a-Ring Chaw," not wanting to take any chance of it being construed as racist.[38] William Warfield and I premiered *Old American Songs II* at Castle Hill Concerts in Ipswich, Massachusetts (24 July 1953).

[38] "Ching-a-Ring Chaw" is number 17 in the Harris Collection of American Poetry and Players, Series of Old American Songs (1833). The title reads: "Ching-a-Ring Chaw or Sambo's 'Dress to He' Bred'trin." The description reads: "The hope that the republic [sic) of Haiti (1822-43) might prove the solution of the negro [*sic*] problem inspired this song, which combines jocularity and pathos in its appeal for emigration to the black paradise."

I arranged both sets of songs for medium voice and small orchestra. Warfield sang the first performance of the orchestral arrangement of *Old American Songs I* with the Los Angeles Philharmonic under Alfred Wallenstein (7 January 1955) and Grace Bumbry premiered II with the Ojai Festival Orchestra, which I conducted; (25 May 1955). Various choral arrangements have been published.[39] It pleases me to know from my publishers that *Old American Songs I* and *II* are in demand by college choral groups around the country.

William Warfield[40]

Shortly after my debut at Town Hall in 1950, I met Aaron and he showed me the Old American Songs I. *I sang them on my second Town Hall recital (28 January 1951). It was the American premiere of the first set, and they were a tremendous success. Aaron was an excellent pianist and, of course, knowing the flavor of them so well, it was a tremendous experience working with him. When we were rehearsing for the recording of the first set, we had a discussion about singing "Simple Gifts." He wanted it simple, almost recitative-like in quality, so you wouldn't feel it as a rhythmic, bouncy thing. The way it is written in the original, it seems obviously very rhythmic, but Aaron even put the chords on the off-accented beat to be sure it wouldn't be sung with that regular rhythmic feeling.*

When we rehearsed "I Bought Me a Cat," I stopped at "I bought me a cow," because the sound written in the score is "bah, bah." I said to Aaron, "It doesn't sound right to me—I think it should be 'moo, moo.'" He grinned and said, "Okay," and that's the way we recorded it. You ask me about "Ching-a-Ring Chaw:" I never thought of it as a minstrel song and never saw the original words. I didn't know until right now that Aaron had changed some of the words.

I did the premiere of the orchestrated sets (eight songs) with the Los Angeles Philharmonic, Wallenstein conducting (7 January, 1955), and I have performed them many times since then: once with Ormandy on tour in Europe (that's when Aaron was in Paris and came to hear them); more recently, I sang a few of the songs with orchestra at the Kennedy Center Honors in Washington when Copland received his award (1979). I don't have a strong preference, but if I had to make a choice, it would probably be toward the orchestrated version, especially for "I Bought Me a Cat," where you have all these wonderful barnyard sounds in the orchestration.

We have had a tremendously wonderful relationship that has lasted all these years. It has included Lincoln Portrait, *which I have narrated with Aaron conducting and with Bernstein also. I was doing* Lincoln *at the Kennedy Center at the time of the Bicentennial, and Lenny said, "Why don't you come on tour with us [the New York Philharmonic] in Europe?" He had someone do the translations so they retained the feeling of Lincoln's words in other languages. We did it in French in Paris, German in Vienna, and English, of course, in England. A videotape was made of the one in Albert Hall, and a record was issued having to do with Bernstein, and it included my narration of* Lincoln *from that tour.*

I was feeling the urge to spend some time in Europe, so I applied for a Fulbright Fellowship for 1951. I was offered two million lira, and for two exciting minutes I thought I was a millionaire! Then I rushed for a pencil, and it turned into $3,250! But the crossing was paid for, and I would be staying at the American Academy in Rome beginning 1 January. Before leaving on the *Queen Elizabeth* (23 December 1950), I had many arrangements to make. First the house: I wanted it lived in while I was away. Victor was in Brazil taking photographs, and Erik Johns hoped his visa would arrive so that he could go along to Italy with me. I wanted to sublet the house to defray some expenses (without Hollywood, my income had returned to a more normal low in 1949 and 1950).[41] I was delighted when Bob Fizdale called to ask whether I knew a place he and Arthur Gold might rent. They needed a place right away, so I suggested they come and stay with me. There was more than enough room. They split some of the bills, helped me during a few violent storms, made sensational meals, rented the house while I was away, and later on, rented it for three years after I moved out.[42]

Erik's exit visa arrived just forty-eight hours before sailing. Gold and Fizdale gave us a going-away party complete with Christmas tree and trimmings and drove us to the boat. I was feeling rather pleased to leave a known life behind for an unknown one ahead. The crossing was surprisingly smooth for that time of year, but the ship was very empty. Erik's dance partner, Luisa Krebs, was with us, and the two of them ate themselves silly. I got some rest, and we all saw a lot of movies.

After landing at Cherbourg, we went on to Paris, and on New Year's Eve, I took the train alone to Rome (Erik and Luisa joined a dance company for a European tour). A representative from the American Academy met me at the station. An hour later, I was dining at a villa with a count and twelve countesses! I was given an apartment that was beautifully situated—overlooking all of Rome. It came with a cook and a good Bechstein grand piano. The main trouble was the barely adequate heating system. Everyone in Rome seemed to take that kind of problem for granted, but I was condemned to cold feet for several months! Sonny Shapero and Lukas Foss were at the Academy when I arrived, and Leo Smit was also in town.[43] They all helped to get me acquainted with things Roman.

I hoped to get started on a piano concerto, commissioned by the Louisville Symphony for William Kapell. The commission fell through, but I continued to compose piano music without a definite plan for its final form. "Life," as I wrote to Esther and Arthur Berger, "was almost too soft." I was to find that there was not much music going on in Italy by American standards, but as I wrote to Claire Reis, "It's a heavenly town."

When Erik and Luisa arrived after their tour, it was a great problem finding a place for them with a wooden floor for dancing—practically every floor in Rome is made of stone or cement. We finally found them a place on Via Margutta, full of artists and sculptors. Then I took a big plunge and bought a car—a green Morris-Minor—on Shapero's advice. I wrote to my sister (3 February 1951); "Dear La: Today I get the tiny car I bought for a

[39] *Old American Songs I*: "The Boatsmen's Song," SATB and TTBB with baritone solo (Fine); "The Dodger," TTBB with baritone solo (Fine); "Long Time Ago," SSA (Straker), SATB (Fine); "Simple Gifts," SA or TB (Fine); "I Bought Me a Cat," SSA (Straker), SATB with tenor or soprano solos (Fine), TBB with TBB solo (Fine). Old American Songs IL "The Little Horses," SA, SA, TTBB (Wilding-White); "At the River," SA, SSA, SATB, TTBB (Wilding-White); "Ching-a-Ring Chaw," TTBB (Copland), SSAA, SATB (Fine).

[40] Interview, William Warfield with Perlis (telephone), 8 February 1989.

[41] Copland's income was $20,092 in 1949; $15,431 in 1950.

[42] See interview with Robert Fizdale.

[43] See interview, Leo Smit with Perlis, 29 January 1981, New York City.

thousand dollars—it's said to get thirty miles on a gallon—and since gas is eighty cents a gallon here, everyone buys small cars for economy sake. Also, many streets are so narrow that a Buick wouldn't fit!" From the time the car arrived, I composed mornings and went exploring most afternoons with Erik, Luisa, and Leo. We went to see and hear the Pope in St. Peter's Square (everybody in Rome kept telling me that the Pope and I looked alike!). We drove to Naples (I had accepted duties for the State Department that included lectures on American music in various cities in Italy), and afterward, down the coast to Pompeii and Paestum. We enjoyed the beautiful Amalfi coast, although my car almost balked on one of those mountains!

It was a small musical world in Italy. When Leo gave a recital at the Academy, there were too many Americans present and not enough Italians. The same situation held when I gave my first lecture on American music, with Leo playing the musical examples. Among the few Italians I saw was Dallapiccola in Florence, who had earlier accepted an invitation to teach at Tanglewood in 1951. I found him personally charming but became less interested in his music the more I heard of it. Edwin Denby, who was living in Ischia, came to visit me in Rome, and once or twice, I went to see Ashley Pettis, who had left the music world to become a priest. I wrote to Arthur Berger, "You ought to see Ashley Pettis in a priest's garb. Complete transformation! When he came to lunch at my place in his priestly robe, he scared my cook!"

As usual, after a short time away, I felt starved for news of New York. When I didn't see the music page of *The New York Times*, I felt deprived. I did hear the news when Gide died. Somehow, I did not feel sad about it—I guess because he had so fully expressed himself in a long lifetime. What more can one ask?

From Rome, I made my first visit to Israel.[44] It had been arranged by Eleazar de Carvalho, then conductor of the Israel Philharmonic Orchestra. Carvalho had conducted *Appalachian Spring* ten times by the end of 1950 in Tel Aviv, Haifa, and Jerusalem, and was planning fifteen more performances during a three-month tour in the States. I found the two and one-half weeks in Israel immensely stimulating. My first lectures were in Tel Aviv. What impressed me most were the young people on the beach on the Sabbath, all jabbering in Hebrew and looking healthy and happy and very un-Jewish. The children were unforgettable. I was moved by merely walking along the beach in Tel Aviv.

I conducted *In the Beginning* at a concert on the shores of the Sea of Galilee—a very appropriate setting. I had never conducted a chorus before, but nobody there seemed to notice. We were only two kilometers away from the Syrian border. At 2:30 A.M., I was awakened by sporadic firing, generally referred to as "border incidents." The radio announced each day that the Festival at Ein Gev would continue, "and Aaron Copland is there." I spent Pesach (Passover) at the kibbutz with six hundred people. For five days, I lived with thirty Israeli composers in an art colony, Zichron Yakov, outside of Tel Aviv, and listened to their music, which was enthusiastic but not exportable. It turned out that I was the first composer to have visited there from abroad, and the reception was very warm. I

[44] See travel diary #7.

Above: Copland planting a tree on his first trip to Israel, April 1951

SATURDAY, APRIL 21, 1951 — OPENING CONCERT

CHORAL CONCERT
by the
TEL-AVIV VOCAL ENSEMBLE
(Eytan Lustig, conducter)

conducted by
AARON COPLAND and EYTAN LUSTIG
Soloist : NAOMI ZURI (mezzo-soprano)

PROGRAMME :

Three Peasants' Songs for mixed chorus and piano (1948) ...
Erich Walter Sternberg (born 1898)
(After ancient folksongs, Hebrew : Joseph Achai)
First Performance.

Cantata No. 4 (composed for Easter Sunday, 1724) ...
Johann Sebastian Bach (1685-1750)
(Original Text by Martin Luther. Hebrew version: Ephraim Dror).

Sinfonia — Chorus — Duet (Soprano, Contralto) — Tenor solo — Chorus — Bass solo — Duet (Soprano, Tenor) — Choral.

—Interval—

In the Beginning (Genesis, ChapterI : 1 — II : 7), for mixed chorus a cappella with mezzo-soprano solo (1947) ...
Aaron Copland (born 1900)
First Performance in Israel.
Conducted by the Composer.
Soloist : Naomi Zuri.

THE OPENING CONCERT

Ein Gev's musical programmes for the 1951 Passover Festival open with a choral concert by a vocal ensemble that has made history in the musical life of Israel. This is the Tel-Aviv Vocal Ensemble (founded and conducted by Eytan Lustig), the nucleus of the larger Tel-Aviv Chamber Choir, to which the country owes the first local performances of a great many Bach Cantatas; of religious works by Pergolesi, Delalande, and Mozart, of ancient operas in concerted form; and of a number of important Israeli compositions, among them works by Sternberg, Ben-Haim, Orgad, and Seter-Starominski. To-night's concert receives special significance by the only guest-appearance as a conductor made in the country by Aaron Copland, who leads the ensemble in the first Israel performance of his recent choral work based on the first chapters of the Bible.

Right: Program of the Ein Gev Music Festival

went to Jerusalem for two days. It is absolutely silent by 9 P.M. each night. From my hotel room at the King David, I could look inside the walls of the Old City, but as the Arabs of Transjordan owned it, it was impossible and frustrating not to be able to get inside! Everyone seemed to be having a terrific adventure, however. I wrote to Victor, "It could make a Zionist out of a Hitler." And when I visited Haifa and Lake Tiberias, everyone seemed so fully alive! In fact, the whole of Israel seemed to be developing at presto speed.

Often questioned about what seemed a lack of "Jewish" material in my compositions, I decided not to dodge the issue: In Jerusalem, I delivered a lecture called "Jewish Composers in the Western World" (15 April 1951)[45] I admitted that the subject was controversial, because it brought into consideration the racial consciousness of the artist, the assimilation theory, and the role of the nonassimilated artist. I made it clear that I was speaking as a composer from my own experience, not as historian, ethnologist, or expert on Jewish

[45] See lecture notes in Copland's files at the Library of Congress.

affairs. I knew in advance that this audience would have liked to hear that Jewish artists who affirm their Jewishness come off best. I pointed out, however, that "The facts are more complex: Of the specifically 'Jewish' composers in Western countries, no leading figure emerged with the possible exception of Bloch."

After opening remarks stating my position, I sketched for the audience the contributions of Jewish composers who wrote music of interest to all the world: in the nineteenth century, Mendelssohn, Meyerbeer, and Offenbach; in the twentieth, Mahler, Schoenberg, Bloch, Milhaud, Gershwin, and Weill. I closed my talk by emphasizing that "a man doesn't create art because he is a Jew but because he is a man. The truly Jewish composer need not worry about his Jewishness—it will be evident in the work."

When I returned to Rome, I conducted a work by another composer for the first time—David Diamond's *Rounds* in a concert also featuring my *Clarinet Concerto* (7 May). When the Rome radio invited me to conduct an all-Copland concert, I accepted, and found the orchestra surprisingly good, so much so that Leo and I decided to program the *Piano Concerto*. The outcome was that we recorded it for the Concert Hall label.

In mid-May, I lectured in Bologna and Genoa, before traveling on to Paris. From Paris, I wrote to Victor, "Every street and shop is full of memories for me." I wanted to stay longer but only had time to see Noel Lee and hear some of his new music. I had to be in London to discuss the renewal of my contract with Boosey & Hawkes. Ralph Hawkes had always looked out for my interests in the past. His sudden death in September 1950 was a serious loss. Leslie Boosey was friendly, but I sensed some opposition among the other Londoners. I spent a week settling the contract satisfactorily and visiting Ben Britten and Peter Pears. I returned to Paris for lunch with Clurman and then took the Simplon Express to Trieste to conduct an all-Copland program (4 June).

Being so far away and traveling from one European city to another as I did in May, I had no idea that Koussevitzky was so seriously ill. I had written him from Rome, saying, "It is slow work to get the Italians interested in American music, but one must begin somewhere. I have been giving lectures." I wrote again from Israel: "Everywhere we spoke of you—in Zichron Yakov, in Ein Gev, in Jerusalem." After hearing the news of Koussevitzky's death, I wrote to Irving (8 June 1951), stating, "I felt sorry that neither Lenny, nor Lukas, nor I were around at the end." What an irreplaceable void Koussevitzky's absence would leave in the world of music! All of the implications would take time to realize.

Taking stock of the six months abroad, I had to admit I hadn't finished composing anything—perhaps because I was traveling so much—somehow, the incentive wasn't there. I arrived home to find many changes. In addition to Koussevitzky's absence (I kept expecting him to appear at Tanglewood), I no longer had the house at Sneden's Landing; Victor was planning to get married to Pearl Kazan; and Lenny Bernstein announced his engagement to Felicia Montealegre Cohn. After seeing Pearl in New York, I wrote to Victor, who was still in Brazil (19 August): "Everybody admired the ring you had sent up. What with Lenny's announcement, everyone agrees there's a trend."

Everyone thought Victor's news was a great surprise, but I had realized long before his marriage that it was important for him to go it alone, or better still, with a woman to help him. I wrote him so, and we continued to stay in touch regularly. Erik suggested that we give Pearl and Victor a special wedding gift—the green Morris-Minor from Italy. I agreed and wrote (14 September 1951), "Dear P & V: No family was ever more excited about a far-off happening than us at the marriage finals. Hope you both like the idea of a Morris-Minor as a wedding gift. It's really a ducky little car—lightish green in color and hasn't given us a day's trouble. I plan to put it in dead storage about October 15 (for you). Please don't ask to have it mailed to Brazil!"

I wrote to Lenny (5 November 1951): "Victor writes very enthusiastic letters from Rio. Seems pleased with himself and Pearl and Rio and job. It's a miracle and I'm awfully pleased." But in less than a year, Pearl and Victor were already parting—before they had even received their wedding gift! I wrote to Victor (15 August 1952), "I will sell the Morris-Minor and split the amount between you."

I was more than surprised to receive a letter while in Rome that I had been chosen to deliver the Charles Eliot Norton Lectures at Harvard during the academic year 1951-1952. Stravinsky had delivered his *Poetics of Music*, and Hindemith *A Composer's World*, but this was the first time a native-born composer had been chosen for the Poetry Chair established a quarter of a century earlier. Although it would mean living in Cambridge for six months, I accepted. After all, the Norton Poetry Chair is one of Harvard's most prestigious honors and a very high responsibility. I immediately began to worry about what I could possibly say! I tried to get started on the lectures while abroad. Fortunately, there was a good library at the American Academy in Rome, and I went often and read on aesthetics, hoping to stimulate my thoughts.

I am not a professional writer. My literary output is a byproduct of my trade. As a kind of salesman for contemporary music, I frequently spoke and wrote (sometimes wrote and then spoke) about issues relating to my product. Although I tended to think that music was either too hard to write about or not worth writing about at all, I periodically published articles and books, sometimes developed from lectures. For example, in 1949 an article appeared in *The New York Times Magazine*—"A Modernist Defends Modern Music"—that was stimulated by a lecture a few months earlier at Town Hall. Looking ahead, I hoped the book to be published from the Norton Lectures could be edited directly from my talks. I took warning from my friend Thornton Wilder, Norton Lecturer the previous year, when he told me he was having a heck of a time writing a book from the sketchy notes he had used for his lectures.

Fortunately, a free interpretation of the title "Norton Professor of Poetics" made it possible for me to discuss the one thing I know something about—music. Nevertheless, it was a bit frustrating and scary because I feared that my words might not be eloquent enough. I gave up composing music entirely and worked on the lectures in much the same way I composed—that is, thinking about ideas in advance and jotting them down for future use. By the time I left for Tanglewood in 1951, I had sketched a rough draft. I wrote and polished the final manuscript after Tanglewood while moving my things out of the attic at Sneden's Landing in the weeks before leaving for Cambridge. Up in the attic at Sneden's, I came across a very stimulating book by I. A. Richards, *Coleridge on Imagination.* It gave me the title of my lectures: "Music and the Imaginative Mind."

An advance trip to Cambridge to see the rooms at Adams House, where I was supposed to stay, convinced me to find something less dreary. I decided to take the top floor of the Edward Forbes house at Gerry's Landing. Mr. Forbes was a grandson of Emerson; furthermore, Stravinsky and Boulanger had both lived in that house while in Cambridge. The place had a nice hidden-away feeling but was only five minutes from Harvard Square. I moved to Cambridge (3 October) and was given the "office" in Widener Library reserved for the Norton Professor. I found a chair in it clearly marked "Charles Eliot Norton"! I never sat in it.

The Norton Professorship Committee gave me a cordial reception. I had known professors Archibald MacLeish and A. Tillman Merritt for many years. It was MacLeish's idea to include a program of music after each lecture—an innovation for the Norton lectures. The programs, which I would arrange, were made possible by the Elizabeth Sprague Coolidge Foundation. I was delighted, for as I pointed out in my second lecture, "The Sonorous Image," music must "sound." The post-lecture concerts would help dispel that vague and unsatisfactory sensation that always follows any mere discussion of music.

It was not so difficult to write the lectures as I had anticipated. I discovered I really did have some fresh things to say and some others that bore repeating. The value of these lectures depended partly on the overall shaping of the material. I thought of them as similar to a musical composition with two large movements (the two sets of lectures), each including three separate but related sections. In the first three lectures, which were delivered in the fall of 1951, I attempted to develop in a logical way the subject of the imagination in connection with musical experience; in the second set, delivered in the spring of 1952, I was concerned with the public rather than the musical imagination.

The audience for my first Norton Lecture (13 November) had applied for tickets far in advance and seemed interested in what I had to say about the art of listening: "Listening is a talent, and like any other talent or gift, we possess it in varying degrees. . . . All musicians, creators, and performers alike think of the gifted listener as a key figure in the musical universe. The ideal listener, above all else, possesses the ability to lend himself to the power of music." The concert following the first lecture featured vocal music by Stravinsky, Berlioz, and Bizet.[46] A week later, the second lecture, "The Sonorous Image," dealt with the overriding preoccupation of the composer with sound, no matter in what age or what the state of technology and engineering. Music by Mozart, Couperin, and de Falla followed. The third lecture (27 November) explored the linkage of creation and interpretation. I described the composer in the throes of composing and the kind of detachment that follows later, after a work is performed. Music following the talk was by Schubert, Ravel, and me.

[46] For a complete list of the performers and the works presented following each Norton Lecture, see Copland, *Music and Imagination*, "Programs," 112-14.

The second set of lectures, "Musical Imagination in the Contemporary Scene," might be considered a guide through Europe and the Americas. I began with "Tradition and Innovation in Recent European Music" (5 March 1952). The music afterward was by Webern and Tippett. The second lecture, "Musical Imagination in the Americas" (12 March), was concerned with Latin America, and appropriately included music by Chávez, Villa-Lobos, and Caturla. The audience also heard recorded music by jazz artists Lennie Tristano, Dave Brubeck, Bud Powell, and Oscar Pettiford (a hoped-for "live" presentation proved impractical). My final presentation, "The Composer in Industrial America" (19 March), dealt with what a composer feels and experiences in twentieth-century America. The musical portion included Ives, Thomson, and me.

I need not go fully into the content of the six Norton Lectures because I can refer the reader to their publication by Harvard University Press. In *Music and Imagination*,[47] my fourth book, the lectures appear substantially in the same form in which they were read to the students and general public at Cambridge. *Music and Imagination* received favorable critical reviews when it was published in 1952.[48]

I also gave a course, "Music in the Twenties," which was open to the public. I was delighted that it drew five hundred people. I could not help but notice that everyone in Cambridge seemed to be over fifty or under twenty-one. I wondered where the middle-agers were! Life was peaceful in Cambridge and I enjoyed the quiet academic atmosphere around Harvard. Widener Library was a big drawing card. There I examined scores of George Chadwick and was surprised to find how varied in style his orchestral works were. I made a note at the time: "I am convinced that there are many amusing discoveries awaiting the more adventurous musicologist."

It was blissful not to travel for a change. I went down to New York only once to attend the League of Composers't "retrospective" in my honor. Otherwise, I stayed in Cambridge and got together with friends in the Boston area—the Fines, Bergers, and Shaperos. Characteristically, Irving was mulling over his notes; Sonny was teaching at Brandeis; and Arthur was putting the finishing touches on his book about my music. My old friend from Fontainebleau days, Melville Smith, played in my *Organ Symphony* (7 February 1952), and Lukas Foss came to town, bringing along his new *Piano Concerto* and a wife, Cornelia. An all-Copland concert was given at Sanders Theater (20 February). I was treated so well at Harvard that when it came time to leave, I regretted departing from Cambridge and the comfort and privacy of Gerry's Landing.

Just as *Music and Imagination* was about to be published, my brother Ralph died. The book is dedicated "to the memory of my brother Ralph Copland, 1888-1952." I knew that Ralph had not been well: he had been depressed for some long time and seemed to be on the verge of a nervous breakdown. In fact, Laurine and I were having lunch to discuss the situation the very day Ralph plunged from his sixteen-story office building (24 March

[47] Copland, *Music and Imagination* (Cambridge: Harvard University Press, 1952; paper, 9th printing, 1979).

[48] One review was by Virgil Thomson, "A Composer's Universe," in the column "Music and Musicians," *Herald Tribune*, 12 October 1952, Section 4, 5.

1952). Ralph was sixty-three, twelve years my senior. He had been practicing law for many years. He and his wife, Dorothy (my old childhood friend), lived in Brooklyn. They had no children. Ralph was such a mild-mannered individual that I could never have dreamed that he—of all people—would do such a thing! My siblings were all older than I, and Ralph was the first to go. I wrote to Victor, "I am shocked and shaken by it."

When I returned from Cambridge to New York, I was again without a home of my own. I had stayed in Greenwich Village with Erik during the midwinter break from Harvard and again in the spring, but the place was really too small for both of us to be working in at the same time. I was looking for a house in earnest and wrote to Victor (28 May): "How does one ever decide where to settle forever!" Erik had hoped to be joining the Martha Graham studio, but an old knee injury was keeping his dance career in the balance. He was painting and working on a project he and I had been talking about—an opera for which Erik would write the libretto. When I left for the MacDowell Colony in June 1952, I took with me a draft of the libretto. Erik wrote (14 June), "Have you let anyone read the lib?" But I was determined to keep it very sub rosa until I knew definitely that we were going ahead. I wrote only to Victor, since he was in Brazil and would keep it to himself (20 July 1952):

> It's an opera for the college trade, about one and a half hours long, I guess. Some of the *Tragic Ground* material can be utilized, which is part of the attraction, since it makes it seem much easier to do. Also, I feel the need of more "trials and errors" before launching into a real "grand opry" . . . I keep telling everyone I'm writing a long piano piece, which I am.

The summer of 1952 was the tenth session of the Berkshire Music Center, as well as my tenth year at Tanglewood. An uneasy feeling that the Center might not survive Koussevitzky's death was dispelled when the trustees voted to continue the school, but it was made clear we were to keep expenses down. After Charles Munch became director, he endorsed the reappointment of the faculty board as constituted the previous summer. I received my usual official letter of appointment from George Judd (1 February 1952): "Your duties will be to serve as teacher of composition and assistant director of the Music Center."[49] I had written an article for *The New York Times*, "Tanglewood's Future," describing a new scholarship program that would remove the burden of tuition fees from any student accepted for work in the advanced departments.[50] Tod Perry, Lenny, and I met at the Harvard Club to discuss the Tanglewood Revolving Scholarship Fund and to work on plans for the upcoming season.

For the first time, a visiting composer was invited to return to the Music Center: Dallapiccola again shared the composition program with me. Among his nine students were Luciano Berio, Salvatore Martirano, and Leonard Rosenman. I had seven.[51] Several foreign countries were represented in 1952: Egypt, New Zealand, Israel, and Turkey. The five Composer Forums of student works, which I led, were performed by other students from the Music Center. The "Aspects of Music" series by the faculty continued, and I delivered three lectures in a new series, "Classical Forms in Modern Music," which was taught once a week.[52]

The senior faculty remained essentially the same, except that Irving Fine was on leave.[53] Lukas took over Irving's work as well as his own. I wrote to the Fines, "One week gone. We miss you. All goes well. A lively crowd of composers. Dallapiccola more relaxed than ever; Lukas inspiring all and sundry. Me—starving at dinnertime—but alive." Ingolf Dahl arrived from California for his first Tanglewood year and accomplished the impossible by revamping Department V, henceforth "The Tanglewood Study Group." Lenny did a terrific job conducting the student orchestra in my *Third Symphony* (9 August).

I stayed on in the Berkshires until mid-September, when I returned to Erik's Greenwich Village apartment to work with him on the opera. On weekends, we went house hunting, and in November, I found a house in Ossining, New York, called Shady Lane Farm. It was a remodeled barn just one hour up the Hudson from New York City, near Croton, with a nice view of the river. Tod Perry wrote from Lenox (10 November): "Congratulations on the house. I didn't know composers ever bought houses. Seems very unusual, but an excellent idea." Erik and I got busy buying furniture and drapes and trying to convince the telephone company to install a phone. I moved in on the first of December 1952. The next day there was a big snowstorm, and there I was snowbound without a telephone! After getting settled, I had a big housewarming party (10 October 1953). I was thrilled to have a place of my own, and I lived at Shady Lane Farm for the next eight years.

I finally owned a house, my opera was beginning to take shape, a piano piece was in the works, and two books about me were in preparation for publication. Nineteen fifty-three held promise of being a fine year. But these were the years of the Cold War, and of Senator Joseph McCarthy. Of all things, I became a victim of a political situation! I tried to carry on as usual. I conducted my *Third Symphony* in Minneapolis (February 1953) and finished *Old American Songs II*. I even attended the opening of Lenny's show, *Wonderful Town*. Afterward, I wrote to Verna: "Looked to me like a smash hit. He was wearing Koussie's cape at the opening!" But I lost a great deal of time and energy (not to mention lawyers' fees) preparing to defend myself against fictitious charges. It was not a happy time. What can one do but go through it and carry on?

[49] The official appointment letter continued: "For your services the Boston Symphony Orchestra will pay you a salary of $1500. In addition the Orchestra will pay you an allowance of $360 for your living expenses in the Berkshires."

[50] Copland, "Tanglewood's Future," *The New York Times*, 24 February 1952; reprinted in *Tempo*, no. 24 (Summer 1952), 22-23.

[51] Copland's students in 1952 were Edward Chudakoff, Halim El-Dabh, Roger Hollinrake, Yehoshua Lakner, Ben-Zion Orgad, Arno Safran, and Raymond Wilding-White; Dallapiccola's other students were Marshall Bialosky, Arnold Freed, Mimi Sandbank Maazel, Mayer Mandelbaum, Robert Pitton, and Ilhan Usmanbas.

[52] Copland's three lectures were: "Variation Form"; "Functional Music I: Music for Films"; "Functional Music II: Music for Ballet, Radio and Theatre."

[53] Ralph Berkowitz's title was changed to Dean of the Music Center; Piatigorsky was on leave due to illness, so for the first time, there was no separate chamber-music head.

INTERLUDE VIII

Everywhere people met, talk turned to the McCarthy hearings: who was being "called," what they said, who they "named." One of Senator Joseph McCarthy's pet peeves was Harvard, and Copland, having just recently delivered the Norton Lectures, was close to the Harvard scene. He and his Boston friends were shocked at the threats to intellectual and academic freedom. The Cold War was escalating rapidly. Revisionist history and post-McCarthy detractors have claimed that the dread of Communist infiltration was exaggerated during the fifties, but historian Irving Howe reminds us that the fear of communism was warranted after the Second World War. In his book *A Margin of Hope*, Howe devotes a chapter, "Ideas in Conflict," to the difficult decisions that intellectuals faced during the Cold War.

> Wherever Stalinism conquered, freedom vanished. . . . The socialist intellectuals either went underground or abandoned socialism. The more thoughtful tried to work out a system of opposing both communism and McCarthyism. The sudden upsurge of McCarthyism was to prove a crucial test for the intellectuals.[1]

Many people Copland knew were called to testify before the House Committee on Un-American Activities (HUAC), including two close friends, Marc Blitzstein and Clifford Odets. Copland became vaguely anxious, knowing he had been connected with Popular Front groups such as the Composers Collective in the thirties. Copland's political thinking derived from a time when it had been a matter of pride for artists and intellectuals to be connected with the socialist movement. Copland was not a registered member of any party; he continued to think of himself as liberal and to depend on Harold Clurman for discussions of a more worldly nature than the music community offered. They talked about literature, ideology, and politics. In an interview, Clurman described his political situation preceding and during the McCarthy years:

> I read more political material than Aaron. I was moving very far to the Left. I never joined any party or anything like that. No intent, no thought of ever doing so. But I was interested and sympathetic to the Soviet Union, what I thought they were going to do, what I thought they believed. And I did read. I read Lenin, some Marx, the literature—and I did feel, yes, the working class must do something. I said to Aaron that there was a political ignorance, an enormous ignorance both of the Left and the Right in this country. I think it's one of the most politically obtuse countries in the world. We talked of these things; I talked to Aaron about everything.[2]

Copland was always impressed with intellectuals, feeling that because he had not gone to college, he did not qualify as one himself. He was somewhat in awe of people such as Arthur Miller and Lillian Hellman; in fact, he had become involved with the pro-Russian film *The North Star* largely because Hellman had written the script. Another left-winger Copland admired and worked with briefly was photographer Ralph Steiner: Copland had helped Steiner edit two films, *H20* and *Surf and Seaweed*.[3] Although Copland thought of himself as a loyal American, even a patriotic one, there was a "new" crime—"guilt by association"—and Copland had associates to whom McCarthy could point: composer Hanns Eisler, who had been deported because of his Communist Party activities; Marc Blitzstein and other former members of the Composers Collective; the Group Theatre crowd; and Copland's liberal-minded colleagues, Bernstein and Diamond. Clurman said, "I used to kid Aaron. 'Oy!' I would say, 'Wait til they hear about "Into the Streets May First," published in *The New Masses* yet!' Aaron didn't think I was so funny."[4]

Copland's involvement with Russian organizations can be traced to Koussevitzky, who tried to help his countrymen whenever possible. When Koussevitzky asked Copland to lend his name or his efforts to a cause, such as the Friends for Russian Freedom, the National Council of American-Soviet Friendship, and its outgrowth the American-Soviet Music Society, Copland never wanted to refuse him. These organizations would be pointed to by McCarthy in 1953 as Communist fronts.[5]

The popularity of Russian composers in America began when Russia was an ally, and sympathy for them continued under the Stalin regime. Copland and other American musicians were impressed with Shostakovich. In 1935, they heard his opera that was banned

[1] Irving Howe, *A Margin of Hope* (San Diego: Harcourt Brace Jovanovich, 1982), 206, 213. See also Victor Navasky, *Naming Names* (New York: Penguin Books, 1981); Fred J. Cook, *The Nightmare Decade* (New York: Random House, 1971); Lillian Hellman, *Scoundrel Time* (Boston: Little, Brown and Co, 1976); Elizabeth Bergman Crist, "Aaron Copland and the Popular Front." JAMS 56, no. 2 (2003), 409-65; Jennifer DeLapp, "Copland in the Fifties; Music and Ideology in the McCarthy Era," PhD diss., University of Michigan, 1997.

[2] See interview, Harold Clurman.

[3] William Alexander, *Film on the Left: American Documentary Film from 1931 to 1941* (Princeton: Princeton University Press, 1981), 15.

[4] See interview, Harold Clurman.

[5] Koussevitzky was chairman of the American-Soviet Music Society; Betty Bean was executive secretary. Among the members were composers Bernstein, Blitzstein, Copland, Cowell, Gould, and Siegmeister. In 1947, Copland became chairman. See Eric A. Gordon, *Mark the Music: The Life and Work of Marc Blitzstein* (New York: St. Martin's Press, 1989).

Board members of the American-Soviet Music Society (*left to right*): Mordecai Bauman, Morton Gould, Betty Bean, Serge Koussevitzky, Elie Siegmeister, Margaret Grant, Copland, and Marc Blitzstein

in Russia, *Lady Macbeth of Mtsensk*, in a production at the Metropolitan Opera House.[6] In 1946, Copland delivered a lecture at Tanglewood on "Shostakovich and the New Simplicity," in which he said, "Shostakovich is enormously musical—not a deep thinker, not strikingly original by comparison with Stravinsky, and sometimes unnecessarily trite. But he has a personal note all his own and enormous facility and brilliance."

When Shostakovich came to the States in 1949, his activities were restricted. Copland was the only composer allowed to meet Shostakovich at the airport, and the two composers were shown together in newspaper photographs (26 March 1949) at the banquet in the Waldorf-Astoria ballroom, where the Russian composer (through an interpreter) addressed delegates of the World Peace Conference (25-27 March). Lillian Hellman, Copland, and Harlow Shapley, chairman of the conference, spoke to the audience of two thousand. Also at the head table were Olin Downes and Henry Wallace. The atmosphere was tense, with heavy police guards at the dinner and anti-Russian war veterans picketing outside the hotel and Carnegie Hall, where the conference continued. Claire Reis described the scene at the Waldorf:

> Shostakovich was guarded by two men from Russia, one who interpreted for him. When he said "Stravinsky is not a good composer—he does not compose for the masses," it was rather a shocking statement. At the end of the program, Arthur Miller made an announcement: "Will all the audience keep their seats, so as to let the honored guests go down in the elevator?" Well, the Waldorf elevators were pretty big, but besides Shostakovich and his guards, nobody was allowed to go. Shostakovich was not allowed to call Koussevitzky or go to Boston to see him, though he was very anxious to do so.[7]

Following the Peace Conference, *Life* magazine published an article, "Red Rumpus," with photographs of fifty people who attended. Under the heading "Dupes and fellow travelers dress up communist fronts," Copland's photograph was included. The Peace Conference of 1949 was one of the Communist-front gatherings attacked by Joe McCarthy.

McCarthyism was a central issue in the 1952 presidential campaign. After Dwight D. Eisenhower was elected, *The Washington Post* announced the program for the inaugural concert, which would take place at Constitution Hall on 18 January 1953:

> The concert will include Jeannette MacDonald and James Melton. A third artist will be either pianist Vladimir Horowitz or violinist Yehudi Menuhin. The master of ceremonies for the concert will be Walter Pidgeon, who will read *Lincoln Portrait*, by Aaron Copland, accompanied by the National Symphony.

On the evening of 16 January 1953 in New York City, Claire Reis picked up her evening newspaper and was shocked to see an announcement that Copland's *Lincoln Portrait* had been removed from the concert because Congressman Fred E. Busbey of Illinois had questioned Copland's political associations. Mrs. Reis immediately called Copland and read him the news. He, too, was shocked. He had not heard that Congressman Busbey had addressed Congress (3 January):

> There are many patriotic composers available without the long record of questionable affiliations of Copland. The Republican Party would have been ridiculed from one end of the United States to the other if Copland's music had been played at the inaugural of a President elected to fight communism, along with other things.

Congressman Busbey's statement had been read into the *Congressional Record*.[8] Claire Reis said to Copland, "We've got to do something quickly. It's only a day and a half before the inaugural concert." She advised Copland to call his lawyer, and with Copland's approval, she sent a wire in the name of the League of Composers protesting the ban. A copy of the telegram to *The New York Times* resulted in an article the following day. It was headed: "Ban on Copland work at Inaugural scored. The League of Composers of 115 West Fifty-seventh Street protested yesterday to the Inaugural Concert Committee in Washington against the dropping of Copland's *Lincoln Portrait*."

Copland noted in his appointment book on 16 January: "Busbey Attack!" A few weeks later, concerned that the League had not had the opportunity to approve what was done in its name, Copland sent a letter to the board (9 February 1953):

[6] See Claire Reis, *Composers, Conductors and Critics* (Detroit: Detroit Reprints in Music, 1974), 143-46.

[7] See interviews, Claire Reis with Perlis, Oral History of American Music, Yale.

[8] Proceedings and Debates of the Eighty-third Congress, First Session, Appendix, volume 99, part 9 (3 January 1953-23 March 1953), 169-71.

Shostakovich and Copland, 1958

> I think I owe our organization a word of explanation. I want it to be known by you that I read of this incident in the papers, after it was called to my attention by Claire Reis. . . . I have no past or present political activities to hide. I have never at any time been a member of any political party: Republican, Democratic, or Communist. . . . We are becoming the targets of a powerful pressure movement led by small minds. It is surely a sign of the times that a musical organization like our own should have become involved in an affair such as this.

Paul Hume, music critic of *The Washington Post*, intending to make the absurdity of the issue plain, informed Congressman Busbey that Air Force bands and other tax-supported orchestras constantly played Copland's works. Busbey professed surprise and shock: "We must look into that!" he cried. Hume followed up with an article headed "Music Censorship Reveals New Peril." Hume's attacks spurred Busbey on to expand his remarks about Copland and to read into the Congressional Record a long list of allegedly suspicious Copland affiliations.[9] Finally, in his review of the inaugural concert (25 January 1953), Hume suggested that some substantial American music was in order for such occasions, ". . . provided, of course, that by 1957 we will have surmounted the idea that music by various American-born composers is to be banned if Congressmen protest."

Several people wrote to music critic Virgil Thomson asking why the *New York Herald Tribune* ignored the Busbey incident. Thomson explained: "I very much fear that public

[9] Under the heading "Copland and Inaugural Concert, extension of remarks of Hon. Fred E. Busbey of Illinois in the House of Representatives, Friday, January 16, 1953." Also in *Daily Record*, vol. 99, part 9, A 169-171.

protests and similar manifestations might result in merely publicizing the incident to Mr. Copland's disadvantage. . . ." To Ernst Bacon, Thomson stated: "Roy Harris has been having similar troubles . . . and I have not publicized them either. . . . I know that agitational or editorial protest can be a two-edged weapon."[10] Copland himself decided to release a statement to newspapers and radio stations.[11] For the usually moderate Copland, the tone was decidedly angry.

> This is the first time, as far as I know, that a composition has been publicly removed from a concert program in the United States because of the alleged affiliations of the composer. I would have to be a man of stone not to have deeply resented both the public announcement of the removal and the reasons given for it. No one has ever before questioned my patriotism. My music, by its nature, and my activities as a musical citizen must speak for me: both have been dedicated to the cultural fulfillment of America. Isn't it strange that if the record of my affiliations in the past were so "questionable" it should have escaped the notice of all the government officials except the representative from Illinois? . . . I cannot for the life of me see how the cause of the free countries of the world will be advanced by the banning of my works. . . . Bad as our situation may be, no American politician has yet called for the banning of an American composer's work because of its aesthetic content, as is the case in Russia today. I'd a thousand times prefer to have my music turned down by Republican congressmen on political grounds (or because I voted for Stevenson) than have it turned down for aesthetic reasons. It is easy to see why this is so: my "politics"—tainted or untainted—are certain to die with me, but my music, I am foolish enough to imagine, might just possibly outlive the Republican Party.

Copland then composed a letter to President Eisenhower:[12]

> I am an American composer of symphonic music and the composer of a musical portrait of Abe Lincoln. I write to you because an incident occurred during the ceremonies attendant upon the inauguration of your administration too small to have come to your attention, certainly, but too large in its implications to be passed over lightly. If I did not think it transcended in importance my own personal stake in the matter, I would not be writing to you now. . . .

Reactions followed: Howard Taubman, chief music critic of *The New York Times*, wrote an article supporting Copland. It was entitled "Portrait of President Deeply Patriotic—Composer's Stature Not in Doubt" (1 February 1953). The ACLU [American Civil Liberties Union] Anti-Censorship Council protested to the inaugural committee about the Copland ban (along with the suppression of Charlie Chaplin's *Limelight*). Historian Bruce Catton wrote a long piece in *The Nation* (31 January 1953), quoted here in part:

[10] See "To a Reader" (29 January 1953) and "To Ernst Bacon" (24 February 1953) in *Selected Letters of Virgil Thomson,* ed. Tim Page and Vanessa Weeks Page (New York: Summit Books, 1988), 262., 266.
[11] See Copland's files in the Library of Congress for pencil draft and typescript.
[12] Telephone requests in October 1988 to the Eisenhower Archive in Abilene, Kansas, revealed no trace of Copland's letter to Eisenhower: The entire documentation of the inaugural ceremonies has disappeared or been removed. The Archivist has no explanation. A draft copy of Copland's letter to Eisenhower is in Copland's files in the Library of Congress.

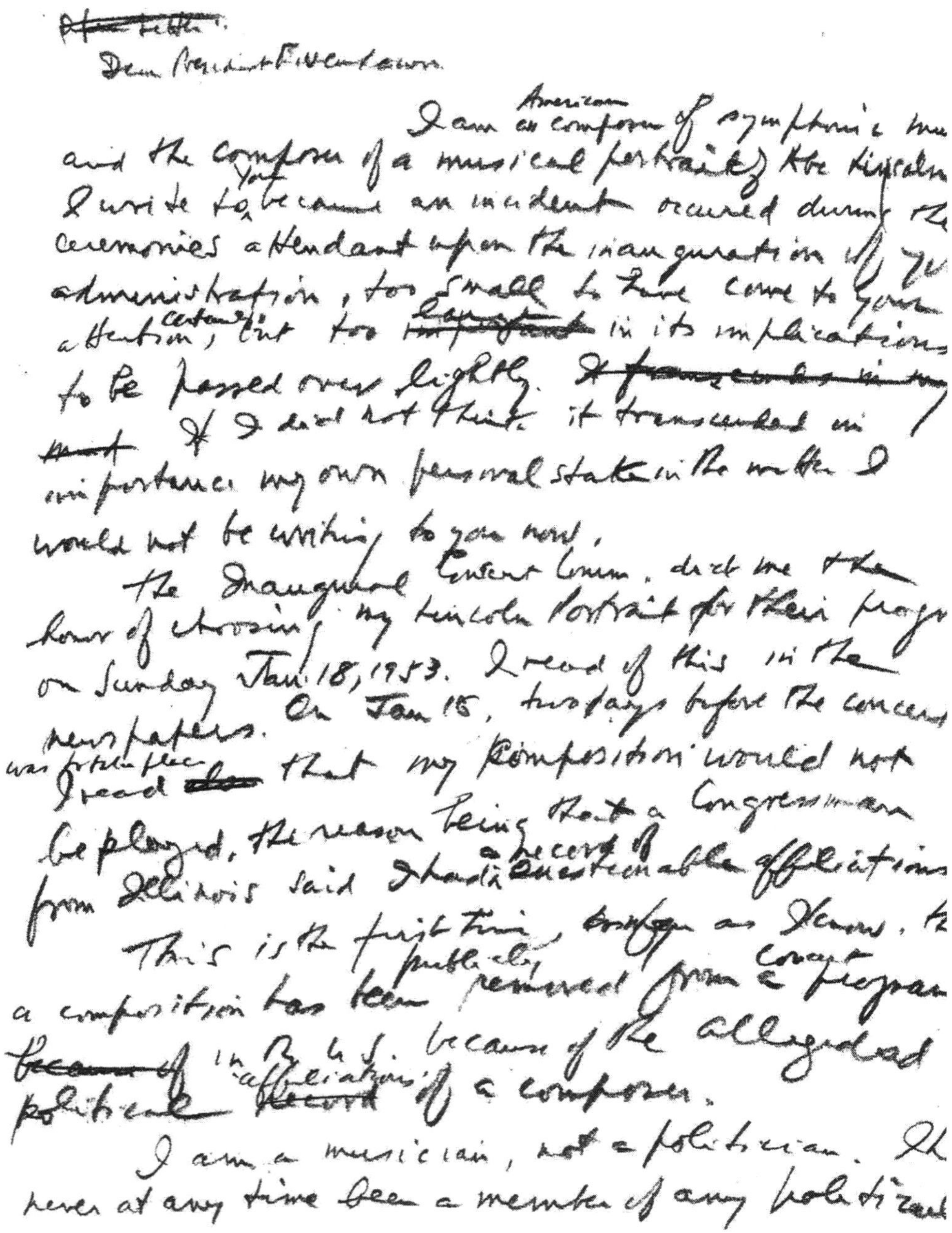
Dear President Eisenhower:

I am an American composer of symphonic music and the composer of a musical portrait of Abe Lincoln. I write to you because an incident occurred during the ceremonies attendant upon the inauguration of your administration, too small to have come to your attention, but certainly too important in its implications to be passed over lightly.

If I did not think it transcended in importance my own personal stake in the matter I would not be writing to you now.

The Inaugural Concert Comm. did me the honor of choosing my Lincoln Portrait for their program on Sunday Jan. 18, 1953. I read of this in the newspapers. On Jan 15, two days before the concert I read that my composition would not be played, the reason being that a Congressman from Illinois said I had a record of questionable affiliations.

This is the first time, insofar as I know, that a composition has been publicly removed from a concert program in the U.S. because of the alleged "affiliations" of a composer.

I am a musician, not a politician. I have never at any time been a member of any political

Draft of an unfinished letter from Copland to President Dwight D. Eisenhower (undated)

> A leading item on the program was to have been Aaron Copland's *A Lincoln Portrait*, for speaker and orchestra. At the last minute, however, this number was quietly expunged because Representative Fred E. Busbey of Illinois lodged a protest, on the grounds that Copland had been accused of associating with Communist front groups. The chairman of the arrangements committee said that the number was dropped as soon as the protest was made, "because we didn't want to do anything to bring criticism." So the Copland number was not heard, and if this was in the end something less than a fatal blow to the evil designs of the men in the Kremlin, it at least saved the assembled Republicans from being compelled to listen to Lincoln's brooding words: "Fellow Citizens, we cannot escape history. We of this Congress and this Administration will be remembered in spite of ourselves."

Copland received many personal letters of support. Composer Elie Siegmeister, who had his own difficulties with HUAC, wrote (21 January 1953):

> Just a few lines to tell you Hannah and I feel with you and are very indignant over the incident of last week. What the hell goes on anyway? Will they soon be forbidding Walt Whitman and the Declaration of Independence?

Edwin Denby wrote to Copland, "Marc B. just came into Minna Daniel's office in a great state about *Lincoln* being taken off the inaugural program." Denby pointed to the fact that "the idea of playing the piece in the first place was *theirs*, not yours."

After the list of alleged affiliations was read into the *Congressional Record* by Congressman Busbey, Copland released another statement:

> I understand that the Un-American Activities Committee has a record of my alleged affiliation with Communist-front organizations. I wish to state emphatically that any interest that I have ever had in any organization has been through my concern with cultural and musical affairs. I had no knowledge or reason to believe, from my own experience, that any such organization was subversive or communistic. I say unequivocally that I am not now and never have been a Communist or member of the Communist Party or of any organization that advocates or teaches in any way the overthrow of the United States Government. As one who has benefited so greatly from the unique opportunities that America offers its citizens, not only on a financial but also on a spiritual and artistic level, I am far too grateful for the privilege of being an American to become a member of any organization that I believed was merely a forum for Communist propaganda.

The National Symphony Orchestra would play Copland's music frequently in years to come; in fact, when his conducting career escalated in the sixties, it was the National Symphony, of all American orchestras, to which Copland felt closest. A decade after the composer was banned from Eisenhower's inaugural concert, Copland conducted the National Symphony from the West Lawn of the White House, facing the nation's Capitol in a Fourth of July concert that began with the national anthem and continued with his own music. Ironically, the National Symphony has never played a Copland piece at an inaugural concert. It seems there is a rule that once a composer is banned by an inaugural committee, he is always banned. At the second Nixon inauguration, *Lincoln Portrait* and "The Promise of Living" from Copland's opera *The Tender Land* were included, but they were played by the Philadelphia Orchestra, brought in at Nixon's request to share the inaugural concert program. Nixon's preference had nothing to do with Copland's situation.

On 1 November 1986, Aaron Copland was awarded the Congressional Gold Medal, an Act of Congress and the highest civilian honor in the land. The citation was read into the Congressional Record, and the award was presented at a concert by the National Symphony Orchestra conducted by Rostropovich.[13] No one seemed to remember the Busbey incident of 1953. At the time, however, it was unpleasant in the extreme and had repercussions into the sixties.

Considering the Busbey incident, Copland could not have been totally surprised when the dreaded telegram arrived from McCarthy. Copland knew that he had been listed in *Red Channels: The Reports of Communist Influence in Radio and Television* and that Henry Moe of the Guggenheim Foundation had been questioned about him by the Select Committee to Investigate Tax-exempt Foundations (11 December 1952). When asked about Copland's affiliations, Mr. Moe spoke in Copland's favor, concluding, ". . . we are not God and we can't foresee the future. But with respect to Mr. Copland, sir, I would not think that there could possibly be anything wrong with him from the point of view of this committee."[14]

Copland's 1953 appointment book shows a memo for 22 May: "McCarthy wire received!" The telegram was telephoned to Copland at 7 P.M. on Friday evening. It instructed him to appear in Washington the following Monday. When Copland responded that he needed time to secure counsel, the hearing was delayed one day. Whoever recommended Oscar Cox (of Cox, Langford, Stoddard & Cutler) did Copland a great favor. Cox's firm was knowledgeable about the hearings, and Cox himself was a gentleman and a music lover who knew about Copland and admired his music. Cox agreed to see Copland Monday evening before the hearing (Tuesday, 26 May). His interest and respect made Copland feel more comfortable with the situation he was facing. Cox explained that he was involved with another case at the time and had to appoint an associate, Charles Glover, to attend the hearing. Copland said later, "My lawyer was a rock-ribbed Republican who understandably did not want to appear himself." Cox kept closely in touch with the proceedings, and when the difficult year of 1953 was ending, Copland wrote to Cox, "It was my lucky day when I walked into your office." Cox responded, "It was our great luck when you walked into our office."[15]

Several fascinating documents exist concerning the dean of American composers and the senator from Wisconsin, foremost among them being the actual transcript of the privately held hearing.[16] Even today, the transcript of the two-hour interrogation makes chilling reading. It shows Copland responding to hostile interrogation in a controlled, proud, and occasionally even humorous way. Furthermore, the document answers the question of

[13] Vivian Perlis accepted the signed bill granting the Congressional Gold Medal to Copland at the Kennedy Center. It was presented by The Honorable Vic Fazio and Morton Gould, president of ASCAP.

[14] See House of Representatives, Select Committee to Investigate Tax-exempt Foundations and Comparable Organizations, 11 December 1952. Transcript, 17, 18.

[15] In 1958, Oscar Cox drafted a bill, "The National Music Act." Its purpose was "to encourage the creation and understanding of serious music."

[16] See stenographic transcript of Hearings, volume 88, which includes Proceedings of the Committee on Government Operations, U.S. Senate, Testimony of Aaron Copland, 47-98.

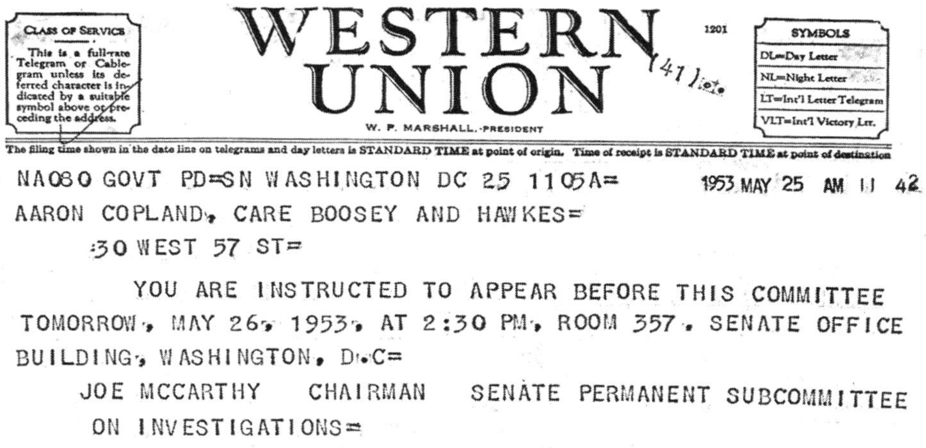

CLASS OF SERVICE
This is a full-rate Telegram or Cablegram unless its deferred character is indicated by a suitable symbol above or preceding the address.

WESTERN UNION

W. P. MARSHALL, PRESIDENT

1201

SYMBOLS
DL=Day Letter
NL=Night Letter
LT=Int'l Letter Telegram
VLT=Int'l Victory Ltr.

The filing time shown in the date line on telegrams and day letters is STANDARD TIME at point of origin. Time of receipt is STANDARD TIME at point of destination

NA080 GOVT PD=SN WASHINGTON DC 25 1105A= 1953 MAY 25 AM 11 42

AARON COPLAND, CARE BOOSEY AND HAWKES=

30 WEST 57 ST=

YOU ARE INSTRUCTED TO APPEAR BEFORE THIS COMMITTEE TOMORROW, MAY 26, 1953, AT 2:30 PM, ROOM 357, SENATE OFFICE BUILDING, WASHINGTON, D.C=

JOE MCCARTHY CHAIRMAN SENATE PERMANENT SUBCOMMITTEE ON INVESTIGATIONS=

Telegram from Senator Joseph McCarthy to Copland, 22 May 1953

why Copland was called to testify at all. Some have claimed it was McCarthy's intention to use Copland to get at others, such as Hellman, Eisler, and Bernstein. Harold Clurman said:

> What they hunted was not Communists but publicity, and Aaron was the music star. . . . I couldn't take seriously any of the "cases" involving my friends and acquaintances. I knew the truth: Communist Party members or not, they were sentimentalists with little practical understanding of any political issue. . . . They were all on the side of the good.[17]

Copland did not keep a personal diary except when traveling, but he felt motivated to write about the McCarthy hearing the following day. From Copland's description and the transcript of the hearing itself, it is clear that McCarthy was really interested in the U.S.I.A. and who in that organization was responsible for choosing Copland to represent America in an educational capacity abroad. The Information Agency controlled the Voice of America and some two hundred information-center libraries in about ninety countries and was responsible for film services, exhibits, lectures, and exchange programs. At the close of 1952 and the beginning of 1953, McCarthy was convinced Communists had infiltrated the propaganda agency. He saw to it that the average number of books shipped abroad monthly dropped dramatically for lack of clearance of the authors and that thirty thousand volumes by what he considered Communist authors were cleared out. Not only was there a blacklist of authors, composers, and artists but a private "graylist" as well—those who were pending screening and clearance. Copland was on that list of 141, along with Dorothy Parker, Malcolm Cowley, Roger Sessions, and Edgar Snow. According to an article in *The Nation* by "Scrutiner" (pen name for the newspaperman who covered the Washington scene for the magazine), the list read like a "Who's Who in the Realm of American culture."[18]

[17] See interview, Harold Clurman.

[18] See Fred J. Cook, *The Nightmare Decade* (New York: Random House, 1971), particularly Chapter 18, "The Witch Hunt Continues," 393-424.

The Copland hearing was comparatively mild. Here is a typical exchange:

> THE CHAIRMAN: I am not criticizing you for joining these organizations. You may have been so naive that you didn't know they were Communist controlled or you may have done it purposely, but I can't believe that this very long list used your name time after time as a sponsor of all these outstanding fronts. I can't believe they forged your name to these petitions—borrowed your name unlawfully time after time. However, I am only interested in knowing why they selected you as a lecturer when we have many other people available as lecturers. . . . We must find out why a man of this tremendous activity in Communist fronts would be selected.
>
> MR. COPLAND: May I reply on two points? I think I was selected because of the fact that my employment as a lecturer had nothing to do with anything but music.
>
> THE CHAIRMAN: If you were a member of the Communist Party, let's assume you were, and you were selected to lecture, you would be bound to try wherever you could to sell the Communist idea, wouldn't you?
>
> MR. COPLAND: No doubt.
>
> THE CHAIRMAN: So that I believe you and I would agree that in selecting a lecturer, even though they are an outstanding musician, before we put our stamp of approval on them, we should find out whether they are a Communist or sympathetic to the Communist cause. Is that right?
>
> MR. COPLAND: Well, I would certainly hesitate to send abroad a man who is a Communist sympathizer or a Communist in order to lecture. My impression was that my political opinions, no matter how vague they may have been, were not in question as far as the Department of State was concerned. I assume if they had been in question, I would have had some kind of going over.
>
> THE CHAIRMAN: You were never asked about these alleged Communist- front activities?
>
> MR. COPLAND: Not to my memory.
>
> THE CHAIRMAN: I may say, for your information, you did get security clearance.
>
> MR. COPLAND: Did I really? How does one get security clearance?

McCarthy did not answer that question, perhaps failing to see the ironic humor in the exchange. After the hearing, Copland released a public statement:

> On late Friday afternoon, I received a telegram from the Senate Permanent Subcommittee on Investigations to appear as a witness. I did. I answered to the best of my ability all of the questions which were asked me. I testified under oath that I never have supported, and am now opposed to, the limitations put on freedom by the Soviet Union. . . . My relationships with the United States Government were originally with the Music Advisory Committee to the Coordinator of Inter American Affairs and later as a lecturer on music in South America and as a Fulbright Professor. In these capacities my work was limited to the technical aspects of music.

More interesting is Copland's entry in his private diary, which concludes with typical Copland humor, comparing McCarthy's entrance into the hearing room with Toscanini's arrival onstage. The entry is published here for the first time:[19]

[19] See diary #3, Copland's files.

> Impressions of the hearing before the Senate Permanent Subcommittee on Investigations, Senator Joseph McCarthy, Chairman, May 26,1953. (Exchange of Persons Program of the State Department under Investigation)
>
> Arrived Washington, D.C., 6 P.M. accompanied by V. K. [Kraft]. Dinner and evening spent with Oscar Cox and two assistant lawyers (C. Glover and H. Packer). I was coached and warned and instructed by the trio after I had outlined my "situation." Subsequent events proved that we were on the right track. Appeared before the subcommittee in private executive session. When we entered the room, only Senator McClelland was present, lounging about. Next arrives the general counsel, Roy Cohn (age twenty-six!), accompanied by a young man in his teens who was introduced to the senator. Finally the "great" man himself, Senator McCarthy, entered. I was inwardly and outwardly calm enough. (C. Glover accompanied me as counsel.) The nervousness of the days previous (I had received the committee's wire only three-and-a-half days before) was gone. One hates to be thought a fool or worse still, a gullible fool. The list of so-called affiliations was long—nervous making. But my conscience was clear—in a free America I had a right to affiliate openly with whom I pleased; to sign protests, statements, appeals, open letters, petitions, sponsor events, etc., and no one had the right to question those affiliations.
>
> The hearing was conducted comparatively politely. McCarthy prefaced by explaining the committee's self-made rules of procedure, which are so much criticized. His manner was direct and patient enough. (It was Cohn who seemed to be chafing under insufficient stimulus for a show of personal animus.) His tough-guy radio manner only showed briefly when he hit upon favorite themes.
>
> It is fascinating to try humanly to estimate such a man as McCarthy on so brief an encounter (two hours to be precise). If I didn't know him by his works, I'd be somewhat disarmed. I suspect he derives strength from a basic simplicity of purpose; power; and a simplicity of rallying cry: the Commies. The power grabbing is subtle—he seems to enjoy his position as if he was himself a spectator of his amazing rise to importance in the world political scene. Something about him suggests that he is a man who doesn't really expect his luck to hold out. It's been too phenomenal, and I suppose, too recklessly achieved. When he touches on his magic theme, the "Commies" or "communism," his voice darkens like that of a minister. He is like a plebian Faustus who has been given a magic wand by an invisible Mephisto—as long as the menace is there, the wand will work. The question is at what point his power grab will collide with the power drive of others in his own party. *A voir.*
>
> My impression is that McCarthy had no idea who I was or what I did, other than the fact I was a part of the State Department's exchange program at one time. He seemed to show little personal animus. The attitude of the others seemed to be one of studied indifference. (It occurred to me to say to Glover as McCarthy entered that it was similar to the entrance of Toscanini—half the battle won before it begins through the power of personality.) During the hearing, McClelland left, and Senator Mundt wandered in. Only McCarthy was present throughout.

In addition to the transcript itself and Copland's diary entry, another interesting document is the list of affiliations put together by the Senate subcommittee. Obviously, a team of thorough researchers went to great lengths compiling such information, with which

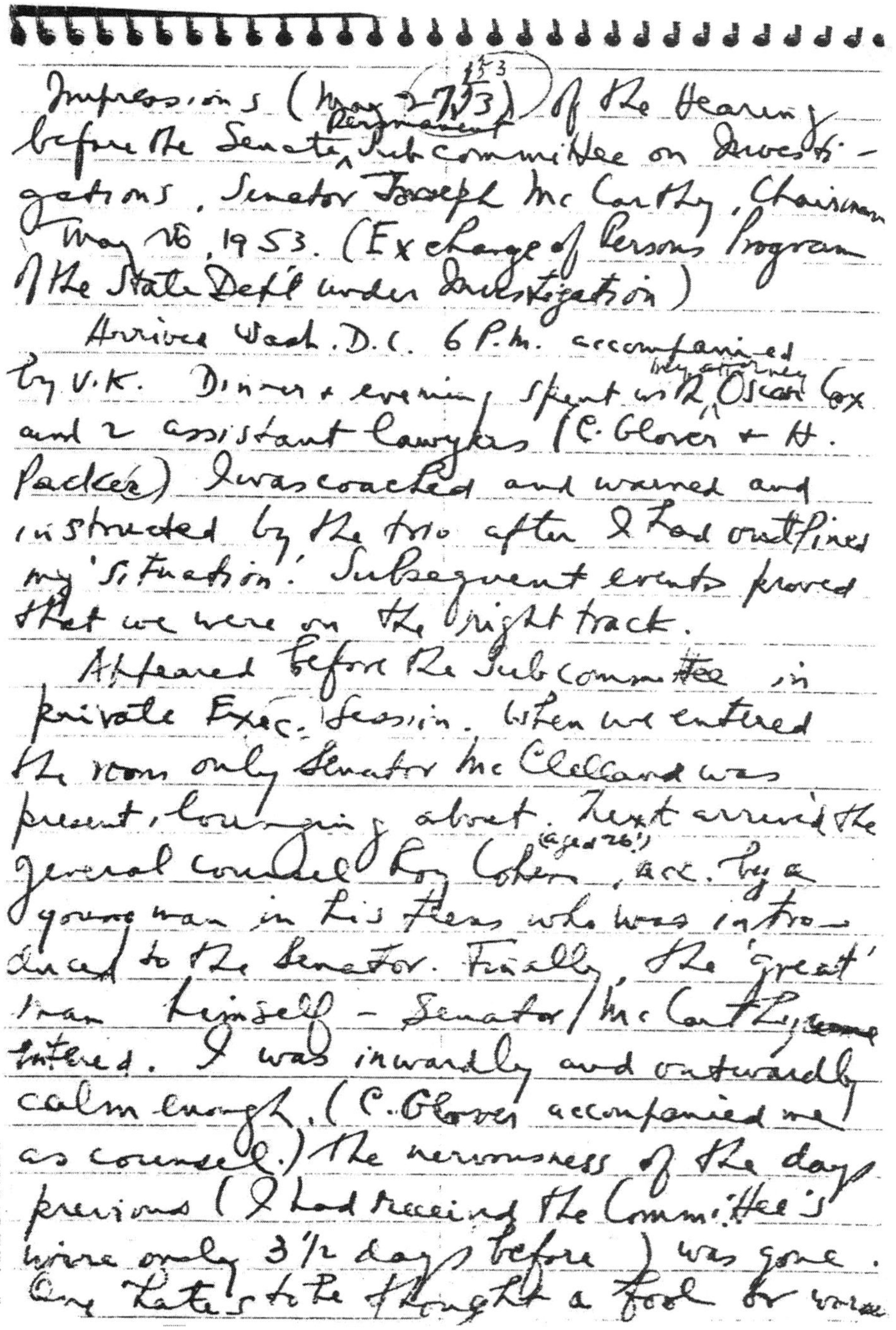
Impressions (May 27 1953) of the Hearing before the Senate Permanent Subcommittee on Investigations, Senator Joseph McCarthy, Chairman May 26, 1953. (Exchange of Persons Program of the State Dep't under investigation)

Arrived Wash. D.C. 6 P.M. accompanied by V.K. Dinner + evening spent with my attorney Oscar Cox and 2 assistant lawyers (C. Glover + H. Packer) I was coached and warned and instructed by the trio after I had outlined my 'situation'. Subsequent events proved that we were on the right track.

Appeared before the Subcommittee in private Exec. Session. When we entered the room only Senator McClelland was present, lounging about. Next arrived the general counsel Roy Cohen (aged 26!) acc. by a young man in his teens who was introduced to the Senator. Finally, the 'great' man himself - Senator McCarthy, came in. I was inwardly and outwardly calm enough. (C. Glover accompanied me as counsel.) The nervousness of the days previous (I had received the Committee's wire only 3½ days before) was gone. Any hate to be thought a fool or worse

The first page of Copland's "Impressions of the Hearing . . . ," 27 May 1953

those called to testify were faced with no time to prepare responses. Copland was astonished when he saw the list, and said, "It was impossible within those few hours to check whether my name appeared with my consent. It was well known that Communists made unauthorized use of well-known names." Copland admitted only to being involved in the World Peace Conference of 1949. He stated, "I had the hope that by demonstrating that relations are possible on a cultural plane, we might encourage talks on a diplomatic plane. I sponsored no further so-called Peace Conferences, being convinced that they were being engineered by Communists."

Following the hearing, Copland's work with his lawyers began in earnest. When Cox's office went through the transcript, they found ninety-seven technical errors.[20] Cox wrote to Copland (20 May), "You will note that there is grave doubt about the accuracy of the transcript, since the stenographer has already admitted that she omitted one entire paragraph." The paragraph in question put the chairman in an embarrassing light: He had been drilling Copland about the notorious Communist Party leader, Eisler. Copland responded, "Surely you must be referring to Gerhart Eisler. . . ." McCarthy continued, demanding to know what Copland knew about this Eisler fellow, "who had jumped bail, gone to East Berlin, and become a minister of information." Copland repeated that he knew only Eisler the composer and author of a book Copland admired, *Composing for the Films*. The interrogation went on for some minutes before McCarthy discovered his error. Harold Clurman describes the incident in his book *All People Are Famous,* calling it, "a good example of the employment of the Big Lie."[21]

Also omitted from the transcript of the hearing was McCarthy's questioning based on the erroneous assumption that Copland wrote an article actually written by Hanns Eisler. It seems extremely unlikely that a stenographer would have made the independent decision to remove these sections. One wonders how far McCarthy's editing went with other transcripts.

Copland had to drop everything to prepare the detailed explanations McCarthy required within one week's time, before a public hearing was to be held. With Victor Kraft's help, Copland went furiously through correspondence and financial files and returned to Washington to work with his lawyers. A letter went from Cox to Roy Cohn (5 June) pointing to the ninety-seven errors in the transcript, and a long and detailed letter was sent from Copland to McCarthy responding to each item that had come up in the hearing. Having been asked by McCarthy to "name names" of Americans at the 1949 World Peace Conference, Copland prepared a separate statement: "I have read over *The New York Times* account of the fine arts panel of the conference. . . . I do not personally remember having seen anyone at the conference who is not listed in those published reports."

Walter Winchell broadcast that the McCarthy committee planned a public hearing on the State Department Interchange of Persons Program (9 June). Copland assumed he would

[20] Correspondence between Cox and Copland and all materials relating to the hearing and its aftermath are in Copland's files in the Library of Congress.
[21] See Harold Clurman, *All People Are Famous* (New York: Harcourt Brace Jovanovich, 1974), 133, for description of McCarthy's questions concerning Hanns Eisler.

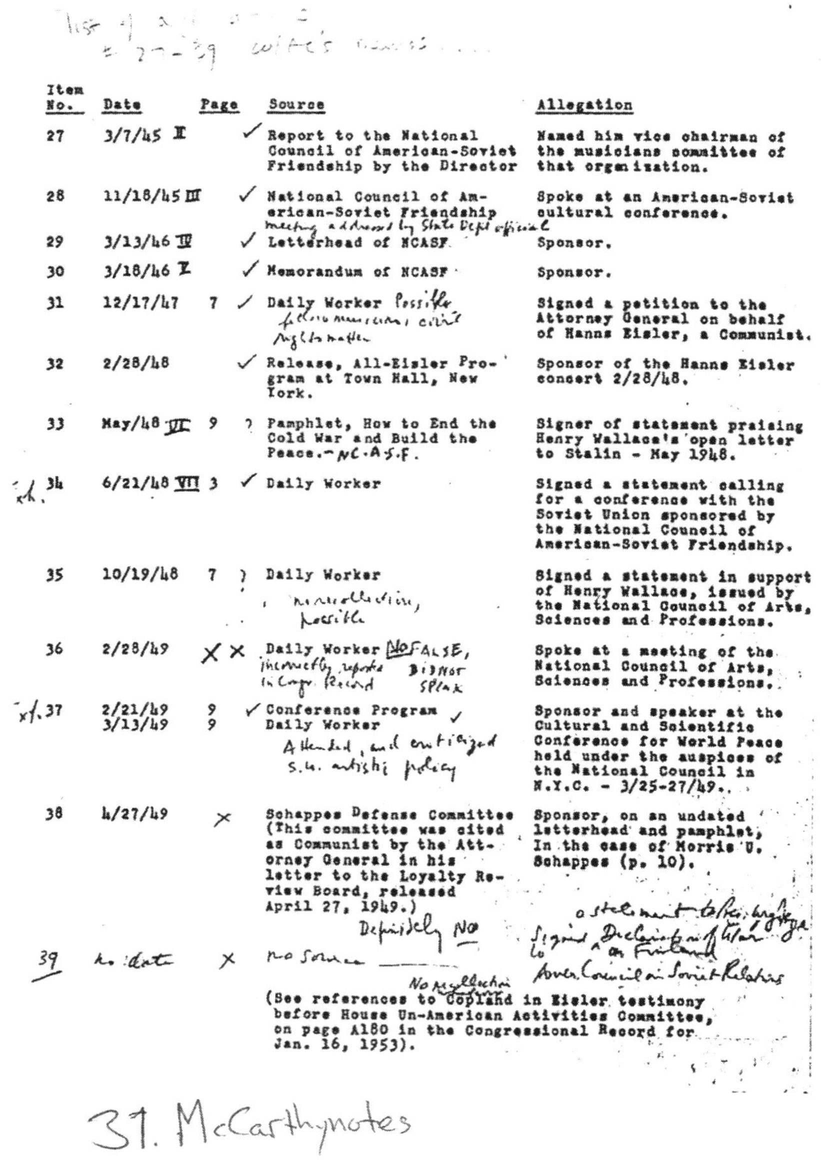

list of ... wife's ...

Item No.	Date	Page		Source	Allegation
27	3/7/45	II	✓	Report to the National Council of American-Soviet Friendship by the Director	Named him vice chairman of the musicians committee of that organization.
28	11/18/45	III	✓	National Council of American-Soviet Friendship *meeting addressed by State Dept official*	Spoke at an American-Soviet cultural conference.
29	3/13/46	IV	✓	Letterhead of NCASF	Sponsor.
30	3/18/46	I	✓	Memorandum of NCASF	Sponsor.
31	12/17/47	7	✓	Daily Worker *possible fellow musicians, civil rights matter*	Signed a petition to the Attorney General on behalf of Hanns Eisler, a Communist.
32	2/28/48		✓	Release, All-Eisler Program at Town Hall, New York.	Sponsor of the Hanns Eisler concert 2/28/48.
33	May/48	VI 9	?	Pamphlet, How to End the Cold War and Build the Peace. - NC.A.S.F.	Signer of statement praising Henry Wallace's open letter to Stalin - May 1948.
34	6/21/48	VII 3	✓	Daily Worker	Signed a statement calling for a conference with the Soviet Union sponsored by the National Council of American-Soviet Friendship.
35	10/19/48	7	?	Daily Worker *no recollection, possible*	Signed a statement in support of Henry Wallace, issued by the National Council of Arts, Sciences and Professions.
36	2/28/49		XX	Daily Worker *NO FALSE, incorrectly reported, DID NOT in Cong Record SPEAK*	Spoke at a meeting of the National Council of Arts, Sciences and Professions.
37	2/21/49 3/13/49	9 9	✓	Conference Program ✓ Daily Worker *Attended, and criticized S.U. artistic policy*	Sponsor and speaker at the Cultural and Scientific Conference for World Peace held under the auspices of the National Council in N.Y.C. - 3/25-27/49.
38	4/27/49		X	Schappes Defense Committee (This committee was cited as Communist by the Attorney General in his letter to the Loyalty Review Board, released April 27, 1949.) *Definitely NO*	Sponsor, on an undated letterhead and pamphlet, in the case of Morris U. Schappes (p. 10). *a statement to be brought, signed Declaration of War to end Communism in Soviet Relations*
39	no date		X	no source ——— *No recollection* (See references to Copland in Eisler testimony before House Un-American Activities Committee, on page A180 in the Congressional Record for Jan. 16, 1953).	

31. McCarthy notes

A sample page from the HUAC list of alleged Copland affiliations, with check marks and notations by Copland

be called to testify, but the hearing came and went, and Copland heard nothing further from the committee. Cox's office kept in touch: "We still have no word about a public hearing. We have not thought it a good idea to check in with them constantly to remind them that you are still under subpoena. . ." As days stretched to weeks, and weeks to months, it seemed less likely that Copland would be called to testify again. However, when Copland

left for Tanglewood, he still feared a telegram from McCarthy might arrive at any moment.

At the end of July, Copland's name was mentioned in *The Washington Post* when the subcommittee questioned Senator Fulbright (25 July 1953):

> FULBRIGHT: "You say you've found one. You've got a whole corps of people looking around for some time and you've found one Communist. . . Nobody is perfect." McCarthy said he has "a sizable number of other cases." Among them . . . composer Aaron Copland, who, McCarthy said, "has a great record of Communist activity." Later, McCarthy corrected that to "Communist front activity," and he called the Fulbright program the "half-bright program."

Copland's philosophical nature kept him from becoming bitter at his treatment during the McCarthy period. His friend Edwin Denby wrote (28 June 1953):

> It is extraordinary [that] even now I can't detect a sign in you that you have been through any trouble. I mean in the sense of wanting comforting. It is only by imagining how grueling it would be to me to be questioned by the police on suspicion, even if I were sure of my innocence, that I can imagine anything. To me, it seems more a hideous humiliation, as far as I can think it, than any sort of objective harm.

Copland admitted to Denby and other friends that the affair was very tiring. Arthur Berger said, "Aaron told me the McCarthy thing took a lot of energy and emotion—that sense of being pursued. . . ."[22]

Copland thought the matter was essentially over with the hearing. Little did he realize how much more time and energy would go into the matter of his passport. When he asked his lawyers about a trip to Mexico planned for the end of August 1953 to help direct a series with the Orquesta Sinfonica Nacional, they saw no reason he should not go, as long as he could be reached easily. Cox wrote (16 August), "There is a slight question as to whether you are still under subpoena. It is true that the State Department has a policy of not issuing passports to individuals who are under subpoena. But, as you point out, the trip which you are taking does not require a passport." Nevertheless, before leaving for Mexico, Copland was required to make sworn statement to a notary: "Aaron Copland of Shady Lane Farm is not a Communist." Copland's passport situation became a long-standing issue, one in which Cox's office played an important role. Reading through the voluminous correspondence, statements from Copland and his lawyers, reports of meetings, and other documentation that continued for several years, until Copland's passport was reinstated, one cannot help but wonder at the extraordinary patience and control displayed by both Copland and Oscar Cox.

The Passport Office requested that Copland furnish evidence of affiliation with avowedly anti-Communist organizations and that he supply affidavits from citizens on his behalf. Copland got to work again, even citing the American character of his music, and he asked Henry Moe and Olga Koussevitzky for supporting letters. Oscar Cox wrote to Copland (7 November 1953), "Mrs. Koussevitzky's affidavit is a jewel." The Passport Office again "tentatively disapproved" Copland's application, "unless Copland could submit evidence that he had not consistently adhered to the Communist Party line." Copland cited an invita-

[22] See interview, Arthur Berger.

tion from the Congress for Cultural Freedom to appear at an International Conference in Rome (5-15 April 1954): "If my passport is not promptly renewed, I will have to withdraw my acceptance." He also mentioned invitations to conduct in Barcelona and London. Finally, Copland compiled a list of twenty-one "American" organizations "of which I was an active member during the period 1935-1952." Along with Copland's request went a lengthy dossier from the firm of Cox, Langford, Stoddard, & Cutler.

Cox personally reviewed all the papers with the Passport Office. Even then, however, questions were posed. At long last, a limited passport renewal of six months was obtained. The irony of Copland's passport difficulties is that they coincided with his appearances as the major representative of American music in Europe and South America during 1954! In January 1955, Copland's passport was renewed for one year, rather than the normal two-year period.

Letters from Oscar Cox and his office were always typed. But a handwritten note from Cox arrived at Shady Lane Farm before Christmas 1953: "To you, Louise and I wish a good Xmas and New Year of even more fruitful production unhampered by the madness of the small hearts and minds." The following year, when Cox had to inform Copland that his passport had not yet been cleared, Cox sent along the following lines paraphrased from Ecclesiastes 12: "The daughters of musick shall not be brought low / Nor the sun, nor the light of the moon, nor the stars be darkened."

Copland was not billed by Cox's office for legal fees until early 1954. The amount was substantial, and when Copland asked whether it could be paid over a period of two years, Cox responded, "From our standpoint, you can take longer if you wish. . . ." Cox so admired Copland that he talked to people he knew on the boards of the National Symphony and the New York Philharmonic to have them invite the composer to conduct his music. Cox had connections in Cuba and Mexico and wrote to highly placed individuals for Copland to be decorated by both countries. Oscar Cox kept in touch with Copland regularly, especially when the Busbey incident and McCarthy hearing came back to haunt the composer. Whenever Copland went to Washington to conduct, he got together with the Cox family.

The first public reactions to the Red-baiting of Copland came from the South. The University of Alabama had invited the composer to speak and conduct at a three-day Composers' Forum planned for April 1953. The withdrawal of the invitation typified the atmosphere of fear and repression in academic institutions at that time. Copland and Gurney Kennedy, chairman of the Composers' Forum Committee, had been in correspondence since October 1952. Kennedy wrote (7 March 1953):

> I regret to inform you that the recent allegations of Communist sympathies on your part as set out on the Extension of the Remarks of the Honorable Fred E. Busbey . . . and the inaugural concert affair in Washington make it inadvisable for us to have you as our guest.

Copland responded with a lengthy letter (12 March) in which he attacked Busbey's tactics and expressed his regret "for the loss of academic independence that such an action implies. It makes clear that freedom of thought is endangered in America if a large university such as yours can be intimidated by the allegations of a single individual." Copland expressed the hope that the university would reconsider its action. He wrote:

> At this juncture it seems enormously important to me that you and I reaffirm our right to talk music to American students without fear of interference on alleged political grounds. The only way to do so is to put it to the test. It goes without saying that I cannot accept an honorarium for work I have not done, and I am therefore returning the check for three hundred dollars.

Gurney Kennedy, a great admirer of Copland and his music, took the liberty of ending his next letter, which informed Copland that the university would not reconsider its withdrawal, with a personal opinion: "Also I want you to know that I, too, deplore the intrusion of a political counterpoint, which to my mind is sadly out of key in any artistic enterprise." Kennedy's supportive sentence caused remarkable difficulty and embarrassment within the university and impelled the dean of music to write a lengthy explanation and apology to his superior, ending with, "May I repeat that all of us in this matter have been motivated by the desire to protect the university from criticism."

In 1967, after Gurney Kennedy moved to Jacksonville University in Florida, the College of Music and Fine Arts there honored Copland with a Contemporary Music Festival and a Doctor of Fine Arts Degree. Dr. and Mrs. Gurney Kennedy were moved by the citation and by their meeting with Copland, and they commented on how far removed the occasion was from the events in Alabama of 1953.[23]

The next reactions came from the West Coast: The Hollywood Bowl Committee canceled a Copland performance scheduled for March 1953 without explanation. Lukas Foss, who was teaching at UCLA and conducting the Los Angeles Chamber Orchestra, had invited Copland to conduct his music. Several members of the board disapproved of Copland's politics. Foss was furious and wrote Copland, "Cornelia and I have stayed up all night talking about whether I should resign. Who wants to be associated with such an organization!" When asked in a recent interview whether he, himself, had had trouble with McCarthy, Foss responded laughingly, "I wasn't famous enough for anybody to bother me! McCarthy liked Mr. America Incorporated. You can't be a better American than Aaron."[24]

The University of Colorado had invited Copland as Reynolds Lecturer for January 1954. The offer was rescinded on the grounds that the university decided not to hold the lecture that year. No reason was given, but Copland learned months later that the decision was due to his alleged Communist front associations. The *Colorado Labor Advocate* printed a story headed "Another Smear Victim," and *The Colorado Daily* sent Copland a telegram: STUDENTS AND FACULTY INTERESTED IN ORGANIZING MOVEMENT FOR YOU TO SPEAK ON CAMPUS. WOULD YOU ACCEPT? UNDER WHAT CONDITIONS? CITY EDITOR. Copland did not go to Colorado in 1954, but he accepted when reinvited in 1961.

In February 1956, citations voted to Copland from the Borough of Brooklyn and ASCAP were canceled. When television personality Ed Sullivan broadcast a performance

[23] The correspondence between Copland and Kennedy, and Dean Marten ten Hoor and Dean J. H. Newman was sent to Perlis by Mrs. Gurney Kennedy, March 1988, along with a program of the 1967 festival and the degree citation.
[24] See interview, Lukas Foss.

of *Lincoln Portrait* in honor of Lincoln's birthday, he did not credit the composer. William Schuman wrote to Sullivan afterward:

> The only disturbing feature was that you neglected to mention the fundamental thing about this composition, namely, that it was composed by Aaron Copland. It is not only that the music for this fine work was written by Copland but that he chose the excerpts from Lincoln's writings and wrote the connecting prose passages which are so effective.

Not surprisingly, the American Legion caused some difficulty. Copland had an appointment as Slee Professor of Music at the University of Buffalo in 1957, and the UB authorities were questioned by the Legion chairman, "Is this the Aaron Copland who. . . ." Cameron Baird, head of the music department, resisted the attack, but the controversy was reported in the *Buffalo Evening News* (2 February 1957). (When the university dedicated their new music building, the letters between Baird and the American Legion were sealed into the foundation stone.)

In 1960, anonymous cards were mailed to the Dallas Symphony trustees and management protesting a Copland concert, causing a board member to cancel a postconcert party. In 1962, the American Legion of San Antonio, Texas, questioned Copland's lectureship appointment at the University of Texas and an award from the San Antonio Symphony, but the activities took place as planned. As late as 1967, a letter was sent to the Rutland, Vermont, newspaper protesting Copland's appearance there as guest conductor of the Buffalo Philharmonic in April 1968. An editorial appeared against the protest, and the concert was given without further incident.

These few disturbances did not change Copland's life. If anything, he was more in demand on the lecture circuit than ever, and invitations to conduct were increasing. Copland's first book, *What to Listen for in Music*, was published in Hebrew and in Italian. *Music and Imagination* appeared in Spanish and Italian versions. He wrote articles for *Musical America*, *Musical Courier*, and *Saturday Review of Literature*. Within a few years of the McCarthy hearing, Copland received prestigious degrees and honors, among them membership to the fifty-member American Academy and Institute of Arts and Letters in 1955 and the Gold Medal in 1956,[25] a year in which he also received an honorary degree from Princeton University, followed by Brandeis in 1957, and Illinois Wesleyan and Oberlin in 1958.

When Copland was asked about the McCarthy hearing by friends at social gatherings, he would treat it lightly, imitating McCarthy's deadly seriousness and Roy Cohn's way of repeating the word *COOOOmmunist*.[26] In private, Copland told friends that it was no joke, and he would bemoan the amount of time the affair had cost him.[27] Most of the people Copland knew and with whom he worked were sympathetic to him and critical of what McCarthy represented. Directly after the hearing, Copland attended a family party and prepared to leave for Tanglewood (he had hoped to take leave in 1953 but thought it might be construed as being connected to the McCarthy hearing). He returned to work. The pace at Tanglewood left little time for anything but music, and afterward, the opera project, which Copland and Erik Johns were already deeply involved with, became enormously demanding. This opera, *The Tender Land,* is counted among Copland's "Americana" works. Except for one moment in the plot, there is no trace of the bitter taste left from the McCarthy hearing and its aftermath. The music for the opera is in Copland's "accessible" style. However, ten years after *Appalachian Spring*, the music and plot seemed nostalgic for a more innocent time in America, a time before the Cold War and Senator Joseph McCarthy.

[25] The Gold Medal from the American Academy and Institute of Arts and Letters was presented to Copland by Virgil Thomson.

[26] See Andrew Porter's mention of "Copland's hilarious account" in *The New Yorker* (2 December 1985), 132.

[27] Only a few of Copland's closest friends were told about a handsome young man who accompanied Roy Cohn and stared into space during the entire hearing (undoubtedly G. David Schine). According to Minna Lederman, Copland told her that no introduction or explanation was made as to his identity or the reason for his presence.

THE TENDER LAND
1953 - 1954

I had hoped to take leave from Tanglewood in 1953 to get to work on my opera, but friends pointed out that my absence might be construed as being connected somehow to the McCarthy business. And Charles Munch was not happy about the idea of my being away for the entire summer, so I decided against it. Lenny Bernstein was also ambivalent about Tanglewood in 1953, but there we were at the opening exercises as usual.[1] I introduced Carlos Chávez as visiting composer to the students and faculty. Chávez' presence cheered me—being used to the erratic political situation in Mexico, he took a philosophical attitude toward the McCarthy hearing. We shared composition students more than when a visiting composer was someone I did not know so well. Chávez and I agreed that the outstanding composition student in 1953 was a young Japanese, Toshi Ichiyanagi.[2] Chávez made a good impression, and there was interest in his music, especially after my lecture in the Aspects of Music course, entitled "Chávez and Mexican Music."

Munch conducted *Appalachian Spring* with the BSO (31 July) and Lenny did *Billy the Kid* with the Music Center orchestra (25 July). I played the piano in my *Piano Quartet* (9 August), and Sam Barber came up that weekend. He wrote afterward (12 August), ". . . you are a marvelous host. Thanks for pepping up a dull midsummer with such glamour—Dear Aaron: Have we become friends, perhaps? It would be nice."

[1] Ingolf Dahl returned to direct the Tanglewood Study Group; Lukas Foss taught the analysis classes, and Irving Fine taught the third group of composition students.
[2] In addition to Ichiyanagi, Copland's students were John (Jack) Brodbin Kennedy, Robert Cogan, Sarah Cunningham, Alvin Epstein, Norman Grossman, Arno Safran, and Joseph Weiss.

Immediately following Tanglewood, I left for Mexico to help direct a festival with the Orquesta Sinfonica Nacional. I wrote to Claire Reis from Mexico, "I have been through the wringer but I am beginning to get my equilibrium back." One of my Tanglewood students, Jack Kennedy, met me for a week of sight-seeing in Oaxaca and Taxco. With no word from the McCarthy committee, I decided to stay in Mexico for another ten days to help open the symphony season (I conducted Roy Harris' *Third Symphony* and Chausson's *Poème*). I wrote to Victor, "The men played like—Mexicans. That is, out of tune half the time with mistakes and flashes of very good sections. . . . I am learning a lot about conducting."

I returned from Mexico refreshed and ready to work on my opera with Erik Johns. I stayed close to home, except for a trip up to Boston for an unusual performance—Lenny Burkat had convinced Munch to revive my *Piano Concerto* after many years of neglect. Leo Smit was the pianist. It was an exciting event. My Boston friends all attended, among them Arthur Berger, who told me that his book *Aaron Copland* was about to be published.[3] An entire book about me! Arthur, an accomplished composer and experienced writer, had discussed various aspects of the book with me over the past few years. *Aaron Copland* is divided into two parts: biographical and musical. Arthur's main focus was on the musical section. He chose a few pivotal works (the *Piano Variations* and the *Third Symphony*) and concentrated on the form and structure of each. Arthur is expert at analyzing music in technical terms, something I have never done very well myself. *Aaron Copland* was reviewed by Harold

[3] Arthur Berger, *Aaron Copland.*

Copland at Tanglewood, 1953

Clurman in *The Saturday Review of Literature* (28 November 1953), and by William Schuman in *The New York Times Book Review* (8 November). I particularly liked the part where Bill wrote that "Mr. Copland is but a promising youngster of fifty-three. We can, therefore, look forward to many more years of his fruitful activity and to exciting additions to his list of major works." I wrote to thank Arthur (9 December): "Think of me the next time you pass those Harvard Sq. bookshops. I went in to buy something and a stranger came up and asked me to autograph your book for a Xmas present! Good sign, no?"

Arthur Berger[4]

Do you ever get Aaron to talk about his music? When I was working on the book, I tried to get him to talk in specific musical terms, but he obviously did not at all relish doing so. Perhaps he did not want to give his secrets away! Stravinsky was the same way about discussing his music. Aaron was critical of what I wrote about the Piano Sonata *in* Partisan Review, *and later about the* Piano Fantasy *in the* Juilliard Review. *I didn't use the most specialized language you find in, say,* Perspectives of New Music, *but nonetheless Aaron made the observation that he was not comfortable with the analytic part of the* Fantasy *article. I always had the feeling he felt that way about the technical side of my book—not that the analysis was on a particularly profound level. Clurman's review of my book reflected the same sentiment. Aaron took exception, furthermore, to the sharp distinction I made between his music for an elite audience and his music for a larger public. He thought I was perhaps responsible for starting the whole idea of a bifurcation in his output.*

I met Aaron through Jerome Moross and Benny Herrmann, my fellow students at NY U, way back in the early thirties when we all got together for those meetings of the Young Composers Group at his place—meetings that were very stormy indeed, both musically and politically.[5] *I refrained from putting the names of the Group's members in my Copland book because it was published during the McCarthy period. Aaron's politics were mild compared with the orientation of some of the Group's members! We young composers worried that Aaron might get away from the strong austere qualities we so much admired. They were difficult to reconcile with Aaron's more popular music. I tried to convince myself that Aaron's writing for a wider audience was just as significant as his other music, but for me, as far as the more popular pieces are concerned, you go through them too fast— they don't last as long.*

I have never considered Aaron to be my teacher—very few can claim him as a teacher, although many composers have studied with him briefly or attended his lectures at Tanglewood. At first, when I showed Aaron my music, he would want to know what organizing principles I thought of when I wrote. I learned certain things from Aaron, but mainly from observing his music; for example, the spacing of intervals and coming back to a given chord for punctuation. My Woodwind Quartet *of 1941, which is dedicated to Aaron, shows a little of his influence, although it is neoclassic in a way that Aaron never was.*

[4] Interview, Arthur Berger with Perlis, 13 November 1981, Cambridge, Massachusetts.

[5] For a description of the Young Composers Group of 1932 of which Berger was an active member, see 83-84.

Copland with Arthur Berger, c.1953

When I was with the Herald Tribune, *I used to go up to Tanglewood as a reviewer quite regularly, and I sometimes stayed with the Fines, with whom Aaron, their neighbor in Richmond, had his meals. My first wife, Esther, and I were in the car behind him in 1949 when he hit the cow, and we were with him when he was severely interrogated by the state police. Aaron was fond of Esther, and he never got used to the idea that she had died. (He kept sending regards to her.) There were so many times I spent with Aaron, I can't remember them all. It's funny how one occasion comes to mind: In 1958, Aaron and I went by train to Illinois to participate in some festival. There was a coal strike, and we couldn't take the train back, so Aaron said, "Let's fly." It was my first time and I was reluctant and scared, but Aaron, in his thoughtful way, kidded me and gave me a silver dollar for luck. You know, I felt very protected because Aaron was there with me.*

I was really up against a deadline: the premiere of my opera was scheduled for 2 April 1954 by the New York City Opera, and I had promised the finished product by the beginning of February. I was still composing in mid-March, and the orchestration was not completed until a few days before the premiere. Jerry Robbins, who directed the opera, thought it was very "cool" of me not to go to rehearsals, but the fact was, I didn't have time!

When I was a student in Paris in the twenties, nobody was interested in opera—nobody, that is, who cared about "new music." We were all interested in ballet. Later, in just the same way, everybody wanted to write an opera. But full-length opera is an enormous challenge for a composer! You spend years on the work, and then it's all over and decided in a few hours. It is such a tremendous effort that I waited until I was over fifty to do it. Even then, my opera, *The Tender Land*, was not meant to be a big dramatic opera. It was for young people to perform, and for that reason, it is rather simple in musical style and story line. I admit that if I have one regret, it is that I never did write a "grand opera."

Composers fall into two categories: those who are "hopelessly" opera composers—such as Rossini, Wagner, and Puccini—and those who debate whether and when to write an opera. To have the courage to cope with it regularly, you have to feel as if you were born to do that particular thing. The urge has to be so strong that because of some inner drive, little else in music attracts you—and then you are an honest-to-God opera composer. I am not such. For me, opera was really a very problematical form—*la forme fatale*—as I called it after my experience with *The Tender Land*.[6] Most composers will agree that opera is a risky medium even before putting a note on paper. However, the reward for writing a good opera, or even one that just brings attention to the composer, is so great that the temptation is to forget the problems and barge ahead.

The basic difficulty of the lyric stage, I think, comes from the fact that there are so many imponderables. Primary among these is the nature of the forces at your command. When I wrote a symphonic work, I had in the back of my mind the Boston the Philadelphia, or the New York Philharmonic—I knew these orchestras and their capabilities in advance. But writing an opera, even for the Metropolitan or City Opera, one never knows what singers

[6] See Copland, "*La forme Fatale*," *Copland on Music*, 129.

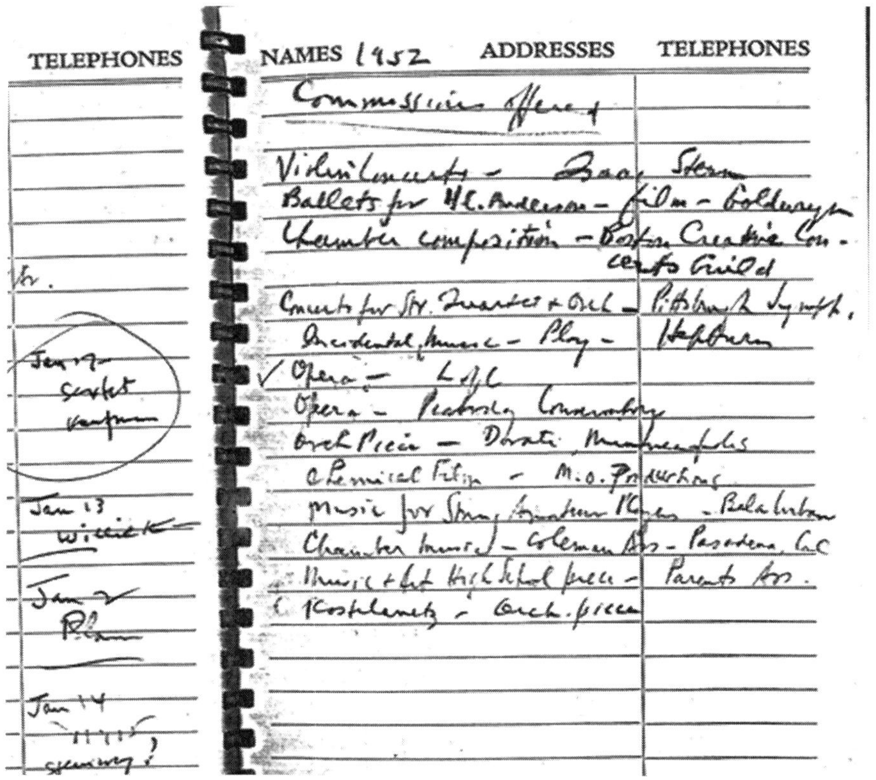

Page from Copland's 1952 appointment book listing commissions offered, with "Opera-L. of C." (League of Composers) checked

might be engaged. Each time you get a group of people together, the resulting production is full of uncertainties. A composer may have some say about who sings for the premiere of his opera, but there is no control over casts in the future. A composer may very well have to put up with tastes that differ from his own. For example, I prefer a voice with a certain objectivity, a certain purity in the presentation of the vocal line. I don't like to feel that I'm

being personally involved in a performer's private emotions. A voice that is deeply emotional makes me cringe! Others may feel differently. (Lenny Bernstein was shocked when I wrote that "I hate an emotion-drenched voice!"—he had never heard me express so strong an aversion to anything in music.)

I once asked Ben Britten what he thought was the most important requisite in composing opera. I was sure he would say a sense of drama, the ability to indicate the meaning of a scene musically in a matter of seconds. What he said was that the most important thing a composer must have is the ability to write many kinds of music—chorus alone, chorus with orchestra, soloists separately, soloists in ensemble, and so on. The needs are so varied that one must have terrific facility to handle them all.

My own feeling is that one of the prime requisites in writing an opera is to keep a sense of the flow of the action. Just as in any long sustained piece of music, it is very hard to keep going in such a way that one feels inevitably carried along. I have noticed with some composers (especially Puccini) that the sense of movement is often supplied not so much by the vocal line as by the orchestral accompaniment. The opera composer has to calculate his accompaniment very carefully. It is one way of solving tricky dramatic problems. The sustained melodic line in operatic vocal writing is comparatively rare in contemporary composition. Britten used it on occasion, as did some of the other British composers, such as Walton and Tippett. But it's not easy for a contemporary composer to write the kind of luscious, long, singing tunes that opera composers used to depend upon.

I believe that opera can be composed in a contemporary musical idiom. Kurt Weill wrote opera in a different style and got away with it, even though not everybody thought it was opera. And I don't think anybody has trouble with Douglas Moore's *Wings of the Dove* or Hugo Weisgall's *Six Characters in Search of an Author*, which has a certain daring about it that I find stimulating. All operas do not have to be done in the same way. I have noticed that it is usually composers with the experience of writing several operas who can bring one off. But the big bottleneck is that so few operas get produced. The cost and complexity of production have escalated to the point where, although younger composers are writing operas, they're wasting their time unless a way is found to get them performed. It is very hard to move on to the next point in one's development without hearing and seeing what has already been done.

Then there is the matter of the libretto. Where and how does one find a really professional librettist? We don't have people in this country who do nothing but write librettos for operas! Librettists usually don't know much about music, unfortunately. I think they would write better librettos if they could imagine what the music is going to do to their words. Composers frequently look at plays in order to find a libretto, but the requisites are different. I was constantly on the lookout for suitable libretto material. I knew and admired the works of several poets and playwrights, and I discussed with them opera librettos and other theatrical projects with music. Among them were Archie MacLeish, Robert Lowell, Bill Inge, and Edward Albee.[7] Clifford Odets was one of the first writers to whom I talked (Clurman always thought that we should collaborate). Cliff and I did some work on his 1938 play *Rocket to the Moon* before abandoning the idea of turning it into an opera. I remember that the main character in the drama was a dentist, and all the action took place in this dentist's office. We also worked on a kind of dramatic concert presentation, *Noah*. Clurman took me to see Arthur Miller to discuss *The Crucible*. I thought about turning Dreiser's *An American Tragedy* into an opera, and I seriously considered a script by Stephen Crane, a writer out in San Francisco. For some reason, I gave that one up, too. In 1948, after seeing a production of my high school opera, *The Second Hurricane*, Thornton Wilder criticized the libretto (6 September 1948): "What I did get from it, though, is—as I would expect—that you have a faultless ear for spoken rhythms and could set the telephone book." I responded by asking Thornton whether he would consider writing a libretto for me. I suggested *The Legends of the Chasidim*, but that did not appeal to him. I wrote to Thornton again in 1950, because Rudolf Bing, then general manager of the Metropolitan Opera, had offered me a commission for making *Our Town* into an opera. Thornton responded (April 1950):

> I'm convinced I write a-musical plays: that my texts "swear at" music; that they're after totally different effects; that they delight in the homeliest aspects of our daily life Music and particularly opera is for the unlocked throat, the outgoing expressive "idea and essence" behind our daily life. I hope my plays don't lack that idea and essence but they singularly shrink from any

[7] For scripts and notes, see folder, "Opera Ideas," in Copland's files at the Library of Congress, which includes a copy of Robert Lowell's play *Benito Cereno*, sent by Lowell when he heard Copland was interested. The play was originally intended as an opera libretto.

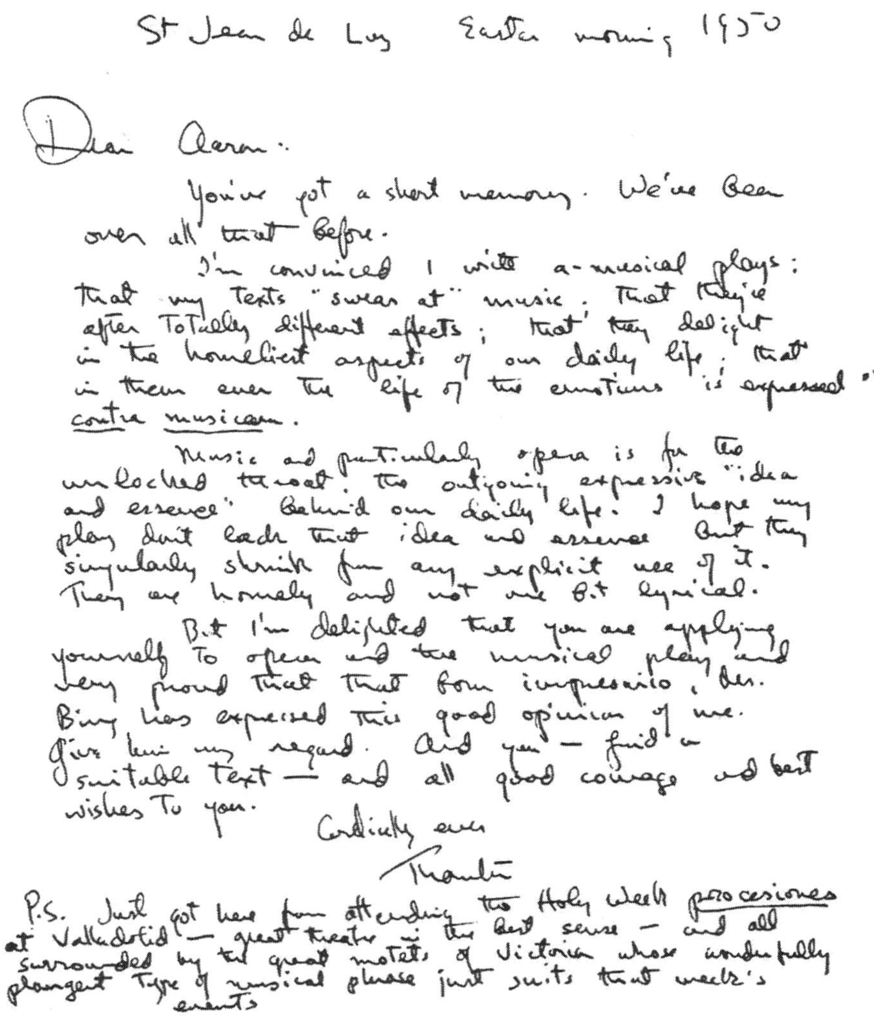

St Jean de Luz Easter morning 1950

Dear Aaron:

You've got a short memory. We've been over all that before.

I'm convinced I write a-musical plays: that my texts "swear at" music. That they're after totally different effects; that they delight in the homeliest aspects of our daily life; that in them even the life of the emotions is expressed "contra musicam."

Music and particularly opera is for the unlocked throat: the outgoing expressive "idea and essence" behind our daily life. I hope my plays don't lack that idea and essence but they singularly shrink from any explicit use of it. They are homely and not a bit lyrical.

But I'm delighted that you are applying yourself to opera and the musical play and very proud that that born impresario, Rud. Bing has expressed this good opinion of me. Give him my regards. And you — find a suitable text — and all good courage and best wishes to you.

Cordially ever

Thornton

P.S. Just got here from attending the Holy Week processiones at Valladolid — great theatre in the best sense — and all surrounded by the great motets of Victoria whose wonderfully plangent type of musical phrase just suits that week's events

Letter from Thornton Wilder, "Easter morning," 1950

explicit use of it. They are homely and not one bit lyrical. . . But I am delighted that you are applying yourself to opera and the musical play.

Mr. Bing said that for once he did not agree with Thornton Wilder and suggested I search for another librettist; but I could not imagine an *Our Town* without Thornton Wilder.[10]

While I was at Harvard delivering the Norton Lectures in the spring of 1952, Claire Reis wrote that I was the League of Composers' first choice for a commission (one thousand dollars) from Richard Rodgers and Oscar Hammerstein II to compose an opera for television.[8] I was intrigued with the idea of composing opera for an exciting new medium. Claire added a personal comment: "It would be wonderful to have you help the League celebrate its thirtieth anniversary and it would be wonderful if I could whisper to Rosenstock [Joseph, general director] perhaps the City Center might have a work of yours in the near future."[9] This seemed like good preparation for the "grand" opera I hoped to write someday. Since Erik Johns and I had been talking about working on a project together, we decided to give it a try. I wanted a simple libretto, and it appealed to me to work with someone I knew without having to worry about changing a famous writer's work or doing damage to a preconceived play or story.

Erik Johns[11]

I took the name "Horace Everett" as a pseudonym because I had a dancing and a painting career at the time of The Tender Land, *and I did not want to confuse the two activities. (Horace Everett was a name that had more to do with my real life than the name Erik Johns, which I had taken as a pen name much earlier, since Horace was my real given name and Everett my father's middle name.) I had never written a libretto or a play, only poems and various stories and sketches. Aaron had had the idea of composing an opera for a long time, and we had often discussed my writing a libretto for him, but as to a specific theme, time, or locale—nothing seemed to materialize. I knew that Aaron felt that opera was uncharted territory for him. "All those notes," he would say, "and that awful bugaboo, dialogue." Then one day he played me several songs from the abandoned folk musical* Tragic Ground, *and he showed me a book he greatly admired,* Let Us Now Praise Famous Men, *by James Agee, with photographs by Walker Evans. They were of a sharecropper's family in the South. Aaron suggested a libretto duplicating the pilgrimage of Agee and Evans, who lived and worked with a poor sharecropper's family. I derived the basic idea of the libretto from the book—two men from an outside world "invading" the inside world of a provincial family. The*

Copland with Erik Johns, 1953

[8] Jerome Moross was second choice for the commission; Foss and Bernstein tied for third. Rodgers and Hammerstein had given similar awards to Leon Kirchner in 1950 and Irving Fine in 1951.

[9] See Perlis for Claire Reis' copy of the piano-vocal score of *The Tender Land* autographed by Copland: "For Claire, the 'Prime Mover' of the opera/ Gratefully and Affectionately, Aaron/ March 1956."

[10] An opera, *Our Town* by Ned Rorem and librettist J. D. McClatchy, was premiered in 2005 by the Indiana University Opera. Rorem received permission from the Thornton Wilder estate.

[11] Interview, Erik Johns with William Owen for Perlis, 3 November 1981, Mt. Carmel, New York. See also Erik Johns, *Center: A Magazine of the Performing Arts* (March 1954), 14-26.

two men became migrant farm workers. I carefully examined the photographs in the book and kept coming back to the faces of the mother and young daughter: one, still a mother but passive and stony; the other, not yet hardened by the grim life. What effect would the entrance of two strangers have upon these lives? The answer to this question came to be my plot.

The locale changed from the south to the midwest in the mid-1930s in June, spring harvest time. The story is about a farm family, the Mosses—a mother, a daughter Laurie about to graduate from high school, her ten-year- old sister Beth, and the grandfather. When the two drifters come along asking for odd jobs, Grandfather Moss is reluctant and the mother is alarmed because she's heard reports of two men molesting young girls in the neighborhood. Nevertheless, and with Laurie's urging, Martin and Top are hired. The first act closes at sunset with the main characters looking forward to Laurie's graduation party. Act II opens with the party. Laurie and Martin fall in love, but there is something of a complication: Laurie associates Martin with freedom, while he associates her with settling down. During the evening, Martin and Top are accused of being the molesters. Although it soon is proven that the accusations are false, Grampa Moss tells them they must leave at daybreak. In the course of the night, Martin and Laurie make plans to run away together, but Top convinces Martin that the roving life is not for Laurie. The two drifters steal off. When Laurie discovers she been jilted, she decides to leave home anyway. At the conclusion, the mother looks to her younger daughter as the continuation of the family cycle that is the reason for their existence.

The action was developed in a series of plot outlines that were quite complex at first, and were then simplified as I went along. I was not used to thinking in terms of time and space plausibilities or of literal justification for actions. I soon discovered another aspect of libretto writing—reading time and singing time are quite different. Also, I learned that the presentation of a "finished" libretto to the composer is not the end of the librettist's job. Aaron might need an extra line to fill out a melodic phrase, and I would find that such a request could take more effort than a dozen verses.

When Aaron returned to Cambridge to deliver the second series of lectures on his Norton Professorship, I stayed in New York to work on the libretto and sent sections off to Aaron. He would cut and make suggestions for changes and additions. By Easter, I had a second draft of the final scene of Act I, which incorporated the quintet "The Promise of Living" for the first-act curtain. I wrote to Aaron, "Lord help you if there are other serious changes." The second act progressed with less difficulty. Aaron came down to New York from Cambridge to play the love duet and a dance number for me, and I made suggestions about the dances, having been a professional dancer myself.

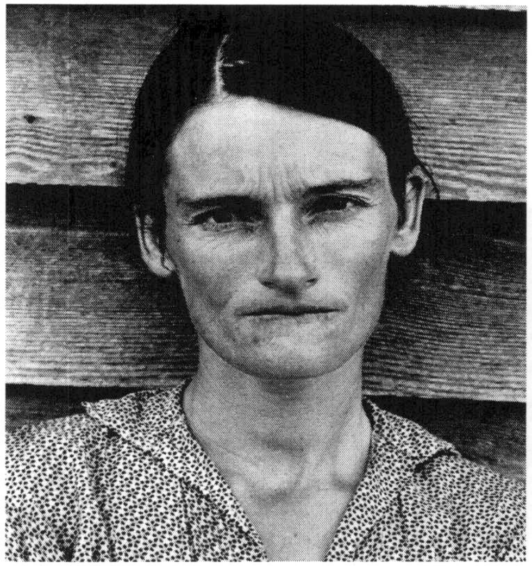

A sharecropper mother and daughter from *Let Us Now Praise Famous Men.* the book that influenced the character and plot of *The Tender Land*

The music for Tragic Ground *was gradually dropped out of the opera.*[12] *It was too popular in style, too folksy. Other changes were made as we went along—a name change, words cut or added as Aaron needed, the title changed twice: from* Graduation Harvest *to* Picket Fence Horizon *to* The Tender Land.[13]*At one time we considered including a murder or rape scene to add dramatic impact, but the idea seemed at odds with the modest pastoral quality of the work. The most dramatic scene was when the drifters are falsely accused, and then discovered to be not guilty. Aaron had just been through the McCarthy business and we were definitely influenced by that. When Grandpa Moss says to the boys, "You're guilty all the same," we were thinking about all the false McCarthy accusations and the effect they had on innocent people.*

[12] See correspondence between Lynn Riggs and Copland, Yale Music Library.

[13] This information is derived from librettos belonging to Erik Johns. Also, see The Library of Congress for a pencil sketch with the title *Picket Fence Horizon*, the dates "1952-54," and timings of each act at the end. Rough sketches contain various memoranda: 14, "murder music," with "murder" crossed out and "rape" written above; 42, "opera ideas" listed; 47, a memo, "no. 198 Cecil Sharp"; "Way Down the Ohio" from *English Folk Songs from the Southern Appalachia.* Other rough sketches contain additional scenes that were added to the original after the first production. A piano-vocal score in the collection is dated "1952-53."

After working separately, Aaron and I got together in the spring of 1954 before he left for the MacDowell Colony, followed by Tanglewood. We went up to Canada for a few weeks, still working on the opera, and returned with a script finally ready to submit to Peter Herman Adler at the NBC television workshop. Well, Adler turned it down cold! We almost gave up the whole thing, but Aaron asked Clurman to read the libretto, and he liked it and made some suggestions, which we incorporated. We decided to go ahead.

In order to give a clear idea of what we had in mind for the opera, we included a memo, "Suggestions Toward Production," in the score:

> The Tender Land *was conceived with an eye to modest production and intimate scale. These increase the effectiveness of the work and make presentation possible for smaller operatic groups. The sets should be poetic rather than naturalistic, simple rather than complex. Overdramatic lighting should be avoided. . . . The nature of the opera allows for varied treatment. Dialogue sections move naturally. . . . The dance should be rustic and "untrained. " Spontaneity is important.*

It was a very exciting time when the opera went into production with the New York City Opera Company. I had never had an experience like it before. Seeing The Tender Land *on the stage, Aaron and I felt that it needed more dramatic tension in various areas. Because the premiere was in the opera house instead of the intimacy of the television screen, our original concept of a very small gentle work, to which Clurman had responded with his suggestions, did not really work. It needed things made more explicit—things that we had in our heads but that weren't shown on the stage. That was just our inexperience. Aaron's commission from the League and the commitment of the City Center had made us go a little faster with the production than we should have. We might have been able to troubleshoot it a little more with more time.*

Many people who know the recording of scenes from The Tender Land *find it very meaningful, as I do.*[14] *Aaron has such a strong lyric gift and his lines sing. He really intended to do another opera; people wanted him to do another; and I thought he should. It just didn't happen.*

In writing *The Tender Land*, I was trying to give young American singers material that they do not often get in the opera house; that is, material that would be natural for them to sing and perform. I deliberately tried to combine the use of traditional operatic set pieces—arias, duets, choruses, etc.—with a natural language that would not be too complex for young singers at opera workshops throughout the country. I wanted simple rhetoric and a musical style to match. The result was closer to musical comedy than grand opera. The music is very plain, with a colloquial flavor. It is primarily diatonic, with dissonance used only in a few instances for dramatic tension. The orchestration is not complex, nor does it call for special effects.

The Tender Land and *The Dickinson Songs*, composed close together in time, were different in intention. Both are recognizably mine, but they are two different solutions to setting texts: the songs are discreet, intellectual; the opera, simple and folklike. *The Tender Land* is not the kind of work to be pulled apart for study of its counterpoint and harmonies. Besides, who cares about tearing an opera apart? It either functions, jells, and works—or it doesn't!

I think of *The Tender Land* as being related to the mood of *Appalachian Spring*. Both the ballet and the opera take place in rural America: one in the southern Appalachians; the other in midwest farm country. Both make use of folk materials to evoke a particular landscape in a real way. I adapted several folk songs for inclusion in the opera, among them "Ching-a-Ring Chaw" for the square dance number and "Zion's Walls" for the quintet that closes Act I. A funny thing happened while I was working with "Zion's Walls:" I began to develop a countermelody of my own and became more interested in my own tune than in the Revivalist one, and the piece ends up being more about my tune than the borrowed one.[15] A more direct arrangement of a folk tune in the opera is "I Was Goin' Acourtin'," sung by Top, one of the migrant workers.[16]

We did not write *The Tender Land* with the City Opera in mind, but nevertheless, I was pleased to have it accepted for production there. The talented Thomas Schippers conducted the premiere (1 April 1954), and the cast included Norman Treigle (Grandpa Moss),

[14] The recording of excerpts by Columbia Records is no longer available. *The Tender Land* was not recorded in its entirety until 1989, concurrent with a production in the Aldeborough Festival (June, 1989), conductor Philip Brunelle, for Virgin Classics featuring the soloists, chorus, and orchestra of the Minneapolis-based Plymouth Music Series who toured with a production directed by Vern Sutton in 1993.

[15] See Copland's *Old American Songs II* for arrangements of "Zion's Walls" and "Ching-a-Ring Chaw" that are closer to the original folk songs.

[16] Copland found "I was Goin' Acourtin'" in *English Folk Songs from the Southern Appalachia*, collected by Cecil J. Sharp and Olive Dame Campbell, ed. Maud Karpeles (New York: Oxford University Press, 1932).

The original production of *The Tender Land*, New York City, 1954

Rosemary Carlos (Laurie), Jean Handzlik (Ma Moss), John Crain (Martin), Andrew Gainey (Top), and Adele Newton (Beth). Jerry Robbins accepted the job of staging the opera, his first work outside of dance. Oliver Smith, who had designed *Rodeo* and was to have done *Tragic Ground*, designed the set.

John Butler was choreographer and Jean Rosenthal was lighting designer. *The Tender Land* was in two acts with two scenes in Act II. The total duration was about an hour and a half. After two years of work, I had an opera that absorbed only two-thirds of an evening. It was necessary to fill out the program. For the premiere, my opera was followed by Menotti's already very successful short opera *Amahl and the Night Visitors*. It was a rather odd combination! As though foreseeing the future, Clurman's good-luck telegram read, "Hope this is a smash and runs at least five performances." The first-night audience must have been a houseful of friends, for despite what seemed like an enthusiastic reception, the reviews were not good. Olin Downes of *The New York Times* criticized the libretto and the second act, describing the ending as "inconclusive and unconvincing." He found the roles of the women undefined and wrote that my music told the audience very little about their feelings and inner lives. As did other critics, Downes praised the production and some of the music, particularly the quintet and the love duet. *Time* magazine concluded: "*The Tender Land* is a step along the road to a full-evening opera." Obviously, this was not the opera the critics were waiting for me to write—if they had been waiting. On the other hand, B. H. Haggin wrote in *The Nation* (24 April 1954):

> I was struck first by the loveliness that was being achieved with the assured mastery one is always aware of in Copland's operation; then as the work continued, by the variety and unfailing adequacy for the dramatic purposes, the power when this was called for; and in the end by the rich profusion of the invention and elaboration.

I considered we had a flop on our hands and told Erik so. I am convinced that the conditions for the initial entry of a particular work into the world of music have a great deal to do with its future. In this country, we put so much emphasis on premieres and reviews of first performances that it can take a long time and a terrific struggle to turn a negative first impression around, if that is possible at all. It is particularly unfortunate when it comes to complicated opera productions where first performances are seldom the most polished. I have often thought that opera companies should copy Broadway, with out-of-town openings and previews in New York before critics are allowed to get their hands on a piece.

I was not sorry to have a legitimate reason to leave town soon after the premiere of *The Tender Land*. (I had agreed to perform in my *Piano Quartet* for the International Society for Contemporary Music in Rome.) I traveled to Milan, Geneva, Zurich (where I conducted an all-Copland radio orchestra program), and London. Erik kept me posted. He wrote (24 April 1954), "After seeing the second performance I am sorry to tell you it was even rougher than the first, which is not surprising considering the lapse of a month and one brush-up rehearsal. I went backstage after, for which the singers were grateful. They had thought they'd been deserted."[17]

[17] See also interviews, Harold Clurman and Jerome Robbins.

Erik, being younger and more energetic than I, was convinced that the opera was worth revising. He began suggesting changes. "What my mistake was," he wrote very honestly, "was not to more clearly develop relationships which were indicated, such as Laurie's 'feeling strange inside,' and her mother's resignation at the end. I'm certain that the motivations must come in the first act. That's what I'm working on." Erik got my enthusiasm going again: "Be prepared for lots of work after May 10th," he warned. After I returned from Europe, we worked on a revised version to be tried out at Tanglewood in August 1954. *The Tender Land* became a three-act opera, with more passion in the romance of Laurie and Martin and a more clearly focused ending. We moved some things around and added a new scene in Act I. The Tanglewood production was directed by Frederick Cohen, acting head of the opera department, with Frederic Waldman conducting.

At Tanglewood, *The Tender Land* fared little better with the critics. Jay C. Rosenfeld of *The Berkshire Eagle* wrote, "Copland can do better and must try again." However, the audience and the cast were enthusiastic and to this day, I have heard people who were at Tanglewood that summer say they were moved by the production. Erik and I were certainly more satisfied with the new version, which seemed closer to our original intentions.

The final revised version was presented by the Oberlin College opera workshop (20, 21 May 1955) under my supervision. I wrote about it to Jack Kennedy, who said, "Make changes now and try them out. . . . This is your last chance! You really should have the help of someone far more competent than Erik or I." With the exception of a few minor changes and more polishing, I felt *The Tender Land* was in its final form and ready for publication. I sent the published score to Richard Rodgers and received a cordial letter of thanks, but I never knew how he felt about the opera, or whether he and Oscar Hammerstein ever saw it.

Certain colleagues admired the opera. Arthur Berger, who had always been an outspoken supporter of my more austere works, surprised me with praise for *The Tender Land.* [18] And Israel Citkowitz wrote:

[18] Arthur Berger, "On First Hearing Copland's 'Tender Land,'" *Center*, vol. I, no 3 (April-May 1954), 6-8.

(*left*) A page from the revised version of *The Tender Land,* Act III, pre-orchestral score with pencil markings toward the orchestration

> The curiously tentative reception accorded *The Tender Land* tempts one to speculate still further on the cognoscenti vs. Aaron Copland. For, is not the opera house still another precinct for the sacred cow? I think Laurie is lovely. It's clear that we weren't dealing with Lulu or Lady Macbeth.

Bill Flanagan found much to his liking (5 May 1956):

> Someone will do this opera again in N.Y. and if the present regime of poisonous criticism dies off—or, better still, is shot to a man—it will be the success that it should be. I couldn't be convinced that there is a composer living who could move me as you do with the music of the mother's closing song.

Soon after the original premiere in 1954, I arranged an orchestral suite from *The Tender Land*. It does not represent a digest of the dramatic action of the opera, but it proceeds from the second act to the first in a three-movement sequence. The first movement, longer than the other two combined, is comprised of the introduction to Act II and the music of the love duet. The second movement is the lively square dance from Act II, and the last movement is the music of "The Promise of Living," the vocal quintet from the end of Act I. Fritz Reiner conducted the premiere of the suite, Chicago Symphony (10 April 1958). When I conducted it with the BSO in Boston (10-11 April 1959) and then New York (21 November), the reviews were far better than they had been for the opera. Even my conducting was praised, which led me to conduct the BSO for a recording in 1959 [Victor]. I prepared arrangements of "Stomp Your Foot" and "The Promise of Living" for chorus (sometimes used with the orchestral suite)[19] and for piano four-hands. "Laurie's Song" is arranged for high voice and piano.

The opera has been produced by various college opera programs through the years.[20] Bill Schuman, as president of Lincoln Center, had the unusual idea of presenting a full concert version of *The Tender Land* during the French-American Festival of 1965 (31 July). I conducted the New York Philharmonic and Norman Treigle sang the grandfather's part as he had in the premiere. From that performance, the recording of excerpts was made that brought *The Tender Land* more public recognition.

It was not until 1975 that *The Tender Land* was heard again in New York, mounted by the Bronx Opera Company at Lehman College. The Michigan Opera Theater of Midland, Michigan, produced the opera at the time of my eightieth birthday and invited me to conduct. The performance was televised and shown nationally on PBS. Unfortunately, what works for an audience in an opera house or theater may not work when a camera comes in close and shows a middle-aged male lead in the role of a very young fellow! The story seemed to lose all sense of reality in the television version.[21]

Surprisingly, it was a summer production in 1976 at Banff, Canada, that was most satisfying. It was a very modest affair with no orchestra and with amateur singers. Nevertheless, the opera seemed to work in a way that I had never seen before. It was very touching. The girl who sang Laurie was sweet and modest and fit the part beautifully. It brought tears to the eyes. I never would have expected I could have been moved that way by it. It all seemed so very real, and everybody seemed to have had the same reaction. It wasn't just myself being satisfied by renewed contact with my own opera.

Murry Sidlin, conductor of the New Haven Symphony, had admired *The Tender Land* for some time and wondered why it was not heard more. In 1985, Sidlin asked whether he could reorchestrate the score in a thirteen-instrument arrangement for a revival of the opera by the Long Wharf Theatre in New Haven, Connecticut.[22] I responded to Sidlin's request (17 May 1986): "I think it is a very good idea, from a creative as well as a practical point of view." Long Wharf Theatre director Arvin Brown was enthusiastic. With Brown as director and Sidlin as musical director,[23] *The Tender Land* was given over fifty perfor-

[19] The arrangement of the *Suite* for chorus and orchestra was first performed at "Tanglewood on Parade" (8 August 1957).

[20] In 1958, the opera was produced at Northwestern School of Music and at the University of Minnesota, Copland directing; in 1962, the first British production took place in Cambridge, England, Philip Ledger conducting, Copland supervising.

[21] Another television production was planned in 1969. According to the script in Copland's files, it was to involve Gower Champion, and the New York Philharmonic or the Chicago Symphony, perhaps with Frank Corsaro as director. Use of the music from the *Suite* (slightly changed) was made by Eugene Loring for a ballet by the Oakland Ballet in California in October 1978. It was conducted by Copland at the Paramount Theatre, Oakland.

[22] See Vivian Perlis, "A New Chance for The Tender Land," *The New York Times*, 26 April 1987, 21, 32; and Perlis, "Aaron Copland and Opera," *Program Book*, Long Wharf Theatre (24 April-7 June 1987), 30-35. The chamber orchestra version was recorded by Sidlin in 1995 and is published by Boosey & Hawkes.

[23] See interviews, Murry Sidlin and Arvin Brown with Perlis, April 1987, New Haven, Connecticut.

Discussing the 1987 Long Wharf Theatre production of *The Tender Land* (left to right): Copland, Vivian Perlis, Arvin Brown, and Murry Sidlin

mances in the spring of 1987.[24] Brown returned to my original two-act form, and he and Sidlin included two songs from my *Old American Songs* in the party scene of Act II: "Zion's Walls" and "Long Time Ago." When I saw a matinee performance, I thought it worked like a charm! Erik Johns accompanied me, and he remembered every word he had written. At first, we missed the full orchestra sound, but then we agreed that Sidlin's version worked exceedingly well.[25] After the performance, when Arvin Brown announced that we were in the audience, everyone stood and cheered while we took our bows. Later, we greeted the cast onstage. These talented young musicians had been living with our work constantly for months. One by one, they came up to see us, and it was clear by the look in their eyes what *The Tender Land* meant to them.[26]

When Erik and I were writing the opera, we had great trouble naming it. When we finally settled on *The Tender Land*, I wrote to Esther and Arthur Berger (9 December 53): "How you like? I've had good reactions to it—so I hope you both approve. It's worse than naming a baby." I was well satisfied with the name and never thought it would be so adaptable to changes. The BSO players sometimes refer to my opera as "The Tender Gland"; and I have received several amusing fan letters: One praises "The Tender City"; another is addressed "To the composer of 'The Tender Hand.'" But the best is the letter that arrived in 1987 referring to the "Tenderloin Suite."

[24] Leading performers in the Long Wharf production were Kristen Hurst-Hyde (Ma Moss), Jamie Louise Baer (Laurie), Bruce Kramer (Grandpa Moss), Craig Schulman (Martin), James Javore (Top), Rebecca Hanson and April Armstrong (Beth). David Bell was choreographer; Michael H. Yeargan set designer.
[25] Copland was seated between Johns and Perlis (30 May 1987). The conversation reported here took place at that time.
[26] *The Tender Land* was produced at the Glimmerglass Opera festival of 2010; director, Tazewell Thompson, conductor Stewart Robertson. Program notes by Vivian Perlis. Performers were all drawn from the Glimmerglass Young Artist Group.

NEW HORIZONS, NEW SOUNDS

1954 - 1957

Nadia Boulanger's 1953 birthday greetings included a request for two songs: "Next year is my fiftieth of teaching. This would be a 'commission' had I the funds. . . . But we are very poor, every year a deficit. . . . Therefore, it is a present I am expecting." I responded, "Of course, of course, I shall write the two songs you ask for as a *petit cadeau*—microscopic *cadeau* is a better word—for such a fifty years. (Fifty? Impossible!)" I heard from Nadia again (May 1954): "This is not to hurry you, but my eagerness to receive your songs cannot be misunderstood. Your music means so much to me, since the old far-gone days when one could see come to light a real composer, even at the very first steps. . . . I am impatient as when one expects a child in a house!" I wrote one song and sent it off in June with an explanation: "Because of revisions in my opera, which must be ready for a Tanglewood production this summer, I was not able to compose more than one song. I hope you will like it, and that it sings well."

The text for Nadia's song, "Dirge in Woods," is by George Meredith. It is for soprano and piano and of about three and one-half minutes duration. "Dirge in Woods," performed first in Paris during the summer of 1954, had its New York premiere in a recital of American music by Adele Addison at Carnegie Recital Hall (28 March 1955). The concert was sponsored by the recently merged League/ISCM. "Dirge in Woods" is not so grim as one might think from the title. As critic Ross Parmenter wrote, "Its mood is hardly sad. Rather, the feeling is one of serene acceptance. . . . The vocal line is long and floating and the piano accompaniment ripples gently under it." Of Adele Addison, Parmenter said, "She sang this and the four other American songs in a quiet and rapt rendition such as few contemporary songs have the luck to receive." Adele included "Dirge in Woods" in several programs after the premiere, but I cannot say that the song has been taken up by other singers.[1]

When the League of Composers' board decided to merge with the U.S. Chapter of the International Society for Contemporary Music in 1954, I was not at all convinced that it was worth continuing under such an arrangement. I felt that the organization had served its purpose well for many years and that perhaps it was time for other groups to take over. However, mine was not the majority opinion. The League/ISCM was established, with headquarters in New York and chapters and juries in various cities around the world. Former board members were invited to stay on the board, such as Roger Sessions, who had been active in the ISCM, and Claire Reis, who continued to work on various committees.

David Walker, who had become my assistant in 1952, went up to Tanglewood with me in 1954. He stayed in Lenox and was given the job of organizing the Sunday night Composers Forum Concerts, acting as general liaison between the composition department and the administration. David also helped with *The Tender Land* production in August. Lenny B., who had been promising to stay away from Tanglewood for a summer, finally did. The place did not seem the same without him.[2] Lenny wrote from Martha's Vineyard, where he and Felicia had a house (29 July):

> I miss you. That's the long and the short of it. I don't miss Berlioz or the crowds or the pewpils or the scenery or the meetings on the green, green furniture of Seranak, or even the hot crowded Sunday forums. I miss you, ecco. And Lukas.

Ingolf Dahl had written to me the previous November: "I have to make a choice of either getting my orchestra piece for Louisville written or coming back to Tanglewood." As a composer, I was sympathetic to the problem, but it seemed a shame to interrupt the successful launching of the Tanglewood Study Group so soon. Lukas Foss took over as acting head, and, along with his composing duties, did a terrific job with the TSG.

Ernst Toch shared the composition department with me. Toshi Ichiyanagi and Jack Kennedy returned in my group; Barney Childs and Jack Gottlieb were among my new students.[3]

[1] The original manuscript of "Dirge in Woods" and two photocopies are at The Library of Congress, sent from the estate of Nadia Boulanger (June 1980). The title page reads "Words by G. Meredith/ music by Aaron Copland/ written especially in honor of Nadia Boulanger's fiftieth year of teaching."

[2] In 1954, Jean Morel was acting head of the orchestral-conducting program assisted by Seymour Lipkin; Boris Goldovsky and Sarah Caldwell were absent (Frederic Cohen was acting head of the opera department); George Judd retired at the end of the season and Tod Perry became Manager of the BSO. The concerts in the Shed formerly presented in the last three weeks of the Festival were spread out over six weeks, expanding these concerts from nine to twelve. The Bach-Mozart chamber-music concerts, formerly presented in the first three weeks of the season, were shifted to Friday evenings.

[3] Other Copland students in 1954 were George Green, Stefan Grove, and Richard Maxfield.

Teaching, lecturing (I spoke on Berlioz), preparations and rehearsals for *The Tender Land,* and Leo's [Smit] performance of the *Piano Concerto* with the BSO (18 July) kept me hopping all summer. I have been asked whether I ever took a vacation that did not have to do with music-making. The idea had always seemed boring to me; but after the schedule of Tanglewood 1954, I did enjoy a brief trip to see Martha's Vineyard, Nantucket, and Newport.

Returning to Ossining refreshed, I tackled some of the things that had been left unattended during preparations for *The Tender Land*, such as lectures for Smith and Amherst colleges and a Town Hall Forum with the musicologist and *Herald Tribune* critic Paul Henry Lang. By November, I was off again to Caracas, Venezuela, for the First Latin American Festival of Contemporary Music. I arrived there to find a very lively scene: Chávez, Varèse, Villa-Lobos, Juan José Castro, Virgil Thomson, plus five of my ex-Tanglewood students.

Within two and a half weeks, forty symphonic compositions from seven Latin American countries were performed in a series of eight concerts. It was a major effort for all concerned, especially the courageous musicians of the Orquesta Sinfonica Venezuela. A prosperous oil economy was being enjoyed, and the festival reflected the Venezuelan largesse. Three prizes totaling twenty thousand dollars were offered for symphonic pieces. They went to Castro, Chávez and Orbón. Villa-Lobos and Chávez confirmed their reputations as leaders of Latin American composition. It was my opinion that the program planners had overemphasized the folklore side of Latin American music. As I pointed out in an article in *The New York Times* (26 December 1954), a few gripes were in order: Chile was inadequately represented; Guarnieri from Brazil was absent, as was the young Chilean Juan Orrego-Salas. Most of all, one missed an experimental note. Of dodecaphonic music, there was not a trace. But all in all, the Festival was a great success and Caracas was already planning another for 1957.

I returned to the States just in time to see Martha Graham and her Company dance *Appalachian Spring* in the full orchestra version conducted by Ormandy in Philadelphia. Back in Ossining, from December 1954 to April 1955, between various lecture, writing, and conducting assignments, I composed a work commissioned for the opening of the new Kresge Auditorium at MIT. I had started to collect some ideas while in Caracas, but now I was pressed for time. I began looking through my notebook and files for something I might use. I came across sketches for a choral work made in 1949 utilizing the lines "Let us now praise famous men, and our fathers that begat us. . . ."[4] These famous biblical words intrigued me, as they had James Agee and Walker Evans, who titled their book *Let Us Now Praise Famous Men.* I used the text and my musical sketches of 1949 as the basis for my new piece for chorus and orchestra.

Canticle of Freedom is fourteen minutes long, and, as I wrote to Victor, "It makes a big noise." I joked about the title to Irving Fine: "Maybe I'll call it 'Inauguration Overture,' and dedicate it to Rep. Busbey!" I wrote to Lenny about it, too (3 April 1955): "It's called *Canticle of Freedom.* Sounds subversive, no?" Lenny responded from Italy, where he was conducting at La Scala:

> It's good to hear that you have a new piece. That's always an occasion for me. *Canticle of Freedom,* though: I thought we had had that era. But this sounds well for the times: A new interpretation can be laid on it. I'm eager to hear it.

The premiere was conducted by the director of music at MIT, Klaus Liepmann, with the Institute's chorus and orchestra at the Kresge Auditorium (8 May 1955). Before leaving for a six-month stay in Europe, I went up to Cambridge for a rehearsal. I inwardly despaired of Liepmann getting results from the forces with which he had to work, even though, knowing the limitations of a nonprofessional chorus, I had confined myself to two-part choral writing and to introducing the chorus only in the final third of the work.

Canticle of Freedom is scored for normal-sized orchestra, with percussion instruments requiring five performers. It is in two main sections: an orchestral prelude followed by a choral portion with orchestral accompaniment. The first part, mainly for brass and percussion, presents the principal melodic material, heard first in imitative fashion in the woodwinds; it concludes with a full orchestral statement of the main material as it appears again later with the chorus added in the final coda. A transition, using chords from the introduction, leads to the choral finale, which brings the materials of the first part to an intense climax.

The first New York performance of *Canticle* was conducted by Lenny Bernstein with the Symphony of the Air (formerly the NBC Symphony) and the Schola Cantorum at Carnegie Hall (9 November 1955). At the rehearsal I attended, the piece seemed to have no conviction; the playing and singing were very tentative because the performers had no chance to familiarize themselves with the music. It was obvious that Lenny had cut the rehearsal time for my work in favor of Mahler's *Resurrection Symphony.* I told him so and threatened not to go to the performance—and didn't. David Diamond was shocked when I wrote to him about it: "AAAAAARON! Not you!"

Critics reviewed *Canticle of Freedom* as a *pièce d'occasion*, which it was. I meant to revise the piece, and when Robert Shaw asked me for a piece to open the 1967-1968 Atlanta Symphony season, I offered him a revision of *Canticle of Freedom.* The revisions were made only in the orchestral introduction; the choral finale was kept intact. Shaw conducted the premiere (19 October 1967). In addition to the revised version, an arrangement of the choral finale with piano accompaniment is available.[5]

I was feeling the need for a change. For whatever reasons, perhaps the McCarthy business and the disappointing reception of *The Tender Land*, I seemed to be having what writers

[4] "Let us now praise famous men, and our fathers that begat us" is from Ecclesiasticus 44:1. The words were used in a fourteenth-century poem, "Freedom," from "The Bruce" by John Barbour (1320-1395). In Copland's files at the Library of Congress are typed pages of the poem and one copy in Copland's hand (pencil), four verses in ink, pencil sketches for a choral work (1949) marked "incomplete," and the chorale from *Canticle* signed "Aaron Copland 1955,"

[5] For the revised *Canticle,* see pencil sketches, pencil score (reproduction), and final score in David Walker's hand, at the Library of Congress. The manuscript for the revised *Canticle of Freedom* bears the memo: "original version not to be played," and "original pp. 1-77; rev. new pp. 1-20; then 33-70 of original."

call a "block." I could not seem to move ahead with the fast sections of the piano piece. Instead, I worked on lectures and articles: One was a response to musicologist Henry Pleasants, who had come to the conclusion that modern music, with the exception of jazz, was finished. *The New York Times Magazine* published an article giving both sides of the story: Pleasants on "Modern Music: 'A Dead Art;'" Copland on "Modern Music: 'Fresh and Different.'"[6] I still could not make headway on the piano piece, so I decided to take the break from Tanglewood that I had been promising myself. I planned a six-month trip to Europe, from April through September 1955.[7]

My friends Bob Cornell, Jack Kennedy, and Victor saw me off at the airport. The first stop was Monaco, where I was on the Olympic Hymn Jury at Monte Carlo (18-25 April). Nadia presided over eight representatives from European countries and me.[8] She seemed her old self— energetic and running the show at age sixty-eight. Nadia did most of the jury work, reading through 389 scores, of which very few were from American entrants. We were all invited to lunch at the palace—quite a show! There were twenty-six guests, pictures of ancestors on the walls, and Prince Pierre himself was host—a nice youngish fellow, seemingly working hard at his job.

I spent all of May in Paris and wrote in my travel diary, "Everything seems the same as in the twenties except for the traffic and the prices—'both of which horrifies an old Parisian resident like me." I stayed in my old *quartier* and kept running into people I knew—Gerald Sykes and his wife Buffie—and Clurman came over from London for a reunion. He couldn't understand why I was spending my time correcting proofs for *The Tender Land*: it aggravated him that I would do such a thing while in Paris! I visited the Musique Concrète studios, which did not seem to have made much progress since I was there last—the same few composers using the same methods. I went to the Paris Opéra with Marcelle de Manziarly to hear a concert in which *Old American Songs* were sung by Warfield, conducted by Ormandy. I noted, "Marcelle was very taken with my orchestration. I rather liked the way it sounded myself." Before leaving Paris, I conducted the Radiodiffusion orchestra in an all-Copland concert, which included the *Third Symphony*. At the end of May, I made a brief but hectic trip to Milan to see Lenny, who was conducting there, and searched in vain for a place to rent at Lake Garda for the summer.

Jack Kennedy met me in London as planned. I gave two BBC talks and conducted the complete ballet version of *Appalachian Spring* twice with the BBC Orchestra. Jack and I attended the opening of a play Clurman was directing, and then we left London for the ISCM Festival at Baden-Baden. I noted:

> Of all the music, the Schoenberg Var. Op 31 left the strongest impression. Boulez' *Le Marteau sans maître* has striking sounds and peculiar rhythms (nonrhythms would describe it better). I worked hard to get him one of the prizes—but lost out in the end.

[6] See *The New York Times Magazine,* 13 March 1955, Pleasants, 14, 57, 59; Copland, 15, 60 62.
[7] See travel diary #5.
[8] The judges were Frank Martin (Switzerland), Lennox Berkeley and Arthur Benjamin (England), Georges Auric (France), Andrze Panufnik (Poland), Necil Aknes (Turkey), Niles Viggo Bentzon (Denmark), Rodolfo Halffter (Spain), and Alexander Spitzmueller (Austria).

I bought a German Ford, and Jack and I drove south in it through Switzerland and into mid-France. We had no luck in finding a villa in Aix-en-Provence, so we continued on to the Riviera and there found a beauty of a place in the hills above Cannes in the small town of Le Cannet. The villa, "L'Orangerie," had two pianos, a cook, a car, and a distant view of the Mediterranean. I wrote to Victor, "Now! Let's see if it brings forth some music." I was finally able to move ahead nicely on the piano piece and wrote again to Victor, saying, "If it turns out well, it should be one of my best things."

I thought about Tanglewood and wrote to Olga Koussevitzky to find out how things were going without me (16 July 1955): "I will be here 'til Aug. 31. How's the Tanglewood season shaping up? Has anyone noticed yet that I am not there??" Olga responded (August 21), ". . . we all missed you at Tanglewood—the season was most successful. . . . Roger Sessions was delighted with and excited by the spirit of Tanglewood, and, I think, put his heart into the task you left him to carry out." (Roger was taking my place as the American composer; Boris Blacher was the visiting European.)

We left France for Venice and a delightful visit with Gian Carlo Menotti and Tommy Schippers. Then on to Munich. Jack returned to New York. Paul Moor was in Munich and he showed me around and took photographs while I was conducting the orchestra. I listened to tapes of music by Hartmann [Karl Amadeus] and Henze [Hans Werner] and was impressed with Hartmann, but Henze put me off. I wrote, "Henze is generally thought of as the white hope of young German music. This tells more about the state of German music than about Henze."

I conducted eleven different works with five orchestras in five weeks— Munich, Baden-Baden, Helsinki, Stockholm, and Oslo. The most enjoyable was the *Short Symphony* in Baden-Baden. I was beginning to feel out of the amateur class as far as conducting was concerned. Helsinki was an odd experience because for the first time ever I couldn't talk to the orchestra at all, except in translation. I gave radio talks, newspaper interviews (which I found frustrating because I couldn't read them), and played chamber music—my *Violin Sonata* three times with three different violinists in three different languages.

In Baden-Baden, I heard radio tapes of the *enfant terrible* of young music—Karlheinz Stockhausen. I wrote my impressions in my diary:

> It seems to me pointless to have an opinion about this sort of music—it is just too soon. Stockhausen is starting music again from the beginning—with notes strewn about like member disjecta. There seemed an end to continuity in the old sense and an end of thematic relationships. In this kind of music, one waits to hear what will happen next without the slightest idea of what will happen, or why what happened did happen once it has happened. Stockhausen's only chance is to mesmerize the listener. No one knows where it will go, and neither do I.

In Helsinki, I gave a talk for a mixed group of Finns and Americans, recorded my *Violin Sonata* with an excellent local violinist, and played the *Piano Variations* for a radio broadcast. Tapes of recent Finnish music were very disappointing. I wrote, "The Finns are rather backward in music, and I suspect that the figure of Sibelius, who is still alive, is overimposing." The boat to Stockholm went through a series of lakes, and then the city appeared at the end of all that inland water. It was more inviting than Helsinki. A nice surprise was to find the Juilliard Quartet there! The American Embassy invited me to a party for them. I rehearsed and recorded the *Clarinet Concerto* with Ib Erikkson, and feeling more confident about my conducting, I did Ives' *Unanswered Question* and felt that it went very well.

In Copenhagen, my lecture at the Royal Conservatory had a very thin audience—no students whatsoever! The interest in new music was very faint, although they had the best orchestra in Scandinavia. I played *The Dickinson Songs* with a singer at an ISCM concert to a small but enthusiastic audience, as well as the *Piano Quartet* and *Violin Sonata*. When I heard Carl Nielsen's music from recordings, I recognized an original mind who thought his own thoughts and I wrote, "What a tragedy that Koussevitzky had not gotten to know his work!"

In Oslo, I found the Norwegian Symphony better than expected: We did *Lincoln Portrait* in Norwegian, *Outdoor Overture*, and *Quiet City* without difficulty. I received compliments on my conducting from the local conductor. I wrote to Victor (6 October 1955):

> This reminds me very much of my two South American tours. I hope the traces I leave are as lasting. Everyone has been very nice and sort of took the attitude that I was honoring them with my visit. In the four main towns, the composers' societies gave me a dinner or lunch—and I said "skol" until I was blue in the face explaining shamefacedly that I'm not much of a drinker. The Norwegians are even worse than the Finns, I think—aquavit, red wine, cognac, and beer all at the same meal, and "skol" by golly, every time.

Victor had returned from Guatemala and was living in Brooklyn, but he made trips out to Shady Lane Farm to keep track of the house and to run the Buick once in a while. David Walker sent important mail on to me. There were three offers for movies: I turned one down because of the script—*Alexander the Great* did not appeal to me, nor did William Wyler's film about the Quakers, *Friendly Persuasion* (it seemed to falsify Quaker ideas as I understood them). I decided to terminate my arrangement with MCA and sign with the William Morris Agency for theatrical contracts and with Arthur Judson for conducting. As a starter, Judson got me a contract ($1,250) for a concert at the Ravinia Festival the following summer. It was about this time I began to realize that I might make good money conducting.

Shady Lane Farm looked grand after six months of traveling! I returned just as a new biography of me was published. It was by Julia Smith and called, not surprisingly, *Aaron Copland*. Julia had been in touch with me since about 1945, when as a young composer and graduate student at New York University, she chose me as her topic for a thesis for the degree of Doctor of Music. We met several times: Julia asked the questions and I responded. I was amazed when she told me that she had also been a pupil of my teacher Rubin Goldmark! Julia worked hard on her thesis, and when it was finished and accepted, she prepared it for publication in book form by E. P. Dutton. Julia Smith's *Aaron Copland* is more a biography than a technical presentation of my music. In that respect particularly, it differs considerably from Berger's book of 1953. Both books have been helpful, each in its own way, in supplying information to the public about my music. I was certainly pleased when, on 30 November 1955, Julia Smith met me at the Harvard Club and presented me with the first published copy of her *Aaron Copland*.

My plan was to stay home from October 1955 to January 1956. I had to get right to work on the revision of the *Symphonic Ode*, commissioned by the Koussevitzky Foundation for the seventy-fifth anniversary of the BSO, to be celebrated with a concert conducted by Munch in Boston (3 February 1956). Koussevitzky had introduced the *Symphonic Ode* twenty-five years earlier. It was a work he had admired. For the new version, the shape and character of the piece remained the same, but the size of the orchestra was reduced and notational changes of the difficult rhythms were made.[9] At the time of the premiere of the revised *Ode*, I was on a conducting and lecturing tour that took me to Washington, San Francisco, Vancouver, and Chicago. Irving Fine sent me the reviews, even though they were awful. The critics' reception for the New York performance that followed was not much better. I wrote to the Fines, "I'm sorry to say the N.Y. performance of the piece was sort of stiff and unconvincing. I guess Munch got self-conscious. Oh well—publication is assured, so it's in the hands of the gods. But I sure do wish I could hear it conducted by an American." (I conducted the *Ode* myself with the New York Philharmonic in June 1980.)

In the spring of 1956, I received two special honors. At the annual May ceremonial of the American Academy and Institute of Arts and Letters, I received the Gold Medal in Music, presented by Virgil Thomson.[10] In June, I became a Doctor of Music for the first time with the honorary degree conferred on me by Princeton University. I felt highly honored. Between conducting and lecture assignments, I was working to finish the piano piece. I had to put it aside again to write a few overdue articles on American music: one for *The Washington Post*, another for *Musical Courier*, and a third for the Associated Press.[11] I was told that the AP piece would be "put on the wires" with a photograph on Sunday, 15 July, and that I would have 47 million potential readers! How could I resist?

David Walker came out to Shady Lane Farm regularly to help with all the paper work and correspondence. Being a composer himself, David knew his way around scores and parts—sometimes I even asked him to write parts out for me.[12] As time went on, David became my loyal and indispensable assistant. He helped organize all my manuscripts and files and is the the most knowledgeable person about my scores and my musical activities. David has composed his own music through the years, never talking much about it. I was amazed when in 1979 I attended a concert in Greenwich Village entirely of music by David Walker!

David went up to Tanglewood with me in 1956. I was surprised (and relieved) to see how little the Music Center had changed—everything seemed the same as when I had left in 1954. I still stayed in the barn in Richmond and had my meals with Verna and Irving Fine

[9] For a full description of the original *Symphonic Ode* and the revised version, see 72ff.
[10] For Virgil Thomson's presentation speech, see *Proceedings*, Second Series, no.7, American Academy and Institute of Arts and Letters.
[11] Copland, "Our Music Isn't Obscure; Most of Its Curators Are," *The Washington Post*, 15 July 1956; Copland, "The Dilemma of Our Symphony Orchestras," *Musical Courier*, 1 November 1956, 6,39; Copland, "Report on American Music, 1956," the Associated Press.
[12] According to David Walker, Copland decided to make all final copies of his scores himself when the Library of Congress informed him that appraisals would be lower for works copied by others.

and their three girls. Most of the regular faculty returned to the Center.[13] The composition department was the largest ever, with four in faculty: Goffredo Petrassi from Italy, Lukas, Irving, and myself. Between us, we had twenty-three students.[14]

One major difference sparked a fresh and lively atmosphere: the involvement of philanthropist Paul Fromm, a successful wine and liquor importer and merchant from Chicago, originally from Germany. Fromm had a passion for contemporary music. Just the man we needed! He had set up a foundation in 1952 to assist the performance of contemporary music and to commission new works. Paul Fromm had written to me (17 February 1956), saying, "You can plan boldly since we do not intend to sponsor contemporary music in economy size over the thrift counter." The Fromm Foundation's two concerts of "modern chamber music" took place on Monday evenings in July in the Theater-Concert Hall with members of the BSO. Four Fromm-commissioned works were played.[15] Enthusiasm ran high; Fromm was so pleased that he promised to continue his support. It was a big step forward for contemporary music. We began to talk about adding a seminar to the contemporary concerts the next season.

The BSO presented my revised *Symphonic Ode* and *First Symphony* as a continuing celebration of the seventy-fifth anniversary of the orchestra. But the event everyone was talking about in the summer of 1956 was Lukas' opera, *Griffelkin*. Friends invited themselves up the first weekend in August to hear it, among them were Erik Johns and Jack Kennedy, and I played host. Unfortunately, *Griffelkin* was not an immediate success.

After Tanglewood, Jack Kennedy and I drove up the Maine coast, visiting Sam Barber in Nantucket on the way. I played some of my new piano piece for him, but I desperately needed some uninterrupted time to bring it all together. That meant the MacDowell Colony. From Peterborough, I wrote to Victor (19 September 1956), "If you're in the midst of new scenes and new faces, I'm in the midst of old ones. The Colony looks just like it always did, but the faces have changed. It's still as conducive to work as ever, and I am plugging away at my piano 'number,' as usual." After a few solitary weeks, I wrote to Verna, "This monster must be tamed!" I made headway at the Colony, but it was not until four months later that I inscribed the date of completion at the end of the last measure of my *Piano Fantasy*: "January 19, 1957."

The *Piano Fantasy* has a long history. Way back in 1951, Bill Schuman had offered a commission from the Juilliard for a work to be premiered during an American Music Festival in

[13] Eleazar de Carvalho took Bernstein's place as head of orchestral conducting and the Department I orchestra, assisted by Lipkin; chamber music became a separate program again under Burgin and Kroll; Hugh Ross was in charge of choral music, assisted by James Aliferis and Lorna Cooke de Varon; Goldovsky and twelve others ran the opera program, and Ingolf Dahl was back and in charge of the Tanglewood Study Group.
[14] Copland's students in 1956 were Hector Campos-Parsi, Carlos Farinas, Thomas Putsche, Jr., Eino Juhani Rautavaara, Michael Sahl, José Serebrier, and Ramón Zupko.
[15] The Fromm composers were Ben Weber, Alvin Epstein, Leland Smith, and Julián Orbón (the Epstein and Smith pieces were premieres). Other composers represented were Stravinsky, Britten, Schoenberg, Webern, de Falla, Petrassi, Barber, Milhaud, and Copland (*Vitebsk* was played by Burgin, Mayes, and Copland). Leonard Burkat handled the Fromm concert arrangements and David Walker assisted.

Manuscript, first page of the ink score of the *Piano Fantasy*

celebration of the school's fiftieth anniversary. I had responded to Bill's request (22 July 1951): "You sure are a planner—to be thinking about 1954-1955 in 1951. But the idea sounds grand. I know what I'd like to do—and the next time I see you I'll discuss it with you. But it needs a text." At that time, I had in mind a choral piece, a kind of cantata, and I was thinking about Walt Whitman (as I had before when composing *The Dickinson Songs*).[16] I made some sketches using sections from *Leaves of Grass*, but occupied as I was with *The Tender Land* in 1952 and 1953, I proceeded no further. In 1953, I received a letter from Bill (17 June): "This note is by way of a gentle, friendly, but firm nudge." I took out the sketches and made a few attempts to move the cantata along, but it soon became clear that the idea was not working. When I had Bill's go-ahead to submit a different type of work for the Juilliard commission, I began to think about the piano piece I had been composing since the early fifties.

I had developed some material for a concerto for William Kapell to play with the Louisville Symphony Orchestra. The commission fell through, but as I wrote to Victor from Italy (28 February 1951), "Perhaps I will do a big piece for piano alone. I have material for it that tempts me—a kind of Fantasy or something." Then Willy Kapell died in an airplane crash, 29 October 1953. I wrote to his wife, Anna Lou:[17]

> When William died he was expecting a new piano work from my pen. It was a promise I had gladly given him. It is a promise I intend to keep, and when the work is written I can only hope that it will be worthy of the best in William Kapell.

The Juilliard anniversary seemed an ideal occasion for the premiere of the *Piano Fantasy* to be dedicated to William Kapell. Bill Schuman suggested a performance date during the American Festival in the spring of 1956. I made some progress on the piece while on my six-month trip to Europe in 1955. I had written to Chávez about it from the Park Lane Hotel in London:

> I have been battling with the piece. It is, as we say, a very hard nut to crack! The no repetitions and no formulas makes the piece hard to get hold of. By the time I have figured out the notes, I cannot hear the music. I have to be inside and outside of the work at the same time—lost in it yet watching the composition being led.

I heard again from Bill Schuman (22 November 1955):

> My great pleasure in seeing you again perhaps covered up my genuine disappointment in learning that there is some question about your piece for the Festival. Surely, as one of your great admirers I would not want you to rush the composition and run the hazard of premature birth. But—couldn't you stop all your other activities, such as baton wielding, lecturing, and committee trotting. Stick to the farm, work long hours and eat Wheaties. Just to make you feel worse, I told the entire faculty that we confidently expected your piece. We will hold up the final copy of our program until December 15 when you should be in a position to know more. As things now stand, your work is scheduled for Monday, February 20. With so much time, I refuse to be discouraged. Just make believe that JSM is MGM and you'll finish.

I was having trouble with the *Fantasy*, particularly the fast sections. To put it plainly, I was stuck! There was nothing to do but take a forced hiatus with the hope that my ideas would be fresh when I returned to it. It was important to me to have a sense of not repeating myself, sorry as I would be to disappoint Bill and the Juilliard. I asked to postpone until late spring and received another of Bill's "gentle but firm" notes (20 January 1956): "Spring begins on March 21 and your work will not be performed until April. I hope you will consider that this is reasonably late spring." But the piece was still not finished—spring and summer came and went and so did Juilliard's American Festival and the date of its fiftieth anniversary. It was the month of September 1956 at the MacDowell Colony when I began to feel the *Piano Fantasy* really begin to come together. When I finally sent the score off to Bill Schuman in February 1957; it had been almost six years after the commission was first offered! Bill wrote (12 March 1957):

> I immediately took it home and placed it next to my writing desk. This was a fatal error.. . . I was in the position of having ten minutes of music to compose in less than a week. And, blast you, in every moment of weakness I would put down my pen and take up your *Piano Fantasy*. Clearly, it is a major Copland work, which is another way of saying, an important addition to music's literature.

Since I had missed the date for which the *Piano Fantasy* was commissioned, Bill arranged a special concert for its presentation (still in honor of Juilliard's fiftieth anniversary) to take place 25 October 1957. Lucky for me that the president of Juilliard was a composer!

I was invited to write an article for *The New York Times* at about the time of the premiere of the *Fantasy*,[18] and I was grateful for the opportunity to explain certain aspects of this work as it related to my career. I was well aware that I had become typecast as a purveyor of Americana in music. I knew this was not the whole story, or even the best of the story. I wrote:

> A composer in our time is comparatively helpless as to the picture of himself that will be presented to the listening public. Commercial exploitation of serious music is by definition plugging the "well known." By and large, performances are restricted to a narrow list of one's most accessible works, and this restriction often obtains in concert and broadcast performances.

As my *Piano Variations* of 1930 and *Piano Sonata* of 1939, the *Piano Fantasy* belongs in the category of absolute music.[19] It makes no use whatever of folk or popular musical materials. My purpose was to suggest the quality of fantasy; that is, a spontaneous and unpremeditated sequence of 'events' that would carry the listener along, while at the same time

[16] Pencil sketches for a choral work with a Whitman text, "Come, Heavenly Death," arc in Copland's files at The Library of Congress..

[17] This letter from Copland to Kapell was printed in the program book of the William Kapell Memorial Concert (26 October 1983 at Symphony Space, New York City).

[18] Copland, "Fantasy for Piano, Composer explains its particular problems," *The New York Times*, 20 October 1957, X 9, reprinted in *Tempo*, no. 46 (Winter 1958), 13, 14. See also Arthur Berger, "Piano Fantasy," *Juilliard Review* (Winter, 1957-1958) and Merilyn Kae Hutchinson, *A Stylistic and Pianistic Evaluation of Aaron Copland's Piano Fantasy*, Master's Thesis, North Texas State University, Denton, 1968.

[19] See the Library of Congress for holograph pencil score; ink score; 113 pages of rough pencil sketches with the title page inscribed "P. F. Piano Fantasy (1951-56 rough sketches)" and various dates on other pages (one dated "Nov 23 '49 for slow section"); a page marked "Plan (Elements) July '55," with the title

Juilliard School of Music
cordially invites you to attend the world premiere of
Aaron Copland's
"PIANO FANTASY"
on Friday evening, October 25, 1957, at 8:30 o'clock
in the Juilliard Concert Hall.

This work, commissioned by Juilliard on the occasion of its fiftieth anniversary, will be performed by William Masselos. The "Piano Fantasy" is the sole work on this program and will be repeated following an intermission.

R.S.V.P.
on the enclosed card.

Invitation from the Juilliard School to the premiere of Copland's *Piano Fantasy*

William Masselos and Copland in the CBS recording studio, New York, 1957

exemplify clear, if somewhat unconventional, structural principles. To give free rein to the imagination without loss of coherence—to be "fantastic" without losing one's bearings—is venturesome, to say the least. Yet a work of art like the *Piano Fantasy* seems to me the ideal proving ground for just such a venture.

I wrote in the program notes for the first performance that the musical framework of the entire piece is based upon a sequence of ten different tones of the chromatic scale. To these are joined, subsequently, the two unused tones of the scale, related throughout as a kind of cadential interval. Thus inherent in the materials are elements able to be associated with the twelve-tone method and also with music tonally conceived. To describe a composer as a twelve-toner, I felt, was much too vague. The *Piano Fantasy* is by no means rigorously controlled twelve-tone music, but it makes liberal use of devices associated with that technique. It seemed to me at the time that the twelve-tone method was pointing in two opposite directions: toward the extreme of total organization with electronic applications, and toward a gradual absorption into what had become a very freely interpreted tonalism. My use of the method in the *Piano Fantasy* was of the latter kind.

I decided not to play the first performance of the *Fantasy* myself, as I had with the *Variations* and the *Sonata*—my friend Lawrence Morton was right on the mark when he said it was too hard for me! I had to practice whenever I played the *Variations*, but as I admitted to Ben Britten when writing to him about the new piece, "The *Fantasy* is quite beyond me." William Masselos, a Juilliard alumnus and one of the most talented young pianists around, was unusually committed to the performance of contemporary American music. He had been responsible for the premieres of several outstanding American works, Ives' *First Piano Sonata* and pieces by Ben Weber, for example. Masselos was without doubt the choice pianist for the premiere of my *Piano Fantasy*, and I was delighted when he agreed to do it. After hearing Bill play through the piece one day while he was testing pianos in Steinway's basement, I really got excited: Masselos was a composer's dream.

William Masselos[20]

I started doing American music in 1939 at my debut. There were the Copland Variations *and the Griffes* Sonata. *When I started working on the* Piano Fantasy *in 1957, I fell in love with the piece. It is a wonderful addition to the big contemporary piano literature, in a Lisztian-Copland style. We performers need big works, ones that can be performed in Carnegie Hall and this is certainly one of them. It seems to me an "American" piece—very open-faced and through-and-through Copland.*

"Fantasy: The Music Within (La Musica por dentro);" 74 pages of a second pencil score that is sketchy at the end but inscribed "Apr 29 '56;" an ink score in a separate envelope with the title page inscribed "Piano Fantasy/Aaron Copland/(1955-57)" and on page two, "Commissioned by the Juilliard School of Music/William Schuman, President on the occasion of its fiftieth anniversary celebration/ and/ dedicated to the memory of William Kapell/finished Jan 19 '57/ duration 30 min."

[20] Interview, William Masselos with Perlis, 3 November 1978, New York City, for the Steinway Project, Oral History of American Music, Yale.

It is the work, of all I have played, that needs the most carefully chosen piano. I put all my body weight into the beginning, into the announcement of the first ten notes of that row. Some of the newer pianos become shocked, jarred by that. There's something that happens—they get paralyzed and there's no sound. I would go to the Steinway basement to see the technician, Bill Hupfer, and say "I need a Copland piano again." He understood what that meant—a piano I could really lean into that would take the thrust. It meant a riper, older piano, one that could take a slugging, particularly in the bass, a piano that's almost ready to go to the piano hospital, one that's in the autumn of its existence, before it gets rehammered. Number fifty-five was like that for a while. That was one of my favorites for Copland's Piano Fantasy.

When I was learning the piece, I asked Aaron to tell me more about it. He said that the row is announced in the first ten notes, and that he'd saved the other two notes for special occasions. Then he said, "It's vaguely in three sections. You don't need to know any more." That's all I got. It wasn't that Aaron couldn't describe the Fantasy, *but he wanted me as the performer to have plenty of room for personal expression.*

I don't remember too much about the premiere.[21] *I have always been a nervous kind of performer. But I remember that the program said "Aaron Copland,* Piano Fantasy *(World Premiere). Intermission. Aaron Copland's* Fantasy." *It was scary, because when I walked out onto the Juilliard stage, I saw that the audience was made up of practically all the great musicians in New York. You're relieved if you get through it the first time and then immediately have to wonder whether you can do it again! Somebody booed from the balcony. I am told it was Morton Feldman.*[22] *Aaron took a bow with me at the end. In the year following the premiere of the* Fantasy, *I traveled fifty thousand miles just doing that piece. And I was the only guy who knew it. For a little while, the* Fantasy *was virtually my exclusive property. As I wrote to Aaron after the premiere, "Now I'm going to be jealous of everyone that plays it. It's my piece."*

I played the Fantasy *for the thirtieth anniversary concert of the Copland-Sessions Concerts (10 May 1958) and at the ISCM Festival in Strasbourg (June) to represent the United States. I even played it in a program of the National Catholic Music Educators Association. Most of the Fathers and Sisters loved the piece—at least, they seemed to—the ending sounds almost biblical. I recall playing it in Mexico City on a beautiful Hamburg Steinway; and for Nadia's seventieth birthday celebration in Washington.*

I recorded the Fantasy *in 1958 and wrote to Aaron, "I think I chose a dreamy piano (the one we used at Juilliard died of a broken plate). 'Course I'm shaking in my boots. Think of all the decisions I'll have to make alone. Recording piano in a studio is so different from a concert hall performance." It was not until 1960 that the record came out together with the* Variations *and then I learned the* Sonata *in time to play all three major works for Aaron's sixtieth birthday celebrations at Tanglewood and at Juilliard. These pieces are always part of me, so Aaron always feels close by, even when we do not see each other or write so often as we did for a while.*

[21] A recording of the Juilliard premiere is in Copland's files. It can be heard on tape at the Recorded Sound Research Center, The Library of Congress.

[22] See interview, Ned Rorem: "Morton Feldman booed from the balcony. That is a fact . . ." Rorem also described Masselos' performance of the *Piano Fantasy* at the 1983 tribute to Kapell: "Masselos was so nervous that he had a student who knew the piece in the wings. All these famous pianists came out and then Masselos made it out. You know how the *Fantasy* begins with an E flat? Masselos took his finger of his right hand and aimed it with the aid of his left hand and hit the note. Once he hit that note, I knew everything was going to be okay. He missed some notes, but I have never heard such piano playing in my life. He is no second Kapell, but he is a major pianist, eccentric as hell, but very big time."

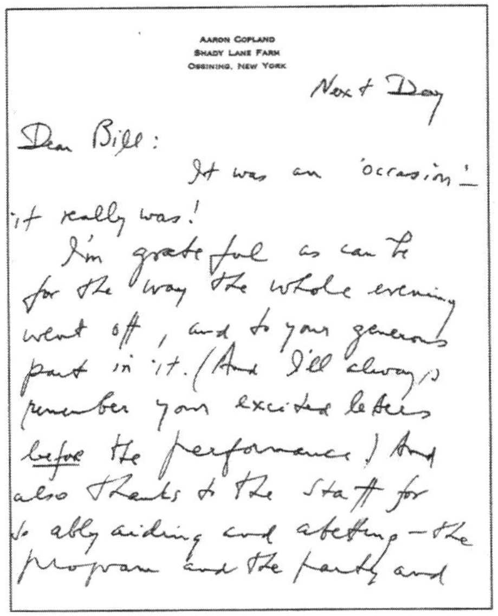

Aaron Copland
Shady Lane Farm
Ossining, New York

Next Day

Dear Bill:

It was an 'occasion'—it really was!

I'm grateful as can be for the way the whole evening went off, and to your generous part in it. (And I'll always remember your excited letters before the performance.) And also thanks to the staff for so ably aiding and abetting—the program and the party and

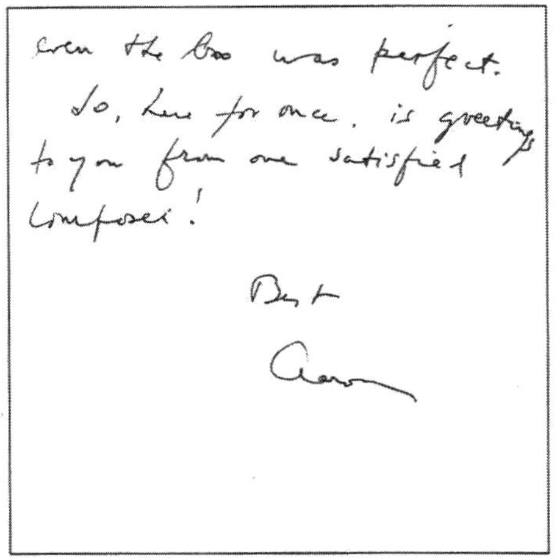

even the boo was perfect.

So, here for once, is greeting to you from one satisfied composer!

Best

Aaron

Above: Letter from Copland to Wiliam Schuman, 26 October 1957
Below: Schuman to Copland, 28 October 1957

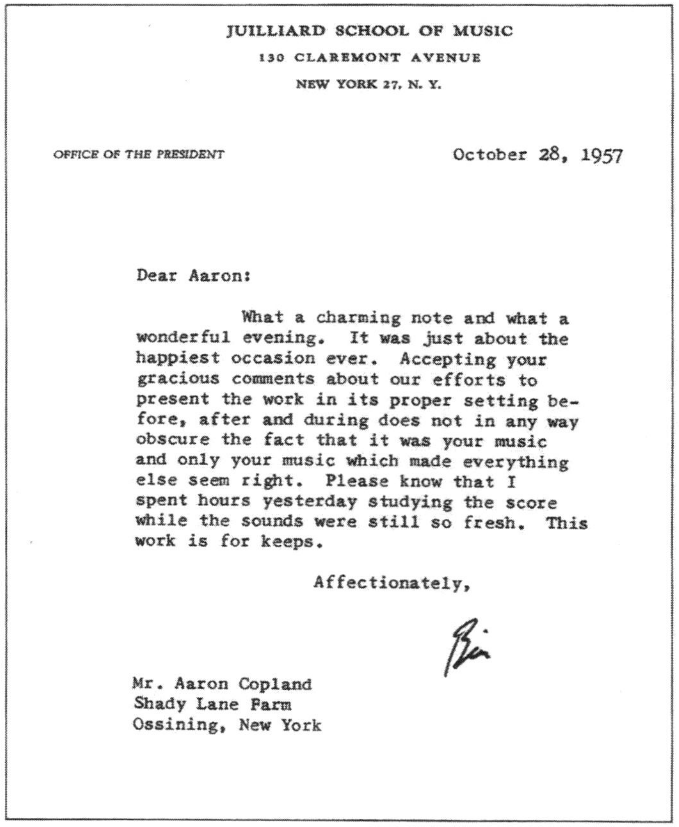

JUILLIARD SCHOOL OF MUSIC
130 CLAREMONT AVENUE
NEW YORK 27, N. Y.

OFFICE OF THE PRESIDENT

October 28, 1957

Dear Aaron:

What a charming note and what a wonderful evening. It was just about the happiest occasion ever. Accepting your gracious comments about our efforts to present the work in its proper setting before, after and during does not in any way obscure the fact that it was your music and only your music which made everything else seem right. Please know that I spent hours yesterday studying the score while the sounds were still so fresh. This work is for keeps.

Affectionately,

Bill

Mr. Aaron Copland
Shady Lane Farm
Ossining, New York

The *Piano Fantasy* is a large-scale work in one movement. If you write a work such as this that lasts half an hour without pause, you would be foolish to imagine that everybody is going to love it—or play it every day. Just for a listener to be able to sit for one half hour, without letup, and connect in his mind what the composer began with from the first note through to where he comes out at the end, takes a considerable amount of concentration and musical sophistication. Such a composition is therefore by its nature not going to win over the kind of audience that a *Salón México* is able to attract. For the composer, a long and continuous one-movement form is one of the most taxing undertakings.

The *Piano Fantasy* was received as I hoped it would be: a serious major work. One always hopes that *The New York Times* review will be favorable. In this case, Howard Taubman seemed to have a good idea of what I was after. He wrote (26 October 1957):

> The *Fantasy* . . . is one of Mr. Copland's most significant compositions. . . .This is an intensely serious work, but it is not forbidding. . . . He has given his imagination wide range, but a cultivated mind and ear have been in control of the selection and development of material. The listener who has any experience with the contemporary world of music and who gives his attention to Mr. Copland is carried along. This *Fantasy* has a largeness of scope that reminds one of the fantasies of Mozart and Schubert, though its idiom is a far cry from theirs.

Taubman went on to praise Masselos. He described the audience as one of the most knowledgeable that could be assembled in New York. "At the end of each performance it hailed composer and performer. There were a couple of boos from avant-gardists who regard Mr. Copland as an old conservative. They couldn't be more wrong." Irving Fine wrote after the premiere (30 October 1957): "I should imagine you must have mixed feelings about being referred to as the grand old master who can show those young whippersnaps a thing or two. We must have the *Fantasy* done up at Brandeis."

Among the many congratulatory notes received after the premiere was one from Anna Lou Kapell, which touched me deeply (19 October): "Willy would have been deeply moved and excited to carry your new *Piano Fantasy* about the world. It is a great privilege of which he was deprived. I was profoundly touched that you should have remembered him in this way. Thank You. Anna Lou."

Leo Smit soon learned the *Piano Fantasy* and gave the West Coast premiere in the Monday Evening Concerts series. Leo wrote (14 January 1958):

> It worked! Cheers, bravos, four calls etc. . . . Your telegram made me so happy. When I finished there was a stunned silence, then a long gasp . . . and finally the outburst. I was thrilled myself.

My friend Lawrence Morton (director of the concert series) wrote (13 January 1958):

> I would call the whole thing a triumph for both you and Leo. And a triumph for Monday Evening Concerts, too—as for myself, I have no words. But I congratulate you with all my heart for this, your "late Beethoven," and I rejoice that you have been able to deliver yourself of a work so tragic as this.

Later, he sent a few reviews:

> I send them with little pleasure. But this is the usual treatment we get for our concerts; we're eggheads. These critics would not be excited by the Crucifixion—they'd say it was not original, too staged, and too stark—even if there were background music by Tiomkin. But everybody who matters knows that the *Fantasy* matters.

Among the pianists who have performed my *Piano Fantasy* are Noel Lee, who played all three of my larger piano works at Hunter College (16 February 1966) and recorded the *Fantasy* and the *Sonata* in France [Valois]; Andor Foldes; Joel Shapiro; Charles Fierro, who played and recorded the *Fantasy* with other of my piano pieces [Delos]; and Shura Cherkassky. Cherkassky wrote from France (22 May 1958) to ask for advice about interpreting the work:

> I will play your *Piano Fantasy* everywhere next season. I am studying the work, and simply crazy about it. However, some markings, changes of tempi, etc. I do not quite understand . . . please be so kind as to drop me a line—your advice how to study it, a general outline. The more I practice it, the more I am becoming thrilled with this piece—it is the most unusual composition I have come across.

In 1965, Leo Smit presented a program in Buffalo, *Keyboard Masterworks of Three Centuries*, on which he included my *Piano Fantasy*. When I was there as visiting lecturer in Morton Feldman's class, Leo played my complete works for piano for the first time (1 June 1977), followed by the same program at Harvard (2 November) and in New York at Carnegie Recital Hall (5 November). In connection with the Harvard program, Leo interviewed me in front of an audience. An edited version of our talk appeared in *Contemporary Keyboard* magazine and was reprinted on the record jacket of Leo's *Aaron Copland: The Complete Music for Solo Piano*, which was released by Columbia Records in 1979.

Leo Smit[23]

I met Aaron for the first time in 1943 after he sent me a copy of the newly published Piano Sonata *in 1941. I played it for him at his sunny loft and was surprised how he seemed to prepare himself for my performance, anticipating a pleasurable experience. He stretched out on his couch, whereas I thought surely he'd pull a chair up to my elbow and watch intently and mutter all kinds of corrections and suggestions. But he didn't say a word. I played through the entire* Piano Sonata. *Then he said that he liked the way I "tasted" the harmonies and the chords, especially in the last movement. When I asked for suggestions, he again expressed his pleasure, his satisfaction. Didn't tell me anything. I was quite frustrated because I was seeking greater authenticity. I wanted some hot tips! He simply expressed his own philosophy—that he was more interested in the variety of performances rather than having everyone play his music the way he thought it should go. That made a very deep impression on me.*

Earlier on, I had worked with Stravinsky, whose ideas were quite different, insisting on strict adherance to his score. But Aaron's way is a more lasting way, because that's the way it ultimately works. With

[23] Interview, Leo Smit with Perlis, 29 January 1981, New York City.

Aaron's dynamics, there's wide margin for personal expression. That's what he's after; especially when it's done with power and conviction and technical backup. Aaron's very different from other composers in that respect. I've heard him express criticism all right, but only when an interpretation went beyond a certain margin—when it really changed the character of a piece.

The next wonderful event was the unveiling of Aaron's new Violin Sonata *at his loft. David Diamond played, and Harold Shapero, Elliott Carter, and Oliver Smith were there—quite a gathering of New York's finest. I played the curtain raiser—a piano transcription of a recently composed orchestral work of my own. Aaron took pleasure in introducing new talent—he was always on the lookout. After Aaron's* Violin Sonata *was performed, Shapero, known for his keen critical ear, sat down at the piano and went through the piece note by note, commenting all the way. Aaron pretended to be scared. He cried out, "Stop that. I didn't write it to be analyzed."*

Aaron introduced me to Lenny Bernstein in 1943 at Carnegie Hall, as I was hurrying backstage to turn pages for Béla Bartók. "You guys ought to know each other," Aaron sang out. Shortly after, I watched Lenny entertain a crowd at a Greenwich Village party, playing everything from El Salón México *to the latest Broadway show tunes—and singing all the words. At that moment, I knew he was going to "make" it big.*

Aaron was interested in my music. I played everything I wrote for him. He was concerned with receiving an overall impression before considering the details. He said to me once, "I like the turn of this cadence." My first ballet was composed in Aaron's loft, which I rented when he went off to Europe. I also made a piano arrangement of The Second Hurricane, *but he thought the music was too simple for concert performance, and he didn't sanction it. And I made a solo piano arrangement of* Danzón Cubano, *which no one has ever played, including me. It's too difficult, but it would be a wonderful program finisher. Aaron has very few pieces that end in a bravura style. You know I helped Aaron make the rehearsal records of* Appalachian Spring *to send to Martha Graham. I stood behind Aaron as he sat and played the main parts, poking away at an inner part or a difficult run, filling out the score, thus approximating the full sound. At the end of the recording, Aaron said, "Martha, here is your ballet." Then he gave the date and said, "This recording was made with the assistance of Leo Smit."*

Don't be fooled when Aaron says, "Oh, did I do that?" He knew what he meant to say. An examination of his sketches, his work in progress, includes strong writing; the impression of the man was powerful in every way. Everything Aaron has written sounds as if it came out in a burst of joy, but actually he's a very slow, painstaking worker. I think it's because he's extremely critical about letting things through that he does not feel convinced of completely. His inner censor works on a very high level. However, when the work is over, he relaxes his extremely fine critical faculties, except when he was writing an article. And how well those evaluations of other composers' music stand up with time!

Aaron's score markings are often unusual: "Crystalline," for example, is one of my favorites.[24] *"Crystalline" had a few chords to go with the word. Aaron built a whole vocabulary to correspond to certain emotions— "searing," for example, had a certain harmony, with minor seconds. The kind of harmony you find in* Night Thoughts *and in the* Piano Fantasy. *I remember Aaron playing the* Fantasy *for me and entire pages were simply incomprehensible in terms of the printed page, but when you realize the words that he used, such as "freely expressive," "hands go two different speeds," he really meant it—like a* Beethoven *crescendo—it goes and goes till it roars. "Uncertain" is one of the words Aaron uses. How do you monumentalize that or put that into concrete tones? Aaron explained: "Well, as if uncertain. I want you to be certain of uncertainness. "Aaron's instructions to the performer in the* Fantasy *are so personalized that it's as though he was standing behind you looking over your shoulder. I know of no other work that is so filled with the physical presence of a composer. "Clangorous" is in there and "brooding." At one point, Aaron indicates— "right hand as background"—which sort of upsets the normal balance between the hands. "Heavy staccato" is one of my favorites, and "muttering" and "musingly." I asked Aaron about that one, and he said, "It suggests the sort of touch that will produce a kind of doodling effect. A toying with the note."*

I always admired Aaron's own piano playing because of the clarity with which he was able to convey the intent of his musical thought, without gorgeous tonal quality or brilliant technique. Yet the rhythmic drive, for one thing, had such an infectious quality of joy. It came out of his whole physical being. And his lonely melodies, the sense of isolation and the stopping of time. I thought his playing unique, extraordinary. I didn't mind the harshness of his tone. I'd rather have that than a crooning, "poetic" touch.

I played with Aaron once when we were in Rome in 1951. I brought over the Bach Chorale Preludes, *and we played them four-hands on his spinet. It was wonderful playing Bach with Aaron. He didn't often play classical music. After we played a particular prelude, "Herr Christ, der ein'ge Gottessohn," I heard him muttering to himself, "He's the best." A rare and precious bow to the great J.S. It sort of stopped me in my tracks. That particular chorale prelude wasn't one everybody would fall for right away. It had a plainness to it that appealed to him. It was in A major—*Appalachian Spring *key, and the intervals were mostly thirds. Aaron didn't talk much about composers. Mahler was definitely one of his favorites. He spoke about his orchestration and his liberating ideas. Once he said a beautiful thing about Wagner. Instead of putting him down, as so many French- trained musicians did, he said that he found a wholeness in every note and measure, and that Wagner sculpted his ideas. Fauré was one of Aaron's very favorites. He mentioned a Fauré song to me, "Diane Selene," the first time we met, and I dashed out and got it right away. Those strange intriguing harmonies. They don't go where they're supposed to. They had a kind of Aaronish quality, and I could understand their appeal to him.*

We had literary discussions, too. Aaron told me once that he read himself to sleep every night. He'd read mostly twentieth-century writers.[25] *He especially liked Gide. One day, he remarked how strange that I loved new music and old books. He referred to me as "a kind of Henry James of music." Isn't that nice? He was also pushing D. H Lawrence then. To Aaron, Lawrence was a liberated writer exploring themes no one else had. I stuck to Tolstoy, Gogol, and Hawthorne.*

The first present I ever gave Aaron was a necktie. He said, "Beautiful. You can pick my ties anytime." I sensed the kind of quality, elegant but subdued. Not sporty, like Stravinsky, who was very daring, wearing polka dot bow ties and navy pea jackets. And Aaron's first present to me back in 1945 was the Harvard Historical Anthology of Music. *Very special.*

[24] See the liner notes for *Complete Works for Solo Piano*, in which Leo Smit reads all of Copland's markings in the *Piano Fantasy*.

[25] When the *Saturday Review of Literature* asked Copland for a list of books he particularly admired, Copland sent the following: *An Anthology of Contemporary American Poetry*, ed. Dudley Fitts; Christopher Isherwood, *Lions and Shadows*; *Journals of André Gide*, ed. Julian Huxley; Paul Collaer, *Darius Milhaud*; Truman Capote, *Other Voices, Other Rooms*; *Don Quixote de La Mancha* (Mexican edition: Editorial Seneca); Alfred Kinsey, *Sexual Behavior in the Human Male*; James Agee, *Let Us Now Praise Famous Men*; and Donald Friede, *The Mechanical Angel*.

Leo Smit and Copland, c. 1945

I have two Stravinsky stories about Aaron. I was riding in a taxi with Stravinsky and Joséph Fuchs in New York, and Joe said, "Copland is a very good American composer." Stravinsky immediately reacted and said, "Why American? He is a very good composer." I told that story to Aaron and he was tickled pink. At a party given by Lawrence Morton one wonderful afternoon in Los Angeles, Stravinsky, Aaron, Lukas Foss, Ingolf Dahl, myself, and a few others were all having lunch, including strawberries hand-picked by Vera [Stravinsky]. Suddenly, out of the blue, Stravinsky raised his glass and offered a toast to Aaron. Aaron almost blushed, he was so pleased; and he was simply delighted that the old master paid him such a sincere compliment.

Aaron's personality, it seems to me, was expressed at the very outset with such power and conviction that even his twelve-tone music is completely his, completely original and not influenced by the atmospheric world of the modern Viennese masters. The emotional integrity has always been constant, and that's the symbol of his great musical power. That voice, the Mosaic voice. What a drive that man was consumed by from the very start—the confidence, the vision, the ambition! The first time I heard the opening of the Piano Concerto, *I thought of Moses blasting away on the mountaintop. How young he was and already filled with the confidence and the power of his own voice.*

I only heard Aaron say "Dear Leo" once at the end of our interview for Contemporary Keyboard. *So when you tell me that you have heard Aaron call me "Dear Leo" when I'm not around, I am very touched.*

I visited Aaron in Peekskill periodically. I went up to see him with Verna Fine in 1988. At lunch, Aaron began to sing to himself and then said with a laugh, "I wonder where that came from!" After lunch, somebody asked me to play, so I did, putting together a medley of Aaron's music, ending with the last pages of Appalachian Spring. *I played the ending very softly and Aaron cut in, "You left out the last three notes!" So I played them again, banging them out for him, fortissimo, and we all laughed like old times.*

INTERLUDE IX

When William Masselos played Copland's *Piano Variations* and *Piano Fantasy* in a retrospective series at the Juilliard in 1960, the spotlight was turned on Copland as a composer of keyboard music. When Noel Lee played all three major piano works at Hunter College Playhouse in 1966, audiences knew that what Virgil Thomson had said in 1946 was true: "Copland has written his most expressive music for the keyboard."[1] Then, along came Leo Smit in 1977, playing all of Copland's solo piano works. Few composers have had the experience of hearing their entire output of piano music played by a talented and knowledgeable performer at a single concert. Pleased as he was, Copland expressed surprise that anyone could play all his piano music at one sitting. He exclaimed afterward, "I thought I'd written more than that!" Smit took his Copland show on the road, and more important, recorded it. *Aaron Copland: Complete Solo Piano Works*, released by CBS Masterworks before Copland's eightieth birthday, is a landmark in the composer's career, demonstrating a fifty-year span in which Copland made use of a wide range of compositional styles. The album makes Copland's entire piano output accessible and points to its dominant role in Copland's work as a whole.

Copland grew up with the piano; he never wanted to play another instrument. Just as other middle-class Jewish immigrant families at the turn of the century, the Harris Coplands viewed their piano as a symbol of culture. Copland was encouraged to play, and when he showed talent, the family was impressed that their youngest might aspire to the heights of professional concert pianist; not that anyone believed he might appear at Carnegie Hall, but a modest performing career or a teaching profession was within the realm of possibility. Even after he knew he wanted to be a composer, Copland continued to study piano. He was practical enough to realize he might need to make some money by playing piano. Also, he would need the piano for score reading, to demonstrate his works to potential performers and conductors, and to play the premieres of his own difficult solos. Copland had no illusions about his pianistic abilities and admits that one reason he gave up composing jazz-oriented works was because he was never able to improvise himself. However, from reports of those who heard him, and from recordings, Copland was more than a passably good pianist. Listening to a recording of the *Piano Variations* many years after it was made, Copland surprised even himself: "I can't believe I ever played it so fast!"

[1] Quoted from Virgil Thomson, "Copland as Great Man," *New York Herald Tribune*, 24 November 1946, 6.

Copland's earliest attempts at composition were simple piano pieces, followed by songs and a few cello pieces with piano accompaniment. In some of the juvenile writings, glimmerings of the mature Copland can be detected, particularly as regards syncopated rhythms and percussive sonorities. He drew from ragtime and "salon" pieces that he heard when the family gathered around the piano in the evening for entertainment, and he never lost track of that tradition, composing short piano pieces throughout his career, which were meant to be played without great difficulty by nonprofessionals for entertainment or for study.

At nineteen and twenty, Copland took lessons from the renowned Rubin Goldmark. His studies culminated with a *Piano Sonata* (Goldmark would not allow the young Copland to leave for France until he had mastered sonata form).[2] When Copland began to compose instrumental works under Nadia Boulanger's tutelage, he included piano parts and continued to include them later on, sometimes giving the piano an unusual or unexpected solo passage.[3] Most of Copland's chamber music includes piano; furthermore, the keyboard is an equal partner rather than mere accompaniment. In fact, the *Violin Sonata*'s full title is *Sonata for Violin and Piano*; and the *Flute Duo* is *Duo for Flute and Piano*.

Copland's use of the piano was so integral to his composing that it permeated his compositional style, not only in the frequent use of the instrument itself but in more subtle and complex ways. Copland's habit of composing at the piano always slightly embarrassed him, until he learned that Stravinsky worked the same way. Copland said, "I can't imagine just sitting at a table and composing." He feels that the layman does not understand what it means when a composer talks about composing at the piano. He explained:

> They tend to think that you touch a chord, then ask yourself, "Do I like this? No." Then you touch another, and perhaps you do like it, and so on. It doesn't work that way. The composer knows in advance what he wants before he tries it out on the piano. It's difficult to explain, but it's certainly not pure chance.

Copland's method of composing was to write down fragments of musical ideas as they came to him. When he needed a piece, he would turn to these ideas (his "gold nuggets"),

[2] The ink score of the early *Piano Sonata* is in Copland's juvenilia file at The Library of Congress.

[3] One example of Copland's unusual use of piano in an orchestral score is in *Connotations* (1962), in which big percusssive chords, normally orchestrated for timpani or percussion instruments, are left to the piano.

On the occasion of the release of *Aaron Copland, Complete Solo Piano Works* by Leo Smit, Columbia Records, 1979. (*Left to right*): producer Thomas Frost, Copland, and Smit

and if he found something appropriate that he thought might develop further, he would write a piano sketch in pencil. For an orchestral piece, he might use three staves, or write it down first for two pianos (for example, *Music for the Theatre,* the ballet *Hear Ye! Hear Ye!,* and *Inscape*). Copland would not think about specific instrumentation until a piece was fully formed and put down on paper. As John Kirkpatrick has pointed out, "It is not difficult to make piano reductions or two-piano arrangements of Aaron's orchestral works, because they can be derived almost directly from his own piano sketches."[4] (Examples of such solo piano arrangements are *Our Town* and "Saturday Night Waltz" from *Rodeo.*) Kirkpatrick made several two-piano arrangements of Copland works—the *Piano Concerto, Billy the Kid* (prior to Bernstein's), and the *Ode.* Kirkpatrick and Copland performed these transcriptions together in the thirties. Several remain unpublished.

Unlike many composers who wrote less well for other instruments than their own, Copland mastered each genre so that it seemed a natural and brilliant vehicle for him. He intuitively adapted his basic pianistic gestures to the particular purpose of each piece. William Schuman has said, "Copland may have composed but one song cycle, one choral work, one piano variations, and so on, but his one is the highest accomplishment of its kind."

[4] John Kirkpatrick to Perlis, 3 September 1986, New Haven, Connecticut.

Copland's three major piano pieces are not among his most popular works, yet they are perhaps his most characteristic: the lean, craggy, and demanding *Piano Variations* (1930), among the composer's most influential works; the lyrical *Piano Sonata* (1942), in a more faithful classical sonata form, yet individualistic and with one of Copland's most beautiful endings; the more atonal *Piano Fantasy*, Copland's last large-scale keyboard piece, disciplined yet wide-ranging, subsuming most of the moods, techniques, and characteristic sounds and rhythms of all his other piano music.[5] Harold Clurman said in an interview:

> These are mysterious works—the way, in a sense, Aaron is mysterious. They reveal some things about him that he never would talk about. Deeply buried things. He said nothing in words that in any way reflects what is in the *Sonata* or the *Fantasy*. But maybe if Aaron could talk these things, he couldn't compose them![6]

When questioned about why he did not write another large piano work after the *Piano Fantasy*, Copland pointed out that the *Fantasy* had taken years of hard work. He frequently remarked, "I have an aversion to repeating myself." Perhaps Copland meant that he had said what was important for him to say (pianistically) in the three big piano works. What was left he would use for short piano pieces during the remainder of his composing career.

In Copland's studio, Ossining, c. 1958

[5] See Douglas Young, "The Piano Music," *Tempo* no. 95 (Winter 1970-1971), 15-22.

[6] See interview with Harold Clurman.

A lifelong aim had been to provide challenging contemporary music for young performers. Copland had done so, starting with *The Young Pioneers* and Sunday Afternoon Music of 1936. Eleven of Copland's short keyboard pieces have been edited by Leo Smit and published together in a Piano Album for "young adventurous pianists" (1981). (One piece, *Petit Portrait*, composed when Copland was twenty-one, appears for the first time in the album.)[7] Copland had planned a three-volume series to be called *Piano Miscellany* (Book I for children; Book II for teenagers; Book III for adults), but the idea never came to fruition. One piece, composed in 1947 and discovered later in Copland's files, was probably meant for that series. It was edited for publication by composer Phillip Ramey in 1977. The title, *Midsummer Nocturne*, was agreed on by Copland and Ramey, to whom the piece is dedicated.[8]

Down a Country Lane (1962) is in the category of "music for young performers," although it is more of a challenge than it may at first seem. Commissioned by *Life* magazine, it was featured in the 19 June 1962 issue with photographs and a homespun type of article headed "Our Bumper Crop of Beginning Piano Players." The article explains, "*Down a Country Lane* fills a musical gap: It is among the few modern pieces specially written for young piano students by a major composer." Copland is quoted: "Even third-year students will have to practice before trying it in public." *Down a Country Lane* begins with instructions to the young performer to play "gently flowing in a pastoral mood;" a brief midsection is slightly dissonant and to be played "a trifle faster;" and the ending returns to the earlier lyric mood. It was orchestrated for inclusion in a Youth Orchestra Series and premiered by the London Junior Orchestra at Royal Festival Hall (20 November 1964).

After the story and music appeared in *Life* magazine, Copland's privacy in Peekskill was temporarily shattered. People searched him out—even for piano lessons! A Texas oil millionaire learned of Copland's whereabouts and sent a telegram: COME DOWN HERE NEXT FRIDAY MORNING AT 9 O'CLOCK TO GIVE MY EIGHT-YEAR-OLD SON A PIANO LESSON. PRICE NO OBJECT.

When the Scribner Music Library commissioned a piece from Copland in 1966, he searched through his files and found a good tune left over from the 1945 documentary film *The Cummington Story*. Copland arranged it for piano and gave it the title *In Evening Air*, after a poem by Theodore Roethke. The theme is pastoral and singable, but the style is undeniably contemporary, with unannounced shifts to new keys, syncopation, and parallel motion of open fifths. Copland so admired the Roethke poem that he chose a few lines to be printed in the score: "I see, in evening air, how slowly dark comes down on what we do."[9]

[7] Copland's *Piano Album* includes *Petit Portrait, Down a Country Lane, Midsummer Nocturne, In Evening Air, Piano Blues No.1 and No.4, Saturday Night Waltz, Sentimental Melody, The Resting-Place on the Hill, The Young Pioneers,* and *Sunday Afternoon Music.*

[8] See Copland's files for ink score copied by David Walker, second copies of original score (with the addition later of the title *Midsummer Nocturne*, and corrected proofs.

[9] *In Evening Air* and *Night Thoughts* were recorded by Meriel and Peter Dickinson in *An American Anthology* (Unicorn).

Another short piano piece, *Night Thoughts*, was composed for the Van Cliburn Competition (1972). It was to be played by each contestant in the 1973 Quadrennial Competition of Fort Worth, Texas. While not a virtuosic work, *Night Thoughts* presented certain difficulties for the three hundred entrants in the competition who were required to sight-read it: unusual chords, wide spacings, and some complicated pedaling.[10] Copland said, "My intention was to test the musicality and the ability of a performer to give coherence to a free musical form." The subtitle, *Homage to Ives*, was added after the music was composed. According to Copland, " This has not prevented performers and critics from finding Ivesian allusions in the music." (A horncall question at the beginning of the piece has been pointed to as reminiscent of *The Unanswered Question.*)

For a few years in the early eighties, a manuscript page in pencil sat on Copland's piano stand. It was dated 1973 and bore the title "Improvisation." When Copland played it, as he did occasionally on request, it seemed to be music that was meant as the opening of an important piano piece. Questioned about taking it further, Copland would laughingly reply, "If only I could!" Composer Phillip Ramey asked Copland whether he could try to make a short piece from "Improvisation," and Copland agreed. It became *Proclamation for Piano.* Bennett Lerner edited a second short piece, based on a sketch from 1944 that was in Copland's files. It was given the title *Midday Thoughts* and was dedicated to Lerner when it was published (1982). Both short pieces were premiered by Lerner in New York (2 February 1983) and recorded in his album *American Piano Music.*

Copland cared little for luxurious living conditions, but he could never tolerate the lack of a piano. In describing various living arrangements, it has always been the room with the piano that was most important—from the family home above the department store in Brooklyn, to a hacienda in the Mexican hills, to the studio in his Peekskill residence. The piano is a prized possession, as it was to Copland's parents. He takes great care with the instrument, watching when it has to be moved and pulling the draperies when the sun shines on the case. Copland's first pianos were Steinways. After moving into his Ossining house, however, Copland took advantage of a good offer from Baldwin: they loaned him pianos, which were replaced periodically, with the agreement that the replaced piano could be sold as "a Copland piano."

For many years, Copland as pianist was a familiar sight to audiences of contemporary music. By the end of the fifties, he was not playing very much in public. However, he accepted with pleasure when Stravinsky asked him to play in a performance of *Les Noces,* 20 December 1959 in New York City. Stravinsky wrote (1 September 1959), "I have never conducted *Les Noces* before, and it has always been my wish that it be performed by four of my esteemed colleagues." (The other three were Samuel Barber, Lukas Foss, and Roger Sessions.) Copland described the event to Victor Kraft: "Strav looked frail, came out on stage slowly with a suggestion of difficulty. The audience stood and greeted him with thunderous applause, and at the end, he was hailed as conquering hero."

DOWN A COUNTRY LANE

by Aaron Copland

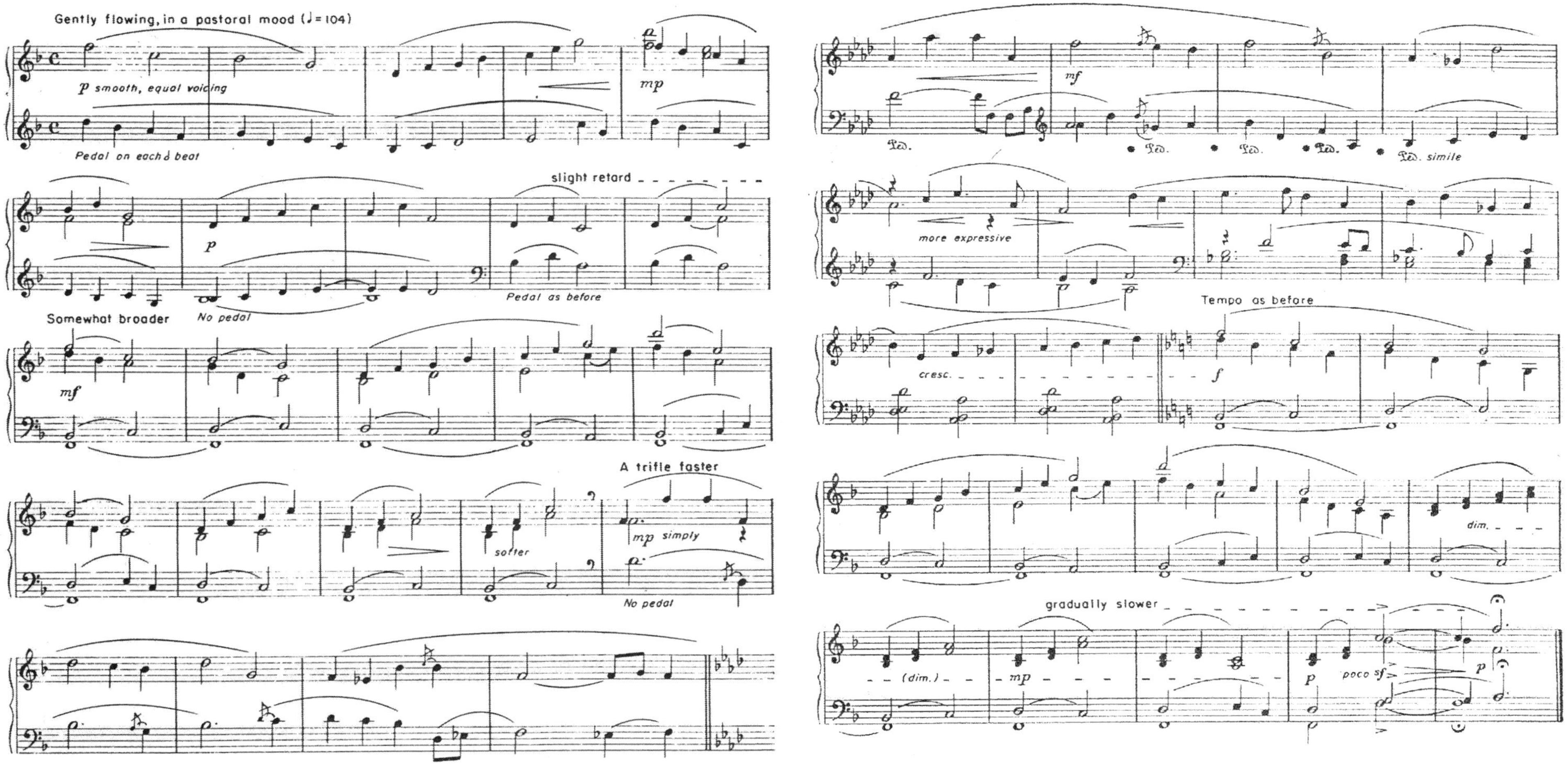

The Premiere of a Noted Composer's Piece for Youngsters

The charming piano piece that makes its debut above is a rarity. It was written especially for LIFE by the dean of American composers, Aaron Copland, a Pulitzer prize winner for music. *Down a Country Lane* helps fill a musical gap: it is among the few modern pieces specially written for young piano students by a major composer. "Yet," warns Copland, "this composition is a bigger challenge than it first looks, and even third-year students will have to practice before trying it in public." It opens in an easygoing pastoral mood, but the middle section is slightly dissonant and takes dextrous fingerwork. "The music," Copland explains, "is descriptive only in an imaginative, not a literal sense. I didn't think up the title until the piece was finished—*Down a Country Lane* just happened to fit its flowing quality."

This is one of the few pieces of its kind that Copland has written in all his 61 years and it is likely, considering the number of young pianists, to be his most widely played composition. His other works of course have become standards in the repertoire of orchestras all over the world—the lyrical *Appalachian Spring*, elegiac *Lincoln Portrait*, dissonant *Piano Fantasy*. Though Copland's style is highly varied, it is always stamped with directness and rhythmic ingenuity—even in so innocent a work as *Down a Country Lane*.

[10] See Copland's files in the Library of Congress for rough sketches, pencil version, ink score, and copies.

(*Above*) At Tanglewood, c. 1965
(*Below*) Copland between his desk and piano, Peekskill, c. 1977

When television made Copland a recognized figure, it was not as pianist but as conductor. His looks and gestures became part of the American consciousness: the lean figure with the wide grin, the long arms akimbo, the informal stance on the podium, a kind of running jump on and offstage at the end of a piece. Only Copland's close friends, who saw him frequently at home, connected him with the piano. The instrument, piled high with music, dominated the studio. Copland's desk was placed so that he could turn directly from it to the piano, which he played regularly until his eighty-fifth year. After that, Copland played only on occasion (when David Diamond visited on Copland's eighty-eighth birthday, the two played piano four-hands ad lib). But even away from the keyboard, when Copland spoke of music, his long fingers moved in pianistic flourishes, left hand over right, or staccato on a tabletop—an imaginary piano at his fingertips.

Copland, c. 1960

RUSSIA AND THE FAR EAST

1957 - 1960

As a young man, one of the writers who had impressed me was Gide. I remember him writing that each person should follow his own natural instincts. For me, it seemed natural and comfortable to do several different things: composing is a solitary pursuit for which I needed uninterrupted periods of time at home or at the MacDowell Colony; conducting took me out to all kinds of places and usually carried with it lecturing and teaching duties; working with organizations, festivals, and competitions that promoted the performance of contemporary music was also very satisfying. Looking through my notebooks and travel diaries, I am amazed to see the number and variety of places I visited during these years—European tours, Mexico, and American cities and college towns, where I conducted, lectured, and taught composition.

1957 began in Caracas, Venezuela, for the Second Latin American Contemporary Festival. I had promised to return after the First Festival in 1954. The Institution José Angel Lamas again planned to hand out twenty thousand dollars in prizes for the best works in a competition for Latin American orchestral pieces. Forty-four works were presented during the nine-day festival (18-27 March). The jurors included Chávez (Mexico), Ginastera (Argentina), Juan Batista Plaza (Venezuela), Domingo Santa Cruz (Chile), and myself. We were required to arrive three weeks in advance to choose the prizewinners, whose pieces would be performed on the concluding program. We decided on four prizes: Blas Galindo (Mexico) and Camargo Guarnieri (Brazil) divided the Lamas Prize of ten thousand dollars; and the two other prizes went to Roque Cordero (Panama) and Enrique Iturriagi (Peru).

No expense was spared in arranging and promoting the festival and life was still luxurious in Caracas. We were put up at the posh Hotel Tamanaco. I wrote to Irving Fine:

> If your ego ever gets low, come to Venezuela. They print your picture in the papers every other day, plug your music on the radio, interview you till you're blue in the face. Finally, even the American Embassy took note, and is arranging a party for the festival personalities. We are all having a fine time reminiscing about Tanglewood days.

Eight programs were devoted to Latin-American music and one to U.S. composers Gail Kubik, Samuel Barber, Roy Harris, Charles Ives, Virgil Thomson, and me. I conducted *Lincoln Portrait*.[1] The quality of the orchestra had deteriorated somewhat since 1954, but the enthusiasm and conviction of the musicians for my piece stirred the audience, so that when the concert was over, they stood and cheered for some time and were reluctant to leave the stone seats in the outdoor amphitheater.

One day during the festival, Ginastera got all fifteen visiting composers together in a large room at the hotel to help Chávez finish a score for an upcoming premiere in New York. We took places at long tables and proceeded to copy 430 pages! *The New York Times* critic Howard Taubman wrote that it was ". . . a practical demonstration of inter-American friendship in action . . . a perfect example of harmony."[2]

Lawrence Morton invited me to participate in the May 1957 Ojai Festival in California, which was to revolve around my music. Lawrence suggested that I conduct works by other composers in addition to my own pieces. So I did: Purcell, Diamond, Britten, Grieg, Haydn, Fauré, and Stravinsky. I wrote to Lawrence afterward, "You really started something!" When invited to return to conduct varied programs again in 1958, I accepted. Ojai was the first.place I was treated like a "real" conductor.[3]

From California, I went directly to the Brandeis Festival (3-10 June 1957), where I was on the jury for the annual Brandeis Creative Arts Awards. We had met during the winter to plan the programs and choose the winners. The festival, which included an all-Copland program,[4] coincided with the Brandeis University commencement. I received a letter from the president of Brandeis informing me that in this one hundredth anniversary year of the birth of Justice Louis Brandeis, the university wished to confer on me a Doctor of Humane Letters degree. The fact that Irving Fine had initiated the idea, and that he, Verna, and other of my Boston friends were in the audience when the honorary degree was bestowed, added to my pleasure in the occasion.

[1] For more on the 1957 performance of *Lincoln Portrait* in Venezuela, see 145.

[2] Howard Taubman, "Composers of 9 Lands Aid Colleague," *The New York Times*, 26 March 1957, 35, and Taubman, "Lavish Festival," *The New York Times*, 24 March 1957, Section II, 7.

[3] Copland conducted Purcell, *Three Fantasias*; Diamond, *Rounds*; Britten, *Serenade*; Grieg, *Holberg Suite*; Haydn, *Symphony No. 95*; Fauré, *Pelléas et Mélisande Suite*; Stravinsky, *Suite No. 2*; Copland, *Clarinet Concerto* and *The Tender Land* (the dance, Act II and the finale, Act I).

[4] The Brandeis Festival program included Copland's *Music for the Theatre, Appalachian Spring* (complete ballet), and *The Tender Land* (the dance, Act II and the finale, Act I).

Carlos Chávez and Copland in Caracas, 1957

During the fall-winter semester of 1957-1958, as Slee Professor of Music at the State University of New York at Buffalo, I made nine visits of two or three days each to Buffalo to teach composition to about ten students. At the end of the semester, I conducted the Buffalo Symphony with Leo Smit as soloist (5 January 1958). In the next few years, I was asked to recommend composers for the visiting Slee Professorship: Chávez followed me, and then Ned Rorem. After my tenure at Buffalo, Slee professors were required to live in Buffalo. Ned wrote, "I've never even dreamed before of having so much money [ten thousand dollars]—but somehow I'd rather skimp along just as a composer being happy and poor in New York than as a professor sad and rich for eight and a half months in Buffalo." Ned asked my advice, I gave it, and off he went to Buffalo. As for myself, I found that I could work while traveling by train. By the end of 1957, I had completed my *Orchestral Variations* (an arrangement of the *Piano Variations* of 1930) and composed music for a television program.

John Houseman and Robert Herridge, producers of the CBS series *Seven Lively Arts*, asked me to compose incidental music for a drama based on five Ernest Hemingway stories that were adapted for television by A. E. Hotchner. The young actor Eli Wallach was to appear in the leading role. I had admired Hemingway since the twenties, when I would see him from a distance in a bookshop or cafe, and I found the idea of composing for the new and exciting medium of television intriguing. I agreed to a contract of fifteen hundred dollars to compose the music for "The World of Nick Adams."

Composing for a television drama was similar in procedure to preparing a film score. I was sent a script with cues to indicate where and for how long music was required: The first music was to follow directly after a voice announcing, "We call it 'The World of Nick Adams'!" I composed a kind of fanfare for the opener and music for such cues as "When a man comes face-to-face with death," and "It's fun all right."[5] I attended the live broadcast at which Alfredo Antonini conducted my music (10 November 1957). Hotchner told me that Hemingway was abroad and could not see the broadcast, but that he was taking a kinescope of the show for Hemingway to view later. I never did hear what Hemingway thought of it.

It was a commission from the Louisville Symphony Orchestra that stimulated me to put into action an idea I had been thinking about— transcribing my *Piano Variations* for orchestra.[6] I found it a challenge to re-create the piano material with orchestral color in mind. Robert Whitney led the Louisville Symphony in the premiere (5 March 1958), and I was astonished to hear catcalls at the end of the piece! At least the perpetrators waited until the work was over. There is something about a boo you can't forget—I seem to remember more vividly the few times my music was booed than the many times it was applauded! About a month after the premiere of the *Orchestral Variations*, I returned to Kentucky for a festival at the University of Louisville School of Music, where the piece was performed again, this time *sans* catcalls. In 1958 at Tanglewood, Charles Munch conducted the *Orchestral Variations* with the BSO, but it was in William Steinberg, conductor of the Pittsburgh Symphony, that the piece found a real champion. Steinberg conducted it in Pittsburgh in 1959 and on tour during the 1959-1960 season.

Working on a freelance basis, I never knew in advance what my total yearly income would be. I listed payments in a notebook as they came along and then added them at the end of each year for tax purposes.[7] When I totaled the amounts for 1957, I realized with surprise that my income had jumped rather suddenly, and it continued to climb in 1958. The change was not, as one might suspect, due to conducting fees or the CBS TV show, but from royalties and performance fees. It amazed me when I looked at the figures—after all, I was paid to compose the music in the first place!

[5] The autograph full score for "The World of Nick Adams" is in the Music Division, the New York Public Library at Lincoln Center; photocopy in Copland's files. Also in Copland's files are a conducting score and pencil sketches of a piano version dated "10 Nov 1957."
[6] For a full description of the *Orchestral Variations,* see p. 80.
[7] Copland's listings of monthly and yearly income are in his diaries. In 1957 his income was $53,799; in 1958, $63,000.

Nineteen fifty-eight got off to an exciting start—my conducting debut with the New York Philharmonic (30, 31 January) and my television debut (1 February). I conducted the *Outdoor Overture* and part of the finale of the *Third Symphony* for the televising, sharing the program with Lenny Bernstein. At Claire Reis' party after the first Philharmonic concert, she commented that I was becoming addicted to conducting. I had to admit that it was pretty heady stuff. Part of me would say, "Stay home and compose," and I would do so. But after a short time, particularly when fresh composing ideas were hard to come by, I would get bored and want to take off again. I heard from people all over the country who saw the television broadcast—even my dentist, who said my new tooth looked fine—and David Diamond, who had heard about the broadcast while living in Florence, Italy. David wrote:

> I hear that you had great success conducting the *Third.* Bravo! But what is this fantastic nonchalance of yours in relation to your own music and performances?. . . . When you clam up . . . especially about your musical activities, your biographers are sure going to have a hard time.

The worst part of the composer's life is the fact that he does not feel himself an integral part of the musical community. I had always enjoyed being with people: Young performers stimulated me; travel was interesting; and conducting puts one in a very powerful position. Best of all, it is a use of power for a good purpose. When Arthur Judson suggested an extensive midwest conducting tour for me during the first few months of 1958, followed by a European tour from August to the end of the year, I agreed. I had no plans to give up composing; in fact, when I left for Europe, I took materials with me for a ballet Jerry Robbins and I had been talking about.

I traveled to Europe by ship.[8] As long as the weather cooperated, I could rest, study scores, and read—a biography of George Sand occupied my attention. After a few days in a London hotel, I took a flat in Mayfair and enjoyed seeing old friends (Ben Britten and Peter Pears) and making new ones. This year of 1958 marked the beginning of a long and satisfying

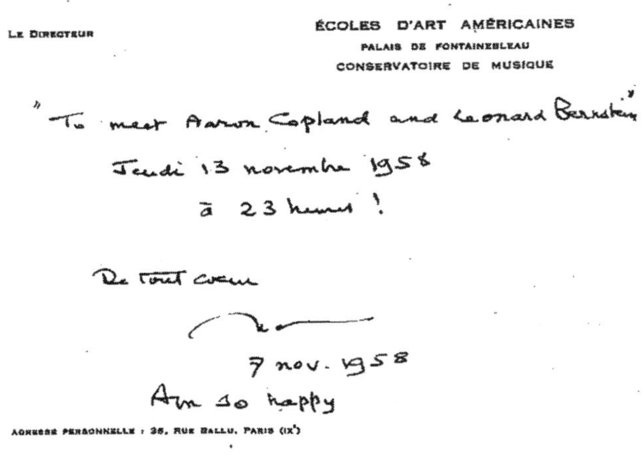
LE DIRECTEUR
ÉCOLES D'ART AMÉRICAINES
PALAIS DE FONTAINEBLEAU
CONSERVATOIRE DE MUSIQUE
"To meet Aaron Copland and Leonard Bernstein"
Jeudi 13 novembre 1958
à 23 heures!
De tout coeur
7 nov. 1958
Am so happy
ADRESSE PERSONNELLE : 36, RUE BALLU, PARIS (IX°)

Invitation to a reception for Copland and Bernstein from Nadia Boulanger, Paris 13 November 1958 with a personal note to Copland

[8] For Copland's memoir of this trip, see travel diary # 6.

relationship with the London Symphony Orchestra. I was the only American composer represented at the Promenade Concerts at the Albert Hall in the summer of 1958. I wrote to Leo Smit from London (3 October 1958):

> My visit started off with a bang in August conducting the *Orchestral Variations* and *Rodeo* at the Proms. London musical life is beyond belief conventional. I wrote an attack in the *Sunday Times* and caused a commotion.[9] Then I taught for ten days at Dartington and heard the Berlin Octet murder my *Sextet* there. I've made two forays to the Continent: one to conduct in Copenhagen, and one to conduct in Stuttgart. Stopped off in Brussels on the way back to do a lecture for USIS. Next week to Paris to lecture, hear *Threni* [Stravinsky], see Lenny, Nadia B., Peggy Bernier, etc. As you can imagine, I don't get much composing done in the midst of all this.

David Walker, who had his own place in New York, went up to Ossining periodically to check my mail and take care of routine correspondence and requests. He forwarded important things to me. The house was looked after by Victor Kraft when he was around, or Jack Kennedy, who went up to Ossining once in a while. I was at Shady Lane Farm only the month of December in all of 1958. I really had to scramble to meet some deadlines: radio talks for WQXR in New York; a lecture, "The Pleasures of Music,"[10] for the Distinguished Lecture Series at the University of New Hampshire for April 1959; a foreword to a book, *Portrait of a Symphony*; and the orchestrations for two of my *Dickinson Songs*. The Ossining house and grounds were attractive, but I was not finding the place perfect for my needs, being a converted barn with one big living room and no separate studio. I could not take care of things by myself when I was there, so people were always around, and I did not have the privacy I needed for composing. Chávez, who was in Cambridge as Norton Lecturer at Harvard, offered me his country house in Acapulco. He arranged to have the piano tuned, and wrote, "Acapulco is waiting for you. My sister Chabela is there and she knows how dear a friend you are to me, so everything will be in order." The house was simple but with everything I could possibly need, including cook and housekeeper, and the separate studio had a spectacular view and a very beautiful garden. I arrived in Acapulco (12 February 1959) and got right to work on a piece for orchestra for the Festival of Two Worlds in Spoleto, Italy. I had promised Gian Carlo Menotti a premiere in July.

The music of Latin America had more than a passing interest for me ever since my first visit to Mexico in 1932. Again in 1958, I was stimulated by my surroundings to compose "Paisaje Mexicano" and "Danza de Jalisco," which when put together became my *Two Mexican Pieces.* As it turned out, only the "Danza" was played at Spoleto. Both pieces were performed together for the first time in the United States under my baton at a private invitation concert given by the Pan-American Union in Washington, D.C. (20 April 1965). In 1968, I made a two-piano arrangement of "Danza de Jalisco," which contains a few revisions (for

[9] Copland, "Performers and New Music," *London Sunday Times,* 12 October 1958, reprinted in *Copland on Music* as "Interpreters and New Music," 261-65.
[10] The lecture was adapted as an article: "Copland, "The Pleasures of Music," *The Saturday Evening Post*, 4 July 1959, reprinted in *Adventures of the Mind*, ed. Richard Thruelsen and John Kohler (New York: Alfred A. Knopf, 1959), 190-205; translated German, 1961, reprinted in *Copland on Music*, 23-51.

example, the handclapping was made optional). In 1971, after I composed a piece derived from Venezuelan sources, "Estribillo," I added it to the others and the collective title became *Three Latin-American Sketches*: "Estribillo" is the vigorous first piece; the lyrical "Paisaje Mexicano" comes next; and the bouncy "Danza de Jalisco," with its contrasting rhythms of 6/8 and 3/4, is the third. I would describe the character of the *Three Latin-American Sketches* as the title indicates: the tunes, the rhythms, and the temperament of the pieces are folksy, while the orchestration is bright and snappy and the music sizzles along—or at least it seems to me that it does. The entire work is scored for a moderate-size orchestra. The world premiere was conducted by André Kostelanetz in a "Promenades" concert with the New York Philharmonic (7 June 1972).

I wanted to stay longer in Mexico, but certain commitments could not be ignored, one being the premiere of the *Suite from The Tender Land* with the BSO (10 and 11 April 1958). Also, I wanted to be back in New York to talk with Jerome Robbins about the ballet we were planning. When Chávez returned to Mexico, he wrote (26 May), "This past Sunday I was in Acapulco and thought a lot of you. I wished you back, anytime, as many times as you can. Please remember the polite Spanish phrase is absolutely literal in your case: 'esa es tu casa.' "

Jerome Robbins and I had hoped to work together since 1954 when he directed the premiere of my opera, *The Tender Land*. Under consideration briefly had been a ballet depicting a bullfight, but, as Lincoln Kirstein wrote, "Jerry decided it is too picturesque and pantomimic. Jerry wants to do only dancing with a very simple program to a four-part symphony." Other commitments intervened, and when we got together one evening at the beginning of 1959 to discuss the possibilities, we discovered that we both leaned toward a non-story ballet. Jerry was particularly interested in waltzes, and he followed up by sending a pageful of ideas. The result was that I accepted a commission from him for a full-length ballet score based on a series of theatrical dances.

At first, I called the music *Ballet for J.R.*, as I had called *Appalachian Spring, Ballet for Martha*. Later, the score bore the title *The Dream*, and later still, it became *Dance Panels, Ballet in Seven Verses*. When the piece was finished, I played the music on the piano for Jerry. There was one section that he couldn't see movement to at all. Jerry explained:

> A strange thing happened. I went straight to rehearsal without the music right after Aaron played the score for me. I tried to remember it, but could only recall the counts. When I began working with the company just with counts, I got interested in what they were doing without music. It fascinated me, and I continued working that way. It really moved along. I was sorry I wasn't able to do *Dance Panels*, but in a very real way, Aaron's music was the accidental genesis of my ballet without music, *Moves*."[11]

Dance Panels sat on the shelf until 1962 when I revised it for a ballet by the Bavarian State Opera in Munich for the opening of their new house in November. The spring before the opening, on a trip to London, Berlin, Munich, and Rome, I met with representatives of

[11] From interview, Jerome Robbins with Perlis. Approved by Robbins for publication in "Critics Mailbag," a response by Perlis to Jack Anderson, *The New York Times*, 19 November 1987, C 29.

Copland playing *Dance Panels* for Jerome Robbins, New York City, 1959

the Opera in Munich and attended an orchestra rehearsal (19 April 1962). It was curious to hear music I had written so long ago (1959) finally being performed. I was invited to return to conduct the premiere. There was much discussion about who would choreograph the work. Heinz Rosen, music director of the Opera House, thought the best solution would still be Robbins. I thought so, too, and tried again, but Jerry could not be interested. Rosen suggested Eugene Loring or Arthur Mitchell, but Mitchell's price was too high, so Rosen decided to do the choreography himself and to engage guest dancers. I was apprehensive, and my worst fears were confirmed when I saw a run-through. I wrote in my diary, "Has good, balletic things in it, but completely without relation to the quality of my music. More or less what I suspected would happen. A ballet seems to be going on, but you could never guess what the music was like from what you see onstage— Damn!" It was essentially a boy-and-girl idea: The Boy was danced by Arthur Mitchell of the New York City Ballet; the Girl was Liane Daydé of the Paris Opera. I hoped that when Mitchell arrived, he might change the atmosphere somehow, but to top the situation off, he turned his ankle and could not dance for a few days, and at the premiere he had to omit his first solo.

The rebuilt Bavarian State Opera House, a replica of the old one, opened 21 November 1963, and the premiere of the ballet took place there on 3 December. Mitchell and Daydé, most appealing dancers, were received well. The designer had devised a set of colored screens with changing patterns that was effective when combined with the unusual lighting.

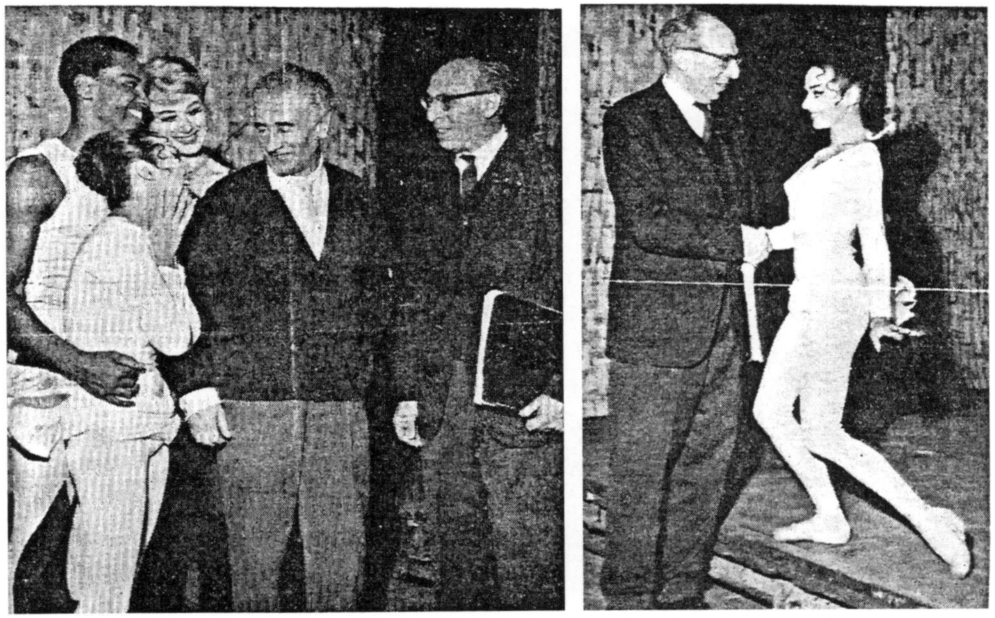

(*Left*): Copland in Munich for the production of the ballet *Dance Panels*, with choreographer Heinz Rosen (center) and dancers (left to right): Liane Daydé, Arthur Mitchell, and Margot Werner. (*Right*): Liane Daydé congratulating Copland after the first performance, 3 December 1964

When it was all over, I wrote in my diary, "Somebody, someday will make a good ballet out of the piece—it's so very danceable, but I'm afraid it's a lost cause here. Still—it's rather fun to be involved in the putting on of a new stage piece—any stage piece." It was rumored that Balanchine was planning to choreograph the music, and I hoped so, since the German affair left much to be desired.

Dance Panels was my sixth ballet score. I seemed to have an affinity for the art of dance, and dancers themselves must have a certain feeling for my music, since each of my ballets, except the first, *Grohg*, was composed at the request of a choreographer. Also, some of my concert music has been considered danceable. *Dance Panels* is a different sort of ballet music from my earlier dance scores. It is more abstract, and it is lyrical and slower in tempo than most of my other ballet music. It does not tell a story as does *Billy the Kid*, or paint a picture of American life as in *Appalachian Spring*. It makes no use of American folk melodies; however, in two of the movements, there is a relationship to familiar genres of our popular music—the quiet sentimental song and a type of stage music used for "tap dancing."[12]

[12] See Copland's files at The Library of Congress for score, pencil sketches with indications for orchestration, photocopy of first version, photocopy of uncorrected copy (38 pages), and pencil revisions dated "Oct '62 new plan."

Dance Panels is in seven contrasting sections: the introduction, with long sustained notes, is in slow waltz tempo; a second section continues the waltz rhythm; the third is a light transparent scherzando; the fourth is a melancholy and nostalgic *pas de trois* featuring solo flute; the fifth is characterized by brisk rhythms and jazzy drum patterns; the sixth is a lyrical episode with a finale in jagged irregular rhythms; and the seventh section ends the piece as quietly as it began. Within these confines, the separate sections are varied in character and easily identifiable, although they are to be played without pause. The score begins and ends with related material. The music is composed in a simple and direct style. The lyrical parts are very diatonic, "white-notey," one might say, while the lively and bouncy portions have more complexity of texture.[13]

Dance Panels as a ballet finally had a production in the United States under the title *Shadow'd Ground*.[14] It was performed by the New York City Ballet at the State Theater at Lincoln Center (21 January 1965). John Taras was choreographer, Robert Irving conductor. The story is about two lovers reading epitaphs in a graveyard. The ballet did not fare well with audience or critics. Walter Terry wrote in the Herald Tribune (22 January 1965):

> Whether one wished to or not, he could not help thinking, while stirred by the Copland music, that perhaps this genre of ballet were better left to an Agnes de Mille or to a Eugene Loring or, perhaps, to a Martha Graham. Taras, who has created some attractive ballets in the past, was just not at home with this type of Americana.

The concert version of *Dance Panels*, which is essentially the same as the ballet score, was played first by the Ojai Festival Orchestra, Ingolf Dahl conducting (24 May 1966). With the pauses in the first dance shortened, *Dance Panels* is approximately twenty-three minutes in duration. It calls for a moderate-size orchestra of six woodwinds, five brass, two percussion (but no timpani), and strings. At first, I had some concern about whether the piece would work on the concert stage, and since I was not able to attend the festival, I was anxious for Ingolf's report (26 May 1966):

> Thanks for your telegram—it was just the thing to cheer me up at the crucial time! I think the performance went very well indeed. You will be happy to hear that the whole orchestra just loved the music from the first rehearsal. As for me, I am crazy about the work. Every detail, every harmonic subtlety, every finesse of melodic phrasing, not to speak of the fabulous orchestral color, seems to me to be inspired and in every way successful. I am tempted to enumerate all the special places that excited me, but that would make this interminable. Not the least admirable about *Dance Panels* is the act of courage on your part, to be so completely "you." Several of my young composer friends shared my admiration for this courage—a ray of light in the present gloom.

[13] Copland's description here is drawn from his liner notes for the Columbia Records recording, LSO, Copland conducting.

[14] The ballet's full title was *Dance Panels: Ballet in Seven Verses*; libretto and Epitaphs by Scott Burton, direction by Robert Mulligan; designed by John Braden. The ballet was first announced under the title "Greenwood." In Copland's files is a page indicating "New Plan for Ballet/TV version-18 min;" the television version was not realized.

When I conducted *Dance Panels* for Columbia Records, I made slight revisions,[15] and in 1965 I approved an arrangement for solo piano made in-house at Boosey & Hawkes. (The first New York concert performance of the orchestral version did not take place until my seventh-fifth birthday celebration at Alice Tully Hall: I conducted *Dance Panels*, and Dennis Russell Davies conducted *Statements for Orchestra* and the *Third Symphony*.)

Tanglewood became an exciting place again for composers, because of Paul Fromm and his Foundation. Beginning in 1957, the Fromm Players (ten instrumentalists and one singer) were in residence and responsible for playing and demonstrating new music in the weekly Composers Forums, the Aspects of Music lecture series, and the Seminar in Contemporary Music envisioned by Fromm in 1956.[16] Ralph Berkowitz, Tod Perry, Gail Rector, and I met during the winter months to choose the Fromm Fellows. Our job was to find top players with an interest in contemporary music who would become a homogeneous ensemble. They had to be able to read almost anything at sight. We were lucky on all counts. The players included a woodwind quintet plus a string quartet, a pianist, and a soprano: all were outstanding performers. I wrote to Leo Smit (25 July 1957), "Tanglewood is hectic as usual, but we have been having lots of fun with our Fromm Players—at our beck and call—playing oodles of modern music from Varèse and Webern to V.T. [Thomson] and S. Revueltas."

The Fromm Seminar in Contemporary Music was held on Friday afternoons. I was responsible for presenting a general outline and background material in the first lecture, and for delivering one lecture during the series. In 1957, I spoke on "Nationalist Trends—American Phase," and the Fromm Players demonstrated by playing my *Sextet*; in 1958, it was "New Music from Latin America"; and in 1959, "Recent European Piano Music," musical examples by pianist Paul Jacobs (Paul joined the Fromm Players that summer). The atmosphere for composers had never been more stimulating. Having Paul Fromm as our patron was like having our own Prince Esterhazy! The Fromm Players gave composers the rare opportunity to have performers right on hand to test out their works. Student composers could hear their pieces played by instruments separately or in combination. They could hear what happens, for example, if a tune is doubled by five instruments rather than four, or hear a five-note chord for woodwind quintet in twenty different ways before deciding the final way. Students don't often get a chance to hear their works before the ink is dry!

Paul Fromm took pleasure from the fact that the composer was again the central figure, a rare occurrence in the twentieth century. As I told a newspaper critic, "Paul Fromm is the ideal patron. He doesn't mix in or give orders, and when he gets enthusiastic about something, he gives money to support his enthusiasm. The Fellowship Players, for instance. It is a vast luxury. Ask anybody. Ask me."

[15] For the recording, measures 8-14 were cut and slight changes made in the percussion ending of the fifth section.
[16] See Arthur Berger, "What Mozart Didn't Have/ The Story of the Fromm Music Foundation," *Hi Fidelity*, vol. 9, no. 2 (February 1959), 41-43,126,128. For description and list of commissioned works from 1952-1972, see Paul Fromm, *The Fromm Music Foundation, 20th Anniversary*, published by The Fromm Foundation. (The Foundation also supported the establishment of a new publication, *Perspectives of New Music*; the first issue was Fall 1962.)

When I went to visit the Fromm Foundation in Chicago in 1958, I did not know what to expect, but whatever it was, I did not find it. Paul Fromm was an importer of liquor and the Foundation offices were in the wholesale wine district. To get there, one walked through the storerooms of crates filled with wine and whiskey. Paul Fromm had a strong German accent; he was not always easy to understand, but what he said about contemporary music was always so passionate that he got his ideas across in no uncertain terms. What he expressed on that day I visited the Foundation was: "I want to help raise the level of advanced musical studies. I am determined to get a project well under way." Fromm's contributions to the Music Center grew to support forty fellowships a year after the program was established. Many new works were commissioned, and in 1964, the annual Tanglewood Festival of Contemporary Music was initiated.

Milton Babbitt was the visiting composer at Tanglewood in 1957 and again in 1958. Although his appointment meant giving up Koussevitzky's idea of a European composer, the need for a leading serialist was pressing, and Milton Babbitt was certainly one of them. Munch was eager to return to the composer-from-abroad tradition; nevertheless, Leon Kirchner was invited in 1959. Leon promptly fell in love with the place. He wrote to me, "It is the most 'gemütlich' atmosphere anywhere."

I was finding the Tanglewood students anxious about their futures. Most were feeling the influence of Webern and his present-day followers. They wanted to learn electronic techniques, but it was very difficult for them to find enough studio time, and they worried about having an audience for their music if they did write it. One of the most talented of these students was a young Argentinian, Mario Davidovsky.[17]

Mario Davidovsky[18]

My friend, Efrain Guigui, went to Tanglewood in 1957, and he took with him a clarinet quintet of mine, which Copland heard and liked very much. Suddenly, out of the blue, I had a letter from Aaron Copland. I almost died!

He was a famous man and one of the most important figures as far as promoting Latin American composers. I doubt that any composers came to the States from Latin America without Copland having something to do with it. Copland's letter asked me to come to Tanglewood, but I had tremendous troubles getting financial help in Argentina. Copland practically solved all my troubles. He really helped more than any Argentinian helped me. Meanwhile, I submitted a score to the 1957 competition in Caracas. I didn't get any prize, but I got a letter from Aaron, saying that he liked the piece, although he criticized the melodic material. He said, "I wish that your material could be less derived from European sources."

[17] Copland's students in 1957 were Egil Hovland, Pohlman Mallalieu, Joel Mandelbaum, Malcolm Peyton, José Serebrier, Gordon Sherwood, and Ramon Zupko. In 1958: Bruce Archibald, Asher Ben-Yohanan, Mario Davidovsky, Michael Kassler, Robert Lombardo, Joseph Lukewitzk, Thea Musgrave, and Rolv Berger Yttrehus. In 1959: Grant Beglarian, Wilson Coker, James Anderson, and Karl Korte.
[18] Interview, Mario Davidovsky with William Owen for Perlis, 22 September 1981, New York City.

At Tanglewood, 1958 (*left to right*): David Walker, Mario Davidovsky, and Copland

I made my way to Tanglewood in 1958. Copland was a wonderful teacher. We argued vehemently about procedures and aesthetics. Copland was very critical of my music derived from Europeans, because he very much believed there were tremendous sources in our Latin American traditions to nourish major compositions. My English was double zero, but Aaron spoke fluent Spanish. Tanglewood, being only for the summer, is not the kind of place where very serious work gets done, but Copland's advice was extremely precise, ranging from general formal troubles to the handling of the orchestra. He was quick to know the shape of a piece, even when it was not his cup of tea. He was very open. If he believed in somebody's talent, he would be a staunch supporter, no matter what kind of aesthetic the composer chose to use.

I was young, idealistic, and intense. One day, Marc Blitzstein came and talked to the composers on what it takes to make an opera. I had no idea who he was. Mr. Blitzstein played on the piano and sang excerpts from his own productions. I remember getting absolutely furious. I just could not understand how I, coming from so far away, should have to use my time listening to that kind of light music! I thought it was a travesty, and I stood up and left in the middle. Copland didn't get angry, but he called me up and asked why I was so upset. I explained about my high standards. Copland very patiently talked to me about what Broadway was and the importance of show music. He took the time and trouble to give me examples of local Argentinian tango and Brazilian samba composers to trace a parallel with what Blitzstein was doing. Aaron didn't act as though I was a spoiled brat from Latin America! I remember that with great affection. I complained to him that many of the composers interested in writing nationalist music, Ginastera and others, were very influenced by Bartók, and that Latin American music was almost one hundred percent Hungarian. He thought that was very funny. I said also that his pieces El Salón México *and* Danzón Cubano, *based on Latin American folk tunes, were so successful that they set the standard of how a good Latin American piece should be written. They became the models, and in the process, to my mind, the music did not sound so Latin American anymore. Aaron didn't see it quite that way.*

Aaron and Milton Babbitt, who was also teaching at Tanglewood, helped me to come back to the States to work at the Columbia University electronic laboratory in 1960. After that, I used to send Aaron studies every three or four months, and he would write me notes with criticism. He would say, "Even if I really find myself unable to discriminate many things musically speaking in this kind of music, I like number one better than number two." And he would tell me reasons. They were always very good reasons why piece number one was better than number two. Aaron was very perceptive. He was interested in the electronic field, but he never could understand it. He said, "How can you people manipulate these machines so elegantly!" He came several times to Columbia University to visit me, and I explained to him step by step, because I wanted very much to interest Aaron in writing some electronic music. I thought it would be a tremendous boost for what we were doing. But Copland was already a completely solidified composer. It is difficult at a certain age to open up to such a radical proposition, and Aaron was already going more and more into conducting. Maybe if the development had come sooner, he might have used it. But he was very much curious and alert to all the developments and came to our concerts. He even commissioned me in the 1960s through the Fromm Foundation to use traditional instruments with electronic sounds. It speaks to his openness and generosity toward composers in whom he believed.

I returned to the barn in Richmond each summer, although I rarely stayed on past the Tanglewood season as I had in earlier years (in 1958, I left immediately for Europe). The BSO trustees were looking at what could be trimmed from the Music Center budget. It seemed to be a matter of who could be kept on. Leonard Burkat had just moved up to become chief administrator of the Center. Irving helped plan and execute a complicated curriculum in 1957, reminding me all along that he had not been given a raise since 1948. Lukas returned in 1958 and 1959. The rest of the faculty remained about the same.[19] Boris Goldovsky was still with us, but the opera program was cut back to four weeks, and in 1959, the trustees decided to suspend the opera program completely, although all agreed that Goldovsky had done fine work for Tanglewood. I called a meeting for the entire faculty (6 July 1959), partly because there had not been one for twelve years, but mostly because of dissatisfaction about the abandonment of the opera program. Also, it seemed the

[19] Eleazar de Carvalho and Seymour Lipkin, orchestra; Burgin and Kroll, chamber music; Ross and deVaron, choral music; Ludwig Zirner, followed by Jacob Avshalomov, the Tanglewood Study Group; Roger Voisin, solfège.

Tanglewood Study Group was in shambles. I had received complaints from several of the faculty about the quality of student talent declining at Tanglewood, and I, myself, felt that the caliber of composition student was not quite as high as in the years when a European guest composer was in residence. A planning committee was elected to deal with the issues before the next Tanglewood season.[20] The time had come for a thorough stock-taking and a rethinking of directions.

In 1960, the State Department wanted two American composers to represent the United States in Russia, with the idea of furthering a cultural exchange program that had begun with five Russian composers and a musicologist touring the United States in 1959. (I took part in a symposium in Boston in November debating with Khrennikov, and in an ASCAP reception for Russian composers in New York.) The State Department chose Lukas Foss and myself as representatives. My plan was to stay in London for a few weeks after touring Russia and then meet up with the BSO as guest conductor for their tour of Japan, the Philippines, and Australia. When the State Department heard about this, they suggested a cosponsored arrangement.

I was required to go to Washington for a "briefing" (2 March 1960). I called Oscar Cox to keep him informed of my activities, since for several years after the McCarthy hearing, I was made to feel anxious about my passport. I would be away for three and one-half months, returning just in time for Tanglewood. Before I left, I had a letter from Sam Barber: "Bon voyage and may the spirit of Olga Koussevitzky see you through such an arduous trip." Sam also thanked me for birthday greetings I had sent for his fiftieth birthday:

> Thank you for your kind wire on that melancholy occasion. It was much appreciated. It was very curious: If you have all the youth of the United States at your feet, at least I have a great following among retired secretaries, janitors, et al.

On 15 March, I left for Amsterdam, where I met Lukas. Together we flew to Moscow via Warsaw.

Lukas Foss[21]

Aaron and I spent four solid weeks together in 1960 when we were chosen to be the two composers to represent the United States in Russia. We had known each other for a long time and were good friends even though there's twenty-two years' difference in our ages. We really got to know each other better on that trip. I first met Aaron when I was only seventeen, but I no longer recall who introduced us. Isn't it amazing the little things one remembers, when so many things are forgotten? Most vivid to me is that I carried with me a bag of dirty laundry to my first meeting with the great American composer at the Empire Hotel! I don't know why—I probably couldn't find a laundry that day—but I recall being embarrassed enough about having that laundry with me that I let Aaron assume the case was full of music. On that first occasion, Aaron played me some excerpts from The Second Hurricane.

It was really via Billy the Kid *that I discovered Aaron. He entrusted me with finding all the mistakes in the galleys before it was published, and I found so many that Aaron began to be irritated and bored by my coming in to see him with more and more mistakes the publishers had made. Then Aaron asked me to do a piano arrangement of* Billy. *When I first heard* Appalachian Spring *played on the piano at a party, Aaron asked, "Well, how do you like it?" I said, "I like it, but it's not like* Billy the Kid.*" I was a creature of habit. Once I got to love something, that was the bible for me, and the next piece was bound to be disappointing until I conducted it or got into it.*

At Tanglewood, I felt like a refugee at first. But a refugee learns to call anything his home, wherever he is, so America very quickly became my home. (I was born in Germany and studied music in Paris before coming to the States at age fifteen.) Aaron had something to do with that, and so did Carl Sandburg, because I discovered his poetry and then got to know him and set "The Prairie" to music. For about five years, before the neoclassicism of Stravinsky took over, my music was American. Aaron was slightly disapproving of my studying with Hindemith at Tanglewood. I remember he said, "Isn't that like bringing coals to Newcastle?" But I didn't agree with him until later. I would probably have been better advised to have studied with Aaron, but in a way I did study with him, because once I got to know him and his music, I asked him for advice and criticism. Aaron's stamp was even stronger than Hindemith's for me during those years. I had fallen in love with America because of people like Aaron.

At Tanglewood, Koussevitzky was very important to me. All of us profited from his interest in American music. Koussevitzky tried to help me—he even gave me his suits after having worn them four or five times. He would ask me to try one, saying, "You feel rich now, don't you?" I probably did. Koussevitzky got me the job of pianist with the BSO in 1944 when I was twenty-two, so I would have some money. After Koussevitzky died, Tanglewood was different. It's an important legacy, but not quite the same.

By the way, I remember Koussevitzky was very critical of Aaron's conducting. I think he did him an injustice. I always thought Aaron conducted very well. It was Aaron who kept the group of us composers together, not Koussevitzky. During the late forties and fifties in New York, a group of us would go to the Russian Tea Room, where there was one table at which we all gathered after concerts, always with Aaron presiding. On Aaron's right was Elliott Carter, and there were a few other faithfuls, such as Bill Schuman and myself.

We were different generations, Aaron and I, but always very good friends. With Aaron good friends doesn't mean necessarily chummy, because Aaron has that composer's aloofness, which I love. He has it when he narrates Lincoln Portrait: *never emoting, absolutely quiet and sober, and his music is quiet and sober much of the time. So he was as a person. I never had chummy sessions with Aaron. There was definitely that generation gap, and I think that is what a boy needs. Aaron's music actually became like a father figure to me.*

Aaron could be very critical. For instance, he felt that the neoclassicism in my Piano Concerto *was really fresh, but a little too schoolish, too classical. He didn't like to see me go that way after* The Prairie. *Stravinsky was foremost in our minds—Shapero, Fine, and myself—but Aaron didn't completely endorse that school. Aaron was not altogether wrong, because in a sense that classicism was something we had to overcome eventually.*

[20] See Copland's files for minutes of full faculty meeting (6 July), and planning committee (20 July).
[21] Interview, Lukas Foss with Perlis, 4 November 1986, New Haven. Also derived in part from a video interview for the television documentary, *Aaron Copland: A Self Portrait.*

The State Department picked Aaron to go to Russia as an example of the older generation, and me as an example of the younger one. We acted out these parts perfectly. Aaron was the proper ambassador, and I was the enfant terrible. *Every evening I would tell him about my exploits, and he would get a vicarious pleasure out of all the naughty things I had done. He enjoyed being what he was, but at the same time, he enjoyed hearing things I was up to. We always had a sort of spy secretary with us—a woman who looked like the kiss of death. She also translated for us at rehearsals. One time, I stole out of the hall, grabbed a cab, handed the driver the Pasternak address Lenny Bernstein had given me.*[22] *He had said, "Lukas, you have got to find out why I don't get any answers, no acknowledgments of the gifts and music I send. . . ." So I handed the address to this driver, but it was in a neighborhood where foreigners are not allowed. The driver didn't like it, but he drove me there anyway and out came Pasternak. I said to him, "Nobody knows I am here." I stayed two hours and the driver came back and dropped me back off in a public place, because I didn't want him to know at which hotel I was staying. I didn't tell anyone except Aaron, but, of course, Pasternak's place was bugged, and when I got back to America, I got a call from the North American Associated News. They said, "We have received a wire with sad news for you. Your friend, Mr. Pasternak, has just suffered a stroke." I said, "What do you mean, my friend?" The wire said: LAST KNOWN WESTERN VISITOR, COMPOSER-CONDUCTOR LUKAS FOSS, KEPT HIS VISIT SO SECRETIVE THAT THE AMERICAN EMBASSY KNOWS NOTHING ABOUT IT All those things I did without permission, I told Aaron about secretly, and the Russians knew about them after all!*

On the Russian trip, I carried a collection of songs around with me and played them for Aaron for his criticism and reactions—these eventually became my Time Cycle. *I played Aaron's music publicly and for composers' meetings in various places we traveled. Once I got terribly mixed up with* El Salón México, *thinking I knew it from memory, and Aaron was really very much like a schoolteacher, shaking his head at me and being very stern.*

I have conducted almost all of Aaron's works. Lincoln *I did with Marian Anderson, Carl Sandburg, and Senator Jacob Javits. For Aaron's eightieth birthday, I did a Copland Festival in Milwaukee, and he came and participated. It was a multimedia festival with film and dance. It was one of the last big trips Aaron took, and he was not feeling very strong, but I noticed how his face suddenly became relaxed when he listened to his music.*

After I returned to the United States, I wrote a report and an article titled "Four Weeks in the Soviet Union—1960."[23] In it, I described our musical activities and my impressions of a friendly and genuine people desiring to do everything possible to further friendly relations, musically and humanly. In addition to the official report, I kept a diary, where I jotted down our day-to-day experiences in a more informal way.[24] I described a visit with the Shostakovich family, seeing

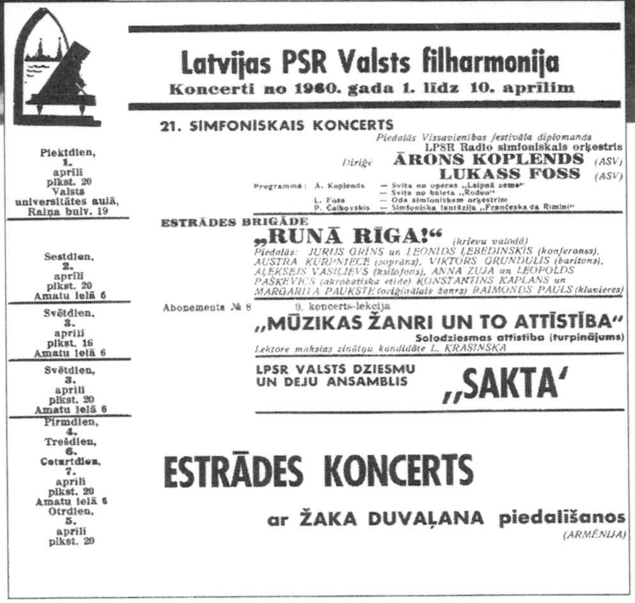

Latvijas PSR Valsts filharmonija
Koncerti no 1960. gada 1. līdz 10. aprīlim

Piektdien, 1. aprīlī pikst. 20 Valsts universitātes aulā, Raiņa bulv. 19

21. SIMFONISKAIS KONCERTS
Piedalās Vissavienības festivāla diplomands
LPSR Radio simfoniskais orķestris
Diriģē **ĀRONS KOPLENDS** *(ASV)*
LUKASS FOSS *(ASV)*
Programmā: Ā. Koplends — Svita no operas „Laipnā zeme"
— Svita no baleta „Rodeo"
L. Foss — Oda simfoniskam orķestrim
P. Čaikovskis — Simfoniskā fantāzija „Frančeska da Rimini"

Sestdien, 2. aprīlī pikst. 20 Amatu ielā 6

ESTRĀDES BRIGĀDE
„RUNĀ RĪGA!" *(krievu valodā)*
Piedalās: JURIS GRĪNS un LEONIDS ĻEBEDINSKIS (konferanss), AUSTRA KURPNIECE (soprāns), VIKTORS GRUNDULIS (baritons), AĻEKSEJS VASIĻJEVS (ksilofons), ANNA ZUJA un LEOPOLDS PAŠKEVIČS (akrobātiska etīde) KONSTANTINS KAPLANS un MARGARITA PAUKSTE (oriģinālais žanrs) RAIMONDS PAULS (klavieres)

Svētdien, 3. aprīlī pikst. 16 Amatu ielā 6

Abonements № 8 — 9. koncerts-lekcija
„MŪZIKAS ŽANRI UN TO ATTĪSTĪBA"
Solodziesmas attīstība (turpinājums)
Lektore mākslas zinātņu kandidāte L. KRASINSKA

Svētdien, 3. aprīlī pikst. 20 Amatu ielā 6

LPSR VALSTS DZIESMU UN DEJU ANSAMBLIS **„SAKTA"**

Pirmdien, 4. Trešdien, 6. Ceturtdien, 7. aprīlī pikst. 20 Amatu ielā 6 Otrdien, 5. aprīlī pikst. 20

ESTRĀDES KONCERTS
ar **ŽAKA DUVAĻANA piedalīšanos** *(ARMĒNIJA)*

Copland conducting the Leningrad Symphony, 7 April 1960; concert announcement for 10 April 1960

the great composer at his own home in a relaxed and charming mood at the dinner table with Kabalevsky, Khrennikov, everyone's wives, and Shostakovich's son, Maxim. I wrote:

> I watched Shostie while Lukas and Kabalevsky played a Haydn symphony four-hands. He loves music with a kind of innocent joy I have rarely seen in a famous composer. Music must have been a great solace to him through the tough days. I was persuaded to play my *Piano Sonata.* At the end, they all said Spasibo (thank you), with no comment of any kind.

[22] Bernstein conducted the New York Philharmonic in 1959 in Moscow, Leningrad, and Kiev. It was the first visit by a major American musical organization after the signing of the United States-Soviet Cultural Exchange Agreement of 1958. Bernstein visited Pasternak in Peredelkino and invited Mr. and Mrs. Pasternak to his concert the next evening. Surprisingly, they were allowed to attend and to speak to Bernstein backstage. See Hans N. Tuch, "A 'Nonperson' Named Boris Pasternak," *The New York Times,* 14 March 1987, 27.

[23] See also article by Copland headed "Copland Finds Composers in Russia Cooperate," *New York Herald Tribune,* 8 May 1960, Section 4, 5, reprinted in BSO *Program Book* (October 1961).

[24] For the trip to Russia and Japan, see Copland travel diary #6.

(*Above*): Copland and Lukas Foss at the State University of New York at Buffalo, 1957

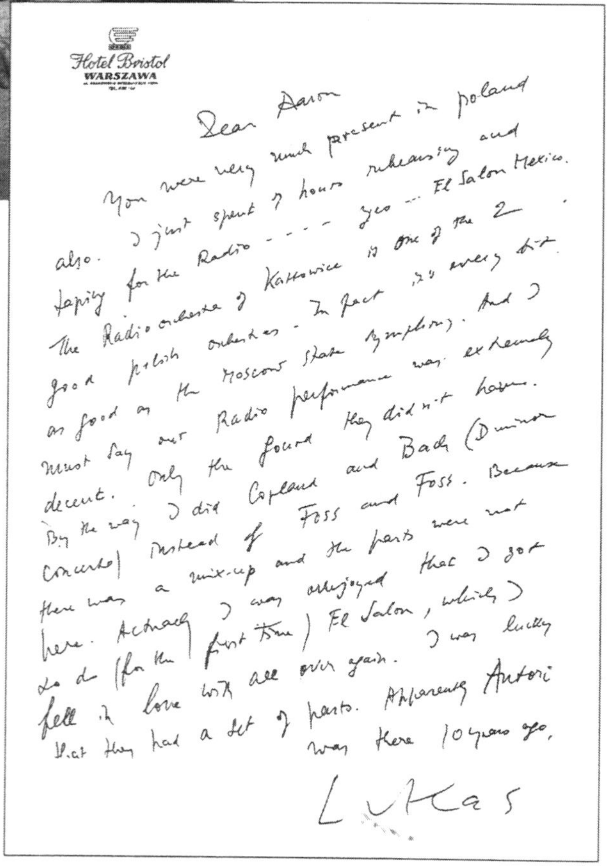

Hotel Bristol
WARSZAWA

Dear Aaron

You were very much present in Poland also. I just spent 7 hours rehearsing and taping for the Radio - - - yes ... El Salon Mexico. The Radio orchestra of Katowice is one of the 2 good polish orchestras. In fact it's every bit as good as the Moscow State Symphony. And I must say our Radio performance was extremely decent. Only the gourd they did not have. By the way I did Copland and Bach (D minor concerto) instead of Foss and Foss. Because there was a mix-up and the parts were not here. Actually I was overjoyed that I got to do (for the first time) El Salon, which I fell in love with all over again. I was lucky that they had a set of parts. Apparently Antoni was here 10 years ago.

Lukas

(*Right*): Letter from Lukas to Copland, Warsaw, 1960 (undated)

The Leningrad Philharmonic was the best of the orchestras with which we worked. They showed not the slightest sign of concern about our "modernisms." I had to repeat the finale of *Red Pony*, and much curiosity was aroused by that title. While walking in the Nevsky Prospect after the concert, a man appeared under the light of one of those beautiful streetlamps they have there and said, "You Copland?" I answered, "Yes." The young man was a musician and he invited us to his apartment to hear some music he had written in the jazz style. We went, and the place was like any little place up in the Bronx and so was the music. The young musician asked me whether I thought jazz was bad. Lukas was impressed by the firmness of my "No!"

In Moscow, I gave a radio talk, the first by an American on the air. At the final concert, I played my *Piano Quartet* with the Borodin Quartet, and the famous pianist Sviatoslav Richter finished the program. Afterward, I gave him all the piano music I had carried with me.

I left Russia with a lasting impression of cooperative spirit at all levels. Our concerts aroused great interest. No surprise was ever shown at dissonance, no matter how severe. But there is active propaganda by those in authority to discredit twelve-tone atonalism and what is referred to as "electronic noises." I was not prepared before our visit as to what degree Russian music is exclusively Russian. There is an extraordinary and all-pervasive unity of expressive ideal: over and over again the pathetic note is struck; the harmonies are fulsome; the melodies clear and singing; the orchestral coloring familiar.

I flew from Moscow to London for a few weeks, where I conducted the LSO and the BBC orchestra.[25] A letter was waiting for me there from Clurman: "I heard from Foss that you were very diplomatic in the U.S.S.R. But I have never known you to be anything but that everywhere." An amusing thing happened in London when I got into a taxicab to go to the Boosey & Hawkes office. As I wrote in my diary at the time:

HE: I see you're an American. What do you do?
ME: Why do you ask?
HE: You look to me like a musician.
ME: That's right.
HE: What sort of musician?
ME: I'm a composer.
HE (in a tone of amazement): Not Walter Piston?!

The opportunity to travel with the BSO as guest conductor in Japan, the Philippines, and Australia was one I could not pass up. I was to meet up with the orchestra in Japan via Seattle and Alaska. I had become quite used to all kinds of flying conditions, but this time I really had a scare. While in the air, a propeller conked out, forcing us to return to Alaska and causing a twenty-four-hour delay. Being late in arriving in Tokyo, I had no time to catch up on sleep. My duties with the BSO began that very day (4 May). Charles Munch and Richard Burgin were alternating as regular conductors, and I filled in at various times with a program

[25] Copland conducted the London Symphony Orchestra in the Royal Festival Hall (19 April 1960): *Statements for Orchestra, Piano Concerto* (Julius Katchen, pianist), *First Symphony*, and *El Salón México*. He conducted the BBC Symphony in a broadcast of *Quiet City* and *TheTender Land Suite* (23 April 1960).

devised by Munch: Purcell, Haydn, and Copland (partway through the trip, I found myself yearning for an alternate program). One concert I conducted was in Osaka. For fun, I traveled there alone by train to Nara, which was packed with kids touring the shrines. It was a strange feeling being the only Westerner in a train full of Japanese.

We went to various one-night stands—Kyoto and then on an Inland Sea boat trip. At times when it rained, I stayed indoors to write letters and to work on an article I had promised to do about Nadia. Everywhere we went, we were greeted with banners: WELCOME BSO. We stayed in hotels where we slept on the floor, Japanese-style. One day, I was awakened by an earth tremor of worrisome proportions. I was concerned, not having asked anyone just what one does in an earthquake! The inland towns in Japan reminded me of Mexico—the people, the mountains, the houses. The small town of Matzuyama had attractions that the big towns lacked. Richard Burgin conducted the evening concert there, including Leon Kirchner's *Toccata* and the *Adagio* from Mahler's *Tenth Symphony,* both big flops. But Tchaikovsky's *Fifth Symphony* always saved the day. Our next stops were Beppu, a dusty resort city; Yawata, a dreary Pittsburgh-like steel center; and Fukuoka, a busy up-and-coming seaport.

In Hiroshima, we stayed in a new hotel surrounded by a park, the former epicenter of the A-bomb. I visited the Museum of the Bomb across from the hotel—it was depressing beyond words, with its photos, statistics, and pieces of clothing—bomb-torn—under glass. I heard half the concert in the new hall, conducted by Munch. It was very strange to sit calmly on the very bomb site listening to a concert! I asked someone what the Japanese audience might be thinking, and the response was chillingly obvious: "These people were not here then." I felt that the Dello Joio piece played by the orchestra sounded sentimental and wooshy under such circumstances.

In Nagoya, the fourth largest city in Japan, I finally caught up on my sleep and on my mail. I walked about and visited a large department store filled with people. Back in Tokyo I had calls from three of Lukas' friends who came to play tapes of music by Takemitsu for me. They were members of the recently formed radical Sogetsu Group of Composers. I wrote in my diary that "Toru Takemitsu was the composer who made the best impression. . . . He chooses his notes carefully and meaningfully. . . . I was pleased also by his personality—typically Japanese and yet a character of his own." I rehearsed and conducted (for a later radio broadcast) the Japan Philharmonic Orchestra in *Appalachian Spring* and "Hoe-Down" from *Rodeo.* I also conducted a piece, *Lyric Ode*, by my friend Jack Kennedy. No opinions were expressed by anyone about anything, but there was a very deferential attitude. Finally, before leaving Japan, I did the things one does in Tokyo—I bought a sport coat from a Singapore tailor, shopped at Takashimaya, and bought an etching.

My impressions of Japan were not clear-cut. I was rather disappointed in the general musical reaction of audiences. However, I wondered whether that might be because they show emotion differently than we do. In part, it makes for the fascination and in part for the dissatisfaction. From my viewpoint, it was the ubiquity of youth in Japan that was quite unique in my travel experiences. I kept wondering, Where are the old people?

Copland conducting a student orchestra in Japan

Copland signing autographs for Japanese fans

We traveled on to Manila, where I made a big impression on the orchestra and the audience by appearing in a Filipino shirt, beautifully embroidered and with the tails hanging out. It was so hot, I was soaked through! In Manila, the audiences applauded during the music when they liked it enough. They only did this once though, for "Hoe-Down," played as an encore. I met with the League of Filipino Composers sponsored by the USIS. They told me I was the first serious composer to come from the United States. I found the heat so exhausting that I stayed in my room working until we left for Brisbane, Australia (5 June).

At some point in our travels, we touched down in the San Francisco airport at 2:30 in the morning. I got out to stretch my legs. There was a bookstand full of paperbacks and standing at the bookstand was a girl who was carrying two books: *What to Listen for in Music* and a volume of Shakespeare plays. I did something I had never done before, but the night was solitary and I was struck by the coincidence. I offered to autograph the book for her. I said, "Would you like me to write my name in that book for you?" She looked down at both of them and said, "Which one?" I answered, "Well, I didn't write the Shakespeare!" "Oh," she said. She just couldn't imagine that the author of the book she was carrying was standing there in front of her!

I do not like to sign autographs much—it gets to be kind of boring, signing your name over and over. I always remember that at one of those post-concert gatherings, some little kid came up to me. I don't know how old he was—eleven or twelve perhaps—with a dirty little piece of paper. He shoved it in front of me and said, "Sign your name." I scribbled my name hastily, handed it back to him, and said, "What are you going to do with that piece of paper?" He looked me straight in the eye and said, "Treasure it." Just like that. I've signed hundreds of autographs, but I'll never forget that kid saying, "Treasure it," with disdain, as if to say, "You're so dumb, you don't even know what I'm going to do with it!"

In Australia, everything suddenly seemed "normal" again—weather, people, language. But I was afraid it would be quite dull compared to Russia and Japan. I had to study the Tchaikovsky *Fifth Symphony* that I was scheduled to conduct in Adelaide. I shared the program with Richard Burgin. We performed in a boxing stadium, open to the night air, and so cold the men wore topcoats over their dress clothes. I had difficulty concentrating. It was all in such strong contrast to sweltering in Manila! Tod Perry was traveling with us, and I said to him as I went offstage, "Can you imagine what Koussevitzky would say if he knew I was conducting his orchestra in Tchaikovsky's *Fifth* in Australia!"

Back in London, I was completely confused as to waking and sleeping hours. My plan was to spend some time in Aldeburgh. I traveled there with composer Harrison Birtwistle and conductor John Carewe. We were put up in rooms without baths or telephones (I always have felt slightly uncomfortable in a room without a phone). My *Piano Quartet* was performed and the Society for the Promotion of New Music sponsored a program at which I spoke. Jack Kennedy met me and we caught up on all the news from home. We were invited to tea chez Benjamin Britten, and it was very posh with the Prince of Hesse and Earl of Harewood present. I was to conduct a new piece at the Aldeburgh Festival, but it was not finished yet; instead, I conducted *Two Pieces for String Orchestra, Quiet City*, and *In The Beginning* at the Blythburgh church. I wrote to Claire [Reis], "The choir sounded like the voice of the Lord!"

Copland in Australia, 1960

Returning to London, I gave a talk for the BBC on Japanese composers. After a visit to Oxford, I flew home and was greeted at the airport by Victor Kraft in my new "buggy"—a Mercedes—bought while I was away (Victor had had an accident with my Buick with "total" damage). I arrived home to find that the country had gotten into a state of excitement and fear over the U2 incident. Everyone was talking about bomb shelters—I was amazed! The subject came up in Ossining, but having only a few days home before leaving for Tanglewood, I was saved from making a decision. Anyway, I did not plan to stay in Ossining. Victor had been searching around for another house. He had found one in Peekskill and took me to see it. One look at the grounds with the Hudson in the distance, the gardens and woods, and the house with the separate studio, and I was sold! When I first saw the studio, I said that it looked like a room where a composer could write music. The house, "Rock Hill," is not a made-over barn as my previous homes had been. I sold Shady Lane Farm in Ossining in August 1960 and moved to Peekskill after Tanglewood, just before my sixtieth birthday. *Time* and *Newsweek* magazines came to interview me for the occasion. They found me surrounded by unpacked cartons of books, papers, recordings, and music.

I am not much of a "backward looker." My head was full of the recent past—my travels in Russia and the Far East. Nevertheless, for Tanglewood's twentieth anniversary in 1960, I allowed myself a bit of nostalgia in my usual opening address to students and faculty. "Only Randall Thompson's 'Allelulia' is the same," I said. I recalled various images from earlier years: "Ben Britten in the wings at *Peter Grimes*; the excitement of Shostie's *Seventh Symphony* played by the student orchestra conducted by Koussevitzky; young conductors such as Thor Johnson, Walter Hendel, and Lenny Bernstein; and the composers from abroad—Hindemith, Martinů, Milhaud, Honegger, Messiaen, Ibert, Dallapiccola, Petrassi, and Chávez."

I introduced Luciano Berio as guest composer for 1960. He would share the program with Leon Kirchner and myself. The famous Italian composer was a coup for Tanglewood. Leonard Burkat had convinced the Ford Foundation's international relations program to give a grant to make his presence possible. I had written to Berio in Milan (5 Feb. 1960): "I have just learned that it is possible to invite you and your wife to be present during these six weeks as house guests of Mrs. Serge Koussevitzky. You probably remember the house itself, which is beautifully situated and should be comfortable. If this plan is agreeable, we would ask you to accept the designation of Composer in Residence." Berio had been a student at Tanglewood in 1951 and 1952 and was familiar with the place. He requested that he have only three or four students (Kirchner had six, I had eight[26]) so that he would be free to produce an open-air electronic concert (8 August). It was the first of its kind in the States.[27] Berio also prepared the premiere of his Fromm-commissioned work, *Circles*, for the Fromm Chamber Music Concert (1 August).

I wrote to Lenny (28 July): "Our summer is considerably enlivened by Luciano Berio who has stirred things up . . . Otherwise, routine reigns. We need you in Tanglewood—but badly!" A few changes in the Music Center in 1960 were the result of the brainstorming meetings in 1959 that had continued during the winter months.[28] Fromm Foundation activities continued with the Sunday Composers Forums. David Walker, who was put in charge of organizing them, described the arrangements:

> It was complicated—a composer would leave a note in my box in the library telling the character of his piece, its duration, instrumentation, and so forth. I would put together the players at the right time in an appropriate space. At one Sunday reading, a young student by the name of Seiji Ozawa conducted a piece.[29]

[26] Copland's students in 1960 were Nicholas Cappabianca, John Duffy, Karl Korte, David Locy, Robert McMahan, Ezra Sims, Timothy Thompson, and Cesar Tort.
[27] Electronic equipment, consisting of an Ampex 300 stereo tape recorder and four groups of speakers (supplied by East Coast Company and the Concert Network, Boston) was placed, along with the necessary transformers and amplifiers, in trees on the lawn and adjoining the Main House. Berio manipulated the console from the Main House. The audience was encouraged to move about the lawns in order to hear the 360-degree perimeter of sound. Composers represented were Berio, Maderna, Boucourchliev, Varèse, Ussachevsky, Ligeti, and Stockhausen.
[28] The Tanglewood Study Group was abandoned in favor of a "Listening and Analysis" program directed by G. Wallace Woodworth and Florence Dunn. Goldovsky produced one-act operas.
[29] David Walker to Vivian Perlis.

The Friday afternoon Seminar in Contemporary Music began with my lecture, "Music in the Twenties," and continued with sessions by composers Berio, Kirchner, Carter, Blomdahl, and Cage.

Paul Fromm was preparing a radio series, "Composers on Composers—Twentieth-Century Profiles," for WFMT in Chicago, which was to be broadcast by over forty affiliated stations nationwide. The programs featured twelve well-known composers about other composers, as well as composers about their own music.[30] Fromm requested that I prepare a tape to give him at Tanglewood in mid-July. The programs were broadcast during the following fall and winter. Fromm had also written to Lenny Burkat expressing his wish for an all-Copland concert to celebrate my sixtieth birthday. I was apprehensive, thinking that it might seem self-serving, but when Paul Fromm was determined, watch out! Fromm's idea was "to show the three compositional phases of Copland." The result was that one of the two Monday-evening concerts was devoted to my three major piano works played by Billy Masselos. At the end of the season, Fromm wrote to me (11 August), "We are again indebted to you for the planning of our Tanglewood project. It is especially gratifying to me that the Copland recital was the high point of our Tanglewood program."

Ralph Berkowitz circulated a memorandum in 1960 suggesting a change in the name of the Center from Berkshire Music Center to Tanglewood Music Center. Most of the faculty agreed, so Tod Perry sent the request on to the trustees. "After all," said Berkowitz, "No one ever has said, 'I'm going to the Berkshire Music Center.' They always say, 'I'm going to Tanglewood.'" The suggestion was not approved, and the BMC did not become the TMC until 1985. For the public, it is not the Center that is the focal point of Tanglewood, but the Festival. I usually conducted one of my own works with the BSO in the Shed each summer; in 1960, it was the *First Symphony* (13 August).

I left the Berkshires directly after the 1960 season for my first visit to the Aspen Festival. Norman Singer, director and dean, had invited me each summer since 1957, but I had not been able to accept because I was committed to Tanglewood. Singer wrote again (August 1959): ". . . to invite you to be with us next summer when it is our intention to feature your music in celebration of your sixtieth birthday." A compromise was reached about the scheduling so I could fly to Aspen a week before the Aspen Festival, immediately after Tanglewood. Aspen offered a different atmosphere of music-making in a very beautiful setting. I conducted the Aspen Festival Orchestra in my *Orchestral Variations* and *Red Pony Suite* and enjoyed it so much that I promised to return if invited.

Every ten years or so, since 1926, I had put myself on the line by naming the most promising young composers in each generation; I attempted a similar assessment of the fifties. However, this decade was more difficult to describe. There were so many more composers active in many parts of the country, and I was that much further away in age from the young composers. Nevertheless, I had a pretty good idea of what was current from summers at Tanglewood and from my travels. I wrote a short article, "1959: Postscript for the Generation

[30] Copies of the Fromm radio series tapes are at the Oral History of American Music, Yale.

of the Fifties," for inclusion in the book I had been working on that was to be published by Doubleday at the time of my sixtieth birthday. In the article I wrote: "The young composer of today seems to be fighting hard to stay abreast of a fast-moving post-World War II European musical scene." By this I meant Pierre Boulez, Karlheinz Stockhausen, and Luigi Nono. I mentioned Elliott Carter as an honorable exception to this trend. The composers I singled out in 1959 as "young talents whose music commands attention" were Billy Jim Layton, Salvatore Martirano, Seymour Schifrin, Edward Miller, Yehudi Wyner, Kenneth Gaburo, and Robert Lombardo. I mentioned Gunther Schuller for his independent use of jazz with serious music and cited others for various reasons: Easley Blackwood, Noel Lee, and Mordechai Sheinkman. After *Copland on Music* was published,[31] I sent copies out to friends and colleagues, including Elliott Carter. He responded, "I rather appreciate never having been singled out in your articles as so many passed-up past masters and dead wood were, since by this it is made more clear than ever that my music has taken an opposite direction—one that can be talked about now and not reminisced about."

Copland on Music includes reprints from earlier publications as well as material written especially for this book (the article on Boulanger, for example).[32] Being away so much of the time prior to publication of *Copland on Music*, I needed an assistant and was fortunate in obtaining the services of Yehudi Wyner, who had given me the original idea for the book. The reception of my book was generally favorable, although there was some criticism that much of the material had appeared elsewhere. My review of Rene Leibowitz' book on Schoenberg and his school drew interest because in it I expressed my attitude to twelve-tone theory. The essays on Mozart, Berlioz, Liszt, and Fauré were praised for their simplicity and directness. Eric Salzman reviewed *Copland on Music* for *The New York Times Book Review*, which appeared the day before my sixtieth birthday. He wrote: ". . . Aaron Copland writes about music in the same way that he composes. The qualities of clarity, liveliness, elegance, precision, and directness which distinguish his music make him a fine essayist."

My sixtieth birthday was a blockbuster, "a deluge," as Nadia Boulanger called it in her congratulatory letter. I had great trouble making a connection with that number—sixty! It seemed to have no relation to how I felt, thank goodness! In an interview at the time, I said that fifty had been worse. I pointed out that since I had no children with whom to compare myself, I couldn't really tell that I was older. However, no one could accuse me of sitting back and taking it easy on my sixtieth. The weekend before my birthday, I conducted the New York Philharmonic at Carnegie Hall in their weekend subscription concerts. The program included my *Symphonic Ode* and *El Salón México*, as well as pieces by Gluck, [Arnold] Franchetti, and the Dvořák *Violin Concerto* (the rather odd program was because the Philharmonic was celebrating violinist John Corigliano's twenty-fifth anniversary with the orchestra, as well as my birthday). Lenny Bernstein had written during the previous summer:

> I have an idea, which will be doing something nobody else can do for your sixtieth, and that is to make a whole TV show for the kids (the Shell series, originating in Carnegie) on the subject of the Venerable Giggling Dean. . . . This will happen on the 12th of November (Sat.) at noon in Carnegie Hall. I want you to participate, do you hear?!

I responded (28 July 1960): "The only thing I don't want to be presented as is grandpa for the kiddies." I appeared with Lenny and William Warfield on the Philharmonic Young People's Concert, "Aaron Copland's Birthday Party." It was taped to be broadcast later on CBS TV (12 February 1961). Lenny was conductor and commentator, and I conducted *El Salón México* at the end of the program. Lenny is a born teacher—he had those young people enjoying every moment.

Television appearances always brought tons of mail from many places. This time, it was the fan letters from kids that delighted me. One twelve-year-old wrote, "My teacher said I should pick someone I don't know anything about for my music assignment. I saw you on TV and don't know anything about you, but I like your fast music. Can you tell me how you write fast music?" Another letter came from a neighbor who had a small store near where I had grown up in Brooklyn:

> Whenever I heard your name mentioned, I always wanted to see you, but I could never see your face until today on Leonard Bernstein's program. It was a great moment for me and my family to see you on television. We all knew you so well. We were such good neighbors. From our little neighborhood came out a lot of geniuses and good people. I am sure that Boys' High School will be happy to know they had a pupil like you. . . . You've made good for everybody.

The major sixtieth birthday event was a two-concert celebration by the Juilliard, one on my birthday and another the following evening. In the audience was a solid representation of the intellectual life of New York, along with many of my friends and colleagues. I dined with Minna Daniel ("Mink" as I call her for reasons known only to us), and she accompanied me to the concert and the Boosey & Hawkes postconcert party at the Gotham Hotel, at which Bill Schuman delighted the guests with a parody of *Lincoln Portrait*—about me, of course.

The first Juilliard program included *In The Beginning*, the score for my early film *The City*, *Sextet*, and three staged excerpts from *The Tender Land*;[33] the second program was devoted to my three major piano works played by Bill Masselos. The celebration did not end with the concerts: the entire issue of *The Juilliard Review* (Winter 1960-1961) was a souvenir album containing the concert programs, photographs, and an essay, "The Copland Festival," by Richard Franko Goldman. All in all, it was the most satisfying kind of celebration for a composer.

In addition to the Juilliard concerts, Benny Goodman played the *Clarinet Concerto* with the Orchestra of the Americas (16 November 1960) and there were concerts held in my honor in other parts of the country.[34] After hearing about the West Coast tribute, I wrote to

[31] Aaron Copland, *Copland on Music* (New York: Doubleday, 1963; paperback, New York: W. W. Norton & Company, 1963); in England (London: André Deutsch,1962); reprinted in U.S. (New York: Da Capo Press, 1976).

[32] Copland, "Nadia Boulanger: An Affectionate Portrait" was written for *Copland on Music* and appeared in advance in *Harper's Magazine* (October 1960), 49.

[33] Performing were the Juilliard String Quartet, Jan DeGaetani, Stanley Drucker, Leonid Hambro, and Juilliard students.

[34] Copland birthday concerts were held in Washington (The Library of Congress), St. Louis, Rochester, and Los Angeles, where a Copland evening was organized at U.S.C. by West Coast friends Leo Smit, Lukas Foss, and Ingolf Dahl.

Leo (24 November), "You've been an angel to engage in all this activity—and I'm forever grateful. Lots of fuss here in the east—especially in the newspapers. So I've been spoiled beyond measure."

Boosey & Hawkes prepared an updated catalogue of my works, and Doubleday published my book *Copland on Music* to coincide with my birthday. Columbia Records released two recordings of my works: Masselos playing the *Piano Fantasy* and Lenny's version of *The Second Hurricane* (with *Rodeo* and *Billy the Kid*).

Lenny wrote after hearing the test pressing of *Hurricane*:

> Mainly I'm writing because I'm so impressed all over again with the music. It is lovely and endlessly fresh: Neither the simplicity nor the grandeur stales. . . . I hope you like it; it will be our November release on Columbia, along with *Billy* and *Rodeo*, making a delightful, gay (though costly) birthday package!

It took me over a month to answer all the tributes and greetings, among them ones from Clurman, Stravinsky, Lenny and Felicia, and even a telegram signed "Papa and Mama of Leonard." Messages arrived from England, France, Russia, Argentina, and other Latin American countries, and David Diamond wrote from Italy about the symphony (his eighth) that he was composing in honor of my birthday (9 November):

> I am on the last measures (orchestration) of "your" symphony. I am sure that by the 14th I shall have it done. I am pleased with the work and hope you will be. What these years of our friendship and sustained faith have been is all there, in those pages.

I heard from all my family as I did every birthday, even my long-silent cousin Percy Uris, who remembered me as "the young man who lived at University Place and played the piano so vigorously that we had to move him to one of our numerous vacant apartments where the piano playing (I was about to call it noise) would not disturb others."

Bill Schuman's "A Birthday Salute to Aaron Copland" in the *Herald Tribune* (30 October) kicked things off in the press. *Time, Newsweek, Musical America,* and *The New York Times Magazine* followed with articles.[35] I was pleased to tell interviewers that I was in the midst of composing a new piece. It was gratifying to be able to bring forth surprise from the press at its unusual instrumentation: three violins, three violas, and three cellos.

Nonet for Solo Strings was commissioned by Dumbarton Oaks in honor of the fiftieth wedding anniversary of Mr. and Mrs. Robert Woods Bliss (Dumbarton Oaks, with its research library and collection, was presented to Harvard University by Mr. and Mrs. Bliss.) The piece was to have been premiered at a special concert celebrating the anniversary and conducted by Nadia Boulanger, who was a longtime friend of the music-loving Bliss family (14 April 1958). In a letter to Mrs. Bliss, I apologized that the pressure of other commitments prevented me from completing the composition in time for the event, but I attended the concert with Nadia and participated in a symposium with Walter Piston. When *Nonet* was finished (December 1960), I conducted it at a private subscription concert at Dumbarton Oaks with nine string players from the National Symphony Orchestra (2 March 1961). I also conducted works by Purcell, Handel, and Bach. The program included my *Piano Variations*, Frank Glazer pianist. I wrote to Chávez (March 1961): "My main news is that I completed my *Nonet*, and it was premiered at Dumarton Oaks last week. I wonder how you will like it? I, myself, thought it had a poignant and elegiac sound—almost autumnal in quality."

Copland demonstrating bowing to string players for *Nonet*. Berlin, 1960

[35] Eric Salzman, "Dean of Our Composers at Sixty," *The New York Times Magazine*, 13 November 1960, 51, 61, 63-64, 66, 68.

Nonet is dedicated to Nadia Boulanger, "after forty years of friendship." When composing it, I had looked through my notebook of musical ideas and found two pages that seemed usable: one that gave me my main tune (undated); the other, a half page (dated "5/22/50"). Perhaps tune does not accurately describe the thematic material: a series of rather darkly colored three-voiced chords. The nature of these chords gives off a crowded, rather sober, and perhaps somewhat lugubrious feeling that is characteristic of this work and no other I have written. The idea of the particular instrumentation for *Nonet* came from these chords, which I "heard" for three solo cellos. Starting with that, I decided to balance the cellos with a combination of strings, which, in its very makeup, would produce a darkly colored sound. Those first three chords generate most of the harmonic and melodic material for the entire composition.

The one-movement *Nonet* is about eighteen minutes in duration. Its general structure is easily grasped: two slow, rather somber sections flanking a livelier midsection. The opening chords are played first by the three cellos with deadened vibrato. After the material rises and subsides in a slow-moving progression, the violas enter one by one, then similarly, the violins. The longer notes give way to shorter ones until the music reaches a complex rhythmic climax in the midsection. The music then broadens and gradually evolves into another lyric section that bears a linear relation to the vertical chordal beginning, leading back to the music of the opening. *Nonet* is introspective and subjective in mood, less diatonic than most of my earlier music and, therefore, freer in its chord relationships. I like to think it shows a continuing development in the type of harmonies and sonorities employed.[36]

In the year of the premiere, 1961, I conducted performances of *Nonet* at Brandeis University, in Chicago, for a BBC broadcast in London, and the New York premiere at a Composers Showcase concert at the Museum of Modern Art (5 April 1962). The occasion was a memorial concert for Theodore Chanler by some of his friends: Nadia Boulanger, Walter Piston, Virgil Thomson, and myself. When Leo Smit was about to conduct *Nonet* at Ojai, he wrote, asking advice, and I replied, "Try to make the beginning real special in color—a moyen-age gloom (but not dull)."[37] Lawrence Morton heard the performance and deferred an opinion: "You took a long time to write the piece and so you must allow me some to learn it."

[36] Copland's description of *Nonet* is from his program notes written at the time of the work's premiere.
[37] A recording of Copland rehearsing *Nonet* is at The Library of Congress, Recorded Sound Reference Center. It was taped before a concert in honor of Nadia Boulanger in 1977.

Most praise for *Nonet* came for its unusual combination of instruments and the string sonorities. Ingolf Dahl and Leon Kirchner both admired and conducted *Nonet* [Dahl in 1969, Los Angeles; Kirchner in 1974, Cambridge]. Ingolf wrote (15 March 1969), "What pleased me particularly was the variety of string color throughout. . . . The passage between four and five is particularly lovely, with that bravely sad rise of the seventh in the melody. . . ."

Nonet was subjected to a rigorous analysis in *Perspectives of New Music*. The article, "Aaron Copland's Nonet: Two Views," was by Eric Salzman and Paul Des Marais: The former treated the piece as a nonserial work; the latter as a serial composition.[38] I cannot say that I recognized my intentions in either discussion, but I appreciated two views being given, which made the point that music can be analyzed according to whatever system the analyst cares to apply. I had a long letter from Leon Kirchner, full of quotes and musical examples, criticizing both of the analyses (17 January 1963).

It seems that the twelve-tone crowd had hoped I would continue in the direction of my *Piano Quartet* (1950) and *Piano Fantasy* (1957), which made use of serial techniques. Then, here I came along and confused the issue again with *Nonet*, a piece that could not be claimed by either the twelve-toners or the diatonic composers. Since the critics could not categorize *Nonet* as belonging to either my "accessible" or my "austere" style, it has been called "transitional." In an article on *Nonet*, Stephen Plaistow concluded, ". . . it must be observed that the *Nonet* does little to advance the expressive boundaries of Copland's style. . . . More positively it can be said that the *Nonet* is a work of charm and immense technical polish . . . a disappointment from Copland is worth more than run-of-the-mill competence from most others."[39]

In concert halls whose size justifies the use of larger groups of strings, specific larger combinations can be employed when performing *Nonet*—up to forty-eight players in all, but, as I stated in the score, "The work should under no circumstances be performed by a string orchestra as normally constituted." William Steinberg conducted the New York Philharmonic in the expanded instrumentation (19, 20, 21 November 1964). Critic Alan Rich wrote in the *Herald Tribune*: "The augmented version detracts not at all from the work's high quality. It is grave, intense music, beautifully constructed and eloquent."

[38] Eric Salzman and Paul Des Marais, "Aaron Copland's Nonet: Two Views," *Perspectives of New Music*, Fall 1962, 172-179.
[39] Stephen Plaistow, "Some Notes on Copland's Nonet," *Tempo*, no. 64; (Spring 1963), 6-11.

INTERLUDE X

Dwight D. Eisenhower had been the oldest President to hold office; by the time of the 1961 election, he and the country seemed immobilized. When John F. Kennedy came into the White House, a cultural revolution was about to begin. The forty-three-year-old Kennedy held out the promise that America would come alive again. Economist John Kenneth Galbraith foretold it in his popular book of 1958, *The Affluent Society*: America had limitless resources, and Jack Kennedy was the man to put them to use.[1] The Kennedy years would be ones of activism, commitment, and, above all, idealism.

The American people fell in love with the handsome young President and his beautiful family, and for artists and intellectuals, it seemed as though the Messiah had arrived. The Kennedys really cared about education and culture. No wonder Washington in the Kennedy years was called "the new Camelot!" The President and First Lady promptly made their artistic interests known by holding a White House Gala in honor of Pablo Casals (13 November 1961) to which they invited outstanding figures in the arts, Copland among them. He described the occasion in a diary:

> I sat between Mrs. Walter Lippmann and Mrs. William Paley. Pierre Salinger and Senator Mike Mansfield were at our table. President Kennedy was in full view the entire time, while ten violins played through dinner. Surprised at his reddish-brown hair. No evil in the face, but plenty of ambition there, no doubt. Mrs K. statuesque. A ceremonial entry with the presentation of colors preceded dinner at which guests were presented to President and Mrs. Kennedy. Seemed to note a glance of recognition from Mr. and Mrs. Kennedy. After dinner we were treated to a concert by Pablo Casals. No American music. The next step.

It did not take long for that "next step." In May 1962, the Kennedys planned a performance of *Billy the Kid* by the Ballet Theatre for a program in honor of the visiting president of the Ivory Coast Republic. With American choreographer Eugene Loring and leading American composer Aaron Copland as honored guests, American dancer John Kriza in the role of the quintessential western cowboy, and the glamorous Kennedys and the handsome entourage from Africa—all in formal attire in the elegant surroundings—the White House proudly displayed American arts and creativity to the world.

[1] John Kenneth Galbraith, *The Affluent Society* (New York: New American Library, 1958).

The Kennedy administration offered hope for the revitalization of the arts in America: Lincoln Center for the Performing Arts was scheduled to open in 1962, and plans were in progress for other large art centers around the country; individual artists were experiencing the heady sensation of support and approval from the top. The "nothing is impossible" Kennedy spirit infiltrated the arts. What could never before mix, could now be tried. Multimedia events became popular, and in all the arts, lines were developing and crossing in many directions.

Those who had lived under the shadow of McCarthyism could finally believe the nightmare was over. For the first time since 1953, Copland renewed his passport without apprehension. As one of the most gifted and articulate musicians of the time, now entering his sixth decade, Copland was refreshed and stimulated by the optimistic atmosphere during the Kennedy years. On behalf of the President, Secretary of State Dean Rusk invited

At the White House on the occasion of the performance of *Billy the Kid* (*left to right*): John Kriza, Eugene Loring, Copland, President Kennedy, Mrs. Felix Houphet-Boigny (wife of the President of the Ivory Republic), and Mrs. Kennedy, May, 1962

Copland to join a small working committee "whose purpose is to prepare a recommendation by July first for the State Department advising on philosophy, concept, and criteria for an international cultural project. They need your wisdom and hope you can serve." Copland was pleased to accept.

The brutal assassination of John Kennedy was a tragedy of such proportion that the circumstances of how and where the news was heard is remembered by every American who heard it that November afternoon in 1963. Copland recalls that he was in the opera house in Munich rehearsing the orchestra for the premiere of the ballet *Dance Panels*. He said, "I stayed on that day to watch the other ballets. The orchestra suddenly became silent. I thought some local person had died. Then the director, Heinz Rosen, came over to tell me, "Your President Kennedy has been killed!" Copland recalls his feelings at the time: "I was shocked. At such a moment one wants to have a fellow countryman nearby. It was sad to be alone and hard to believe. Even when I attended a memorial service at Amerika House the next day."

The sixties are described as a decade of radical change and upheaval. The most profound changes followed in the wake of the Kennedy assassination, which caused sustained and debilitating trauma to the country. In the aftermath of the nation's grief, "the Kennedy legend" was kept alive for a while, a fact that Lyndon Johnson had to live with during much of his administration, sometimes uncomfortably. Johnson did not care greatly for the arts, and he rated low with intellectuals. Nevertheless, the National Council on the Arts was established in Johnson's administration (1964) and following the inauguration, under pressure from former Kennedy supporters, Johnson agreed to hold The First White House Festival of the Arts (24 March 1965). When several prominent artists refused to participate as a gesture of protest against the Vietnam War (poet Robert Lowell in the forefront), Johnson was so incensed, he vowed to stay clear of "those people" during the remainder of his time in office.[2] Copland, who had received the Medal of Freedom the previous September and had attended the Johnson inauguration concert in January 1965, was not invited to participate in the Festival of the Arts. Because of the Vietnam protests, the Johnson people were being careful about associating with those who had confrontations with McCarthy. (Ironically, the liberal playwright Arthur Miller had been asked to speak at the festival before the political implications surfaced, and his invitation could not be rescinded without embarrassment to the President.)

During the ensuing Johnson years, there was a good deal of discussion about government support of the arts, but it was known and felt that the President himself was not committed. As the decade progressed, Copland, as an artist and public figure, was affected by the changed spirit and the upheavals in the country, but his personal life and career were neither turbulent nor changeable. The pattern of his life had been set earlier, and it continued: conducting tours, lecture and teaching engagements in the United States and abroad, interspersed with quiet periods at home among familiar faces and unchanging surroundings.

[2] Eric F. Goldman, *The Tragedy of Lyndon Johnson* (New York: Alfred A. Knopf, 1969), Chapter Sixteen, "The President and the Intellectuals," 418-75.

At the start of each new year, a red leather appointment book, with "Aaron Copland" and the year imprinted in gold, arrived mysteriously at Copland's house in Peekskill. (No one can recall who was responsible for sending it.) One year, the diary failed to arrive, and Copland exclaimed in mock horror, "*Mon dieu*, how can I go on without it?" (It was a great relief when delivery resumed the following year.) After Copland transcribed fixed dates, such as quarterly tax payments and birthdays of friends and relatives, into his new diary, the year was ready to begin. Taken individually, these appointment books reveal useful details of time and place; over the decade, they show the continuity and stability that was essential to Copland's sense of well-being. The diaries also demonstrate a gradual change of emphasis away from the solitary life of composer toward a more public one of conductor.

The pattern of Copland's day-to-day existence can be reconstructed from the regularity of certain diary entries: trips to New York—"reserve at Harvard Club," "Philharmonic rehearsal," "B & H meeting," "ASCAP." For out-of-town dates—"Pick up plane tickets and tux," "pack scores." Or for times at home in Peekskill—"DW coming to work," "meet Clurman at train." At the back of each appointment book, Copland listed the commissions offered, marking rejections with an X, acceptances with a checkmark. These lists make interesting reading, considering some of the music that might have been. Asked whether he regretted not accepting more of the commissions, Copland responded, "Good Heavens, no! I'm lucky to have composed the one or two a year I did accept."

The birthdates marked by Copland into his appointment books were of the same friends and colleagues every year: "Clurman, Mink [Minna Daniel], Claire [Reis], LB [Bernstein], BS [Schuman], DD [Diamond], Alvin [Ross], DW [David Walker], V [Victor Kraft], Chávez, Olga [Koussevitzky]." The list changed only when someone died, which occurred with increasing frequency as Copland grew older. The greatest shock was the sudden death of Irving Fine in 1962. Fine was a younger colleague and dear friend. Irving, Verna, and their three daughters were the closest Copland had to a family of his own.[3] He wrote to Boulanger (September 1962): "Now—after Teddy Chanler and Mel Smith—another sad loss— Irving Fine." When Clifford Odets died in 1963, Copland heard from David Diamond (17 August): "I am just sick about Cliff; and I know how you must feel." Then Colin McPhee and Marc Blitzstein both died in 1964. In a tribute to Blitzstein, Copland wrote, "I feel saddened to realize how little his music was known by the current generation. It was ironic, with all Blitzstein's accomplishments, to think that his fame rested on his talent as translator of *The Threepenny Opera*."[4]

Copland's own health was excellent, and his yearly checkups with his doctor, Arnold Salop, duly notated in his appointment books, were routine. Only once during the sixties

[3] For family letters and photographs, some with Copland, see the Verna and Irving Fine archive at the Library of Congress. For tributes to Fine, including Copland's "A Composer's Praise," see Brandeis University newspaper, *The Justice*, 30 October 1962. Copland helped organize a committee to endow a studio at the MacDowell Colony, the "Fine Studio," in Irving Fine's memory.

[4] Copland, "In Memory of Marc Blitzstein (1905-1964)," *Perspectives of New Music* (Spring/Summer 1964), 6-7, reprinted in Blitzstein Memorial Program Book, see Copland's files.

Copland with great-grandnephews Matthew and Daniel Levey, and the dog Nadja, 1972

was he hospitalized, for a prostate operation, from which he recovered rapidly. Copland's doctor, lawyer, accountant, dentist, publisher—all stayed the same through the years. David Walker, who became Copland's assistant in 1952, was his close friend and colleague. Victor Kraft, an intimate friend for many years, remarried in 1960. The couple had a baby boy and Copland was named godfather. They lived close by, and Victor continued to take care of the grounds and the car at Rock Hill when Copland traveled. Even when Victor became difficult and demanding, Copland would never abandon him. As for Copland's family, he sent checks on birthdays and for special occasions and he helped take care of his sister-in-law Dorothy. "Dot" appears regularly in the appointment books, as does "La" (sister Laurine). Not having a family of his own, nieces and nephews (nine in all) received his attention, and as time went on, grandnieces and nephews. The oldest of these, Roger Levey, said:

> Uncle Aaron was never too busy or too far away to remember the family. When I got married, he wrote from the Connaught Hotel in London, and we heard from him when each of the children was born. We went to see Uncle Aaron conduct at Tanglewood several times. Once (I must have been about ten years old), I was impressed with seeing him wearing a white tuxedo and conducting in the Shed and the next thing, we were all back at his place and he had on a white apron and was carving a turkey, acting as host. He liked to do that kind of thing at home.
>
> There was always a very warm feeling between Uncle Aaron and the family. If he thought any of us was interested in music, he went all out. He left his Steinway at our apartment once when he was between houses, and there it stayed because I was taking lessons.

After settling into his new home in Peekskill, Copland gave one big housewarming party in the fall of 1961. Thereafter, he enjoyed inviting friends and colleagues individually or a few at a time for lunch or dinner. He took pride in showing the place and liked to walk around the grounds or in the woods with his guests. For several years, a Belgian couple (Mireille and Gaston Varaertenryck and their poodle "Poupette") kept the house and grounds in good order. Copland was upset when they decided to leave, and delighted when they returned after a brief stint with another employer.

Few changes were ever made in the Peekskill house: If something wore out, it was likely to be replaced with the same or a similar item. When Copland moved in, he brought with him from Ossining his favorite desk, which someone had put together from a large piece of wood balanced on carpenters' "horses." Copland used it in his studio ever since. He had one of each piece of clothing—a black overcoat, a beret, one dark suit, a tuxedo. His car, once a Mercedes, remained a Mercedes.

Copland never considered staying anywhere in New York City but the Harvard Club, his "home away from home." One day when he entered the dining room and heard recorded music being piped in, he was appalled to think he might have to find a new place to take guests to lunch or dinner. (Perhaps other members complained, too, since a week later, the Harvard Club dining room was silent as usual.)

Boosey & Hawkes was Copland's publisher from the time Benjamin Britten introduced Copland to Ralph Hawkes in 1938. This longstanding association, so much in character

Copland at his desk in the seventies

Copland and Ralph Hawkes at Tanglewood, c. 1949

with Copland, has been an important one in his career. Through the years, various people at Boosey & Hawkes were in charge of Copland's catalogue,[5] but no one was as knowledgeable about rights, royalties, contracts, and the myriad details surrounding Copland's music as Sylvia Goldstein.

Sylvia Goldstein[6]

I began working at Boosey & Hawkes in 1940 and have been concerned with Copland's account since then. In 1945, I attended law school at night and got my law degree, but I never left the firm as I had intended. This is a different kind of firm. We represent only a small number of important composers. My contract work has been with all of them, but Aaron has always been an important part of our activities. Working with him was different from the other composers. Aaron liked to stay out of the limelight. He was a good businessman, precise and careful. He always wanted copies of his contracts, and he knew where everything was. He was easy to deal with, but not easily led. Aaron always knew what he wanted.

I remember he used to work very hard on titles, from Lincoln Portrait *to* Inscape. *Not that they meant a lot in terms of the music, but he was convinced titles have a lot to do with the way the public reacts to a piece. Only the ballets he left to the choreographers to name.* Appalachian Spring *was always Ballet for Martha until Martha Graham named it. Aaron gave it to her as a gift, and as long as Martha danced it, she didn't pay for it.*

Aaron brought back thoughtful gifts when he traveled, and he gave them to me along with nice notes: a painting, Jensen jewelry from Europe, a bowl, bangle bracelets. And when he returned from his first trip to Israel, he gave me a shofar.

Aaron came to rely on my judgment. He would ask my opinion about requests to use his music. One time when we were having a change in personnel, he said, "If Sylvia goes, I go!" He wanted to know there were people he could trust taking care of his music. Aaron was worried about the continuity. He liked the sameness of things.

Stuart Pope, president of the American branch of Boosey & Hawkes from 1964 to 1984, became closely involved with Copland's music and career.

Stuart Pope[7]

Aaron was the most civilized person with whom to work. He was certainly the most businesslike of composers. He understood the business aspects of music publishing, which is most unusual in composers. The first question Aaron would ask when a proposal concerning his music came up was "Can we make any money out of it?" If the answer was yes, we would then look further and deal with the matter seriously. When Aaron got his annual financial statements, he went through them and then made an appointment to go

Copland with Stuart Pope, 1979

[5] Hans Heinsheimer, followed briefly by Betty Bean, was in charge early on. David Adams was president of Boosey & Hawkes in the United States until Stuart Pope replaced him in 1964. Robert Holton was also associated with Copland's music at Boosey, as were Robert Wharton, David Huntley, James M. Kendrick, Linda Golding, Jenny Bilfield, and current president Zizi Mueller. See Helen Wallace, *The Story of Boosey & Hawkes* (London, Boosey & Hawkes Publishing Ltd., 2007).

[6] Interview, Sylvia Goldstein with Perlis, 5 January 1989, New York City.

[7] Interview, Stuart Pope with Perlis, 6 July 1988, New York City.

through them with us. I mean he went through them from line to line with questions. "Why have we sold this piece more this year than last?" "Can't we do something about the Dance Symphony*?" And so on.*

Aaron's contract had been standard, with his royalties higher than they would be for an unknown or unestablished composer. Not long after I arrived at Boosey & Hawkes' New York office, Aaron's contract was due for renewal. It was in 1965 or 1966, and Aaron's lawyer, Abe Friedman, and I negotiated a rather special deal, under which we took a kind of mercenary attitude, gambling on Aaron's longevity. Not having heirs to be concerned about, he was to receive higher royalties for ten years or life, and on his death, the royalties would drop below normal. (This is, of course, aside from ASCAP, which is the usual 50-50 arrangement.) It has worked out far better for Aaron than for B & H, but they have done very well with Aaron. Everything of Aaron's has been published, so they no longer have major expenses with his music.

We always had a lot to talk about, and most of our meetings were at the Harvard Club. I was a musician, but Aaron really only cared that his publisher be a good businessman, as was Ralph Hawkes, who was not a musician. It is a disappointment to me that so few of the remaining serious music publishers today cannot see the responsibility to do more promotion of their composers—so many publishers take on a piece rather than a composer.

I made an effort to develop the American list at B & H. I inherited two composers and brought ten others in. I recall that Aaron met me on my first visit to Tanglewood. Roger Sessions was with him, and they showed me around. In the course of conversation, I said to both of them, "Who are the young composers I should be hearing?" Sessions said, "Never mind about the younger ones, how about me?! " A year or so later at Tanglewood, Aaron asked, "Do you know the music of Jacob Druckman?" He advised me to hear the concert on which Jacob's Dark Upon the Harp *was being played. I signed Jacob as a B & H composer that very day. Aaron also recommended David Del Tredici and Barbara Kolb. He cared deeply about other peoples' work.*

Copland tried to keep au courant with what was happening in the music world, no easy task at a time when there were many composers and no dominant musical style. His thinking at the time can best be discerned from his own writings. From an unpublished journal entry, when it seems Copland was in an introspective mood (1961):

> On "depth" in music: How can notes—mere notes—project philosophically profound thoughts? And yet, certain composers by comparison with other composers do appear to be more deeply serious, more able to handle "thoughts" that dig deeper, seeming to reflect ideas that evoke a world of philosophy. I have thought of this more than once, curiously enough, while listening to the works of Shostakovich. Whatever else I might say about Shostakovich's many musical qualities, it strikes me that he is not at all the deep thinker in the sense I indicate here. It is all the more strange in that he often puts on the role of the "philosopher," musically speaking. . . . What is "deep" in music? My mind thinks first of all of the *Orgelbuchlein* of Bach. But why are these short organ pieces "deep?" How does Beethoven break "depth" in the slow movements of the late string quartets? Or Mozart or Palestrina or Purcell? It would seem that they touch within each of us some deep well of sensitivity, an area of musical empathy that even their own music does not always reach.These thoughts of mine suggest that when musicians insist that music is "just music," and that one shouldn't attempt to read "meanings" into mere note patterns, they are not probing "deep" enough.

In an unpublished article, "Where Are We?" (1963), Copland compared the contemporary situation to earlier years:

> The preoccupations we had in the twenties find almost no echo today. For example, the desire some of us had to establish America's voice in the context of serious concert music. The use of folk tunes and jazz as a basis for a specifically native music has been completely abandoned. It was established and so it isn't needed any longer.

Copland told Walter Piston (1963), "People always want to shove me into the Americana idea more than I really want. Nobody wants to be an `American' composer now as they did."[8] To another friend, he said, "Young composers today wouldn't be caught dead with a folk tune!"[9] An unpublished typescript, prepared for a lecture in Buenos Aires, "The Aesthetic Climate of Today," shows Copland questioning the validity of music journals that were filled with analyses and theories understandable only to those with scientific knowledge. He wrote (1963), "The composer asks himself whether he ought not go back to school to study physics, acoustics, and higher mathematics, if only to save music from being 'taken over' by the engineers and technicians."

Copland's conducting career was escalating: city orchestras and college groups around the country; European tours almost every year, sometimes twice yearly; Mexico periodically. With London as his European base (where many of Copland's recordings were made), Copland frequently toured elsewhere: Yugoslavia, Portugal, and Spain (spring 1961);[10] Japan (1962); a State Department tour of Latin America (1963), where Copland was surprised

Copland at a recording session, London, c. 1960

[8] From a taped dialogue between Copland and Piston at the Recorded Sound Reference Center, The Library of Congress.
[9] See interview with Paul Moor.
[10] See travel diary #6.

to see many of his old friends;[11] and Israel (1968).[12] When Copland returned from these trips, his mail was awesome. That he continued to answer it all personally is little short of astonishing—the number of requests for Guggenheim Fellowship recommendations alone was staggering!

One of the continuing activities in Copland's life was Tanglewood. For twenty-one years, since 1940, he knew that come spring, it was time to prepare for the upcoming session of the Music Center. Retirement from Tanglewood in 1965 would be a major change, one that was to be accomplished gradually. Tanglewood was Copland's channel to young composers. Teaching was a learning process for him as well as for his students. Copland may have heard more serial music than he might have wished, but by constant exposure, he became genuinely interested in what the system might do for his own music.

Tanglewood was the closest Copland ever had to a steady teaching position. There were many offers, but only one had seriously tempted him: in 1945, William Schuman, recently appointed president of Juilliard, had invited Copland to join the faculty. Copland accepted, but when it came to actually fixing his name to the agreement, he had second thoughts. What Copland wrote to Schuman at that time held true for the rest of Copland's career (2 January 1946):

> I've been having the great inner struggle of all time. At the eleventh hour, faced with the prospect of tying myself down to a thirty-hour-week job, I got the jitters. . . . My deepest inner concern seems to be a need to think of myself as free to move about when and where I please and to let my mind dwell solely on my own music if I happen to feel that way. I hope this won't come as too great a shock. You'll probably think it uncharacteristic of me to not know my own mind for so long but put it down to my real wish to work with you and your own potent charm.

Copland knew that the decision was right for him, but he admitted to feeling a sharp pang of regret when the Juilliard bulletin appeared without his name. Similarly, in 1965, Copland knew the time had come to retire from Tanglewood. He would miss the exposure to young composers at the Music Center, the Berkshires, and his barn in Richmond. 1961 was Copland's last full season at the Music Center;[13] in 1962, when Erich Leinsdorf came in to replace Munch as music director, Copland took a leave of absence, and when he returned, it was on part-time basis. Leonard Burkat left to take a position with Columbia Records, and his assistant, Harry Kraut, took over as administrator of the Music Center.

[11] See travel diary #7.
[12] See travel diary #8.
[13] In 1961, the composition faculty included Roberto Gerhard, Wolfgang Fortner, and Lukas Foss. Copland had three students: Enrique Diaz, Michael Horvit, and Ben-Zion Orgad. In 1962, Iain Hamilton and Witold Lutoslawski taught composition. Ralph Berkowitz filled in as acting chairman of the faculty. For listings of yearly activities, faculty and students, see bound reports, Director's Office, Main House, Tanglewood, prepared at various times by Ralph Berkowitz, Leonard Burkat, Viola Aliferis, and Daniel Gustin.

Harry Kraut[14]

An alienation took place between Aaron and Tanglewood, which everyone tended to blame on Erich Leinsdorf, but actually it preceded him somewhat. In 1960, Aaron went on tour with the BSO to Japan. Aaron enjoyed it no end; the orchestra thought it was about okay, but unfortunately, no one, not even the public, was enthusiastic about Aaron in the role of conductor. Everyone loved him as a composer and was appreciative of what he had done at Tanglewood, but, at the price of inviting him to conduct the BSO, there was great hesitation. So by the time Leinsdorf came on, the decision was already pretty much made: with Aaron embarked on a conducting career, it would be too embarrassing for him to be at Tanglewood but not invited to conduct in the Shed. I was a partisan of Aaron's, because he played a really vital role (that wasn't filled at Tanglewood by Munch) by conducting his own music and other American music. And Leinsdorf had too much of an eye on the box office to want to do an awful lot of American music.

Leinsdorf was deeply interested in the school, if not much interested in Aaron's kind of music. The structure had remained the same all during Munch's time, and it was getting harder each year to maintain a high level of student quality. There was not the volume of good string players then, and many were going to other summer places. They were given the impression by their teachers that if they were really good, God forbid they should show interest in playing in an orchestra! There were not so many good composition students applying, either.

Leinsdorf was given a mandate by the BSO trustees to do something about the Center. My juggling the numbers persuaded them it would not cost that much more money to keep it going. The simple change that was made between 1963 and 1964 was that Paul Fromm's money was used as the main support for the entire performance program, and all the contemporary music activities were melded into the performance program rather than being separate. Fromm approved, agreed, and increased his support. This enabled the underwriting of the new Fellowship Program, and attracted the best students.

Tod Perry stayed through all the changes . . . a remarkable man and a great fan of Aaron's. It was Tod who offered me a full-time job with the BSO in 1958. Beginning as Burkat's assistant, I got to meet with Aaron Copland to discuss the student applications and scores, and was impressed with just sitting in the same room with him! As I came to know him, I saw what we all found—a very nice fellow who would listen to whatever one wanted to discuss—music, management, organization, public relations. Aaron was able to strike right to the core of an issue and set us straight. He was never self-promoting or egotistical about his own work. In fact, very much to the contrary: if someone suggested a whole Copland program, he would recommend incorporating other works.

I hired Dan Gustin as my assistant in 1965, and he carried on the continuity: Dan is also a great Copland admirer. With Ozawa as director, it became a different scene again. Aaron was invited back after he retired, but there were fewer invitations than he might have liked. Perhaps he thought that his friends in the BSO had deserted him, and in fact there were few of them left around Tanglewood, except for Tod, Dan, and myself. The new people were interested in the international music scene rather than anything nationalistic and American. Aaron was having a wonderful time conducting all over the world, and it may have been hard for him to understand why Boston and New York did not pay the same attention to him as a conductor.

[14] Interview, Harry Kraut with Perlis, 26 July 1987, New York City.

Being a good disciple of Aaron Copland and taking his writings on musical meaning seriously, I felt like the wrong guy in the wrong job, trying to like (let alone promote) some of the serial, atonal music better. When William Steinberg came in as director of the Boston Symphony, he wasn't interested at all in the school. I finally left Boston myself to work for Leonard Bernstein in 1971. I remember what Aaron said when I told him I was going to work for Lenny. "Well! That will keep you busy!" I was never quite sure what he meant, but he was right, as usual.

In 1963, when Copland announced to Erich Leinsdorf that he wished to be in residence for the month of August only, Leinsdorf's reaction was "Since you really exploded a bomb by saying you wished to devote only half the summer to Tanglewood, I am most anxious to see you and discuss that problem and what becomes of your position as chairman of the faculty." Copland suggested that Gunther Schuller become acting head of the composition department. In addition to Schuller and Copland, the composition faculty included Foss, Paul Jacobs, and visiting Greek composer Iannis Xenakis from Paris.

After a hiatus in Paul Fromm's involvement during the changeover from Munch to Leinsdorf, fourteen Fromm Players were reinstated in 1963, and Fromm began working toward a major Festival of Contemporary Music to begin the following season.[15] Copland, aware that offerings at the Center in the past were in need of updating, drafted ideas for courses in electronic music, serial techniques, and percussion. In the summer of 1963, David Del Tredici was a composition student at Tanglewood, and Copland recognized in him a special talent.

David Del Tredici[16]

I might be the last composer Aaron supported in a tremendous way. I had just come to New York from California and was floundering around in the usual way. On a lark, I sent a tape of my music to Aaron. A few months later, mysteriously, I received a letter offering me a Fromm commission. So I was off to Tanglewood in 1963 and met for the first time the great man who was to become a friend. To this day, Aaron has never said there was a connection between the tape I sent and the commission, but I have a strong feeling there was.

Aaron was using serialism when I first got to know him. By then, I think he'd tired of his tonal Tender Land *style and serial procedures seemed fresh. The way Aaron made serialism work for him was interesting. He had just written* Connotations, *and in our class, talked about the opening pages. The piece begins with three statements and each gets a little louder than the last. The idea, Aaron said, was to suggest that the music was as loud as it could possibly be each time, while at the same time saving something in reserve for an even stronger second and third repetition. It was a simple concept that made a big impact on me.* No *one had stated musical principles so simply before.*

[15] Fromm support was withdrawn for the Fromm Week at Tanglewood in 1983 and given to the Aspen Festival in 1985; the Fromm Foundation continued to support the Fellowship program at the Tanglewood Music Center.
[16] Video interview, David Del Tredici with Perlis, August 1985 for *Aaron Copland: A Self Portrait*; also, interview with Mark Carrington, December 1981, for Oral History of American Music, Yale.

Copland greeting David Del Tredici in New York City, 1984

Every time I wrote a piece after that summer of 1963, I went with it up to Rock Hill. Aaron would never say much, and often I would have to draw out a comment, but what he did say was always frighteningly accurate. If I played a piece, he'd say something noncommittal at first, such as "It's very nice." Maybe an hour or so later, at dinner, he would turn to me, apropos of nothing, and say, "I think the bass line is too regular, and the percussion should not always underline the main beat and would you pass the butter. . . ." It would always be something I had been worrying about—Aaron was usually right on target and went to the musical core; but he preferred what he said to be by indirection. He didn't ever want to seem to know too much. There was an enigmatic quality to Aaron: his knowing yet not expressing. Aaron was the same way about his own music. If I asked specific questions, he'd be reluctant with answers. Aaron once told me that when he was composing and with a close friend, he'd like to carry on a conversation while continuing to improvise at the piano. I asked him what he got from that, and he said that his musical ideas often took surprising turns, just because part of his brain was casually involved. All Aaron really cared about was what got him to get the music out. It had nothing to do with some regular procedure. It has nothing to do with understanding the process or being able even to describe it. *One day, while talking about the* Piano Concerto, *Aaron said, "No one plays this right." He jumped up and played the opening of the second movement for me. I realized when I heard him that there was no way to write it down exactly as he played. It was so idiosyncratic—like trying to write down a jazz improvisation; there's no notational equivalent.*

Aaron was nurtured by the French school, but he didn't have the terrifically quick ear that is supposed to be part of French compositional technique. Lenny has it. Aaron had of course a wonderful ear, but it didn't show in any facile way. My ear is more like Aaron's—very different when I am composing than when I am not. (One's ear gets good when it must.) When Aaron is through with the struggle of composing a piece, he sort of floats away from it—disengages. Maybe it's been too personal, too upsetting. Or maybe he's just glad to be rid of it! Also, Aaron never seemed to be much of a reviser. Because I revised an awful lot when I was younger, I asked Aaron about himself, hoping to make myself feel better. Aaron's reply, however, was simply that he worked on a piece until he was satisfied and rarely felt the need to revise afterward.

Aaron conducted one of my earliest orchestral pieces, The Lobster Quadrille, *in London on November 25, 1969, while he was on a conducting tour of Europe. I went over the score with him beforehand and he was very open to suggestions. As might be expected, he had none of the typical conductorial vanities.*

When people ask me who influenced me, I always say Aaron. Ironically though, when critics accuse me of sounding like this or that composer, they have yet to mention Aaron! I suppose it was not so much his music that shows up in mine, but his way of dealing with music and composing that had a profound effect on me. Aaron trusted his musical instincts completely. He was untouched by academic ways. He never let the enormous effort of composition show. It all just seemed to happen. "Remember, David, it is the illusion of inevitability that we are all after, as though all those notes just fell from heaven." I have tried to emulate that.

In 1964, Copland spent only the month of August in the Berkshires. He relinquished his position as head of the composition department at Tanglewood to Gunther Schuller. Thirteen composition students were taught by Copland, Schuller, Foss, Jacobs, and Berger. As usual, a few Copland works were performed by students and by the BS0.[17] The Fromm Fellows now numbered twenty-two, and Fromm supported a group of nine composers to be commissioned for works to be performed in the week-long Festival of Contemporary Music. The "Fromm Week," supervised by Schuller, became an important annual event in contemporary music. After the first festival, critic Eric Salzman wrote, "For once, the composers really are young . . . and all but a couple have something to say. There's talent in these here hills and there's a music of the future and it's here right now."[18] A feature of the festival in 1964 was a panel of five composers, with Copland as moderator, discussing "Problems of Materials."

A festive dinner was held after the gala concert celebrating Tanglewood's twenty-fifth year, which opened with *Fanfare for the Common Man* and included *Outdoor Overture.* Lukas Foss wrote to Copland afterward (18 September), "I knew then that it was a farewell dinner as well. . . . Sad as it is for Tanglewood, I cannot blame you. Enough is enough. Your time will be spent better without all that summer activity." In 1965, the "Fromm Week" featured music by composers who had attended the Music Center in past summers. One of the highlights was a retrospective Copland concert (17 August).[19] During intermission, Leinsdorf announced Copland's retirement from the Music Center and the appointment of Gunther Schuller, age thirty-nine, as head of contemporary music and composition. The thirty-three-year-old concertmaster of the BSO, Joseph Silverstein, was named chairman of the faculty. Many in the audience viewed Copland's retirement as the end of an era at Tanglewood. He was given a standing ovation, but he made no speech of farewell, choosing to allow his music to speak for him.

[17] Copland works performed in 1962: *Violin Sonata, Outdoor Overture* (students), *Quiet City* (BSO under Munch); 1963: *El Salón México, Music for the Theatre, Sextet* (Fromm Players), *Two Pieces for String Quartet* (Juilliard Quartet); 1964: "As It Fell Upon a Day;" four *Dickinson Songs; Music for the Theatre* (students); 1965: *Music for a Great City* (BSO under Leinsdorf).

[18] Eric Salzman, "Music," *Herald Tribune,* 23 August 1964, 23.

[19] The five pieces were "As It Fell Upon a Day," *Vitebsk, Sextet, In The Beginning,* and *The Piano Fantasy.*

A reception to celebrate Copland's recording contract with Columbia Records, at Leonard Burkat's apartment, New York City, 28 April 1964. (*Left to right*): Bernstein, Burkat, Copland, and Felicia Bernstein

Copland wanted to spend more time on the recording of his music. He recognized the importance of recordings to a composer's career, and he always tried to accommodate his schedule when a recording opportunity was involved. Leonard Burkat's new position at Columbia Records was fortunate for Copland; Burkat saw to it that Copland's music was systematically recorded by Columbia. He said, "Aaron's series of Columbia Masterworks Records was something I thought up when I was head of the label. It was approved by the president, Goddard Lieberson, and produced by John McClure. Public announcement was made (28 April 1964) in my apartment with press and lots of friends from the music world in attendance."[20]

Copland received major awards in the sixties, among them the Edward MacDowell Medal for lifetime achievement (1961) and the Medal of Freedom (1964). Among the honorary degrees,[21] one from Harvard in 1961 was especially meaningful, considering Copland's long association with the university. Also in 1961, Copland was voted president of the MacDowell Colony, a position he held until 1967. Toward the end of the decade, two books about Copland for young readers were published.[22]

[20] See interview with Leonard Burkat. Among the composers present were Babbitt, Bernstein, Carter, Diamond, and Mennin.

[21] Degrees received by Copland in the sixties were Harvard (1961); Syracuse, Michigan, Rhode Island (1964); Kalamazoo College (1965); Utah (1966); Jacksonville, Rutgers (1967); Fairfield (1968); Peabody Institute (1969).

[22] Arnold Dobrin, *Aaron Copland: His Life and Times* (New York: Thomas Y. Crowell, 1967); and Catherine Owens Peare, *Aaron Copland: his Life* (New York: Holt, Rhinehart and Winston, 1969).

Following the brief glory years for the arts during the Kennedy administration, contemporary American music retreated to its familiar position: a sharp division between popular music (almost completely rock by the end of the sixties) and concert music (serial, electronic, and chance operations). Diversification and experimentation continued to an extent, but the best of Kennedy's intentions to create an atmosphere of artistic and academic freedom ended with the student riots of 1968. Many composers, who depended on university positions, suddenly found themselves in uncertain and unsympathetic situations. Small groups were formed in the cities to promote the performance of contemporary music. Not unlike the 1920s and 1930s, they drew from the limited segment of the population that had a particular interest in new music.

Young composers were not very much interested in Copland's music. Paul Moor described the difference between going to concerts with Copland in the sixties and what it had been earlier:

> In the forties Aaron was like a magnet and had to stay in his seat for fear of being overwhelmed at intermission, but not so, later on. At one concert of his music in the sixties, Copland commented almost wistfully, "Do you realize that there is not a single young composer in the audience!"[23]

[23] See interview with Paul Moor.

Leonard Bernstein recalls a similar remark from Copland backstage after he conducted the premiere of Copland's *Inscape* in 1967. Bernstein said, "I recognized that as the moment Aaron really stopped composing."[24]

Removed as young composers might have felt from Copland as the generation gap widened, they looked to him with wonder: an American composer whose music got played regularly by the major orchestras, almost all of it recorded; a composer making a substantial living from being a musician without a regular teaching position. If Copland was no longer the enormous influence he had been on younger composers in terms of actual composition, he was a role model, an example of the good citizen in music, a man tolerant and open to what others might want to do.

No one replaced Copland as the leader among younger composers. Perhaps a single figure was no longer appropriate or necessary. But the enduring qualities in Copland's music and the stability of his personality took on special meaning in the fast-changing, violent sixties, when values changed from day to day and heroes disappeared as suddenly and quickly as the shot of a gun.

[24] Bernstein to Perlis, 6 February 1989.

Copland leading the London Philharmonic in a concert of his works as well as those by Ives, Barber, and Harris. Daytona Beach, Florida, 16 August 1966

THE MUSIC WITHIN

1961 - 1969

Early in 1961, a young director by the name of Jack Garfein approached me about composing the music for his film *Something Wild.* I explained how busy I was, and so forth, but Garfein said, "Please! Just see it before you decide." Well, the film was already shot, and I was curious and thought it couldn't hurt just to see it before refusing. I went to United Artists and sat in the projection room watching this unusual production. It was so vivid that it gripped my imagination. Then I saw it a second time. Garfein was so eager for me to compose the score that he agreed to anything I asked—yes, he was willing to wait until I had an opening in my schedule; yes, he would supply a Moviola so I could work at home in Peekskill; and yes, he would hire wonderful musicians, almost twice as many as was usual for a film. Finally, I agreed to spend about six weeks on the score and to supervise the recording.

Something Wild was my eighth film score and the first since *The Heiress* twelve years earlier.[1] I had been offered seven movies during that time, but none seemed to give opportunity for musical treatment that could serve the picture in a meaningful way. In my view, Garfein's film had that potential. Based on a novel, *Mary Ann*, by Alex Karmel, *Something Wild* was adapted for the screen by Karmel and Garfein, produced by Prometheus, an independent company, in collaboration with United Artists. In the starring role of Mary Ann Gates was the young and beautiful actress Carroll Baker (Garfein's wife), who had made a big hit in the movie *Baby Doll.* Ralph Meeker was Mike, the co-star in this psychological drama set in New York City. Also in the cast were Mildred Dunnock as the girl's mother and Jean Stapleton in the role of a prostitute.

Something Wild was about feelings—the loneliness and despair of a young girl learning to live with violence—and it was about the moods of the city; in fact, the original title of the film had been *Something Wild in the City.* The story was basic: On the way home from school choir practice one summer evening, young Mary Ann is raped. She runs away from home and exchanges her safe, ordinary life for a job in a chain store and a room in a squalid part of the city. When she attempts a suicide jump from a bridge, she is saved by a man who then offers her the spare bed in his basement room. He keeps her a prisoner, something like Beauty and the Beast. By the end, they have fallen in love and get married.

Something Wild had lengthy stretches of silent action without dialogue, which invited musical comment in a way that imbues the whole picture with a certain musical "tone." It goes without saying that the composer must have a free hand for this kind of score. Jack Garfein assured me of this, as did George Justin, the producer assigned to the film from United Artists.

In most films, the composer's prime opportunity comes at the very beginning, for the so-called "title music." The composer is expected to do his best work accompanying the long list of screen credits. At this point, the audience, of course, knows nothing about the film but its name. In the case of *Something Wild*, I was given something more tangible, since the title and credits were superimposed on action shots of the city and on some drawings. I had the chance to compose the equivalent of a big-city profile. The opening chord taken by itself was meant to give a sense of power and tension. I worked on that chord to make it sum up what the picture is all about.

Having been shot on location in New York City, the film was interspersed with every variety of city noise—trucks, taxis, subways, police sirens, slum kids shouting. In one scene I tried to outshout a bulldozer and bridge traffic. It proved a hopeless task, so I decided to work with the sounds by allowing the percussion to improvise along with it. For the bucolic scenes set in Central Park, I also had to use some ingenuity. Take, for example, the segment where our star is discovered asleep in the park in the early hours, against a background of skyscrapers. What I tried for there were pastoral sounds edged with a steely quality, hoping thereby to suggest the country in the midst of the city.

The most difficult hurdle of all in *Something Wild* was keeping the audience guessing as to the underlying emotions and intentions of the two principal characters. For much of the film, we don't know what their relationship implies. The trouble with music is that when it speaks, it can tell too much. I had to exercise continual discretion in order not to give away the real motives of the characters too soon. It is comparatively easy to reflect physical action in musical terms; more challenging are those moments when one attempts

[1] The Copland text on *Something Wild* here is adapted from an unpublished article of December 1961, "Composing for Something Wild." Also in Copland's files is a page with two measures marked "Violent/ Apr 21 '47/ used in 'Something Wild'and miscellaneous sketch pages. Materials at the Library of Congress include a reproduction of the conducting score with autograph pencil markings, complete piano score marked "short version" and dated "Apr-Sept 10, 1961," and cue sheets with timings.

to think unspoken thoughts musically. *Something Wild* took the question even further: what consecutive thoughts, such as when Ralph Meeker returns to his apartment one night completely drunk? Natural musical sequences would not convey the foggy, disjointed nature of his mental processes. I decided on an unconventional solution: unexpected silences that abruptly disconnect the musical texture. When we recorded that scene, the musicians were perplexed at why they were expected to stop and start so fitfully. Another scene where I made explicit use of silence was the rape of the heroine. Garfein was surprised when he heard what I intended, but he went along with it. I thought that the girl's shock suggested a kind of "stop dead" treatment. I wrote about that in my diary at the time:[2]

> Study clinical reaction to rape. The music, if possible, should enter and leave curiously; as if in a series of non sequiturs (somewhat "confused" perhaps.) The sudden outbursts of shouted dialogue may well be reflected in sudden bursts of music, like a radio turned on too loud. A moment of discomfort for the audience, followed by relief at return of normal sound levels.

David Walker, as a composer familiar with electronic music techniques, was copying out the orchestration for me. I suggested to him that the score could possibly be enhanced by a few electronic segments subtly layered over the orchestral sound. A perfect spot was the scene on the bridge when Carroll Baker is close to throwing herself into the swirling water. David composed two or three electronic sections and played them for me while we were at Tanglewood in 1961. Unfortunately, Garfein vetoed the idea for financial reasons.[3] He had agreed so readily until then to everything I requested, I could not insist.

Jack Garfein[4]

The famous literary agent Audrey Wood brought Mary Ann *to me. From the first reading, it had an emotional impact. I kept thinking about that girl. The idea of invisible forces in the city and how they affect a person fascinated me. I optioned the book and started on the script myself. I was thirty-one years old and had done only one other film. It was difficult to convince Hollywood to support such a film, but finally United Artists agreed, if we could do it on an acceptably low budget.*

Usually you choose the composer before shooting a film, but I knew that the music would give the viewer a sense of the soul of this girl and that we needed to find a great composer. Someone recommended Morton Feldman, and we met a few times and Morty played some music for me, but I couldn't imagine his kind of music for this story. I got in touch with Aaron Copland, and although he was all booked up with his own projects, I convinced him to see the film. It was one of the first screenings I ever had for anyone, and was I nervous! I was completely in awe of Copland. He said he liked it and would think about it: "Call me tomorrow." When I called, Copland told me he couldn't get the film out of his head, but if we wanted him, we would have to wait six months and pay a hefty fee. The music costs came to almost ten percent of the budget—unheard of then. United Artists thought it was insane, but it worked out in an unusual way. Carroll [Baker] was by then a star at Warner Brothers. She wanted Aaron also, and she agreed to guarantee his fee through her contract at Warners.

Above: Copland at the Moviola with director Jack Garfein, discussing *Something Wild*, Peekskill, 1961

Right: Garfein, Carroll Baker, and Copland in the recording booth

Aaron and I went over the script together, and he put me at ease by asking questions that I hesitated to answer. I was afraid he would compose something just to please me. When I told Aaron that, he just laughed and said, "Don't worry. I've never done anything just to please someone." Only at one point did we disagree. That was the rape scene, where Aaron said, "No music here. Not until she gets home." That turned out to be absolutely masterful. And in the drunk scene, where Aaron wanted the music to stop and start abruptly, I at first thought it was mirroring the action too much, but again, his instincts were dead right.

We shipped the Moviola up to Peekskill and Aaron got to work. I only talked to him twice during the six months. Once he called to ask about the segment when the girl escapes from the apartment and wakes up in Central Park: he thought there should be contrasting music between the park and the city, and wanted to discuss it with me. The next time he called, it was to tell me the score was ready and would I come up to Peekskill to hear him play through some of it on the piano. I couldn't get the sense of it at all from that, but Aaron just said, "Don't worry. We'll take care of everything at the recording session. Whatever time you give me, we'll do it with corrections and everything."

[2] "Notes on Making a Movie Score" in Copland journal # 6 (March 1961) includes a listing of various scenes and a script with inserts of musical ideas and remarks about the score and film.
[3] David Walker to Perlis.
[4] Interview, Jack Garfein with Perlis, 7 May 1987, New York City.

Copland conducting the film score of *Something Wild,* 1961

I was so taken just seeing Aaron Copland conducting for my film and listening to the music that I had to remind myself to pay attention to the screen. Every decision Aaron made was right—his timings, his use of the real city sounds. Extraordinary. Somehow Aaron had locked into the girl's feelings and touched on some things I couldn't express in the film. It is not too much to say that Aaron made me realize things about my life I had not confronted.

Carroll Baker[5]

When Jack and I formed our production company, Prometheus, *it was at a time when films were beginning to cost a great deal. Movie studios wanted some low-budget films. One of our ideas was to make a quality film in New York City and bring it in with a budget of about $100,000. We made the deal through United Artists, and if we wanted anything beyond actual production costs, we had to go to them and ask. It was Jack's idea that Aaron Copland could add something specifically to a story about New York City. When Copland showed an interest, it was partly because New York was like another character in the story. Copland named his price and we went to United Artists, but they did not feel that such a film as ours warranted a pricey big-name composer. We wanted Copland so much that I agreed United Artists could take my services as collateral: I would have to make a film for them for whatever amount* Something Wild *went over budget. I actually ended up having to do* Mister Moses *with Robert Mitchum in Africa in exchange for Copland's fee for* Something Wild! *But at the time, I was very happy to find a way for Copland to do it.*

[5] Interview, Carroll Baker with Perlis (telephone), 10 June 1987.

In all truthfulness, I do not believe that the story was quite as strong as it should have been. It was a mood piece more than an exciting story. If one takes on something like this, it is usually a financial loss. That style of film was something the French had an easier time selling. In America, you either hit success immediately with a film or it's dead. But we believed in it and were not in it for the money. Our producer, George Justin, used to laugh at me about the fact that I did not feel free to use the hairdresser, and he'd say, "Carroll was in there counting the bobby pins." I had never been to a recording session before, and I was ecstatic at what the music added to the film. Afterward, I went over to Mr. Copland and told him what I felt: "Your music makes me a wonderful actress."

A limousine arrived each day to take David Walker and me to the Fine Studios in Bayside, Long Island, where I conducted and recorded the sound track. Four television monitors were placed around the room so the musicians could follow the action and mood as we played. In three days, we recorded 40 minutes of music, a little more than one-third of the total 100-minute film. United Artists wanted to invite representatives from the record companies to these sessions, but I suggested we play tapes for them afterward. When *Something Wild* was ready for its first screening in New York, the music was played at a high level to emphasize my involvement to the press.

Something Wild met with mixed reviews. Bosley Crowther, film critic of *The New York Times*, found the story unconvincing. He claimed it was hard to believe that a girl like Mary Ann would not find one person to sympathize with her in the whole city of New York. *Something Wild* was a commercial flop, probably because it was ahead of its time, although serious filmgoers recognized its remarkable qualities. Garfein and Miss Baker were awfully disappointed. Harold Clurman wrote a review for *Show* magazine, claiming that it was the only existentialist film in the United States, but the magazine's editor refused to run it, and Harold told me later that he always felt guilty about not insisting.

United Artists refused to record my music after the film was released. It seems that they never thought the film had a chance commercially. I asked Garfein to set up a meeting with the producers and told them, "Every recording of mine has been successful and has made money." But when the head of the music department was called in for an opinion, he said, "It won't sell." Garfein asked what kind of music was selling, and the response was, *Birdman of Alcatraz*. When we went down in the elevator from that meeting, I told Jack, "Don't worry. I will do whatever I can about the music."

I retrieved the rights to my score from United Artists and had a studio recording made of the sound track. A copy was sent to Senator Jacob Javits, because after seeing the film, he had written:

> I wanted to let you know how much we loved the score of the Carroll Baker movie, *Something Wild*. It would be wonderful if it could be made into a symphonic suite called "New York"—what could I do to help bring that dream into reality? If you'd let me know, I'd do my best to do it.

As it turned out, the music for *Something Wild* was not used for New York, but to satisfy a commission I had received from the London Symphony Orchestra for a piece in honor of their sixtieth anniversary season in 1964. I wrote to Ernest Fleishmann, manager of the LSO: "My intention is to incorporate parts of the film score in a new composition composed for the L.S., somewhat in the manner of Vaughan Williams in his *Antarctica Symphony*, in which work he also makes use of previously composed film material." Fleishmann agreed, but when I sent the title, "Music for New York," he countered with, "How about *Symphony No. 4*?" We compromised, choosing the title *Music for a Great City*. I felt that the music could be thought to portray any large city, even though it had been composed with New York in mind: to me the "great" in the title meant large and noisy. In any case, I did not intend to follow the cinematic action of *Something Wild* when adapting the music for the London commission.[6]

The four movements of *Music for a Great City* alternate between evocations of big-city life with its external stimuli and personal reactions to the city experiences. The first movement, *Skyline*, opens with a broad introduction for full orchestra, followed by a percussion solo to introduce the jazz-oriented theme presented by brass, piano, and pizzicato strings. For the second movement, *Night Thoughts*, I reduced the full orchestra scoring to chamber music orchestra for what might be called a series of free contrapuntal variations. The reality of big city life returns in the third movement scherzo, *Subway Jam*, which, as one might suspect, includes a great deal of brass and percussion. (One reviewer wrote, "There is not a string player to be found in this rush-hour crowd.") The final movement, *Toward the Bridge*, presents contrasting ideas, some jazz-inspired, that build to a big climax, followed by a coda with material from the introduction to the first movement. *Music for a Great City* calls for an extra complement of percussion, such as slapstick, cowbells, sandpaper, maracas, ratchet, and conga drum. The work is dedicated to the members of the London Symphony Orchestra.[7]

Before the premiere, Victor Kraft met me in London. He was to take photographs of the preparations for the premiere, to be used along with interviews and rehearsals for a television documentary by the BBC. From the time we arrived in London, the director, Humphrey Burton, had the cameras follow us everywhere. I found the LSO responsive and well prepared. They had looked at their parts in advance and the general atmosphere was of keen interest. In addition to the new piece, I conducted Stravinsky's *Ode*, Britten's *Sinfonia da Requiem*, my *Lincoln Portrait*, with Sam Wanamaker narrating, and the *Clarinet Concerto*, with Gervase de Peyer. I described the concert, which took place at Festival Hall, 26 May 1964, in my journal:

> The LSO played a beautiful Britten [he sent a wire from Aldeburgh]. They seemed to be playing both for me and with me. De Peyer did an excellent *Clar. Concerto*. Wanamaker couldn't be heard in the *LP* (mike mismanagement), and he muffed one whole section. (Oy!) Rapt attention during the *Ode*. The new piece was very well played, much public enthusiasm at the end. All-round my best public appearance as conductor thus far.

The audience gave a terrific ovation, so I was a little surprised when I saw in the papers the next morning that the critics were not thoroughly pleased. They thought I had not done myself justice by playing the more popular side of my output. If they only knew how programs are really made! Sure enough, every critic mentioned that the precise locale of the "great city" in the title was Manhattan, not London.

A few weeks after the premiere, I recorded the piece with the LSO for Columbia Records (John McClure in charge), together with *Statements for Orchestra*. Reviewers gave varying opinions of *Music for a Great City*, but all agreed that the fresh recording of *Statements* was welcome. On my last day in London, I saw the BBC documentary and was pleased with the editing. I commented at the time, "One watches oneself for sixty minutes and is never quite the same. A rare form of egomania results!"

I conducted the London Symphony for the American premiere of *Music for a Great City* at Constitution Hall, Washington, D.C. (13 October 1964), and Antal Dorati conducted it with the BBC Symphony Orchestra at Carnegie Hall (15 May 1965). Howard Klein wrote in *The New York Times*: "It is tight as a drum and a potently dramatic work . . . it reflects the anxiety and tension of the present." *Music for a Great City* did not catch on quickly. I was reminded again how much the fate of a work depends on the circumstances surrounding its launching. A work composed for a special occasion is not as likely to be taken up by conductors for regular programs. I programmed *Music for a Great City* whenever I could—it seemed to have a freshness, but that may be precisely because it was not played as often as my other works.

The offer of a commission from the New York Philharmonic to compose a work for performance at the opening concert in its new home sparked my writing *Connotations for Orchestra*. It was the first purely symphonic work since my *Third Symphony* of 1947. I worked on sketches during 1961, and promised myself to stay home in 1962 for uninterrupted composing time. But I could not resist an invitation to return to Japan for a State Department conference at the beginning of the year to be combined with conducting in Seattle and Vancouver. To gain some composing time, I took leave from Tanglewood in 1962. As I wrote to Chávez (25 June): "I am working day and night on my symphony for the Philharmonic commission. It is in three movements and I have just finished the last, the first being more than half done." Chávez invited me to Mexico for some conducting, but mostly to continue composing. From there, I wrote to Leo Smit (4 July), "I'm not finished with my piece and so I have a very hectic five weeks ahead of me after my return from Mexico, Rio, and Montevideo. Damn! Having a hell of a time trying to find a title, and they need it tomorrow."

Connotations was completed just in time for orchestra rehearsals. Carlos Moseley, then managing director of the New York Philharmonic, wrote (12 September 1962), "My sigh of relieved joy at hearing from you that the work is completed was probably registered on seismographs throughout the Northern Hemisphere."

Knowing that other music on the gala Philharmonic program would represent earlier and more traditional aspects of musical culture, I preferred to compose a work expressing something of the tensions, aspirations, and drama inherent in contemporary living. I have frequently been asked why I decided to make use of twelve-tone principles in this particular

6 See Copland's files for rough pencil sketches identified as "concert suite from *Something Wild*."
7 Copland's description here of *Music for a Great City* derives from his program notes of 1964.

Manuscript, first page from the sketch of *Connotations*

work. I can only say that the method seemed appropriate for my purpose. I had used it for my *Piano Quartet* of 1950 and again in 1957 for the *Piano Fantasy* and both seemed to work. In those two works, the row is first presented as a theme; in *Connotations*, the row is first heard vertically in terms of three four-voiced chords with, needless to add, no common tones. When spelled out horizontally, these chords supplied me with various versions of a more lyrical discourse.[8]

After I wrote to David Diamond about *Connotations*, he responded from Italy (14 August 1962): "Is it a variation form? It will confuse some, I am sure, and wish you could come up with a better title. It's not—it seems to me—even provoking as a title—and somewhat forced, no?" An early sketch reminds me that my temporary working title had been *Music for a New Hall,* and that other titles had been considered.[9] The dictionary states that the verb connote means "to imply," to signify meanings "in addition to the primary meaning." In the case of *Connotations*, I explained (to David Diamond, and to Chávez, who thought the title too abstract) that the skeletal frame of the row is the "primary meaning;" it denotes the area of exploration. The subsequent treatment seeks out other implications—connotations that come in a flash or connotations that I might have only gradually uncovered. The listener, on the other hand, is free to discover his or her own connotative meanings, including perhaps some not suspected by the author.

The twenty-minute work was dedicated to the members of the New York Philharmonic and to its music director, Leonard Bernstein. It is scored for large orchestra, including a percussion group of five performers to deal with various special percussion effects and a piano solo. David Diamond had not been far off in speculating about the structure of *Connotations*, which comes closest to a free treatment of the baroque form of the chaconne with a succession of variations, based on the opening chords and their implied melodic intervals, supplying the basic framework. The variations are sometimes recognizably separate, one from another, sometimes not. As in the *Orchestral Variations,* the problem was to construct an overall line that had continuity, dramatic force, and an inherent unity. It has been pointed out many times that the dodecaphonic method supplies the building blocks but does not create the edifice. The composer must do that.[10]

The gala opening week of Lincoln Center's Philharmonic Hall (later Avery Fisher Hall) featured thirteen concerts (23-30 September 1962). The first program was conducted by Bernstein and included works by Beethoven, Vaughan Williams, Mahler, and my *Connotations.*

[8] At the Library of Congress: rough pencil sketches dated "1961-62" that include a theme labeled "violent" and dated "Feb 10/60"; sketches of tone rows; a page marked "10/20/61 for end/sudden entrance piano allegretto/violent"; and an open score sketch (complete) with titles on the verso dated "Sept 11, '62."

[9] Other titles considered were *Chaconne for Orchestra* (on 3 four-voiced chords); *Connotations and Distillations; Pregnancies; Composition No. 80; Chaconne on 3 four-voiced Chords; Symphonic Connotations;* and *Orchestral Connotations.*

[10] The description here is quoted from Copland's program notes for the premiere. See also Peter Evans, "Copland on the Serial Road, An Analysis of *Connotations*," *Perspectives of New Music* 2 (Spring—Summer 1964), 141-149, and Evans, "Copland's *Connotations*, a Review of the First Performance," *Tempo*, no. 64 (Spring 1963), 30-33.

Above: Copland discussing the score of *Connotations* with Bernstein at rehearsal for the premiere at Philharmonic Hall (later named Avery Fisher Hall), New York City, 1962

Left: Jacqueline Kennedy and Copland backstage at Philharmonic Hall after the premiere of *Connotations*

In the fourth concert of the celebration week, *Lincoln Portrait* was performed with Adlai Stevenson narrating and Eugene Ormandy conducting.

Since Philharmonic Hall was the first of the Lincoln Center complex to be completed, the opening concert was a momentous occasion, happening amid gaping holes and construction rubble. The Metropolitan Opera House was no more than an excavation. There would be other openings, but this being the first, was special. There was an air of glamour

and excitement as an imposing array of national and international celebrities arrived by limousine. They included John D. Rockefeller III (chairman of Lincoln Center), Jacqueline Kennedy (looking particularly stunning), Secretary of State Dean Rusk, Governor and Mrs. Nelson Rockefeller, Mayor Wagner, and many other dignitaries. Harold Schonberg of *The New York Times* wrote the following day, "It was a highly formal audience, the kind that quite naturally said, 'There's Jackie,' or 'There's Adlai'—not because it was namedropping, but because to this audience they are Nelson, Jackie and Adlai."

General agreement was that the premiere was not a congenial circumstance for *Connotations for Orchestra.* It was an occasion when the music was not as important as the hall itself; the interest was on acoustical sound. The critics also were less involved with the music than with questions such as: "Did the sound work?" "Was it as good as Carnegie?" and so forth. I had not wanted to present something bland and traditional for this occasion and to such a distinguished audience. My gesture was not appreciated at the time: *Connotations* was not what was expected. The piece does have, after all, a rather severe and somewhat intellectual tone, but my hope was that it is also intense and dramatic. When it was over, a confused near silence ensued.

The evening's gala tone quickly resumed and it all ended with champagne being served to the entire audience of 2,588 guests. Leo Smit told me afterward that he was impressed when Governor Rockefeller shook his hand, until he realized that the governor didn't know who he was and was shaking everyone's hand, campaign style! I had arranged for my closest friends and family to attend, and Laurine wrote afterward, "I still haven't come down to earth. It was most exciting for us to be there in person." The event was televised by NBC and broadcast nationwide.[11] I was asked to speak to the television audience while the cameras alternated between me and a shot of the music manuscript. I said:

> It seems to me that there are two things you can do when listening to any new work. The most important thing is to lend yourself—or to put it another way—try to be as sensitive as you can to the overall feeling the new piece gives off. The second way is to listen with some awareness of the general shape of the new piece, realizing that a composer works with his musical materials just as an architect works with his building materials in order to construct an edifice that makes sense. Let me show you the opening manuscript page of my *Connotations for Orchestra.* At the very start, you will hear three rather harsh-sounding brass chords that climax almost immediately into silence. Each of these three chords contain four different tones, so that they add up to the twelve tones of the chromatic scale. These form the basic working materials of the entire composition. Later on, after a passage for the solo piano, the tension subsides. At this point you should watch for the moment when all the strings of the orchestra except for the basses, sing these same twelve tones as a melodic line. Here you have a page of my score as illustration. These are the same tones as those in my three primary chords, spelled out horizontally. In listening to the work as a whole, some of you may wonder why I chose to create a work that reflects drama and tension and even desperation on so gala an occasion as this. The

[11] "Opening Night at Lincoln Center," broadcast from 9 to 11 P.M., produced by Robert Saudek and hosted by Alistair Cooke; intermission featured interviews with Governor Nelson Rockefeller and William Schuman, President of Lincoln Center.

> reason is simple: in inaugurating this beautiful new hall, I wanted to remind our listeners that we are dedicating it not only to the rehearing of the great music of the past but also to the more challenging music of our own day. I wanted to speak in a musical idiom of our own day in a hall of our own making.

To my great surprise, my little talk was interpreted by some as an apology for the piece. I certainly did not mean it that way. Moreover, I was surprised at the vehemence of the letters that began to arrive from across the country after the broadcast. For example: "If last night is any criterion of what can be expected in Lincoln Center, it should be called 'Center of Jungle Culture';" "Dear Mr. Copland, Shame Shame Shame!" *Connotations* did not fare quite so poorly with the critics. Louis Biancolli wrote in the *New York World Telegram,* "It struck me as a turning point in his career, a powerful score in twelve-tone style that has liberated new stores of creative energy." John Molleson wrote in the *Herald Tribune*:

> This is a difficult work and like most music difficult to understand at one hearing . . . this listener had the feeling that these connotations are couched in terms of a present crisis over what to do with serialism. But this piece has flesh where others have only skin, and there was a good deal of arresting lyricism.

Virgil Thomson commented that counterpoint was totally lacking in *Connotations*. I wrote to him (27 November 1962), saying, "You must have been in a homophonic mood not to have heard the pages of two-part counterpoint in the fast section (and sometimes maybe even three-part)."[12] Reviewers had only praise for Lenny's conducting of the entire program.

Connotations was certainly not an immediate success, but then, I did not expect it to be. I had gone through this kind of thing earlier in my career and was not concerned about the piece itself in the long run, although I did make some minor modifications after the premiere. I am reminded that once, when crossing the Atlantic several decades earlier, I was approached by a fellow passenger. "Mr. Copland," he announced, "I don't like your music." "Well," I said, "I don't think any more highly of you for that!" No matter how much recognition I have received, there always have been my tough pieces I can't seem to sell to audiences. There were at least some who understood my intentions with the new piece. Claire Reis, who attended a rehearsal in addition to the premiere, and Minna Daniel, who wrote to me afterward:

> I think *Connotations* was exactly the right piece for the place and occasion— indeed the only one properly related to them. It sounds a good deal like certain aspects of the building—big, spacious, clear, long-lined, and it sounds very like you . . . To those familiar with your music, the characteristic, identifying moods are perfectly apparent. The special Copland eloquence is there.

Marc Blitzstein wrote from Bennington College, where he was teaching, that he was "all for *Connotations* as a work, and as a picture of growth. It makes me happy." Composer Bill Flanagan wrote (1 February):

> You were swallowed up by the blue and gold reaches of Philharmonic Hall yesterday before I had the chance to tell you how glad I was finally to hear *Connotations* . . . the work makes perfect sense to me; I reject the Total Gloom descriptions that I've heard. . . . I think it's an impressively vital and absorbing piece of music.

Lenny programmed *Connotations* again a few months after the premiere for the regular Philharmonic subscription concerts during the first week of 1963, and on the orchestra's February tour in London. The European premiere was more successful than the New York reception. Lenny explained at a press conference, "*Connotations* is Copland looking back at earlier works from the vantage of 1962—and the 1962 point of view is a twelve-tone one." In response to the lengthy ovation after the piece in London, Lenny announced he would conduct another Copland work. To cries of "Oh oh," he said, "But this will be a very different style." He then conducted "Hoe-Down" from *Rodeo*.

I conducted *Connotations* myself in 1966, 1967, and 1968 around the United States, including the Musica Viva series in San Francisco, the Baltimore Symphony, the National Symphony in Washington, and the Buffalo Philharmonic. I spoke to the audiences with humorous accounts of the work's adverse effect on droves of letter writers, who had heard the original performance, in person or on TV. Then I asked the brass section to illustrate the opening chords, and the strings to show how they sounded. Before they knew it, the audience was sympathetic. My purpose was not to sell the work but to demonstrate it.

Connotations was recorded on the commemorative album of the opening of Lincoln Center, along with an impressive booklet containing articles and photographs (Lenny recorded *Connotations* again in 1973 with the Philharmonic for Columbia, paired with my 1967 *Inscape* and Elliott Carter's *Concerto for Orchestra*.)

A decade after the premiere, Pierre Boulez conducted *Connotations* with the New York Philharmonic (1973-1974). The auspices were similar, but ten years had changed audience perception enough so that *Connotations*' revival was a different story. In a review in *The New York Times* headed "'62 Copland Piece Gets Cheers This Time," Harold Schonberg wrote, "Connotations is Boulez' kind of music." Nevertheless, the piece is not programmed often. After a 1987 hearing at Juilliard's "Focus!" series at Tully Hall conducted by Joel Sachs, critic John Rockwell stated, "*Connotations* holds up very well indeed—a genuinely powerful piece that once again reveals Mr. Copland's exploration of Serialism to have been an extension, not a denial of his musical personality."

Choreographer John Neumier asked for permission to use *Connotations* for a ballet, *Der Fall Hamlet* (*The Hamlet Affair*), in which he would also use some of the *Piano Variations*. Baryshnikov danced Hamlet, and other stars danced various parts: Marcia Haydee, Gelsey Kirkland, and Erik Bruhn. The world premiere was by the Ballet Theatre (6 January 1976). Despite the impressive roster of dancers, the ballet was not successful and has not been staged again.

Soon after the Philharmonic premiere of *Connotations*, I accepted an invitation to participate in a Latin American conference at the Huntington Hartford estate in Nassau, and I admit to using it as an excuse to recover from the excitement and to celebrate my sixty-second birthday by basking in the sun for five days.

[12] For Copland letters to Virgil Thomson, see Beinecke Rare Book and Manuscript Library, Yale University.

I have often called myself "a work-a-year man:" 1963 was the year of the ballet *Dance Panels* in Munich and 1964 belonged to the band piece *Emblems*. Among the invitations I received to compose new pieces was one from clarinetist Keith Wilson, who was president of the College Band Directors National Association (CBDNA), for a work to be played at the organization's national convention (December 1964). Wilson wrote, "The purpose of this commission is to enrich the band repertory with music that is representative of the composer's best work, and not one written with all sorts of technical or practical limitations." I hesitated for a moment but accepted when I was told that the piece would be bought sight unseen by at least two hundred bands!

I began the piece in the summer of 1964 (after conducting in Holland and Scotland in June) and finished it a few weeks before the premiere (while on a guest-conducting tour of Washington, Rochester, Chicago, and Pittsburgh). The premiere was played by the University of Southern California band, The Trojans, conducted by director William Schaefer.

I tried to keep Keith Wilson's injunction in mind while still making *Emblems* challenging to young performers. Schaefer made a few recommendations: substitution of bass clarinet for my original baritone sax; and cueing of the piano part. After receiving the score, he wrote (7 December), "We find it challenging, but hope to have it well prepared. The item of greatest resistance is the blending and resolution of intonation problems in the doubling of high E-flat clarinet and flute. We trust that we shall live up to the honor of giving the first performances of this significant work." I explained the title *Emblems* in the program notes:

> An emblem stands for something—it is a symbol. I called this work *Emblems* because it seemed to me to suggest musical states of being: noble or aspirational feelings, playful or spirited feelings. The exact nature of these emblematic sounds must be determined for himself by each listener.

Emblems is tripartite in form: slow-fast-slow, with the return of the first part varied.[13] Embedded in the slow sections may be heard a brief quotation of the well-known hymn tune "Amazing Grace." Curiously, the harmonies had been conceived without reference to the tune. It was only by chance perusal of an anthology of tunes that I realized a connection existed between my harmonies and "Amazing Grace!"

Schaefer sent me a tape of the premiere, which took place in Tempe, Arizona (18 December 1964), and he expressed gratitude on behalf of The Trojans, but I sensed that the work was received with some disappointment. I did not hear *Emblems* played until the New York performance by the combined bands of Columbia and Harvard universities at Carnegie Hall (10 February 1965). Alas, my new band piece was not taken up by two hundred bands! I had purposely avoided serial composition; nevertheless, *Emblems* was at first considered dissonant and angular. In time, it has come into the college-band repertory.

[13] See Copland's files: "rough sketches" dating in part from 1946 with pages that include marginalia and comments such as "firm, somewhat drugged," and working titles, *Composition for Band, Band Piece*; complete pencil score with orchestral markings signed "Aaron Copland/ Nov 1964" and title page, "Chant/ Emblems for Band;" original ink manuscript. See also uncatalogued materials at the Library of Congress: 42-page pencil score with title page, "Piece for Band/Emblems for Band/ begun 8/24/64."

When in Cleveland in November 1965 to conduct the orchestra there, it happened that the Baldwin–Wallace College Band was rehearsing *Emblems* for a performance, so I went to Berea to hear them. The band director had posted a notice— "Aaron Copland will attend rehearsal." One student was heard to mutter, "Yeah, and next week, Shostakovich." I had the opportunity to say a few words to the players:

> You must always play absolutely in tune when you play dissonance. We composers take a chance when we write it, because if it is not played absolutely in tune, it sounds like a mistake. . . . Everybody knows a band can play loud. The question here is, How soft can you play?

When rehearsal was over, I told a reporter from *The Cleveland Plain Dealer*, "Baldwin-Wallace has a swell band."

President Lyndon Johnson sent a telegram informing me of his intention to award me a Presidential Medal of Freedom. I was told that it was the highest civilian honor that could be conferred by the President of the United States in peacetime.[14] The citation reads:

> To those men and women prominent in public affairs, business, science, education, journalism and the arts who collectively have made man's world safe, his physical body more durable, his mind broader, his leisure more delightful, his standard of living higher and his dignity important. They are creators; we are the beneficiaries.

The Medal of Freedom was conferred at a White House ceremony (14 September 1964). Among the thirty prominent recipients were Secretary of State Dean Acheson, John Steinbeck, Helen Keller, Edward R. Murrow, T. S. Eliot, Walter Lippmann, and Carl Sandburg. We were all invited to return to Washington early in 1965 for the inauguration of Lyndon Johnson.

I had been impressed with being invited to the White House from my first visit in 1945, after Franklin Roosevelt was re-elected. Twenty years later, I was still impressed, although the only American music played at the Johnson inaugural concert were excerpts from *Porgy and Bess* and "America the Beautiful." I no longer recall much about the inaugural ball, but I see from my diary that I danced until the wee hours of the morning. I wrote, "Lucy danced the frug, and the President danced."

Directly after receiving the Medal of Freedom, I went to Ann Arbor, Michigan, where I found myself onstage with Lenny Bernstein as we both received honorary doctorates from the University of Michigan (19 September 1964). Traveling home, Lenny was inspired to write a sonnet for the occasion, which he sent to me.

Television, as a new medium for promotion of the performance of contemporary music, interested me, just as radio and film had earlier. An offer to host my own television series on the music of the twenties was too tempting to pass up. I wrote the scripts, conducted

[14] The Medal of Freedom had been initiated in wartime. In 1952, its scope was broadened to include civilian contributions to national security.

WESTERN UNION TELEGRAM

CT WWY005 WWZ3 WWZ3 GOVT PD=WUX THE WHITE HOUSE 1 NFT=
AARON COPLAND=
ROCK HILL RFD #1 PEEKSKILL NY=

I AM HAPPY TO INFORM YOU OF MY INTENTION TO AWARD YOU THE PRESIDENTIAL MEDAL OF FREEDOM. THIS IS THE HIGHEST CIVIL HONOR CONFERRED BY THE PRESIDENT OF THE UNITED STATES FOR SERVICE IN PEACETIME. THE CRITERIA FOR THIS AWARD INCLUDE MERITORIOUS CONTRIBUTION TO THE SECURITY OR NATIONAL INTEREST OF THE UNITED STATES, WORLD PEACE, CULTURAL OR OTHER SIGNIFICANT PUBLIC OR PRIVATE ENDEAVOR. THE FORMAL ANNOUNCEMENT FROM THE WHITE HOUSE OF THE THIRTY RECIPIENTS FOR THIS YEAR WILL BE MADE ON JULY FOURTH. THE PRESENTATION OF THE MEDAL WILL TAKE PLACE IN SEPTEMBER AT THE WHITE HOUSE.
¶ WITH WARM BEST WISHES AND CONGRATULATIONS=
LYNDON B JOHNSON.

Above: Telegram from President Lyndon Johnson offering Copland the Medal of Freedom, 1964

Left: Announcement of Medal of Freedom awards in the *Herald Tribune* (Copland third row down, far right)

LEONARD BERNSTEIN 1964

Sonnet on receiving an honorary doctorate with Aaron Copland

This day, my will demurring, I grew old.
I could have written memoirs on that stage
For the first time. A longwave had unrolled,
And beached me, spent with swimming and with age.

Doctor honoris causa. First for him,
A craggy cedar planted by the sea
Since Adam. Then they called on me to swim
Ashore, and simulate that salty tree.

A poor impostor, I. Not even brave,
A plotter with no plan, and less than bold.
They fished me, red-eyed flounder, from the wave,
Wounded, rigid, open-mouthed, and cold.

With velvet bait they plucked me from the sea
And dropped me, panting, near a cedar tree.

Much love,
L.

19 Sept 1964

"Sonnet" from Leonard Bernstein to Copland (previously unpublished), 1964

the music, and appeared as host. Station WGBH in Boston taped the presentations during 1965 and 1966, and they were broadcast on public television across the country[15] under the title "Music in the Twenties." While I enjoyed doing the series, it was more demanding than I had envisioned. Because of various conducting engagements (Europe in the fall, including Warsaw), I did not compose anything in 1965. That always made me slightly uneasy. I was determined to get back to writing music in 1966. The results were the piano piece *In Evening Air*; an arrangement of *Eight Songs* from *Twelve Poems of Emily Dickinson* for voice and orchestra; a school-orchestra version of *Variations on a Shaker Melody* from *Appalachian Spring*; and music for a television series to be presented on CBS' "Television Playhouse."

The scope of the CBS series was impressive. It was produced by Fred Coe, and I was to compose "signature" music to announce each play. What little music there is to talk about, I would describe as being in the style of a fanfare for brass and percussion. I also composed music for the opening play, Ronald Ribman's *The Final War of Olly Winters*. Seven takes of various short segments were recorded (5 December 1966).[16] To my surprise, the CBS "signature" music received a nomination for an Emmy from The National Academy of Television Arts and Sciences.

I was puzzled when people asked why I bothered composing for television. Although I never accepted assignments that did not interest me, there was another factor to consider: somebody had to pay the rent! It was ironic that when I was younger and really needed commissions, they were few and far between; now, I had ten times more than I could accept. Since it could take a year or two to honor a commission for a major work, I occasionally accepted something that did not take long to write but paid well, such as the CBS "signature" music.

In celebration of its one hundred and twenty-fifth anniversary, the New York Philharmonic commissioned eighteen new works, each to be included on a program during the 1967-1968 season. (The actual anniversary was marked by a gala reproduction of the 1842 inaugural concert (7 December 1967). My commission would be the first symphonic piece I had tackled since *Connotations*, five years earlier. Searching through my notebooks, I came upon several quotations from poets I particularly admired, which I had transcribed into a diary. Among these were the words of the nineteenth-century English poet-priest Gerard Manley Hopkins. Hopkins interested me because of his originality and his experiments with prosody and meter, language and structure. He had also tried his hand at musical composition. Hopkins wrote, "No doubt my poetry errs on the side of oddness. . . . Melody is what strikes me most of all in music and design in painting, so design, pattern, or what I am in the habit of calling 'inscape' is what I above all aim at in poetry."[17]

[15] Copies of the television tapes are at WNET, Channel 13, New York City; audio tapes and transcripts are in Copland's files in the Library of Congress.

[16] See NYPL for script copies with autograph marginalia.

[17] Gerard Manley Hopkins, *The Letters of Gerard Manley Hopkins to Robert Bridges*, ed. Claude Colleer Abbott (London: Oxford University Press, 1935, rev. 1955), 66.

Rosamund ("Peggy") Bernier and Copland at the "Gala" celebrating the New York Philharmonic's 125th anniversary

As I reread some of Hopkins' poetry, I found that his term seemed to apply more truly to the creation of music than to any of the other arts. What appealed to me was Hopkins' ability to see beyond the outward appearance of things to their innermost being and his genius in making the outer appearance itself reflect the inner reality. My idea was to write music that would attempt to do just that, music that seemed to be moving inward upon itself, and (as I wrote in the score of my new piece) "a quasimystical illumination, a sudden perception of that deeper pattern, order and unity which give meaning to external forms." I was reminded recently that these were the principles Nadia Boulanger talked to me about so long ago—order, unity, discipline. I set out to find a different way of expressing these principles. I felt that I could accomplish this with serialism, which had opened a wide range of possibilities and combinations.

The material for *Inscape* comes from two different series of twelve tones that give rise to several subsidiary serial patterns of less importance. One of these dodecaphonic tone rows, heard as a twelve-tone chord, opens and closes the piece. All twelve notes of the row are equal and free of either tonal or serial considerations, while frequent use of thirds and triadic groupings creates a sense of diatonic center, giving *Inscape* more tonal orientation than is usual in serial composition; indeed, there is quite a lot of two-voice writing that suggests tonality. *Inscape*, scored for large orchestra, is in one continuous movement of about twelve minutes duration. It begins simply in an andantino tempo, becomes more complex as it proceeds to an allegretto, before gradually returning to the opening tempo and material.

Copland's diagram of a twelve-tone series used for *Inscape*, 1967

Examining the rough sketches of *Inscape* in my files, I see that I drew on some materials from 1963.[18] When I began to put the piece together, I found that I needed more time, so having accepted various conducting dates, I carried the *Inscape* materials along with me and composed whenever I could—on planes, trains, in hotel rooms, and in college practice rooms. *Inscape* was completed in Peekskill (August 1967).

I am not certain when I made the decision to use Gerard Manley Hopkins' privately invented word for my title. In any case, I have never felt audiences should attach too much significance to titles. *Inscape* is a suggestive word, that's all. The idea of a "scape" of any kind—a landscape, or an inscape, or an escape—seemed to lend itself in a general way to a music piece, because it is so general. To the uninitiated, the word "inscape" may suggest a kind of shorthand for "inner landscape." Hopkins, however, meant to signify a more universal experience. *Inscape* shares an extramusical relationship with *Connotations* insofar as both compositions derive motivation from literary sources. Because I allowed myself more tonal implications within the twelve-tone procedure with *Inscape*, it is a more relaxed piece than *Connotations* and therefore has been compared to *Quiet City* and even *Our Town* in feeling, although it is considerably more dissonant than either.

Lenny Bernstein wrote to me from Italy (August 1967):

> A letter from the Philharmonic contains programs, rehearsal schedules, etc., wherein I find the word *Inscape*. Nobody told me, least of all you—good title. You might conceivably drop a line about it and what it's like and how it goes and how it feels to be writing an inscape at almost sixty-seven.

Lenny had good reason to be interested, since it was he who would conduct the premiere performances with the New York Philharmonic on their preseason tour, beginning 13 September 1967 in Ann Arbor, Michigan, where the university was celebrating its sesquicentennial. Thirteen performances were given in all, including five upon the orchestra's return to New York. *Inscape* was positioned between Beethoven's *Eighth Symphony* and Tchaikovsky's *Second Symphony*. The audience reception was warm and enthusiastic, and for once, the critics seemed to understand right off that my intention was to make a piece of music in my own way, with my own sound, using the twelve-tone method, instead of creating an example of a perfect serial composition. Irving Kolodin wrote in *The Saturday Review*, "What Copland had undertaken . . . in a search for making Schoenberg's precepts the means not merely for expression, but for self-expression, he has done convincingly." In *The New York Times,* Allen Hughes wrote, "You will admire the workmanship and will respect the composer's ability to make the twelve-tone technique as though it had been invented to create the Copland sound." Although there was some criticism regarding melodic and rhythmic elements, the critics unanimously praised the sonorities and textures.

The serial aspects of *Connotations* and *Inscape* have been commented on more than I consider necessary, but that was due to the time-lag factor between the listener and the composer. For us composers, serialism was hardly a new thing. I was always interested in what Stravinsky was up to, and of course I heard his pieces of the early fifties (*Cantata* and *Septet*) in which he used serial elements. By the sixties, serialism had been around for over fifty years; young composers were not so fascinated with it anymore. It was taking its place with the passage of years. As I told an interviewer for *Music and Musicians* in 1966, "I imagine serial technique is going into history like the fugue form." New things arrived to be ingested and digested before becoming part of the musical vocabulary. We composers have access to each new development, and I, for one, never wanted to be limited to one kind of musical language.

When I conducted *Inscape* at Tanglewood (23 August 1968), it made at least one member of the audience happy. Thornton Wilder wrote to me the next day:

[18] See Copland's files: rough sketches (1963-1967); first complete sketch (1967); piano reduction (1967); final sketch with orchestral indications (1967). For analysis and description of source materials, see David Joseph Conte, "A Study of Aaron Copland's Sketches for *Inscape*," dissertation, Cornell University, Ithaca, N.Y., 1983.

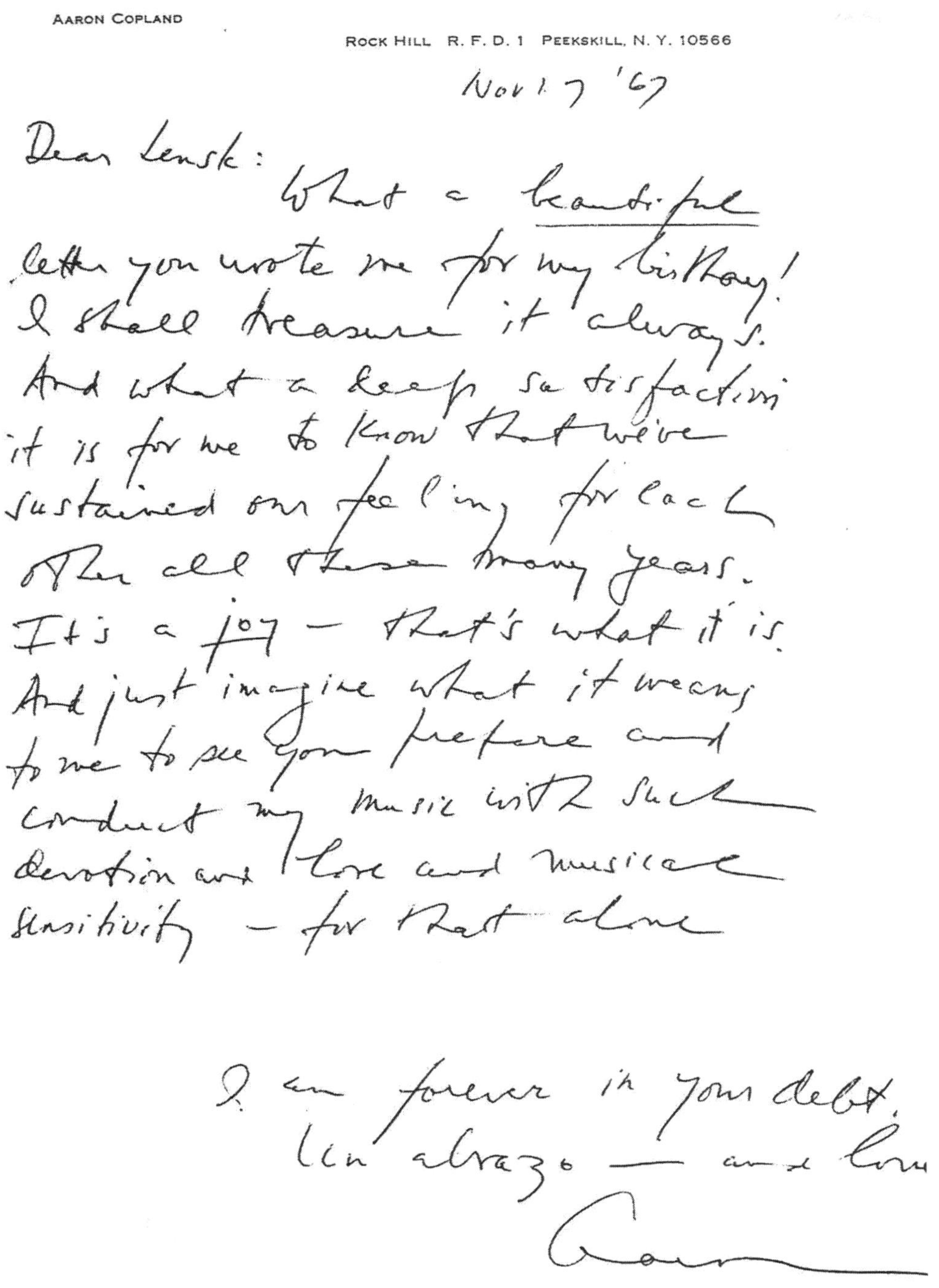

AARON COPLAND

ROCK HILL R. F. D. 1 PEEKSKILL, N. Y. 10566

Nov 17 '67

Dear Lensk:

What a beautiful letter you wrote me for my birthday! I shall treasure it always. And what a deep satisfaction it is for me to know that we've sustained our feeling for each other all these many years. It's a joy — that's what it is. And just imagine what it means to me to see you prepare and conduct my music with such devotion and love and musical sensitivity — for that alone

I am forever in your debt.
Un abrazo — and love
Aaron

Letter from Copland to Bernstein, 17 November 1967

> Just a word to say that *Inscape* is a very fine piece. It mounts to a wonderfully eloquent urgency . . . The orchestration is of the richest and all so clearly signed by you. Of course, I was shocked to hear that you don't obey one of Schoenberg's first rules (but no one else does either): in stating a row do not repeat a note until you have given all the other eleven! Cheers. Felicitations. Gratefully, Thornton.

I conducted the first European performance of *Inscape* with the London Symphony on their International Series (24 October 1968). The work elicited no comment whatever from the players but received a good review from the *London Sunday Times*.[19] While I was composing *Inscape*, I got to know the young composer Phillip Ramey. I invited him to the first rehearsal of the new piece and to the premiere.

Phillip Ramey[20]

When Aaron heard that big crashing first chord of Inscape *at rehearsal, his eyes gleamed with pleasure and excitement. Despite so many years of experience, it was all new to him, every time. I went with him to Ann Arbor, Michigan, for the world premiere. Lenny Bernstein, who conducted, had never been enthusiastic about Aaron's twelve-tone music; but backstage after the concert, he exclaimed, "Aaron, it's amazing how, even when you compose in a completely 'foreign' idiom, the music still comes out sounding like you!" Aaron thought that first performance excellent, the tempi and so on. Then the New York Philharmonic continued its tour and played* Inscape *several times more, on the same program with the Mahler* Fifth Symphony, *before introducing it to New York. Upon hearing his piece again, Aaron grumbled, "Lenny's been conducting too much Mahler.* Inscape *has gotten too slow." By the time of the recording session, Lenny's version of* Inscape *was somewhat longer than the premiere. Aaron was not pleased but he didn't fuss about it to Lenny.*

I was introduced to Aaron by David Del Tredici at a piano recital in New York early in 1967, and I boldly asked whether I might show him some of my music. "Sure," he replied. "Give me a ring." I did, and he invited me to Rock Hill. There, I played for him a recent piece, Piano Sonata No.2. *The dean of American composers told me my sonata, though well made, sounded too like Prokofiev and therefore lacked freshness. The judgment was delivered firmly but not unkindly, for he also pointed out things he liked. (Aaron tends not to be unduly kind to young composers; he's too objective for a grandfatherly role.) The high point of that first visit was his read-through at the keyboard, at my request, of his own* Piano Variations— *which does not sound like Prokofiev, or, for that matter, anyone else.*

As our friendship grew, I often reflected how lucky I was to have one of the century's great composers to consult whenever I wrote a new piece. When I asked for Aaron's opinion, I always found everything he said

[19] Other programs on which *Inscape* was included under Copland's direction: Musica Viva Concert by the San Francisco Symphony (15 June 1968); The National Symphony at Lincoln Center, New York City (16 February 1969); the New York Philharmonic in honor of Copland's seventieth birthday. The first performance in France was part of an all-Copland concert, the Orchestre National, Jean Martinon conducting. Chávez conducted *Inscape* at Cabrillo (1970), and Mehta conducted it during the Philharmonic's 1983-1984 season.

[20] Interview, Phillip Ramey with Perlis, 10 November 1987, New York City.

Above: Copland and Phillip Ramey en route from Budapest to Bucharest, 14 November 1969

Above: Copland at the Teatro Communale, Bologna, Italy, 1969

Right: Signing copies of the Hungarian translation of *The New Music*, Hungary, 1969

extremely helpful, even in those few instances when I couldn't agree. He seldom suggested solutions to compositional problems; rather, he took note of material he felt worth keeping and that which might be discarded. He emphatically conveyed to me his ideal of how tightly constructed and economical pieces should be; and his special kind of chord spacing had a certain influence on me. His neojazzy rhythms did not, though I liked them, and he sometimes expressed amazement that such a "warlike character" (his favorite description of me) didn't write more rhythmic music.

When Aaron went to Dartmouth College as composer-in-residence in the fall of 1967, I went with him, for he wanted a musician as a general assistant. That was the first of our many trips, most of them conducting tours. After Dartmouth, he asked me to go to Europe. In Vienna, during grueling rehearsals of his Third Symphony, *I had my first demonstration of the famous Copland patience. I remember Aaron complaining about the musicians: "They're so arrogant. Not only can't they play the irregular rhythms accurately, they won't even try." He suspected that their obstructiveness was motivated in part by anti-Semitism. In London, where Aaron's concert with the London Symphony Orchestra was sold out and the musicians played enthusiastically for him, he was more relaxed, always charming (I used to tell him he would have made a fine diplomat, and he would respond, "Or psychiatrist") whether conversing with a young British composer, Peter Maxwell Davies or with a future prime minister, Edward Heath.*

Two years later, in November 1969, Aaron and I went to Europe again. In Bucharest, he was somewhat annoyed to discover that his agent had neglected to tell him his fee would be in Roumanian lei and couldn't be taken out. [21] *I said, "Well, then let's live it up: champagne—morning, noon, and night! And we can buy lots of souvenirs." But Aaron graciously— and cannily—decided to use the money to establish a prize in his name for young composers.*

Aaron is one of the few friends with whom I've never had a falling-out. We took to each other immediately, and we remain close twenty-two years later. Of course, he's a patient man, which may account for the phenomenon, and he's incredibly loyal to friends. Aaron is most drawn to a different kind of personality from his own. Lenny Bernstein, for instance—how very unlike Aaron he is. By different, I don't mean stronger, for under all the cordiality he is strong as can be, but rather a more assertive, even acerbic, type. There's no cruel or vindictive side to Aaron; he's genuinely well-meaning, but he likes people who are more opinionated and outspoken than he is. I filled that bill.

In 1968, with the Stravinsky–Robert Craft books in mind, I decided to conduct interviews with Aaron on the subject of his music, focusing on specific works, and more than a dozen were eventually published, most of them as liner notes for the CBS Records series "Copland Conducts Copland." All those interviews were tape-recorded, put together from transcripts by me and then carefully edited by Aaron. He was enthusiastic about the project, for he thought it important to leave his own commentary for future generations. Later, when I became the New York Philharmonic's program editor, I found our interviews invaluable for my many Copland annotations.

As an example of how private and emotionally contained Aaron is, there was the weekend in the early 1970s when I was at Rock Hill with two composer friends, David Del Tredici and Robert Helps. After lunch on Saturday, we played tapes of our latest pieces, and Aaron followed the scores. Then he disappeared

[21] Copland's agents in Europe were Robert Paterson as sole representative for Great Britain and Europe and Thea Dispeker for the choice of local managers in Europe.

for a while and reentered the studio dressed in a suit. "I've got to go out for a couple of hours," he said, and off he went in his Mercedes-Benz. When he returned, he was a bit subdued and would not tell us where he'd been, but we had a lively dinner and played four-hand piano music afterward. The following week, a small article appeared in The New York Times *concerning the funeral, Saturday, of Aaron's beloved sister Laurine, and it noted that Aaron had been present. I wondered then just how well I actually knew Aaron, since I hadn't realized that something was very wrong. Aaron is given to concealing his innermost feelings and, even so, he wouldn't have wanted to subject friends to a personal trauma.*

In recent years, one of my duties on trips was to make certain Aaron did not become overtired, along with keeping careful watch over appointments and rehearsal schedules. At the colleges, he always agreed to listen to works by student composers. In Kansas in 1982, I wouldn't have wanted to be one of them. Aaron didn't much like anything he heard and was cool and a bit clipped. He said to me afterward, "They really should be doing better. "I replied, "You made that quite clear." "Did I?" he asked, concerned. "I meant to get it across but I hope I didn't sound mean." Yet he had been intimidating. Aaron won't take the easy way out and be politely noncommittal when asked to evaluate a score, even with friends. Music is too important to him, and he's always serious about it. He has extraordinary integrity. That's the real gist of Copland.

In June 1967, I spent four days on the Oberlin campus for the celebration of the conservatory's one hundredth anniversary, conducting, attending recitals, listening to student composers, and speaking informally, in addition to delivering the convocation address. I enjoyed spending time with the students. By this time, I had talked about twentieth-century music so often, I could do it blindfolded! For the serious presentations, I did as other speakers do in similar situations—adapted notes and outlines from my files. At about this time, I began to curtail lecturing. There is some danger in that you begin to find yourself believing everything you say! With conducting, no matter how many times one might conduct a piece, there would be the excitement of different players, a different atmosphere, the uncertainty of what might or might not happen. But with lecturing, as with composing, if indulged in over a very long period of time, one runs the risk of repeating oneself.

My trip to Europe in the fall of 1967 was scheduled to coincide with Nadia Boulanger's eightieth birthday party in Monaco, hosted by Prince Rainier and Princess Grace. Much of the music world was there for the occasion. I sat with my old friend from the Paris days, Marcelle de Manziarly, for the concert at the Monte Carlo Theatre. Nadia looked more fragile than I remembered but otherwise her old self. I had written an article about her, just published by the Associated Press (3 September) and released worldwide. It had been seen by many people at the party. I wrote to Nadia afterward, "It was a never-to-be-forgotten occasion."

On my return to London, I conducted a recording of the *Dance Symphony, the Symphonic Ode, Our Town,* and *Outdoor Overture.* Phillip Ramey and I had a pleasant country visit with Michael Tippett before returning to Paris. The weather was sunny and warm, and I walked everywhere—St. Germain des Près hangouts from my old days in Paris, Brentanos, the rue de Rivoli, the whole Champs Elysées. I had dinner with Virgil at his place on the quai Voltaire, with Peggy Bernier and Earle Brown. As pleasant as it was to be in Paris, it seemed that the French had lost all contact with my music. I wrote, "All is *a refaire*, a rather glum prospect."

From Paris I went to Köln [Cologne] to conduct my *Orchestral Variations* with the Köln Radio Orchestra, which had too small a string section and rather weak brass. They also had the same sense of reluctant cooperation, though the discipline was somewhat better than most radio orchestras. Phillip and I traveled on to Venice via Frankfurt and Milan, and from Venice to Bologna, where I had to conduct a third-rate orchestra. Bologna was plastered with posters announcing my arrival. We had a lot of rehearsals for the concert, which went off fairly well. It was repeated the next night to a pitifully small house. I wrote, "Stupid of the management to have thought they could get two audiences for a modern American music program in Bologna. It was an 'experiment' that failed!"

Back in Peekskill by the end of October, I hoped to stay home for a while. A quiet sixty-seventh birthday was enjoyed with friends. I finished the revision of *Canticle of Freedom* and tried to make some headway on a commission for a string quartet I had promised Bill Schuman for the Juilliard back in 1962. It was not moving along, and much as I would like to have had a string quartet in my catalogue, I eventually relinquished the commission.[22]

In 1966, Victor Kraft had suggested I update my 1940 book, *Our New Music.* He wrote, "Isn't it a waste to have it lying around unsold? Wouldn't it be worthwhile to redress the whole thing—maybe even alter the title a bit . . . people are really exposed to our new music in a way you never dreamt of then." I thought Victor had a good idea, so I got to work writing "second thoughts." The revision gave me the opportunity to admit I had not foreseen the enormous influence the twelve-tone system would have on postwar composers. I caught readers up on recent developments, such as chance operations and electronic music, and updated my autobiographical sketch. The title became *The New Music: 1900-1960.*[23]

In connection with the publication, I was invited to appear on NBC's "Today" show with Hugh Downs (13 March 1968) and on WOR radio with the actress Arlene Francis. I don't know how many books were sold as a result, but my family sure was impressed! My sister-in-law Mildred wrote, "You should have seen Leon's face when he watched that wonderful interview." When the family visited me in Peekskill about a month later, they were amazed when I told them that the television show was unrehearsed—except for Leon, who said, "Aaron, you were always that way—when you were three years old you got up on the pulpit at temple— people could just see the top of your head—and you recited 'How would you like to be a dog?'"

After conducting varied programs with the BSO and the Music Center orchestra at Tanglewood (20-25 August 1968), I wrote to Lenny (26 August): "I'm just back from conducting at Tanglewood, where your spirit hovers. But it always hovers wherever I go. American music would have a different 'face' without you!"

The Israel Philharmonic invited me to conduct a series of concerts at the end of 1968 and beginning of 1969. Victor Kraft, recently separated from his wife, went with me. I had

[22] See Copland's files for sketches toward the string quartet: two pages of tone rows dated "June '48"; a page from *The Tender Land*, Act III; two pages from "The World of Nick Adams"; a page titled "Folk Trilogy."

[23] Copland, *The New Music: 1900-1960* (New York: W. W. Norton & Company [paperback], 1968).

not been to Israel since 1951, and not surprisingly, I discovered some changes: a luxurious guest house for visitors of the orchestra and the Mann Auditorium, which seated three thousand. The subscription audience numbered twenty-four thousand for each set of concerts in Tel Aviv, which was calculated to be about ten percent of that city's population! Therefore, the same program had to be repeated eight times, with a ninth in Jerusalem. I wrote in my diary:[24]

> The mere prospect of all those repetitions of the same program is exhausting! The orchestra is cooperating well. Weak elements—horns, some woodwind players. The program [Stravinsky, *Symphony in C*; Ives, *Decoration Day*; Copland, *Orchestral Variations*] is too hard for four rehearsals—my error—damn!

In addition to conducting, I played the piano in *Vitebsk* in a chamber music concert arranged by the American consul. Local composers attended and afterward I listened to some of their works and talked with them. My impression was that they had gained considerable self-confidence in an organizational way since 1951.

In Jerusalem, Victor and I stayed at the King David Hotel and visited the Old City, which I found incredibly picturesque. After a visit to Bethlehem, I commented, "The usual sense of unreality about these ancient sites and legends. Most impressed with the *paysage*. Kept puzzling over how it happened that this was the Holy Land." During one three-day weekend, we rented a car and toured the countryside, accompanied by a young guide. I wrote:

> Our first stop was again Jerusalem, then Jericho by way of an impressive ride down from the heights to the subsea-level ruins of ancient Jericho and a distant view of the Dead Sea. Unforgettable terrain. Drove for more than three hours back to Jerusalem and on to the kibbutz through rather scary Arab towns and lovely stretches of mountainous roads. Reached the kibbutz in time for dinner. . . . We were shown the children being put to bed in an underground shelter (because of the danger of Jordanian shelling). . . After a communal breakfast, we were taken to visit a kibbutz right on the border with Jordan. . . . An heroic atmosphere since they are under continual strain of possible attack. We dropped our guide at his kibbutz and headed for Safed on a narrow bumpy road through remote areas of empty hill country—left an impression!

Back in Tel Aviv for the remaining concerts, we spent a quiet New Year's Eve, and then made a one-day excursion to Eilat on the Red Sea. On our return to Tel Aviv, I was greeted by Julius Rudel, who had arrived for the next series of nine concerts. After my final concert, I was presented with candlesticks made in Israel, as a momento. Victor was so taken with the country, he decided to stay for a while, but as my plane touched ground in New York (5 January), I wrote in my diary, "glad to be home."

I composed three short musical works in 1969, all of a celebratory nature. One was for the dedication of a very large red stabile by Alexander Calder in a plaza in downtown Grand Rapids, Michigan. The sculpture, *La Grande Vitesse*, was the first work of art in American history to be jointly commissioned and financed by federal and private funds. I knew and admired Sandy Calder and this was a spectacular sculpture, so I accepted the commission.[25] The result was *Inaugural Fanfare*, composed for twenty-four instruments—woodwinds, brass, and percussion—in three sections. The opening is characterized by biting harmonic chords; the middle section is for ad-lib snare drum against a quiet melodic line played by two trumpets; and the closing material resembles the opening.

Calder attended the unveiling of *La Grande Vitesse* in Grand Rapids (14 June 1969), but I could not be at the dedication ceremony. Reviews and a tape were sent to me afterward. One critic quipped, "Copland's *Inaugural Fanfare* was unfortunately gone with the wind." I had aimed for something more than a conventional fanfare, and it seems that the nuances of the piece were lost in the open air. Such events are rarely very satisfactory in a musical sense, and for the Calder dedication, several factors combined to dull the effect of the music, which was played by the Grand Rapids Symphony under their conductor, Gregory Millar. I decided not to release *Inaugural Fanfare* for publication until it could be revised.[26] Other commitments intervened, and I did not get around to doing anything about it.

In 1974, the powers that be in Grand Rapids were installing another Calder, an enormous rooftop painting close to the sculpture in the plaza, which was about to be renamed "Calder Plaza." When they looked for "their" Copland piece in order to perform it again, they found no sign of a score or parts in their files. Gregory Millar had a photocopy of the score; Boosey & Hawkes had nothing; and I had only the sketches from which I had planned to revise the work. The newspapers made a thing about it, joking that at least Grand Rapids could not misplace the Calder sculpture as it had its Copland piece! The situation spurred me on to compose the new version for wind ensemble. I apologized to Grand Rapids for letting so much time pass and soon presented them with the new score, dedication intact: "Composed for the City of Grand Rapids. Inauguration of Calder Statuary, revised 1975."

Another *pièce d'occasion* of 1969 was *Happy Anniversary*, an arrangement for symphony orchestra of the well-known tune "Happy Birthday," in honor of Eugene Ormandy's seventieth birthday.[27] It was first performed as part of a *Variations on Happy Birthday* by famous composers, which I conducted in Philadelphia (24 January 1970) at the orchestra's seventieth anniversary concert (Ormandy's birthday was actually in November). The date was planned to coordinate with President Nixon's presentation of the Medal of Freedom to Ormandy at the concert. My score, dedicated to the conductor, was presented in a bound book containing the twenty variations. I never expected to hear anything further about *Happy Anniversary*, but it was published by Boosey & Hawkes in 1972, although it is only about one minute in duration, and the idea was turned around by the National Symphony Orchestra when they played the arrangement for my seventy-seventh birthday, on an all-

[24] See travel diary # 11. See also "Aaron Copland: A Visit to Israel," in *Boosey & Hawkes Newsletter*, vol. III, no. 2 (Spring 1969) 1.

[25] The commission of $1,000 was offered by letter (19 May 1969).
[26] See Copland's files for the original pencil score with indications for orchestration. The envelope is marked, in Copland's hand, "not to be published as is."
[27] See Copland's files for pencil sketches, original full-orchestra pencil score, photocopy ink score.

Copland concert, Rostropovich conducting. It was used in the same way at the "Wall-to-Wall Copland" eightieth birthday party at Symphony Space in New York City.

The third tribute I had promised was for the Metropolitan Museum of Art centennial, which was to be celebrated with the performance of an original fanfare to open each exhibit during the 1969-1970 season. (Commissions went also to Virgil Thomson, Walter Piston, William Schuman, and Leonard Bernstein.) I composed it immediately after returning from my 1969 fall trip to Europe (Phillip Ramey accompanied me to Baden-Baden, Budapest, Bucharest, and London, where I reviewed tapes for recordings made the previous year). *Ceremonial Fanfare* is for brass ensemble of eleven instruments and is three minutes and twenty seconds in duration. The piece falls into three connected sections: The first begins with a trumpet line echoed in the trombone, followed by the horns building to a big climax; the middle section is a more flowing passage with canonic and quasicanonic imitation; and the final section is basically a recapitulation of the beginning, except for the final half-dozen bars, which bring the short piece to a quiet close. *Ceremonial Fanfare* is tonal in feeling, using key signatures and a home base of B major/minor.[28] The first performance took place at the museum on my seventieth birthday, for the opening of the exhibit "Masterpieces of Fifty Centuries."

[28] See Copland's files for original piano manuscript, sketches dating from 1942 and 1944, and a photocopy of the orchestral score, marked "unedited copy."

INTERLUDE XI

Following the assassinations of the Kennedys and Martin Luther King, the Vietnam War and Watergate further diminished American pride and self-respect. A loss of confidence in democratic ideals resulted in severe setbacks in education and civil rights. Social historians have compared the disillusionment that characterized the seventies to the Depression, but for the first time in American history, traditional values faltered to such a degree that schools and colleges closed at an alarming rate around the country.[1] As educational standards lowered, the arts were in turn affected. Discouraged by Vietnam and embarrassed by government corruption, American artists preferred to follow international styles rather than ones that would be perceived as national or American.

A key word of the period was *cool*, a term borrowed from bebop and modern jazz. An outward show of emotion or vitality was not admired. Visual artists produced abstract forms and shapes; literature and poetry explored words as sounds, not commentary; and most composers used atonal styles that referred to nothing extramusical: serialism, electronic sounds, chance operations, and minimalism. The fragmentation and pluralism (terms used by historians to describe the diversity of musical activities)[2] would show little change until the eighties, when the prevailing aesthetic would finally swing back toward figurative art, and an old "ism" would reappear in music as "the new romanticism."

Aaron Copland at seventy was cool and contained, tall and spare, craggy- featured and bespectacled, grayer of hair, but still sure of step, speech, and purpose. For his major works of the sixties, he had used serialism, but in ways that are unmistakably Copland. As Ned Rorem, a composer who wrote tonal music during the years when it was not in fashion, explains about *Connotations* and *Inscape*: "We are now far enough away from those pieces to see that, in fact, they still contain the leanness that Copland has always had—like when an airplane leaves the earth, and things get smaller and smaller in the distance and become more and more one color." [3]

[1] See Paul Johnson, *Modern Times* (New York: Harper & Row, 1983), Chapter Eighteen, "America's Suicide Attempt," 613-58.

[2] See Kyle Gann, "Our Pluralistic Post-Modern Era: Since the Mid-1970s," in H. Wiley Hitchcock, *Music in the United States*, Fourth Edition (New Jersey: Prentice Hall, 1988).

[3] See interview with Ned Rorem.

Inscape was Copland's last major work, although he continued to compose into the seventies. Whether the decline in Copland's composing was connected to the disenchantment of the times is speculation, as are other possibilities—the increasing gap in time between Copland and young composers, the natural effects of aging, or a combination of these. Copland continued to be very actively involved in the music world, and when he turned seventy and was told he hardly looked his age, he responded, "I hardly feel it." He said to interviewers (as he would at seventy-five and eighty), "I just don't relate to that number!" Indeed, he was about to go through such a round of birthday tributes that one journalist wrote, "Copland concerts are outnumbered only by Beethoven's."

No manager or public relations firm had ever organized a Copland birthday celebration, but Claire Reis, who was a consummate organizer, discussed Copland's seventieth with William Schuman and Stuart Pope at Boosey & Hawkes in order to coordinate the New York events. Claire's idea was to put together an album of composer tributes from all over the world to be presented to Copland at a birthday dinner after the Juilliard concert.[4] The gala dinner at the Essex House, hosted by Boosey & Hawkes, was described by Ned Rorem: "The feast . . . followed by *louanges* and presentations from the Great, terminated with *Danzón Cubano* performed at two pianos by Copland and Bernstein with the élan of a pair of drunken sailors, all harmless fun. . . ."[5] Bernstein evidently was feeling no pain, playing exuberantly and smiling away, while Copland looked up and over in alarm at the fusillade of wrong notes. The "presentations from the Great" included the album of composers' letters, the Handel Medallion, "the highest award given by New York City for a contribution to its cultural life," and remarks by Schuman and Bernstein.[6] Copland wrote to Claire Reis afterward:

> Thank you for that magnificent book of letters from my fellow composers. I've just finished reading them. If any composer of serious music has ever been more generously praised by his

[4] See interviews, Claire Reis with Perlis, Oral History of American Music, Yale University, 1976-1977, New York City.

[5] Ned Rorem, "Copland's Birthday (at Seventy)," *Settling the Score* (New York: Harcourt Brace Jovanovich, 1988), 21-24

[6] See Copland's files at the Library of Congress for the seventieth birthday tribute book.

Copland at seventy

peers, I can't imagine who it might have been. Verily, my cup runneth over! And I have a very good idea as to who it was that first raised the cup.[7]

According to Claire Reis, every request brought forth a response, except for those sent to Russia. One that particularly pleased Copland read, "Dear Aaron, Seventy is pretty good. Congratulations, Stravinsky."

Copland conducted The New York Philharmonic in a concert of his music, and received honorary membership in the Philharmonic Society of New York, conferred by Carlos Moseley, who said, "Aaron Copland's music has been represented on the Society's programs more than that of any American composer during its history." In addition to the Philharmonic, Copland himself conducted seventeen orchestras during that year.[8] In Minneapolis, he wryly reminded the newspaper critics, who were referring to him as "The Dean of American Music," that many years earlier a Minneapolis critic had called him "Copland the Ogre." Yale University awarded Copland its prestigious Howland Medal (30 January 1970), and honorary degrees were given by the Peabody Conservatory, Columbia, Brandeis, and York universities, as well as by the New York University School for Continuing Education. In July, when the Interlochen Music Camp students presented their annual "Man of Music" plaque to Copland and asked the secret of his success, Copland responded, "These things just happen to you!"

[7] Copland's letters to Claire Reis are at the Music Division, the New York Public Library at Lincoln Center.

[8] Orchestras conducted by Copland in 1970 were: Minneapolis, Toledo, Columbus, Chicago, St. Louis, Rochester, Interlochen, BSO, BMC, Cleveland, Los Angeles Philharmonic, Los Angeles Chamber Orchestra, BBC, Berlin, Bamberg, New York Philharmonic, and LSO.

Left: Claire Reis presents a book of composers' letters to Copland at his seventieth birthday dinner, the Essex House, New York city. William Schuman, master-of-ceremonies, is at the right

Right: Looking at the tributes with Copland (*left to right*) Claire Reis, Michael Tilson Thomas, Mari and Robert Cornell, Olga Koussevitzky, Leonard Bernstein

Below: Letter from Copland to Claire Reis, 21 November 1970

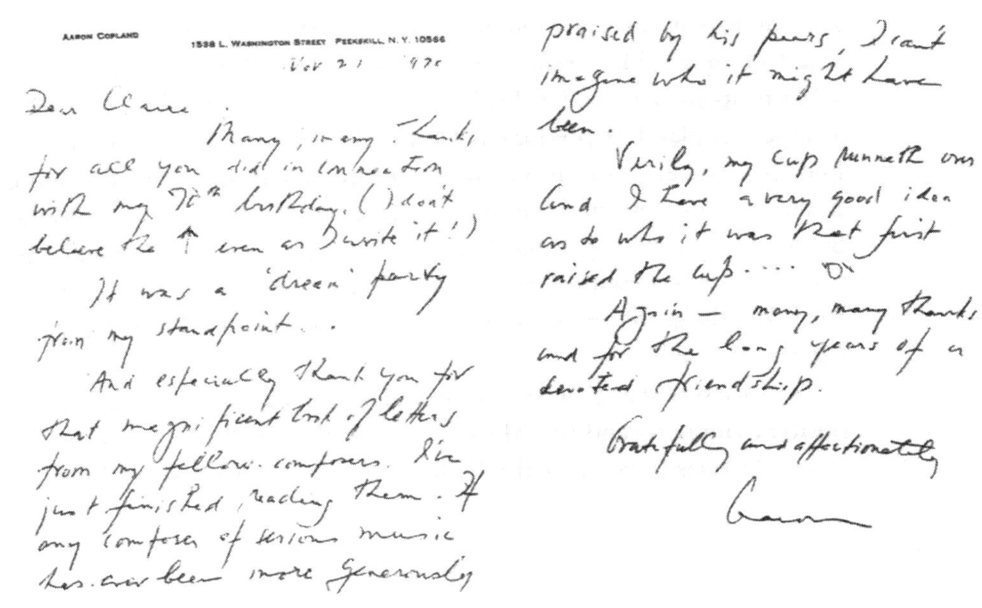

AARON COPLAND   1538 L. WASHINGTON STREET PEEKSKILL, N.Y. 10566

Nov 21 1970

Dear Claire:

Many, many thanks for all you did in connection with my 70th birthday. (I don't believe it even as I write it!)

It was a 'dream' party from my standpoint...

And especially thank you for that magnificent book of letters from my fellow-composers. I've just finished reading them. If any composer of serious music has ever been more generously praised by his peers, I can't imagine who it might have been.

Verily, my cup runneth over and I have a very good idea as to who it was that first raised the cup...

Again — many, many thanks and for the long years of a devoted friendship.

Gratefully and affectionately,

Aaron

Festivities at Tanglewood in July included Copland conducting the Boston Symphony and the Music Center orchestras.[9] In August, he flew to Los Angeles to conduct the Philharmonic in the Hollywood Bowl and the Los Angeles Chamber Ensemble in the premiere of *Appalachian Spring* in its original orchestration. Lawrence Morton wrote in the program book of this concert of Copland's early music (14 August), "This is not inappropriate, for it is only chronologically that he approaches seventy. In heart and spirit he remains the youngest of them all."

In October, the British rolled out the red carpet. André Previn, then director of the London Symphony Orchestra, had been asked to play Copland's *Piano Concerto*, but he demurred, saying it was "because of a lack of time to learn the solo part of your fiendish piano concerto—much as I admire the work." Copland played it himself, afterward vowing not to do so again: "I didn't enjoy it. Hit too many wrong notes. Other people don't notice it, but I do." After the concert at the Festival Hall, Copland received honorary membership in the Royal Philharmonic Society, and a dinner was held in his honor by Ambassador Walter Annenberg, with Prime Minister Edward Heath attending. As critic Peter Heyworth noted in *The Observer* (15 November): "No American composer has made such an impact on English musical life as Aaron Copland. . . ." Copland was so taken with the British, he told Harold Clurman that he was considering buying a flat in London.

Copland's career as composer, conductor, and representative of American music was discussed and evaluated in articles, reviews, radio programs, and on television.[10] He enjoyed it all, except for part of an article by Leonard Bernstein, "An Intimate Sketch," in *Hi Fidelity* magazine (November 1970). Lenny praised his close friend, but in the closing paragraphs, he wrote about Copland's current status and situation as composer:

> . . . So Copland stopped composing. How sad for him. How awful for us. . . . All it will take, it seems to me, is another musical turn, this time to a rediscovery of the basic simplicities of art, in which Copland will once more be looked to as a leader, will once again feel wanted as a composer. Happy Birthday, Aaron. We miss your music.

Someone other than Bernstein placed a heading on the article. It read, "Why Has Copland Stopped Composing?" Copland had made no decision or public pronouncements about his composing; evidently, he did not want anyone else doing so, although he had admitted to friends that he was in a composing slump. As he wrote to Carlos Chávez (22 August): "I wish I could tell you of new works of my own—but the truth is that the urge to compose seems to be tapering off. I hope not permanently. Perhaps you have a 'cure' to suggest?" In response to Bernstein's article, Copland was quoted in the the *Daily News*: "Don't know where Lenny got the idea I was stopping composing. I never told him that." Donal Henahan of *The New York Times* described an interview with Copland in Peekskill:

> Copland said, "Did you see the piece that Lenny Bernstein wrote about me in the new *Hi Fi*? 'Happy Birthday, Aaron. We miss your music.' " Copland breaks out in a giggle. "I thought it was rather naïve of him to imagine that you can just happily go on doing what you always had been doing and get away with it. . . . Also, the picture he paints of me at the end of the article of having been abandoned by the young composers. Why, that's nothing at all like what I feel." An incredulous laugh. "It's perfectly natural, after all, that when you get to your seventies you're not going to have the same hold on a younger generation as when you were forty or fifty! Why he should seem unhappy for me, I don't know."

Phillip Ramey sent a response to the editor of *Hi Fidelity*, after showing it to Copland. Ramey wrote, "Copland is presently writing, on commission, a sizable three-movement work for flute and piano." (This became Copland's *Duo for Flute and Piano*.)

The relationship between Copland and Bernstein was of such long standing that the contretemps was soon forgotten. Bernstein's own birthday salute to Copland was "A Copland Celebration" (27 December), similar to the sixtieth birthday tribute. It was a broadcast of a Young People's Concert on CBS featuring the *Clarinet Concerto* and excerpts from *Billy the Kid*. Bernstein said, "It's almost impossible to believe that time has rushed by so fast that this year Copland is suddenly seventy. Copland has often been called the 'Dean of American composers,' whatever that means. I guess it's supposed to mean that he's the oldest, but he isn't the oldest—he's just the best." Bernstein also played a major role in a MacDowell Colony dinner and concert in Copland's honor (24 November), along with Isaac Stern and others. (After seven years as president, Copland turned the leadership of the Colony over to Schuman in 1968).

With birthday festivities extending into 1971 (a vocal concert in February by Phyllis Curtin and Jan DeGaetani, films with Copland's music at the Metropolitan Museum), Copland was more than ready to leave for Europe in June, first to Paris, where he had not been for several years.[11] Perhaps because of having reached his seventieth year, Copland was nostalgic in France. He conducted a concert of his works at the Théâtre des Champs Elysées, where he had spent his first night in Paris in 1921, watching the Ballet Suédois in Milhaud's *L'Homme et son désir*, and saw friends from the twenties, including Marcelle de Manziarly and Nadia at Fontainebleau. Copland wrote of Nadia in his diary, "I was struck by the fact that she couldn't see anything anymore. Otherwise, she seemed very much alive. I visited the outside of my 1921 abode. The town of Fontainebleau in general and the house in particular looked all spruced up— younger than in 1921!"

Between conducting tours, Copland stayed at home, catching up with correspondence and organizations with which he was involved,[12] and working on various publications and

[9] Copland conducted the BSO (24 July): Busoni (*Rondo Arlechinesco*); Copland (*Dance Panels, Clarinet Concerto*); Schubert (*Symphony No. 5*); he conducted the BSO at "Tanglewood on Parade" (28 July): Bernstein (*Overture to Candide*); Tchaikovsky (*Romeo and Juliet*); and he led the Music Center Orchestra: Hindemith (*Metamorphosis on Weber*); Copland (*The Tender Land Suite*).

[10] A sampling of seventieth birthday tributes: "The Kid from Brooklyn," *Newsweek* (23 November 1970); Donal Henahan, "He Made Composing Respectable Here," *The New York Times*, 8 November 1970; articles by Wilfrid Mellers, Hugo Cole, and Norman Kay in a Copland birthday issue of *Tempo*, no. 95 (Winter 1970-71); Phillip Ramey in *Boosey & Hawkes Newsletter* (November 1970).

[11] See travel diary #11.

[12] Organizations Copland was actively working with in the early seventies included The American Academy of Arts and Letters (Copland was president from 1971-1974); The Pulitzer Prize Committee (chairman); The MacDowell Colony (president); and board member of American Music Center, Koussevitzky Music

presentations. Ten years at his Peekskill home, Rock Hill, was enough for him to know that the place really suited his needs: a country house close enough to the city for his purposes and for visitors to come out easily by train or car in little over an hour. Copland managed to keep his housekeepers, Gaston and Mireille, with him until 1973. Once, when he was with Harold Lawrence, manager of the London Symphony Orchestra, Copland pointed out that he could not stay away from home too long. "My rare and wonderful cook and gardener get lonely when I am away," Copland told Lawrence. "Touring is one thing, but a bachelor-composer needs someone to look after him."[13] When Gaston and Mireille finally returned to Europe, Copland found another couple for a short time; then in 1974, a young man who was a talented cook, Sophronus Mundy, came to take over the kitchen and the driving. Professional equipment was installed in the old-fashioned kitchen, and Sophronus proceeded to cook gourmet meals that meant not so much to Copland but were a delight to his guests. Sophronus sometimes accompanied Copland on trips and to concerts in New York, driving him home afterward.

Invitations and requests continued to fill Copland's mailbox. His name alone on a program or announcement was good publicity for any organization or performing group. His attractive style of public speaking accounted for the many requests to appear as master of ceremonies or toastmaster for special occasions. Copland would always supply the perfect blend of seriousness and wit. He could be relied on to be straightforward and insightful, not to ramble or mumble, and always to get a good laugh or two. As with most people who speak with ease and spontaneity, Copland always thought carefully about what he wanted to say, then delivered the message in his inimitably breezy and impromptu fashion. He and Schuman frequently hosted each other's special parties, and Schuman, an exceptional speaker himself, would joke, "I have a second occupation—introducing Aaron Copland at his own birthday parties. It's not lucrative, but it's fun!"

Included in Copland's speaking engagements were the inevitable memorial tributes, such as the opening remarks at a concert in William Flanagan's memory (14 April 1970). Others close to Copland died in the seventies. In 1972, his sister Laurine and her husband Charles Marcus, composer Ingolf Dahl, and Copland's lawyer Abe Friedman. (Copland's *Piano Sonata* was played by Leo Smit at Friedman's memorial service.) Abe Friedman's music clients were turned over to an associate, Ellis J. Freedman, who reported that Copland was wary at first and had asked him, "Do you think you can handle composers' affairs?"[14] (Before long, Copland came to rely on Ellis Freedman as he had Abe Friedman.) Composer Israel Citkowitz and Copland's sister-in-law Dorothy ("Dot") died in 1974; and a year later, the last member of Copland's immediate family, his older brother Leon. In 1979, Andre Kostelanetz died, and Copland appeared in the New York Philharmonic's concert tribute to the

Foundation, Brandeis Committee, Naumburg Foundation (until 1973), Ives Society (1973-1978), American branch of the Aldeburgh Festival, and ASCAP.

[13] See Harold Lawrence in *The LSO Diary* (October-November 1972).

[14] Ellis Freedman to Perlis, 16 February 1989.

Accepting the Laurel Leaf Award from the American Music Center, 1968

Speaking about "Music in the Thirties" on stage with Minna Daniel, Graduate Center, City University of New York, 8 May 1979

conductor as narrator in the work "Kosty" had commissioned from him, *Lincoln Portrait*. In the late seventies, Copland lost two people who had been closest to him throughout much of his life: Harold Clurman in 1978 and Nadia Boulanger in 1979. Copland never got used to the idea. He would comment, "I just think of them as still being out there."

Copland with Harold Clurman, Lotos Club Dinner, New York City, 1978

Copland's own health continued to be excellent. He had rarely been seriously ill, and in all the years of traveling, on only one trip (to Prague in 1973) did Copland need to consult a physician and go to bed for a few days. It caused him to miss an ambassador's dinner and a meeting with Prague's composers, the latter with great disappointment; the former not at all.

Copland continued to travel extensively during the seventies and well into the eighties. He became a familiar and popular figure on the conducting circuit. He had developed his own style on the podium: relaxed, economical; and informal, but with zest and vitality. Audiences liked his obvious physical enjoyment of the music. The English particularly

Copland in London, 1975

found him a refreshing contrast to their own more restrained conductors. Above all, Copland's performances possessed rhythmic energy. When an interviewer asked how it felt to be conducting in his seventies, Copland responded, " I don't feel weighed down by seventy years. Every time I finish conducting, I come off exhilarated, like a boxer after a good ring workout."

Copland was beginning to think about writing an autobiography. He made some notes and an outline, and even considered a title— "The Music Within." Several publishers were interested.[15] Copland promised himself that as soon as the birthday celebrations were over, he would do two things: begin to write his life story and get back to composing.

[15] See Copland's files at the Library of Congress for notes toward an autobiography and letters from publishers Knopf, Harcourt Brace Jovanovich, and Braziller.

COMPOSER AS CONDUCTOR
1970 - 1982

I had a few promises to keep: one was to write a brief salute for the fortieth birthday celebration of the Music Library Association in 1971. I sent off eight measures, a sort of inversion of "Happy Birthday," in fanfare style "for a single brass instrument or several in unison." I see from the markings on my score that it was meant to be played *larghetto pomposo* and *marcatissimo*. After the Music Library Association's conference, Bill Lichtenwanger, head of the reference section of the music division at the Library of Congress, sent me the program on which my salute was printed, and he wrote (2 February 1971):

> In case the ghost of Joe McCarthy is hovering around, I had better explain that the ink is not pink but ruby. I had hoped to get together a Russian horn band to give the piece its first performance . . . but the meeting was so big and busy and formal that I couldn't get a rehearsal going—so the first performance is still to come.

As far as I know, the first performance is still to come.[1]

This commitment fulfilled, I composed a short piece requested by my friend Andre Kostelanetz—"Estribillo," which when added to my two *Latin-American Sketches* of 1959 make a three-part work. It was played in that form for the first time by the New York Philharmonic, conducted by Kostelanetz (10 June 1972).

In draft stage since 1969 had been a work for flute and piano, commissioned by seventy pupils and friends of William Kincaid, first flutist of the Philadelphia Orchestra from 1921 to 1960.[2] After Kincaid died in 1967, John Solum, a former student, organized the committee, and they offered me the commission.[3] Solum and Elaine Shaffer, also a Kincaid pupil, corresponded with me and were most helpful when it came to preparation of the final score, which is dedicated to the memory of William Kincaid.[4] I composed the slow movement first and sent it off to Elaine Shaffer. When I had the second movement in hand, I asked the two flutists to meet with me—after all, this was my first extensive writing for the flute. In one spot, I had asked the flutist to play with a "thin tone" and was told in no uncertain terms that one never invites a flutist to do that! Instead, Solum recommended some harmonic fingerings that gave just the veiled quality I had in mind.[5]

Duo for Flute and Piano is in three movements, with the following indications: Flowing; Poetic, somewhat mournful; Lively, with bounce. My *Duo* is a lyrical piece, in a somewhat pastoral style. Almost by definition, it would have to be a lyrical piece, for what can you do with a flute in an extended form that would not emphasize its songful nature? Lyricism seems to be built into the flute. Some colleagues and critics expressed surprise at the tonal nature of *Duo*, considering that my recent works had been in a more severe idiom; however, the style was naturally influenced by the fact that I was composing for Kincaid's students, not for future generations (although I hoped younger flutists would play *Duo* eventually). Also, I was using material from earlier sketches in my notebooks, and that may have influenced the style of the piece.[6] For example, the beginning of the first movement, which opens with a solo passage for flute, recalls the first movement of my *Third Symphony*.

The first movement is altogether a rather easygoing pastoral sort of movement, while the second uses harmonic and melodic language more akin to my later works, with the principal idea in the flute projecting a whole-tone sound similar to the opening of the *Piano Quartet*. The second movement has a certain mood that I connect with myself—a rather sad and wistful one, I suppose. The last movement is lively, with a triadic theme in a free form. The whole is a work of comparatively simple harmonic and melodic outline, direct in expression. Being aware that many of the flutists who were responsible for commissioning the piece would want to play it, I tried to make it grateful for the performer, but no amateur could handle the *Duo*— it requires a good player.

The world premiere of *Duo for Flute and Piano* took place in Philadelphia, performed by Elaine Shaffer with Hephzibah Menuhin, pianist (3 October 1971). The concert was a benefit for Philadelphia's Settlement Music School, and I was pleased to attend. The

[1] The Institute for Studies in American Music, Brooklyn College, printed the salute on the cover of the *ISAM Newsletter*, Vol. X, no. 1 (November 1980) as a tribute to Copland on his eightieth birthday.
[2] See *Duo* folder, Copland's files in the Library of Congress, for the list of supporters.
[3] Also on the committee were John Knell and Kenton Terry.
[4] See Edward Blakeman and John Solum, "William Kincaid (1895-1967) a Tribute," *Pan* (December 1987), 4, 5.

[5] For details on changes and suggestions, see *Duo* folder, Copland's files in The Library of Congress.
[6] Several sketch pages, from which segments of *Duo* derive, are dated December 1943 and are for a trio of clarinet, flute, and bassoon. Other pages dated 1944 and 1945 are for flute and piano.

Duo was played twice: before intermission and again after. The New York premiere followed at the Hunter College Playhouse with the same players (9 October). The piece was warmly received in both cities. I wrote to Chávez (25 December 1971), "I have finished a fourteen-minute *Duo for Flute and Piano*, which was premiered in October, but the musical ideas date from the forties, and so, naturally, the piece is not at all 'avant-grade' in sound. *Eh bien, tant pis*! But it would be nice to get some '1970' ideas to work on."

After *Duo* was played for the first time in Boston, Michael Steinberg of the *Boston Globe* wrote (25 January 1972):

> Hearing *Duo* was also an occasion for gratefully remembering how extraordinarily and evenly high Copland's standard of achievement has been. He has composed at greater and lesser levels of musical density, but he has never written inattentively nor, for that matter, without huge signs saying "only by Aaron Copland." The *Duo* is a lightweight work of a masterful craftsman. It is going to give pleasure to flutists and their audiences for a long time.

When Elaine and I rehearsed for the Columbia recording of *Duo*, 1 missed several of my own notes, but Elaine just smiled sweetly and missed none at all! I was shocked when I heard later that she was terminally ill at the time. I am told that our recording was the very last time Elaine ever played. Other fine flutists have taken up the piece from time to time, among them Jean-Pierre Rampal, John Solum, Paula Robison, and Doriot Dwyer.[7] After hearing *Duo*, Leo Smit wrote (19 January 1972), "Flute piece simply lovely, Emilyish with tiny touches of *Piano Fantasy*. Happy for all flutists."

The flute part was edited for violin by Bobby (Robert) Mann of the Juilliard Quartet. He played the first performance of *Duo for Violin and Piano* at the Library of Congress with pianist André-Michel Schub (5 April 1978). The new version was well received; in fact, some critics have preferred the violin arrangement to the flute original.

After Doriot Anthony Dwyer (first flutist of the BSO) played *Duo*, she wrote (4 January 1973), "Everyone I know welcomed your *Duo*, because it was the first composition of yours in a long time, and because of its own lovely spirit." Doriot then asked to arrange my early "Vocalise" for flute and piano. We met and I suggested sonic adjustments. Doriot had been asking me to compose a work for her instrument for years, and even after *Duo*, she spoke to me about a concerto for flute and orchestra or a chamber piece. I composed neither but was pleased to approve Doriot's flute version of "Vocalise." After the first performance, she wrote (9 April 1973), "Well, the 'Vocalise' is launched! I got the right climax to it, and it was all a great deep pleasure to play. I knew everyone would love it and they did!"

[7] Some other notable performances of *Duo* were by Jean-Pierre Rampal and Robert Veyron-Lacroix, the Library of Congress (25 Feb 1972); Louise Ditullio and Ralph Grierson, West Coast premiere, Los Angeles Monday Evening Concerts (20 March 1972); Jayne Rosenfeld and Cheryl Selzer, Copland Retrospective, Performers' Committee for Twentieth Century Music (1974); John Solum and Ann Schein, Copland seventy-fifth birthday program, the Library of Congress; Doriot Dwyer and Gilbert Kalish, fiftieth anniversary of Copland-Sessions Concerts, Tanglewood. Others who have performed *Duo*: Harvey Sollberger and Charles Wuorinen; Karl Kraber and Paul Jacobs; Paula Robison and Charles Wadsworth. The first movement of *Duo* was played at the Memorial Service for Harold Clurman (18 September 1980), Shubert Theatre, New York City, with Samuel Baron, flutist.

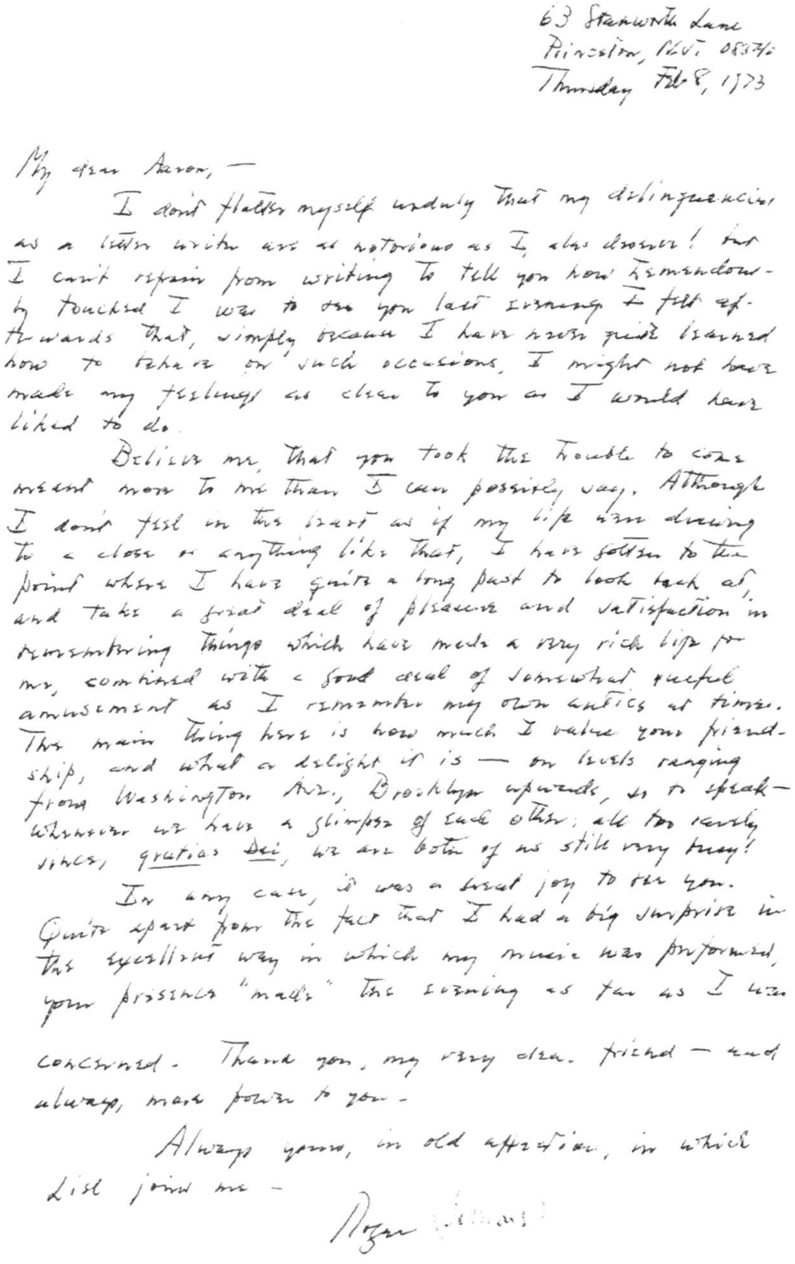
63 Stanworth Lane
Princeton, N.J. 08540
Thursday Feb. 8, 1973

My dear Aaron, —

I don't flatter myself unduly that my delinquencies as a letter writer are as notorious as I, alas, deserve! but I can't refrain from writing to tell you how tremendously touched I was to see you last evening. I felt afterwards that, simply because I have never quite learned how to behave on such occasions, I might not have made my feelings as clear to you as I would have liked to do.

Believe me, that you took the trouble to come meant more to me than I can possibly say. Although I don't feel in the least as if my life were drawing to a close or anything like that, I have gotten to the point where I have quite a long past to look back at, and take a great deal of pleasure and satisfaction in remembering things which have made a very rich life for me, combined with a good deal of somewhat rueful amusement as I remember my own antics at times. The main thing here is how much I value your friendship, and what a delight it is — on levels ranging from Washington Ave., Brooklyn upwards, so to speak — whenever we have a glimpse of each other; all too rarely since, gratias Dei, we are both of us still very busy!

In any case, it was a great joy to see you. Quite apart from the fact that I had a big surprise in the excellent way in which my music was performed, your presence "made" the evening as far as I was concerned. Thank you, my very dear friend — and always, more power to you —

Always yours, in old affection, in which Lisl joins me —

Roger

Letter from Roger Sessions, 8 February 1973

There were other memorable occasions in the early seventies that stand out in my mind: One was the opening of the Kennedy Center in Washington. The first concert, in memory of the late President Kennedy, featured the premiere of Lenny Bernstein's *Mass*, which caused quite a sensation (8 September 1971). I sat in the box with members of the Kennedy and Bernstein families.

In March 1972, I enjoyed my first visit to Mexico in ten years. It had the pleasant feeling of a homecoming. I conducted the Orquesta Filarmonica de la Universidad, regularly directed by Eduardo Mata. As usual in Mexico, the enthusiasm of the players and audience made up for a certain lack of polished technique. After visiting with Chávez, I returned to enjoy spring in Peekskill until the end of May, when I was off again, this time to London to conduct the LSO for recordings of *The Red Pony, Latin-American Sketches*, and *Music for the Movies*. I also conducted a concert in that enormous barn of a Royal Albert Hall, gave a talk for the BBC, and visited with Victor Kraft, who was living in Cambridge.

I was home when the Composers Committee put on a retrospective concert for Roger Sessions (7 February 1973) and was pleased to be able to attend. Roger and I had not seen each other much in recent years. Since the time when we had put on the Copland-Sessions Concerts, I had never been sure how Roger felt about me. I was pleasantly surprised to receive a warm and friendly letter from him the day following his concert. Roger wrote (8 February):

> . . . I can't refrain from writing to tell you how tremendously touched I was to see you last evening. I felt afterwards that, simply because I have never learned how to behave on such occasions, I might not have made my feeling as clear to you as I would have liked to do. Believe me, that you took the trouble to come meant more to me than I can possibly say. . . . The main thing here is how much I value your friendship. . . Thank you, my very dear friend. . . Always yours, in old affection. . . Roger

We had another reunion (30 September 1981): Roger, Virgil, and I performed in Stravinsky's *Histoire du Soldat* for a Composers Showcase concert at the Whitney Museum. Virgil took the part of the devil, Roger was the soldier, and I the narrator. Andrew Porter wrote in *The New Yorker* (19 October 1981):

> It was a nostalgic, affectionate runthrough of the piece; it was not without wit, and offered the unusual spectacle of one of America's greatest composers calling another a "lousy, rotten cheat." Mr. Copland was the most coherent speaker and Mr. Thomson the most perky, but Mr. Sessions' soft, bewildered protestations won the heart.

It was not the first such appearance: In 1966, Bill Schuman planned a summer series of Stravinsky programs at Lincoln Center in which *Histoire du Soldat* was included (15 July). Lukas Foss conducted, Elliott Carter was the soldier, and John Cage the devil. Cage recalls that Stravinsky was in the audience, and Elliott remembers exactly what Stravinsky said to Cage: "You are the only sensible composer I know—you don't write any notes." Elliott described the occasion.:

Copland in rehearsal, c. 1972

> Aaron and I had never done this kind of thing before, so we rehearsed and practiced at his home. Cage could not be there until the final rehearsal. When he heard us, he said, "What you are doing is so beautiful, it makes me cry. I don't know how I will be able to do this with you." Then he upstaged us terribly and stole the show! We were rather cross with him. The performance was sold out, and I remember Cage calling it, "the history of the sold-out."[8]

After the death of Stravinsky in 1971, Boosey & Hawkes invited sixteen composers to write brief commemorative canons and epitaphs in his memory to be published in two issues of their quarterly, *Tempo*. Each composer was asked to use some or all of the instruments Stravinsky had used for two works in 1959: *Epitaphium* for flute, clarinet and harp and *Double Canon* for string quartet. I composed *Threnody Igor Stravinsky: In Memoriam,* later called *Threnody I*. It is a two-minute piece for flute and string trio, consisting of a canonic ground in the strings over which a flute melody is spun. I used a theme from my notebook of musical ideas dated "February 1942," which was originally intended "for a passacaglia."[9] *Threnody* was first performed on a Radio 3 concert conducted by Elgar Howarth (6 April 1972).

[8] From a telephone conversation, Elliott Carter to Perlis, 1 June 1989.

[9] Copland noted on the manuscript, "A Spanish tune from Schindler." He was probably referring to Kurt Schindler, *Folk Music and Poetry of Spain and Portugal* (New York: Hispanic Institute in the United States, 1941).

"Composers Showcase" performance of Stravinsky's *Histoire du Soldat* at the Whitney Museum, New York City, 30 September 1981. (*Front, left to right*): Roger Sessions, Aaron Copland, and Virgil Thomson; (*rear*): Speculum Musicae musicians and conductor Robert Craft (left of Copland)

Threnody II was composed in 1973 as an elegy to Beatrice Cunningham (Mrs. Robert W. Cunningham), sister of Lawrence Morton and supporter of the Ojai Festival, In this piece, alto flute replaces the C flute of *Threnody I.* It is made up of successions of rich homorhythmic chords with intermittent solos, brief canonic passages, and various transpositions of a quickly ascending figure. *Threnody II* is somewhat more complex than *Threnody I.* Since both are short, I recommended they be paired. The premiere of *Threnodies I* and *II* took place at Ojai under Michael Tilson Thomas, director of the twenty-seventh Ojai Festival (2 June 1973). In 1972, between the threnodies, I composed a piano piece for the Van Cliburn piano competition: *Night Thoughts (Homage to Ives).*

I had an exciting five-week conducting tour in the fall of 1973, which included Budapest, Istanbul, Ankara, Prague, and Madrid (23 September-28 October).[10] Upon my return, I found in my usual flood of mail an item that caused some consternation. It was from Richard Nixon's office requesting that some of my music be played at his inaugural concert. I

[10] For programs and schedules, see "Trips" and "Programs" in Copland's notebook (compiled by David Walker) in the Library of Congress..

Manuscript, first page of *Night Thoughts (Homage to Ives)*, composed in 1972

was in a quandary, since I did not admire Mr. Nixon, but I had no desire to take a stand against him by refusing to have my music played. My decision was to allow the performances but not to attend. Afterward I heard from a few colleagues who thought I should have objected.[11] (For Jimmy Carter's inauguration in 1977, I not only attended but conducted the Atlanta Symphony in part of the program.[12])

After a quiet seventy-third birthday celebration in New York (lunch with David Del Tredici, dinner with Alvin Ross), I went up to Boston: how could I resist an invitation to participate in a Harvard Law School forum!"[13]

Boulez programmed *Connotations* with the New York Philharmonic the weekend before Christmas, and I spent the week in the city at rehearsals and performances. My friends asked me to reserve tickets—they all seemed very interested in hearing Boulez' interpretation of *Connotations*. I had Christmas dinner with Minna and Mel Daniel as usual; this year, Chávez, Victor, and David Walker joined us. One evening, I went to visit Paul Jacobs, taking along my new piano piece, *Night Thoughts*, so I could hear how it sounded played by a really good pianist.

Invitations to conduct were plentiful; the ones that interested me most, after the major orchestras, were those that came from places I wanted to see, such as Scotland (August 1974), Hawaii (November), and El Salvador (1975). Nineteen seventy-four was Koussevitzky's centennial, and I joined in the celebration by conducting the BSO at Tanglewood in *Appalachian Spring* and Prokofiev's *Classical Symphony*. On Koussevitzky's birthday, I shared the program with Lenny (16 July), and while conducting *Quiet City*, I felt the presence of Koussevitzky. As I walked around the grounds, I wished he could have been there to see Tanglewood that day.

Until my seventy-fifth birthday, there had been ten years between major birthdays, but now the celebrations were almost continuous, beginning the spring and summer preceding it and continuing into the following year. To those who mentioned my next birthday in advance, I complained, "Please don't rush me!" Gunther Schuller, who had his fiftieth birthday in 1975, expressed my own feelings exactly when he wrote, "I'm about birthday'd out, how about you?" I was not fond of being reminded of my age, but I felt a lot better than I thought I would at seventy-five. I responded to questions from interviewers by saying, "If I had known in advance how well I would be treated, I would not have taken so long to get here!" Donal Henahan of *The New York Times* reported that I was "as old as the century, but in much better shape."

No one wants to be reminded about the passage of time, certainly not me, but when the Bicentennial festivities of 1976 promised to expand the number of performances of American music, we composers managed to bear with it. I detected more interest in American music abroad than there had been in the past. In addition to the Bicentennial, I attributed it to a renewed interest in Charles Ives, which had been sparked by the Ives centennial of October 1974. A Festival-Conference was held in honor of that occasion, with many concerts and presentations, among them a performance by David Barron and myself of the seven Ives songs I had helped introduce at Yaddo in 1932.[14]

Entries in my date books for 1974-1976 piled up beyond feasible listing. I toured Europe in the early fall (31 August-8 October 1975), going first to Copenhagen to conduct American works at the Tivoli, then on to Paris. In the former, it was Roy Harris' *Third Symphony* that was most admired; in the latter, Gershwin's *Piano Concerto* was preferred. As usual when in Paris, I stayed at the Pont Royal Hotel. Noel Lee gave a party for me and our French friends. Lenny Bernstein was also in Paris, making recordings. He and Harry Kraut were in a studio in the same building where I was rehearsing the Nouvelle Orchestra Philharmonique. When Harry came over to see me, he was shocked at how rude and inattentive the players were. Harry was so furious that he went to get Lenny, who raised hell with the manager of the orchestra.[15] It was not a pleasant

Copland's seventy-fifth birthday dinner in New York City: Bernstein, Schuman, and Copland

[11] See letter from John Vinton in Copland Collection (14 January 1973): "I was very much disturbed to read that a piece of yours would be played . . . honoring Richard Nixon. Nothing I have ever read about you would lead me to believe that you want to support this man's actions."
[12] Copland conducted the first half of the Carter inaugural concert; Robert Shaw the second half. Copland was responsible for "The Star Spangled Banner," *Fanfare for the Common Man*, Bernstein's *Overture* to *Candide*, Barber's *Essay No. I*, and *Rodeo*.
[13] The Harvard Law School Forum was cosponsored by the music department; panel members were chosen by Arthur Berger.

[14] The Ives Festival-Conference was coproduced by H. Wiley Hitchcock and Vivian Perlis and held in Brooklyn, New York City, and New Haven (17-21 October 1974). Barron and Copland performed at the opening event at the American Academy and Institute of Arts and Letters, New York City. Copland also appeared on a panel moderated by Gilbert Chase (18 October). See *An Ives Celebration*, edited by Hitchcock and Perlis (Urbana: University of Illinois Press, 1977), 16-28. For tape recordings of the Festival-Conference, see Historical Sound Recordings, Yale.
[15] See interview with Harry Kraut.

experience, and I was relieved to get to London, where I was welcomed warmly by the LSO. I conducted a Proms concert (16 September), and the new director of Boosey & Hawkes, Tony Fell, gave a reception in my honor before I left for conducting dates in Norway.

I wrote to Chávez, "Watch out, here come the birthday fireworks at home!" In October, I played in my *Piano Quartet* with the Juilliard Quartet at the Coolidge Auditorium in Washington, and then went to Cleveland for a celebration called "Mr. Copland Comes to Town." On my birthday, I conducted the first New York concert performance of *Dance Panels* at the Juilliard, sharing the program with Dennis Russell Davies, who led the Juilliard Orchestra in *Statements* and the *Third Symphony*. Concurrently, an exhibit, "Copland and the Theater," was being shown in the Music Division of the Lincoln Center Library for the Performing Arts. Two days earlier, a celebration had taken place in Alice Tully Hall, followed by a supper in the Library for the benefit of the MacDowell Colony.

I had the pleasure of conducting the American Symphony Orchestra and the Orpheon Chorale at Carnegie Hall (7 December) in an all-Copland program. During intermission, Daniel P. Moynihan, United States Representative to the United Nations, presented me with a scroll signed by members of the orchestra.

I have not even touched upon the soloists who were kind enough to do me honor, such as Leo Smit and Charles Fierro in all-Copland piano recitals.

The Schwann record catalogue published an all-Copland issue, with articles by Nadia, Clurman, Olga Koussevitzky, Bill Schuman, and Lenny Bernstein. Other writings ranged from the local Croton-on-Hudson weekly, to the powerful *Frankfurter Allgemeine Zeitung*, to a tribute from Tod Perry in the *BSO Newsletter*, sent on to me with personal messages from Seiji Ozawa, Dan Gustin, and others. Columbia Records released "Aaron Copland: a 75th Birthday Celebration," with the LSO and the New Philharmonia of London, which I conducted. Bill Moyers interviewed me at Aspen for National Public Radio. The BBC's Humphrey Burton put together a special television program and a documentary film was made by Terry Sanders for the United States Information Agency (USIA). I appreciated all the attention at the time, and now that I stay closer to home and have more time, I take great pleasure in looking at the television programs periodically. I particularly enjoy the conducting segments and the American landscape scenes in the Sanders film.

I accepted a commission for a major Bicentennial work. The plan had been worked out by Tod Perry and others: composers were each assigned to one of six orchestras—the Philadelphia was to be mine, with a premiere at the Grand Opera House, Wilmington, Delaware, scheduled for May 1976. I heard from Ormandy in the summer of 1974: "I like to learn a work one year before it is to be performed"; later, he said, "Aaron, as an old friend, I ask you to sit down and make an outline for this commission and give me an idea of its context, the approximate length as well as its orchestration and whether any soloists or chorus will be involved." I was sorry to disappoint Ormandy, but I was not able to come up with fresh ideas; rather than repeat myself, I decided not to compose the work. I was bogged down in terms of composing, but there was always the hope I would bog up again! In the meantime, I had enough conducting dates scheduled to keep me hopping.

While in Minneapolis with the Minnesota Orchestra over the Fourth of July 1976, I received the news that Victor Kraft died while vacationing in Maine a few days earlier. Victor had a history of heart ailment and had had a few serious attacks earlier. Still, it was hard to believe—Victor had been part of my life for so many years! David Diamond wrote to me after Victor died, "He was a beautiful young man. I could never understand what happened to Vic. Please remember Aaron—if there is anything at all I can do, let me know. Anything."

During the Bicentennial, interviewers were asking questions about the state of my career, as well as my views about the musical arts in general. I stated that I was not worried about what I saw in the world of contemporary music, except for so many composers going into academia. They took themselves so far from the larger public! I saw a danger of exclusivity, of composing only for the most knowledgeable audiences. But then, where were our composers to go—except perhaps abroad—in the relatively unreceptive cultural milieu of America in the seventies? I never felt I could criticize those composers with families to support who found academia the only recourse for a steady income.

To questions about my composing, I answered honestly that one tends to slow down in composition after fifty years of it. There seems to be so much more that has to be said at twenty! The creative impulse, the need, was no longer strong with me. That part of creativity is very mysterious. There are people who have every reason in the world to go on, but they just stop writing, while somebody else with no encouragement, no technique, no need—you can't stop him. Very strange. I was thinking of doing a study on the output of composers after the age of seventy. Of course, most composers in the past did not live long enough to have had to face that problem.

As I developed my conducting skills, I always remembered what an elderly Bostonian lady told me years earlier: "Aaron, it is important to engage in an activity when you get older that you didn't do when you were young, so you will not be in competition with yourself as a young man." Aside from that, there is a certain satisfaction in leaving a "document" for the future. For once, I wanted to stand up there and conduct my own music the way I originally thought it should go. It's not that I want to be imitated, and other conductors may reveal something about my music of which I might not have thought, but every composer thinks he knows how a piece he wrote should sound, even if it's not the same every time. (For example, you may change your tempi from one time to the next.)

If there are advantages for a composer in conducting, it seems to me the opposite also holds true: A conductor can benefit from knowing how to compose. It gives insight into the structure of a piece, the high and low points, and an intimate sense of the formal structure. It is mainly in the overall shaping that being a composer can help a conductor.

I had not suddenly become a conductor, nor did it come about without patience and effort. I don't remember very much about my earliest conducting, probably because it must have been *terrible*! Koussevitzky required all young composers at Tanglewood to do some con-

Performance of *Lincoln Portrait*, Marian Anderson, speaker, Copland, conductor, c. 1975

Walter Cronkite and Copland before a performance of *Lincoln Portrait*, Nebraska, 1977

ducting, like it or not. He was not flattering about mine and soon urged me not to take time away from composing. I recall a turning point in 1946 when conductor Eugene Goossens was taken ill and the manager of the Cincinnati Symphony asked me to conduct *Appalachian Spring*. I was embarrassed to have to say that I didn't know the piece from the conductor's point of view. I decided then that I would become able to conduct my own works adequately. At about the same time, Stravinsky reinforced my resolve when he told me, "My dear, you should conduct your own music, every composer should." But I always felt hesitant to conduct while Koussevitzky was alive. Conducting was a suppressed passion.

I accumulated experience gradually, but it is hard to find an orchestra to practice on. I found a few in Mexico and Latin America in the forties. After conducting my first major orchestra, the Chicago Symphony, at Ravinia in 1956, I began to feel out of the amateur class. It was only when they invited me to return, however, that I knew my conducting had been satisfactory. David Diamond used to ask me whether Lenny was giving me pointers, but Lenny did not think much more of my conducting than Koussevitzky had. He wrote in 1960, "The notion that we're competing is positively quaint!" However, later that year, he wrote again:

> I watched and heard you conduct the BSO for ninety minutes on TV, and it was a joy. Man, you've improved incredibly! Clarity, meaningfulness of beat. . .only problem—die head too much in die score. You must to know die musik better (or at least trust yourself more) if you want to succeed me at the Phil.

By my sixtieth birthday, I had conducted thirty orchestras in the previous five years; by 1963, the count was up to about one hundred. Of course, I had to go pretty far afield for some of them—Japan and Australia, for example. By June 1972, I had conducted 28 of a possible 30 major American orchestras, in addition to 9 "Metropolitan," 58 foreign, and 17 university groups: a total of 112.[17] Conducting fees improved as I improved. I could make as much as five thousand dollars plus expenses for two appearances with an orchestra. I once said to a friend after receiving a check for conducting the New York Philharmonic, "If only Papa could see me now!" When I was still teaching at Tanglewood in the sixties, I pulled up to the Main Gate one day in my Mercedes, and when Tod Perry saw me, he said, "Aaron, that doesn't look like a composer's car!" I answered jokingly, "Well, it's not! It's a conductor's car."

I admitted to having been bitten by the conducting bug, and once bitten, it gets into your blood and is the very devil to get rid of. I always felt that composing was the really serious business; conducting was for fun. But it has other advantages: it keeps one young, and it pays the bills. Furthermore, conducting is good for the ego. Nobody can make a move until you move your arm!

[16] This paragraph and some other material in Copland's discussion of his conducting career are drawn from Aaron Copland and Leon Kirchner, "The Composer as Conductor and Performer," *The American Symphony Orchestra*, ed. Henry Swoboda (New York: Basic Books, 1967), 75-89. See also Copland recorded interview, "Composer as Conductor," Oral History of American Music, Yale.

[17] See conducting folders and scores in Copland's files at the Library of Congress.

Conducting was not *all* fun and prosperity. Orchestras in far-off places were not always up to playing some of the music I programmed. While on tour to Hungary and Turkey in 1973, I wrote to Verna Fine, "The orchestras in Turkey oy! Less said, etc. But it's all plenty exotic. . . ." I wrote in my diary:

> The orchestra in Ankara, alas, is not much better than in Istanbul. Not much interested in their jobs, and only a mild sign of interest in the new music they were reading—Bernstein's *Candide* and *Billy*. I get a kick out of *Billy the Kid* in Turkish *Billy Tohid*. . . . I talked to the orchestras in German at their request but really had little idea what was understood. I took a certain satisfaction at rehearsal in getting the orchestra to play better than they know how.

A composer has to contend with orchestra players who are potentially the conductor's severest critics. They put up with it when you conduct your own works. It seems like something "authentic"—you wrote it, so they assume you know best how it goes. But when you tackle works by other composers, watch out! It was my friend Lawrence Morton who first urged me to conduct music by composers other than myself. I developed a core repertoire: my European list included a piece or two by Haydn, Fauré, Roussel, Mahler, Tchaikovsky, Busoni, Mozart, Britten, and Hindemith; of American composers, I included Ives, Schuman, Harris, Diamond, Gershwin, Carter, Sessions, and Del Tredici. I planned three types of programs: all-Copland; all-American; American with standard repertoire.[18] I conducted all of my own works at one time or another, welcoming the opportunity to program those that were not chosen regularly by other conductors.

I was never tempted to accept a regular conducting position. I liked being able to choose from a wide range of offers. Also, I could have some leeway as to what I could conduct. To lead the great orchestras of the world and accompany top performers, such as Isaac Stern and Itzhak Perlman, was one kind of thrill. Another was conducting young performers. It was a challenge to build their confidence while at the same time get them to play better than they thought they could. I tended to look for a clean sound and to avoid the sentimental, overly romantic approach. I may have been influenced by Stravinsky, whose conducting seemed to me dry and precise, and I thought that Hindemith had been admirably businesslike when conducting.

When I went into universities, in addition to conducting, I would get together with young composers, listen to their music and have a powwow. So it was not just waving a stick. I had that experience, for example, when visiting Yale University in 1977 to receive the Howland Medal from the School of Music. I was in residence for a few days, ostensibly working, but really enjoying the college atmosphere. I conducted *Appalachian Spring* with the Orchestra of New England in an informal concert in the Morse College dining hall and became an associate fellow of the college (24 January 1977). In the evening, I accompanied my friend Phyllis Curtin in *The Dickinson Songs* and had an opportunity to answer questions from the audience in Yale's recital hall. It was the kind of experience I enjoyed many times over. I found that youngsters in school orchestras could play complicated rhythms as though they had grown up with them—which they had! Seasoned professionals sometimes lost their enthusiasm for the music. I recall conducting Howard Shanet's Columbia University Orchestra (3 December 1973) and the obvious pleasure and enthusiasm the group took in playing *Billy the Kid* under my direction. There was a reception after the concert, and I don't think a single player missed coming up to talk to me.

Of all the orchestras I conducted outside the United States, I most enjoyed the London Symphony Orchestra. They, in turn, treated me with a high degree of respect. Though they are more formal than Americans, they are a great joy to work with, because they are such gentlemen. Part of my success in England is that I have a British publisher who spreads the word about my works. The British seem to have special feeling for American music. After all, there is a kind of Anglo-Saxon connection there that a German or a French orchestra wouldn't have in quite the same way.

France was an unrequited love, since they paid little attention to my music in spite of my early connections there. The Italians were not much interested in American composers, either. In Germany and Holland, I felt that it was difficult to communicate our rhythms and our sense of discretion in the expression of emotion. The long impassive line, without crescendo or decrescendo, is difficult to achieve with a foreign orchestra. Audiences are different, too. Americans look for a more glamorous sound, more brilliant, one that is more precise in the jazz-band sense, with more bite. They want to be "wowed."

Another reason I had more success in England than in other countries is due to the fact that many of my recordings were made in London. In fact, the LSO, under my direction, recorded more of my music than any other orchestra anywhere, with the New York Philharmonic holding second place. For me, recording was more nervous-making than live performances, But the advantages for a composer are enormous! Every work of mine has been recorded, except for the complete version of *The Tender Land*. Some pieces have been recorded many times, frequently with my participation as conductor and/or pianist. (*Lincoln Portrait* is the piece that has been most recorded under my baton.)

Each year in London, I would review the tapes made the previous year as well as make fresh recordings. For example, in 1969 I listened to the *Ode* recorded in 1968. I would get so involved with the music I had to remind myself constantly to pay attention to the sound of the recording! In one day, we recorded the *Orchestral Variations, Rodeo, Letter from Home*, and *John Henry*. About the last, I wrote in my diary: "Was amused at the railroad sounds in the orchestration. I had quite forgotten what the piece sounded like." On another day, we recorded *Lincoln, Fanfare* and *Down a Country Lane*, which I heard in my orchestral arrangement for the first time while conducting the recording in 1969.

I became aware of a phenomenon at concerts I was conducting, which was corroborated by concert managers, who would speak to me with considerable surprise at the number of school and college-age youngsters who filled the top balcony seats

[18] In Copland's files are lists of typical programs, such as: "Type A: *Statements, Our Town, El Salón México, Music for the Theatre, Appalachian Spring*. Or *Third Symphony, Quiet City, Old American Songs*."

Copland enjoying the informal atmosphere at Interlochen Music Camp, summer 1970

and responded with unconcertlike enthusiasm to the music. I first noticed it when I was conducting the Houston Symphony and I was mystified about it. But I hit upon a plausible sible reason for their presence: many of these young people were record collectors. In that way, they became familiar with music at home through repeated hearings on their own turntables or cassettes. That is a very different relationship from hearing a new work played once at a concert. I have every reason to be particularly grateful to the creator of the phonograph. We composers owe a profound debt to Thomas Edison!

I had been promising to return to Australia, not having been there since 1961. Australian composer Vincent Plush had interviewed me during the Bicentennial and, at that time, he began making advance arrangements for my visit in 1978. I arrived in March and enjoyed spending some time with Plush and Peter Sculthorpe (both had promoted first performances of some of my works in Australia). I conducted in Sydney and found the new Sydney Opera House on the harbor impressive—the sailboats were right by one's dressing-room windows! In Sydney and in Melbourne, I sensed a very warm reception from the audiences.[19]

[19] See correspondence of Vincent Plush to Perlis for description of Copland's visit to Australia. The concerts were not totally successful from a musical standpoint, but Copland's presence was greatly appreciated by musicians and audiences. See also Jill Sykes, "Exchanges with Aaron Copland," *The Sydney Morning Herald*, 18 March 1978, 16.

Whenever I am asked about high points in my conducting career, I mention the National Symphony's concert at the Kennedy Center, which elicited a review from Paul Hume that was reprinted in the Congressional Record (5 April 1975). The McDonald's restaurant sponsorship at first struck me as rather odd, but the concert really took off and I wanted to take that particular audience home in my pocket!

Of them all, it would be difficult to top the experience of Decoration Day [Memorial Day] with the National Symphony in Washington, D.C. (28 May 1979). It was in the open air on the grounds of the Capitol, with admission free to the public. I chose works that were serious but approachable: Ives' *Decoration Day* was an obvious choice; Gershwin's *An American in Paris* supplied the infectious bounce of our popular music; and Samuel Barber's *Overture to The School for Scandal* provided the lively opening. Of my own, I chose *Fanfare for the Common Man*, the *Clarinet Concerto*, and *Lincoln Portrait*, which I narrated (guest conductor Gerhardt Zimmerman). The usual preconcert suspense was heightened by the rain that threatened to cancel the concert; but luck was with us. By 6 P.M. the heavens had begun to clear and by 7, the public began to arrive. People seemed to be streaming in from every possible direction. The *Washington Post* the next morning estimated that audience at twenty-two thousand. Imagine standing up to conduct in front of such an audience! As night descended, the lit-up dome of the Capitol spread a soft light on the thousands of music enthusiasts gathered on the lawn below. I could not recall ever having conducted a concert for so numerous and enthusiastic audience before. The orchestra responded by playing three encores: Sousa marches, of course, and we ended the evening with a bang-up rendition of "Hoe-Down" from *Rodeo.* It was truly a night to be remembered.

I must confess, in all honesty, that I have had more than my share of honors awarded me over the years. I am referring primarily to honorary doctorates from universities. My records show that from 1956 to 1979 I accepted degrees from thirty-two American universities.[20] Also, in 1975 and 1976, I received the Brandeis Creative Arts award, the Chancellor's Medal from Syracuse University, the Governor's Medal of the State of New York, and the National Arts Club Award. In 1978, the mayor of New York, Edward Koch, decided to invite composers to Gracie Mansion after I told him I had never been there. He said, "But you were born in Brooklyn and are one of our great composers. I am shocked!" Mayor Koch invited me to be guest of honor at a reception (22 May 1978) at which my music was performed, and a plan to give commissions to young composers was announced by John Duffy, head of Meet the Composer.

I was also guest of honor at a 1979 "State Dinner" given by the Lotos Club of New York City, with Bill Schuman as master of ceremonies. I received the Award for Distinguished Achievement from the Third Street Music School Settlement. The gala lunch took place

[20] During Copland's seventy-fifth birthday and Bicentennial years, honorary degrees were received from Brooklyn College, Tulane, and Rochester universities; in 1979, from Catholic University; in 1976 and 1979, respectively, from two British schools, University of Leeds and York University.

At the White House reception during the Kennedy Center Honors, 1979. (*Left to right below*): Copland, Tennessee Williams, First Lady Rosalynn Carter, Ella Fitzgerald, and Henry Fonda

on my seventy-fifth birthday in the grand ballroom of the Plaza Hotel, with Bill Schuman as keynote speaker. I am amazed that Bill never seemed to tire of introducing me! The program included the most unusual of hundreds of performances I have heard of *Appalachian Spring*. It was played by very young students from the school on various percussion instruments.

A signal honor was to be chosen as the first composer in the field of concert music to receive a Kennedy Center Honor in 1979. These awards were inaugurated the previous year "to give appropriate recognition to individuals who throughout their lifetime have made significant contributions to American culture through the performing arts." It was a special pleasure to receive a Kennedy Center Honor along with Martha Graham, Henry Fonda, Ella Fitzgerald, and Tennessee Williams. The weekend, full of exciting events, included a gala reception in honor of the awardees, which was hosted by Mrs. Carter at the White House.

I stayed at the Watergate Hotel with a few friends who had come to Washington with me.[21] On the day of the festivities, we were escorted by a female Marine lieutenant who was assigned to drive us in a large black limousine. We soon left all the traffic and drove right up to the front portico of the White House. The spacious rooms and corridors of the executive mansion were packed with people. "Everybody" was there, with the exception of President Carter; he was absent due to the strain of the Iran hostage crisis. The fact that the President was upstairs grappling with an international situation was a dramatic contrast to the festivities.

The White House reception was followed by an evening's entertainment at the Kennedy Center (2 December). The entire program opened with *Fanfare for the Common Man.* Each awardee had a section of the program devoted to a celebration of his or her own artistic production. Bill Schuman wrote a tribute to me in the impressive program book, and Lenny Bernstein hosted "my" segment of the program in typical Lenny fashion. I heard him say things about me that I hope are true—"Copland is a mentor I trust completely as my master, idol, sage, guide, shrink, counselor . . . and beloved friend." Then Lenny conducted "Hoe-Down" from *Rodeo* and Bill Warfield sang "The Dodger" and "The Boatman's Dance" from *Old American Songs I.*

I had the pleasure of being seated in a box between Rosalynn Carter and Ella Fitzgerald. I shall not soon forget the extraordinary contrast between the quiet charm of the President's wife and the unalloyed joy of Ella listening to the singing of songs from her repertoire. We all wore our impressive medals, not designed to be pinned on but to hang around one's neck on a multicolored ribbon. A gala dinner and dance to music by Count Basie and his orchestra followed. I wrote the description above of the Kennedy Center Honors in my journal when I returned home, with a note at the top of the page—"For autobiog."

I had proceeded no further on my autobiography than a few scribbled ideas and part of a beginning chapter about my youth in Brooklyn. And then in 1975 Vivian Perlis invited me to participate in the oral history project in American music that she directs at Yale University, I thought it a good idea on its own terms (preservation of material in a composer's own voice) and also as a necessary stimulus toward gathering my ideas together.[22] Contrary to music composition, which is best done in solitude, this kind of project benefits from the stimulus of another person asking questions and assisting in organizing one's thoughts. Vivian and I worked together every few weeks through 1976. A year or so later, I was amazed to see the transcripts of the interviews, which in size resembled nothing less than two very large Manhattan telephone books. And the process was absolutely painless! In 1978, we agreed to put our heads together to prepare a coauthored autobiography, using the oral history transcripts and adding to them from my files of correspondence, notebooks, and music manuscripts. This is the result.

[21] Joining Copland at the Kennedy Center Honors were Verna Fine, David Del Tredici, Vivian and Sandy Perlis, and Copland's niece, Felice Copland Marlin.

[22] An arrangement between Oral History of American Music, Yale University and the Oral History Research Office at Columbia University allows for transcripts of Copland's oral history to be available through both collections.

Aaron Copland and Leonard Bernstein at the home of their mentor, conductor Serge Koussevitsky

INTERLUDE XII

The winding, heavily wooded driveway is marked with a discreet sign: ROCK HILL. Copland's house is revealed slowly, perched on a ledge looking out toward the Hudson in the distance. The low, long building of natural wood with dark green trim seems almost part of the landscape. There is nothing conspicuous or grand about it, except perhaps the grounds and plantings. Rock Hill is a comfortable place, with a kind of unstudied natural elegance, not unlike Copland himself. From 1974 on, I visited there regularly, first to interview Copland for the Yale oral history project, later to work on his autobiography.[1] During the interviewing, I would drive the distance every few weeks, going over in my mind what I planned to cover in each session. I never feared what kind of reception I would receive (except from Sophronus' enormous great dane, Dido). Copland was always the same—the wide grin, a gesture of mock surprise—"Gee Lucifer! You came all this way just to see me?" He was always gracious and welcoming, never rushed or begrudging of his time.

Interviews were written into the current appointment book and were taken as seriously as other professional commitments. Copland's informal and genial manner could be misleading: he was not an easy person to interview. Never polite for politeness' sake, or chatty to keep things going, he would not embellish what he had to say. If a question was too general or not phrased to his liking, he would point it out, tactfully but firmly: "Aren't you taking a rather broad view?" or "Are you asking me or telling me?" If Copland's memory would fail, he might say jokingly, "Do you realize that was almost fifty years ago!" or "Fill me in on that, will you?" It was not long before the similarity between the man and his music became evident: outspoken and straightforward, quick and intelligent, introspective, witty, dependable.

Copland's papers, consisting of correspondence, programs, reviews, lectures, journals, photographs, and music manuscripts were at Rock Hill, to be moved to the Library of Congress gradually. The extensive collection, organized through the years by David Walker, proved useful during the interviewing and invaluable for the autobiography. As a composer known for not speaking freely about his music, Copland could be stimulated to comment about various aspects of composition by looking at manuscripts or by reading through a sketch or score at the piano. If asked about a particular piece in a more formal way, his answer was likely to be, "I prefer to leave analysis to those who really know how to do it."

Copland at Rock Hill, Peekskill, New York

[1] For Copland oral history interviews (1974-1976) and video interviews (1978) by Perlis, see Oral History of American Music, Yale.

Work sessions were punctuated by cheerful lunches, the most memorable on the terrace overlooking the Hudson when weather allowed. Three, perhaps four or five, would be seated: Copland, David Walker, and myself, and whoever else happened to be there—Sophronus with his delicious food (until he left in 1983 and Victor Basso arrived), or another of Copland's staff: Michael O'Connor, Chris Cole, or later on, Petey Neyland or Ron Caltabiano, or my assistant Janice Fournier. In the seventies, Clurman and Edwin Denby both came to try to recuperate from the illnesses that would claim them. On weekends, Verna Fine, David Del Tredici, or Phillip Ramey might take the train and be picked up at the Croton station. Other friends visited regularly: David Diamond, Helen and Elliott Carter, Minna Daniel, or Leo Smit and Paul Moor when in New York from out of town. Conversation was always lively. While Copland was still conducting, he would tell about his latest trip, and visitors would relate the latest music news and gossip. Lunch over, his cheerful but inevitable "*au travail*" would send everyone home or back to work.

When I was a newcomer to Copland's home, Victor Kraft's stormy appearances were puzzling. Who was this odd person who could shatter the peaceful atmosphere by bursting noisily into a conversation or interview in Copland's studio? He was a burly, heavily bearded, barrel-chested man, often carrying a camera; he either talked constantly and noisily or sat morosely and silently before stomping out of the room. Friends explained that Victor had been Copland's intimate friend for many years. Copland had always tried to help Victor and had bailed him out of difficulty more times than he liked to remember. After Victor died, Copland was sad, but he was never gloomy or brooding for long; he described himself as being "optimistic by nature."

In the long afternoons working through Copland's papers (the files were unpretentiously stored in the basement next to the laundry machines), I occasionally heard him at the piano: one day practicing *Vitebsk* for an upcoming concert in Santa Fe (31 July 1982); another time, *The Dickinson Songs* for a performance with Jan DeGaetani (1978): while playing, Copland sang "Going to Heaven!" with great gusto, laughing out loud at himself as he went along. Occasionally, young performers came to visit, seeking advice or approval for a new instrumentation or arrangement. At such times, David and I would join as audience in the studio, as we did when the Alexander String Quartet arrived to play the movement of an early quartet I had unearthed at the Library of Congress. "Did I write that?" Copland queried with a chuckle. Then he listened intently and offered suggestions. (*Movement for a String Quartet* was premiered by the Alexander String Quartet and subsequently published.)[2] Copland always enjoyed hearing young people make music. He would say jokingly, "especially my music." Youngsters from the Aaron Copland Music and Arts Program in Westchester County came to see and perform for him every summer.

[2] *Movement for String Quartet* was performed by the Alexander String Quartet at the press party for *Copland: 1900 Through 1942,* in the Amsterdam Gallery, the New York Public Library at Lincoln Center (18 October 1984); the public premiere was at Merkin Concert Hall in New York City (19 December 1985). The work was recorded by the Alexander String Quartet and is dedicated to Vivian Perlis.

Youngsters from the Aaron Copland Music and Arts Program in Westchester County visit their distinguished sponsor, summer 1987.

After Copland's oral history interviews were completed, we worked together on a ninetieth birthday tribute to Nadia Boulanger for *The New York Times*,[3] and then progressed naturally to the coauthored autobiography. A literary agent and publisher[4] were chosen and I began to accompany Copland to rehearsals and concerts in order to collect firsthand information. Of these many special occasions in the late seventies and eighties, I will describe only a few.

One involved Copland and Bernstein. After a video interview session with both composers in Washington for the Kennedy Center Honors archive, we all rode together by taxi to the Lincoln Memorial (February 1979). As we drove by the White House, Copland napped and Bernstein talked emotionally about his friendship with the Kennedys and their lost dreams for the arts in America. At the Lincoln Memorial, Copland showed evidence of his patient and even temperament, waiting in the bitter cold, Lenny's white duffle coat over his shoulders, while cameras and lights were set up to film them together in that historic place, the statue and the spirit of Lincoln hovering over all.

Another special occasion was when Copland received an honorary doctorate from Brown University (June 1980). The ritual was extraordinary: the commencement ceremony

[3] Copland and Perlis, "Boulanger—20th Century Music Was Born in Her Classroom," and "Copland Salutes Boulanger," *The New York Times,* 22 September 1977, D 25-26.

[4] Literary agents for Copland's autobiography were Robert Lantz and his associate Joy Harris. *Copland: 1900 Through 1942*, St. Martin's/Marek, 1984, and *Copland Since 1943*, St. Martin's/Griffin, 1989. *Copland Since 1943*, Marian Boyars, Ltd., 1992; paperback, 1994. Paperbacks, St. Martin's/Griffin, 1999.

(which occupied most of a day) parties and dinners, an all-Copland vocal concert that he conducted, an onstage "class" about American music by Copland and me, and finally, a festive dance held outdoors on the campus. Copland was delighted when a vivacious student approached and invited him to dance. They moved at a brisk pace across the dance floor, and he had a wonderful time while other students watched with a mix of pleasure and surprise. During a lively fox-trot, Copland explained to me that he had enjoyed dancing ever since his sister Laurine had taught him when he was a boy in Brooklyn.

Copland rehearsed the Brown Chorus, which included the captain of the football team, for a performance of *In The Beginning*. Among other things, he told them, "Be tough and not sentimental." After I wrote about that rehearsal in an article for *Keynote* magazine (November 1980), a letter arrived from Robert Reichley, vice-president of Brown University:

> One footnote to the piece. The football captain/chorus member and I were talking about his summer of singing in bars in San Francisco and working out with the Stanford football team to stay in shape for the Brown season. He mentioned that of all the football games he has played in and even the great trip to China with the Brown Chorus, one of his greatest moments at Brown will be the last measure of *In The Beginning*, Aaron Copland conducting.

Another memorable occasion in 1980 was the joint celebration of Tanglewood's fortieth anniversary and Copland's eightieth birthday on the Fourth of July weekend. Seiji Ozawa, music director of the BSO, said, "Copland really made this place. It is really his." Reviewers of the Saturday evening concert, conducted by Copland (6 July), commented on the fact that the program contained only his accessible music,[5] but as John Rockwell wrote, "The distinction of the evening lay in its symbolic function. What was notable about the program was its reflective cast, its persistently autumnal, lyrical flavor."[6] Copland was concerned about the rainy weather, "and the poor dears out on the lawn." Although the conditions kept attendance down to 8,479, those outside seemed content to huddle under umbrellas. The next day, the kickoff party for Copland's birthday was made official. It took place at Koussevitzky's former home, Seranak. Copland, Bernstein, and Ozawa stood in front of the full-length portrait of Koussevitzky as a large birthday cake arrived. Lenny played "Happy Birthday" and some lively measures from *Rodeo*.

Copland, having given interviews through so many years, was used to dealing with tape recorders and in more recent years, videocameras. Interviews for television productions frequently took place at Copland's home; for example, those made in December 1979 for the documentary "Aaron Copland: A Self Portrait," broadcast by PBS for Copland's eighty-fifth birthday.[7] At such times, the house would be in disarray for days to accommodate wiring and lighting, but Copland took it all in stride. Like a professional actor, he could

[5] The Tanglewood program included: *Fanfare, El Salón México, Clarinet Concerto* (Harold Wright, soloist), *Suite from The Tender Land*, and *Four Dance Episodes from Rodeo*.
[6] John Rockwell, "Music: Copland Conducts Copland at Tanglewood," *The New York Times*, 7 July 1980, C
[7] *Aaron Copland: A Self Portrait* was coproduced by Ruth Leon Productions, and Vivian Perlis; Leon and Allan Miller, directors; Perlis, writer and interviewer. Released by PBS as the first in the series "American Masters" (16 October 1985), as a Copland eighty-fifth birthday tribute.

Above: Copland receiving Doctor of Music honorary degree from Brown University, 1980

Below: Copland dancing with a happy student at Brown's commencement party

Above: David Walker and Copland on the terrace, with Dido

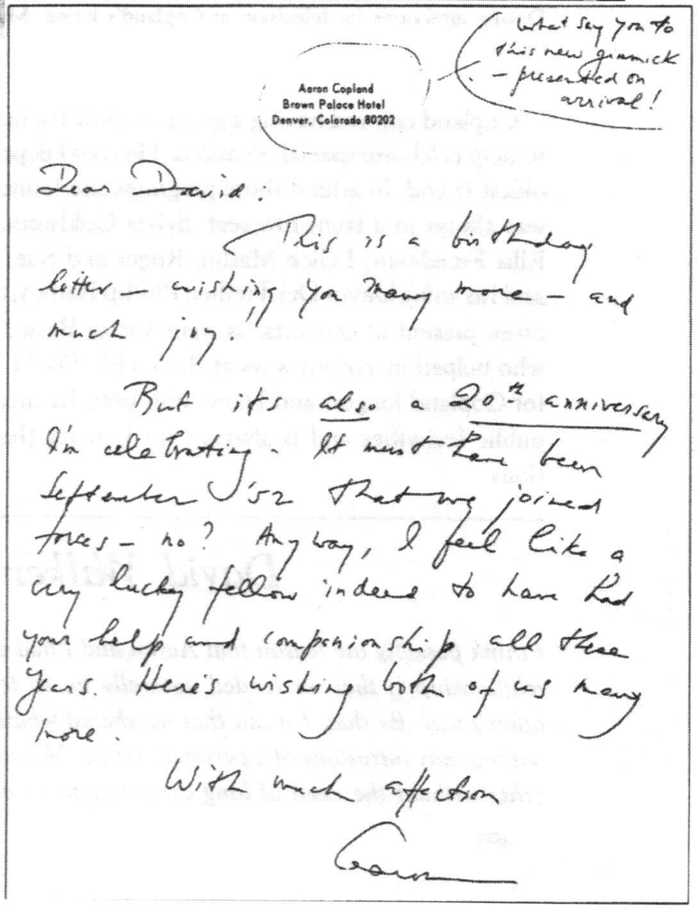

Aaron Copland
Brown Palace Hotel
Denver, Colorado 80202

What say you to this new gimmick – presented on arrival!

Dear David:

This is a birthday letter—wishing you many more—and much joy!

But it's also a 20th anniversary I'm celebrating. It must have been September '52 that we joined forces—no? Anyway, I feel like a very lucky fellow indeed to have had your help and companionship all these years. Here's wishing both of us many more.

With much affection

Aaron

Right: Letter from Copland to David Walker, 1972

repeat his favorite stories until the take was just right, yet each telling seemed fresh and spontaneous.

Copland enjoyed having a group of close friends and colleagues on hand to help celebrate special occasions. He could depend on Minna Daniel, his oldest friend, to attend those programs she found interesting. Verna Fine was always in a front-row seat. Sylvia Goldstein, Doris and Stuart Pope, Ellis Freedman, Felice Marlin, Roger and Sue Levey (his great-nephew and wife), David Del Tredici, Phillip Ramey, and Bennett Lerner were often present at concerts, as were Victor Basso, Irene Wiley, and others who helped in various ways at Rock Hill. David Walker, who worked for Copland longest and knew him best, frequently accompanied him to public festivities and was always with him for the quieter private celebrations.

David Walker[8]

I think possibly the reason that Aaron and I had such a long and workable relationship is that we tended naturally to, so to speak, stay out of each other's way. By that, I mean that we shared whatever work was to be done without any intrusions of a personal nature. We seemed to understand each other without the need of long explanations or any setting down of rules.

I understood instinctively the times he needed privacy and his wish not to discuss any compositional works that were in progress. Sometimes he would play sections of a new piece, asking me to sit in and listen; but usually what I heard when he was at the piano in the evenings was a phrase here, a chord there, realizing silently that these were the makings of a Copland piece that eventually the world would hear and become familiar with.

Aaron was an almost constant worker. There was always a project or two underway—if not composing, he was studying scores, planning programs, working on a lecture, an article, a book, and travel plans. Even on trips to far-off countries, when the musicmaking was over, Aaron was ready to come back home.

There were fun times and serious times, but I never once found him to be "difficult." He knew what he wanted and could make that quite clear. Yet he always had time to listen to others, and in so many, many instances over the years he advised and assisted friends and strangers alike—with a mere phone call, a letter or two, or a series of meetings.

The houses in Ossining and Peekskill were, first of all, places where Aaron lived as privately as possible and worked in as much comfort as possible—which to Aaron meant a good piano, a large desk, ample space, and quiet. The atmosphere was a mixture of an easygoing day-to-day routine interspersed with frequent visits of a business or personal nature. There were times of entertainment with a few guests—drinks and meals, walks in the woods, and, of course, music talk and listening.

Although I worked with Aaron on a business basis, we were good friends in the best sense of that word. An ongoing thirty-five years does make a long and fascinating relationship, and I'm happy now to say it was one that worked. On social occasions, instead of being introduced as his assistant, I was "a composer friend." How grateful I will always be for the many dimensions and meanings of this friendship.

[8] Interview, David Walker with Vivian Perlis, October 1988, Weston, Conn.

The music world and the media were hard put not to repeat themselves as, year after year, one special Copland event followed another, and each tribute seemed more honorific than the last. It would be misleading to focus on these occasions as the fabric of Copland's life. He accepted each degree with pleasure, invitations to the White House with almost boyish wonder (he continued to present his Social Security card, even when he was an honored guest), every black-tie dinner hosted by Bill Schuman or Lenny Bernstein, every celebrity interview (such as the 1978 "Dick Cavett Show"). They were all special. Copland had a kind of naive sense of wonder about such things. But life was not held together by major birthdays or the awarding of honors. In fact, Copland usually paid less attention to them than others did. He was always respectful and grateful, but he did not take them so very seriously.

As medals and satin hoods from honorary degrees accumulated, and scrolls and awards were received, Copland would comment on each with appreciation (sometimes amusement). The item would then be displayed for a respectable time before being put away in a drawer or closet with a multitude of similar artifacts. A few presidential medals and photographs had permanent places in Copland's living room and studio, and the famous Oscar always stood on a mirrored shelf in the hallway. For Copland, the real events were the musical ones, when he could face an expectant group of musicians ready to play when he lifted the baton.

Always willing to try a new experience, Copland agreed when pianist and friend, the late Paul Jacobs, said "Let's appear at the rock club, the Bottom Line." The owners of the club showed a willingness to experiment by presenting some non-rock acts occasionally. Jacobs and Copland were invited to do a program about the influence of jazz on classical music in the twentieth century (15 December 1979). Jacobs played, and then he and Copland chatted onstage, ending with a performance of *Danzón Cubano* together. Copland confessed to being a little nervous about playing piano in public after a hiatus of several years, but he said, "Paul's an old friend and he talked me into it."

Copland's eightieth birthday began with an official announcement from Washington: "The Congress of the United States joins in honoring this extraordinary American on this occasion with the reading of the following into the Congressional Record: 'Aaron Copland, this country's greatest living composer, is the classic American success story: a man from modest beginnings who has reached the top of his profession solely by his own efforts.'"The entry, which continued for several pages, concluded:

> Aaron Copland, always at the frontier of American music, has become its most distinguished elder statesman. He has won every honor in the book, including thirty-three honorary doctorates, the Pulitzer Prize, the Presidential Medal of Freedom and the Kennedy Center Honor. We salute this fine American for his music and for his tireless efforts on behalf of all of American music.

When Copland received notification and a copy of the Congressional Record entry, he asked Lawrence Morton, "Has anyone told Roy Cohn?"

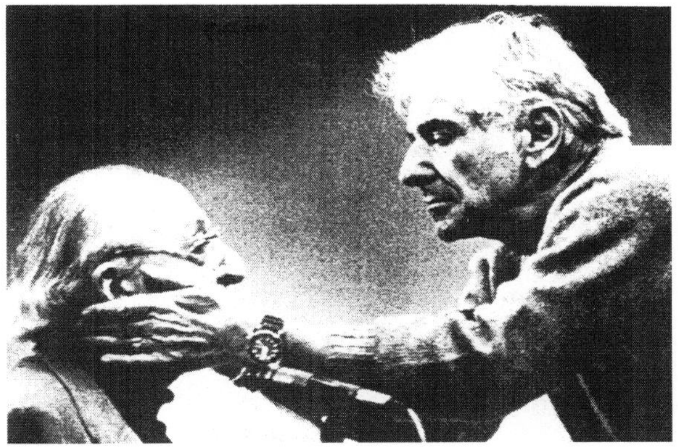

Bernstein and Copland at rehearsal for the Carnegie Hall eightieth birthday tribute to Copland

Considering Copland's close relationship with the National Symphony Orchestra and his friendship with its director, Mstislav Rostropovich, it is not surprising that the major eightieth birthday celebration was planned by Rostropovich and took place in Washington.[9] Several spectacular times were yet to come (such as the eighty-fifth birthday gala in New York), but Washington 1980 was the last big event in which Copland took an active role. He has always preferred being involved in the musicmaking to being a spectator, or as he put it, "merely gracing the occasion." Since it is not possible to include in detail all of the special events of Copland's eightieth birthday, or those that followed,[10] perhaps a full account of the Washington festival will convey the quality of excitement and exuberance that characterized a Copland celebration.

A group of friends and family joined Copland at his favorite Washington hotel, the Watergate. The kickoff event, a National Press Club Symposium, took place between rehearsals for the concert. Leo Smit, who took part in the symposium, asked Copland whether he had a secret formula that made him never lose his temper or use harsh words (Smit explained that one of Copland's most unusual characteristics was an extraordinary equanimity in face of difficult situations). Copland looked out at the audience with a serious expression, hesitated for a moment, and said, "Sounds dull." The audience broke up with laughter, he grinned, and the symposium continued in the relaxed mood everyone had hoped for.

Behind-the-scenes rehearsals at the Kennedy Center Opera House offered glimpses of private moments as memorable as the glamorous public ones. When Leo Smit and Copland were rehearsing the *Piano Concerto*, Bernstein came onstage and stood behind Leo, making suggestions. Asked about this afterward, Leo said, "It was fine. It had the feeling of a reunion for the three of us." And there was something touching about the solitary look of Copland as he sat quietly onstage listening to the plaintive trumpet player during the rehearsal of *Quiet City*.

9 The eightieth birthday celebration at Kennedy Center was edited for public television as "A Copland Celebration" and broadcast in the series "Kennedy Center Tonight" (1 April 1981); Stephen Dick, writer; Hal Holbrook, narrator; Rodney Greenberg, director.

10 Events were coordinated by Toni Greenberg for Boosey & Hawkes.

During interviews for television at Copland's home. Mike Wallace and Copland

President and Mrs. Carter had not planned to attend the gala evening concert; the presidential box was reserved for Copland's guests. At the last moment, the Carters decided to go after all (Bernstein had something to do with the change). Guests were greeted by President and Mrs. Carter and their guest, Sol Linowitz (a central figure in the Middle East peace negotiations), in the receiving room attached to the presidential box. After conversation and refreshments, the Secret Service seated everyone before the President and First Lady entered. The Carters had not been seen in public since the landslide election of Ronald Reagan eight days earlier. When the audience saw the presidential party, they rose and cheered for several long moments.

The program began with Bernstein leading Copland onstage as the orchestra played *Fanfare for the Common Man*, and it was Bernstein who read a letter to the composer from the President: "Wherever music is played and loved—at home and abroad, among your fellow composers, among musicians and among ordinary listeners—you are justly recognized as America's foremost composer. We are proud to join in this fanfare for a most uncommon man." Then Rostropovich conducted the audience in "Happy Birthday, dear Aaron!" and enrolled Copland as honorary member of the National Symphony, presenting him with a book of greetings from musicians across the land.[11] Copland took the conductor's stand and led *Appalachian Spring*, which was followed by Rostropovich conducting *El Salón México*. At intermission, more presentations were made.[12] When Copland responded, it was with characteristic simplicity: "I've had some very good evenings in my life, but this is something special—a birthday festival for me. I'm very touched and moved, and I feel like a very lucky fellow."

[11] The book of tributes is in Copland's files at the Library of Congress.

[12] Leonard Silverstein, president of the National Symphony Orchestra board, also spoke.

Backstage at the Kennedy Center. (*Left to right*): Sol Linowitz, Rosalynn Carter, President Jimmy Carter, and Copland

After intermission, the program continued with Rostropovich conducting *Quiet City*, Copland and Leo Smit performing the *Piano Concerto*, and finally *Lincoln Portrait*. Copland stood tall and erect and his voice was firm as he read the text. *Lincoln Portrait* has been narrated by hundreds of speakers, professional and amateur, political and theatrical, and before presidents and kings, in high school auditoriums, in English and in Spanish, and even once by Rosalynn Carter. Lincoln's words have carried different meanings for each new generation and with every hearing; under the circumstances of 14 November 1980, as spoken by Aaron Copland on his eightieth birthday from the stage of the Kennedy Center, facing the Presidential party, Lincoln's words took on special meaning. "Fellow citizens, we cannot escape history. We hold the power and bear the responsibility. . . ."

Following the concert, Copland's dressing room was filled with people, telegrams, red roses, and colorful balloons, all of which went along to a lavish dinner dance hosted by the orchestra. Copland, a late-night person, was reported to have been at the bar drinking coffee with Slava [Rostropovich] after 2 A.M.

Copland left for New York the following day for a gala Boosey & Hawkes reception at the St. Regis Hotel. New York birthday concerts preceded and followed Washington: each was extraordinary in its own right.[13] One was "Wall-to-Wall Copland," a ten-hour Copland

[13] Among the many tributes in 1980 the New York Philharmonic performed *Symphonic Ode*, Copland conducting (18 January); The National Orchestral Association presented *Clarinet Concerto* and *Music for a Great City*, Copland conducting, Michael Webster clarinetist (5 February); The Chamber Music Society of Lincoln Center performed two concerts of *Nonet* and six choral works (31 October, 2 November);

program (20 November), planned and executed by Allan Miller, artistic director of Symphony Space, with my participation. The program featured many of Copland's friends and colleagues and a great deal of his music, and it had the relaxed atmosphere and quality performances typical of Symphony Space's "Wall-to-Wall" celebrations. Copland's lawyer, Ellis Freedman, commented during the eightieth birthday festivities, "I bet you'll be glad when this is over!" And Copland answered, "Young man, you underestimate my capacity for adulation."

Copland had not been to Europe since 1975. When his agent, Basil Douglas, asked whether he would visit in 1978, Copland responded, "I have no reason to be going to Europe in 1978 or 1979. I'm pleased to say that I've been happily busy with American symphonies in various parts of the country." An invitation followed from the LSO for 1980. Copland accepted and LSO manager Peter Hemmings wrote, "We are delighted to renew our association with you." Copland heard from his old friend John Kenworthy-Browne: "I know what a splendid thing it is to know and to have known you. We met just twenty-two years ago! I hope to see a little of you, as well as coming to your concert. That, too, will be an emotional event."

Copland left for London, Brussels, and Paris (28 November-22 December)[14] accompanied by a young lawyer, William (Bill) Conroy, who spoke French and could assist Copland with arrangements and schedules.

William Conroy[15]

The LSO could not have been more delighted to have Aaron there. At the first rehearsal, the first thing they did was play "Happy Birthday" to Aaron. It was very touching because it was unexpected. It was not a banal gesture; their warmth was clear throughout rehearsals and performances.[16] *Aaron had a terrifically arduous schedule. He just loved it. At the end of the day when everyone else was tuckered, he seemed chipper. One of the musicians commented, "He's not tired at all—only the rest of us.!" I think it was the reception in London that did it.*

There was an astounding difference between London and Brussels. The Brussels Philharmonique was only a few years old, but that was no excuse for their impolite and downright rude behavior. Aaron could always take the other side. He said, "Well, how would you feel if you had to play the same things over and over again for years?" Much of the difficulty revolved around the fact that the Short Symphony *had been scheduled for performance, and at rehearsal, it was clear that there was not time for the orchestra to prepare*

(*Above*) Copland and Rostropovich at the party following the eightieth birthday concert

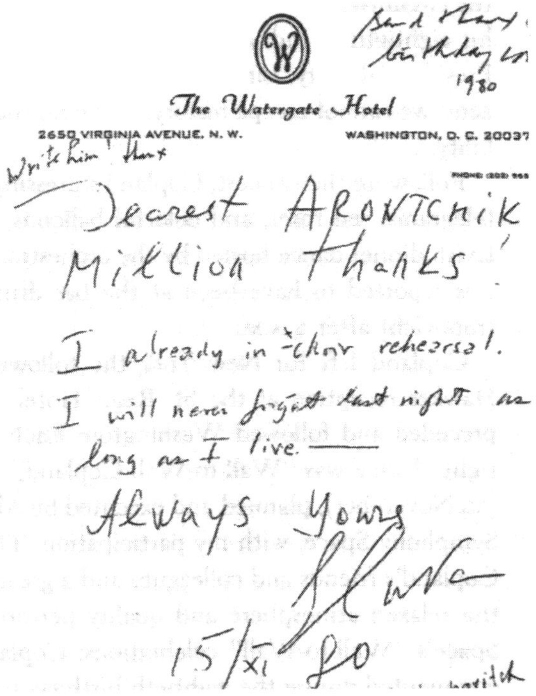

Sent Many
birthday
1980

The Watergate Hotel
2650 VIRGINIA AVENUE, N. W.
WASHINGTON, D. C. 20037

Write him! thanx

Dearest ARONTCHIK
Million thanks!

I already in choir rehearsal.
I will never forget last night as
long as I live.——
Always Yours
Slava
15/XI 80

(*Right*) Letter from Rostropovich to Copland the day after the birthday concert

Brooklyn College featured The American Symphony Orchestra, Copland conducting the Oratorio Society of New York with soprano Linda Wall (9 November); The American Symphony at Carnegie Hall, Bernstein conducting all-Copland (9 November) with a festive party afterward at the Hampshire House; piano concerts by John Kozar in London and Leo Smit in New York (18 November); American Composers Orchestra played *Orchestral Variations*, Jorge Mester conducting (24 November).

[14] See folder, "Europe, 1980," Copland's files at The Library of Congress.

[15] Interview, William Conroy with Perlis, 26 March 1981, New York City.

[16] The London program included *Fanfare, Appalachian Spring, Three Latin American Sketches, Clarinet Concerto,* and *Suite from The Tender Land.*

it, particularly since the concert was to be broadcast nationwide on radio and television.[17] *A compromise was reached—the* Short Symphony *was included in the concert but not the broadcast. One highlight for Aaron in Brussels was seeing his former cook and gardener, Mireille and Gaston, again. They could not go to the concert but saw the broadcast, and Mireille said when she saw Aaron at the podium, "Monsieur Copland is in his element." They came to see us off, and Aaron was absolutely delighted.*

We arrived in Paris and settled into the Hotel Concorde Lafayette. After the Brussels experience, I decided not to go to the rehearsals. The concert was held at the Palais des Congrès (18 December), and it included Pelléas et Mélisande *by Fauré, which Aaron had requested to be in memoriam for Nadia Boulanger. The printed program asked that there be no applause after it. The silence was touching.*

Aaron and I went to see some of his old haunts in Paris, including the Boulevard Raspail, where he had lived with Harold Clurman in the twenties. Aaron said he wished Harold could be there. We went by metro and had a distance to walk, and Aaron complained that his sore foot (a minor chronic complaint) was bothering him. After I said, "ne kvetchez pas," Aaron laughed and repeated that many times. I was again amazed at his stamina and energy as he went sightseeing, gave interviews, and went to rehearsals. Other than his brief remark about Harold Clurman, the only sign of nostalgia was that Aaron repeatedly asked, "Whatever happened to the red taxis?"

As birthday tributes spilled over into 1981,[18] Copland's energy and health remained strong, and for a while after the European trip, travel and conducting continued. In 1981, he conducted the New York Philharmonic and other groups in Las Vegas, Wolf Trap, and Dallas. Copland conducted *Appalachian Spring* for the spring gala of the Graham Company (16 June 1982), explaining, "I never could refuse Martha!"[19] He delighted musicians and audiences as composer-in-residence at the Santa Fe Chamber Music Festival in the summer of 1982. However, conducting was beginning to be a strain, and Copland was limiting the invitations he accepted. As with composing, he made no dramatic decision to stop conducting. It was simply the natural time to do so. Copland's last concert was with the New Haven Symphony Orchestra (7 December 1982), conducting *Outdoor Overture* and the piece that had introduced him to American audiences in 1924, *Symphony for Organ and Orchestra* (organist William Owen).

In 1983 and 1984, Copland attended some of the concerts in his honor,[20] but most of his time was spent at home working on the first volume of his autobiography. He was pleased that his friends and colleagues were contributing interviews and exclaimed, "I can't wait to read what they have to say about me!" While working with Copland, I experienced what others have frequently described: his total confidence that you can do the job makes you do more than what at first seemed possible. Copland would always listen to my ideas with an open mind. He was puzzled when I said his family background and genealogy should be in the book: "Will people be interested? It's not about music!" He also agreed, but without enthusiasm, that his socialist connections in the thirties and the McCarthy hearing in the fifties must be included, but he never wanted to deal with unpleasant situations at great length. He would say, "Agonizing is not my thing!"

Copland read all of the book material carefully and made comments, corrections, and additions. When we drew on writings and speeches from earlier times, as we often had to, it was necessary for me to add missing lines or connective links. Our procedure was for him to read these sections out loud. He never failed to stop at what he had not written and ask, "Did I say that?" I would answer, "No, but how would you say it?" Then Copland would supply in his own words what had been missing.

Copland: 1900 Through 1942 was published in the late summer of 1984. A special book party was given by Minna Daniel. It took place at a country inn at Lake Waramaug, Connecticut, where Minna stayed summers. The day was sparkling clear, the setting like an old-fashioned lawn party, and Minna saw to it that the guest list was as brilliant as the rest of the event. There were two surprises: a cake that exactly duplicated the cover of the book, and the first copies of the book itself, off the press just in time for the party. When our editor, Richard Marek, first showed us the book, Copland asked, "But when will it actually be in Brentanos?" An official press party for Copland was given by St. Martin's Press in New York at the Library at Lincoln Center, attended by the music and publishing world (18 October 1984). The Alexander String Quartet played the movement that I had recently found among Copland's papers.The many favorable reviews that followed book publication gave both authors the impetus to work toward completion of the second volume.

Copland could not attend many of the birthday salutes during his eighty-fifth birthday year, but Lenny Bernstein planned a very special one at Tanglewood and convinced his old friend to be there. Copland arrived by limousine at Seranak, where he was greeted by friends and introduced by Bernstein to the composition and conducting students. An all-Copland concert by the Music Center Orchestra included the *Third Symphony*, conducted masterfully by Bernstein (20 July 1985). Performers have described the concert as one of the memorable experiences of a lifetime. When Copland entered the Shed, the entire audience including those on the lawn, rose and cheered. The reception was extraordinary.

The New York Philharmonic planned to celebrate Copland's eighty-fifth year in the way composers like best: sixteen Copland works performed at twenty-six concerts in the 1985-1986 season by Bernstein, Mehta, James Conlon, Charles Dutoit, and Raymond Leppard. The Philharmonic's plans included the major birthday gala, which Copland attended as guest of honor on his birthday.[21] The event was televised from Avery Fisher Hall and seen

[17] The Brussels program also included: *Quiet City, El Salón México, Clarinet Concerto,* and *Billy the Kid.*

[18] Some special tributes to Copland in 1981: The New York Philharmonic, Bernstein conducting *Appalachian Spring, Clarinet Concerto,* and *Dance Symphony* (29, 30, 31, January, 3 February); a Doctor of Humane Letters degree from Queens College and the renaming of the school as "The Aaron Copland School of Music" (2. June); *Stereo Review*'s 1981 Award of Merit (15 January); Century Association, "Musical evening honoring Copland, Luening and Schuman" (17 February); Da Capo Chamber Players, "Aaron Copland and His Friends," Carnegie Hall, included works by Del Tredici, Schuman, Carter, Berger, Thomson, and Fauré (16 March); Library of Congress, "A Copland Celebration," Coolidge Auditorium (14 November).

[19] For Copland's conducting of *Appalachian Spring* in 1982, see p.179ff.

[20] Among the Copland concerts and tributes of 1983 and 1984: American Chamber Orchestra, Charles Baker conducting an all-Copland program, Carnegie Hall (28 November 1983); Mayor Koch presentation of the New York City Seal of Recognition (15 November 1983); Jan DeGaetani and Gilbert Kalish, premiere of an early Copland song, "Alone," at Carnegie Hall (4 December 1984).

[21] The eighty-fifth birthday program by The New York Philharmonic included *Fanfare for the Common Man, Letter From Home, John Henry; Piano Concerto* (Bennett Lerner), *Proclamation for Orchestra* (orchestrated by Phillip Ramey), *Prairie Journal,* and *Symphony No. 1.*

by millions on "Live from Lincoln Center." It was announced that a Copland scholarship fund was established by Boosey & Hawkes and ASCAP "to be presented annually to an outstanding composer attending an American high school for the arts."

Among the many tributes of 1985[22] was one that particularly interested Copland: the revival of his opera *The Second Hurricane*, which had a substantial run at the Henry Street Settlement House, where it had first been produced in 1937. Copland attended a matinee performance and was delighted with the new production.[23]

Since Copland was no longer traveling by air, he asked me to represent him in Washington on two very impressive occasions in 1986. To receive Copland's awards for him was an honor, but most enjoyable was taking them back to him, along with a full description of the events and greetings from his friends and admirers. The Medal of the Arts was conferred by President Reagan on nine artists and three patrons at a White House luncheon (14 July 1986).[24] It was special—from the dinner for recipients the evening before, to the front entry of the White House and the Marine escorts, to the luncheon itself, with the President and Mrs. Reagan presiding at the two tables reserved for those receiving the honor. A festive State Department reception was held later in the day.

The House of Representatives voted Copland a Congressional Gold Medal, the highest honor that can be awarded a civilian. First given to George Washington, Copland's was the 120th Gold Medal to be approved by Congress. The ceremony (11 November), which preceded Copland's eighty-sixth birthday, was on the stage at the Kennedy Center during a concert conducted by Copland's friend Rostropovich. He conducted *Fanfare for the Common Man* to announce the presentation, made by Representative Vic Fazio. Morton Gould spoke for ASCAP, and I accepted the framed bill, signed by members of the House, granting the Gold Medal to Copland.[25] A single gold medal was designed and struck by the Treasury in 1989, with bronze medals to be minted and made available to the public.

Copland's life at Rock Hill contiued in its familiar pattern: friends visiting and pleasant lunches being the focal point of the day. Copland still wanted to hear talk about music. He would ask, "Who are the new composers?" and "What are they writing?"

[22]Some highlights of the 1985 Copland year: Chicago Symphony performances of the *Third Symphony*, Leinsdorf conducting (March); "Meet the Moderns," Brooklyn Philharmonic in "Music by, for and about Aaron Copland," Foss conducting, Smit soloist in *Piano Concerto* (14 May); concerts by the Philadelphia, Atlanta, St. Louis symphonies; The National Chorale, Merkin Concert Hall (13 November); The American Symphony Orchestra in an all-Copland program, Gould conducting, Walter Cronkite narrating *Lincoln Portrait,* Madison Square Garden (13 November); the First Annual Paul Jacobs Memorial Lecture, Avery Fisher Hall, delivered by Perlis (6 November 1985).

[23] *The Second Hurricane* ran from 13 November-1 December, Tazewell Thompson, director and choreographer; Charles Barker, conductor; David Walker, consultant; artist contributors to the sets: Willem de Kooning, Louise Nevelson, John Cage, Elaine de Kooning, Red Grooms, David Katz, Larry Rivers, and Rudy Burckhardt.

[24] The six other artists who could not attend the awards ceremony due to age or ill health were Marian Anderson, Frank Capra, Copland, Willem de Kooning, Eva Le Gallienne, and Lewis Mumford. Attending were Agnes de Mille, John Lomax, and Eudora Welty. The patrons honored were Dominique de Menil, Seymour H. Knox, and the Exxon Corporation.

When told the minimalists, he said, "Well, by defintion they can't do much harm!" Copland's composer friends reported about the "new romanticism" (the term introduced by Jacob Druckman in 1983 to denote the return of a more accessible compositional style), and Copland was bemused to think that tonality could be making news.

Copland's career ran parallel to the century. He saw musical styles come and go. It was no surprise to him that music in the eighties returned to a style that would reach larger audiences. He had seen a similar shift in the thirties, when composers strove for a more accessible kind of music after the exclusiveness of the avant garde in the twenties. Copland had always been affected by the world around him. His music was influenced by current aesthetics, yet the core remained undeniably Copland. By the eighties, he could afford to be philosophical about another swing in musical style, and it interested him to know that young composers were producing a more expressive music, frequently with extramusical connotations, a kind of music that had been scorned for decades.

Copland enjoyed hearing about performances and recordings of his own music. When compact discs arrived, he exclaimed with typical enthusiasm, "What will they think of next!" He was delighted to know that the summer of 1989, as Tanglewood celebrated its fiftieth anniversary, was being dedicated to him with many performances of and lectures about his music.[26] At the conclusion of the festival, Leonard Bernstein saluted his friend by conducting *Music for the Theatre* and *Music for Movies* at a most appropriate occasion—Tanglewood's annual Serge and Olga Koussevitsky Memorial Concert.

Copland has been part of the world of music for over seventy years, most of the time in the public eye. Those who have become acquainted with him only recently might be reminded that within the familiar genial, avuncular figure is a fighter for American music, a strong leader, one who has done more for composers and for American music than any other single person in this century. By now, it is rare to find anyone connected to twentieth-century music who has not had a Copland experience. William Schuman wrote in the Kennedy Center Honors program book,

> This erudite man of music with the hearty laugh is asked everywhere, and he accepts. He is a peripatetic conductor of America's symphonies large and small, not to mention those abroad, and he is a familiar figure on college campuses. Everywhere he goes, the visit ends with the same question, 'When can you return?'

Each of the many places Copland visited treasures its own set of Copland memories and anecdotes, ready to be told as though unique. It was a Copland talent to face each

[25] A reception was hosted by the Equitable Life Assurance Society.

[26] The season-long Copland tribute was planned and organized by Daniel Gustin, Richard Ortner, Costa Pilavachi, Oliver Knussen, and Vivian Perlis. In addition to the many performances of a wide range of Copland's music by the BSO and the faculty and fellows of the Music Center were some unusual events: the presentation of the score for the early ballet *Hear Ye! Hear Ye!* and "Skyline" from *Music for a Great City* by the Music Center orchestra under Knussen; and songs from the film *The North Star* (lyrics by Ira Gershwin) sung by Lisa Saffer. Highlights of this summer included the *Piano Variations* played by Gilbert Kalish, the *Piano Quartet* by Kalish and the Juilliard Quartet, and *Sextet* by members of the Boston Symphony Chamber Players. A lecture series presented by Steven Ledbetter and Vivian Perlis concluded with

Copland traveling in Europe, 1981

Copland greeting the audience with conductor Zubin Mehta and members of the New York Philharmonic from the stage of Avery Fisher Hall, New York City, 14 November 1985

occasion with anticipation, fresh spirit, and genuine pleasure. He has shared himself with so many musicians and listeners that he has become part of the American consciousness. The media helped to make familiar the tall, lanky figure with the spectacles and quick grin, but the enduring affection of the public for Copland has more to do with the vast accumulation of his sharing of himself, the continuous sound of his music in the collective ear, and the successful transference of his own pleasure in making music. The American people are fond of Aaron Copland, and when he says, "I'm a lucky fellow to have lived my life in music," they believe it and like him all the more.

a panel discussion moderated by Ledbetter with Perlis, Lukas Foss, and Tod Perry.

A Public Law Bestowing

The Congressional Gold Medal

awarded to

Aaron Copland

accepted on his behalf by

Vivian Perlis

presented by

The Hon. Vic Fazio

Morton Gould

and

Marvin Hamlisch

The Congressional Gold Medal is being awarded to Aaron Copland in recognition of his special achievement in creating a uniquely American style of composition, making a vital contribution to American artistic life.

Aaron Copland's

"Fanfare for the Common Man"

National Symphony Orchestra
Mstislav Rostropovich, *Music Director*
Concert Hall
The John F. Kennedy Center for the Performing Arts

November 11, 1986

REFLECTIONS ON MY LIFE IN MUSIC

Being a composer is a great privilege.[1] I find a profound satisfaction in the fact that the works I composed in my own home have found a response in the outside world. To write an extended composition, and to evoke those sounds from an orchestra of a hundred men playing different instruments, can certainly be considered one of the grander experiences of mankind.

An artist can crystallize his personal sadness or his fear or his anger or his joy. Thus he is released from his emotion as others cannot be. The arts offer the opportunity to do something that cannot be done anywhere else. It is the only place where one can express in public the feelings ordinarily regarded as private. It is the place where we can say whatever is in our hearts or minds, where we never need to hide from ourselves or from others.

Early in life, I set myself certain standards. I studied works of the great masters and found common denominators; one is the fact that a truly great work of art will never look tired. To keep my ideas fresh, I was able to adjust to different occasions and to different kinds of musical materials. I consider myself fortunate; some composers are stuck with the style they adopt in the first place and go on writing in that style. But I had the feeling that I was living in a continuing state of self-discovery: I wished others could share in that adventure. I always wanted to take the average man in the street by the arm and say, "Look, here is a wonderful living art," and let him know that without it, he's missing something worthwhile.

Some people are more ear-minded than others. We must seem mesmerized to our less musically inclined friends! All of us, however, can understand and feel the joy of being carried forward by the flow of music. It is one of the great pleasures of the world, and those people who react to music and enjoy it are privileged people.

Part of the joy of involving oneself with the arts is the excitement of exploring its contemporary manifestations. But a strange thing happens in the field of music. The same people who find it quite acceptable for modern books, plays, or paintings to be controversial find these qualities unacceptable in music. Composers don't write music to console their audiences as though they were composing lullabies. They write music to stir people up, to make them think about the varieties of human experience reflected in their work. Moreover, the American public suffers from what might be called a masterpiece complex. They are willing to concern themselves only with music that is perfect, but not with music in the process of becoming so.

One hears a great deal of pessimistic talk these days not only about the arts but about the world in which we live. I think that in music we are not doing so badly. I do not subscribe to the notion that the symphony orchestra will soon disappear or that opera is dead. True, orchestras are having a difficult time with escalated production costs, and recent American operas have not fared well. However, in composition, I see a trend toward something that has been missing in music for a long time. It worried me that one did not meet up with the kind of composer we used to think of as being "musical." Years ago, if you said of someone, "He or she is terribly musical," that was the highest compliment you could pay. More recently, to stress "musicality" would seem to be pinning a bad name on a composer or making him or her look uninteresting. I am pleased to see that "musicality" has been making a comeback.

Artists have also become skeptical about inspiration. Perhaps the word has become meaningless through being used too loosely. But the composer has to believe in inspiration. It means being well disposed toward the thing you're doing—it is the time when the theme comes clearly, when the path opens up, when the process almost does itself.

I have often been asked, "Why become a composer?" It is a question to which there is really no answer—composers have no choice. It is a peculiar thing to be born a composer. It doesn't happen to everyone and it comes as rather a surprise to those to whom it does happen. The rewards are likely to be small from a practical point of view. No money in the bank. No good reviews in the papers the next day. You really have to be strong. By that I mean in the sense that you must be sure that what you are doing is absolutely what you must do. You can't worry about whether audiences will love you right away—that has never been the story with new music.

[1] These reflections are drawn from various Copland sources: an unpublshed typescript for a lecture, "The Composer's Experience," presented during the late fifties and sixties at eleven universities; an article,, "The Pleasures of Music," first publshed in *The Saturday Evening Post*, reprinted in *The Adventures of the Mind* (New York: AlfredA. Knopf, 1959); an unpublished lecture written for NBC's "Comment" program, Edwin Newman host; and interviews with Bill Moyers and Vivian Perlis.

Copland in his study, Peekskill, summer 1978

Composing is a lonely occupation and perhaps there is an advantage to the fact that many composers must add other, more sociable activities to their schedules in order to make a living. I was able to devote myself almost exclusively to composition during most of my career, although there were some difficult years before I became financially secure. The fact is that the creative artist is a kind of gambler, since there are no guarantees of success. Look at Charles Ives—the courage he had, to compose without hearing his music played! But he knew within himself what he was. I think it is for this reason that I have given so much time and energy to advancing the interests of my fellow composers by doing what I could to help them get their music performed.

Some people have a sense of where they are in the world more than others. They absorb it better, feel it more. Something inside them makes them want to reflect on the life that they live. And that, I think, is essential for those who create works of art. The world badly needs its artists, if only because the artist's life affirms the individual and the importance of the individual. Such artists symbolize the free man, the man who must decide for himself what is right, who must be free to make his own mistakes.

Music is a world of the emotions, feelings, reactions. It can be very strong, it can be very heroic. It can reflect deep religious feeling. But it cannot write programs for the future. The language of music exists to say something—something that constitutes essential emotions seized and shaped into meaningful forms. The feelings are like feelings *are*—emotional, and sort of vague. It shouldn't always be possible to put them into words. If it was, you wouldn't need poems or paintings and all the other ways in which people express themselves.

I think that my music, even when it sounds tragic, is a confirmation of life. If there is a unifying core in it all, it is a sense of affirmation. I would also like to think that my music enlarges the listener's sphere of reference; when I listen to a work by Bach or Palestrina, I have a *larger* sense of what it means to be alive. That is one of the great things about art, of course, that it does enlarge the sense of who you are and what life is all about.

Perhaps the answer to why a man like me composes is that art summarizes the most basic feelings about being alive. Just as we look to eighteenth-century works to try to experience that time, our arts mirror the atmosphere of the present. By reflecting the time in which one lives, the creative artist gives substance and meaning to life as we live it. Life seems so transitory! It is very attractive to set down some sort of permanent statement about the way we feel, so that when it's all gone, people will be able to go to our art works to see what it was like to be alive in our time and place: twentieth-century America.

POSTLUDE

Copland was not the sort to talk about "immortality," but when asked how he would like to be remembered, he said simply, "I would like to be remembered through my music." More than twenty years have passed since the composer's death, and it is safe to say his wish has been granted. *Fanfare for the Common Man* continues to be what Bernstein called "America's greatest hit"; the bouncing rhythms of *Billy the Kid* and *Rodeo* still bring to mind cowboys, Indians, and the western plains; and *Appalachian Spring* is loved for its lyricism, especially Copland's treatment of "The Gift to Be Simple." The popular pieces that caused Copland to be called the "President of American Music" are still among the most performed and admired classical works worldwide, and Copland continues to be a beloved American icon. There are no signs of the customary silence that follows a composer's death.

The revival of a forgotten composer may come about in many ways: admiring students, relatives, performers in search of new material, or an event, such as a centennial. Circumstances vary and serendipity usually plays a role.[1] For Copland, there has been no break in popularity and no lack of performances—at least of the accessible pieces. The lively rhythms of "Hoedown" still set feet tapping, the trumpet blasts of *Fanfare* tempt listeners to stand and salute, the dissonant chord that accompanies the crunch of Curly's hand in *Of Mice and Men* continues to make film audiences cringe, and Emily's appearance in *Our Town* still brings forth tears. Copland did not expect his more thorny and intellectual pieces, those he dubbed his "neglected children," to be accepted immediately; he knew they would be heard eventually and never lost confidence that all were deserving. The *Piano Variations* and the *Third Symphony* have joined *Lincoln Portrait* and *El Salón México* in the standard concert repertoire; *Quiet City* and the *Piano Sonata* are heard more and more. Copland's place in the concert hall is secure.

We left Copland in his mid-eighties.[2] He had ceased composing in the 1970s and stopped conducting in the 1980s. Throughout his career, he had been stimulated by new music and fresh ideas. He loved being part of the avant-garde and the movement for modern music. Copland was determined not to repeat himself in his music, and this may account for the size of his catalogue, which shows one or two examples of each genre—a symphony, one piano quartet. a trio, a nonet, a few ballet suites, one song cycle, a choral piece, film scores. Copland's catalogue is not large —he considered himself a slow worker, a "one work-a-year-man," but his oeuvre is varied, and as William Schuman pointed out, "There may be only one of each kind of music, but it's likely to be the very best of its kind."

Following the excitement of the 80th birthday, Copland limited his appearances to daytime events; for example, the dedication of the Queens College music department as the Aaron Copland School of Music. It was 1981, the same year the College presented him with an honorary doctorate. Claire Brook recalls William Schuman, who frquently introduced Copland at such events, saying (when Copland stumbled briefly) "Aaron, you have forgotten more than most of us will ever remember." Another meaningful occasion was a matinee performance of *The Tender Land* at the Long Wharf Theater in New Haven. Copland was thrilled to know there were fifty-one performances of his neglected opera. He attended a matinee with Erik Johns, Verna Fine, and me. The audience stood and the cast cheered when the composer's presence was announced.

Until the mid-1980s, Copland's life was full: his extensive collection of manuscripts and papers was always in need of attention, he responded to all queries and mail personally (with the assistance of David Walker), and the demands of his autobiography escalated. He was determined to read, comment, add, and correct, as

[1] Twentieth-century examples include: Sibelius, Hindemith, Mahler, and Leo Ornstein. The Centenary celebrations of Charles Ives stimulated interest in 1974. Closer to the present, the significant figures of William Schuman, Roger Sessions, Samuel Barber, Lukas Foss, and Jacob Druckman are yet to be rediscovered. However, Barber's music, long considered old-fashioned, is being performed more often and even the much maligned Schoenberg is finally being accepted as the great revolutionary who changed the basic elements of composition.

[2] See Composer as Conductor, Interlude XII, and Reflections on My Life in Music.

Perlis, Copland, Erik Johns, and Verna Fine at performance of *Tender Land*.

work progressed. Copland's files were stored in the basement of his house between the washer and dryer (a shaky experience during "spin" cycles). One day a folder with over forty papers in Copland's hand surfaced. These items (and many more) were valuable in reconstructing earlier times and are vivid examples of the wide range of Copland's thinking, the depth of his knowledge, and the quality of his writing. However, Copland's memory had been failing for some time. Whether his condition affected musical connections or impacted his creativity is not known, nor is an exact date of his earliest symptoms. Copland's physician, Arnold Salop, diagnosed a hereditary dementia that was confirmed after an appointment with Bernstein's physician. The results were sent to Copland by mail. He read the letter aloud, then said quietly to me and David Walker, "Doesn't sound good, does it?" He became increasingly isolated. Clurman, Boulanger, Britten, Victor Kraft, and most of his family were gone; those still alive and able, found visits difficult. Toward the end, Bernstein was the only one Copland remembered, and even that memory was finally lost.[3]

The daily walk down the wooded path to the mailbox became the singular event of Copland's day. He had described himself as "optimistic in nature"; one of his favorite sayings was "Agonizing is not my thing." Yet, as life would have it, his final years were quiet and lonely.

Copland's wish was for the chronicle of his life to be told in the context of American music. Placing him in his time frame, setting the scene, attempting to

[3] See Perlis, "Dear Aaron, Dear Lenny, A Friendship in Letters," in *Aaron Copland and His World*, ed. Carol J. Oja and Judith Tick. (Princeton, New Jersey: Princeton University Press, 2005).

picture him at various ages—these were the challenges. As historian George Kennan said: "History is not what happened in the past, but what it felt like to be there when it happened." Copland lived through chaotic and turbulent times in history and was aware of the fast-moving cultural and political changes. He said, "In my one lifetime, I was witness to the lighting of the gas lamps outside my window and to a man walking on the moon!" He was not part of the computer age, he never knew about the cell phone and barely touched upon the CD revolution in recorded sound. "Digital" was not in his vocabulary (computers were not yet in use for the first volume of the autobiography and electronic files did not exist for this revision). Copland belonged to a very different time, pre-dating the sexual revolution and gay rights. If "digital" was not in his vocabulary, the word "gay" had a completely different meaning. It was a time when homosexuals lived in "the closet." Copland's friend Lenny said, "Aaron came out early," and he explained, "Aaron came out to himself. He always knew who he was and he lived accordingly." In fact, far in advance, he lived the way most gay men desired, then and now—like other normal and private individuals. When he described a particular time or event, his "partner" or "roommate" was always named, never hidden. Copland assumed he could live with whomever he pleased, as he assumed he could choose his own politics during the Cold War. Minna Lederman said, "Aaron protected himself for the sake of his music. Everything else was on a different level." He was, indeed, like a conduit for the music. Copland could compose *Billy the Kid* in Paris and *Appalachian Spring* in Mexico, as long as he had a piano. He was rarely seen outwardly angry or openly affectionate. He did not want anyone making a "fuss." This need for tranquility was crucial to his creativity. On the other hand and paradoxically, Copland was willing to take chances with new music and inventive ideas. Looking back, he would bemoan in mock misery, "Nobody remembers me as the 'wild-eyed modernist. . .'"

When Leonard Bernstein died at the age of seventy-three, seven weeks before his older friend, it was decided that Aaron (for his own peace of mind) was not to be told. Copland's 90th birthday was the same day of the Bernstein's Carnegie Hall memorial. On that day, Copland was at home, surrounded by drawings sent to him by local elementary school children. When we (my husband, Sandy Perlis, and I) arrived for a visit, we celebrated with a single candle placed on an apple pie and sang "Happy Birthday to Aaron." We believe he knew something special was happening.

Copland died a few weeks later (2 December 1990) in Phelps Memorial Hospital, North Tarrytown, New York. The cause was listed as respiratory failure following pneumonia and two strokes. Copland and Bernstein both died at the start of the final decade of the 20th century. They had been among the few composers who had given American music its place on the international scene for the first time in history.

Copland's papers and manuscripts were sent to the Library of Congress. Rock Hill was closed and put up for sale. Ellis Freedman and I, together with Roger Levey, Sylvia Goldstein, David Walker and Ronald Caltabiano (who had succeeded David Walker) made the many contacts and announcements necessary at such times, not only out of a sense of duty and responsibility but with genuine admiration for a great composer and heartfelt affection for the man we had known and worked with for so long. Arrangements were soon underway for the Copland Memorial Concert at Alice Tully Hall, 20 April 1991. The event was co-produced by Harry Kraut (Bernstein's long-time manager) and featured Lukas Foss conducting the American Composers Orchestra.[4] Family and friends were invited to a gathering at the Century Club following the concert. One might say, life went on without Aaron Copland. But while he would no longer be seen in person or at concerts, or heard "live" on radio and TV, the central core of Copland—his music— has stayed alive and well.

Some time later, Roger Levey (Copland's great nephew and closest relative) called to discuss a time and place for burial of Copland's ashes. We agreed that Tanglewood was appropriate, and Daniel Gustin, Tanglewood's director and Copland's friend, arranged for a site in the maze of hedges close to the Theatre-Concert Hall where Copland had spent so much time with students, composers, faculty, and audiences. Dan Gustin's sensitive touch was evident in the simple and elegant event. Copland's "As It Fell Upon a Day" was performed by gifted students as they walked slowly down the pathway by the grape arbor to a circle enclosed by green hedges that sparkled in the bright Berkshire sunshine. Following a brief welcome (Copland had requested no eulogy or religious service), guests were invited to sprinkle ashes around the grass fringe of the circle. At the entrance to the space there are three flat rectangular stones inconspicuously embedded in the grass. From top to bottom they read:

BEQUEATHED BY FAMILY AND FRIENDS
AARON COPLAND
1900-1990
THE FIRST THREE NOTES OF "FANFARE FOR THE COMMON MAN"

Praised for its eloquent simplicity, Copland's burial place was not known to the public and rarely visited. Indeed, even on the Tanglewood staff, few knew such a tribute space existed. On 30 June, 2011, a handsome bronze bust of Copland was unveiled and placed in the center of Tanglewood's hidden Copland circle. Lighting was installed to lead visitors to the burial place. The sculptor is Penelope Jenks; the tribute was sponsored by conductor John Williams, who hopes to place similar sculptures in appropriate places at Tanglewood to honor Serge Koussevitsky and Leonard Bernstein.

Copland's Centenary coincided with the millennium, precipitating a flood of events in and around 2000. To name a few: Howard Pollack's excellent biography, *Aaron Copland, The Life and Works of an Uncommon Man*, was published in 1999. The landmark occasion continued with concerts and festivals that featured American music, celebrated with a wide range of genres in various locations. The New York Philharmonic kicked off a year-long party with three weeks of "Completely Copland"; An all-Copland salute at Yale

[4] The program: Variations and Finale from *Appalachian Spring*; *Duo for Flute and Piano* (Fenwick Smith, Gilbert Kalish); *Four Piano Blues; Three Moods* (Leo Smit); Two Songs from *Twelve Poems of Emily Dickinson* (Roberta Alexander and David Del Tredici); *Two Preludes for Violin and Piano* (Isaac Stern, Lukas Foss); *Old American Songs* (Kurt Ollman, the Harvard Glee Club); *Lincoln Portrait* (Narrated by Wiliam Warfield).

featured two premieres—the composer' s arrangement of *Music for the Theatre* for piano four-hands and his trio version of *Prelude* from the *First Symphony* for violin, piano, and cello; Boosey & Hawkes published an impressive brochure, featuring drawings by Al Hirshfeld, my annotations of Copland's published music, and commentary by historian Carol Oja; critic Tim Page wrote a five-part series in the *Washington Post.* Among several video documentaries, a standout is Michael Tilson Thomas' "Copland and the American Sound" with the San Francisco Symphony.

There is a particular satisfaction for researchers in the field of American music—the possibility of fresh discovery. One would think that the Copland mine would long have been exhausted, but performers and researchers are still tapping new areas and finding unexamined gems. With each "find" the balance shifts and the biography of Aaron Copland changes slightly. For example, "Music in the Twenties," a DVD, has been released by Kultur; in it, Copland, filmed in 1965 at station WGBH in Boston, makes use of his lecture notes about the twenties discovered at the Library of Congress. It is a vivid mix of music and words about the 1920s, using the 1960s "new" technology of the video camera; the original score of *Appalachian Spring* has been located and has been examined for the first time in sixty years; an alternate text for the final aria of Copland's only opera will alter future studies of *The Tender Land;* and someone will finally perform the two-piano arrangements of orchestral works made by Copland and John Kirkpatrick. Researchers will find that there is a Copland peak in Antarctica, a Copland Court in Maryland (between Stravinsky and Strauss Lanes), and a Copland stamp issued by the island of Grenada. The legend lives and grows, aided by Copland himself who bequeathed a large part of his estate to the support of new American music in the future. Younger composers, struggling to make their way in a difficult profession admire Copland's legacy. His "rags to riches" story did not end with his death but has continued, providing proof positive that it is possible for a composer to "make it" on his own.

The Fund established in Copland's name was first called The Aaron Copland Fund for Composers, but as its scope became clear, the title was broadened. Copland's directives in his will were general and open to change: he asked only that his estate be used for the support of American music and composers, preferably under the age of forty. Copland's Last Will and Testament was finalized with his attorney, Ellis J. Freedman, in 1984 (updating an earlier will of 1970).

The first meeting of the Aaron Copland Fund for Music took place on 29 April 1991 at Ellis Freedman's office. Freedman acted as temporary chairman. Copland had smoothed the way by naming the board in his will: Arthur Berger, Leonard Bernstein (deceased), Elliott Carter, David Del Tredici, Jacob Druckman, Ellis Freedman, Vivian Perlis, William Schuman, and Leo Smit. The first official act of the board was the election of officers: Jacob Druckman was chosen president; Perlis vice president, Freedman Secretary, and John Grozier treasurer[5]

[5] Others have worked with the Fund for many years in addition to Grozier: Norman Feit, treasurer, Anthony Schmidt, accountant, and Allen Jacobi of Wilmington Trust.

The will and by-laws were read, and Freedman reported on the financial status of the estate. An executive committee was chosen (Druckman, Freedman, Perlis, and Del Tredici) for decisions and discussions between meetings of the full board. Thus, the basic structure of the Fund was in place from the start and has remained constant: an executive director, president and officers, an executive committee with voting powers, and the board of directors comprised mostly of composers.

At the start, the expertise of Freedman and Schuman provided a smooth continuation and transition from Copland's life and career. Freedman had learned his way around the music world, his contacts with Boosey & Hawkes in the U.S. and U.K. were strong, and he drew investment and security representatives who have stayed with the Fund from its inception. William Schuman, a brilliant administrator, was a close friend and colleague to Copland. As a young president of Juilliard followed by the first presidency of Lincoln Center, Bill knew his way around boards, and he shared his knowledge with his customary grace and enthusiasm. Jacob Druckman, the first president, had studied with Copland at Tanglewood and was at the height of an internationally successful career as educator and composer, admired especially for the brilliant colors of his orchestral pieces. (Druckman was awarded the Pulitzer Prize in Music in 1972.) Jacob chaired the board from its second meeting 11 June 1991. Discussions revolved around basic principles: should the prime purpose be to support established organizations and institutions, mostly in New York City? Or ought the major thrust be smaller amounts to many musicians in diverse locations nation-wide? Schuman leaned toward the former; Druckman the latter. These were important decisions that would set the guidelines for the future. Four meetings were required in 1991 and several extra in the next few years to create guidelines and put the protocol in place for carrying them out.

Bill Schuman chaired the meeting of 5 February 1992 in his New York City apartment. Sadly, later that month, the board was called together again, this time in Freedman's office, to note the passing of William Schuman.

Soon thereafter, the decision was made to continue the support of major performing organizations and institutions, particularly those Copland had contributed to in his lifetime, but to focus largely on smaller grants to lesser-known musical efforts nationwide. Thus, a door was opened to the many proposals that began to pour in as news of a new source of support was released to the public and spread rapidly through the world of new music. The Copland Fund has distributed approximately a million dollars annually for over twenty years and continues at that level of giving.

Considering the wide range of ages and personalities on the board, members are aware of their common purpose, and they have a strong bond of mutual admiration and devotion to the cause of new music. Copland, who had been on innumerable committees and boards, considered it a great pleasure to be in a room full of composers for several intense hours. Short of being "fun," Copland Fund board members enjoy a congenial atmosphere and the opportunity to reunite with colleagues. The most heated debates of the early years revolved around gifting directly to individual composers: a few directors were strongly in favor of what they considered Copland's original intentions, while others opposed the idea, because of a tax rule that would complicate direct giving. The subject remained open and resurfaces from time to time, but even when there is not agreement, discussions are always respectful.

By the end of 1992, the division of the Fund into three areas of giving was adopted: performing ensembles, recording, and supplemental. It was recognized that independent review panels were necessary for assessing the performing and recording proposals. The rotating panels of five individuals, examine and make their choices, which are then voted on by the board of directors. This system works but demands a great deal of advance preparation and attention, not the least being a continuous search for appropriate panelists.

In April 1992 the American Music Center suggested a plan to exchange administrative assistance for support. The arrangement brought composer Wesley York of the AMC staff into the Copland Fund where he has become essential to subsequent grant-giving activities, including the recent conversion of the Fund's pocesses to on-line technology.

The supplemental fund was meant to cover proposals that do not fit into the performing or recording categories. It has grown to include a wide range of projects. The proposals are arbitrarily divided and distributed to a few board members in advance, who meet to discuss them and subsequently recommend their choices to the full board. The supplementary program requires frequent attention and "tweaking" by the executive committee, and success depends strongly on advance preparation. The in-progress change to on-line technology, a huge effort and responsibility, is already proving efffective to the complex procedures of all three areas of giving.

In 1996, Copland's legendary "lucky" timing kicked in again when James W. (Jim) Kendrick "inherited" most of Ellis Freedman's music clients. Jim Kendrick first entered the board in 1996 as joint secretary with Norman Feit. In 1997 he became an officer as secretary and Feit became treasurer. Jim Kendrick is a musician (oboist); he served as director of the American office of Boosey & Hawkes for five years (1985-1990) and came to the Copland Fund knowledgeable about its operations. As a lawyer, he specializes in intellectual properties. Jim is deeply involved in the world of music, as it goes along its turbulent and fast-moving way, especially in the areas of foundations, recording and publishing. As executor of the Copland estate and secretary of the board of the Fund, Jim is at the center of operations and is frequently in contact with the officers and the executive committee on a wide range of subjects, among them requests for use of Copland's music and writings, which have continued to escalate. Jim's expertise in working with the board, officers, and executive committee and his up-to-date familiarity with the technological changes in the music industry is formidable. He has steered the Fund through rough and smooth times; hopefully, he will continue to do so in the unforeseeable crises ahead.

[5] In addition to Grozier, others have stayed with the Fund for many years, among them: Norman Feit, Treasurer, Anthony Schmidt, accountant, and Allen Jacobi of Wilmington Trust.

Wesley York became Jim Kendrick's assistant and is director of funding programs. Wes has seen the Fund through growth and change in the years since his first board meeting in September 1993. He is largely responsible for the countless arrangements and preparation of materials for the board meetings. The smoothness of its operations are due to Wes' conscientious attention. With Kendrick, he is central to the task of adopting the on-line technology for the entire Copland Fund operation, a project that requires skill and knowledge, patience and determination. Wes goes about his role with a quiet mien that can rightfully be described as "Coplandesque."

In 1994, the directors made a decision about Copland's house in the town of Cortlandt. Since Rock Hill did not attract a buyer, a project was proposed by local citizens to renovate the house into a space that would be available for public events. This was an appealing idea but did not seem practical; nevertheless, the good citizens of Cortlandt deserved a try; the house was deeded to them for $1 a year and after the result proved highly successful, ownership was transferred to Copland House. It is a grass roots movement and has become an admired entity, first as a composers' retreat and subsequently as a thriving center for activities in American music. Much of its success can be traced to the energetic leadership of noted pianist, Michael Boriskin, Artistic Director (1996) and Executive Director (2003). Boriskin has forged ahead with amazing energy, generous with his considerable musical knowledge and with dynamic optimism. He and his dedicated board maintain a high level of musical quality and ideas—first with the residency awards (six to eight annually), followed by the formation of "Music from Copland House (MCH)," an unusual resident chamber ensemble.[6]

Jacob Druckman's sudden death (24 May 1996) was a shock to the music world and a challenge to the Copland Fund. His final appearance at a board meeting was 12 April 1996. 15 November that year, John Harbison was named president. His first act was to request a vote of thanks to Jacob Druckman and Ellis Freedman for their efforts "reflective of Copland's spirit . . . in great part due to their devotion and guidance."

The range and demands of presidential duties are known to very few—they are mostly offstage—Copland style. The Fund has had three presidents in twenty-one years, each with a strong distinctive personality, each a composer with an international reputation and Pulitzer Prize winners in music—and each with a history of pedagogy at the highest level. Without a stated term as president, Jacob Druckman's tenure lasted until his death and has a special place of honor as the Copland Fund's first president. John Harbison's tenure stands for the period when the Copland Fund was fully established as the preeminent foundation of its kind. In an interview, Harbison said:

> I watched Jacob closely. He was broader, in the deep sense, than I am. He was genuinely wide open. His attitude seems to me to be absolutely the right one; that is. don't make any snap judgments that might close off an avenue. And he was very concerned to make sure there was wide representation of many strands of music, because it's hard from a historical perspective to know which ones are going to be valuable. . .you have to go by your own ears. If you are arrested by something, it's important to go with it.[7]

Harbison remembered his own early years and how difficult it was to actually get someone to listen to a young composer's work. Harbison reognized that the Copland Fund provides the chance for countless composers to be heard and by more than one set of ears. For thirteen years, he succeeded in maintaining Copland's emphasis on the art of music and balancing it with the innumerable practical matters related to bringing new music to new audiences. John announced his resignation effective November 2010. Composer Christopher Rouse, president since then, in his close and continuing involvement with composers and orchestras, brings his own exuberant vitality to the position; his inclusive approach to popular music is likely to bring a lively panorama of views to the office of president.

Additions to the board are made occasionally to maintain a quorum: Lukas Foss and John Harbison in 1992, and others through the years: Marin Alsop, Bill Bolcom, Jim Kendrick, Ursula Oppens, Christopher Rouse, Steve Stucky, and Ellen Taaffe Zwilich. Elliott Carter was an active member of the board until his death in 2012. Only Del Tredici and Perlis remain from the original board.

The Copland Fund is an excellent example of the truism that organizations tend to take on the personality of those who establish them. Survivors who knew Copland have commented that the Copland Fund comes as close as possible to the composer's intentions and aims during his lifetime. Frequently described as "modest," Copland did not sponsor his own music, nor does the Fund exclude or include proposals on that basis. Its officers have leadership qualities in common with Copland. It was a very long time ago at a summer camp in the Adirondacks when the question, "What does Aaron think?" began to be heard. Throughout much of the twentieth-century, composers and colleagues repeatedly asked, "What does Aaron think?" The question still gently echoes at Copland Fund board meetings, "What would Aaron think?"

[6] See website, Copland House, for more on the founding of Copland House and its resident peforming group—Music from Copland House (MCH) and the addition of Merestead, an estate on a large and impressive property in lower Westchester County. The elegant manor house is in active use for concerts. Expansion for use of the small buildings on the property is under consideration.

[7] Interview, John Harbison with Perlis, May 1998, Tarrytown, New York, See Oral History of American Music, Yale.

Acknowledgments

I welcome the opportunity to thank those who contributed to the research and publication of *The Complete Copland.* I am also pleased to repeat my thanks to the many who made the original two volumes of Aaron Copland's autobiography possible. *Copland: 1900 to 1942*, released in 1984, and *Copland Since 1943*, which followed in 1989, were distinguished by reminiscences of Copland himself and enhanced by many interviews with friends, family and colleagues of the composer,. These testimonies have not diminished with time and are deserving of recognition again in this revised edition. While it is not feasible to repeat the names of all who gave so generously in the past, know that you continue to be remembered and appreciated.

The remarkably high standard maintained throughout Copland's life and career continues to inspire performers, scholars, composers and audiences. I am grateful to those who have been involved with *The Complete Copland* for their determination to achieve a similar quality of excellence.

Prior to the untimely death of Claire Brook in June 2012, I wrote the following, intended for this space:

"First and foremost among those to be thanked for the revision of Copland's autobiography is Claire Brook, editor extraordinaire of Pendragon Press. Claire's unique hands-on approach, her patience, imagination, and experience, all contributed toward turning *The Complete Copland* from an idea into reality."

While Claire's passing is an irreplaceable loss, I am extremely grateful to Robert (Bob) Kessler, Claire's co-publisher (and brother). As managing editor and publisher of Pendragon Press, Bob took on the challenge of adapting Claire's iconoclastic methods toward the completion of this publication and its guidance through the transformation from computer files to book chapters. Bob Kessler has not only satisfied Copland's high standards, he has produced a *Complete Copland* that would have had Claire's approval. Bob's efforts to bring the publication to fruition is nothing less than an act of heroism. Others at Pendragon Press who assisted in the project from behind the scenes also deserve heartfelt thanks.

It has been my great good fortune to have the cooperation of Yale University Library and School of music, especially the Oral History of American Music project and the long-standing support of Libby Van Cleve, director of OHAM, who is a trusted friend and valued colleague; Anne Rhodes, Jef Wilson, students Paul Kereke, and especially Claire Donnelley for research assistance and for her remarkable good humor.

Copland's music publisher, Boosey & Hawkes, Inc., supplied advice, historical information, and permissions. Copland's story and "Boosey" run parallel and his autobiography has had many assists along the way, from Sylvia Goldstein to Zizi Mueller, president of the classical music division, and to John White who has provided assistance with permission to use excerpts. See list on the following pages.

For cooperation and support. are the Library of Congress, The New York Public Library, and the archives of the Boston Symphony Orchestra and the New York Philharmonic, The Koussevitzky Foundation, and the estates of Emily Dickinson, Benny Goodman, Paul Whiteman, Hart Crane, John Steinbeck, and Thornton Wilder.

The Copland Fund for Music, Inc. shares author's ownership of *The Complete Copland.* The cooperation of its executor and board of directors have been invaluable in far too many ways to enumerate, but I am especially grateful to James (Jim) Kendrick for guidance and friendship and to Wesley York whose presence and advice have been evident throughout. The Copland Fund, in its position of co-authorship, has been responsible for the index by Alexa Selph, who went far beyond creating the index to become an advisor and valued reader.

Special thanks go to the American Musicological Society for a generous grant in 2011 to Pendragon Press for aid with publishing costs.

Several individuals supplied unique materials or valuable information. They include Mather Pfeiffenberger, Daniel Mather, Stephen Gottlieb, Jennifer De Lapp, Aaron Sherber, and Elizabeth Blaufox.

The memory of Sandy Perlis has provided an enduring spirit of cooperation and optimism, and my family continues in their support with patience and encouragement: Missy and Michael Perlis, Lauren and David Ambler, Amy and Jonathan Perlis, Morgan, Steve, and Ben Perlis, and Charlie and Melanie Ambler.

Finally, posthumous thanks to Aaron for the beauty of his music, which transcends mortality and allows his presence to be felt from afar.

Vivian Perlis

Grohg by Aaron Copland
© Copyright 1992 by The Aaron Copland Fund for Music, Inc.
Boosey & Hawkes, Inc., sole licensee.
Reprinted by permission of Boosey & Hawkes, Inc.

Symphony for Organ and Orchestra by Aaron Copland
© Copyright 1931, 1963 by The Aaron Copland Fund for Music, Inc. Copyright renewed.
Boosey & Hawkes, Inc., sole licensee.
Reprinted by permission of Boosey & Hawkes, Inc.

First Symphony by Aaron Copland
© Copyright 1931, 1958 by The Aaron Copland Fund for Music, Inc. Copyright renewed.
Boosey & Hawkes, Inc., sole licensee.
Reprinted by permission of Boosey & Hawkes, Inc.

Music for the Theatre by Aaron Copland
© Copyright 1932 by The Aaron Copland Fund for Music, Inc. Copyright renewed.
Boosey & Hawkes, Inc., sole licensee.
Reprinted by permission of Boosey & Hawkes, Inc.

Vitebsk by Aaron Copland
© Copyright 1934 by The Aaron Copland Fund for Music, Inc. Copyright renewed.
Boosey & Hawkes, Inc., sole licensee.
Reprinted by permission of Boosey & Hawkes, Inc.

Symphonic Ode by Aaron Copland
© Copyright 1957 by The Aaron Copland Fund for Music, Inc. Copyright renewed.
Boosey & Hawkes, Inc., sole licensee.
Reprinted by permission of Boosey & Hawkes, Inc.

Piano Variations by Aaron Copland
© Copyright 1932 by The Aaron Copland Fund for Music, Inc. Copyright renewed.
Boosey & Hawkes, Inc., sole licensee.
Reprinted by permission of Boosey & Hawkes, Inc.

The Second Hurricane by Aaron Copland and Edwin Denby
© Copyright 1938 by The Aaron Copland Fund for Music, Inc. Copyright renewed.
Boosey & Hawkes, Inc., sole licensee.
Reprinted by permission of Boosey & Hawkes, Inc.

Billy the Kid by Aaron Copland
© Copyright 1941 by The Aaron Copland Fund for Music, Inc. Copyright renewed.
Boosey & Hawkes, Inc., sole licensee.
Reprinted by permission of Boosey & Hawkes, Inc.

Fanfare for the Common Man by Aaron Copland
© Copyright 1944 by The Aaron Copland Fund for Music, Inc. Copyright renewed.
Boosey & Hawkes, Inc., sole licensee.
Reprinted by permission of Boosey & Hawkes, Inc.

Appalachian Spring by Aaron Copland
© Copyright 1945 by The Aaron Copland Fund for Music, Inc. Copyright renewed.
Boosey & Hawkes, Inc., sole licensee.
Reprinted by permission of Boosey & Hawkes, Inc.

Third Symphony by Aaron Copland
© Copyright 1947 by The Aaron Copland Fund for Music, Inc. Copyright renewed.
Boosey & Hawkes, Inc., sole licensee.
Reprinted by permission of Boosey & Hawkes, Inc.

Concerto for Clarinet and String Orchestra by Aaron Copland
© Copyright 1949, 1952 by The Aaron Copland Fund for Music, Inc. Copyright renewed.
Boosey & Hawkes, Inc., sole licensee.
Reprinted by permission of Boosey & Hawkes, Inc.

Quartet for Piano and Strings by Aaron Copland
© Copyright 1951, 1952 by The Aaron Copland Fund for Music, Inc. Copyright renewed.
Boosey & Hawkes, Inc., sole licensee.
Reprinted by permission of Boosey & Hawkes, Inc.

Going to Heaven! By Aaron Copland and Emily Dickinson

© Copyright 1951 by The Aaron Copland Fund for Music, Inc. Copyright renewed.

Boosey & Hawkes, Inc., sole licensee.

Reprinted by permission of Boosey & Hawkes, Inc.

The Tender Land by Aaron Copland and Horace Everett

© Copyright 1954, 1956 by The Aaron Copland Fund for Music, Inc. Copyright renewed.

Boosey & Hawkes, Inc., sole licensee.

Reprinted by permission of Boosey & Hawkes, Inc.

Piano Fantasy by Aaron Copland

© Copyright 1957 by The Aaron Copland Fund for Music, Inc. Copyright renewed.

Boosey & Hawkes, Inc., sole licensee.

Reprinted by permission of Boosey & Hawkes, Inc.

Connotations by Aaron Copland

© Copyright 1962, 1963 by The Aaron Copland Fund for Music, Inc. Copyright renewed.

Boosey & Hawkes, Inc., sole licensee.

Reprinted by permission of Boosey & Hawkes, Inc.

Night Thoughts by Aaron Copland

© Copyright 1965 by The Aaron Copland Fund for Music, Inc. Copyright renewed.

Boosey & Hawkes, Inc., sole licensee.

Reprinted by permission of Boosey & Hawkes, Inc.

LIST OF ILLUSTRATIONS, CREDITS, PERMISSIONS, AND COPYRIGHTS

Abbreviations

AC: Aaron Copland
VP: Vivian Perlis
CC LC: Copland Collection Library of Congress
L: left column, R: right column, C: between the two columns
l: lower, u: upper
ACFM: Aaron Copland Fund for Music, Inc.
B & H: Boosey & Hawkes, Inc.
UP: unidentified photographer

PRELUDE

1.Photograph Mittenthal store on wheels 1889 CC LC UP 2 L
2. Photograph Sarah Mittenthal circa1885 CC LC UP 3 L
3. Photograph Harris M.Copland 1890 CC LC UP 3 L
4. Photograph AC family group CC LC UP 3 R
5. Photograph Kaplan grandparents and three daughters 1899 CC LC UP 4R
6. Photograph Sarah and Harris Copland circa 1922 CC LC UP 5 L

BROOKLYN

7. Photograph AC circa 1914 CC LC ACFM UP 6 C
8. Three photographs AC at two, six and nine CC LC ACFM UP 7 R
9. Photograph family in auto circa 1916 Courtesy Selma Furman UP 9 L
10. *Zenatello* circa 1911 CC LC copyright 1984 AC 9 R
11. *Lola* CC LC copyright 1984 AC 10 R
12. *Night* 1918 CC LC copyright 1984 AC 13 L, R
13. *A Love Poem* 1918 CC LC copyright 1984 AC 14 R
14. Photograph High School graduation CC LC UP 14 R
15. *The Cat and the Mouse* CC LC copyright 1921 by MM Durand and Company, a Universal Music Publishing company. All rights reserved. Reprinted by permission . 16 R

FONTAINEBLEAU

16. Photograph AC circa 1920 CC LC UP 17 C
17. Page from letter home CC LC permission ACFM UP 18 R
18. Photograph AC with landlady circa 1921 CC LC UP 19 R
19. Manuscript page *Old Poem* circa1921 CC LC copyright 1923 Editions M. Sénart renewed 1951 AC 21 L
20. Photograph Nadia Boulanger with students circa 1922 CC LC UP 22 L

PARIS

21.Photograph AC circa 1923 CC LC UP 23 C
22. Page from AC letter home 1921 CC LC permission ACFM 24 L
23. Photograph AC with friends CC LC UP 25 R
24. Photograph Piano UP Courtesy Howard Clurman 26 L
25. Photograph Boulanger in studio CC LC UP 27 R
26. Photograph Boulanger and students CC LC UP 28 L
27. Photograph AC and Boulanger 1976 CC LC UP 29 R
28. First page of AC letter home, CC LC permission ACFM 33 R
29. Proof page *Scherzo humoristique: Le chat et las souris* CC LC copyright 1921 by MM Durand and Company, a Universal Music Publishing company. All rights reserved. Reprinted by permission . 34 R
30. Proof page from *Grohg* CC LC copyright 1984 AC renewed B & H 36 R
31. Photograph AC and Clurman, courtesy VP 36 R
32. Letters Boulanger to and from AC 1923 CC LC Courtesy Nadia Boulanger 38 R
33. Caricature AC by Olga Koussevitsky, permission Koussevitzky Foundation 39 C

INTERLUDE I

34. Photograph AC early twenties CC LC UP 42 R

NEW YORK

35. Photograph AC circa 1925 CC LC UP 43 C
36. Sketch Scherzo *Symphony for Organ and Orchestra* CC LC copyright AC 1963 B & H Sole Publishers and Licensees 45 L
37. Program New York Symphony 1925 CC LC 45 L

INTERLUDE XII

REFLECTIONS ON MY LIFE IN MUSIC

POSTLUDE

Index

Page numbers in italics indicate illustrative material.